Introductory Algebra
for College Students

Robert E. Dressler
Professor of Mathematics,
Kansas State University

Isidore Dressler
Adjunct Assistant Professor
of Mathematics and
Mathematics Education,
Pace University

AMSCO COLLEGE PUBLICATIONS
315 Hudson Street   New York, N.Y. 10013

ISBN 0-87720-975-8
Specify CR 180 P or INTRODUCTORY ALGEBRA

Published in 1976 by Amsco College Publications,
a division of Amsco School Publications, Inc.

Printed in the United States of America

PREFACE

Introductory Algebra for College Students was written to be used as a textbook in a college course for students who have not previously studied algebra and for students who have studied elementary algebra but need to refresh and strengthen their knowledge of the subject before taking more advanced courses.

This book has two major purposes: (1) to aid the student in understanding the basic concepts of elementary algebra, and (2) to help the student acquire competence in the manipulative algebraic skills necessary in the application of mathematics in other fields such as physical science, social science, statistics, and business. Although this textbook presents a modern structural approach, the authors have avoided an extremely rigorous treatment of the subject matter. The degree of rigor can be determined by the instructor, depending upon the mathematical sophistication of the students, without in any way interfering with their ability to master the manipulative skills.

In addition to the usual topics covered in an elementary algebra course, this text treats the basic language and concepts of sets, the number line, properties of numbers, absolute value, the ordering of numbers, the function concept, inequalities, and deductive proof of algebraic theorems. The metric system and metric units are introduced early and used in a variety of problems throughout the book.

An unusual feature of the book is its organization, which is directed toward encouraging and helping students to learn by studying and comprehending the book on their own. Each chapter contains a set of learning units, which, with proper application, a student should be able to master independently. The basic concepts of each unit are carefully developed with simple language and symbolism. New words and terms are defined clearly. Explanations and teaching problems lead to the clear and concise statement of important general principles and procedures. Numerous model problems, whose solutions are accompanied by step-by-step explanations, demonstrate how to apply the principles and follow the procedures. Students complete their mastery of the unit by doing the series of many carefully graded exercises, which involve a variety of challenges. These exercises test the students' understanding and mastery of the basic concepts and manipulative skills dealt with in the unit.

Answers to the odd-numbered exercises appear at the back of the book. A separate pamphlet with answers to the even-numbered exercises is available to teachers.

Introductory Algebra for College Students can be used effectively to train students to read a mathematics textbook with courage, comprehension, and enjoyment.

The authors dedicate this book to their wives Leona and Hilda, whose encouragement, patience, and understanding were towers of strength during its creation.

Robert E. Dressler
Isidore Dressler

CONTENTS

Chapter 1. Symbols, Numbers, and Numerals

Chapter 2. Sets

Chapter 3. Open Phrases, Open Sentences, and Truth Sets

Chapter 4. Properties of Operations

Chapter 5. Signed Numbers

Chapter 6. Operations With Polynomials

Chapter 7. First-Degree Equations and Inequalities
in One Variable

Chapter 8. Solving Problems by Using First-Degree Open Sentences in One Variable

Chapter 9. Special Products and Factoring

Chapter 10. Operations With Fractions

Chapter 11. First-Degree Equations and Inequalities Involving Fractions

Chapter 12. The Formula

Chapter 13. Graphs of Linear Open Sentences in Two Variables

Chapter 14. Systems of Linear Open Sentences in Two Variables

Chapter 15. Ratio, Proportion, and Variation

Chapter 16. The Real Numbers

Chapter 17. Quadratic Equations

Chapter 18. Trigonometry of the Right Triangle

Chapter 19. Relations and Functions

Chapter 1

Symbols, Numbers, and Numerals

1. Symbols and Numerals

SYMBOLS FOR NUMBERS

In your study of arithmetic, you used symbols to represent numbers. In algebra, we will work with the numbers of arithmetic and we will use their customary names and symbols. Number names or number symbols are called *numerals* or *numerical expressions*.

Remember that a numeral and the number it represents are not the same thing. A number is an idea that we can talk about and think about; a numeral is a name or symbol for a number. We know, for example, that the number 8 is larger than the number 6. In the figure, however, the numeral "6" is larger than the numeral "8."

SYMBOLS FOR OPERATIONS

The symbol "+" is used to indicate the operation of *addition*. The numeral "6 + 2" represents the result obtained when 2 is added to 6. The result, 8, is called the *sum*.

The symbol "×" is used to indicate the operation of *multiplication*. The numeral "6 × 2" represents the result obtained when 2 is multiplied by 6. The result, 12, is called the *product*.

The symbol "−" is used to indicate the operation of *subtraction*. The numeral "6 − 2" represents the result obtained when 2 is subtracted from 6. The result, 4, is called the *difference*.

The symbol "÷" is used to indicate the operation of *division*. The numeral "6 ÷ 2" represents the result obtained when 6 is divided by 2. The result, 3, is called the *quotient*. The fraction "$\frac{6}{2}$" also indicates a quotient which is the result of dividing 6 by 2.

Since addition, multiplication, subtraction, and division are operations which are performed on two numbers, each of these operations is called a *binary operation*.

A number may be represented by many numerals. For example, each of the following numerals may be used as a number name to count a collection of eight objects:

"8"	"eight"	"VIII"	"ocho"
"6 + 2"	"18 − 10"	"4 × 2"	"6400 ÷ 800"

Note that "8" is probably the simplest looking of all the preceding numerals, each of which represents the number 8.

EXERCISES

In 1–6, each sentence contains an underlined symbol. State whether the sentence refers to the object, person, or idea, or whether the sentence refers only to the symbol itself.

1. A <u>house</u> has a roof.
2. <u>House</u> ends with an *e*.
3. <u>Buffalo</u> is a word which has two *f*'s.
4. A <u>buffalo</u> is an animal.
5. Robert spelled <u>beauty</u> incorrectly.
6. She walks in <u>beauty</u> like the night.

In 7–10, tell which number every numeral in each exercise represents.

7. $3 + 1$ $6 - 2$ 4×1 $12 \div 3$ IV
8. $12 - 3$ $36 \div 4$ $8\frac{1}{2} + \frac{1}{2}$ $36 \times \frac{1}{4}$ IX
9. $5 - 5$ 7×0 $\frac{1}{2} - \frac{1}{2}$ $.7 - .7$ 0×1
10. $.5$ $\frac{1}{4} + \frac{1}{4}$ $1\frac{1}{2} - 1$ $\frac{25}{50}$ 50%

11. Write five different numerals for each of the following numbers:

    a. 6   b. 20   c. 100   d. 1   e. 0   f. $\frac{1}{4}$

In 12–19, state whether the two numerals represent the same number.

12. $5 + 3$, $16 \div 2$ 13. 8×1, 12×1 14. 8×0, 4×0
15. $\frac{1}{3} + \frac{1}{3}$, $\frac{1}{2} + \frac{1}{4}$ 16. $6 + 4$, $4 + 6$ 17. 5×7, 7×5
18. $8 \div 2$, $2 \div 8$ 19. 7×0, $7 - 0$

In 20–23, four of the five numerals in each exercise represent the same number. Select the numeral which represents a number different from this number.

20. $8 + 4$ $36 - 24$ 12×0 $24 \div 2$ $6 \div \frac{1}{2}$
21. 8×1 $8 - 0$ $1.5 + 6.5$ $80 \div 100$ 800%

22. $5 \times \frac{1}{5}$ $\frac{1}{2} + \frac{1}{2}$ $3\frac{2}{3} - 2\frac{2}{3}$ $1.25 \div 1.25$ 1%
23. $2 \times .15$ $\frac{1}{10} + \frac{1}{5}$ $.03 \times 10$ $\frac{4}{15} - \frac{1}{5}$ 30%

In 24–35, write a simpler looking numeral for each given numeral.

24. $\frac{3}{5} + \frac{7}{5}$ 25. $75 + 1.25$ 26. $\frac{3}{4} + \frac{5}{8}$ 27. $\frac{12}{7} - \frac{5}{7}$
28. $4.65 - 2.25$ 29. $\frac{15}{3} - \frac{1}{2}$ 30. $\frac{21}{2} \times \frac{1}{7}$ 31. $2.5 \times .64$
32. $6 - .35$ 33. 1.25×4 34. $6.28 \div 4$ 35. $60 \div 1.25$

2. The Numbers of Arithmetic

Let us recall the numbers with which you became familiar when you studied arithmetic. We shall refer to these numbers as the *numbers of arithmetic*.

COUNTING NUMBERS OR NATURAL NUMBERS

In your study of arithmetic, you learned how to count. You know that when we count, we start with a first number, which is named "one," or "1." The number which follows 1 is named "two," or "2." The number 2 is called the *successor* of the number 1. The number 2 in turn has a successor which is named "three," or "3." Each counting number has a successor which is one more than the number. Because of this, the process of counting is endless; there is no last counting number.

The *counting numbers*, which are also called *natural numbers*, are represented by the symbols:

$$1, 2, 3, 4, 5, 6, 7, 8, 9, 10, 11, 12, \ldots$$

The three dots after the 12 indicate that the numbers continue in the same pattern without end.

The first ten natural numbers may be represented by the symbols:

$$1, 2, 3, 4, \ldots, 10$$

The three dots after the 4 indicate that the numbers continue in the same pattern until 10 is reached.

WHOLE NUMBERS

If the only numbers of arithmetic at our disposal were the counting numbers, then we would not be able to subtract any counting number from itself. For example, there is no counting number that is the answer to the problem "Subtract 6 from 6." Later, when we study the solution of equations, we will have occasion to subtract a number from itself. To perform such subtractions, we need the number zero, written 0. Zero has the important property that if we subtract any number from itself, the answer is zero. For example, $6 - 6$ is 0 $(6 - 6 = 0)$, $1 - 1$ is 0 $(1 - 1 = 0)$, and $0 - 0$ is 0 $(0 - 0 = 0)$.

The number 0 is not one of the counting numbers. That is, 0 is not a natural number. Zero, together with all the natural numbers, forms a new collection of numbers called *whole numbers*. The whole numbers are represented by the symbols:

$$0, 1, 2, 3, 4, 5, 6, 7, 8, 9, 10, 11, 12, \ldots$$

FRACTIONS

If the only numbers of arithmetic at our disposal were the whole numbers, then we would not, in all cases, be able to divide a whole number by a counting number. For example, we would be able to divide 6 by 3 because the answer is 2; however, we would not be able to divide 7 by 3 because there is no whole number which is the answer. Later, when we study the solution of equations, we will have occasion to divide a whole number by a natural number. To perform such divisions we need numbers called *fractions*. The answer to the problem "Divide 7 by 3" is represented by the fraction $\frac{7}{3}$. We shall say that *a fraction is a symbol which indicates the quotient of two numbers*. You are familiar with fractions like $\frac{1}{2}, \frac{3}{4}, \frac{7}{3}, \frac{12}{5}, \frac{8}{8}$, and $\frac{20}{10}$.

Many different fractions may name the same number. For example, each of the different symbols $\frac{6}{3}, \frac{10}{5}, \frac{12}{6}$, and $\frac{36}{18}$ is a fraction which names the number 2.

Mixed numbers are numbers that are named by symbols such as $1\frac{1}{4}$, $4\frac{2}{3}, 5\frac{3}{8}$. Note that a mixed number is the sum of a whole number and a proper fraction. A mixed number may be named by many different fractions. For example, the number named by $1\frac{1}{4}$ can be represented by the fractions $\frac{5}{4}, \frac{10}{8}, \frac{15}{12}$, etc.

Decimal fractions are numbers that are named by symbols such as .4, .23, .035, 2.5. They can also be represented by quotients. For example, the number named by .4 can be represented by $\frac{4}{10}, \frac{2}{5}, \frac{8}{20}$, and so on.

RATIONAL NUMBERS

If a number can be represented by a fraction which indicates the quotient of a whole number divided by a natural number, the number is called a *rational number*.

For example, $\frac{1}{2}, \frac{2}{3}, 1\frac{1}{2}, .4, 3$, and 0 are rational numbers.

The whole numbers are included among the rational numbers because any whole number can be represented as a fraction which indicates the quotient of that number and 1. For example:

$$0 = \tfrac{0}{1} \qquad 1 = \tfrac{1}{1} \qquad 2 = \tfrac{2}{1} \qquad 3 = \tfrac{3}{1} \qquad 5 = \tfrac{5}{1} \qquad 10 = \tfrac{10}{1}$$

We see, therefore, that all the numbers of arithmetic which we have discussed are rational numbers.

For reasons that we shall learn later, we may not divide a number by zero (0). For example, $\tfrac{5}{0}$ has no value because it does not name any number. We say that division by zero is meaningless.

We shall learn later that not all fractions represent rational numbers. We shall also learn to work with additional rational numbers which are not among the numbers of arithmetic we have studied.

EXERCISES

1. Name the first counting number.
2. Name the successor of each of the following natural numbers:
    a. 75   b. 120   c. 999   d. 514,621   ·   e. 64,499,999
3. State a rule for finding the successor of a given natural number.
4. Name a number which is a whole number but is not a natural number.
5. Write four fractions that are different names for each of the following numbers:
    a. 4   b. 9   c. 12   d. 50   e. 0
6. Write four fractions that are different names for each of the following fractions:
    a. $\tfrac{1}{2}$ b. $\tfrac{3}{4}$ c. $\tfrac{4}{6}$ d. $\tfrac{8}{5}$ e. $\tfrac{7}{1}$
7. Write four fractions that are different names for each of the following decimal fractions:
    a. .6   b. .25   c. .80   d. 1.5   e. 2.75
8. Write four fractions that are different names for each of the following mixed numbers:
    a. $1\tfrac{1}{4}$ b. $2\tfrac{1}{2}$ c. $4\tfrac{3}{4}$ d. $10\tfrac{1}{5}$ e. $12\tfrac{2}{3}$
9. State which of the numbers $0, 3, 5, \tfrac{1}{5}, 1\tfrac{1}{4}$ are (a) natural numbers (b) whole numbers (c) rational numbers.
10. State which of the symbols $0, 1, \tfrac{0}{1}, \tfrac{1}{0}$ represent (a) natural numbers (b) whole numbers (c) rational numbers.

In 11–22, state whether the sentence is true or false.

11. Every counting number is a natural number.
12. Every natural number is a whole number.
13. Every whole number is a natural number.
14. Every natural number has a successor.

15. There is a first counting number.
16. There is a last natural number.
17. A whole number may be represented by many different fractions.
18. Every fraction names a whole number.
19. Every whole number is a rational number.
20. Every rational number is a whole number.
21. Every rational number may be represented as a fraction.
22. Every fraction represents a rational number.

3. The Number Line

If we think of a straight line as a collection or set of points, we can *associate* (make correspond) all the numbers of arithmetic (each of which is a rational number) with points on the line. Such a line is called a *number line*.

To construct a number line, we choose two points on a straight line. We label the point at the left "0" and the one at the right "1." We use the length of the segment from 0 to 1 as a unit of measure to mark off equally spaced points to the right of 1. The numbers 2, 3, 4, and so on, are assigned to these points as shown.

The arrowhead indicates that the number line extends without end to the right. Therefore, it is possible to associate every whole number with a point on the line. Note that every point that we have located on the line is associated with a whole number.

Consider a number line on which points have been associated with whole numbers. If we divide the intervals between whole numbers into halves, thirds, quarters, and smaller subdivisions, we can label additional points as shown.

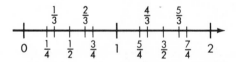

On the number line, each point that has been located is associated with a rational number. The number associated with a point on the number line is called the *coordinate* of that point. The point on the number line which is associated with a number is called the *graph* of that number.

Notice that on a number line the point which is associated with the smaller of two numbers is to the left of the point associated with the larger of the two numbers. For example, the number 1 is less than the number 2; the point labeled 1 lies to the left of the point labeled 2. Any number less than 1 corresponds to a point to the left of 1. On the other hand, any number greater than 1 corresponds to a point to the right of 1.

When we say that 1 is *between* 0 and 2, we mean that 1 is greater than 0 but less than 2; also, the graph of 1 is to the right of the graph of 0 but to the left of the graph of 2.

No matter how close two points may be on a number line, there is always an infinite number of points between them. Some of these points can be graphed (determined) by dividing the interval between the points which are associated with the whole numbers into more and more equal parts. For example, the interval between the points associated with the numbers 0 and 1 can be divided first into halves, then into thirds, then into fourths, then into smaller subdivisions, thus obtaining an infinite number of points. Therefore, there are infinitely many numbers that can be named between any two given numbers, no matter how close together they may be. For example, since $\frac{1}{2}$ may also be named $\frac{12}{24}$, and $\frac{2}{3}$ may also be named $\frac{16}{24}$, the numbers $\frac{13}{24}$, $\frac{14}{24}$, and $\frac{15}{24}$ are between $\frac{1}{2}$ and $\frac{2}{3}$. Similarly, since $\frac{1}{2}$ may also be named $\frac{24}{48}$, and $\frac{2}{3}$ may also be named $\frac{32}{48}$, the numbers $\frac{25}{48}$, $\frac{26}{48}$, . . . , $\frac{31}{48}$ are between $\frac{1}{2}$ and $\frac{2}{3}$. You can see that this process is endless.

From our previous discussion, it appears that every rational number can be associated with a point on a number line. It may also appear that every point on a number line has been associated with some rational number. However, this is not true. Later we will learn that there are infinitely many points on a number line which cannot be associated with rational numbers. We will associate these points with other collections of numbers that we will study.

Model Problems

Use the number line in the figure to answer questions 1–10.

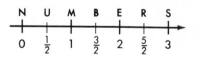

1. Name the number assigned to point *S*.   *Ans.* 3
2. Name the coordinate of point *M*.   *Ans.* 1
3. Name the point which is the graph of $\frac{1}{2}$.   *Ans.* U
4. Name the point which is the graph of $1\frac{1}{2}$.   *Ans.* B
5. Name the points which are associated with
    natural numbers.   *Ans.* M, E, S

6. Name the points which are the graphs of
   whole numbers.   *Ans.* N, M, E, S
7. Name the points which are the graphs of
   fractions.   *Ans.* U, B, R
8. Name the points which are the graphs of
   rational numbers.   *Ans.* N, U, M, B, E, R, S
9. Name the point which is the graph of a
   whole number that is not a natural
   number.   *Ans.* N
10. Give three additional numerals which can   *Ans.* $\frac{2}{2}, \frac{3}{3}, \frac{4}{4}$
    be used to represent the coordinate of   (There are many other
    point M.   possible answers.)
11. On the number line shown at the right,
    locate the points that can be asso-
    ciated with the numbers   (a) $\frac{1}{3}$
    (b) .5   (c) $\frac{20}{20}$ (d) $1\frac{2}{3}$ (e) 1.8.

Answer:
a. Point G, which is $\frac{1}{3}$ of the way from
   M to A.

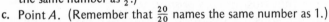

b. Point R, which is $\frac{1}{2}$ of the way from
   M to A. (Remember that .5 names
   the same number as $\frac{1}{2}$.)
c. Point A. (Remember that $\frac{20}{20}$ names the same number as 1.)
d. Point P, which is $\frac{2}{3}$ of the way from A to T. (Remember that $1\frac{2}{3}$ names
   the same number as $\frac{5}{3}$.)
e. Point H, which is $\frac{4}{5}$ of the way from A to T. (Remember that 1.8
   names the same number as $\frac{18}{10}$ or $\frac{9}{5}$.)
12. a. How many whole numbers are there be-
       tween 3 and 6?   *Ans.* Two
    b. List these numbers.   *Ans.* 4, 5
13. a. How many numbers are there between
       3 and 6?   *Ans.* Infinitely many
    b. List four numbers between 3 and 6.   *Ans.* 3.5, $\frac{13}{3}$, 5, $5\frac{1}{2}$
                                                 (There are many other
                                                 possible answers.)

EXERCISES

In 1–4, name the number that can be associated with each of the
labeled points on the number line.

1.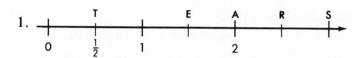

2.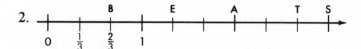

3.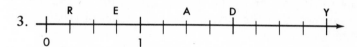

4.

5. Draw a number line and locate on it the points whose coordinates are:

   a. $\frac{1}{4}, \frac{3}{4}, \frac{6}{4}, \frac{8}{4}, \frac{13}{4}, \frac{16}{4}$

   b. $\frac{1}{10}, \frac{5}{10}, \frac{9}{10}, \frac{13}{10}, \frac{25}{10}, \frac{30}{10}$

   c. $\frac{1}{5}, \frac{3}{5}, \frac{9}{5}, \frac{10}{5}, 2\frac{1}{5}, 3\frac{2}{5}$

   d. .1, .3, .7, 1.0, 2.7, 3.4

   e. $\frac{1}{4}, \frac{1}{2}, \frac{3}{8}, 1\frac{1}{4}, 2.25, \frac{25}{8}$

   f. $\frac{1}{4}, \frac{1}{3}, \frac{5}{12}, \frac{9}{6}, 2\frac{1}{2}, 3.75$

   g. rational numbers represented by fractions whose denominators are 3, beginning with $\frac{1}{3}$ and ending with $\frac{15}{3}$

   In 6–11, use the following number line:

   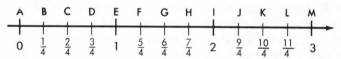

6. Name the point which is the graph of the number:

   a. 1   b. $\frac{8}{4}$ c. $1\frac{3}{4}$ d. $2\frac{1}{2}$ e. .5   f. 1.25   g. 2.75

7. Give three different names for the coordinate of each of the following points:

   a. E b. C c. D d. G e. L

8. Name the points which are associated with natural numbers.

9. Name the points which are the graphs of whole numbers.

10. Name the points which are the graphs of rational numbers.

11. Name the point which is the graph of a whole number that is not a natural number.

12. State the number of natural numbers that are between:

    a. 0 and 1   b. 2 and 3   c. 2 and 6   d. 1 and 10

13. List the natural numbers between:

    a. 2 and 6   **b.** 3 and 8   **c.** 1 and 10   **d.** 12 and 17

    In 14-17:   **(a)** State the number of rational numbers between the given numbers.   **(b)** List three numbers between the given numbers.

14. 5, 6   **15.** $\frac{5}{100}$, $\frac{6}{100}$ **16.** .4, .5   **17.** .24, .25

    In 18-29:   **(a)** State whether on a number line the graph of the first number lies to the left or to the right of the graph of the second number.   **(b)** State whether the first number is smaller or greater than the second number.

18. 12, 18	**19.** 29, 23	**20.** $\frac{9}{2}$, $\frac{4}{2}$	**21.** $\frac{1}{4}$, $\frac{1}{8}$
22. $3\frac{2}{3}$, $5\frac{1}{3}$	**23.** 3.9, 1.3	**24.** 3.1, 9.3	**25.** .5, .05
26. 11, 110	**27.** .47, 4.7	**28.** 6.4, 6.45	**29.** .95, .905

30. Name a number between:

    a. 8 and 9   **b.** .8 and .9   **c.** 3.21 and 3.22   **d.** 4.666 and 4.667

4. Comparing Numbers

SYMBOL OF EQUALITY

    The equal sign, =, is read "equals" or "is equal to." When the symbol = is placed between two numerals, it indicates that the numerals represent the same number. To indicate that the numerals "7 + 2" and "5 + 4" both represent the same number, 9, we write "7 + 2 = 5 + 4" which is read "seven plus two equals five plus four."

    A statement that two numerals represent the same number is called an *equality*. Such a statement may be a true statement or a false statement. For example, 7 + 2 = 5 + 4 is a true statement because 7 + 2 represents the number 9 and 5 + 4 also represents the number 9. But 7 − 2 = 5 − 4 is a false statement because 7 − 2 represents the number 5, whereas 5 − 4 represents the number 1.

EXERCISES

    In 1-12, state whether the statement is true or false. Give a reason for your answer.

1. 5 + 4 = 4 + 5	**2.** 12 × 4 = 4 × 12	**3.** 5 − 3 = 3 − 5
4. 12 ÷ 4 = 4 ÷ 12	**5.** 6 + 0 = 6	**6.** 6 × 0 = 6
7. 6 − 0 = 6	**8.** 0 ÷ 6 = 0	**9.** 6 ÷ 0 = 6
10. .5 + .4 = .09	**11.** 5 × .4 = 10 × .2	**12.** $5 \times \frac{1}{5} = 2 \div 2$

In 13–18, replace the question mark with a numeral which will make the resulting statement true.

13. $8 + ? = 4 + 6$ **14.** $8 - ? = 5 \times 1$ **15.** $7 - ? = 7 \times 1$
16. $\frac{1}{4} + ? = 1 - \frac{1}{4}$ **17.** $.8 + .2 = 4 \times ?$ **18.** $4 \times .5 = 12 \div ?$

SYMBOLS OF INEQUALITY

The false statement $3 + 6 = 5$ may be changed to a true statement by replacing the symbol $=$ with the symbol $\neq$, read "is not equal to." Thus, $3 + 6 \neq 5$ is a true statement. A statement that one number is not equal to another number is called an *inequality*.

For any two numbers of arithmetic, we can say that one must be greater than the other, equal to the other, or less than the other. This statement is called the *law of trichotomy*. To compare unequal numbers, we use the following symbols:

$>$ is read "is greater than." Thus, $4 > 2$ is read "4 is greater than 2."

$<$ is read "is less than." Thus, $1 < 3$ is read "1 is less than 3."

$\not>$ is read "is not greater than." Thus, $2 \not> 7$ is read "2 is not greater than 7."

$\not<$ is read "is not less than." Thus, $5 \not< 4$ is read "5 is not less than 4."

Notice that in an inequality which is a true statement involving the symbol $>$ or $<$ (for example, $4 > 2$ or $1 < 3$) the symbol points to the *smaller* number.

An inequality, just like an equality, may be a true statement or a false statement.

Model Problems

In 1–8, tell whether the statement is true or false.

1. $6 + 7 \neq 15$	*Ans.* True		**2.** $0 \neq 8 - 8$	*Ans.* False
3. $8 + 6 > 10$	*Ans.* True		**4.** $3 \times 6 \not> 10$	*Ans.* False
5. $20 \div 5 < 8$	*Ans.* True		**6.** $15 - 13 \not< 7$	*Ans.* False
7. $\frac{1}{2} \times \frac{1}{2} < 1$	*Ans.* True		**8.** $8\frac{6}{7} + \frac{1}{5} \not> 9$	*Ans.* False

EXERCISES

In 1–5, state whether the inequality is true or false.

1. $8 + 5 \neq 6 + 4$ **2.** $9 + 2 \neq 2 + 9$ **3.** $6 \times 0 \neq 4 \times 0$
4. The sum of 8 and 12 is not equal to the product of 24 and 4.

5. The product of 5 and 4 is not equal to 5 divided by 4.

In 6–11, write the inequality using the symbol $>$ or the symbol $<$.

6. 25 is greater than 20.   7. $12 + 3$ is less than 20.
8. $6 - 3$ is less than $5 + 4$.   9. $80 \div 4$ is greater than $6 + 3$.
10. The sum of 9 and 4 is less than the product of 10 and 5.
11. The sum of 8 and 7 is greater than the quotient 20 divided by 5.

In 12–14, express each inequality in words.

12. $9 + 8 > 16$ 13. $12 - 2 < 4 \times 7$ 14. $5 + 24 \not> 90 \div 3$

In 15–23, state whether the inequality is true or false.

15. $20 - 4 < 5 + 8$ 16. $6 \times 0 > 3 + 5$ 17. $18 + 0 > 4 + 0$
18. $2.05 < 20.5$ 19. $\frac{1}{2} + \frac{1}{8} < .8$ 20. $3 - .25 > 2\frac{1}{2}$
21. $4.6 - 2.1 > 1.5 + .9$ 22. $8 \times .5 \not< 6 \div \frac{1}{2}$ 23. $\frac{1}{2} + \frac{1}{3} \not> 1 - \frac{1}{4}$

In 24–29, replace the question mark with a numeral which will make the resulting statement true.

24. $5 + ? \neq 11$ 25. $? - 7 > 3$ 26. $15 \div 5 < ? \div 2$
27. $8 \times \frac{1}{2} \neq 6 - ?$ 28. $10 \div ? \not> 10$ 29. $4 - .7 \not< 1 \times ?$

In 30–35, state which of the symbols $+, -, \times, \div$ can replace the question mark to make the resulting statement true.

30. $4 ? 2 \neq 6$ 31. $20 ? 5 > 10$ 32. $12 ? 6 < 10$
33. $\frac{1}{2} < 1 ? \frac{1}{4}$ 34. $6 - 4 > 6 ? 4$ 35. $3 + 1.5 > 3 ? 2$

ORDERING NUMBERS ON A NUMBER LINE

On a number line, the smaller of two numbers appears to the left of the larger, and the larger of the two numbers appears  to the right of the smaller. Thus, the true statement $2 < 4$ tells us that on a number line the graph of 2 is to the left of the graph of 4. The true statement $4 > 2$ tells us that the graph of 4 is to the right of the graph of 2. We say that the phrases "less than" and "greater than" express an *order relation*, as is illustrated by the order in which the numbers appear on a number line.

We know that the statement "4 is between 2 and 6" means that 4 is greater than 2 $(4 > 2)$ and also that 4 is less than 6 $(4 < 6)$. On a number line, 2 is to the left of 4 and also 4 is to the left of 6. Hence, we can combine the symbols $4 > 2$ and $4 < 6$ into a single symbol "$2 < 4 < 6$." This symbol is read "2 is less than 4 and 4 is less than 6" or "4 is between 2 and 6." We may also express the statement "4 is between 2 and 6" as follows: "$6 > 4 > 2$." This symbol is read "6 is greater than 4 and 4 is greater than 2."

EXERCISES

In 1–5, state how you can tell from a number line that the statement is true.

1. $1 < 7$ **2.** $10 > 5$ **3.** $0 < 6$ **4.** $\frac{3}{4} < 1$ **5.** $2\frac{1}{2} > 1.5$

In 6–15, arrange the numbers in proper order so that they will appear from left to right on a number line.

6. 5, 8   **7.** 16, 4   **8.** $\frac{1}{2}, \frac{1}{4}$ **9.** 2.5, 3.2
10. $2\frac{3}{5}$, 2.8   **11.** 2, 3, 9   **12.** 9, 6, 11   **13.** $\frac{1}{4}, \frac{7}{8}, \frac{2}{3}$
14. 3.2, 2.6, 4.3   **15.** $3\frac{1}{3}$, 3.75, $3\frac{1}{4}$

In 16–19, select the number that is between the other two numbers, and use the symbol $<$ to write that the selected number is between the other two.

16. 13, 17, 9   **17.** $5\frac{1}{3}, 4\frac{1}{2}, 6\frac{1}{4}$ **18.** 4.7, 6.6, 5.3   **19.** $4\frac{7}{8}, 4.5, 5\frac{1}{4}$

5. Order of Operations

Sometimes a numeral is enclosed in parentheses to indicate clearly that it is a numeral. For example, "$(5 + 3)$" is another numeral for 8.

A *numerical phrase*, sometimes called a *numerical expression*, is any numeral written as an expression that involves numerals together with signs of operation. For example, "$4 + 3$," "5×7," "$(8 + 6) - 3$," and "$(9 + 7) - (3 + 6)$" are numerical phrases. Since a numerical phrase must name a number, the symbol "$(5^+) \times (3_-)$" is not a numerical phrase.

The symbol "$5 + 3 \times 2$" does not name a definite number. "$5 + 3 \times 2$" might mean $5 + 6$, or 11; or it might mean 8×2, or 16. To give a single meaning to this symbol and others like it, mathematicians have agreed to follow a procedure which gives the order of operations in such expressions.

Procedure. In numerical expressions involving numerals along with signs of operation:

1. **Do all multiplications and divisions first, performing them in order from left to right.**
2. **Then do all additions and subtractions, performing them in order from left to right.**

By following the above procedure, expressions such as "$5 + 3 \times 2$" may be used as numerical phrases.

Model Problems

1. Give the meaning of the numerical phrase $15 - 12 \div 2$.

   Solution: $15 - 12 \div 2$ means that the quotient of 12 and 2 is to be subtracted from 15.

2. Find a simpler name for the numerical phrase $28 - 4 \times 2$.

How to Proceed	*Solution*
1. Write the numerical phrase.	$28 - 4 \times 2$
2. Do the multiplication first.	$= 28 - 8$
3. Then do the subtraction.	$= 20$ *Ans.*

3. Simplify the numerical phrase $30 - 10 \div 5 + 6 \times 2$.

How to Proceed	*Solution*
1. Write the numerical phrase.	$30 - 10 \div 5 + 6 \times 2$
2. First do the multiplication and division from left to right.	$= 30 - 2 + 12$
3. Then do the addition and subtraction.	$= 40$ *Ans.*

EXERCISES

In 1–9: (a) Give the meaning of the numerical phrase. (b) Find a simpler name for the numerical phrase.

1. $5 + 3 \times 7$
2. $6 + 8 \times 2$
3. $15 - 6 \times 2$
4. $14 - 2 \times 5$
5. $10 + 8 \div 2$
6. $16 \div 4 + 4$
7. $26 - 14 \div 2$
8. $72 \div 8 - 2$
9. $9 \times 2 + 3 \times 4$

In 10–15, simplify the numerical phrase.

10. $6 \times 5 - 8 \times 2$
11. $20 + 20 \div 5 + 5$
12. $36 - 12 \div 4 - 1$
13. $36 + \frac{1}{2} \times 10$
14. $24 - 4 \div \frac{1}{2}$
15. $28 + 0 \div 4 - 10 \times .2$

6. Using Grouping Symbols

In mathematics, parentheses are used to indicate the meaning of an expression. For example, if we wish "$4 \times 6 + 7$" to mean that the number represented by "4×6" and the number represented by "7" are to be added, we write "$(4 \times 6) + 7$." However, if we wish "$4 \times 6 + 7$"

to mean 4 times the number represented by "6 + 7," we write "4 × (6 + 7)," or merely "4(6 + 7)." Notice that the part of the expression which is to be considered as a numeral is enclosed in the parentheses.

Thus, 30 − (6 + 5) means 30 − 11, or 19.

Also, 6(4 + 1) means 6(5), which means 6 × 5, or 30.

To simplify a numerical phrase which involves parentheses, first perform the operations indicated on the numbers within the parentheses.

Observe that the use of a grouping symbol makes it possible to give a numerical phrase a meaning other than the meaning it would have according to the agreement on the order of operations. For example, we have agreed that 4 × 6 + 7 means 24 + 7, or 31. However, 4 × (6 + 7) means 4 × 13, or 52.

In addition to the parentheses, another symbol of grouping is used to show that a given expression is to be considered as a numeral. This symbol is called *brackets*, and is written [ ].

The expressions 2(5 + 9) and 2[5 + 9] both mean that the sum of 5 and 9 is to be multiplied by 2.

A bar may also be used below an expression that is to be considered as a numeral. In the fraction $\frac{20 - 8}{3}$, the bar, or fraction line, indicates that the number (20 − 8) is to be divided by 3. Therefore, $\frac{20 - 8}{3} = \frac{12}{3} = 4$.

When there are two or more grouping symbols in an expression, we perform the operations on the numbers in the innermost symbol first. For example:

$$5 + 2[6 + (3 - 1) \times 4]$$
$$= 5 + 2[6 + 2 \times 4]$$
$$= 5 + 2[6 + 8]$$
$$= 5 + 2 \times 14$$
$$= 5 + 28$$
$$= 33$$

Model Problem

Simplify the numerical expression 80 − 4(6 − 4).

How to Proceed	Solution
1. Write the expression.	$80 - 4(6 - 4)$
2. Simplify the expression within the parentheses.	$= 80 - 4(2)$
3. Do the multiplication.	$= 80 - 8$
4. Do the subtraction.	$= 72$ *Ans.*

EXERCISES

In 1–8, state the meaning of the symbol in part **a** and the meaning of the symbol in part **b** and give the most common (the simplest) name for each symbol.

1. **a.** $20 + (6 + 1)$ **b.** $20 + 6 + 1$
2. **a.** $18 - (4 + 3)$ **b.** $18 - 4 + 3$
3. **a.** $17 + (6 - 4)$ **b.** $17 + 6 - 4$
4. **a.** $12 - (3 - \frac{1}{2})$ **b.** $12 - 3 - \frac{1}{2}$
5. **a.** $15 \times (2 + 1)$ **b.** $15 \times 2 + 1$
6. **a.** $.4 \times (8 + 2)$ **b.** $.4 \times 8 + 2$
7. **a.** $(12 + 8) \div 4$ **b.** $12 + 8 \div 4$
8. **a.** $48 \div (8 - 4)$ **b.** $48 \div 8 - 4$

In 9–14, use parentheses to express the sentence in symbols.

9. The sum of 10 and 8 is to be found and then 5 is to be subtracted from this sum.
10. 15 is to be subtracted from 25, and 7 is to be added to the difference.
11. 8 is to be multiplied by the difference of 6 and 2.
12. 12 is to be subtracted from the product of 10 and 5.
13. The difference of 12 and 2 is to be multiplied by the sum of 3 and 4.
14. The quotient of 20 and 5 is to be subtracted from the product of 16 and 3.

In 15–35, simplify the numerical expression.

15. $10 + (1 + 4)$ 16. $36 - (10 - 8)$ 17. $(6 - 1)10$
18. $20 \div (7 + 3)$ 19. $48 \div (15 - 3)$ 20. $15 - (15 \div 5)$
21. $26 - 4(7 - 5)$ 22. $25 \div (6 - 1) + 3$ 23. $3(6 + 4)(6 - 4)$

24. $\dfrac{12 - 5 + 14}{3}$ 25. $\dfrac{39}{8 + 7 - 2}$ 26. $\dfrac{10 + 14}{10 - 2}$

27. $\dfrac{7(6 + 14)}{2}$ 28. $\frac{3}{2}(6 + 9)$ 29. $\frac{1}{2}(8)(12 + 14)$

30. $10[4 + (7 - 1) \times 5]$ 31. $75 - [6(8 - 6) + 3]$
32. $36 + 4[1 + (12 - 8) \times 2]$ 33. $[6(5\frac{1}{2}) - 4](\frac{3}{8} + \frac{5}{8})$
34. $[.2 + 1.3][3.2 - \frac{1}{2}(.9 + .7)]$ 35. $(6\frac{1}{4} + 11\frac{6}{8}) \div 4(4 - 2.5)$

7. Expressing Verbal Phrases and Sentences by Using Mathematical Symbols

Study the following model problems to learn how to express verbal phrases and number relationships by using mathematical symbols.

Model Problems

Use mathematical symbols to express each of the following:

1. Four increased by the product of two and one.

   Ans. $4 + 2 \times 1$, or $4 + (2 \times 1)$

2. Twelve decreased by the quotient of six and three.

   Ans. $12 - 6 \div 3$, or $12 - (6 \div 3)$

3. The product of nine and five is to be decreased by the sum of eight and seven.

   Ans. $9 \times 5 - (8 + 7)$, or $(9 \times 5) - (8 + 7)$

4. When nine is added to the quotient of eight and four, the result is eleven.

   Ans. $8 \div 4 + 9 = 11$, or $(8 \div 4) + 9 = 11$

5. When twice the difference between sixteen and four is decreased by three, the result is greater than zero.

   Ans. $2(16 - 4) - 3 > 0$

EXERCISES

In 1–15, express the phrase or sentence by using mathematical symbols.

1. Five increased by the product of six and seven.
2. One hundred decreased by the product of eight and four.
3. The sum of one and eight, added to ten.
4. Eighteen decreased by twice the sum of three and four.
5. When eight is added to four times six, the result is thirty-two.
6. When twenty-seven is decreased by the sum of seven and three, the result is seventeen.
7. When fourteen is increased by twice the sum of four-tenths and six-tenths, the result is sixteen.
8. The sum of six and twelve is not equal to twenty.
9. Sixteen reduced by fourteen is greater than one.
10. The quotient of thirty and two, decreased by the product of two and four, is less than twenty-five.

11. The difference between eighteen and ten, divided by five, is not equal to nine.
12. When twice the sum of seven and four is decreased by the product of ten and zero, the result is twenty-two.
13. When the product of fifty and ten is added to twice the sum of eight and fifteen, the result is less than one thousand.
14. The difference between sixteen and one, divided by the sum of two and three, is not equal to seven.
15. When five-tenths of three hundred is added to three-tenths of the difference between eight hundred and three hundred, the sum equals three hundred.

In 16–25, express the symbol as a verbal phrase or a verbal sentence.

16. $5 \times 6 - 4$

17. $(.5 + .3) - .4$

18. $20 \div 5 - (2 + 1)$

19. $(15 + 5) - (15 - 5)$

20. $2 \times (7 + 3) - 10$

21. $20 - (5 + 1) = 40 \times .3$

22. $(28 + 12) \div 5 = 8(6 - 1)$

23. $2 \times (6\frac{1}{2} + \frac{5}{2}) \neq 20$

24. $20 - .2(3 + 1) > 9$

25. $(5 - 1) \div (4 + 3) < 10 - 9$

Chapter 2

Sets

The concept of a *set* plays an important role in the study of algebra. Two nineteenth-century mathematicians, George Boole and Georg Cantor, were early pioneers in the development of many ideas concerning the theory of sets.

1. The Meaning of a Set and Set Notation

When a collection of distinct objects is so clearly described that it is always possible to tell whether or not an object belongs to it, we call the collection a **well-defined set**, or a **set**. For example, the odd counting numbers less than 10 form a set. The numbers 1, 3, 5, 7, and 9 belong to this set, whereas 2, 4, and 6 do not.

Every object that belongs to a set is called a **member**, or an **element**, of the set. For example, a trumpet is a member of the set of wind instruments; the number 5 is an element of the set of counting numbers.

HOW TO INDICATE A SET

One way of indicating a set is to list the names of its elements between braces, { }. For example, to indicate the set whose elements are 2, 4, 6, 8, we can write {2, 4, 6, 8}. This method of representation is called **tabulating** the set, or giving a **list**, or **roster**, of the set.

By using a capital letter, such as A, to represent the set, we can write $A = \{2, 4, 6, 8\}$. This is read "A is the set whose elements are 2, 4, 6, and 8." To indicate that the number 4 is an element of set A, we use the symbol $\in$ and write $4 \in A$. To indicate that the number 5 is not an element of set A, we use the symbol $\notin$ and write $5 \notin A$.

The elements of a set may be listed in any order. For example,

{2, 4, 6, 8} and {8, 6, 4, 2} represent the same set whose elements are listed differently.

It is not necessary for the elements of a set to be related to one another in any way other than that they are listed together. If we wish certain objects to be the elements of a set, we simply list them as members of the set. Thus, in the set {golf, Saturday, cow, football} the elements of the set are related to each other in no obvious way other than that they are listed as the members of a set.

To write the word "keep," four symbols are used. However, the set of letters to which these symbols refer has only three elements, the letters k, e, and p. Therefore, we say that the word "keep" is composed of the letters of the set {k, e, p}. Observe that when we use the roster method of describing a set, the same element is listed only once.

It is sometimes inconvenient to list the elements of a set. For example, if we wish to indicate the set of even whole numbers between 1 and 999, we would have to list {2, 4, 6, . . . , 998}, a total of 499 numbers. In such a case we can describe the set using words, that is, state a rule which describes the elements of the set. We may do this as follows: {even whole numbers between 1 and 999}.

There is still another way of describing a set, by using a new symbol, as shown in the following example:

This is read:

{ n | n is an even whole number between 1 and 999}.

the set   all   such n is an even whole number between 1 and 999.
  of   elements   that
            n

This method of describing a set is called the **set-builder notation**.

In the sentence, "n is an even whole number between 1 and 999," the letter n does not name a specific number as do the symbols 1 and 999. The letter n is a **placeholder** for any element of a given set of numbers. When a symbol such as n, x, y, or $*$ is used in this way, it is called a **variable**. We shall discuss variables in greater detail in a later chapter.

Some familiar sets of numbers whose elements were studied in arithmetic are:

the set of counting (or natural) numbers: {1, 2, 3, 4, . . .}.
the set of whole numbers: {0, 1, 2, 3, 4, . . .}.
the set of even whole numbers: {0, 2, 4, 6, . . .}.
the set of odd whole numbers: {1, 3, 5, 7, . . .}.

Model Problems

1. Indicate the set of letters a, b, c, d, e by **(a)** listing the elements, **(b)** describing the set in words using a rule, and **(c)** using set-builder notation.

   Solution:

   a. $\{a, b, c, d, e\}$.
   b. {first 5 letters in the English alphabet}.
   c. $\{* \mid *$ is one of the first five letters in the English alphabet$\}$.

2. a. Using set-builder notation, write a symbol that represents the set of all odd numbers.
   b. Using the result obtained in part **a**, indicate that 5 is an odd number.
   c. Indicate that 8 is not an odd number.

   Solution:

   a. $\{n \mid n$ is an odd number$\}$.
   b. $5 \in \{n \mid n$ is an odd number$\}$.
   c. $8 \notin \{n \mid n$ is an odd number$\}$.

EXERCISES

In 1–6, describe two sets whose elements are:

1. women   2. fish   3. tools
4. buildings   5. ships   6. numbers

In 7–14, tell whether the collection may be regarded as a set.

7. hat, top, day   8. 1, 2, 3, 5, 6   9. some even numbers
10. all pretty girls   11. all odd natural numbers
12. all honest men   13. 2, 4, 6, 8, 10   14. all small numbers

In 15–17, the elements of a set are given. Indicate the set by listing its members.

15. June, Tuesday, Easter   16. 11, 13, 15, 17   17. violin, piano, drum

In 18–20, (a) indicate the set by using set-builder notation and (b) name the variable used.

18. {Sunday, Monday, Tuesday}   19. $\{2, 4, 6, 8\}$ 20. $\{1, 3, 5, 7\}$

In 21–29, state whether the sentence is true or false.

21. Paul is an element of the set {Cary, Paul, Harold}.
22. 4 is an element of the set $\{14, 24, 34, 44\}$.
23. 8 is not an element of the set of odd natural numbers.
24. $12 \in \{10, 12, 14, 16, 18, 20\}$.
25. $\triangle \in \{\circ, \varangle, \square, \square\}$.

26. bat $\notin$ {base, glove, bat, ball}.
27. $\frac{1}{2} \notin \{1, \frac{3}{2}, \frac{2}{3}\}$.
28. $0 \in \{n \mid n$ is a whole number}.
29. $1 \notin \{n \mid n$ is an odd whole number}.
30. Select from the following those which are elements of the set of counting numbers:

    a. 7   b. $\frac{2}{3}$ c. 22   d. 0   e. 1

    In 31–37, represent the set that is described by listing its members.
31. The set of United States Presidents since Franklin D. Roosevelt
32. The set of letters in the word "prevail"
33. The set of letters in the word "Missouri"
34. The set of months that have 31 days
35. The set of odd natural numbers greater than 70 and less than 80
36. The set of even natural numbers between 11 and 19
37. The set of odd numbers by which 36 is exactly divisible
38. Write the set whose elements are the digits used in writing the number:

    a. 100   b. 1000   c. 5756   d. 9999

    In 39–42, describe by a rule the set that is indicated.
39. {Alaska, Arizona, Alabama, Arkansas}
40. {21, 23, 25, 27, 29}
41. {3, 6, 9, 12, 15, 18}
42. {Huron, Ontario, Superior, Michigan, Erie}

    In 43–45, state whether the sentence is true or false.
43. {horse, mule, pony} is the same set as {mule, pony, horse}.
44. {trout, salmon, bass} is the same set as {pike, bass, salmon, trout}.
45. {6, 12, 18} is the same set as {all counting numbers between 1 and 20 that are exactly divisible by 6}.

    In 46–48, represent the set by listing its members.
46. $\{x \mid x$ is a whole number less than 6}.
47. $\{n \mid n$ is an even whole number less than 10}.
48. $\{y \mid y$ is a natural number greater than 4 and less than 11}.
49. a. Using set-builder notation, write a symbol that represents the set of all natural numbers.
    b. Using the result obtained in part a, indicate that 0 is not a natural number.
    c. Indicate that 4 is a natural number.

    In 50–53, restate the sentence using set-builder notation.
50. 6 is an even whole number.
51. 7 is not an even whole number.
52. 20 is a whole number which is greater than 13.
53. 19 is not an even number less than 20.

2. Kinds of Sets and Relations Between Sets

FINITE SETS

We have learned that the set of odd natural numbers less than 10,000, a set which has a large number of elements, may be indicated as follows:

$$\{1, 3, 5, 7, 9, 11, \ldots, 9999\}$$

Since there is an end to the tabulation of the elements of this set, the number of elements in the set can be counted. We call a set whose elements can be counted a *finite set*. Some examples of finite sets are:

1. the set of professional basketball players
2. the set of natural numbers less than 100

THE EMPTY SET

It is possible for a set to have no elements. For example, the set of women more than 10 feet tall has no members. Such a set is called the *empty set*, or *null set*. It is usually designated by the symbol $\emptyset$. The empty set may also be expressed by a pair of empty braces { }. Other descriptions of the empty set are:

1. the set of months that begin with the letter B
2. the set of odd numbers exactly divisible by 4

Since the empty set is a set with no elements, it is a finite set.

Note that $\{0\}$ is not the null set because it is a set that has one element, the number 0.

INFINITE SETS

Sometimes the listing of the elements of a set is an endless process. For example, it is impossible to tabulate all the elements of the set of odd numbers. In this case, we indicate the set as follows:

$$\{1, 3, 5, 7, 9, \ldots\}$$

Since there is no end to listing the members of this set, there is no end to counting its members. We call such a set an *infinite set*. That is, an infinite set is one that is not finite. Some examples of an infinite set are:

1. the set of natural numbers
2. the set of even numbers
3. the set of whole numbers greater than 1 billion

EXERCISES

In 1–4, tabulate the elements of the set that is described. Use three dots when convenient or necessary.

1. {odd numbers between 300 and 310}
2. {multiples of 5 between 1 and 49}
3. {even natural numbers less than 500 that are exactly divisible by 4}
4. {whole numbers exactly divisible by 3}

In 5–22, state whether the set is the empty set, a finite but non-empty set, or an infinite set.

5. The set of all people who live in the United States today
6. The set of all animals in the world
7. The set of men who weigh a ton
8. The set of all natural numbers greater than 1 million
9. The set of all natural numbers less than 1 million
10. The set of odd natural numbers
11. $\{x \mid x$ is a number less than 2$\}$.
12. $\{n \mid n$ is a natural number between 8 and 9$\}$.
13. $\{1, 3, 5, 7, 9, \ldots, 49\}$
14. $\{10, 20, 30, 40, 50, 60, \ldots\}$
15. {vowels in the English language}
16. {0}
17. {rectangles}
18. {triangles having two, and only two, sides}
19. {months of the year having 40 days}
20. {two-digit numbers between 1 and 100}
21. $\{y \mid y$ is a whole number which is a multiple of 9$\}$.
22. {all fractions whose numerator is 1}

SUBSETS AND THE UNIVERSAL SET

Let U be a set of students who are members of a committee.

$$U = \{\text{Harry, Marie, Susan, Ted, William}\}$$

Let M be the set of men who are members of this committee.

$$M = \{\text{Harry, William, Ted}\}$$

Notice that every element of set M is also an element of set U. In such a case, we say: "Set M is a *subset* of set U" (and "set U is a *super-set* of set M") and we write: "$M \subset U$."

The set $U = \{$Harry, Marie, Susan, Ted, William$\}$ from which we chose elements to form a new set is called the *universe*, or *universal set*. In different discussions we will start with different universal sets as the situation dictates. For example, if we are discussing rodents, the universal set might be the set of all animals or the set of all mammals, but it would not be the set of all fish.

The universal set $U = \{1, 2, 3\}$ has several subsets. Every subset of U which does not contain all the elements of U is called a *proper subset* of U. For example, the sets $\{1\}$ and $\{2, 3\}$ are proper subsets of U. We can write $\{1\} \subset \{1, 2, 3\}$ and $\{2, 3\} \subset \{1, 2, 3\}$.

The subset $\{1, 2, 3\}$ which contains every element of U is called an *improper subset* of U. We can write $\{1, 2, 3\} \subset \{1, 2, 3\}$. This example illustrates that *every set is a subset of itself*. In general, if A is any set, then $A \subset A$ because every element of A is an element of A.

Although the empty set $\emptyset$ does not contain any elements of a universal set U, it is still a subset of U ($\emptyset \subset U$). This is so because there is no element in $\emptyset$ which is not a member of U.

EXERCISES

In 1–11, state whether the sentence is true or false. Justify your answer.

1. $\{10, 11, 12, 13\}$ is a subset of $\{10, 11, 12\}$.
2. $\{5, 8, 7\}$ is a subset of $\{7, 8, 9, 10\}$.
3. $\{10, 20, 30\}$ is a subset of $\{30, 20, 10\}$.
4. $\emptyset$ is a subset of $\{$tent, cabin, house$\}$.
5. $\{$athletes in your college$\}$ is a subset of $\{$baseball players in your college$\}$.
6. $\{a, b, c\} \subset \{a, b, c, d, e\}$.
7. $\{10, 11, 12, 13\} \subset \{13, 12, 11, 10\}$.
8. $\emptyset \subset \{a\}$.
9. $\{a\} \subset \emptyset$.
10. $\emptyset \subset \{0\}$.
11. $A \subset A$.

In 12–15, state whether the first set is a proper or improper subset of the second set.

12. $\{10, 15, 20\} \subset \{10, 15, 20, 25\}$.
13. $\{r, s, t\} \subset \{t, s, r\}$.
14. $\{6, 8, 10\} \subset \{6, 8, 10, 12\}$.
15. $\{n \mid n$ is a natural number exactly divisible by 4$\} \subset \{y \mid y$ is an even natural number$\}$.

In 16–21, list all the subsets (including the empty set) of the given set.

16. $\{5\}$
17. $\{5, 6\}$
18. $\{5, 6, 7\}$
19. $\{5, 6, 7, 8\}$
20. $\{a\}$
21. $\{w, x, y, z\}$

22. Find the number of subsets (including the empty set) of set A if the number of elements in set A is:

    a. 1   b. 2   c. 3   d. 4

23. Give two examples of sets X and Y such that X is a subset of Y and Y is not a subset of X.

24. Give two examples of sets R and S such that R is not a subset of S and S is not a subset of R.

25. a. Give two examples of sets G and H such that G is a subset of H and H is a subset of G.

    b. What relationship exists between the sets G and H?

EQUAL SETS

A set may be represented by different names. For example, $A = \{3, 5\}$ and $B = \{$odd numbers between 2 and 6$\}$ are different names for the same set. When we list the elements of set B, we find that $B = \{3, 5\}$. Since both set A and set B have exactly the same elements, we say that A and B are *equal sets* and write $A = B$. Other ways of saying this are:

Set A is equal to set B if every element of A is an element of B and every element of B is an element of A.

or

Set A is equal to set B if set A is a subset of set B and set B is a subset of set A.

If $R = \{3, 4\}$ and $S = \{2, 3\}$, set R does not equal set S because set R and set S do not have the same elements. In this case, we write $R \neq S$, which is read "R does not equal S."

EXERCISES

In 1-10, use either the symbol $=$ or the symbol $\neq$ to write a true sentence about the two sets.

1. $A = \{5, 7, 9, 10\}$ and $B = \{9, 7, 5, 10\}$.
2. $C = \{6, 8, 4, 3\}$ and $D = \{6, 8, 4, 2\}$.
3. $E = \{4, 6, 8\}$ and $F = \{4, 6, 8, 10\}$.
4. $G = \{$spring, summer, autumn, winter$\}$ and $H = \{$four seasons of the year$\}$.
5. $K = \{4, 8, 12, 16\}$ and $L = \{$counting numbers less than 20 that are exactly divisible by 4$\}$.
6. $M = \{0, 1, 2, 3, 4, 5, 6, 7, 8, 9\}$ and $N = \{$all one-digit counting numbers$\}$.

7. R = {all birds that have fins} and $S = \emptyset$.
8. $X = \emptyset$ and Y = {0}.
9. T = {7, 8, 9} and V = {$x \mid x$ is a natural number that is greater than 7 and less than 10}.
10. I = {$n \mid n$ is a natural number less than 1} and
    J = {$y \mid y$ is a whole number greater than 10 and less than 11}.

EQUIVALENT SETS

Let us consider the two sets A = {1, 3, 5} and B = {2, 4. 6}. Since their elements are different, set A does not equal set B. However, both sets have the same number of elements. We can see this when we pair, in different ways, the elements of set A (1, 3, 5) with the elements of set B (2, 4, 6) as follows:

$$A = \{1, 3, 5\} \qquad A = \{5, 3, 1\} \qquad A = \{1, 5, 3\}$$
$$\updownarrow \updownarrow \updownarrow \quad or \quad \updownarrow \updownarrow \updownarrow \quad or \quad \updownarrow \updownarrow \updownarrow$$
$$B = \{2, 4, 6\} \qquad B = \{2, 6, 4\} \qquad B = \{6, 4, 2\}$$

Notice that in each of the pairings, every element of set A has been matched with a unique element of set B, and that every element of set B has been matched with a unique element of set A. When two sets can be matched in this way, we say that there is a *one-to-one correspondence* between the two sets; such sets are called **matching sets**, or **equivalent sets**. The symbol $A \sim B$ means "set A is equivalent to set B."

A simple way to determine whether or not two finite sets are equivalent sets is to count the number of elements in each set. If both sets have the same number of elements, they are equivalent sets.

Note that two equal sets must always be equivalent sets. However, two equivalent sets need not always be equal sets.

It may also be possible to match two infinite sets, for example, the set of *all odd natural numbers* and the set of *all natural numbers*.

Let A = {1, 3, 5, 7, 9, 11, 13, 15, 17, 19, . . .} and B = {1, 2, 3, 4, 5, 6, 7, 8, 9, 10, . . .}. Then we can match the elements of set A and set B as follows, and we could continue the process endlessly:

$$A = \{1, 3, 5, 7, 9, 11, 13, 15, 17, 19, . . .\}$$
$$\downarrow \downarrow \downarrow \downarrow \downarrow \downarrow \quad \downarrow \quad \downarrow \quad \downarrow \quad \downarrow$$
$$B = \{1, 2, 3, 4, 5, 6, \quad 7, \quad 8, \quad 9, \quad 10, . . .\}$$

We see that there is a one-to-one correspondence between the set of all odd natural numbers and the set of all natural numbers. Therefore, we can say that {all odd natural numbers} $\sim$ {all natural numbers}.

EXERCISES

In 1–6, tell whether or not there is a one-to-one correspondence between the two sets.

1. $\{5, 6, 9, 4, 8\}$ and $\{1, 3, 5, 6, 7\}$ 2. $\{a, b, c, d\}$ and $\{x, y, z\}$
3. $\{M, E, A, T\}$ and $\{T, E, A, M\}$ 4. $\{5, 6, 7, 8\}$ and $\{\frac{1}{8}, \frac{1}{7}, \frac{1}{6}, \frac{1}{5}\}$
5. {odd numbers between 50 and 60} and {odd numbers between 60 and 70}
6. {all even natural numbers} and {all natural numbers}

In 7–10, tell whether or not the given sets are equivalent sets.

7. $\{\triangle, \bigcirc, \square\}$ and $\{1, 2, 3, 4, 5\}$
8. $\{2, 4, 6, 8, 10, 12\}$ and $\{12, 14, 16, 18, 20\}$
9. {counting numbers between 30 and 40} and {odd counting numbers between 30 and 40}
10. {even counting numbers} and {odd counting numbers}

In 11–13, state whether the two sets are (a) equivalent and (b) equal.

11. $\{1, 2, 3, 4\}$ and $\{a, b, c, d\}$
12. $\{B, A, T\}$ and $\{T, A, B\}$
13. {even natural numbers between 1 and 10} and {odd natural numbers between 1 and 10}
14. Describe two finite sets that are equivalent sets but not equal sets.
15. Describe two finite sets that are not equivalent sets.
16. Describe two infinite sets that are equivalent sets.

3. Picturing a Universal Set and Its Subsets

We have learned that the set from which we choose elements to form a new set is called the universal set, or the universe. For example, if we are considering the set of members of the United Nations, we can write the universal set, represented by U, as $U = $ {members of the United Nations}. If we are considering the set of even numbers between 1 and 17, we can write $U = \{2, 4, 6, 8, 10, 12, 14, 16\}$. We can represent the universal set pictorially by a rectangle and its interior.

The Universal Set U

We will now see how we can picture a subset of a universal set.

If from the universal set $U = \{2, 4, 6, 8, 10, 12, 14, 16\}$ we select the set of numbers, A, each of whose elements is exactly divisible by 4, we get $A = \{4, 8, 12, 16\}$. Set A is a subset of set U. We can picture

**Set *A* Is a Subset of
Universal Set *U***

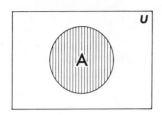

this fact by representing *U* by a rectangle
and its interior, and by representing the subset *A* by a circle and its interior. Notice that
the circle is placed within the rectangle.
Such a picture is called a ***Venn diagram***.

EXERCISES

1. a. If the set of objects under consideration is the collection of
United States coins of different denomination in use, list the
elements of the universal set *U*.
   b. If set *A* is a set each of whose elements is a United States coin
worth less than 25 cents, list the elements of set *A*.
   c. Draw a Venn diagram to show pictorially that set *A* is a subset
of the universal set *U*.

2. a. If the set of objects under consideration is the set of odd counting numbers less than 20, tabulate the elements of the universal
set *U*.
   b. If set *C* is a set each of whose elements is an odd number less
than 20 that is divisible by 5, list the elements of set *C*.
   c. Draw a Venn diagram to show pictorially that set *C* is a subset
of set *U*.

3. a. If the universal set *U* is $\{x \mid x$ is a natural number which is greater
than 10 and less than 20$\}$, use set-builder notation to represent
a set *E* which is a proper subset of *U*.
   b. Draw a Venn diagram to show pictorially that set *E* is a subset of
set *U*.

4. Two sets under consideration are the set of even natural numbers
less than 5 and the set of natural numbers less than 5. One of these
sets is the universal set; the other is a subset of the universal set.
   a. Tabulate the elements of the universal set *U*.
   b. Tabulate the elements of the subset *A*.
   c. Draw a Venn diagram to show pictorially that set *A* is a subset of
set *U*.

4. Intersection of Sets

Let us suppose that the universal set is the set of natural numbers.
If *A* is the set of natural numbers greater than 4 and less than 12, then

$A = \{5, 6, 7, 8, 9, 10, 11\}$. If B is the set of natural numbers greater than 8 and less than 15, then $B = \{9, 10, 11, 12, 13, 14\}$. Notice that the numbers 9, 10, 11 are elements of both set A and set B. The set whose elements belong to both set A and set B, $\{9, 10, 11\}$, is called the *intersection* of set A and set B.

The intersection of two sets, A and B, is the set containing those and only those elements of set A that are also elements of set B.

$A \cap B$ When A and B Intersect

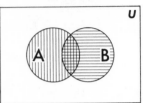

The intersection of set A and set B is represented by the symbol $A \cap B$, read "*A* intersection *B*." Thus, if $A = \{5, 6, 7, 8, 9, 10, 11\}$ and $B = \{9, 10, 11, 12, 13, 14\}$, then $A \cap B = \{9, 10, 11\}$. The intersection of set A and set B, $A \cap B$, can be shown pictorially by a Venn diagram. The cross-hatched part of the circles represents $A \cap B$.

$A \cap B$ When A and B Are Disjoint Sets

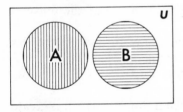

Suppose $U = \{$natural numbers$\}$. If A is the set of even natural numbers less than 10, then $A = \{2, 4, 6, 8\}$. If B is the set of odd natural numbers less than 10, then $B = \{1, 3, 5, 7, 9\}$. Notice that set A and set B have no common elements. Therefore, the intersection of set A and set B is the empty set, $\emptyset$, written $A \cap B = \emptyset$. Two sets such as set A and set B, which have no common elements, are called *disjoint sets*. The intersection of set A and set B, $A \cap B$, when A and B are disjoint sets, can be shown pictorially by a Venn diagram. Since A and B have no common elements, no part of the circles is crosshatched.

Suppose $U = \{$natural numbers$\}$. If A is the set of natural numbers less than 10, then $A = \{1, 2, 3, 4, 5, 6, 7, 8, 9\}$. If B is the set of odd natural numbers less than 10, then $B = \{1, 3, 5, 7, 9\}$. Notice that set B is a subset of set A. The intersection of set A and set B, $A \cap B$, when set B is a subset of set A, can be shown pictorially by a Venn diagram. The crosshatched part of the circles represents $A \cap B$. When B is a subset of A, then $A \cap B = B$.

$A \cap B$ When B Is a Subset of A

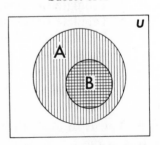

EXERCISES

1. If R = {6, 7, 8} and S = {3, 4, 5, 6, 7}, find $R \cap S$.
2. If C = {5, 10, 15, 20} and D = {5, 6, 7, 8, 9, 10}, find $C \cap D$.
3. U = {natural numbers}, A = {10, 11, 12, 13, 14, 15}, and B = {13, 14, 15, 16, 17}.
   a. Tabulate the elements of $A \cap B$.
   b. Picture $A \cap B$ with a Venn diagram.
4. U = {natural numbers}, A = {even natural numbers less than 20}, and B = {natural numbers less than 20 that are divisible by 4}.
   a. List the elements of set A and set B.
   b. List the elements of $A \cap B$.
   c. Picture $A \cap B$ with a Venn diagram.
5. U = {$n \mid n$ is a natural number less than 20}, A = {$n \mid n$ is a natural number less than 10}, and B = {$n \mid n$ is a natural number greater than 10 and less than 20}.
   a. List the elements of the universal set U, set A, and set B.
   b. How many elements are common to set A and set B?
   c. Describe the set $A \cap B$.
   d. Picture $A \cap B$ with a Venn diagram.
6. The universe is the set of men who are members of the Best College athletic teams. A is the set of men on the Best College football team. B is the set of men on the Best College basketball team. C is the set of men on the Best College tennis team. D is the set of men on the Best College baseball team.
   a. Make a Venn diagram for $A \cap B$ when some of the Best College men who are on the football team are also part of the basketball team.
   b. Make a Venn diagram for $B \cap D$ when none of the Best College men who are on the basketball team is also on the baseball team.
   c. Make a Venn diagram for $B \cap C$ when every man on the 10-man tennis team is also a member of the 15-man basketball team.
7. Set U represents the universe and set A and set B are subsets of set U. In a Venn diagram that pictures $A \cap B$, the circle representing set A coincides with the circle representing set B. What relationship must exist between set A and set B?

In 8–12, state whether the given sets are disjoint. Justify your answer.

8. {1, 4} and {2, 4}
9. {1, 3, 5} and {13, 5}
10. {odd natural numbers} and {even natural numbers}
11. {$x \mid x$ is a whole number greater than 40} and {$x \mid x$ is a whole number less than 40}.

12. $\{x \mid x$ is exactly divisible by $2\}$ and $\{x \mid x$ is exactly divisible by $3\}$.
13. If $U = \{$all fish in a particular farm pond$\}$, $A = \{$all fish in the pond which are bass$\}$, and $B = \{$all fish in the pond which weigh at least 5 pounds$\}$, tell what each of the following diagrams means:

a.
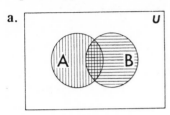

b.
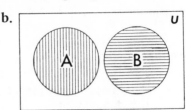

c.
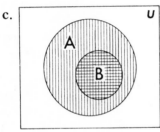

d.
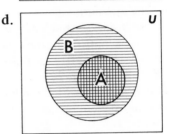

14. If U is the universe, set A is a subset of U, and $\emptyset$ is the null set, represent with a Venn diagram:
   a. $A \cap U$ b. $A \cap A$ c. $A \cap \emptyset$

In 15–18, $A = \{2, 4, 6\}$, $B = \{4, 6, 8, 10\}$, and $C = \{5, 7, 9, 11\}$. Find the indicated set.

Hint: In $(A \cap B) \cap C$, the parentheses are used to indicate that $A \cap B$ is to be found first, then the intersection of the resulting set with C is to be found.

15. $(A \cap B) \cap C$ 16. $A \cap (B \cap C)$
17. $(B \cap A) \cap C$ 18. $(C \cap B) \cap A$

In 19–22, complete the statement when A represents any set.

19. $A \cap A = ?$ 20. $A \cap \emptyset = ?$
21. $(A \cap A) \cap A = ?$ 22. $A \cap (A \cap A) = ?$
23. Complete the statement if D is a subset of C. $C \cap D = ?$
24. Complete the statement if A is a subset of B and B is a subset of C.
   a. $A \cap C = ?$ b. $(A \cap B) \cap C = ?$ c. $A \cap (B \cap C) = ?$

5. Union of Sets

The *union* of two sets A and B is the set containing all the elements of both set A and set B. (Any elements present in both set A and set B are listed only once.)

The union of set A and set B is represented by the symbol $A \cup B$, read "A union B." Thus, if $A = \{5, 6, 7, 8, 9, 10, 11\}$ and $B = \{9, 10, 11, 12, 13, 14\}$, then $A \cup B = \{5, 6, 7, 8, 9, 10, 11, 12, 13, 14\}$. Note that both set A and set B are subsets of the set $A \cup B$. The union of set A and set B, $A \cup B$, can be shown pictorially by a Venn diagram in which U is the set of natural numbers. The shaded region represents $A \cup B$.

$A \cup B$ When A and B Intersect

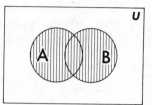

Suppose $U = \{\text{natural numbers}\}$. If A is the set of even natural numbers less than 10, then $A = \{2, 4, 6, 8\}$. If B is the set of odd natural numbers less than 10, then $B = \{1, 3, 5, 7, 9\}$. The union of set A and set B can be written $A \cup B = \{1, 2, 3, 4, 5, 6, 7, 8, 9\}$. The union of set A and set B, $A \cup B$, can be shown pictorially by a Venn diagram. Both shaded regions together represent $A \cup B$.

$A \cup B$ When A and B are Disjoint Sets

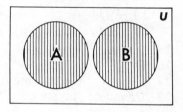

$A \cup B$ When B Is a Subset of A

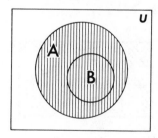

Suppose $U = \{\text{natural numbers}\}$. If A is the set of natural numbers less than 10, then $A = \{1, 2, 3, 4, 5, 6, 7, 8, 9\}$. If B is the set of odd natural numbers less than 10, then $B = \{1, 3, 5, 7, 9\}$. The union of set A and set B can be written $A \cup B = \{1, 2, 3, 4, 5, 6, 7, 8, 9\}$. A Venn diagram can be used to represent $A \cup B$ pictorially. The shaded region represents $A \cup B$. When B is a subset of A, then $A \cup B = A$.

EXERCISES

1. If $A = \{0, 2, 4\}$ and $B = \{1, 2, 3, 4\}$, find $A \cup B$.
2. If $C = \{1, 2, 3, 4, 5\}$ and $D = \{2, 4, 6, 8, 10\}$, find $C \cup D$.
3. If $R = \{1, 3, 5\}$ and $S = \{0, 2, 4, 6\}$, find $R \cup S$.
4. $U = \{\text{natural numbers}\}$, $A = \{10, 11, 12, 13\}$, $B = \{11, 12, 13, 14\}$.
   a. List the elements of $A \cup B$.
   b. Picture $A \cup B$ with a Venn diagram.
5. $U = \{\text{letters of the English alphabet}\}$, $A = \{a, e, i, o, u\}$, $B = \{r, s, t\}$.
   a. List the elements of $A \cup B$.

    b. Picture $A \cup B$ with a Venn diagram.

6. $U = \{x \mid x$ is a natural number$\}$, $A = \{x \mid x$ is a natural number less than 30 that is divisible by 5$\}$, $B = \{x \mid x$ is a natural number less than 30 that is divisible by 10$\}$.

    a. List the elements of set A, set B, and $A \cup B$.

    b. Picture $A \cup B$ with a Venn diagram.

7. If U is the universe, set A is a subset of U, and $\emptyset$ is the empty set, represent with a Venn diagram: **a.** $A \cup U$ **b.** $A \cup A$ **c.** $A \cup \emptyset$

In 8–12, $A = \{2, 4, 6\}$, $B = \{4, 6, 8, 10\}$, and $C = \{5, 7, 9, 11\}$. Find the indicated set. [*Hint:* In $(A \cup B) \cup C$, the parentheses are used to indicate that $A \cup B$ is to be found first, then the union of the resulting set with C is to be found.]

    8. $(A \cup B) \cup C$ **9.** $A \cup (B \cup C)$ **10.** $A \cup (B \cap C)$

11. $(B \cup C) \cap A$ **12.** $(A \cup B) \cap (A \cup C)$

In 13–16, complete the statement when A represents any set.

13. $A \cup A = ?$ **14.** $(A \cup A) \cup A = ?$ **15.** $(A \cup A) \cap A = ?$

16. $(A \cap A) \cup A = ?$

17. Complete the statement if D is a subset of C. $C \cup D = ?$

18. Complete the statement if A is a subset of B and B is a subset of C.

    a. $A \cup B = ?$ **b.** $(A \cup B) \cup C = ?$ **c.** $A \cup (B \cup C) = ?$

6. The Complement of a Set

If U is a universal set and A is a subset of U, then the **complement of A in U**, or more simply the **complement of A**, is the set of elements of U which are not elements of A. The complement of set A is represented by 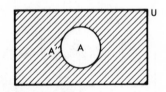 A'. For example, if $U = \{2, 4, 6, 8, 10, 12\}$ and $A = \{2, 4, 8, 10\}$, then the elements of U which are not elements of A are 6 and 12. Hence, $A' = \{6, 12\}$. The shaded region in the Venn diagram contains the elements of A'.

Observe the following two things about the sets A and A':

1. Set A and set A' are disjoint sets. Hence, $A \cap A' = \emptyset$.
2. $A \cup A' = \{2, 4, 6, 8, 10, 12\}$. Hence, $A \cup A' = U$.

In general, if A' is the complement of a given set A when the universal set is U, then

$$A \cap A' = \emptyset \text{ and } A \cup A' = U$$

Note that in order to determine the complement of a given set, we must know which set is the universal set.

Model Problems

1. If $U = \{5, 10, 15, 20, 25\}$ and $A = \{5, 15, 25\}$, determine A', the complement of A.

   Solution:
   $U = \{5, 10, 15, 20, 25\}$, and $A = \{5, 15, 25\}$. A' is the set of elements contained in U which are not elements of A. In this case, these elements are 10 and 20.
   Hence, $A' = \{10, 20\}$ *Ans.* $A' = \{10, 20\}$

2. If $U = \{1, 2, 3, 4, 5, 6, 7, 8, 9\}$, $A = \{8, 9\}$, $B = \{5, 7, 9\}$, determine
   (a) $A' \cap B'$.   (b) $(A \cup B)'$

   Solution:
   a. $U = \{1, 2, 3, 4, 5, 6, 7, 8, 9\}$.
      Since $A = \{8, 9\}$, $A' = \{1, 2, 3, 4, 5, 6, 7\}$.
      Since $B = \{5, 7, 9\}$, $B' = \{1, 2, 3, 4, 6, 8\}$.
      Hence, $A' \cap B' = \{1, 2, 3, 4, 5, 6, 7\} \cap \{1, 2, 3, 4, 6, 8\} = \{1, 2, 3, 4, 6\}$
                                              Ans. $A' \cap B' = \{1, 2, 3, 4, 6\}$
   b. Since $A = \{8, 9\}$ and $B = \{5, 7, 9\}$, $A \cup B = \{5, 7, 8, 9\}$.
      $(A \cup B)'$ is the set of elements contained in U which are not elements of $A \cup B$.
      Since $A \cup B = \{5, 7, 8, 9\}$, $(A \cup B)' = \{1, 2, 3, 4, 6\}$.
                                              Ans. $(A \cup B)' = \{1, 2, 3, 4, 6\}$

EXERCISES

In 1–5, determine A', the complement of the given set A, when the universal set is $\{1, 3, 5, 7, 9, 11\}$.
1. $A = \{1\}$ 2. $A = \{3, 9, 11\}$ 3. $A = \{3, 5, 7, 11\}$
4. $A = \emptyset$ 5. $A = U$

In 6–11, determine the indicated set when $U = \{1, 2, 3, 4, 5, 6, 7, 8, 9\}$, $A = \{1, 3, 5\}$, and $B = \{6, 8\}$.
6. A' 7. B' 8. $A' \cap B$
9. $A \cup B'$ 10. $(A \cap B)'$ 11. $(A \cup B)'$

In 12–15, describe in words the complement of the given set when U is the set of all natural numbers.

12. $A = \{1, 2, 3, 4, 5\}$ 13. $A = \{2, 4, 6, \ldots, 40\}$ 14. $A = \{2, 4, 6\}$
15. $A = \{$odd natural numbers$\}$.
16. If U is the set of letters of the English alphabet, and A is the set of consonants, describe in words the complement of A.
17. If $U = \{$natural numbers$\}$, and $A = \{$natural numbers divisible by 9$\}$, determine A'.
In 18–20, state whether the statement is true or false.
18. The complement of the empty set is the universal set.
19. A set and its complement may have an element in common.
20. If U is an infinite set, and A is a finite subset of U, then A' is an infinite set.

7. De Morgan's Laws

Suppose the universal set is the set of all students receiving a grade in a particular course (grades are A, B, C, D, and F). Let A be the set of students in the course who received an A and let B be the set of students in the course who received a B. Then, $A \cup B$ is the set of students in the course whose grade was A or B. The complement of $A \cup B$, written $(A \cup B)'$, is the set of students in the course whose grade was neither an A nor a B. Thus, $(A \cup B)'$ is the set of students in the course whose grade was C, D, or (perish the thought) F.

Also, A' is the set of students in the course whose grade was not an A; that is, their grade was B, C, D, or F. Likewise, B' is the set of students in the course whose grade was A, C, D, or F. Observe that $A' \cap B'$ is the set of students in the course whose grade was C, D, or F. Hence, $(A \cup B)' = A' \cap B'$. This example illustrates the following principle, which is one of *De Morgan's* laws:

Law 1. If A and B are both subsets of a universal set U, then the complement of the union of A and B is equal to the intersection of the complements of A and B. That is, $(A \cup B)' = A' \cap B'$.

Now, let us suppose that the universal set is $U = \{1, 2, 3, 4, 5, 6, 7, 8, 9, 10\}$, $A = \{1, 3, 7, 10\}$, and $B = \{1, 2, 7, 9, 10\}$. Then, $A \cap B = \{1, 7, 10\}$, and $(A \cap B)' = \{2, 3, 4, 5, 6, 8, 9\}$. Also, $A' = \{2, 4, 5, 6, 8, 9\}$, $B' = \{3, 4, 5, 6, 8\}$, and $A' \cup B' = \{2, 3, 4, 5, 6, 8, 9\}$. Hence, $(A \cap B)' = A' \cup B'$. This illustrates another of De Morgan's laws:

Law 2. If A and B are both subsets of a universal set U, then the complement of the intersection of A and B is equal to the union of the complements of A and B. That is, $(A \cap B)' = A' \cup B'$.

Notice that if we begin with either of De Morgan's laws and interchange the words "intersection" and "union," then we have formed the other De Morgan law.

EXERCISES

1. Let $U = \{1, 2, 3, 4, 5, 6, 7, 8, 9\}$, $A = \{1, 2, 3\}$, and $B = \{2, 4, 6, 8\}$. Use one of De Morgan's laws to find $(A \cup B)'$. Then, check your answer by first finding $A \cup B$ and then finding its complement.

In 2-7, let $U = \{$natural numbers$\}$. Use one of De Morgan's laws to find $(A \cup B)'$. Check your answer by first finding $A \cup B$ and then finding its complement.

2. $A = \{2, 4, 6\}, B = \{1, 3, 5, 7\}$
3. $A = \{1, 2, 3\}, B = \{$even natural numbers$\}$
4. $A = \{$odd natural numbers$\}, B = \{$even natural numbers$\}$
5. $A = U$ and $B = U$
6. $A = U$ and $B = \emptyset$
7. $A = \emptyset$ and $B = \emptyset$
8. Let $U = \{1, 2, 3, 4, 5, 6, 7, 8, 9\}$, $A = \{7, 8, 9\}$, $B = \{1, 3, 5, 7\}$. Use one of De Morgan's laws to find $(A \cap B)'$. Then, check your answer by first finding $A \cap B$ and then finding its complement.

In 9-14, let $U = \{$natural numbers$\}$. Use one of De Morgan's laws to find $(A \cap B)'$. Check your answer by first finding $A \cap B$ and then finding its complement.

9. $A = \{1, 3, 5\}, B = \{2, 4, 6, 8\}$
10. $A = \{1, 2, 3\}, B = \{$odd natural numbers$\}$
11. $A = \{$even natural numbers$\}, B = \{$odd natural numbers$\}$
12. $A = U$ and $B = U$
13. $A = U$ and $B = \emptyset$
14. $A = \emptyset$ and $B = \emptyset$
15. Use a Venn diagram to illustrate:
    a. De Morgan's law 1: $(A \cup B)' = A' \cap B'$
    b. De Morgan's law 2: $(A \cap B)' = A' \cup B'$

8. Graphing Sets of Numbers

The **graph of a set of numbers** is the set of points on a number line which are associated with the numbers in the set. When we make such a graph, we use:

1. a darkened circle • to represent a point on the number line which is associated with the number in the set.
2. a nondarkened circle ∘ to represent a point which does not belong to the graph.
3. a darkened line ▬▬▬ to indicate that every point on the line is associated with a number in the set.

Model Problems

1. Draw the graph of each set.
   a. $\{2, 4, 6\}$

   Answer: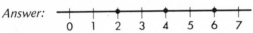

   b. $\{x \mid x$ is a number between 2 and 5$\}$

   Answer: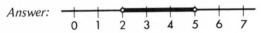

   c. $\{3\frac{1}{2}$ and numbers greater than $3\frac{1}{2}\}$

   Answer: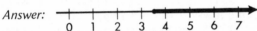

2. If set $A = \{1, 3, 5, 7\}$ and set $B = \{0, 2, 3, 4, 5, 6, 8\}$, (a) write and graph the intersection of set A and set B, $A \cap B$; (b) write and graph the union of set A and set B, $A \cup B$.

   Solution:

   a. Since the intersection of set A and set B is a set whose elements are numbers that are elements of both set A and set B, $A \cap B = \{3, 5\}$.

   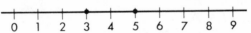

   b. Since the union of set A and set B is a set whose elements are numbers that are elements of set A, of set B, or of both set A and set B, $A \cup B = \{0, 1, 2, 3, 4, 5, 6, 7, 8\}$.

   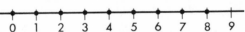

EXERCISES

In 1–14, name the points on the pictured line which form the graph of the given set of numbers.

1. $\{1, 3, 5, 7\}$ 2. $\{10, 0, 6\}$ 3. $\{11, 12\}$ 4. $\{0\}$ 5. $\emptyset$
6. {whole numbers between 1 and 10}
7. {even whole numbers between 1 and 10}
8. {whole numbers between 8 and 14}
9. {multiples of 3 between 1 and 15}
10. {whole numbers greater than 10 but less than 15}
11. {odd whole numbers between 3 and 13, and including 3 and 13}
12. {multiples of 2 between 14 and 15}
13. $\{n \mid n$ is a whole number less than 7$\}$.
14. $\{n \mid n$ is an odd whole number between 5 and 11$\}$.

In 15–28, draw the graph of the given set of numbers.

15. $\{0, 2, 4\}$ 16. $\{1, 2\frac{1}{2}, 3.5\}$ 17. $\{1, 2, 3, \ldots, 10\}$ 18. $\{0\}$
19. {whole numbers between 3 and 10}
20. {even whole numbers greater than 4 but less than 12}
21. {odd whole numbers less than 14 and greater than 9 or equal to 9}
22. a. {whole numbers less than 7}   b. {numbers less than 7}
23. a. {numbers greater than 4}   b. {numbers greater than $1\frac{1}{2}$}
24. {numbers less than 3 and including 3}
25. {numbers between 4 and 6}
26. $\{x \mid x$ is a number between 6 and 10$\}$.
27. $\{y \mid y$ is a number not greater than 8 and not less than 7$\}$.
28. $\{s \mid s$ is a number greater than 7 and not greater than 8$\}$.
29. If set $U = \{1, 2, 3, \ldots, 20\}$, write and graph a subset of U whose elements are:
    a. odd numbers   b. even numbers
    c. numbers exactly divisible by 4

In 30 and 31: (a) Write and graph the set which is the intersection of set P and set $Q, P \cap Q$. (b) Write and graph the set which is the union of set P and set $Q, P \cup Q$.

30. $P = \{1, 3, 4, 6, 7, 8\}, Q = \{2, 4, 5, 6, 8, 9\}$
31. $P = \{0, 1, 4, 6, 8, 9, 10\}, Q = \{0, 1, 3, 4, 5, 6\}$

Chapter 3

Open Phrases, Open Sentences,

and Truth Sets

1. Open Sentences and Truth Sets

Consider the following sentence: It is the capital of New York State. We cannot tell whether this sentence is true or false until more information, the name of the particular city that is to replace "It," is known. Such a sentence is called an *open sentence*. Let us assume that "It" can be replaced by an element of the set {New York, Rochester, Albany, Buffalo}. If "It" is replaced by Albany, the resulting sentence, "Albany is the capital of New York State," is a true sentence. Suppose "It" is replaced by any other element of the given set of cities, for example, Rochester. Now the resulting sentence, "Rochester is the capital of New York State," is a false sentence.

In the sentence "It is the capital of New York State," "It" does not refer to a definite city, but to any one of a set of cities. "It" is a symbol which holds a place for, or represents, any one of a given set of cities. Recall that such a symbol is called a *variable*.

The set from which the replacements for the variable are selected is called the *replacement set,* or *domain,* of the variable. In the previous discussion, {New York, Rochester, Albany, Buffalo} is the replacement set.

The subset of the domain of the variable consisting of those elements of the domain which make the open sentence true is called the *truth set,* or the *solution set,* of the open sentence. In our previous discussion, {Albany} is the truth set of the open sentence.

We have seen that a letter such as n or x can be used to represent a variable. For example, the open sentence "A number + 3 = 7" may be written "$n + 3 = 7$" if we use the letter n to represent "A number." If the domain of the variable n is {1, 2, 3, 4, 5}, then 4 is the only element of the domain which makes the open sentence a true sentence.

$$n + 3 = 7$$
If $n = 1$, then $1 + 3 = 7$ is a false sentence.
If $n = 2$, then $2 + 3 = 7$ is a false sentence.
If $n = 3$, then $3 + 3 = 7$ is a false sentence.
If $n = 4$, then $4 + 3 = 7$ is a *true* sentence.
If $n = 5$, then $5 + 3 = 7$ is a false sentence.

Therefore, the truth set of the sentence $n + 3 = 7$ is $\{4\}$.

This is sometimes written as $\{n \mid n + 3 = 7\} = \{4\}$, and is read "The set of all numbers n such that $n + 3 = 7$ is the set consisting of the number 4." We must remember that $n \in \{1, 2, 3, 4, 5\}$.

The elements of the domain of a variable are called the **values** of the variable. Thus, in the previous problem the values of the variable n were 1, 2, 3, 4, and 5. If a variable has only one value, it is called a **constant**.

If no member of a replacement set will make a sentence a true sentence, we say that the truth set is the **empty set**, represented by the symbol $\emptyset$.

Model Problems

1. Using the domain $\{0, 1, 2, 3\}$, find the truth set for the open sentence $2n > 3$.

   Solution: Replace the variable n in the open sentence $2n > 3$ by each member of the replacement set.

   $$2n > 3$$
   If $n = 0$, then $2 \times 0 > 3$, or $0 > 3$, is a false sentence.
   If $n = 1$, then $2 \times 1 > 3$, or $2 > 3$, is a false sentence.
   If $n = 2$, then $2 \times 2 > 3$, or $4 > 3$, is a *true* sentence.
   If $n = 3$, then $2 \times 3 > 3$, or $6 > 3$, is a *true* sentence.

   Answer: Since $n = 2$ and $n = 3$ are replacements that make $2n > 3$ a true sentence, the truth set is $\{2, 3\}$.

   The answer may also be written as follows:

   $$\{n \mid 2n > 3\} = \{2, 3\} \text{ when } n \in \{0, 1, 2, 3\}$$

2. Using the domain $\{1, 2, 3\}$, find the solution set for the open sentence $y + 5 = 9$.

   Solution: Replace the variable y in the open sentence $y + 5 = 9$ by each member of the replacement set.

   $$y + 5 = 9$$
   If $y = 1$, then $1 + 5 = 9$ is a false sentence.

If $y = 2$, then $2 + 5 = 9$ is a false sentence.
If $y = 3$, then $3 + 5 = 9$ is a false sentence.

Answer: Since no member of the replacement set changes the open sentence $y + 5 = 9$ into a true statement, we say that the solution set has no members. In other words, the solution set is the empty set, or null set, symbolized $\emptyset$.

3. If $x \in \{1, 2, 3\}$, determine the elements of $\{x \mid 3x - 1 < 8\}$.

Solution: Replace the variable x in the open sentence $3x - 1 < 8$ by each member of the domain.

$$3x - 1 < 8$$
If $x = 1$, then $3 \times 1 - 1 < 8$, or $2 < 8$ is a *true* sentence.
If $x = 2$, then $3 \times 2 - 1 < 8$, or $5 < 8$ is a *true* sentence.
If $x = 3$, then $3 \times 3 - 1 < 8$, or $8 < 8$ is a false sentence.

Answer: $\{x \mid 3x - 1 < 8\} = \{1, 2\}$ when $x \in \{1, 2, 3\}$

EXERCISES

In 1-8, tell whether or not the sentences are open sentences.

1. Franklin D. Roosevelt was a President of the United States.
2. She is pretty.
3. $6 - 3 = 5 + 1$ 4. $x + 10 = 14$ 5. $y - 4 = 12$
6. $3 + 2 < 10 \times 0$ 7. $r < 5 + 2$ 8. $2t > 5$

In 9-17, tell what the variable is.

9. She has blue eyes.
10. It is the longest river in the United States.
11. The highest mountain in the world is R.
12. $x + 5 = 9$ 13. $4y = 20$ 14. $.5x = 30$
15. $n + 1 < 3$ 16. $2d > 7$ 17. $14 < h + 9$

In 18-29, use the domain $\{0, 1, 2, 3, 4, 5\}$ to find all the replacements that will change the open sentence to a true sentence. If no replacement will make a true sentence, write *None*.

18. $5 - n = 2$ 19. $2x = 4$ 20. $5z = 0$ 21. $2x + 1 = 5$
22. $x - x = 0$ 23. $2n < 6$ 24. $n + 3 > 9$ 25. $2n + 1 < 8$
26. $\dfrac{n + 1}{2} = 2$ 27. $\dfrac{2n + 1}{3} = 4$ 28. $\dfrac{n}{4} > 1$ 29. $\dfrac{3x}{2} < x$

In 30-33, using the replacement set $\{1, 2, 3, 4, 5, 6, 7, 8, 9, 10\}$, find the truth set.

30. $2x + 1 = 24$ 31. $16 = 18 - x$ 32. $4 < m$ 33. $2x - 1 > 50$

In 34-37, using the domain $\{2, 2\frac{1}{2}, 3, 3\frac{1}{2}, 4, 4\frac{1}{2}\}$, find the solution set.

34. $5 - r = \frac{1}{2}$ **35.** $\frac{x}{2} = 2.25$ **36.** $2x > 8$ **37.** $3a < 4.5$

In 38-41, using the domain $\{3, 3\frac{1}{2}, 4, 4\frac{1}{2}, 5, 5\frac{1}{2}\}$, find the truth set.

38. $y - 2 = 3.5$ **39.** $2x - 1 = 5$ **40.** $2n > 8$ **41.** $2n < 7$

In 42-45, using the domain $\{2.1, 2.2, 2.3, 2.4, 2.5\}$, find the solution set.

42. $3x - 4 = 2.3$ **43.** $\frac{y}{2} = 3.6$ **44.** $z < 2\frac{1}{3}$ **45.** $2x + 3 < 6.5$

In 46-53, determine the elements of the set if the domain of the variable is the one indicated.

46. $\{n \mid n + 2 = 5\}$, $n \in \{0, 1, 2, 3, 4, 5\}$
47. $\{x \mid x - 4 = 6\}$, $x \in \{7, 8, 9, 10\}$
48. $\{r \mid r > 4\}$, $r \in \{3, 4, 5, 6\}$
49. $\{y \mid y - 1 < 8\}$, $y \in \{7, 8, 9, 10\}$
50. $\{x \mid 2x + 1 = 8\}$, $x \in \{0, 2, 4, 6\}$
51. $\{r \mid 2r + 1 > 4\}$, $r \in \{1, 2, 3, 4\}$
52. $\{d \mid 9 - d = 5\}$, $d \in \{0, 1, 2, 3, 4, 5\}$
53. $\{x \mid 3x + 1 < 12\}$, $x \in \{0, 1, 2, 3, 4, 5\}$

2. Graphing the Truth Set of an Open Sentence Containing One Variable

After we have found the truth set of an open sentence, we can graph the truth set by using the procedure we have already learned for graphing sets on a number line.

Model Problems

1. Using the replacement set $\{0, 1, 2, 3, 4\}$, find and graph the truth set for $2x + 1 = 5$.

Solution:

Step 1. Replace the variable x in the open sentence $2x + 1 = 5$ by each element of the replacement set.

$$2x + 1 = 5$$
If $x = 0$, then $2 \times 0 + 1 = 5$ is a false sentence.
If $x = 1$, then $2 \times 1 + 1 = 5$ is a false sentence.

If $x = 2$, then $2 \times 2 + 1 = 5$ is a *true* sentence.
If $x = 3$, then $2 \times 3 + 1 = 5$ is a false sentence.
If $x = 4$, then $2 \times 4 + 1 = 5$ is a false sentence.

Step 2. Since 2 is the only element of the replacement set that changes the open sentence to a true sentence, the truth set is $\{2\}$.

Step 3. Graph the truth set $\{2\}$.

2. Find and graph the solution set of $n + 1 > 2$ when the domain is $\{0, 1, 2, 3, 4\}$.

Solution:

Step 1. Replace the variable n in the open sentence $n + 1 > 2$ by each element of the domain.

$$n + 1 > 2$$
If $n = 0$, then $0 + 1 > 2$ is a false sentence.
If $n = 1$, then $1 + 1 > 2$ is a false sentence.
If $n = 2$, then $2 + 1 > 2$ is a *true* sentence.
If $n = 3$, then $3 + 1 > 2$ is a *true* sentence.
If $n = 4$, then $4 + 1 > 2$ is a *true* sentence.

Step 2. Since the values 2, 3, and 4 are the elements of the domain that change the open sentence to a true sentence, the solution set is $\{2, 3, 4\}$.

Step 3. Graph the solution set $\{2, 3, 4\}$.

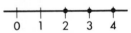

3. If the domain is $\{$numbers of arithmetic$\}$, graph the truth set of $x > 2$ or $x = 2$ (meaning x is greater than 2 or x is equal to 2). $x > 2$ or $x = 2$ may be written more compactly $x \geq 2$.

Solution:

Step 1. We see that 2 or any number greater than 2 is an element of the domain that changes the open sentence to a true sentence. Therefore, the truth set is $\{2$ and the numbers greater than 2$\}$.

Step 2. Graph the truth set $\{2$ and the numbers greater than 2$\}$.

4. Graph the truth set of $1 < x \leq 4; x \in \{$ numbers of arithmetic$\}$.

Solution:

Step 1. We see that 4 or any number that is greater than 1 and also less than

4 is an element of the domain that changes the open sentence to a true sentence. Therefore, the truth set is {4 and the numbers between 1 and 4}.

Step 2. Graph the truth set {4 and the numbers between 1 and 4}. Note that the nondarkened circle at 1 indicates that 1 is not an element of the truth set.

EXERCISES

In 1-4, find and graph the truth set when the replacement set is {0, 1, 2, 3, 4, 5}.

1. $2x + 1 = 7$ 2. $5x = 0$ 3. $t + 3 > 1$ 4. $3t + 1 \leq 7$

In 5-8, find and graph the solution set when the domain is {0, 1, 2, 3, 4, 5, 6, 7, 8, 9, 10}.

5. $2z + 8 = 8$ 6. $3a + 1 = 26$ 7. $s + 2 < 11$ 8. $14 > 5x + 1$

In 9-24, if $x \in$ {coordinates of points on the number line}, graph the truth set.

9. $x + 7 = 10$ 10. $2x = 14$ 11. $2x + 1 = 13$
12. $3x - 1 = 8$ 13. $2x > 6$ 14. $3x < 8$
15. $x \geq 5$ 16. $x \leq 8$ 17. $1 < x < 5$
18. $2 \leq x < 6$ 19. $4 < x \leq 8$ 20. $0 \leq x \leq 7$
21. $x + 3 = x + 3$ 22. $x + 3x = 4x$ 23. $x + 4 = 4 + x$
24. $x - 1 = x + 4$

3. Translating Verbal Phrases Into Algebraic Language

An expression or mathematical phrase that contains one or more variables is called an *open expression,* or an *open phrase.* For example, $2n$ is an open phrase because we do not know what number $2n$ represents until we know what number n represents, that is, the value of n. An open phrase such as $2n$ is also called an *algebraic expression.*

In Chapter 1 on page 17 we saw how number relationships could be expressed with mathematical symbols. Now we will see how to translate verbal phrases into the language of algebra. Recall that in algebra we usually use letters to represent variables and we use symbols to represent operations on numbers.

VERBAL PHRASES INVOLVING ADDITION

$5 + 4$ means that 5 and 4 are to be added.
$a + b$ means that a and b are to be added.

All of the verbal phrases "a plus b," "the sum of a and b," "a and b are added," "a increased by b," "b more than a" are written $a + b$ in algebraic language. Notice that many different verbal phrases can be expressed by a single algebraic expression.

When we say "7 exceeds 5 by 2," we mean that 7 is 2 more than 5, $7 = 5 + 2$. If we wish to write a number which exceeds 10 by 4, we write a number that is 4 more than 10: $10 + 4$, or 14. To write a number which exceeds a by b, we write a number that is b more than a, or $a + b$.

VERBAL PHRASES INVOLVING SUBTRACTION

$5 - 4$ means from 5 subtract 4.
$a - b$ means from a subtract b.

All the verbal phrases "the difference between a and b," "a minus b," "b subtracted from a," "a decreased by b," "a diminished by b," "b less than a," "a reduced by b" are written $a - b$ in algebraic language.

VERBAL PHRASES INVOLVING MULTIPLICATION

5×4 means that 5 and 4 are to be multiplied.
$a \times b$ means that a and b are to be multiplied.

Phrases such as "the product of a and b" and "a times b" mean that a and b are to be multiplied.

In algebra, multiplication may be indicated in several ways. For example, to write in symbols that 7 and t are to be multiplied, we can use the following methods:

1. $7 \times t$, using the symbol $\times$ between 7 and t.
2. $7 \cdot t$, using a raised center dot between 7 and t. (Be careful not to confuse the dot with a decimal point.)
3. $7t$, omitting the multiplication symbol and placing 7 and t next to each other. Note that this cannot be done with numbers of arithmetic. If we wish to multiply 5 and 4, we *may not* place the 5 next to the 4 and write 54. We know that 54 means the

number fifty-four, whereas 5 × 4 is a numeral which names the same number as twenty.

4. $7(t)$, $(7)t$, (7) (t), placing the 7 and t next to each other and enclosing one or both in parentheses.

Similarly, there are six ways in which we may write in symbols that a and b are to be multiplied: $a \times b, a \cdot b, ab, a(b), (a)b, (a)$ (b).

VERBAL PHRASES INVOLVING DIVISION

$5 \div 4$ and $\frac{5}{4}$ mean that 5 is to be divided by 4.

$a \div b$ and $\frac{a}{b}$ mean that a is to be divided by b.

In some verbal phrases, we can use a comma to prevent misreading. For example, in "the product of x and y, decreased by 2," the comma after y tells us that the phrase means $(xy) - 2$ and not $x(y - 2)$.

4. Units of Measure in the United States System and the Metric System

We will be solving problems which involve units of measure. In some we will use what were previously known as English units; in others we will use metric units. Since England has adopted the *metric system*, we will no longer refer to English units. Instead, we will refer to these units as United States units since they are still being used in the United States.

The metric system, which is a decimal-based system, was developed in France by the French Academy in the latter part of the 18th century. Most countries are abandoning the system of measurement now used in the United States and are adopting the metric system. All over the world the metric system is used almost exclusively in chemistry, physics, and medical sciences. As time marches on, the metric system is being used more and more widely in industry and in the home.

Recall the following:

UNITS OF LENGTH

United States system: inch (in.), foot (ft.), yard (yd.), mile (mi.)

Metric system: meter (m), millimeter (mm), centimeter (cm), kilometer (km)

UNITS OF WEIGHT OR MASS

United States system: pound (lb.), ounce (oz.), ton (T.)
Metric system: gram (g), milligram (mg), centigram (cg), kilogram (kg)

UNITS OF LIQUID VOLUME

United States system: ounce (oz.), pint (pt.), quart (qt.), gallon (gal.)
Metric system: liter (l), milliliter (ml), centiliter (cl), kiloliter (kl)
We will deal more comprehensively with the metric system on pages 404 and 412–413.

Model Problems

1. Use mathematical symbols to translate each of the following verbal phrases into algebraic language:

   a. w more than 3   *Ans.* $3 + w$
   b. r decreased by 2   *Ans.* $r - 2$
   c. the product of $5r$ and s *Ans.* $5rs$
   d. 4 divided by x *Ans.* $4 \div x$

   e. twice x decreased by 10, divided by 3   *Ans.* $\dfrac{2x - 10}{3}$

   f. 25, diminished by 4 times n *Ans.* $25 - 4n$

   g. the sum of t and u, divided by 6   *Ans.* $\dfrac{t + u}{6}$

   h. 100 decreased by twice $(x + 5)$ *Ans.* $100 - 2(x + 5)$

2. Represent in algebraic language:

   a. a number which exceeds 5 by m *Ans.* $5 + m$
   b. a number which x exceeds by 5   *Ans.* $x - 5$
   c. twice the sum of x and y *Ans.* $2(x + y)$
   d. a weight which is 40 kg heavier than p kg   *Ans.* $p + 40$ kg
   e. a distance which is 20 m shorter than f m   *Ans.* $f - 20$ m
   f. a sum of money which is twice d dollars   *Ans.* $2d$ dollars

   g. the number of yards in x ft.   *Ans.* $\dfrac{x}{3}$ ft.

EXERCISES

In 1–22, use mathematical symbols to translate the verbal phrase into algebraic language.

1. the sum of b and 8
2. x diminished by y
3. the product of x and y
4. the quotient of s and t
5. 12 increased by a
6. 5 less than d
7. 8 divided by y
8. y multiplied by 10
9. the product of $2c$ and $3d$
10. t more than w
11. d less than c
12. twice the difference of p and q
13. $\frac{1}{3}$ of z
14. x subtracted from 5
15. a number that exceeds m by 4
16. $\frac{1}{2}$ the sum of L and W
17. 5 times x, increased by 2
18. 10 decreased by twice a
19. 36 divided by the sum of t and u
20. 7 less than one-half d
21. the product of x and y decreased by $\frac{1}{2}$ the sum of x and y
22. 4 less than twice the sum of a and 5

In 23–40, using the letter n to represent the variable "a number," write the verbal phrase in algebraic language.

23. a number increased by 2
24. 20 more than a number
25. 8 increased by a number
26. a number decreased by 6
27. 2 less than a number
28. 12 decreased by a number
29. 3 times a number
30. $\frac{3}{4}$ of a number
31. 4 times a number, increased by 3
32. 10 times a number, decreased by 2
33. 30 increased by 4 times a number
34. 8 more than the product of 3 times a number
35. 3 less than twice a number
36. 30 decreased by a number
37. $\frac{1}{3}$ the product of 5 times a number
38. $\frac{1}{2}$ of 10 more than a number
39. the product of 5 more than a number, and 4
40. twice the sum of $\frac{1}{2}$ a number and 1

In 41–46, represent the answer in algebraic language, using the variable mentioned in the problem.

41. The number of kilometers traveled by a bus is represented by x. If a car traveled 100 kilometers farther than the bus, represent the number of kilometers traveled by the bus.

42. Mr. Gold invested $1000 in stocks. If he lost d dollars when he sold them, represent the number of dollars he received for them.

43. The cost of a fur coat is 5 times the cost of a cloth coat. If the cloth coat costs x dollars, represent the cost of the fur coat.

44. The length of a rectangle is represented by L. If the width of the rectangle is $\frac{1}{2}$ its length, represent its width.

45. After 2 meters had been cut from a piece of lumber, there were f meters left. Represent, in meters, the length of the original piece of lumber.

46. Saul is 25 years old. Represent his age x years ago.

In 47–50, translate the verbal phrase into algebraic language, representing the two numbers by L and W, with L being the larger.

47. the sum of twice the larger number and twice the smaller number

48. the sum of the larger number and the smaller number, doubled

49. 10 times the smaller number, decreased by 6 times the larger number

50. 1 less than 5 times the larger number, this result divided by 3 times the smaller number

In 51–66, write a verbal phrase which gives a meaning of the symbol, if n in the symbol represents "a number."

51. $3n$ 52. $n + 4$ 53. $n - 3$ 54. $\frac{1}{2}n$
55. $2n + 1$ 56. $3n - 1$ 57. $5 - n$ 58. $10 + n$
59. $\dfrac{n}{4}$ 60. $\dfrac{n + 2}{2}$ 61. $\dfrac{n - 8}{3}$ 62. $\dfrac{20 - 2n}{5}$
63. $2(n + 1)$ 64. $4(3n - 1)$ 65. $\frac{1}{2}(2n + 1)$ 66. $4 + 2(n - 1)$

In 67–72, state the difference in meaning between the two symbols.

67. $x - 10; 10 - x$ 68. $2(x + 3); 2x + 3$ 69. $a - b; b - a$

70. $3(a + b); 3a + b$ 71. $\dfrac{x}{4}; \dfrac{4}{x}$ 72. $\frac{1}{2}(x - 6); \frac{1}{2}x - 6$

5. Problems Involving Variables Represented by Letters

Those students who find it difficult to solve problems in which letters represent variables will find the following procedure helpful.

Procedure. To solve problems in which letters represent variables:

1. **Write a similar problem involving numbers of arithmetic.**
2. **Solve this arithmetic problem.**
3. **Use the same method to solve the problem involving the letters.**

Model Problems

1. Represent, in dollars, the value of *n* hats, each worth *d* dollars.

   Solution: First write a similar problem. Represent the value of 5 hats, each worth $10. We can solve this problem by multiplying the number of hats, 5, by the value of each hat, 10 dollars, giving 5 × 10, or $50. Similarly, in the original problem, the value of all the hats will be the number of hats, *n*, times the value of each hat, *d*, which is *n* × *d*, or *nd* dollars.

   Answer: *nd* dollars

2. Express the number of grams in *k* kilograms.

   Solution: First write a similar problem. Represent the number of grams in 2 kilograms. We can solve this problem by multiplying the number of kilograms, 2, by the number of grams in each kilogram, 1000, giving 2 × 1000, or 2000 grams. Similarly, in the original problem, the number of grams will be the number of kilograms, *k*, times the number of grams in each kilogram, 1000, which is *k* × 1000, or 1000*k* grams.

   Answer: 1000 *k* grams

3. Express the number of yards in *d* feet.

   Solution: First find the number of yards in 15 feet. Since each yard contains 3 feet, find the number of yards in 15 feet by dividing 15 by 3, giving $\frac{15}{3}$, or 5, yards. Similarly, to represent the number of yards in *d* feet, divide *d* by 3, giving $\frac{d}{3}$.

   Answer: $\frac{d}{3}$

EXERCISES

1. A ballpoint pen sells for 39 cents. Represent, in cents, the cost of *x* pens.
2. Represent, in cents, the cost of *t* feet of lumber which sells for *g* cents a foot.
3. If Sam started on a trip with *w* dollars and spent $50 on the trip, represent, in dollars, the amount he had left at the end of the trip.
4. If Helen weighs *p* pounds, represent her weight after she has gained 8 pounds.
5. Ronald, who weighs *c* pounds, is *d* pounds overweight. Represent the number of pounds Ronald should weigh.

6. Toby is n years old now. Represent his age 4 years from now.
7. Saul is b years old now. Represent his age x years from now.
8. Pauline is x years old. Represent her age 10 years ago.
9. A man is x years old. Represent his age b years ago.
10. Helen is 35 years old. If Sue is x years younger than Helen, represent Sue's age.
11. The sum of the length and the width of a rectangle is 20 meters. If the length is represented by x meters, represent the width in meters.
12. A car travels r kilometers per hour. The rate of a train exceeds the rate of the car by 50 kilometers per hour. Represent the rate of the train in kilometers per hour.
13. A man bought an article for c dollars and sold it at a profit of \$25. Represent, in dollars, the amount for which he sold it.
14. A man gave a total of w dollars to his son and to his daughter. If the boy received m dollars, represent the number of dollars the girl received.
15. The length of a rectangle is represented by L meters. Represent, in meters, the width of the rectangle if it is 5 meters less than the length.
16. The width of a rectangle is x meters. Represent, in meters, the length of the rectangle if it exceeds twice the width by 3 meters.
17. Represent the number of cents in q quarters.
18. Represent the number of cents in d dimes and h half-dollars.
19. Represent the number of cents in x nickels and $(25 - x)$ dimes.
20. If a plane travels 350 kilometers per hour, represent, in meters, the distance it will travel in h hours.
21. If an auto traveled for 5 hours at an average rate of r kilometers per hour, represent, in kilometers, the distance it has traveled.
22. A ship sailed for t hours at an average rate of r kilometers per hour. Represent the number of kilometers it sailed.
23. Represent, in centimeters, the length of a diameter of a circle whose radius measures r centimeters.
24. Represent algebraically the number of:
    a. centimeters in m meters   b. meters in i centimeters
    c. days in w weeks   d. weeks in d days
    e. hours in d days   f. days in h hours
25. Represent, in dollars, the cost of a foot of lumber if a yard of lumber costs m dollars.
26. A boy weighs y kilograms. Represent the number of kilograms he must gain to weigh 45 kilograms.
27. Represent the number of baseballs you can buy with c dollars if each baseball costs m dollars.
28. Represent the number of candy bars you can buy with n nickels and d dimes if each candy bar is worth 15 cents.

6. Understanding the Meaning of Some Vocabulary Used in Algebra

TERM

A *term* is a numeral, a variable, or a product of any of these. For example, 5, x, $4y$, $7rs$, and $\frac{1}{2}abc$ are terms. In an algebraic expression such as $4a + 2b - 5c$, which has more than one term, the terms $4a$, $2b$, and $5c$ are separated by $+$ and $-$ signs.

FACTORS OF A PRODUCT

If two or more numbers are to be multiplied, each of the numbers, as well as the product of any of them, is a *factor* of the product. For example, in the product $3xy$, the factors are $1, 3, x, y, 3x, 3y, xy$, and $3xy$. Note that when we factor whole numbers, we usually concern ourselves only with factors that are whole numbers.

COEFFICIENT

In a product, any factor is the *coefficient* of the remaining factor. In the product $4ab$, 4 is the coefficient of ab, $4a$ is the coefficient of b, and $4b$ is the coefficient of a.

When a constant and variables are factors of a product, the constant is called the *numerical coefficient* of the product. For example, in $4ab$, the numerical coefficient is 4.

Since x names the same number as $1 \cdot x$, we sometimes say that the coefficient of x is understood to be 1. Likewise, we may say that the coefficient of ab is understood to be 1.

BASE, EXPONENT, POWER

We know that 4×4 may be written 4^2, which is read "four squared" or "4 to the second power." The product $s \times s$ may be written s^2, which is read "s squared" or "s to the second power."

In 4^2, the small ^{2} above and to the right of 4 tells us that 4 is to be used as a factor 2 times. Similarly, in s^2, the small ^{2} above and to the right of s tells us that s is to be used as a factor 2 times.

The product $4 \times 4 \times 4$ may be written 4^3, which is read "4 cubed" or "4 to the third power." The product $e \times e \times e$ may be written e^3, which is read "e cubed" or "e to the third power."

In 4^3, the small ^{3} above and to the right of 4 tells us that 4 is to be used as a factor 3 times. Similarly, in e^3, the small ^{3} above and to the right of e tells us that e is to be used as a factor 3 times.

The product $3 \times 3 \times 3 \times 3$ may be written 3^4, which is read "3 to the fourth power." Since $3 \times 3 \times 3 \times 3 = 81$, 3^4 names the same number as 81. We say that the value of 3^4 is 81. We can also say that 81 is the fourth power of 3.

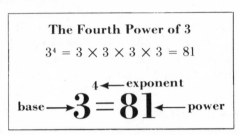

In $3^4 = 81$, the 3 is called the base, the 4 is called the exponent, and the 81 is called the power. A *base* is a number which is used as a factor two or more times. An *exponent* is a number which tells how many times the base is to be used as a factor. A *power* is a number which can be expressed as a product in which all the factors are the same.

We will agree that 4 means 4^1 and that, in general, a means a^1.

Note that an exponent refers only to the base which is directly to the left of it. Thus:

$c^3 d^4$ means $cccdddd$ cd^4 means $cdddd$ $5d^2$ means $5dd$

If we wish to use $5d$ as a factor 2 times, that is $(5d)(5d)$, we write $(5d)^2$. Notice how the meanings of $5d^2$ and $(5d)^2$ differ: $5d^2$ means $5dd$, whereas $(5d)^2$ means $(5d)(5d)$.

Model Problem

Name the coefficient, base, and exponent in the term $4x^5$.

Answer: The coefficient is 4, the base is x, and the exponent is 5.

EXERCISES

In 1–6, name the factors (other than 1) of each product.

1. xy 2. $3a$ 3. $5n$ 4. $7mn$ 5. $13xy$ 6. $11st$

In 7–12, name the numerical coefficient of x.

7. $8x$ 8. $(5 + 2)x$ 9. $\frac{1}{2}x$ 10. x 11. $1.4x$ 12. $2 + 7x$

In 13–18, name the base and exponent in the expression.

13. m^2 **14.** s^3 **15.** t **16.** 10^6 **17.** $(5y)^4$ **18.** $(x + y)^5$

In 19–27, write each product using exponents.

19. $m \cdot m \cdot m$ **20.** $b \cdot b \cdot b \cdot b \cdot b$ **21.** $10 \cdot 10 \cdot 10 \cdot 10$
22. $2 \cdot 2 \cdot 2 \cdot 2 \cdot 2 \cdot 2$ **23.** $4 \cdot x \cdot x \cdot x \cdot x \cdot x$ **24.** $a \cdot a \cdot a \cdot a \cdot b \cdot b$
25. $7 \cdot r \cdot r \cdot r \cdot s \cdot s$ **26.** $9 \cdot c \cdot c \cdot c \cdot d$ **27.** $(6a)(6a)(6a)$

In 28–33, write the term without using exponents.

28. r^6 **29.** $5x^4$ **30.** $x^3 y^5$ **31.** $4a^4 b^2$ **32.** $3c^2 d^3 e$ **33.** $(3y)^5$

7. Evaluating Algebraic Expressions

The algebraic expression $3n + 1$ represents an unspecified number. It is only when we replace the variable n by a specific number that $3n + 1$ represents a specific number. For example, suppose that the domain of n is $\{1, 2, 3\}$. The specific numbers that $3n + 1$ represents (the values of $3n + 1$) can be found as follows:

If $n = 1$, $3n + 1 = 3(1) + 1 = 3 + 1 = 4$.
If $n = 2$, $3n + 1 = 3(2) + 1 = 6 + 1 = 7$.
If $n = 3$, $3n + 1 = 3(3) + 1 = 9 + 1 = 10$.

When we determine the number which an algebraic expression represents for specified values of its variables, we are *evaluating the algebraic expression;* that is, we are finding its value or values.

Procedure. To evaluate an algebraic expression:

1. **Replace the variables by their specific values.**
2. **Simplify any number expressions that may be included within symbols of grouping such as parentheses. Remember to simplify the number expression in the innermost symbols of grouping first.**
3. **Simplify any powers and roots. (Roots will be studied later.)**
4. **Do all multiplications and divisions, performing them in order from left to right.**
5. **Do all additions and subtractions, performing them in order from left to right.**

8. Evaluating Algebraic Expressions Involving Addition, Subtraction, Multiplication, and Division

Model Problems

1. Evaluate $50 - 3x$ when $x = 7$.

How to Proceed	Solution
1. Write the expression.	$50 - 3x$
2. Replace the variable by its given value.	$= 50 - 3 \times 7$
3. Do the multiplication.	$= 50 - 21$
4. Do the subtraction.	$= 29$ *Ans.*

2. Evaluate $\dfrac{5r}{3} + \dfrac{7s}{2} - \dfrac{t}{5}$ when $r = 6, s = 4,$ and $t = 15$.

How to Proceed	Solution
1. Write the expression.	$\dfrac{5r}{3} + \dfrac{7s}{2} - \dfrac{t}{5}$
2. Replace the variables by the given values.	$= \dfrac{5 \times 6}{3} + \dfrac{7 \times 4}{2} - \dfrac{15}{5}$
3. Do the multiplications.	$= \dfrac{30}{3} + \dfrac{28}{2} - \dfrac{15}{5}$
4. Do the divisions.	$= 10 + 14 - 3$
5. Do the addition and subtraction.	$= 21$ *Ans.*

EXERCISES

In 1–18, find the numerical value of the expression. Use $a = 8$, $b = 6, d = 3, x = 4, y = 5,$ and $z = 1$.

1. $5a$
2. $\frac{1}{2}x$
3. $.3y$

4. ax
5. $3xy$
6. $\dfrac{2b}{3}$

7. $\dfrac{3bd}{9}$
8. $2x + 9$
9. $3y - b$

10. $20 - 4z$
11. $5x + 2y$
12. $ab - dx$

13. $a + 5d + 3x$
14. $9y + 6b - d$
15. $ab - d - xy$

16. $\dfrac{7y}{5} + \dfrac{b}{2}$
17. $\dfrac{dy}{3z} - \dfrac{z}{d}$
18. $\dfrac{xy}{z} - \dfrac{y}{x} - \dfrac{dy}{xz}$

9. Evaluating Algebraic Expressions Involving Powers

Model Problems

1. Evaluate $4x^3y^2$ when $x = 2$ and $y = 3$.

How to Proceed	*Solution*
1. Write the expression.	$4x^3y^2$
2. Replace the variables by their given values.	$= 4(2)^3(3)^2$
3. Evaluate the powers.	$= 4(2 \times 2 \times 2)(3 \times 3) = 4(8)(9)$
4. Do the multiplication.	$= 288$ *Ans.*

2. Evaluate $x^2 - 5x + 4$ when $x = 7$.

How to Proceed	*Solution*
1. Write the expression	$x^2 - 5x + 4$
2. Replace the variable by its given value.	$= (7)^2 - 5(7) + 4$
3. Evaluate the power.	$= 49 - 5(7) + 4$
4. Do the multiplication.	$= 49 - 35 + 4$
5. Do the addition and subtraction.	$= 18$ *Ans.*

3. Evaluate $4x^2 + 9y^2$ when $x = 1$ and $y = 4$.

How to Proceed	*Solution*
1. Write the expression.	$4x^2 + 9y^2$
2. Replace the variables by their given values.	$= 4(1)^2 + 9(4)^2$
3. Evaluate the powers.	$= 4(1) + 9(16)$
4. Do the multiplications.	$= 4 + 144$
5. Do the addition.	$= 148$ *Ans.*

EXERCISES

In 1–33, find the numerical value of the expression. Use $a = 8$, $b = 6, d = 3, x = 4, y = 5$, and $z = 1$.

1. a^2	2. b^3	3. d^4
4. $4d^3$	5. $6z^5$	6. $\dfrac{b^2}{9}$
7. $\frac{3}{4}x^3$	8. xy^2	9. $2a^2b^3$
10. $\frac{1}{5}x^2y^3z^3$	11. $a^2 + b^2$	12. $b^2 - y^2$
13. $a^2 + b^2 - d^2$	14. $x^2 + x$	15. $b^2 + 2b$

16. $y^2 - 4y$ **17.** $2b^2 + b$ **18.** $2y^2 - y$
19. $9a - a^2$ **20.** $5z - 3z^2$ **21.** $x^2 + 4y^2$
22. $x^2 + 3x + 5$ **23.** $y^2 + 2y - 7$ **24.** $2a^2 - 4a + 6$
25. $2b^2 - 5b - 10$ **26.** $15 + 5z - z^2$ **27.** $36 + 5y - 2y^2$
28. $x^3 \cdot x^2$ **29.** $x^2 \cdot x^3$ **30.** x^5
31. $d^1 \cdot d^5$ **32.** $d^5 \cdot d^1$ **33.** d^6

10. Evaluating Expressions Containing Parentheses or Other Symbols of Grouping

Model Problems

1. Evaluate $2[a + (n - 1)d]$ when $a = 40, n = 10$, and $d = 3$.

How to Proceed	*Solution*
1. Write the expression.	$2[a + (n - 1)d]$
2. Replace the variables by their given values.	$= 2[40 + (10 - 1)(3)]$
3. Simplify the expression within the parentheses (the innermost grouping symbol).	$= 2[40 + (9)(3)]$
4. Do the multiplication.	$= 2[40 + 27]$
5. Simplify the expression with the bracket.	$= 2[67]$
6. Do the multiplication.	$= 134$ *Ans.*

2. Evaluate $(2x)^2 - 2x^2$ when $x = 4$.

How to Proceed	*Solution*
1. Write the expression.	$(2x)^2 - 2x^2$
2. Replace the variable by its given value.	$= (2 \times 4)^2 - 2(4)^2$
3. Simplify the expression within the parentheses.	$= (8)^2 - 2(4)^2$
4. Evaluate the powers.	$= 64 - 2(16)$
5. Do the multiplication.	$= 64 - 32$
6. Do the subtraction.	$= 32$ *Ans.*

3. Evaluate $\dfrac{b^2 + c^2 - a^2}{2bc}$ when $a = 5, b = 4$, and $c = 3$.

How to Proceed	*Solution*
1. Write the expression.	$\dfrac{b^2 + c^2 - a^2}{2bc}$

2. Replace the variables by their given values.

$$= \frac{(4)^2 + (3)^2 - (5)^2}{2 \times 4 \times 3}$$

3. Since the fraction line is a symbol of grouping, evaluate the numerator and denominator separately.

$$= \frac{16 + 9 - 25}{24}$$

$$= \frac{0}{24}$$

4. Do the division.

$$= 0 \quad Ans.$$

EXERCISES

In 1–27, find the value of the expression. Use $w = 10, x = 8, y = 5$, and $z = 2$.

1. $2(x + 5)$
2. $3(2x + z)$
3. $4(2x - 3y)$
4. $\frac{x}{2}(y + z)$
5. $\frac{1}{2}x(y + z)$
6. $\frac{5}{9}(4y - z)$
7. $4x + (y + z)$
8. $2[3y - (x - 3)]$
9. $2x + 5(y - 1)$
10. $30 - 4(x - y)$
11. $[(w + x)(y + z) - 2]z$
12. $(w - z)x - y$
13. $3x^2$
14. $(3x)^2$
15. $y^2 + z^2$
16. $(y + z)^2$
17. $w^3 - x^3$
18. $(w - x)^3$
19. $3w^2 - 2x^2$
20. $(3w - 2x)^2$
21. $(3w)^2 - (2x)^2$
22. $(yz)^2$
23. $(y^2)(z^2)$
24. $(zy)^2$
25. $(xw)^2$
26. $(x^2)(w^2)$
27. $(wx)^2$

In 28–40, find the value of the expression. Use $a = 8, b = 6, d = 3$, $x = 4, y = 5$, and $z = 1$.

28. $\dfrac{x + 2a}{4}$
29. $\dfrac{3a - 2x}{3x - a}$
30. $\dfrac{a + b + x}{y - d + z}$

31. $\dfrac{dx - yz + a}{bx - ad + dy}$
32. $\dfrac{a^2 + b^2}{y^2}$
33. $\dfrac{x^2}{y^2 - d^2}$

34. $\dfrac{d^2 + x^2 - y^2}{2dx}$
35. $\dfrac{b^3 - d^3}{(b - d)^3}$
36. $\dfrac{(4y)^2 - (3x)^2}{4y^2 - 3x^2}$

37. $4y^2 - 3(2y + 1)(3y - 12)$
38. $4(2a^2 + b^2) - 6(4a - 3b)$

39. $\dfrac{x^2 + 2xy + y^2 - z^2}{(x + y + z)(x + y - z)}$
40. $\dfrac{x^4 - 2x^2 + 1}{(x - 1)^2 (x + 1)^2}$

In 41 and 42, evaluate the expression. Use $r = .2, s = .3$, and $n = .5$.

41. $r^2(s + 4n)$
42. $(r + s)^2 - (r^2 + s^2)$

Chapter 4

Properties of Operations

From past experience you have probably noticed that numbers have various properties. For example, if someone told you that 178,432 + 902,871 = 1,081,303, and then asked you to find the sum 902,871 + 178,432, you would probably give the answer 1,081,303 immediately, without actually performing the addition. In doing this, you would have been assuming the truth of the principle that *the order in which two numbers are added does not affect the sum.* Actually, you do not know that this is always true. No matter how many times you might test this principle, it would always be possible that in some instance the order in which two numbers are added does affect the sum. Mathematicians can prove that this property of addition is true. However, we will assume its truth.

In this chapter we will deal with some important properties of addition and multiplication. These properties will play a vital role in the algebra we are to study.

1. Understanding the Meaning of Closure Under an Operation

From your experience you know that if two elements of the set of natural numbers are added, the result is always another natural number. Further, the result is always unique; there is one—and only one—natural number which represents the result when two natural numbers are added. For example, 6 + 2 = 8, and only 8. We say that *the set of natural numbers is closed under addition.*

In general, for all *a* and *b* which are elements of the set of natural numbers, there is a unique natural number *c* such that:

$$a + b = c$$

If two elements of the set of natural numbers are multiplied, the result is always a unique natural number. For example, $6 \times 4 = 24$, and only 24. We say that *the set of natural numbers is closed under multiplication.*

In general, for all a and b which are elements of the set of natural numbers, there is a unique natural number c such that:

$$ab = c$$

However, when one element of the set of natural numbers is subtracted from another element of the set, the result does not always represent a natural number. For example, $4 - 6$ does not represent a natural number. Hence, we say that *the set of natural numbers is not closed under subtraction.*

Likewise, since $6 \div 4$ does not represent a natural number, we say that *the set of natural numbers is not closed under division.*

A set is closed under an operation when the number that results from performing the operation on any two elements of the set is always a unique member of the set.

Closure under an operation depends on two things: the operation and the domain of numbers being used. We have seen that the set of natural numbers is closed under multiplication but is not closed under division. Thus, closure depends on the operation.

When the operation is addition, the set of even numbers is closed, but the set of odd numbers is not closed. Thus, closure depends on the domain.

THE SUBSTITUTION PRINCIPLE

An indicated sum or product of numbers is not dependent upon the numerals that are used to represent the numbers. For example:

$$88(65 + 35) = 88(100) \text{ because } 65 + 35 = 100$$
$$37(24 - 14) = 37(10) \text{ because } 24 - 14 = 10$$

These examples illustrate the substitution principle:

For every number a and every number b, if $a = b$, then b may be substituted for a, and a may be substituted for b in any expression without changing the value of the expression.

Model Problem

State whether or not {natural numbers which are multiples of 4} is closed under
(a) addition   (b) subtraction   (c) multiplication   (d) division.
Give a reason for your answer in each part.

Solution: The set {natural numbers which are multiples of 4} is the same as the set {4, 8, 12, . . .}.

a. Closed under addition—because the sum of any two elements in the set is also an element of the set.

b. Not closed under subtraction—because 4 − 8 does not name a number which is an element of the set.

c. Closed under multiplication—because the product of any two elements of the set is also an element of the set.

d. Not closed under division—because 12 ÷ 4 does not name a number which is an element of the set.

EXERCISES

In 1–8, state whether the numerical phrase names a natural number.

1. $8 + 2$ 2. $2 + 8$ 3. $8 - 4$ 4. $4 - 8$
5. 8×4 6. 4×8 7. $8 \div 4$ 8. $4 \div 8$

9. If x and y represent natural numbers, select the phrases that always represent natural numbers.

   a. $x + y$ b. $x - y$ c. xy d. $x \div y$

In 10–19, state whether the set is closed under the indicated operation.

10. {1}; multiplication   11. {4}; subtraction
12. {0}; addition   13. {1}; division
14. {0, 1}; multiplication   15. {0, 2, 4}; subtraction
16. {2, 4, 8}; division   17. {0, 1, 2}; multiplication
18. {2, 4, 6, 8, . . .}; addition 19. {1, 3, 5, . . .}; multiplication

In 20–31, state whether the set is closed under **(a)** addition, **(b)** subtraction, **(c)** multiplication, **(d)** division. Give a reason for your answer in each part.

20. {0}   21. {1}
22. {10}   23. {0, 1}
24. {1, 3, 5}   25. {2, 4, 6}
26. {all even numbers}   27. {all odd numbers}
28. {all multiples of 3}
29. $\{\frac{1}{2}, 1, 1\frac{1}{2}, 2, 2\frac{1}{2}, . . .\}$
30. $\{\frac{1}{3}, \frac{2}{3}, 1, 1\frac{1}{3}, 1\frac{2}{3}, 2, . . .\}$
31. {.1, .01, .001, .0001, . . .}
32. Describe a set which is closed under: **a.** addition   **b.** subtraction   **c.** multiplication   **d.** division

2. Properties of Addition

COMMUTATIVE PROPERTY OF ADDITION

When we add numbers of arithmetic, we assume that we may change the order in which two numbers are added without changing the sum. For example, $4 + 5 = 5 + 4$, and $\frac{1}{2} + \frac{1}{4} = \frac{1}{4} + \frac{1}{2}$. These examples illustrate the *commutative property of addition.*

In general, we assume that for every number a and every number b:

$$a + b = b + a$$

Notice that subtraction does not have the commutative property because $5 - 4 \neq 4 - 5$.

ASSOCIATIVE PROPERTY OF ADDITION

When adding three numbers, we assume that we may group the numbers in different ways without changing the sum. For example, $2 + 5 + 8$ can be found by first adding 2 and 5, getting 7, and then adding 7 to 8, getting 15. In the symbols of mathematics, this is written $(2 + 5) + 8 = 15$. Or, we may add 5 and 8, getting 13, and then add 13 to 2, getting 15. This is written $2 + (5 + 8) = 15$. Therefore, we see that $(2 + 5) + 8 = 2 + (5 + 8)$. This example illustrates the *associative property of addition.*

In general, we assume that for every number a, every number b, and every number c:

$$(a + b) + c = a + (b + c)$$

Notice that subtraction is not associative because $(10 - 8) - 2 \neq 10 - (8 - 2)$.

USES OF PROPERTIES OF ADDITION

When we check addition by adding in the opposite direction, we are using the commutative property.

Adding	Checking
3489 ↓	3489 ↑
1546 ↓	1546 ↑
5035	5035

The commutative and associative properties may be used to find an indicated sum quickly and easily. Study the following steps that make it simple to add $78 + 64 + 22$ mentally:

Step	Reason
1. $(78 + 64) + 22 = (64 + 78) + 22$	1. Commutative property of addition

2.	$= 64 + (78 + 22)$	2. Associative property of addition
3.	$= 64 + 100$	3. Substitution principle, $(78 + 22) = 100$
4.	$= 164$	4. Substitution principle, $64 + 100 = 164$

Since the commutative and associative properties of addition make it possible to add numbers in any order, grouped in any way, parentheses may be omitted in indicated sums. For example, $(78 + 64) + 22$, or $78 + (64 + 22)$ may be written $78 + 64 + 22$.

In general, $(a + b) + c$, or $a + (b + c)$ may be written:

$$a + b + c$$

Model Problems

1. Name the property illustrated in each true sentence.

   a. $5 + 13 = 13 + 5$ *Ans.* Commutative property of addition

   b. $(5 + x) + y = 5 + (x + y)$ *Ans.* Associative property of addition

2. State the reason that justifies each step in the following sequence of related equalities:

Step	*Reason*
a. $3\frac{1}{2} + (x + 9\frac{1}{2}) = 3\frac{1}{2} + (9\frac{1}{2} + x)$	*Ans.* Commutative property of addition
b. $\quad\quad = (3\frac{1}{2} + 9\frac{1}{2}) + x$	*Ans.* Associative property of addition
c. $\quad\quad = 13 + x$	*Ans.* Substitution principle

EXERCISES

In 1–6, name the property illustrated in each true sentence.

1. $7 + 2 = 2 + 7$ **2.** $(9 + 3) + 7 = 9 + (3 + 7)$

3. $8 + (6 + t) = (8 + 6) + t$ **4.** $m + 2n = 2n + m$

5. $(r + s) + t = t + (r + s)$ **6.** $(x + y) + 2z = x + (y + 2z)$

In 7–10: **(a)** Give a replacement for the question mark which makes the sentence true for all values of the variable. **(b)** Name the property illustrated in the sentence that is formed when the replacement is made.

7. $2 + x = x +$?

8. $(4 + a) + 7 = 4 + (a +$?$)$

9. $23 +$? $= x + 23$

10. $(8 +$?$) + 2 = 8 + (x + 2)$

In 11–16, use properties of addition and the substitution principle to perform the indicated addition mentally in the simplest way.

11. $275 + 83 + 125$

12. $398 + 124 + 102 + 376$

13. $.79 + .63 + .21$

14. $1.41 + .49 + 2.59 + .26$

15. $2\frac{3}{4} + 1\frac{1}{3} + 4\frac{1}{4}$

16. $1\frac{1}{6} + 2\frac{1}{8} + 2\frac{5}{6} + 3\frac{3}{8}$

In 17–20, state the reason that justifies each step in the sequence of related equalities.

17. a. $(31 + 89) + 69 = (89 + 31) + 69$
    b. $\qquad = 89 + (31 + 69)$
    c. $\qquad = 89 + 100$
    d. $\qquad = 189$

18. a. $7 + (78 + 13) = 7 + (13 + 78)$
    b. $\qquad = (7 + 13) + 78$
    c. $\qquad = 20 + 78$
    d. $\qquad = 98$

19. a. $5 + (x + 1) = 5 + (1 + x)$
    b. $\qquad = (5 + 1) + x$
    c. $\qquad = 6 + x$

20. a. $(x + z) + y = x + (z + y)$
    b. $\qquad = x + (y + z)$
    c. $\qquad = (x + y) + z$

In 21–24:   (a) Develop the steps of a sequence of related equalities which show that the sentence is true.   (b) Name the property or principle used in each step.

21. $(592 + 649) + 408 = 649 + (592 + 408)$

22. For every y, $12 + (y + 6) = (12 + 6) + y$.

23. For every t, $(10 + t) + 13 = t + 23$.

24. For every a, every b, and every c, $(a + c) + b = c + (b + a)$.

3. Properties of Multiplication

COMMUTATIVE PROPERTY OF MULTIPLICATION

When we multiply numbers of arithmetic, we assume that we may change the order of the factors without changing the product. For example, $5 \times 4 = 4 \times 5$, and $\frac{1}{2} \times \frac{1}{4} = \frac{1}{4} \times \frac{1}{2}$. These examples illustrate the *commutative property of multiplication*.

In general, we assume that for every number a and every number b:

$$a \times b = b \times a$$

Notice that division does not have the commutative property because $8 \div 4 \neq 4 \div 8$.

ASSOCIATIVE PROPERTY OF MULTIPLICATION

To find a product which involves three factors, we first multiply any two factors and then multiply this result by the third factor. We assume that we do not change the product when we group the numbers differently. For example, to find the product $5 \times 4 \times 2$, we can multiply as follows:

$$5 \times 4 \times 2 = (5 \times 4) \times 2 = 20 \times 2 = 40$$

We can also multiply in a different way as follows:

$$5 \times 4 \times 2 = 5 \times (4 \times 2) = 5 \times 8 = 40$$

Therefore, $(5 \times 4) \times 2 = 5 \times (4 \times 2)$.

This example illustrates the *associative property of multiplication.*

In general, we assume that for every number a, every number b, and every number c:

$$(a \times b) \times c = a \times (b \times c)$$

In general, $(a \times b) \times c$ or $a \times (b \times c)$ may be written:

$$a \times b \times c$$

Notice that division is not associative because $(8 \div 4) \div 2 = 2 \div 2 = 1$, whereas $8 \div (4 \div 2) = 8 \div 2 = 4$. Therefore, $(8 \div 4) \div 2 \neq 8 \div (4 \div 2)$.

USES OF PROPERTIES OF MULTIPLICATION

When we check multiplication by changing the order of the factors, we are using the commutative property.

Multiplying	Checking
57	23
X 23	X 57
171	161
114	115
1311	1311

The commutative and associative properties may be used to find an indicated product quickly and easily. Study the following steps that make it simple to find the product $4 \times 89 \times 25$ mentally:

Step	Reason
1. $(4 \times 89) \times 25 = (89 \times 4) \times 25$	1. Commutative property of multiplication
2. $\qquad = 89 \times (4 \times 25)$	2. Associative property of multiplication
3. $\qquad = 89 \times 100$	3. Substitution principle
4. $\qquad = 8900$	4. Substitution principle

Model Problems

1. Name the property illustrated in each true sentence.
   a. $6 \times 13 = 13 \times 6$ *Ans.* Commutative property of
   multiplication
   b. $(4 \times a) \times b = 4 \times (a \times b)$ *Ans.* Associative property of
   multiplication

2. Give a sequence of related equalities which show that $(4a) \times 5 = 20a$ is a true sentence, and name the property or principle used in each step.

   Solution:

Step	Reason
1. $(4a) \times 5 = 4 \times (a \times 5)$	1. Associative property of multiplication
2. $\quad\quad = 4 \times (5 \times a)$	2. Commutative property of multiplication
3. $\quad\quad = (4 \times 5) \times a$	3. Associative property of multiplication
4. $\quad\quad = 20\,a$	4. Substitution principle

EXERCISES

In 1–6, name the property illustrated in each true sentence.

1. $8 \times 12 = 12 \times 8$
2. $\frac{1}{2} \times (2 \times 4) = (\frac{1}{2} \times 2) \times 4$
3. $y \times 5 = 5 \times y$
4. $(y + 6) \times 3 = 3 \times (y + 6)$
5. $4 \times (\frac{1}{4} \times d) = (4 \times \frac{1}{4}) \times d$
6. $(r \times s) \times t = r \times (s \times t)$

In 7–10: **(a)** State a replacement for the question mark which makes the sentence true for all values of the variable. **(b)** Name the property illustrated in the sentence that is formed when the replacement is made.

7. $z \times 4 = 4 \times ?$
8. $(9 \times b) \times 7 = 9 \times (b \times ?)$
9. $5 \times ? = g \times 5$
10. $? \times (10 \times c) = (\frac{1}{10} \times 10) \times c$

In 11–19, use properties of multiplication and the substitution principle to perform the indicated multiplication mentally in the simplest way.

11. $50 \times 93 \times 2$
12. $4 \times 876 \times 250$
13. $125 \times 798 \times 8$
14. $12\frac{1}{2} \times 87 \times 8$
15. $2\frac{1}{2} \times 49 \times 40$
16. $3 \times 73 \times 33\frac{1}{3}$
17. $2.5 \times 6.9 \times 4$
18. $5 \times 63 \times 1.2$
19. $125 \times 7.66 \times 8$

In 20–23, state the reason that justifies each step in the sequence of related equalities.

20. a. $250 \times (9.6 \times 4) = 250 \times (4 \times 9.6)$
    b. $= (250 \times 4) \times 9.6$
    c. $= 1000 \times 9.6$
    d. $= 9600$

21. a. $\frac{3}{4} \times (86 \times \frac{4}{3}) = \frac{3}{4} \times (\frac{4}{3} \times 86)$
    b. $= (\frac{3}{4} \times \frac{4}{3}) \times 86$
    c. $= 1 \times 86$
    d. $= 86$

22. a. $8d \times 7 = 8 \times (d \times 7)$ **23. a.** $(f \times g) \times h = f \times (g \times h)$
    b. $= 8 \times (7 \times d)$ **b.** $= (g \times h) \times f$
    c. $= (8 \times 7) \times d$ **c.** $= (h \times g) \times f$
    d. $= 56d$ **d.** $= h \times (g \times f)$

In 24–27: **(a)** Develop the steps of a sequence of related equalities which show that the sentence is true. **(b)** Name the property or principle used in each step.

24. $8 \times (736 \times 125) = 1000 \times 736$
25. $\frac{5}{9} \times (731 \times \frac{9}{5}) = 1 \times 731$
26. For every r, $25r \times 4 = 100r$.
27. For every c and every d, $dc \times 8 = 8 \times cd$.

In 28–35, name the properties of addition or multiplication that are illustrated or involved in the true sentence. Include the substitution principle when necessary.

28. $18 + 2e = 2e + 18$ **29.** $4 \times (9 \times r) = (4 \times 9) \times r$
30. $17 + (23 + x) = (17 + 23) + x$ **31.** $2 \times (t + 8) = (t + 8) \times 2$
32. $12.25 + (x + 37.75) = 50 + x$ **33.** $\frac{1}{3} \times (y \times 3) = 1 \times y$
34. $p \times (q + 7) = (7 + q) \times p$ **35.** $(ba + c) + d = d + (ab + c)$

4. The Distributive Property

We know that $2(20 + 3) = 2(23) = 46$ and that $2 \times 20 + 2 \times 3 = 40 + 6 = 46$. Therefore, we see that $2(20 + 3) = 2 \times 20 + 2 \times 3$.

This example illustrates the ***distributive property of multiplication over addition***, also called the ***distributive property***. This means that the product of one number times the sum of a second and a third number equals the product of the first and second numbers plus the product of the first and third numbers.

Thus, $5(6 + 4) = 5 \times 6 + 5 \times 4$.

In general, we assume that for every number a, every number b, and every number c:

$$a(b + c) = ab + ac \qquad and \qquad ab + ac = a(b + c)$$

Since multiplication is commutative, the distributive property can be written in other forms:

$$(b + c)a = ba + ca \quad and \quad (b + c)a = ab + ac$$

The distributive property is assumed to be true for more than three numbers:

$$a(b + c + d + \ldots + x) = ab + ac + ad + \ldots + ax$$

The distributive property is also assumed to be true for subtraction:

$$a(b - c) = ab - ac \quad and \quad ab - ac = a(b - c)$$

USING THE DISTRIBUTIVE PROPERTY

Observe how the distributive property may be used to find the following indicated products:

1. $6 \times 23 = 6(20 + 3) = 6 \times 20 + 6 \times 3 = 120 + 18 = 138$
2. $20(\frac{1}{4} + \frac{1}{5}) = 20 \times \frac{1}{4} + 20 \times \frac{1}{5} = 5 + 4 = 9$
3. $9 \times 3\frac{1}{3} = 9(3 + \frac{1}{3}) = 9 \times 3 + 9 \times \frac{1}{3} = 27 + 3 = 30$
4. $6.5 \times 8 = (6 + .5)8 = 6 \times 8 + .5 \times 8 = 48 + 4 = 52$

The distributive property can be used to *transform*, or change, the form of an algebraic expression. When a given expression is an indicated product, note how it may be transformed to an equal expression which is an indicated sum, or an indicated difference:

1. $5(a + b) = 5a + 5b$
2. $7(x - y) = 7x - 7y$
3. $r(m + n + t) = rm + rn + rt$
4. $6(3x + 5) = 6 \cdot 3x + 6 \cdot 5 = 18x + 30$
5. $(x + y)(m + n) = (x + y)m + (x + y)n = xm + ym + xn + yn$

In 5, notice that in the first transformation $(x + y)$ is considered as one number, whereas $(m + n)$ is considered as the sum of two numbers. If we wish, we may consider $(m + n)$ to be one number and $(x + y)$ to be the sum of two numbers. The result will be the same.

The use of the distributive property also makes it possible to transform an algebraic expression which is an indicated sum, or an indicated difference, to an equal expression which is an indicated product. Study the following examples:

1. $3c + 3d = 3(c + d)$
2. $xa + xb + xc = x(a + b + c)$
3. $5L + 3L = (5 + 3)L = 8L$
4. $9y - 4y = (9 - 4)y = 5y$

EXERCISES

In 1–14, state whether the sentence is a correct application of the distributive property. If you believe that it is not, state your reason.

1. $6(5 + 8) = 6 \times 5 + 6 \times 8$
2. $10(\frac{1}{2} + \frac{1}{5}) = 10 \times \frac{1}{2} + \frac{1}{5}$
3. $(7 + 9)5 = 7 + 9 \times 5$
4. $3(x + 5) = 3x + 3 \times 5$
5. $2(y + 6) = 2y + 6$
6. $(b + 2)a = ba + 2a$
7. $4a(b + c) = 4ab + 4ac$
8. $4b(c - 2) = 4bc - 2$
9. $8m + 6m = (8 + 6)m$
10. $14x - 4x = (14 - 4)x$
11. $2.7a + 5.3a = 8a$
12. $7\frac{1}{2}r - 2\frac{1}{2}r = 5r$
13. $7r + 7s = 7(r + s)$
14. $\frac{1}{2}hb + \frac{1}{2}hc = \frac{1}{2}h(b + c)$

In 15–20, complete the sentence so that it is an application of the distributive property.

15. $9(7 + 3) = $ _____
16. _____ $= 12 \times \frac{1}{2} + 12 \times \frac{1}{3}$
17. $4(p + q) = $ _____
18. _____ $= 2x - 2y$
19. $8t + 13t = $ _____
20. _____ $= (15 - 7)m$

In 21–28, find the value of the numerical phrase by using the distributive property to simplify the computation.

21. $15 \times 36 + 15 \times 64$
22. $3 \times 89 + 5 \times 89 + 2 \times 89$
23. $128 \times 615 - 28 \times 615$
24. $1\frac{3}{4} \times 576 + 8\frac{1}{4} \times 576$
25. $937 \times .8 + 937 \times .2$
26. $36(\frac{1}{3} + \frac{1}{4})$
27. $50 \times 8\frac{3}{5}$
28. $73 \times 632 + 47 \times 632 - 20 \times 632$

In 29–34, use the distributive property to transform the expression to an equal expression without parentheses.

29. $4(m + n)$
30. $(x - y)8$
31. $12(\frac{2}{3}x + 2)$
32. $(\frac{1}{3}m - \frac{3}{5}n)30$
33. $3a(7 - b)$
34. $(a + b)(s + t)$

In 35–40, use the distributive property to express each indicated sum as a product.

35. $2p + 2q$
36. $8p - 8m$
37. $12y - 4y$
38. $4a + 5a + 3a$
39. $2bc + 4b$
40. $9r + 6d$

In 41 and 42, name the property that justifies each step in the sequence of related equations. Use the substitution principle if necessary.

41. a. $s(m + n) = s(n + m)$
    b. $ = sn + sm$
    c. $ = ns + ms$

42. a. $5x + (3x + 4) = (5x + 3x) + 4$
    b. $ = (5 + 3)x + 4$
    c. $ = 8x + 4$

5. Combining Like Terms

Terms having the same variables as factors, with corresponding variables having the same exponent, are called *like terms*. For example, $3L$ and $5L$, $5x^2$ and $7x^2$, $9ab$ and $2ab$, $4(x + y)$ and $6(x + y)$ are pairs of like terms. On the other hand, $2x$ and $3y$, $3ab$ and $4cd$, $3x^2$ and $5x^3$ are examples of *unlike terms*.

We have seen that the distributive property enables us to transform an indicated sum or difference into an indicated product:

1. $9x + 2x = (9 + 2)x = 11x$
2. $16cd + 3cd = (16 + 3)cd = 19cd$
3. $18y - y = 18y - 1y = (18 - 1)y = 17y$

When we express the indicated sum or the indicated difference of like terms as a single term, we *combine like terms*.

Notice that in each of the preceding examples when two like terms are combined:

1. The result has the same variable factors as the original terms.
2. The numerical coefficient of the result is:
   (a) the sum of the numerical coefficients of the terms when the terms are to be added

or

   (b) the difference of the numerical coefficients of the terms when the terms are to be subtracted.

The indicated sum or difference of two unlike terms cannot be expressed as a single term. For example, $2x + 3y$ and $4ac - 5bd$ cannot be simplified.

Model Problems

1. Show that $4x + 5x = 9x$ is a true sentence when $x = 10$.

How to Proceed	Solution
1. Write the sentence.	$4x + 5x = 9x$
2. Replace the variable by its value.	$4 \times 10 + 5 \times 10 \stackrel{?}{=} 9 \times 10$
3. Do the multiplication.	$40 + 50 \stackrel{?}{=} 90$
4. Do the addition. The result is a true sentence.	$90 = 90$ (true)

In 2-6, simplify the expression by combining like terms.

2. $8a + 3a$

Solution: $8a + 3a = (8 + 3)a = 11a$ Ans. $11a$

3. $3.9c - 3.9c$

Solution: $3.9c - 3.9c = (3.9 - 3.9)c = 0 \cdot c = 0$ Ans. 0

4. $3\frac{1}{2}xy + 4\frac{1}{4}xy$

Solution: $3\frac{1}{2}xy + 4\frac{1}{4}xy = (3\frac{1}{2} + 4\frac{1}{4})xy = 7\frac{3}{4}xy$ Ans. $7\frac{3}{4}xy$

5. $9t + 4t - t$

Solution: $9t + 4t - t = (9 + 4 - 1)t = 12t$ Ans. $12t$

6. $7a + 6b + 5a - 2b$

Solution:

$7a + 6b + 5a - 2b = 7a + 5a + 6b - 2b$	Commutative property
$= (7a + 5a) + (6b - 2b)$	Associative property
$= (7 + 5)a + (6 - 2)b$	Distributive property
$= 12a + 4b$	Substitution principle

Answer: $12a + 4b$

EXERCISES

1. Show that $5y^2 - 2y^2 = 3y^2$ is a true sentence when y equals:
    a. 3 **b.** 12 **c.** $.2$ **d.** $\frac{1}{3}$ **e.** 0

2. Show that $6c + 9d + c + 2d = 7c + 11d$ is a true sentence when:
    a. $c = 10, \ d = 7$ **b.** $c = 1.2, \ d = .1$ **c.** $c = \frac{3}{4}, \ d = \frac{2}{3}$

In 3-14, simplify the expression by combining like terms.

3. $7x + 3x$ **4.** $9t - 5t$ **5.** $10c + c$
6. $2\frac{1}{2}d + 1\frac{1}{2}d$ **7.** $3.4y + 1.3y$ **8.** $9ab + 2ab$
9. $8m + 5m + m$ **10.** $9w + 8w - 3w$ **11.** $8s + 5\frac{1}{2}s + 6\frac{3}{4}s$
12. $8.2b + 3.8b - 12b$ **13.** $2\frac{3}{4}xy - 2xy + \frac{1}{2}xy$ **14.** $9d^2 - 6d^2 - d^2$

In 15 and 16, simplify the sentence by combining like terms.

15. $P = 5x + 5x + 5x$ **16.** $P = x + \frac{3}{2}x + x + \frac{3}{2}x$
17. Express the perimeter of each of the following figures and simplify the result by combining like terms:

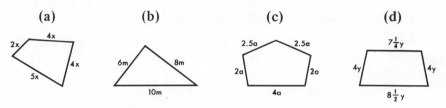

(a)   (b)   (c)   (d)

In 18–25, simplify the expression by combining like terms.

18. $8m + 5m + 7n + 6n$

19. $a + 5m + 2a - 4m$

20. $5a + b + 3c + 1\frac{1}{3}a + b + \frac{3}{4}c$

21. $2x + 9 + 3x + 1 + 5x - 8$

22. $5y^2 + 25 + 2y^2 - 10$

23. $6ab + 5ac + 3ac - ab$

24. $2(x + y) + 3(x + y)$

25. $5(2c + 9) + 3(4c - 7)$

In 26 and 27, simplify the sentence by combining like terms.

26. $P = 4r + 5s + 4r + s$

27. $S = 6a + 2\frac{1}{2}b + 3\frac{1}{4}a + \frac{3}{4}b$

28. Express the perimeter of each of the following figures and simplify the result by combining like terms:

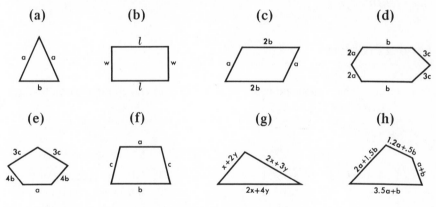

(a)   (b)   (c)   (d)

(e)   (f)   (g)   (h)

6. Properties of Zero and One

ADDITION PROPERTY OF ZERO

The true sentences $5 + 0 = 5$ and $0 + 8 = 8$ illustrate that the sum of any number and zero is that number itself. These examples illustrate the *addition property of zero*.

In general, we assume that for every number a:

$$a + 0 = a \quad and \quad 0 + a = a$$

We call 0 the *identity element of addition*, or the *additive identity*. We will also agree that: *If* a + x = a *for some number* a, *then* x = 0.

MULTIPLICATION PROPERTY OF ZERO

The true sentences $4 \times 0 = 0$ and $0 \times 3 = 0$ illustrate that the product of any number and zero is zero. These examples illustrate the *multiplication property of zero*.

In general, we assume that for every number a:

$$a \times 0 = 0 \quad and \quad 0 \times a = 0$$

MULTIPLICATION PROPERTY OF ONE

The true sentences $5 \times 1 = 5$ and $1 \times 9 = 9$ illustrate that the product of any number and one is that number itself. These examples illustrate the *multiplication property of one*.

In general, we assume that for every number a:

$$a \times 1 = a \quad and \quad 1 \times a = a$$

We call 1 the *identity element of multiplication*, or the *multiplicative identity*.

Model Problems

1. Evaluate the number expression $3 \times 1 + (8 + 0)$ and give the reason for each step of the procedure.

   Solution:

Step	Reason
1. $3 \times 1 + (8 + 0) = 3 \times 1 + 8$	1. Addition property of 0
2. $\qquad\qquad\quad = 3 + 8$	2. Multiplication property of 1
3. $\qquad\qquad\quad = 11$	3. Substitution principle

   Answer: 11

2. Express $6t + t$ as a product and give the reason for each step of the procedure.

   Solution:

Step	Reason
1. $6t + t = 6t + 1t$	1. Multiplication property of 1
2. $\quad\quad = (6 + 1)t$	2. Distributive property
3. $\quad\quad = 7t$	3. Substitution principle

   Answer: $7t$

EXERCISES

In 1–6, evaluate the number expression and give the reason for each step in the procedure.

1. $10 \times 0 + 6 \times 1$
2. $(7 + 0) + 7 \times 0$
3. $(0 + 6) + 1 \times 8$
4. $(6\frac{1}{2} + 0) - (0 + 5)$
5. $4 \times 1 - (0 + 2)$
6. $12(8 - 7) + 6 \times 0 - (1 + 0)$

In 7–11, write the algebraic expression as a product and give the reason for each step in the procedure.

7. $10x + x$ 8. $3b + b$ 9. $8y - y$ 10. $7ab + ab$ 11. $8x^2 - x^2$

12. The following sequence of equations can be used to show that $y \cdot 0 = 0$ for all numbers y. State the reason for each of the steps from 1 through 5.

    1. $y(1 + 0)$ $= y \cdot 1$
    2. $y(1 + 0)$ $= y \cdot 1 + y \cdot 0$
    3. $y \cdot 1 + y \cdot 0 = y \cdot 1$
    4. $y + y \cdot 0$ $= y$
    5. $y \cdot 0$ $= 0$

Chapter 5

Signed Numbers

If the numbers of arithmetic were the only numbers at our disposal, we could represent a temperature of 80 degrees above zero by 80, but we would have no symbol to represent the opposite, a temperature of 80 degrees below zero. Moreover, we would not be able to subtract one number from another in all cases. For example, we would be able to find a value, the number 3, for the indicated difference $10 - 7$; but we would not be able to find a number to represent $7 - 10$. In order to deal with situations such as these, we will develop a new set of numbers. These numbers will be essential in the solution of many algebraic problems.

1. Extending the Number Line

Until now, we have dealt only with a number line like the one shown. It starts at zero and extends indefinitely to the right.

Since a line extends indefinitely in both directions, we can begin at 0 and mark off unit intervals to the left as well as to the right. We label successive points to the right of zero $^+1$, $^+2$, $^+3$, and so on; we label successive points in the opposite direction, to the left of zero, $^-1$, $^-2$, $^-3$, and so on.

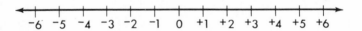

The entire number line which extends both to the right of zero (in a positive direction) and to the left of zero (in a negative direction) is called the *real number line*. The coordinate of each point on the line is called a *real number*. The numbers which are coordinates of points to the right of zero are called *positive real numbers*; those to the left are called *negative real numbers*. The numbers which are either 0 or positive are called ***non-negative***; the numbers which are either 0 or negative are called ***non-positive***. Since signs that indicate direction are used to distinguish between numerals that represent positive and negative numbers, these numbers are called ***signed numbers***, or ***directed numbers***. Although 0 is not written with a sign, we include it in the set of signed numbers. There are points on the real number line which are associated with real numbers that we have not yet discussed, but which we will discuss in later chapters. All statements we will make about the properties of real numbers in this chapter will also be true for these other real numbers; that is, they will be true for *all* real numbers.

We will make frequent use of the set of signed numbers

$$\{\ldots,\ ^-4,\ ^-3,\ ^-2,\ ^-1,\ 0,\ ^+1,\ ^+2,\ ^+3,\ ^+4,\ \ldots\}$$

called the set of ***integers***. The numbers $^+1$, $^+2$, $^+3$, ... are called ***positive integers***; the numbers $^-1$, $^-2$, $^-3$, ... are called ***negative integers***.

Observe that $^+1$ and 1 are considered as numerals which represent the same number, because they are associated with the same point on a number line. Likewise, 2 is another name for $^+2$, and $^+3$ is another name for 3. Actually, the positive numbers do not represent new numbers; only the negative numbers do.

We must be careful not to confuse the "$^+$" and "$^-$" with the "+" and "−." The "$^+$" and "$^-$", placed slightly above the numbers, are used in signed numbers to indicate direction; the "+" and "−" are used to indicate addition and subtraction.

EXERCISES

In 1–3, draw a real number line. Then locate the points whose coordinates are given.

1. $^+4$, $^-2$, 0, $^-5$, $^+3$ **2.** $^+\frac{1}{2}$, 0, $^-1\frac{1}{2}$, $^+3\frac{1}{2}$, $^-\frac{3}{4}$ **3.** $^+1$, $^-\frac{1}{3}$, 0, $^+1\frac{2}{3}$, $^-\frac{5}{6}$

In 4–6, graph the set of numbers on a real number line.

4. $\{2, ^-1, 0, 3, ^-4\}$ **5.** $\{^-\frac{1}{2}, \frac{3}{4}, 0, 1\frac{1}{2}, ^-1\frac{3}{4}\}$ **6.** $\{3, ^-\frac{2}{3}, \frac{5}{6}, ^-2\frac{1}{3}, 0\}$

In 7–14, state whether or not the signed numbers are on the same side of 0 on a number line.

7. $^+9$, $^+4$ **8.** $^-9$, $^-4$ **9.** $^+9$, $^-4$ **10.** $^-9$, $^+4$
11. $^+3$, $^+6$ **12.** $^-5$, $^-4$ **13.** $^+10$, $^-3$ **14.** $^-8$, $^+7$

15. Which part of the numeral for a signed number reveals whether the number is to the right or to the left of 0 on a number line?

In 16–23, select the number which is farther from 0 on a number line.

16. $^+10$, $^+4$ **17.** $^-10$, $^-4$ **18.** $^+10$, $^-4$ **19.** $^-10$, $^-4$

20. $^+9, ^+3$ **21.** $^-6, ^-8$ **22.** $^-7, ^+5$ **23.** $^+8, ^-1$

24. What part of the numeral for a signed number reveals its distance from 0 on a number line?

In 25–30, graph the numbers on a number line. Then tell which point is to the right of the other.

25. $^+5, ^-2$ **26.** $^-5, ^+2$ **27.** $^+7, ^+3$ **28.** $^-7, ^-3$ **29.** $0, ^-4$ **30.** $^+4, 0$

In 31–37: **(a)** Graph the number on a number line. **(b)** Locate a point on the number line which is the same distance from 0 as the given point but on the opposite side of 0. **(c)** Name the number located in **(b)**.

31. $^+4$ **32.** $^-5$ **33.** 7   **34.** $^-3$ **35.** $1\frac{1}{2}$ **36.** $^-3\frac{1}{4}$ **37.** $^+2.5$

In 38–42, use a real number line which extends from $^-10$ to $^+10$ to answer the question. Moving a given distance to the right is represented by a positive number; moving a given distance to the left is represented by a negative number.

38. Start at 0 and move a distance represented by $^+3$. From that point, move a distance represented by $^+5$. At what point on the number line have you arrived?

39. Start at 0 and move a distance represented by $^-3$. From that point, move a distance represented by $^-6$. At what point on the number line have you arrived?

40. Start at 0 and move a distance represented by $^+9$. From that point, move a distance represented by $^-3$. At what point on the number line have you arrived?

41. Start at 0 and move a distance represented by $^+4$. From that point, move a distance represented by $^-9$. At what point on the number line have you arrived?

42. Start at 0 and move a distance represented by $^+8$. From that point, move a distance represented by $^-8$. At what point on the number line have you arrived?

2. Using Signed Numbers to Represent Opposite Situations

In daily life, we frequently talk about "opposite situations." For example, we talk about traveling east and traveling west, gaining weight and losing weight, latitudes north of the equator and latitudes south of the equator. The following examples illustrate the use of signed numbers in such situations:

    1. If traveling 10 miles east is indicated by $^+10$, then traveling 10 miles west is indicated by $^-10$.

2. If winning $5 is represented by $^+5$, then losing $5 is represented by $^-5$.

3. If a temperature reading of $^+8°$ means 8° above zero, then a temperature reading of $^-8°$ means 8° below zero.

Model Problem

If the temperature changes from 2° below zero to 4° above zero, represent the change as a signed number.

Solution: If the temperature changes from 2° below zero to 4° above zero, it has risen 6°, which is represented by $^+6°$.

Answer: $^+6°$

EXERCISES

In 1–6, describe the opposite of each situation.

1. a rise in price   2. south of the equator
3. traveling west   4. below average
5. a gain in weight   6. making a profit
7. If $^+8$ means a profit of $8, what does $^-8$ mean?
8. If $^+12$ means a gain of 12 kilograms, what does $^-12$ mean?
9. If $^+40$ means 40° north of the equator, what does $^-40$ mean?
10. If $^-75$ means withdrawing $75 from a bank, what does $^+75$ mean?
11. If $^-90$ means 90 kilometers east, what does $^+90$ mean?

In 12–19, represent each situation by a positive number, a negative number, or zero.

12. 75° above zero   13. 12° below zero
14. sea level   15. 1200 feet above sea level
16. a gain of $100.50   17. a fall of $1\frac{1}{2}$ meters
18. the latitude of the equator   19. a withdrawal of $25 from a bank
20. If sea level is represented by 0, by what signed number would 100 meters below sea level be represented?
21. What is meant by the statement that the altitude of the Dead Sea is $^-1290$ feet?
22. What is meant by the statement that the net change in the value of a stock is $^+2$ dollars?
23. If the temperature changes from 15° above zero to 28° above zero, represent the change as a signed number.

24. If the temperature changes from 3° below zero to 12° below zero, represent the change as a signed number.
25. If the temperature changes from 10° above zero to 2° below zero, represent the change as a signed number.
26. If the temperature changes from 8° below zero to 5° above zero, represent the change as a signed number.
27. One day the following Fahrenheit temperatures were reported:

Time, P.M.	1	2	3	4	5	6	7	8	9
Temperature (degrees)	⁻5	⁻3	⁻2	0	⁺3	⁺1	⁻2	⁻4	⁻7

   a. Give the meaning of the temperature at each hour.
   b. What was the highest temperature reported?
   c. What was the lowest temperature reported?
   d. Between what hours was the temperature rising?
   e. Between what hours was the temperature falling?
28. By means of a signed number, indicate for each child the difference between the actual weight and the normal weight:

	Tom	Bill	John	Sam	Mary	Sue	Bess	Ann
Actual weight	23	28	36	50	39	46	42	43
Normal weight	21	29	39	43	35	46	37	49
Difference	⁺2							

3. Ordering Signed Numbers on a Number Line

A temperature of ⁺4° is higher than a temperature of ⁺2°. That is, ⁺4 is greater than ⁺2, written ⁺4 > ⁺2. On a number line, ⁺4 is to the right of ⁺2.

$$\xleftarrow{\quad} \underset{\substack{-4 \ -3 \ -2 \ -1 \ 0 \ +1 \ +2 \ +3 \ +4}}{\overline{|\ |\ |\ |\ |\ |\ |\ |\ |}} \xrightarrow{\quad}$$

A temperature of ⁻3° is lower than a temperature of ⁻1°. That is, ⁻3 is less than ⁻1, written ⁻3 < ⁻1. On a number line, ⁻3 is to the left of ⁻1.

These examples illustrate the fact that *all signed numbers are ordered on the real number line.* Any number is greater than every number to its left and is less than every number to its right.

If we wish to indicate that ⁻3 is between ⁻4 and ⁻2, we write ⁻4 < ⁻3 < ⁻2 or ⁻2 > ⁻3 > ⁻4.

Model Problems

1. State whether each of the following sentences is true or false and give the reason for your answer:
   a. ⁺7 > ⁻2 *Ans.* True because ⁺7 is to the right of ⁻2 on a number line.
   b. ⁻5 > ⁻3 *Ans.* False because ⁻5 is to the left of ⁻3 on a number line.
   c. ⁻4 < ⁺1 *Ans.* True because ⁻4 is to the left of ⁺1 on a number line.

2. If the domain of x is {⁻3, ⁻2, ⁻1, 0, ⁺1, ⁺2, ⁺3}, graph the solution set for the sentence $x \geq$ ⁻2.

   Solution: When any element of the
   domain except ⁻3 replaces x in the
   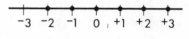
   sentence $x \geq$ ⁻2 (which means
   $x >$ ⁻2 or $x =$ ⁻2), the resulting statement is true. Therefore, the solution set
   of $x \geq$ ⁻2 is {⁻2, ⁻1, 0, ⁺1, ⁺2, ⁺3}.

3. Using the set of signed numbers as the replacement set, graph the solution set of each of the following sentences:
   a. $y >$ ⁻4   b. $m \leq$ ⁻2   c. ⁻3 $\leq t <$ ⁺2

   Solution:

   a. The graph of $y >$ ⁻4 consists of all points to the right of ⁻4. The non-darkened circle shows that ⁻4 is not included.

   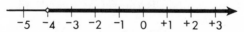

   b. The graph of $m \leq$ ⁻2 consists of
   the point ⁻2 and all points to the
   left of ⁻2. The darkened circle
   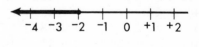
   shows that ⁻2 is included.

   c. The graph of ⁻3 $\leq t <$ ⁺2 consists of the point ⁻3 and all points between ⁻3 and ⁺2. The point ⁺2 is not included.

   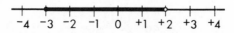

EXERCISES

In 1–8, state whether the sentence is true or false. Give the reason for your answer.

1. $^+5 > {}^+2$ 2. $^-3 < 0$ 3. $^+2 < 0$ 4. $^+8 > {}^-2$
5. $^-7 > {}^-1$ 6. $^-4 > {}^+2.5$ 7. $^-1\frac{3}{4} > {}^-1\frac{7}{8}$ 8. $0 < {}^-\frac{1}{4}$

In 9–14, use the symbol $<$ to order the numbers.

9. $^-4, {}^+8$ 10. $^-3, {}^-6$ 11. $^+1\frac{1}{2}, {}^-1\frac{1}{2}$
12. $^+3, {}^-2, {}^-4$ 13. $^-2, {}^+8, 0$ 14. $^-3\frac{1}{2}, {}^+6, {}^+2\frac{1}{2}$

In 15–20, use the symbol $>$ to order the numbers.

15. $^+7, {}^-4$ 16. $^-12, {}^+12$ 17. $^-1\frac{1}{2}, 0$
18. $^+3, {}^-3, {}^+5$ 19. $^-5, {}^-1, 0$ 20. $^-1.5, {}^+3\frac{1}{2}, {}^-2\frac{1}{2}$

In 21–23, state which number is between the other two.

21. $^+8, {}^-2, {}^+2$ 22. $^+9, {}^-9, {}^-4$ 23. $^+.6, {}^+1.1, {}^-.8$

In 24–27, state whether the sentence is true or false.

24. $^+5 \geq {}^+2$ 25. $^-2 \leq {}^+5$ 26. $^-9 \leq {}^-12$ 27. $^-3 \geq {}^-3$

28. If x is a positive number and y is a negative number ($x > 0$ and $y < 0$), tell whether each statement is true or false.
    a. $x = y$ b. $x > y$ c. $y > x$ d. $x < 0$ e. $y < 0 < x$

In 29–40, if the replacement set is $\{^-4, {}^-3, {}^-2, {}^-1, 0, {}^+1, {}^+2, {}^+3, {}^+4\}$, graph the truth set of the open sentence.

29. $x > 0$ 30. $x < 0$ 31. $x \geq 0$
32. $x \leq 0$ 33. $y > {}^-1$ 34. $t < {}^+2$
35. $m \geq {}^+1$ 36. $c \leq {}^-1$ 37. $^-1 < d < {}^+3$
38. $^-1 \leq x < {}^+2$ 39. $^-1 < y \leq {}^+2$ 40. $^-3 \leq t \leq {}^+3$

In 41–55, if the domain is the set of signed numbers, graph the solution set of the sentence.

41. $x > {}^+6$ 42. $y < {}^-3$ 43. $r > 0$
44. $s \leq 0$ 45. $m \geq {}^-1$ 46. $m \leq {}^-4$
47. $x \neq {}^+2$ 48. $z \geq {}^+2\frac{1}{2}$ 49. $^-3 < x < {}^+2$
50. $^-2 \leq x < {}^+4$ 51. $^-1 < y \leq {}^+3.5$ 52. $^-3\frac{1}{3} \leq m \leq {}^-3$
53. $x \neq {}^+1$ and $x \neq {}^-1$ 54. $x \geq {}^+2\frac{1}{4}$ and $x \not> {}^+2\frac{1}{4}$ 55. $x \geq 0$ and $x \leq 0$

In 56–59, graph the set when the domain is the set of signed numbers.

56. $\{x \mid x > 0\}$ 57. $\{y \mid y \leq {}^-2\}$
58. $\{z \mid {}^-3 \leq z < 3\}$ 59. $\{x \mid {}^-5 < x \leq {}^-3\frac{1}{2}\}$

4. The Opposite of a Directed Number

On a real number line, any nonzero number can be paired with a unique number which is the same distance from 0 and on the opposite side of 0. We call such a pair of numbers *opposites*. For example, ⁻1 is

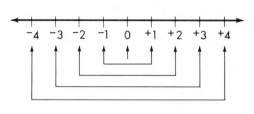

the opposite of ⁺1, and ⁺2 is the opposite of ⁻2. We say that the opposite of 0 is 0. A centered dash "−" placed before a numeral is used as a symbol for "the opposite of."

$-(^+1) = {}^-1$ is read, "the opposite of ⁺1 is ⁻1"
$-(^-2) = {}^+2$ is read, "the opposite of ⁻2 is ⁺2"

We know that ⁺4 and 4 name the same number. Hence, the opposite of ⁺4, written −(⁺4), and the opposite of 4, written −4, both name the same number. Since −(⁺4) = ⁻4, then −4 = ⁻4. Notice that −4 and ⁻4 are really two different names for the same number. Therefore, we will use only one symbol, −4, to represent that number.

In the future, we will simplify our mathematical notation by not using the symbols "⁺" and "⁻". The number represented by the symbol ⁺4 will be written 4 or +4. The number represented by the symbols ⁻4 and −(⁺4) will be written −4. The equation −(⁺4) = ⁻4 will be written −(+4) = −4 or, even more simply, −4 = −4.

If y is a real number, the opposite of y is written $-y$. The symbol $-y$ is also frequently read "negative y." However, this does not mean that $-y$ is always a negative number. When y is a positive number, its opposite, $-y$, is a negative number; when y is a negative number, $-y$ is a positive number. When y is 0, $-y$ is also 0. When y is non-negative, $-y$ is non-positive; when y is non-positive, $-y$ is non-negative.

The opposite of the opposite of a number is always the number itself. For example, the opposite of the opposite of 5, −(−5), is 5. The opposite of the opposite of −6, −[−(−6)] is −6.

In general, if y is a real number, then:

$$-(-y) = y$$

Model Problems

In 1–4, write the simplest symbol which represents the opposite of the number.

1. 15   *Ans.* −15   2. −10   *Ans.* 10 or +10

3. $(4 + 8)$　　　　*Ans.* −12　　　　4. $-[-(9 - 3)]$　　　　*Ans.* −6
5. Graph the solution set of $-c > 1$ if the domain is $\{-2, -1, 0, 1, 2\}$.

　Solution:

　　Step 1. In the open sentence $-c > 1$, replace c by the elements of the domain.

　　　　　　　$-(-2) > 1$, or $2 > 1$ is a *true* sentence.
　　　　　　　$-(-1) > 1$, or $1 > 1$ is a false sentence.
　　　　　　　$-(0) > 1$, or $0 > 1$ is a false sentence.
　　　　　　　$-(1) > 1$, or $-1 > 1$ is a false sentence.
　　　　　　　$-(2) > 1$, or $-2 > 1$ is a false sentence.

　　　　Therefore, the solution set of $-c > 1$ is $\{-2\}$.

　　Step 2. Graph the solution set $\{-2\}$.
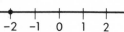

EXERCISES

In 1–12, write the simplest symbol which represents the opposite of the number.

1. 8　　　　　　2. −8　　　　　3. $+3\frac{1}{2}$　　　　4. −6.5
5. $(10 + 9)$　　6. $(24 - 10)$　7. $(9 - 9)$　　8. 8×0
9. $-(-7)$　　10. $-(-\frac{3}{4})$　11. $-[-(+5)]$　12. $-[-(6 + 8)]$

In 13–16, select the greater of the two numbers.

13. $10, -5$　　　14. $-1, 7$　　　15. $-8, -4$　　16. $-12, 0$

In 17–28, graph the solution set of the open sentence if the domain of the variable is $\{-4, -3, -2, -1, 0, 1, 2, 3, 4\}$.

17. $-w > 2$　　18. $-t < 1$　　19. $-m > 0$　　20. $-y \leq 0$
21. $-x \geq 1$　　22. $-x > -1$　23. $-x < -3$　24. $-y < y$
25. $-c \geq -2$　26. $-d \leq -1\frac{1}{2}$　27. $-4 < x < 4$　28. $-2 < -x < 1$

In 29–40, graph the solution set of the open sentence if the domain of the variable is the set of real numbers.

29. $x < -3$　　30. $y > -6$　　31. $m \geq -1$　　32. $y \leq -2.75$
33. $-t \geq 4$　　34. $-s \leq 0$　　35. $-c < -2$　　36. $-d > -3.5$
37. $-m \geq -2\frac{1}{2}$　38. $-r \leq -4$　　39. $-8 < s < 3$　40. $-3 < -y < 1.25$

In 41–48, tell whether the statement is true or false.

41. If a is a real number, then $-a$ is always a negative number.
42. If a is a negative number, then $-a$ is always a positive number.
43. The opposite of a number is always a different number.

44. On a number line, the opposite of a positive number is to the left of the number.

45. On a number line, the opposite of any number is to the left of the number.

46. If *a* is a positive number, then *a* is greater than its opposite.

47. If *a* is greater than its opposite, then *a* is positive.

48. The opposite of the opposite of a number is that number itself.

5. The Absolute Value of a Number

In every pair of opposite numbers, other than 0 and 0, the positive number is the greater. On a real number line a positive number is always to the right of the negative number which is its opposite. For example, 10 is greater than its opposite −10; on a number line, 10 is to the right of −10. The greater of a nonzero number and its opposite is called the *absolute value* of the number. Since 10 is the greater of the two opposite numbers 10 and −10, the absolute value of 10 is 10, symbolized $|10| = 10$. Also, the absolute value of −10 is 10, written $|-10| = 10$. Likewise $|+8| = 8$, and $|-8| = 8$. We use the symbol "$|x|$" to represent the absolute value of the number x. The absolute value of 0 is 0, written $|0| = 0$.

Notice that the absolute value of a positive number is the number itself; the absolute value of a negative number is always its opposite; the absolute value of zero is zero.

In general, using the absolute value symbol, we can say: For every number x,

$$|x| = x \text{ when } x > 0,$$
$$|x| = -x \text{ when } x < 0, \text{ and}$$
$$|x| = 0 \text{ when } x = 0.$$

Note that for any nonzero number x, $|x|$ is a positive number ($|x| > 0$). Hence, since $|0| = 0$, it follows that for every number x, $|x| \geq 0$.

If P is the graph of the number 3 on any real number line, then the distance between P and O, the graph of 0, is 3. Observe that this dis-

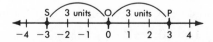

tance 3 is equal to the absolute value of 3, written $3 = |3|$. Also, if S is the graph of the number −3 on this real number line, the distance between S and O is 3. Observe that the distance 3 is equal to the absolute value of −3, written 3 = |−3|. We see, therefore, that the concept of absolute value expresses the idea of *undirected distance* from the zero point on a real number line.

Since |3| = 3 and |−3| = 3, then |3| = |−3|. This example illustrates that, for a pair of opposite numbers, the absolute value of one member of the pair is the same number as the absolute value of the second member.

In general for any number x,

$$|x| = |-x|$$

Model Problems

1. Find the value of the number expression |12| + |−3|.

   Solution: |12| + |−3| = 12 + 3 = 15   *Answer:* 15

2. Find the solution set of |x| = 4, if the domain is the set of signed numbers.

   Solution: We know that 4 and −4 are the only numbers whose graphs on a number line are an undirected distance of 4 from the zero point. If x is replaced by 4, |x| = 4 becomes |4| = 4, a true sentence. If x is replaced by −4, |x| = 4 becomes |−4| = 4, a true sentence. No other signed number can replace x and result in a true sentence. Therefore, the solution set of |x| = 4 is {4, −4}. *Answer:* {4, −4}

EXERCISES

In 1–10: **(a)** Give the absolute value of the given number. **(b)** Give another number which has the same absolute value.

1. 3	2. −5	3. +18	4. −13	5. −20
6. $1\frac{1}{2}$	7. $-3\frac{3}{4}$	8. $-1\frac{1}{2}$	9. +2.7	10. −1.4

In 11–18, state whether the sentence is true or false.

11. |20| = 20	12. |−13| = 13	13. |−15| = −15	14. |−9| = |9|
15. |−7| < |7|	16. |−10| > |3|	17. |8| < |−19|	18. |−21| > 21

In 19–27, find the value of the number expression.

19. |9| + |3|	20. |+8| − |+2|	21. |−6| + |4|
22. |−10| − |−5|	23. |4.5| − |−4.5|	24. |+6| × |−4|
25. |(8 − 4)| + |−3|	26. |+12| − |−8| − |+4|	27. −(|−9| − |7|)

In 28–35, state whether the sentence is true or false.

28. |+5| − |−5| = 0   29. |+9| + |−9| = 0

30. $|3| \times |-3| = -9$ **31.** $2 \times |-4| = |-2| \times |-4|$

32. $\dfrac{|-8|}{|-4|} = -|+2|$ **33.** $|4| \times |-2| - \dfrac{|-16|}{|2|} = 0$

34. $|-6| \times |4| > 0$ **35.** $|6| + |-4| < 6 - 4$

In 36–43, find the solution set of the open sentence if the domain is the set of signed numbers.

36. $|x| = 5$ **37.** $|m| = 6$ **38.** $|t| = 0$

39. $|-x| = 8$ **40.** $|x| + 2 = 12$ **41.** $|y| + |7| = 13$

42. $|x| - 5 = 10$ **43.** $|t| - |4| = 2$

In 44–47, graph the solution set of the open sentence if the domain is the set of signed numbers.

44. $|x| = 2$ **45.** $|x| > 2$ **46.** $|x| < 2$ **47.** $-1 < |x| < 2$

6. Adding Signed Numbers on a Number Line

Addition of signed numbers may be interpreted on a number line as a sequence of directed moves. We will represent "moving to the right" by a positive number and "moving to the left" by a negative number.

Model Problems

1. Add +3 and +2.

   Solution: Start at 0 and move 3 units to the right to +3; then move 2 more units to the right, arriving at +5.

   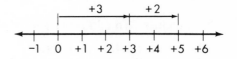

   Answer: $(+3) + (+2) = +5$

2. Add −3 and −2.

   Solution: Start at 0 and move 3 units to the left to −3; then move 2 more units to the left, arriving at −5.

   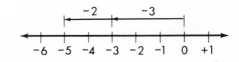

   Answer: $(-3) + (-2) = -5$

3. Add +3 and −2.

> *Solution:* Start at 0 and move 3 units
> to the right to +3; then move 2
> units to the left, arriving at +1.
>
> *Answer:* $(+3) + (-2) = +1$

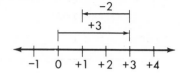

4. Add −3 and +2.

> *Solution:* Start at 0 and move 3 units
> to the left to −3; then move 2 units
> to the right, arriving at −1.
>
> *Answer:* $(-3) + (+2) = -1$

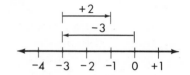

5. Add + 3 and −3.

> *Solution:* Start at 0 and move 3 units
> to the right to +3; then move 3
> units to the left, arriving at 0.
>
> *Answer:* $(+3) + (-3) = 0$

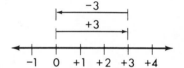

6. Add 0 and −3.

> *Solution:* Start at 0 and move neither
> to the right nor to the left; then
> move 3 units to the left, arriving at
> −3.
>
> *Answer:* $(0) + (-3) = -3$

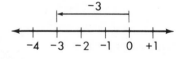

Procedure.   To add two signed numbers on a number line:

1. **Graph the first number.**
2. **From this point, move to the right a number of units equal to
   the absolute value of the second number if the second number is
   positive; move to the left if the second number is negative; do
   not move if the second number is 0. The number at the point
   that is reached is the sum of the two signed numbers.**

Model Problem

Use positive and negative numbers to do the following problem:

Helen gained 3 kilograms during one month and lost 2 kilograms during the next
month. What was the net change in her weight over the two-month period?

Solution: A gain of 3 kilograms can be represented by +3, a loss of 2 kilograms by −2. The net change can be represented by $(+3) + (-2)$. Using a number line, or adding mentally, $(+3) + (-2) = +1$.

Answer: The net change in her weight was a gain of 1 kilogram.

EXERCISES

In 1–13, use a number line to find the sum of the signed numbers.

1. $(+3) + (+4)$ 2. $(-5) + (-3)$ 3. $(+7) + (-4)$
4. $(-6) + (+5)$ 5. $(+4) + (-4)$ 6. $(-7) + (+7)$
7. $(0) + (+4)$ 8. $(0) + (-6)$ 9. $(-8) + (0)$
10. $[(+3) + (+4)] + (+2)$ 11. $[(+8) + (-4)] + (-6)$
12. $[(-7) + (-3)] + (+6)$ 13. $[(-5) + (+2)] + (+3)$

In 14–16, find the sum in both parts and state the relationship between the two results.

14. a. $(+1) + (+6)$ b. $(+6) + (+1)$
15. a. $(-5) + (-4)$ b. $(-4) + (-5)$
16. a. $(-7) + (+3)$ b. $(+3) + (-7)$
17. Judging from the answers obtained in exercises 14–16, what property of addition seems to hold true for signed numbers?

In 18–20, find the sum in both parts and state the relationship between the two results.

18. a. $[(+3) + (+2)] + (+4)$ b. $(+3) + [(+2) + (+4)]$
19. a. $[(-1) + (-2)] + (-4)$ b. $(-1) + [(-2) + (-4)]$
20. a. $[(-5) + (+6)] + (-3)$ b. $(-5) + [(+6) + (-3)]$
21. Judging from the answers obtained in exercises 18–20, what property of addition seems to hold true for signed numbers?

In 22–24, find the sum of the signed numbers.

22. $(+8) + (-8)$ 23. $(-6) + (+6)$ 24. $(-20) + (+20)$
25. Judging from the answers obtained in exercises 22–24, what seems to be the sum of any two signed numbers which are opposites?

In 26–29, find the sum of the signed numbers.

26. $(0) + (+3)$ 27. $(0) + (-8)$ 28. $(+7) + (0)$ 29. $(-5) + (0)$
30. Judging from the answers obtained in exercises 26–29, if a signed number and 0 are added, what seems to be true of the sum?

In 31–35, use signed numbers to solve the problem.

31. In one hour the temperature rose 4° and in the next hour the temperature rose 3°. What was the net change in temperature during the two-hour period?

32. An elevator started on the ground floor and rose 30 floors. Then it came down 12 floors. At which floor was it at that time?

33. A plane started in New York and flew 400 kilometers south in one hour. During the next hour, it flew 350 kilometers farther south. At the end of two hours, where was the plane with reference to New York?

34. A football team gained 7 yards on the first play, lost 2 yards on the second, and lost 8 yards on the third. What was the net result of the three plays?

35. During a four-day period, the value of a share of stock rose $1\frac{1}{2}$ on the first day, dropped $\$\frac{5}{8}$ on the second day, rose $\$\frac{1}{8}$ on the third day, and dropped $\$1\frac{3}{4}$ on the fourth day. What was the net change in the stock during this period?

36. What type of number does the sum of two positive numbers always appear to be?

37. What type of number does the sum of two negative numbers always appear to be?

38. Is it possible for the sum of a positive and a negative number to be **(a)** a positive number? **(b)** a negative number?

39. If two given signed numbers (not opposites) are to be added, how can you tell whether the sum is a positive number or a negative number?

40. Is it possible for the sum of two numbers of arithmetic to be less than each of the numbers?

41. **a.** Is it possible for the sum of two signed numbers to be less than each of the numbers?
    b. If your answer in part **a** is yes, give an example.

7. Addition of Signed Numbers

In Chapter 4, we learned that the numbers of arithmetic have various properties of addition. Now we will define the operation of addition so that these properties are also true for signed numbers. Thus, we will be able to add signed numbers without the use of a number line.

ADDITION OF TWO POSITIVE NUMBERS

If $+2$ and $+4$ are added on a number line, the sum is $+6$. We write $(+2) + (+4) = +6$, or $2 + 4 = 6$. This example illustrates that we can add positive numbers in the same manner that we added the numbers of arithmetic.

The sum $(+2) + (+4)$ can also be written vertically as shown at the right.

$+2$	The absolute value of $+2$ is 2.
$+4$	The absolute value of $+4$ is 4.
$+6$	The sum of the absolute values is 6.

Observe that the sum $+6$ is a positive number whose absolute value 6 is the sum of 2 and 4, the absolute values of $+2$ and $+4$.

Rule 1. The sum of two positive numbers is a positive number whose absolute value is found by adding the absolute values of the numbers.

In general, if both a and b are positive numbers; that is, $a > 0$ and $b > 0$, then:

$$a + b = |a| + |b|$$

Model Problems

In 1-4, add the two numbers.

1. $\begin{array}{r} +\ 8 \\ +10 \\ \hline +18 \end{array}$
   2. $\begin{array}{r} +\ 9.1 \\ +\ 7.5 \\ \hline +16.6 \end{array}$
   3. $(+8) + (+4) = +12$
   4. $1\frac{1}{3} + 8\frac{1}{3} = 9\frac{2}{3}$

ADDITION OF TWO NEGATIVE NUMBERS

If -2 and -4 are added on a number line, the sum is -6. We can write $(-2) + (-4) = -6$, or we can arrange the addition vertically as shown at the right.

-2	The absolute value of -2 is 2.
-4	The absolute value of -4 is 4.
-6	The sum of the absolute values is 6.

Observe that the sum -6 is a negative number whose absolute value 6 is the sum of 2 and 4, the absolute values of -2 and -4.

Rule 2. The sum of two negative numbers is a negative number whose absolute value is found by adding the absolute values of the numbers.

In general, if both a and b are negative numbers; that is, $a < 0$ and $b < 0$, then:

$$a + b = -(|a| + |b|)$$

Model Problems

In 1–5, add the two numbers.

1. $\begin{array}{r} -4 \\ \underline{-3} \\ -7 \end{array}$ 2. $\begin{array}{r} -8 \\ \underline{-10} \\ -18 \end{array}$ 3. $\begin{array}{r} -7.4 \\ \underline{-8.7} \\ -16.1 \end{array}$ 4. $(-6) + (-13) = -19$

5. $(-5\frac{1}{2}) + (-3\frac{1}{4}) = -8\frac{3}{4}$

ADDITION OF A POSITIVE NUMBER AND A NEGATIVE NUMBER

If $+5$ and -3 are added on a number line, the sum is $+2$. We can write

$(+5) + (-3) = +2,$

or we can arrange the addition vertically as shown at the right.

$\begin{array}{ll} +5 & \text{The absolute value of } +5 \text{ is } 5. \\ \underline{-3} & \text{The absolute value of } -3 \text{ is } 3. \\ +2 & \text{The difference of the absolute values is } 2. \end{array}$

Observe that the sum $+2$ is a positive number and that $+5$, the number with the larger absolute value, is also a positive number. Observe that 2, the absolute value of the sum $+2$, is the difference of 5 and 3, the absolute values of $+5$ and -3. The difference of the two absolute values is simply the larger absolute value minus the smaller absolute value.

If -5 and $+3$ are added on a number line, the sum is -2. We can write

$(-5) + (+3) = -2,$

or we can arrange the addition vertically as shown at the right.

$\begin{array}{ll} -5 & \text{The absolute value of } -5 \text{ is } 5. \\ \underline{+3} & \text{The absolute value of } +3 \text{ is } 3. \\ -2 & \text{The difference of the absolute values is } 2. \end{array}$

Observe that the sum -2 is a negative number and that -5, the number with the larger absolute value, is also a negative number. Observe that 2, the absolute value of the sum -2, is the difference of 5 and 3, the absolute values of -5 and $+3$.

If $+6$ and -6 are added on a number line, the sum is 0. We write $(+6) + (-6) = 0$.

Rule 3. To find the sum of two numbers, one of which is positive and the other negative, find a number whose absolute value is the difference of the absolute values of the numbers. The sum is positive when the positive number has the greater absolute value; the sum is negative when the negative number has the greater absolute value; the sum is 0 if both numbers have the same absolute value.

In general, if a is a positive number, that is, $a > 0$; and if b is a negative number, that is, $b < 0$, then:

$$\text{if } |a| \geq |b|, \text{ then } a + b = |a| - |b|$$

and

$$\text{if } |b| > |a|, \text{ then } a + b = -(|b| - |a|)$$

If b is a positive number, that is, $b > 0$; and if a is a negative number, that is, $a < 0$, then:

$$\text{if } |b| \geq |a|, \text{ then } a + b = |b| - |a|$$

and

$$\text{if } |a| > |b|, \text{ then } a + b = -(|a| - |b|)$$

Model Problems

In 1–5, add the numbers.

1. $+9$	2. -8	3. -6	4. $-7\frac{3}{4}$	5. -1.8
-2	$+3$	$+8$	$5\frac{1}{4}$	7.2
$+7$	-5	$+2$	$-2\frac{1}{2}$	5.4

In Chapter 4, we studied the addition properties of the numbers of arithmetic. Now let us apply these properties to signed numbers also.

CLOSURE PROPERTY OF ADDITION

The sum of two signed numbers is always a unique member of the set of signed numbers. For example, the sum of -7 and $+2$ is -5, a signed number.

In general, for every signed number a and every signed number b:

$$a + b \text{ is a unique signed number}$$

COMMUTATIVE PROPERTY OF ADDITION

We know that $(-8) + (+6) = -2$ and that $(+6) + (-8) = -2$. Therefore, $(-8) + (+6) = (+6) + (-8)$. This example illustrates that the commutative property of addition holds for signed numbers. That is, signed numbers may be added in any order.

In general, for every signed number a and every signed number b:

$$a + b = b + a$$

ASSOCIATIVE PROPERTY OF ADDITION

We know that $[(+3) + (-1)] + (-4) = -2$ and that $(+3) + [(-1) + (-4)] = -2$. Therefore, $[(+3) + (-1)] + (-4) = (+3) + [(-1) + (-4)]$. This example illustrates that the associative property of addition holds for signed numbers. That is, in adding signed numbers, we may group them as we please.

In general, for every signed number a, every signed number b, and every signed number c:

$$(a + b) + c = a + (b + c)$$

ADDITION PROPERTY OF ZERO

The true sentences $(-5) + 0 = -5$ and $0 + (+8) = +8$ illustrate that the sum of 0 and a signed number is that number itself. For this reason, 0 is called the *identity element of addition*, or the *additive identity*.

In general, for every signed number a:

$$a + 0 = a \quad and \quad 0 + a = a$$

We will agree that:

If $a + x = a$ for some signed number a, then $x = 0$.

ADDITION PROPERTY OF OPPOSITES

The true sentence $(+7) + (-7) = 0$ illustrates that the number $+7$ has an opposite number -7 such that their sum is 0.

In general, every signed number a has a unique opposite $-a$ such that:

$$a + (-a) = 0$$

Note that if a is positive, then $-a$ is negative; if a is negative, then $-a$ is positive; if a is 0, then $-a$ is also 0.

The opposite of a number is also called the *additive inverse* of the number. The additive inverse of $+7$ is -7; the additive inverse of -7 is $+7$. Every signed number x has a unique additive inverse $-x$ such that the sum of the number x and its additive inverse $-x$ is 0.

Since the sum of a number and its additive inverse is 0, it follows that *the additive inverse of $-x$ is x*. This statement is symbolized as follows:

$$-(-x) = x$$

Observe that another interpretation of the statement "$-(-x) = x$" is *the additive inverse of the additive inverse of x is x*.

PROPERTY OF THE OPPOSITE OF A SUM

We know that $-[(+5) + (-2)] = -[+3] = -3$. We also know that $(-5) + (+2) = -3$. Therefore, $-[(+5) + (-2)] = (-5) + (+2)$. This example illustrates that the opposite of the sum of two signed numbers is equal to the sum of their opposites.

In general, for every signed number a and every signed number b:

$$-(a + b) = (-a) + (-b)$$

ADDING MORE THAN TWO NUMBERS

Since the commutative and associative properties of addition hold for signed numbers, these numbers may be arranged in any order and grouped in any way when we are adding them. It may be helpful to add all the positive numbers first, all the negative numbers second, and then add the two results.

Model Problems

1. Add: $(+5) + (+2) + (-4)$

How to Proceed	Solution
1. Write the expression.	$(+5) + (+2) + (-4)$
2. Use the associative property.	$[(+5) + (+2)] + (-4)$
3. Add the positive numbers.	$(+7) + (-4)$
4. Add the positive number and the negative number.	$+3$ *Ans.*

2. Add: $(+6) + (-2) + (+7) + (-4)$

How to Proceed	Solution
1. Write the expression.	$(+6) + (-2) + (+7) + (-4)$
2. Use the commutative and associative properties and add the positive and the negative numbers separately.	$[(+6) + (+7)] + [(-2) + (-4)]$ $\begin{array}{cc} +\,6 & -2 \\ +\,7 & -4 \\ \hline +13 & -6 \end{array}$
3. Add the positive and the negative sums.	$(+13) + (-6) = +7$ *Ans.*

USING ADDITION PROPERTIES IN PROOFS

Model Problems _____

1. Using only the associative and commutative properties of addition, show that:

$$[(+5\tfrac{2}{3}) + (-7)] + (+8\tfrac{1}{3}) = [(+5\tfrac{2}{3}) + (+8\tfrac{1}{3})] + (-7)$$

Solution:

Step	Reason

1. $[(+5\tfrac{2}{3}) + (-7)] + (+8\tfrac{1}{3}) = (+5\tfrac{2}{3}) + [(-7) + (+8\tfrac{1}{3})]$ 1. Associative property

2. $\qquad\qquad\qquad = (+5\tfrac{2}{3}) + [(+8\tfrac{1}{3}) + (-7)]$ 2. Commutative property

3. $\qquad\qquad\qquad = [(+5\tfrac{2}{3}) + (+8\tfrac{1}{3})] + (-7)$ 3. Associative property

2. To show that for any signed number x, $[(-3) + x] + 3 = x$, the following chain of equations can be used. State the reason for each step from 1 through 5.

Solution:

Step	Reason

1. $[(-3) + x] + 3 = -3 + [x + 3]$ 1. Associative property
2. $\qquad\qquad = -3 + [3 + x]$ 2. Commutative property
3. $\qquad\qquad = [(-3) + 3] + x$ 3. Associative property
4. $\qquad\qquad = 0 + x$ 4. Property of opposites (additive inverse)
5. $\qquad\qquad = x$ 5. Property of 0 (additive identity)

EXERCISES

In 1–77, add.

1. $+15$	2. -17	3. -28	4. $+8$	5. -15	6. 34
$\underline{+9}$	$\underline{-8}$	$\underline{-38}$	$\underline{+17}$	$\underline{-15}$	$\underline{66}$

7. $+6\tfrac{2}{3}$	8. $-5\tfrac{1}{2}$	9. $+3\tfrac{1}{4}$	10. $-8\tfrac{2}{3}$	11. $9\tfrac{1}{2}$	12. $-6\tfrac{5}{6}$
$\underline{+1\tfrac{1}{3}}$	$\underline{-3\tfrac{1}{2}}$	$\underline{+7\tfrac{1}{4}}$	$\underline{-4\tfrac{2}{3}}$	$\underline{8\tfrac{3}{4}}$	$\underline{-1\tfrac{2}{3}}$

13. -5.6 14. $+6.8$ 15. $+5.4$ 16. -8.8 17. 5.7 18. -5.4
    $\underline{-2.2}$ $\underline{+3.2}$ $\underline{+2.9}$ $\underline{-7.5}$ $\underline{8.3}$ $\underline{-2.6}$

19. $+70$ 20. -55 21. -15 22. 18 23. $+10$ 24. -30
    $\underline{-20}$ $\underline{+20}$ $\underline{+42}$ $\underline{-32}$ $\underline{-10}$ $\underline{0}$

25. $+9\frac{1}{2}$ 26. $23\frac{5}{6}$ 27. $-10\frac{1}{2}$ 28. $+7$ 29. $-33\frac{1}{3}$ 30. $-5\frac{3}{4}$
    $\underline{-3}$ $\underline{-9\frac{1}{6}}$ $\underline{8\frac{1}{2}}$ $\underline{-8\frac{3}{4}}$ $\underline{+19\frac{2}{3}}$ $\underline{8\frac{1}{2}}$

31. 7.9 32. -8.7 33. -6.9 34. -8.5 35. 8.3 36. $+7.1$
    $\underline{-5.6}$ $\underline{+3.7}$ $\underline{9.4}$ $\underline{+6.1}$ $\underline{-8.3}$ $\underline{-9.4}$

37. $(+15) + (+19)$ 38. $(+13) + (-32)$ 39. $(-41) + (-9)$
40. $(+8) + (-14)$ 41. $(-12) + (+37)$ 42. $(+40) + (-17)$
43. $(-18) + (0)$ 44. $(0) + (-28)$ 45. $(+15) + (-15)$
46. $(-15) + 34$ 47. $14 + 17$ 48. $(-19) + 7$
49. $|-34| + |+20|$ 50. $-|7| + (-10)$ 51. $|15| + (-|-15|)$

52. $+27$ 53. -45 54. 15 55. $+20$ 56. -1.5 57. $8\frac{1}{2}$
    -9 $+12$ -28 -12 $+3.7$ $-4\frac{1}{4}$
    $\underline{-12}$ $\underline{+13}$ $\underline{13}$ $\underline{-8}$ $\underline{-8.3}$ $\underline{7\frac{3}{4}}$

58. $+9$ 59. -21 60. 14 61. -24 62. $-.7$ 63. $8\frac{1}{6}$
    $+7$ -13 -9 15 $+3.1$ $-13\frac{1}{6}$
    -3 $+17$ -13 19 -9.6 $-3\frac{1}{3}$
    $\underline{-5}$ $\underline{+10}$ $\underline{+8}$ $\underline{-12}$ $\underline{+.5}$ $\underline{-9\frac{5}{6}}$

64. $(+18) + (-15) + (+9)$ 65. $30 + (-18) + (-12)$
66. $(-19) + (+8) + (-15)$ 67. $(-17) + (-19) + 40$
68. $(+12) + (-18) + (-4) + (+7)$ 69. $(-19) + 8 + (-5) + 16$
70. $(+36) + (-49) + (-31) + (+20)$ 71. $48 + (-32) + 19 + (-41)$
72. $(-1.5) + (+3.1) + (+6.8) + (-3.4)$
73. $9.6 + (-7.7) + (-5.6) + 2.2$
74. $(+5\frac{1}{4}) + (-8) + (+6\frac{3}{4}) + (-1\frac{1}{2})$ 75. $(-4\frac{1}{3}) + 7 + 8\frac{1}{3} - 11$
76. $|+7| + |-8| + |0|$ 77. $|-13| + |7| + (-|-20|)$

In 78-82, name the signed number which represents the sum of the quantities.

78. a rise of 4 meters and a rise of 6 meters
79. a loss of 6 yards and a loss of 2 yards
80. a rise of 4 meters and a fall of 2 meters
81. a loss of $20 and a profit of $20
82. a gain of 8 kilograms, a gain of 4 kilograms, and a loss of 7 kilograms

In 83-88, give the additive inverse of the given expression.

83. $+10$ 84. -8 85. $15\frac{3}{4}$ 86. -2.5 87. C 88. $-d$

In 89-100, give a replacement for the question mark which will make the resulting sentence true.

89. $(+4) + (?) = 0$ 90. $(-2) + (?) = 0$
91. $(0) + (?) = 0$ 92. $(12) + (?) = 0$
93. $(b) + (?) = 0$ 94. $(-y) + (?) = 0$
95. $(+8) + (?) = (+12)$ 96. $(+10) + (?) = 7$
97. $(6) + (?) = -4$ 98. $(-4\frac{1}{2}) + (?) = -9\frac{1}{2}$
99. $(-\frac{6}{7}) + (?) = (+\frac{2}{7})$ 100. $(-3.75) + (?) = -3.75$

In 101-106, give a replacement for the variable which will make the resulting sentence true.

101. $9 + y = 0$ 102. $x + (-12) = 0$ 103. $5 + c = 1$
104. $x + 4 = -2.5$ 105. $x + (-6) = 8\frac{1}{2}$ 106. $d + (-\frac{5}{2}) = -3\frac{1}{2}$

In 107-111, name the addition property which makes each sentence true.

107. $(-3) + (+8) = (+8) + (-3)$ 108. $(+50) + (-50) = 0$
109. $(-8) + 0 = -8$ 110. $-[8 + 9] = (-8) + (-9)$
111. $(-6) + [(-4) + (+2)] = [(-6) + (-4)] + (+2)$
112. The following chain of equations can be used to show that $9 + (-5) = 4$. State the reason for each step from 1 through 4.
    1. $9 + (-5) = (4 + 5) + (-5)$
    2. $\qquad\quad = 4 + [5 + (-5)]$
    3. $\qquad\quad = 4 + 0$
    4. $\qquad\quad = 4$

In 113-116, use a chain of equations like the one used in exercise 112 to show that the statement is true. Give the reason for each step.

113. $15 + (-8) = 7$ 114. $12 + (-3) = 9$
115. $(-3) + 9 = 6$ 116. $(-8) + 5 = -3$

In 117-127, use only the properties of addition to prove that the sentence is true. Give the reason for each step of the proof.

117. $(8 + 9) + 5 = (8 + 5) + 9$
118. $[(-3) + (-4)] + 6 = [(-3 + 6)] + (-4)$
119. $[(-5) + (-6)] + (-2) = [(-2) + (-5)] + (-6)$
120. $(x + 5) + (-5) = x$ 121. $[y + (-4)] + 4 = y$
122. $(7 + c) + (-7) = c$ 123. $[(-8) + 2d] + 8 = 2d$
124. $(x + y) + z = (x + z) + y$ 125. $r + [x + (-r)] = x$
126. $(-c) + (y + c) = y$ 127. $(x + y) + [(-x) + (-y)] = 0$

In 128-131, state whether the sentence is true or false.

128. $|x| + |-x| = 0 \ (x \neq 0)$ 129. $(-c) + (-d) = -(c + d)$
130. $-(-b) = b$ 131. $(a + b) + [-(a + b)] = 0$

8. Subtraction of Signed Numbers

When we were dealing with the numbers of arithmetic, we were able to subtract 3 from 7. The result was 4. We wrote $7 - 3 = 4$. However, we were not able to subtract 7 from 3 because we had no number to represent $3 - 7$. The set of numbers of arithmetic was not closed with respect to subtraction. We will now see that we can always subtract one number from another when we are dealing with the set of signed numbers.

In arithmetic, to subtract 3 from 7, we find a number which, when added to 3, will give 7. That number is 4. We know that $7 - 3 = 4$ because $3 + 4 = 7$.

Subtraction in the set of numbers of arithmetic may be viewed as the inverse operation of addition.

In general, for every number c and every number b, the expression $c - b$ represents a number a such that $b + a = c$.

In the set of signed numbers, subtraction may also be viewed as the inverse operation of addition. To subtract (-2) from $(+3)$, written $(+3) - (-2)$, we must find a number which, when added to -2, will give $+3$. We write $(-2) + (?) = +3$.

We can use a number line to help us find the answer to $(-2) + (?) = +3$. Think as follows: From a point two units to the left of 0, what motion must be made to ar-

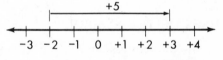

rive at a point three units to the right of 0? We must move five units to the right. This motion is represented by $+5$.

Therefore, $(+3) - (-2) = +5$ because $(-2) + (+5) = +3$. We can write $(+3) - (-2) = +5$ vertically as follows:

$$\begin{array}{ccl} (+3) & or & \textit{Subtract:}\ (+3)\ \text{minuend} \\ \underline{-(-2)} & & \underline{(-2)}\ \text{subtrahend} \\ +5 & & +5\quad \text{difference} \end{array}$$

Check each of the following examples by using a number line to answer the related question: subtrahend + (?) = minuend.

Subtract:	+9	−7	+5	−3
	+6	−2	−2	+1
	+3	−5	+7	−4

Now we will consider another way in which addition and subtraction are related. In each of the following examples, compare the result obtained when subtracting the signed number with the result obtained when adding the additive inverse or the opposite of that signed number:

Subtract	Add	Subtract	Add	Subtract	Add	Subtract	Add
$+9$	$+9$	-7	-7	$+5$	$+5$	-3	-3
$\underline{+6}$	$\underline{-6}$	$\underline{-2}$	$\underline{+2}$	$\underline{-2}$	$\underline{+2}$	$\underline{+1}$	$\underline{-1}$
$+3$	$+3$	-5	-5	$+7$	$+7$	-4	-4

Observe that in each example adding the additive inverse of a signed number gives the same result as subtracting that signed number. It therefore seems reasonable to define subtraction as follows:

If a is any signed number and b is any signed number, then:

$$a - b = a + (-b)$$

Procedure. **To subtract one signed number from another, add the additive inverse of the subtrahend to the minuend.**

Notice that it is always possible to subtract one signed number from another. Therefore, the set of signed numbers is closed with respect to subtraction.

USES OF THE SYMBOL "−"

In the expression $7 - (-5)$, the symbol "−" is used in two different ways. The first "−," which stands between the two numerals 7 and (-5), indicates the operation of subtraction. The second "−," which is part of the numeral (-5), indicates the additive inverse of 5.

Since $7 - 4 = 7 + (-4)$, the symbol $7 + (-4)$ is sometimes written $7 - 4$.

Similarly, $(+9) + (-2) + (-4)$ is sometimes written $9 - 2 - 4$.

Likewise, $-3 - 4 - 2$ can mean the sum of $-3, -4$, and -2; this may be written $(-3) + (-4) + (-2)$.

Model Problems

In 1-4, perform the indicated subtraction.

1. $(+30) - (+12) = (+30) + (-12) = +18$
2. $(-19) - (-7) = (-19) + (+7) = -12$
3. $(-4) - (0) = (-4) + (0) = -4$
4. $0 - 8 = 0 + (-8) = -8$

In 5-7, subtract the lower number from the upper number.

5. $+45$ 6. -19 7. -5
   $\underline{-20}$ $\underline{17}$ $\underline{-5}$
   $+65$ -36 0

[*Note:* In each problem the signed number is subtracted by adding its additive inverse to the minuend.]

EXERCISES

In 1–6, use a number line to do the subtraction.

1. $(+6)-(+2)$ 2. $(+5)-(-3)$ 3. $(-1)-2$
4. $(-3)-(-4)$ 5. $(-3)-(+3)$ 6. $(-3)-(-3)$

In 7–30, subtract the lower number from the upper number.

7. $+50$ 8. $+18$ 9. $+15$ 10. $+36$ 11. -39 12. -26
  $\underline{+30}$ $\underline{+29}$ $\underline{+15}$ $\underline{-15}$ $\underline{+15}$ $\underline{-18}$

13. $+27$ 14. -45 15. -6 16. -8 17. 0 18. $+7$
   $\underline{-8}$ $\underline{+17}$ $\underline{+6}$ $\underline{-8}$ $\underline{-15}$ $\underline{0}$

19. $+8.7$ 20. $+8.3$ 21. -6.9 22. 6.9 23. -3.6 24. 5.9
   $\underline{+6.5}$ $\underline{-6.2}$ $\underline{+3.7}$ $\underline{9.5}$ $\underline{-5.2}$ $\underline{7.2}$

25. $+9\frac{1}{2}$ 26. $-3\frac{1}{4}$ 27. $-3\frac{1}{6}$ 28. $7\frac{3}{4}$ 29. $-6\frac{5}{6}$ 30. $-8\frac{7}{8}$
   $\underline{+6\frac{1}{2}}$ $\underline{-7\frac{3}{4}}$ $\underline{8\frac{5}{6}}$ $\underline{-2\frac{1}{4}}$ $\underline{+3\frac{1}{3}}$ $\underline{-3\frac{1}{4}}$

In 31–39, perform the indicated subtraction.

31. $(+19)-(+30)$ 32. $(-12)-(-25)$ 33. $22-(-8)$
34. $(+6.4)-(+8.1)$ 35. $(-3.7)-(-5.2)$ 36. $(-9.2)-8.3$
37. $(+5\frac{1}{3})-(+3\frac{1}{3})$ 38. $6\frac{1}{2}-(-2\frac{1}{4})$ 39. $(-8\frac{1}{6})-(-5\frac{2}{3})$
40. Subtract $+5$ from:
    a. $+15$ b. -15 c. $+3$ d. -2 e. $+5$ f. 0
41. Subtract -9 from:
    a. $+20$ b. -30 c. $+5$ d. -6 e. -9 f. 0
42. How much is 18 decreased by -7?
43. How much greater than -15 is 12?
44. How much greater than -4 is -1?
45. How much less than 6 is -3?
46. What number is 6 less than -6?
47. From the sum of 25 and -10, subtract -4.
48. Subtract 8 from the sum of -6 and -12.

In 49–54, state the number that must be added to the given number to make the result equal to 0.

49. $+5$ 50. -3 51. $+8.5$ 52. -3.7 53. $+1\frac{7}{8}$ 54. $-\frac{9}{2}$

In 55–60, find the value of the given expression.

55. $(+7) + (+9) - (-4)$ **56.** $(-5.1) - (-8.4) - (-1.7)$

57. $(+6\frac{1}{4}) + (+9\frac{1}{2}) - (+7\frac{3}{4})$ **58.** $(-8\frac{5}{6}) - (+2\frac{1}{3}) - (-5\frac{2}{3})$

59. $32 - 49 - 21 + 10$ **60.** $-5\frac{1}{3} + 8 + 9\frac{1}{3} - 12$

In 61 and 62, use signed numbers to do the problem.

61. Find the change when the temperature changes from:
   a. $+5°$ to $+8°$ b. $-10°$ to $+18°$ c. $-6°$ to $-18°$ d. $+12°$ to $-4°$

62. In a game, Sid was 35 points "in the hole." How many points must he make in order to have a score of 150 points?

63. State whether the following sentences are true or false:
   a. $(+5) - (-3) = (-3) - (+5)$
   b. $(-7) - (-4) = (-4) - (-7)$

64. If x and y represent numbers:
   a. Does $x - y = y - x$ for all replacements of x and y?
   b. Does $x - y = y - x$ for any replacements of x and y? For which values of x and y?
   c. What is the relation between $x - y$ and $y - x$ for all replacements of x and y?
   d. Is the operation of subtraction commutative? That is, does $x - y = y - x$ for all signed numbers x and y?

65. State whether the following sentences are true or false:
   a. $(15 - 9) - 6 = 15 - (9 - 6)$
   b. $[(-10) - (+4)] - (+8) = (-10) - [(+4) - (+8)]$

66. Is the operation of subtraction associative? That is, does $(x - y) - z = x - (y - z)$ for all signed numbers x, y, and z?

67. State whether the following sentences are true or false:
   a. $5(7 - 3) = 5 \cdot 7 - 5 \cdot 3$
   b. $8[(+4) - (-2)] = 8 \cdot (+4) - 8 \cdot (-2)$

68. Does it appear that the operation of multiplication is distributive over subtraction? That is, does it appear that $x(y - z) = xy - xz$ for all signed numbers x, y, and z?

9. Multiplication of Signed Numbers

We will define multiplication of signed numbers in such a way that the properties of multiplication of numbers of arithmetic will still hold. Our own experiences will be used to illustrate the various situations that arise in the multiplication of signed numbers. We will represent a gain of weight by a positive number and a loss of weight by a negative number, a number of weeks in the future by a positive number and a number of weeks in the past by a negative number.

Case 1. Multiplying a Positive Number by a Positive Number.

If a girl gains 1 kilogram each week, 4 weeks from now she will be 4 kilograms heavier. Using signed numbers, we may write:

$$(+4) \times (+1) = +4$$

Notice that the product of the two positive numbers is a positive number.

Case 2. Multiplying a Negative Number by a Positive Number

If a girl loses 1 kilogram each week, 4 weeks from now she will be 4 kilograms lighter than she is now. Using signed numbers, we may write:

$$(+4) \times (-1) = -4$$

Notice that the product of the negative number and the positive number is a negative number.

Case 3. Multiplying a Positive Number by a Negative Number

If a girl has gained 1 kilogram each week, 4 weeks ago she was 4 kilograms lighter than she is now. Using signed numbers, we may write:

$$(-4) \times (+1) = -4$$

Notice that the product of the negative number and the positive number is a negative number.

Case 4. Multiplying a Negative Number by a Negative Number

If a girl has lost 1 kilogram each week, 4 weeks ago she was 4 kilograms heavier than she is now. Using signed numbers, we may write:

$$(-4) \times (-1) = +4$$

Notice that the product of two negative numbers is a positive number.

Observe that in all four cases the absolute value of the product, 4, is equal to the product of the absolute values of the factors, 4 and 1.

Now let us look at the multiplication of signed numbers in a more mathematical manner.

Suppose we wish to multiply +4 by +2. We know that +4 and 4 represent the same number; that +2 and 2 represent the same number; and that +8 and 8 represent the same number. Since 4 × 2 = 8, it must be true that (+4) × (+2) = +8.

In general, we will assume that if a and b are any two positive numbers, then:

$$a \cdot b = |a| \cdot |b| \qquad (a > 0, b > 0)$$

Notice that the product of any two positive numbers is a positive number.

In order to deal with the multiplication of $+4$ by -2, let us keep in mind that, for signed numbers, we wish to preserve the multiplication property of zero and the distributive property of multiplication. Consider the following sequence of equations:

$$(+4)\,(0) = 0$$
$$(+4)\,[(+2) + (-2)] = 0 \qquad \text{Addition property of opposites}$$
$$(+4)\,(+2) + (+4)\,(-2) = 0 \qquad \text{Distributive property}$$
$$+8 + (+4)\,(-2) = 0$$

Thus, $(+4)\,(-2) = -8$, since the only number that can be added to $+8$ to give 0 is -8.

In general, we can use the same procedure to find the product of any positive number a and any negative number b:

$$a\,(0) = 0$$
$$a\,[b + (-b)] = 0 \qquad \text{Addition property of opposites}$$
$$a \cdot b + a \cdot (-b) = 0 \qquad \text{Distributive property}$$

But, $a \cdot (-b) = |a| \cdot |b|$. (If b is negative, then $-b$ is positive.) Hence, $a \cdot b + |a| \cdot |b| = 0$. Therefore, $a \cdot b$ is the additive inverse of $|a| \cdot |b|$. This can be symbolized as follows:

$$a \cdot b = - |a| \cdot |b| \qquad (a > 0, b < 0)$$

We already know that $(+4) \times (-2) = -8$. Since we will want the multiplication of signed numbers to be commutative, it must be true that $(-2) \times (+4) = -8$. In general, we have:

$$a \cdot b = - |a| \cdot |b| \qquad (a < 0, b > 0)$$

Notice that the product of any two numbers one of which is positive and the other is negative is a negative number.

Now let us deal with the product of two negative numbers, for example, $(-4) \times (-2)$. Consider the following sequence of equations:

$$(-4)\,(0) = 0$$
$$(-4)\,[(+2) + (-2)] = 0 \qquad \text{Addition property of opposites}$$
$$(-4)\,(+2) + (-4)\,(-2) = 0 \qquad \text{Distributive property}$$
$$-8 + (-4)\,(-2) = 0$$

Thus, $(-4)\,(-2) = +8$, since the only number that can be added to -8 to give 0 is $+8$.

In general, we can use the same procedure to find the product of any negative number a and any negative number b.

$$a\,(0) = 0$$
$$a\,[b + (-b)] = 0 \qquad \text{Addition property of opposites}$$
$$a \cdot b + a \cdot (-b) = 0 \qquad \text{Distributive property}$$

But, $a \cdot (-b) = -|a| \cdot |b|$ (a is negative and $-b$ is positive).
Hence, $a \cdot b + (-|a| \cdot |b|) = 0$.
Therefore, $a \cdot b$ is the additive inverse of $-|a| \cdot |b|$. Since the additive inverse of $-|a| \cdot |b|$ is $|a| \cdot |b|$, it follows that:

$$a \cdot b = |a| \cdot |b| \qquad (a < 0, \, b < 0)$$

Notice that the product of any two negative numbers is a positive number.

The previous discussion dealing with the multiplication of nonzero signed numbers can be summarized in the following rules.

RULES FOR MULTIPLYING SIGNED NUMBERS

Rule 1. The product of two positive numbers or of two negative numbers is a positive number whose absolute value is the product of the absolute values of the numbers.

Rule 2. The product of a positive number and a negative number is a negative number whose absolute value is the product of the absolute values of the numbers.

In general, if a and b are both positive or both negative, then:

$$ab = |a| \cdot |b|$$

If one of the numbers a and b is positive and the other is negative, then:

$$ab = -(|a| \cdot |b|)$$

Model Problems

In 1-5, multiply the two numbers.

1. $+12$	2. -13	3. $+18$	4. -15	5. -7
$+4$	-5	-3	6	1
$+48$	$+65$	-54	-90	-7

In Chapter 4, we studied the multiplication properties of the numbers of arithmetic. Now let us see how these properties are preserved for the set of signed numbers.

CLOSURE PROPERTY OF MULTIPLICATION

The product of two signed numbers is always a member of the set of signed numbers. For example, the product of -7 and $+3$ is -21, a signed number.

In general, for every signed number a and every signed number b:

ab is a unique signed number

COMMUTATIVE PROPERTY OF MULTIPLICATION

We know that $(+5) \times (-2) = -10$ and $(-2) \times (+5) = -10$.
Therefore, $(+5) \times (-2) = (-2) \times (+5)$.

This example illustrates that the commutative property of multiplication holds for signed numbers. That is, signed numbers may be multiplied in any order.

In general, for every signed number a and every signed number b:

$$ab = ba$$

ASSOCIATIVE PROPERTY OF MULTIPLICATION

We know that $[(-5) \times (+2)] \times (+4) = -40$ and that $(-5) \times [(+2) \times (+4)] = -40$.
Therefore, $[(-5) \times (+2)] \times (+4) = (-5) \times [(+2) \times (+4)]$.

This example illustrates that the associative property of multiplication holds for signed numbers. That is, in multiplying signed numbers, we may group them as we please.

In general, for every signed number a, every signed number b, and every signed number c:

$$(ab)c = a(bc)$$

DISTRIBUTIVE PROPERTY OF MULTIPLICATION

We know that $(-5)[(-4) + (+6)] = (-5)(+2) = -10$ and that $(-5)(-4) + (-5)(+6) = (+20) + (-30) = -10$.
Therefore, $(-5)[(-4) + (+6)] = (-5)(-4) + (-5)(+6)$.

This example illustrates that the distributive property of multiplication over addition holds for signed numbers. This means that the product of one signed number times the sum of a second and a third signed number equals the product of the first and second numbers plus the product of the first and third numbers.

In general, for every signed number a, every signed number b, and every signed number c:

$$a(b + c) = ab + ac \quad and \quad ab + ac = a(b + c)$$

The distributive property is also assumed to be true for subtraction of signed numbers:

$$a(b - c) = ab - ac \quad and \quad ab - ac = a(b - c)$$

MULTIPLICATION PROPERTY OF THE NUMBER ONE
AND THE NUMBER NEGATIVE ONE

The true sentences $(+5) \times 1 = +5$ and $1 \times (-4) = -4$ illustrate that the multiplication property of 1 holds for signed numbers. That is, the product of 1 and any signed number is that number itself. For this reason, 1 is called the *identity element of multiplication,* or the *multiplicative identity*.

In general, for every signed number a:

$$a \times 1 = a \quad and \quad 1 \times a = a$$

Also, for every signed number a:

$$(a) \times (-1) = -a \quad and \quad (-1) \times (a) = -a$$

For example, $(-1) \times (+5) = -5$ and $(-1) \times (-5) = +5$.

MULTIPLICATION PROPERTY OF ZERO

We will now see that the multiplication property of zero extends to the set of signed numbers. We already know that $0 \times 0 = 0$. Now suppose that a is any nonzero signed number. Consider the following chain of equations:

$a \times 0 = a \times [1 + (-1)]$	Addition property of opposites
$a \times 0 = a \times 1 + a \times (-1)$	Distributive property
$a \times 0 = a + (-a)$	Multiplication property of 1 and -1
$a \times 0 = 0$	Addition property of opposites

Hence, in general, for any signed number a:

$$a \times 0 = 0 \quad and \quad 0 \times a = 0$$

For example, $(+8) \times 0 = 0$ and $0 \times (-6) = 0$.

Model Problem

Use the properties of multiplication to show that:

$$5 \times [(-4) + 9] = (-4) \times (5) + (9) \times (5)$$

Solution:

Step	*Reason*
1. $5 \times [(-4) + 9] = (5) \times (-4) + (5) \times (9)$	1. Distributive property
2. $ = (-4) \times (5) + (9) \times (5)$	2. Commutative property

MULTIPLYING MORE THAN TWO SIGNED NUMBERS

Since the commutative and associative laws of multiplication hold for signed numbers, signed numbers may be arranged and multiplied in any order we choose. If more than two numbers are to be multiplied, we first multiply any two of them, then multiply this product by one of the remaining factors. We continue this until all factors have been used. See how the product of -2, $+3$, and -4 can be found in several ways:

$$(-2)(+3)(-4) = [(-2)(+3)](-4) = (-6)(-4) = +24$$

$$(-2)(+3)(-4) = (-2)[(+3)(-4)] = (-2)(-12) = +24$$

$$(-2)(+3)(-4) = (+3)[(-2)(-4)] = (+3)(+8) = +24$$

Study the following examples:

$$(+3)(-1)(+3) = -9 \qquad \text{(1 negative factor)}$$
$$(-1)(+3)(-3) = +9 \qquad \text{(2 negative factors)}$$
$$(+3)(-1)(-3)(-1) = -9 \qquad \text{(3 negative factors)}$$
$$(+3)(+1)(-1)(-3)(-1)(-1) = +9 \qquad \text{(4 negative factors)}$$

The preceding examples illustrate the following rules:

Rule 1. When a product of nonzero factors contains an *odd* number of negative factors (1, 3, 5, and so on), the product is *negative.*

Rule 2. When a product of nonzero factors contains an *even* number of negative factors (2, 4, 6, and so on), the product is *positive.*

Model Problems

1. Find the value of $(-2)^3$.

   Solution: $(-2)^3 = (-2)(-2)(-2) = -8$ *Ans.*

   Note: The answer is negative because there is an odd number of negative factors (3 negative factors).

2. Find the value of $(-3)^4$.

   Solution: $(-3)^4 = (-3)(-3)(-3)(-3) = +81$ *Ans.*

   Note: The answer is positive because there is an even number of negative factors (4 negative factors).

EXERCISES

In 1–30, find the product of the numbers.

1. $+9$	2. -11	3. -17	4. 0	5. 15	6. $+9$
$+8$	-7	$+3$	-5	-9	0

7. $+1.5$	8. $-.25$	9. $+8$	10. -15	11. $-\frac{1}{2}$	12. $+16$
-2.4	80	$+\frac{1}{2}$	$+\frac{3}{5}$	$-\frac{1}{3}$	$-2\frac{1}{4}$

13. $(+8)$ and $(+6)$ 14. (-12) and (-5)
15. $(+11)$ and (-7) 16. (-10) and $(+9)$
17. (0) and (-3) 18. (15) and $(-.6)$
19. $(+8)(+\frac{1}{4})$ 20. $(-\frac{3}{5})(-20)$
21. $(2)(\frac{1}{2})$ 22. $(+\frac{3}{8})(-\frac{32}{27})$
23. $(-4\frac{1}{2})(+\frac{2}{3})$ 24. $|-15|\cdot(-3\frac{1}{5})$
25. $(+4)(+3)(+2)$ 26. $(-1)(-7)(-8)$
27. $(-3)(-5)(+4)(-1)$ 28. $(-7)(+2)(0)$
29. $|+10|\cdot|-3|\cdot(-4)$ 30. $(+8)(-9)(0)(-10)$
31. Multiply each of the following numbers by $+5$:
     a. $+7$ b. -3 c. -9 d. $8\frac{1}{5}$ e. -15.3 f. 0
32. Multiply each of the following numbers by -8:
     a. $+9$ b. -12 c. -15 d. $+50\frac{3}{4}$ e. 100.5 f. 0

In 33–44, find the value of the expression.

33. $(+4)^2$ 34. $(-3)^2$ 35. $(+5)^3$ 36. $(-4)^3$ 37. $(-5)^3$ 38. $(-1)^4$
39. $(+\frac{1}{2})^2$ 40. $(-\frac{1}{2})^2$ 41. $(+\frac{2}{3})^3$ 42. $(-\frac{3}{5})^3$ 43. $(-\frac{1}{4})^3$ 44. $(-1)^{51}$

In 45–50, fill in the blanks so that the resulting sentence is an illustration of the distributive property.

45. $5 \cdot (9 + 7) = $ _____   46. $(-4)(x + y) = $ _____
47. _____ $= (6) \cdot (-3) + 6 \cdot (-5)$ 48. _____ $= 7a + 7b$
49. $8 \cdot ($ ____ $) = ($ ____ $) \cdot 5 + ($ ____ $) \cdot (-3)$
50. $3 \cdot ($ ____ $) = ($ ____ $) \cdot r + ($ ____ $) \cdot (-s)$

In 51–54, use the distributive property to find the value of the expression.

51. $15 \times 87 + 15 \times 13$
52. $34 \times 26 + 34 \times (-6)$
53. $93 \times (-\frac{3}{4}) + 93 \times (-\frac{1}{4})$
54. $(-5) \cdot (-13) + (-5) \cdot (+4) + (-5) \cdot (+9)$

In 55–59, name the multiplication property illustrated.

55. $(-6) \times (-5) = (-5) \times (-6)$
56. $[(-3) \cdot 4] \cdot 7 = (-3) \cdot [4 \cdot 7]$

57. $-8 \cdot [4 + (-1)] = (-8) \cdot (4) + (-8) \cdot (-1)$

58. $5x + 5 \cdot (-y) = 5 \cdot [x + (-y)]$

59. If we know that $(5)(6) = 30$, the following chain of equations can be used to show that $(5)(-6) = -30$. State the reason for each step from 1 through 5.

    1. $5(0) = 0$

    2. $5[6 + (-6)] = 0$

    3. $(5)(6) + (5)(-6) = 0$

    4. $30 + 5(-6) = 0$

    5. $(5)(-6) = -30$

60. Use a chain of equations like the one used in exercise 59 to show that each of the following equalities is true. Give the reason for each step. Assume that $(a) \cdot (b) = ab$ when a and b are both positive.

    a. $(8)(-3) = -24$ **b.** $(7) \cdot (-6) = -42$

    c. $(-4)(3) = -12$ **d.** $(a) \cdot (-b) = -ab$ (a and b are positive)

61. If we know that $(-5)(6) = -30$, the following chain of equations can be used to show that $(-5)(-6) = +30$. State the reason for each step from 1 through 5.

    1. $(-5)(0) = 0$

    2. $-5[6 + (-6)] = 0$

    3. $(-5)(6) + (-5)(-6) = 0$

    4. $-30 + (-5)(-6) = 0$

    5. $(-5)(-6) = +30$

62. Use a chain of equations like the one used in exercise 61 to show that each of the following equalities is true. Give the reason for each step. Assume that $(-a) \cdot (b) = -ab$ when a is positive and b is positive.

    a. $(-6)(-2) = +12$ **b.** $(-9)(-3) = +27$

    c. $(-4)(-8) = 32$ **d.** $(-a)(-b) = ab$ (a and b are positive)

10. Division of Signed Numbers

USING THE INVERSE OPERATION IN DIVIDING SIGNED NUMBERS

Division may be defined as the inverse operation of multiplication, just as subtraction is defined as the inverse operation of addition. To divide 6 by 2 means to find a number which, when multiplied by 2, gives 6. The number is 3, because $3 \times 2 = 6$. We can write $\frac{6}{2} = 3$, or

$6 \div 2 = 3$. The number 6 is the **dividend**, 2 is the **divisor**, and 3 is the **quotient**.

It is impossible to divide a signed number by 0. That is, division by zero is undefined. For example, to solve $(-9) \div 0 = ?$, we would have to find a number which, when multiplied by 0, would give -9. There is no such number, since the product of any signed number and 0 is 0.

In general, for every signed number a and every signed number b $(b \neq 0)$:

$$a \div b, \text{ or } \frac{a}{b}, \text{ represents a number } c \text{ such that } cb = a$$

In dividing nonzero signed numbers, there are four possible cases. Consider the following examples:

Case 1. $\frac{+6}{+3}$ means $(?)(+3) = +6$. Since ? is $+2$, $\frac{+6}{+3} = +2$.

Case 2. $\frac{-6}{-3}$ means $(?)(-3) = -6$. Since ? is $+2$, $\frac{-6}{-3} = +2$.

Case 3. $\frac{-6}{+3}$ means $(?)(+3) = -6$. Since ? is -2, $\frac{-6}{+3} = -2$.

Case 4. $\frac{+6}{-3}$ means $(?)(-3) = +6$. Since ? is -2, $\frac{+6}{-3} = -2$.

In the preceding examples, observe:
1. When the dividend and divisor are both positive, the quotient is positive; when the dividend and divisor are both negative, the quotient is positive.
2. When the dividend is positive and the divisor is negative, or when the dividend is negative and the divisor is positive, the quotient is negative.
3. In all cases, the absolute value of the quotient is the absolute value of the dividend divided by the absolute value of the divisor.

The previous examples illustrate the following rules of division.

RULES FOR DIVIDING SIGNED NUMBERS

Rule 1. The quotient of two positive numbers or of two negative numbers is a positive number whose absolute value is the absolute value of the dividend divided by the absolute value of the divisor.

Rule 2. The quotient of a positive number and a negative number is a negative number whose absolute value is the absolute value of the dividend divided by the absolute value of the divisor.

In general:

For every signed number a and every signed number b such that $a > 0$ and $b > 0$, or $a < 0$ and $b < 0$:

$$\frac{a}{b} = \frac{|a|}{|b|}$$

For every signed number a and every signed number b such that $a > 0$ and $b < 0$, or $a < 0$ and $b > 0$:

$$\frac{a}{b} = -\left(\frac{|a|}{|b|}\right)$$

RULE FOR DIVIDING ZERO BY A NONZERO NUMBER

The expression $\dfrac{0}{-5}$ means (?) $(-5) = 0$. Since ? is 0, $\dfrac{0}{-5} = 0$. This illustrates that when zero is divided by any nonzero number the quotient is zero.

In general, if b is a nonzero number ($b \neq 0$):

$$\frac{0}{b} = 0$$

Model Problems

In 1–5, perform the indicated division.

1. $\dfrac{+60}{+15} = +\left(\dfrac{60}{15}\right) = +4$　　　　2. $\dfrac{+90}{-10} = -\left(\dfrac{90}{10}\right) = -9$

3. $\dfrac{-27}{-3} = +\left(\dfrac{27}{3}\right) = +9$　　　　4. $(-45) \div 9 = -(45 \div 9) = -5$

5. $0 \div (-3) = 0$

USING THE RECIPROCAL IN DIVIDING SIGNED NUMBERS

When the product of two numbers is 1, either number is called the *reciprocal,* or *multiplicative inverse,* of the other. For example, since $(+8) \cdot (+\frac{1}{8}) = 1$, we say $+\frac{1}{8}$ is the reciprocal, or multiplicative inverse, of $+8$. Also, $+8$ is the reciprocal, or multiplicative inverse, of $+\frac{1}{8}$.

Since $(\frac{3}{5}) \cdot (\frac{5}{3}) = 1$, we say $\frac{5}{3}$ is the reciprocal, or multiplicative inverse, of $\frac{3}{5}$.

Since $(-\frac{1}{2}) \cdot (-2) = 1$, we say -2 is the reciprocal, or multiplicative inverse, of $-\frac{1}{2}$.

Since there is no number which, when multiplied by 0, gives 1, the number 0 has no reciprocal.

In general, for every nonzero signed number $a\,(a \neq 0)$, there is a unique signed number $\dfrac{1}{a}$ such that:

$$a \cdot \frac{1}{a} = 1$$

Notice that if a number is positive, its reciprocal is positive; if a number is negative, its reciprocal is negative.

The reciprocal of the reciprocal of a nonzero number is that number itself. For example, the reciprocal of the reciprocal of 8 is 8, because the reciprocal of 8 is $\frac{1}{8}$ and the reciprocal of $\frac{1}{8}$ is 8.

For nonzero numbers, the reciprocal of the product of two numbers is equal to the product of their reciprocals. For example, consider the numbers 5 and 3.

The product of 5 and 3 is $5 \cdot 3$, or 15; the reciprocal of the product is $\dfrac{1}{5 \cdot 3}$, or $\dfrac{1}{15}$.

The reciprocals of 5 and 3 are $\dfrac{1}{5}$ and $\dfrac{1}{3}$. The product of the reciprocals is $\dfrac{1}{5} \cdot \dfrac{1}{3}$, or $\dfrac{1}{15}$.

We see that $\dfrac{1}{5 \cdot 3} = \dfrac{1}{5} \cdot \dfrac{1}{3}$.

Using the reciprocal of a number, we can define division in terms of multiplication as follows:

For every signed number a and every nonzero signed number $b\ (b \neq 0)$, "a (the dividend) divided by b (the divisor)" means "a multiplied by the reciprocal of b," or:

$$\frac{a}{b} = a \cdot \frac{1}{b} \ (b \neq 0)$$

Procedure. To perform a division, multiply the dividend by the reciprocal (multiplicative inverse) of the divisor.

Notice that if we exclude division by 0, the set of signed numbers is closed with respect to division because every nonzero signed number has a reciprocal, and multiplication is always possible.

Model Problems

In 1-5, perform the indicated division.

1. $\dfrac{+10}{+2} = (+10)\left(+\dfrac{1}{2}\right) = +(10)\left(\dfrac{1}{2}\right) = +5$

2. $\dfrac{-12}{+6} = (-12)\left(+\dfrac{1}{6}\right) = -(12)\left(\dfrac{1}{6}\right) = -2$

3. $\dfrac{-28}{-7} = (-28)\left(-\dfrac{1}{7}\right) = +(28)\left(\dfrac{1}{7}\right) = +4$

4. $\dfrac{0}{-3} = (0)\left(-\dfrac{1}{3}\right) = 0$

5. $(+18) \div \left(-\dfrac{1}{2}\right) = (+18)(-2) = -(18)(2) = -36$

EXERCISES

In 1-8, name the reciprocal of the given number.

1. 9   2. -7 3. 1   4. -1
5. $\frac{1}{5}$ 6. $-\frac{2}{3}$ 7. $x \, (x \neq 0)$ 8. $-x \, (x \neq 0)$

In 9-35, find the indicated quotients.

9. $\dfrac{+18}{+6}$ 10. $\dfrac{-36}{-3}$ 11. $\dfrac{+52}{-4}$ 12. $\dfrac{-84}{+12}$ 13. $\dfrac{-30}{-6}$ 14. $\dfrac{-144}{9}$

15. $\dfrac{75}{15}$ 16. $\dfrac{0}{3}$ 17. $\dfrac{+4}{-8}$ 18. $\dfrac{-6}{-9}$ 19. $\dfrac{-15}{-12}$ 20. $\dfrac{+18}{-4}$

21. $\dfrac{-16}{+6}$ 22. $\dfrac{-34}{4}$ 23. $\dfrac{0}{-4}$ 24. $\dfrac{8.4}{-4}$ 25. $\dfrac{-9.6}{-.3}$ 26. $\dfrac{-3.6}{1.2}$

27. $(+48) \div (-6)$ 28. $(+12) \div (-\frac{1}{3})$ 29. $(-4.8) \div (-4)$
30. $(-75) \div (-15)$ 31. $(-\frac{3}{4}) \div (+6)$ 32. $(+9.6) \div (-3)$
33. $(-50) \div (+10)$ 34. $(-\frac{3}{4}) \div (-\frac{2}{3})$ 35. $(-1.8) \div (+.9)$
36. a. Find the value of x for which the denominator of the fraction

$\dfrac{1}{x-2}$ has a value of 0.

b. State the value of x for which the multiplicative inverse of
$(x - 2)$ is not defined.

In 37–40, give the multiplicative inverse of the expression and state the value of x for which the multiplicative inverse is not defined.

37. $x - 5$ **38.** $x + 3$ **39.** $2x - 1$ **40.** $3x + 1$

41. State whether the following sentences are true or false:
   a. $(+10) \div (-5) = (-5) \div (+10)$
   b. $(-16) \div (-2) = (-2) \div (-16)$

42. If x and y represent signed numbers:
   a. Does $x \div y = y \div x$ for all replacements of x and y?
   b. Does $x \div y = y \div x$ for any replacements of x and y? If your answer is yes, give an example.
   c. What is the relation between $x \div y$ and $y \div x$ when $x \neq 0$ and $y \neq 0$?
   d. Is the operation of division commutative? That is, does $x \div y = y \div x$ for every nonzero signed number x and every nonzero signed number y?

43. State whether the following sentences are true or false:
   a. $[(+16) \div (+4)] \div (+2) = (+16) \div [(+4) \div (+2)]$
   b. $[(-36) \div (+6)] \div (-2) = (-36) \div [(+6) \div (-2)]$

44. Is the operation of division associative? That is, does $(x \div y) \div z = x \div (y \div z)$ for every signed number x, y, and z, when $y \neq 0$ and $z \neq 0$?

45. State whether the following sentences are true or false:
   a. $(12 + 6) \div 2 = 12 \div 2 + 6 \div 2$
   b. $[(+25) - (-10)] \div (+5) = (+25) \div (+5) - (-10) \div (+5)$

46. Does it appear that the operation of division is distributive over addition? That is, does $(x + y) \div z = x \div z + y \div z$ for every signed number x, y, and z when $z \neq 0$?

47. Does it appear that the operation of division is distributive over subtraction? That is, does $(x - y) \div z = x \div z - y \div z$ for every signed number x, y, and z when $z \neq 0$?

11. Evaluating Algebraic Expressions by Using Signed Numbers

When we evaluate an algebraic expression by replacing the variables with signed numbers, we follow the same procedure that we used when we evaluated algebraic expressions by replacing the variables with the numbers of arithmetic.

Model Problems

1. Find the value of $-3x^2y^3$ when $x = +2$ and $y = -1$.

How to Proceed	*Solution*
1. Write the expression.	$-3x^2y^3$
2. Replace the variables by the given values.	$= -3(+2)^2(-1)^3$
3. Evaluate the powers.	$= -3(+4)(-1)$
4. Multiply the signed numbers.	$= +12$ *Ans.*

2. Find the value of $x^2 - 3x - 54$ when $x = -5$.

How to Proceed	*Solution*
1. Write the expression.	$x^2 - 3x - 54$
2. Replace the variable by its given value.	$= (-5)^2 - 3(-5) - 54$
3. Evaluate the power.	$= 25 - 3(-5) - 54$
4. Do the multiplication.	$= 25 + 15 - 54$
5. Do the addition and subtraction.	$= -14$ *Ans.*

EXERCISES

In 1–40, find the numerical value of the expression. Use $a = -8$, $b = +6, d = -3, x = -4, y = 5$, and $z = -1$.

1. $6a$
2. $2xy$
3. $-4bz$
4. $\frac{1}{3}d$
5. $-\frac{2}{3}b$
6. $-\frac{3}{4}ab$
7. a^2
8. d^3
9. $-y^2$
10. $-d^2$
11. $-z^3$
12. $2x^2$
13. $-2z^3$
14. xy^2
15. $2d^2y^2$
16. $\frac{1}{2}db^2$
17. $-2d^3z^2$
18. $a - x$
19. $2x + z$
20. $a - 2d$
21. $5x + 2y$
22. $7b - 5x$
23. $x^2 + x$
24. $2b^2 + b$
25. $2d^2 - d$
26. $2a + 5d + 3x$
27. $8y + 5b - 6d$
28. $9b - 3z - 2x$
29. $x^2 + 3x + 5$
30. $z^2 + 2z - 7$
31. $a^2 - 5a - 6$
32. $d^2 - 4d + 6$
33. $.2x^2 - .3x + 5$
34. $15 + 5z - z^2$
35. $2(a + b)$
36. $3(2x - 1) + 6$
37. $10 - 3(x - 4)$
38. $(x + 2)(x - 1)$
39. $(a - b)(a + b)$
40. $(x + d)^2(x - 4z)$

In 41–48, find the value of the expression. Use $a = -12, b = +6$, and $c = -1$.

41. $\dfrac{a}{6}$
42. $\dfrac{b}{-2}$
43. $\dfrac{2a}{b}$
44. $\dfrac{ac}{-3b}$

45. $\dfrac{b^2c}{a}$
46. $\dfrac{3a^2c^3}{b^3}$
47. $\dfrac{a - b^2}{-2c^2}$
48. $\dfrac{b^2 - a^2}{b^2 + a^2}$

Chapter 6

Operations With Polynomials

1. The Vocabulary of Polynomials

A polynomial is an expression that can be formed from variables and numerical coefficients, using only the operations of addition, subtraction, and multiplication. Thus, 5, $6x + 5$, $x + y + z$, and $.4x^3 - \frac{2}{3}xy + 11$ are all polynomials. Every polynomial can be written as a sum of terms. For example, the polynomial $2x^3 - 11y^2 + 9z - 1$ is the sum of the four terms $2x^3$, $-11y^2$, $9z$, and -1. Hence, we may write

$$2x^3 - 11y^2 + 9z - 1 = 2x^3 + (-11y^2) + (9z) + (-1).$$

Notice that $\frac{2}{x} + 5$ is *not* a polynomial because the variable x appears in the denominator of a fraction. Remember that when we are dealing with polynomials, the variable may never appear in the denominator of a term and all exponents of the variable must be positive integers.

A polynomial may have any number of terms. A polynomial with one term is called a ***monomial***. For example, each of the expressions $5x$, $-9y^3$, and $\frac{1}{2}$ is a monomial. A polynomial that has two terms is called a ***binomial***. For example, $4x - 1$, $-2x^2 + x$, and $17x^3 - 11y^4$ are binomials. As you might suspect, a polynomial with three terms is called a ***trinomial***. Thus, $2x^2 - 9x + 4$ and $z + x^2 - y^3$ are trinomials.

A *polynomial in one variable* is a polynomial that has only one variable.

A polynomial in which the only variable is x is called a ***polynomial in x***. Examples are $x^4 - 8x^2$, $x + 1 - 2x^3$, and $\frac{1}{2}x^2 + x^3$.

We have seen that we may classify polynomials according to the number of terms which they have. Another way of classifying polynomials in one variable is according to their *degree*. The *degree of a polynomial* in one variable is the same as the greatest exponent of the variable which appears in it. The degree of the polynomial $5x^3 - 4x^2 + 3x$ is 3, and the degree of the polynomial $\frac{1}{2}a - 2a^5 + 1$ is 5. The degree of a nonzero constant polynomial is 0. For example, the degree of the polynomial 7 is 0. The zero polynomial has no degree.

A polynomial in one variable is written in *standard form* when the term with the greatest exponent of the variable appears at the extreme left and the other terms are arranged in *descending order* of the exponents of the variable as we move from left to right. The polynomials $8x^3 - 2x^2$, $\frac{1}{2}y^2 + y - 2$, and $-a^5 + 20a^4 + 9$ are in standard form; the polynomials $8z^3 - 2z^2 + z^4$, $1 + x$, and $y^5 + y^4 - y^2 + 2y^3$ are not in standard form.

A polynomial is arranged in *ascending order* when the exponents of a particular variable increase as we move from left to right. Thus, $x^2 + 2xy + y^2$ is arranged in ascending powers of y because the exponents of y increase as we move from left to right.

A polynomial is arranged in *descending order* when the exponents of a particular variable decrease as we move from left to right. Thus, $b^2 + 5ba + 4a^2$ is arranged in descending powers of b because the exponents of b decrease as we move from left to right.

2. Adding and Subtracting Like Monomials

We have already learned how to add like monomials whose numerical coefficients were numbers of arithmetic. We applied the distributive property of multiplication; for example, $5x + 4x = (5 + 4)x = 9x$.

Now we will use a similar procedure to add like monomials whose numerical coefficients are signed numbers:

$$(+9t) + (-3t) = [(+9) + (-3)]t = +6t$$

$$-3ab + 7ab - 2ab = (-3 + 7 - 2)ab = +2ab$$

In the preceding examples, the middle step may be done mentally.

The subtraction of like monomials is very similar to the subtraction of signed numbers. To subtract like monomials, we add the additive inverse of the subtrahend to the minuend. Thus,

$$+6t - (-7t) = (+6t) + (+7t) = 13t.$$

Procedure. To add like monomials, use the distributive property of multiplication, or find the sum of the numerical coefficients and multiply this sum by the common variable factor. To subtract like monomials, add the additive inverse of the subtrahend to the minuend.

Model Problems

In 1-6, add.

1. $+7x$	2. $-3y^2$	3. $-15abc$	4. $+8x^2y$	5. $-9y$	6. $+2(a+b)$
$\underline{-3x}$	$\underline{-5y^2}$	$\underline{+6abc}$	$\underline{-x^2y}$	$\underline{+9y}$	$\underline{+6(a+b)}$
$+4x$	$-8y^2$	$-9abc$	$+7x^2y$	0	$+8(a+b)$

In 7-12, subtract.

7. $+8y$	8. $-5x^2$	9. $+15rst$	10. 0	11. $-8m$	12. $+4(m+n)$
$\underline{+3y}$	$\underline{-3x^2}$	$\underline{-8rst}$	$\underline{-5t}$	$\underline{-8m}$	$\underline{-5(m+n)}$
$+5y$	$-2x^2$	$+23rst$	$+5t$	0	$+9(m+n)$

EXERCISES

In 1-6, simplify the expression by adding the monomials.

1. $(+8c) + (+7c)$ 2. $(+10t) + (-3t)$ 3. $(-4a) + (-6a)$
4. $(-20r) + (5r)$ 5. $(-7w) + (+7w)$ 6. $(5ab) + (-9ab)$

In 7-12, simplify the expression by subtracting the monomials.

7. $(+9r) - (+2r)$ 8. $(+15s) - (-5s)$ 9. $(-5q) - (-7q)$
10. $(-17n) - (11n)$ 11. $(-15t) - (-15t)$ 12. $(0) - (-30c)$

In 13-37, add.

13. $+7c$	14. $-39r$	15. $+14c$	16. $-1.5m$	17. $+2x^2$
$\underline{+8c}$	$\underline{-22r}$	$\underline{-c}$	$\underline{+1.2m}$	$\underline{+9x^2}$

18. $-48y^2$	19. $-d^2$	20. $.5y^3$	21. $+\frac{5}{3}c^4$	22. $-6mn$
$\underline{-13y^2}$	$\underline{+7d^2}$	$\underline{.8y^3}$	$\underline{-\frac{7}{3}c^4}$	$\underline{-mn}$

23. $-4xyz$	24. $+.4cd$	25. $-8xy$	26. $+6a^2b$	27. $-xy^2$
$\underline{+5xyz}$	$\underline{-.8cd}$	$\underline{+8xy}$	$\underline{+7a^2b}$	$\underline{-3xy^2}$

28. $-8c^2d^2$	29. $+\frac{3}{4}x^2y^2$	30. $+.5r^2s^2$	31. $-4(c+d)$	32. $+8a$
$\underline{9c^2d^2}$	$\underline{-2x^2y^2}$	$\underline{-.5r^2s^2}$	$\underline{+2(c+d)}$	$-6a$
				$\underline{+7a}$

33. $-16x^2$	34. $-4rst$	35. $-6xy^2$	36. $9c^2d^2$	37. $+5(r+s)$
$-x^2$	$+8rst$	$+9xy^2$	$3c^2d^2$	$-6(r+s)$
$\underline{+15x^2}$	$\underline{+9rst}$	$\underline{-3xy^2}$	$\underline{-7c^2d^2}$	$\underline{+(r+s)}$

In 38-41, tell whether the sentence is true or false.

38. $5^3 + 5^3 = 2(5)^3$ 39. $2^3 + 2^5 = 2^8$
40. $3^2 + 3^2 = 6^2$ 41. $2^2 + 2^3 = 4^5$

In 42–65, subtract.

42. $\begin{array}{r} +9a \\ +7a \\ \hline \end{array}$ 43. $\begin{array}{r} -9b \\ -3b \\ \hline \end{array}$ 44. $\begin{array}{r} -8c \\ +2c \\ \hline \end{array}$ 45. $\begin{array}{r} +7d \\ -d \\ \hline \end{array}$

46. $\begin{array}{r} -5.1x \\ +2.3x \\ \hline \end{array}$ 47. $\begin{array}{r} -7r \\ -7r \\ \hline \end{array}$ 48. $\begin{array}{r} 3x^2 \\ 5x^2 \\ \hline \end{array}$ 49. $\begin{array}{r} -9y^2 \\ -6y^2 \\ \hline \end{array}$

50. $\begin{array}{r} 7d^2 \\ -3d^2 \\ \hline \end{array}$ 51. $\begin{array}{r} -8t^3 \\ +t^3 \\ \hline \end{array}$ 52. $\begin{array}{r} -1.5y^3 \\ +.7y^3 \\ \hline \end{array}$ 53. $\begin{array}{r} +9(m+n) \\ +5(m+n) \\ \hline \end{array}$

54. $\begin{array}{r} +7cd \\ +9cd \\ \hline \end{array}$ 55. $\begin{array}{r} -8mn \\ -9mn \\ \hline \end{array}$ 56. $\begin{array}{r} -6rs \\ +5rs \\ \hline \end{array}$ 57. $\begin{array}{r} -3ab \\ 7ab \\ \hline \end{array}$

58. $\begin{array}{r} .4cd \\ -.9cd \\ \hline \end{array}$ 59. $\begin{array}{r} -5(x+y) \\ -3(x+y) \\ \hline \end{array}$ 60. $\begin{array}{r} +3y^2z^2 \\ +2y^2z^2 \\ \hline \end{array}$ 61. $\begin{array}{r} -5xy^2 \\ +2xy^2 \\ \hline \end{array}$

62. $\begin{array}{r} -5a^2b^2 \\ -a^2b^2 \\ \hline \end{array}$ 63. $\begin{array}{r} +8c^2d^2 \\ -8c^2d^2 \\ \hline \end{array}$ 64. $\begin{array}{r} +.1x^2y^2 \\ +.9x^2y^2 \\ \hline \end{array}$ 65. $\begin{array}{r} +3(a+b) \\ -7(a+b) \\ \hline \end{array}$

In 66–77, simplify the expression by combining like terms.

66. $(+6x) + (-4x) + (-5x) + (+10x)$ 67. $-5y + 6y + 9y - 14y$
68. $(+7c) - (-15c) + (+2c) - (+12c)$ 69. $4m + 9m - 12m - m$
70. $(+8x^2) + (-x^2) + (-12x^2) - (+2x^2)$
71. $-13y^2 - 15y^2 - y^2 - 8y^2$
72. $(-9c^2) + (-5c^2) + (+8c^2) + (+2c^2)$
73. $d^2 - 9d^2 - 5d^2 + 13d^2$
74. $(+10ab) - (-15ab) - (+18ab) + (-6ab)$
75. $-7cd - 5cd + 4cd - 2cd$
76. $(-13x^2y^2) + (+6x^2y^2) + (-2x^2y^2) - (+7x^2y^2)$
77. $-10rs^2 + 3rs^2 + 8rs^2 - rs^2$
78. What must be added to $+6x$ to give the result $+10x$?
79. What must be added to $-3y$ to give the result $+7y$?
80. What must be subtracted from $+9d$ to give the result $+5d$?
81. What must be subtracted from $-8z$ to give the result $+3z$?
82. From the sum of $-5xy$ and $+12xy$, subtract the sum of $+9xy$ and $-15xy$.

3. Simplifying, Adding, and Subtracting Polynomials

To simplify a polynomial that has several terms, we collect like terms, making use of the commutative, associative, and distributive properties:

Step	Reason
$4x + 3y - 9x + 6y$	
1. $= 4x - 9x + 3y + 6y$	1. Commutative property of addition
2. $= (4x - 9x) + (3y + 6y)$	2. Associative property of addition
3. $= (4 - 9)x + (3 + 6)y$	3. Distributive property of multiplication
4. $= -5x + 9y$	4. Substitution principle

To add two polynomials, we use the commutative, associative, and distributive properties to combine like terms. For example:

Step	Reason
1. $(3x + 5) + (6x + 8)$ $= (3x + 6x) + (5 + 8)$	1. Commutative and associative properties
2. $= (3 + 6)x + (5 + 8)$	2. Distributive property
3. $= 9x + 13$	3. Substitution principle

To find the sum of the polynomials $4x^2 + 3x - 5$, $3x^2 - 6 - 5x$, and $-x + 3 - 2x^2$, we can write the polynomials vertically, first arranging them in descending (or ascending) powers of x. Then we can add the like terms in each column. As shown at the right, the sum is $5x^2 - 3x - 8$.

$$\begin{array}{r} 4x^2 + 3x - 5 \\ 3x^2 - 5x - 6 \\ -2x^2 - x + 3 \\ \hline 5x^2 - 3x - 8 \end{array}$$

To subtract one polynomial from another, we use a procedure similar to that used to subtract like terms; we add the additive inverse of the subtrahend to the minuend.

We can write the additive inverse of a polynomial using the symbol "−." For example, the additive inverse of $2x^2 - 5x - 3$ can be written $-(2x^2 - 5x - 3)$.

We can also write the additive inverse of a polynomial by forming a polynomial each of whose terms is the additive inverse of the corresponding terms of the original polynomial. For example, the additive inverse of $2x^2 - 5x - 3$ is $-2x^2 + 5x + 3$. Thus:

$$(5x^2 + 8x - 7) - (2x^2 - 5x - 3) = (5x^2 + 8x - 7) + (-2x^2 + 5x + 3)$$
$$= 5x^2 + 8x - 7 - 2x^2 + 5x + 3$$
$$= (5 - 2)x^2 + (8 + 5)x + (-7 + 3)$$
$$= 3x^2 + 13x - 4$$

The solution of a subtraction example can also be arranged vertically as shown at the right. We mentally add the additive inverse of each term of the subtrahend to the corresponding term of the minuend.

$$\begin{array}{r} 5x^2 + 8x - 7 \\ 2x^2 - 5x - 3 \\ \hline 3x^2 + 13x - 4 \end{array}$$

Subtraction can be checked by adding the subtrahend and the difference. The result should equal the minuend.

Procedure. To add polynomials, combine like terms by adding their numerical coefficients. For convenience, arrange the polynomials in descending or ascending powers of a particular variable so that like terms are in vertical columns. Then add each column separately.

To subtract polynomials, add the additive inverse of the subtrahend to the minuend.

Model Problems

1. Add and check: $4x + 3y - 5z$, $3x - 5y - 6z$, $-2x - y + 3z$

   Solution:

   $$\begin{array}{r} 4x + 3y - 5z \\ 3x - 5y - 6z \\ -2x - y + 3z \\ \hline 5x - 3y - 8z \end{array}$$

   Answer: $5x - 3y - 8z$. Check by adding in the opposite direction.

2. Add: $+7x^2 - 5xy + 4y^2$, $+3xy - x^2$, $-9y^2 + 2xy$

How to Proceed	Solution
1. Arrange in descending powers of x.	$+7x^2 - 5xy + 4y^2$
2. Arrange like terms in the same column.	$- x^2 + 3xy$
3. Add like terms in each column.	$\underline{ + 2xy - 9y^2}$
	$+6x^2 + 0 - 5y^2$

   Answer: $6x^2 - 5y^2$. Check by adding in the opposite direction.

3. Subtract and check: $(5x^2 - 6x + 3) - (2x^2 - 9x - 6)$

   Solution:

   $$\begin{array}{ll} 5x^2 - 6x + 3 & \text{minuend} \\ 2x^2 - 9x - 6 & \text{subtrahend} \\ \hline 3x^2 + 3x + 9 & \text{difference} \end{array}$$

   Check:

   $$\begin{array}{ll} 2x^2 - 9x - 6 & \text{subtrahend} \\ 3x^2 + 3x + 9 & \text{difference} \\ \hline 5x^2 - 6x + 3 & \text{minuend} \end{array}$$

   Answer: $3x^2 + 3x + 9$

4. Simplify: $9x - [7 - (4 - 2x)]$

Solution:

$$\begin{aligned}
9x - [7 - (4 - 2x)] &= 9x - [7 + (-4 + 2x)] \\
&= 9x - [7 - 4 + 2x] \\
&= 9x - [3 + 2x] \\
&= 9x + [-3 - 2x] \\
&= 9x - 3 - 2x \\
&= 7x - 3
\end{aligned}$$

(First perform the subtraction involving the expression within the innermost grouping symbol.)

Answer: $7x - 3$

5. Simplify: $6a - [5a + (6 - 3a)]$

Solution: When one grouping symbol appears within another grouping symbol, first perform the operation involving the algebraic expression within the innermost grouping symbol.

$$\begin{aligned}
6a - [5a + (6 - 3a)] &= 6a - [5a + 6 - 3a] \\
&= 6a - [2a + 6] \\
&= 6a - 2a - 6 \\
&= 4a - 6
\end{aligned}$$

Answer: $4a - 6$

EXERCISES

In 1–4, simplify the polynomials.

1. $9y + 6w + 3w + y$ 2. $-4a + 6b + 3a - b$
3. $7ab - bc - 4ab - 5bc$ 4. $3x^2 - 5x + 7 + 2x^2 + 3x - 9$

In 5–11, add and check the result.

5. $\begin{aligned} 4a - 6b \\ 9a + 3b \end{aligned}$ 6. $\begin{aligned} -6m + n \\ -4m - 5n \end{aligned}$ 7. $\begin{aligned} 9x^2 + 5 \\ -2x^2 - 8 \end{aligned}$ 8. $\begin{aligned} -4x^2y^2 + 2r^2s^2 \\ -6x^2y^2 - 5r^2s^2 \end{aligned}$

9. $\begin{aligned} x^2 + 3x + 5 \\ 2x^2 - 4x - 1 \\ -5x^2 + 2x + 4 \end{aligned}$ 10. $\begin{aligned} 5c^2 - 4cd + 6d^2 \\ - c^2 + 3cd + 2d^2 \\ -3c^2 + cd - 8d^2 \end{aligned}$ 11. $\begin{aligned} 2.1 + .9z + z^2 \\ - .7z - 2z^2 \\ -.9 + 2z \end{aligned}$

In 12–15, write the additive inverse of the expression.

12. $-5x + 3$ 13. $-6x - 6y$ 14. $7ab - 3bc$ 15. $-2x^2 + 3x - 2$

In 16–22, subtract and check.

16. $\begin{aligned} 5b + 3c \\ 4b + c \end{aligned}$ 17. $\begin{aligned} 4r - 7s \\ 5r - 7s \end{aligned}$ 18. $\begin{aligned} 0 \\ 8a - 6b \end{aligned}$ 19. $\begin{aligned} 5xy - 9cd \\ -3xy + cd \end{aligned}$

20. $x^2 - 6x + 5$ 21. $3a^2 - 2ab + 3b^2$ 22. $x^2 \qquad - 9$
     $\underline{3x^2 - 2x - 2}$ $\underline{-a^2 - 5ab + 3b^2}$ $\underline{-2x^2 + 5x - 3}$

In 23–42, simplify the expression.

23. $7b + (4b - 6)$ 24. $3y - (5y - 4)$ 25. $-5x^3 + (4 - x^3)$
26. $8r - (-6s - 8r)$ 27. $6xy + (5xy + 7)$ 28. $-(5x + 6) - 2x$
29. $(-6y + 7) + (6y - 7)$ 30. $(-4x + 7) - (3x - 7)$
31. $(5a + 3b) + (-2a + 4b)$ 32. $(5x^2 + 4) - (-3x^2 - 4)$
33. $(5x^2 + 6x - 9) - (x^2 - 3x + 7)$
34. $(d^2 + 9d + 2) + (-4d - d^2)$
35. $-9a - (2b - 4a) + 4b$
36. $(x^2 - 3x) + (5 - 9x) - (5x^2 - 7)$
37. $8 + [5 + (6 - x)]$
38. $12 - [-3 + (6x - 9)]$
39. $[-4x + (10 - 5x)] + 5x$
40. $x^2 - [-3x + (4 - 7x)]$
41. $3x^2 - [7x - (4x - x^2) + 3]$
42. $9a - [5a^2 - (7 + 9a - 2a^2)]$
43. Find the sum of $6p - 3q + z, -3p + 2q - z$, and $-p + q$.
44. Subtract $2y + 5y^2 - 8$ from $4y^2 - 5y + 1$.
45. What algebraic expression must be added to $2x^2 + 5x + 7$ to give $8x^2 - 4x - 5$ as the result?
46. What algebraic expression must be added to $-3x^2 + 7x - 5$ to give 0 as the result?
47. From the sum of $y^2 + 2y - 7$ and $2y^2 - 4y + 3$, subtract $3y^2 - 8y - 10$.
48. Subtract the sum of $c^2 - 5$ and $-2c^2 + 3c$ from $4c^2 - 6c + 7$.
49. Represent the perimeter of a geometric figure whose sides are represented by **(a)** $6x - 4, 5x - 5, 8x + 3$.   **(b)** $8a + 3b, 9b - 2a, 3a - 2b, 2a - b$.
50. Represent the perimeter of a square each of whose sides is represented by $x^2 + 4x - 3$.
51. Represent the perimeter of a rectangle whose width is represented by x and whose length is represented by **(a)** $4x + 5$.   **(b)** $6x - 4$.

In 52–57, use grouping symbols to write an algebraic expression which represents the verbal phrase. Then simplify the expression.

52. the sum of $4x - 9$ and $5 - x$ 53. $9x + 2y$ decreased by $-3x + 5y$
54. 50 decreased by $20 - 2x$ 55. $3x^2 - 1$ less than $5x^2 + 7$
56. $5x - 7y$ more than $9y - 7x$ 57. $9x + 5$ subtracted from $3x - 4$

4. Multiplying Powers of the Same Base

FINDING THE PRODUCT OF POWERS

We know that y^2 means $y \cdot y$ and y^3 means $y \cdot y \cdot y$. Therefore:

$$y^2 \cdot y^3 = \overbrace{(y \cdot y)}^{2} \cdot \overbrace{(y \cdot y \cdot y)}^{3} = \overbrace{y \cdot y \cdot y \cdot y \cdot y}^{5} = y^5$$

Similarly, $c^2 \cdot c^4 = \overbrace{(c \cdot c)}^{2} \cdot \overbrace{(c \cdot c \cdot c \cdot c)}^{4} = \overbrace{c \cdot c \cdot c \cdot c \cdot c \cdot c}^{6} = c^6$, and

$$x \cdot x^3 = \overbrace{(x)}^{1} \cdot \overbrace{(x \cdot x \cdot x)}^{3} = x^4 \text{ (Remember that } x \text{ means } x^1.)$$

Observe that the exponent in each product is the sum of the exponents in the factors. These examples illustrate how the exponent of a product is obtained from the exponents of the factors.

In general, when x is a signed number and a and b are positive integers:

$$x^a \cdot x^b = x^{a+b}$$

Procedure. In multiplying powers of the same base, find the exponent of the product by adding the exponents of the factors. The base of the power which is the product is the same as the base of the factors.

Note that this procedure does not apply to the product of powers that have different bases. For example, $c^2 \cdot d^3$ cannot be simplified because $c^2 \cdot d^3 = c \cdot c \cdot d \cdot d \cdot d$, an expression that does not have five identical factors.

FINDING A POWER OF A POWER

Since $(x^3)^4 = x^3 \cdot x^3 \cdot x^3 \cdot x^3$, then $(x^3)^4 = x^{12}$. Observe that the exponent 12 can be obtained by addition, $3 + 3 + 3 + 3 = 12$, or by multiplication, $4 \times 3 = 12$.

In general, when x is a signed number and a and c are positive integers:

$$(x^a)^c = x^{ac}$$

FINDING A POWER OF A PRODUCT OF POWERS

We know that $(x^5 y^2)^3 = (x^5 y^2) \cdot (x^5 y^2) \cdot (x^5 y^2)$
$$= x^5 \cdot x^5 \cdot x^5 \cdot y^2 \cdot y^2 \cdot y^2 \qquad \text{Commutative}$$
$$= (x^5 \cdot x^5 \cdot x^5) \cdot (y^2 \cdot y^2 \cdot y^2) \qquad \text{and}$$

$$= (x^5)^3 \cdot (y^2)^3 \qquad\qquad \text{associative}$$
$$= x^{5 \cdot 3} \cdot y^{2 \cdot 3} \text{ or } x^{15} y^6 \qquad\qquad \text{properties}$$

Observe that 15, the exponent of x, is obtained by multiplication, $5 \times 3 = 15$; and 6, the exponent of y, is also obtained by multiplication, $2 \times 3 = 6$.

In general, when x is a signed number and a and c are positive integers:

$$(x^a \cdot y^b)^c = x^{ac} \cdot y^{bc}$$

Model Problems

In 1–5, simplify the expression by multiplying the powers.

1. $x^5 \cdot x^4 = x^{5+4} = x^9$ 2. $m^6 \cdot m = m^{6+1} = m^7$
3. $10^3 \cdot 10^2 = 10^{3+2} = 10^5$ 4. $m^{4a} \cdot m^{3a} = m^{4a+3a} = m^{7a}$
5. $(a^2)^3 = a^2 \cdot a^2 \cdot a^2 = a^{2+2+2} = a^6$ or $(a^2)^3 = a^{2 \cdot 3} = a^6$
6. $(c^4 \cdot d^5)^3 = c^{4 \cdot 3} \cdot d^{5 \cdot 3} = c^{12} \cdot d^{15}$

EXERCISES

In 1–25, multiply.

1. $a^2 \cdot a^3$ 2. $b^3 \cdot b^4$ 3. $c^2 \cdot c^5$ 4. $r^3 \cdot r^3$
5. $r^2 \cdot r^4 \cdot r^5$ 6. $x^3 \cdot x^2$ 7. $a^5 \cdot a^2$ 8. $s^6 \cdot s^3$
9. $t^8 \cdot t^4 \cdot t^2$ 10. $x \cdot x$ 11. $a^2 \cdot a$ 12. $c \cdot c^5$
13. $e^4 \cdot e \cdot e^5$ 14. $3^4 \cdot 3^3$ 15. $5^2 \cdot 5^4$ 16. $(\frac{1}{4})^3 \cdot (\frac{1}{4})$
17. $2^4 \cdot 2^5 \cdot 2$ 18. $(x^3)^2$ 19. $(a^4)^2$ 20. $(z^3)^2 \cdot (z^4)^2$
21. $(x^2 y^3)^2$ 22. $(ab^2)^4$ 23. $(rs)^3$ 24. $(2^2 \cdot 3^2)^3$
25. $[\frac{2}{5} \cdot (\frac{1}{3})^3]^4$

In 26–30, multiply. (The exponents in each exercise are positive integers.)

26. $x^a \cdot x^{2a}$ 27. $y^c \cdot y^2$ 28. $c^r \cdot c^2$ 29. $x^m \cdot x$ 30. $(3y)^a \cdot (3y)^b$

In 31–38, state whether the sentence is true or false.

31. $10^4 \cdot 10^3 = 10^7$ 32. $2^4 \cdot 2^2 = 2^8$ 33. $3^3 \cdot 2^2 = 6^5$
34. $3^3 \cdot 2^2 = 6^6$ 35. $5^4 \cdot 5 = 5^5$ 36. $2^2 \cdot 2^2 = 2^3$
37. $(2^2)^3 = 2^5$ 38. $(2^3)^5 = 2^{15}$

5. Multiplying a Monomial by a Monomial

We know that the commutative property of multiplication makes it possible to rearrange the factors of a product and that the associative property of multiplication makes it possible to multiply the factors in any order. Therefore:

$$(5x)(6y) = (5)(6)(x)(y) = (5 \cdot 6)(x \cdot y) = 30xy$$
$$(-2x^2)(+5x^4) = (-2)(x^2)(+5)(x^4)$$
$$= [(-2) \cdot (+5)][(x^2) \cdot (x^4)] = -10x^6$$
$$(-3a^2 b^3)(-4a^4 b) = (-3)(a^2)(b^3)(-4)(a^4)(b)$$
$$= [(-3) \cdot (-4)][(a^2) \cdot (a^4)][(b^3) \cdot (b)] = +12a^6 b^4$$

In the preceding examples, the factors may be rearranged and grouped mentally.

Procedure. To multiply monomials:

1. **Use the commutative and associative properties to rearrange and group the factors. This may be done mentally.**
2. **Multiply the numerical coefficients.**
3. **Multiply the variable factors that are powers having the same base.**
4. **Multiply the products previously obtained.**

Model Problems _____

In 1-5, multiply:

1. $(+8xy)(-3z) = -24xyz$ 2. $(-4a^3)(-5a^5) = +20a^8$
3. $(-5x^2 y^3)(-2xy^2) = +10x^3 y^5$ 4. $(+6c^2 d^3)(-\frac{1}{2}d) = -3c^2 d^4$
5. $(-3x^2)^3 = (-3x^2)(-3x^2)(-3x^2) = -27x^6$ or
   $(-3x^2)^3 = (-3)^3(x^2)^3 = -27x^6$

EXERCISES

In 1-36, multiply.

1. $(+6)(-2a)$ 2. $(-4)(-6b)$ 3. $(+5)(-2)(-3y)$ 4. $(-8r)(-2s)$
5. $(+7x)(-2y)(3z)$ 6. $(+6x)(-\frac{1}{2}y)$ 7. $(-\frac{3}{4}a)(+8b)$
8. $(-6x)(\frac{1}{2}y)(-\frac{1}{3}z)$ 9. $(+5ab)(-3c)$ 10. $(-2)(+6cd)(-e)$
11. $(+9xy)(-2cd)$ 12. $(3s)(-4m)(5cd)$ 13. $(+5a^2)(-4a^2)$
14. $(-7y^2)(5y^5)(-2y^3)$ 15. $(18r^5)(-5r^2)$ 16. $(-\frac{1}{2}s^4)(-\frac{1}{4}s^2)(8s^3)$

17. $(+3z^2)(+4z)$
18. $(+6x^2y^3)(-4x^4y^2)$
19. $(-7a^3b)(+5a^2b^2)$
20. $(2r^2s^3)(3r^3s^2)(-r^5s^5)$
21. $(-2r^4s)(+8rs)$
22. $(3ab^3)(-4a^4b)(8ab)$
23. $(-6m^2n)(+5m^2)$
24. $(+\frac{2}{3}x^2)(-6x)$
25. $(-15ab^2)(-\frac{3}{5}a^2b)$
26. $(\frac{1}{3}xy)(\frac{1}{2}x)(-12x^2y^2)$
27. $(+7a)^2$
28. $(-3a)^2$
29. $(-.5x)^2$
30. $(+5a^2)^3$
31. $(-\frac{2}{5}c^2d)^3$
32. $(+2x)^2(+3y)^2$
33. $(-4x)^2(-y)^2$
34. $(\frac{1}{2}x^2)^3(-4y^3)^2$
35. $-5(-3y)^3$
36. $10(2x)^2(-y^2)^3$

37. Express the area of a rectangle whose length is $5w$ and whose width is $3w$.
38. Express the area of a square each of whose sides is $5x$ centimeters.

6. Multiplying a Polynomial by a Monomial

We know that the distributive property of multiplication states:

$$a(b + c) = ab + ac$$

Therefore, $x(4x + 3) = (x)(4x) + (x)(3)$

$$x(4x + 3) = 4x^2 + 3x$$

To find the product $5(3x + 2y)$, we apply the distributive property of multiplication: $5(3x + 2y) = 5(3x) + 5(2y)$.

$$5(3x + 2y) = 15x + 10y$$

The multiplication may also be arranged vertically as shown at the right.

$$\begin{array}{r} 3x + 2y \\ 5 \\ \hline 15x + 10y \end{array}$$

Procedure. To multiply a polynomial by a monomial, use the distributive property: multiply each term of the polynomial by the monomial and add the resulting products.

Model Problems

In 1–3, multiply.

1. $8(3x - 2y + 4z) = 24x - 16y + 32z$
2. $-5x(x^2 - 2x + 4) = -5x^3 + 10x^2 - 20x$
3. $-3a^2b^2(4ab^2 - 3b^2) = -12a^3b^4 + 9a^2b^4$

EXERCISES

In 1–28, multiply.

1. $3(6c + 3d)$
2. $-5(4m - 6n)$
3. $-2(8a + 6b)$
4. $10(2x - \frac{1}{5}y)$
5. $12(\frac{2}{3}m - 4n)$
6. $-27(\frac{2}{9}x - y)$
7. $-16(\frac{3}{4}c - \frac{5}{8}d)$
8. $4x(5x + 6)$
9. $5d(d^2 - 3d)$
10. $-5c^2(15c - 4c^2)$
11. $mn(m + n)$
12. $-ab(a - b)$
13. $3ab(5a^2 - 7b^2)$
14. $-r^3s^3(6r^4s - 3s^4)$
15. $10m^4n(-5n^3 + 3m^2)$
16. $-a^4(10b^2 - a)$
17. $-8(2x^2 - 3x - 5)$
18. $3d(d^2 - 2d + 8)$
19. $-5s(2s^2 - 6s + 7)$
20. $3xy(x^2 + xy + y^2)$
21. $5r^2s^2(-2r^2 + 3rs - 4s^2)$
22. $-15xyz(3xz - 5xy - yz)$
23. $-24(\frac{1}{2}t^2 - \frac{3}{4}t + \frac{2}{3})$
24. $\frac{1}{2}(4x^2 - 6x + 14)$
25. $\frac{3}{4}(12 - 8x + 4x^2)$

26. $x^2 - 5x + 4$
    $\underline{3x\qquad\qquad}$

27. $2y^2 - 5y - 3$
    $\underline{-2y\qquad\qquad}$

28. $y^2 - 3yz + z^2$
    $\underline{3yz\qquad\qquad}$

In 29–33, use grouping symbols to write an algebraic expression which represents the answer. Then simplify the expression.

29. Express the area of a rectangle whose length is $3x + 4y$ and whose width is $5z$.
30. Express the area of a rectangle whose length is $\frac{2}{3}r$ and whose width is $9r - 6s$.
31. A car travels $2x + 5$ kilometers per hour. Express the distance it travels in:
    a. 4 hours   b. 8 hours   c. 20 hours   d. h hours   e. x hours
32. A boy is y years old now. His father is 5 times as old as the boy will be 3 years from now. Express the father's present age.
33. If the length of one side of a square is represented by $3a + 4b$, represent the perimeter of the square.

7. Using Multiplication to Simplify Algebraic Expressions Containing Symbols of Grouping

To simplify the expression $3x + 7(2x + 3)$, we use the distributive property and then collect like terms. Thus:

$$3x + 7(2x + 3) = 3x + 7(2x) + 7(3) = 3x + 14x + 21 = 17x + 21$$

Model Problems

In 1 and 2, simplify the expression by using the distributive property of multiplication and collecting like terms.

1. $-2(3 - 2x) - (6 - 5x)$

   Solution

   $-2(3 - 2x) - (6 - 5x)$
   $= -6 + 4x - 6 + 5x$
   $= 9x - 12$ *Ans.*

2. $6x - [+3x - 2x(x - 5)]$

   Solution

   $6x - [+3x - 2x(x - 5)]$
   $= 6x - [+3x - 2x^2 + 10x]$
   $= 6x - 3x + 2x^2 - 10x$
   $= 2x^2 - 7x$ *Ans.*

EXERCISES

In 1–20, simplify the expression.

1. $5(d + 3) - 10$
2. $3(2 - 3c) + 5c$
3. $7 + 2(7x - 5)$
4. $-2(x - 1) + 6$
5. $-4(3 - 6a) - 7a$
6. $5 - 4(3e - 5)$
7. $5x(2x - 3) + 9x$
8. $12y - 3y(2y - 4)$
9. $7c - 4d - 2(4c - 3d)$
10. $3a - 2a(5a - a) + a^2$
11. $4(2x + 5) - 3(2 - 7x)$
12. $5x(2 - 3x) - x(3x - 1)$
13. $y(y + 4) - y(y - 3) - 9y$
14. $-2c(c + 2d) + 4d(2c - 3d)$
15. $ab(7a - 3c) - bc(2a - b)$
16. $mn(4m^2 - 2n^2) - 2mn(2m^2 - n^2)$
17. $7[5x + 2(x - 3) + 4]$
18. $-4[8y - 7 - 3(2y - 1)]$
19. $4x[2x^2 - 2x(x + 3) - 5]$
20. $x^2z - x[xy - x(y - z)]$
21. A carpenter has a piece of lumber which is $x + 2$ yards in length and another piece which is $2x - 1$ feet in length. Represent in simplest form the total number of inches of lumber that he has.
22. A girl has $3x - 4$ nickels and $2x + 2$ dimes. Represent in simplest form the total number of cents she has.

8. Multiplying a Polynomial by a Polynomial

To find the product $a(x + 3)$, we used the distributive property of multiplication: $a(x + 3) = a(x) + a(3)$. Now let us find the product of two polynomials: $(x + 4)(x + 3)$.

Since $a(x + 3)$ $=$ $a(x)$ $+$ $a(3)$, if we replace a by $x + 4$, then

$(x + 4)(x + 3) = (x + 4)(x) + (x + 4)(3)$ Distributive property
$= x^2 + 4x + 3x + 12$ Distributive property
$= x^2 + 7x + 12$ Combining like terms

In general, for all numbers a, b, c, and $d, (a + b)(c + d) = (a + b)c + (a + b)d$, or

$$(a + b)(c + d) = ac + bc + ad + bd$$

Notice that each term of the first polynomial is multiplied by each term of the second.

At the right, we see a convenient vertical arrangement of the previous multiplication, similar to the arrangement used in arithmetic multiplication. Multiply from left to right.

$$
\begin{array}{rl}
& x \;+ 4 \\
& x \;+ 3 \\
\hline
(x + 4)x \longrightarrow & x^2 + 4x \\
(x + 4)3 \longrightarrow & + 3x + 12 \\
\hline
\text{Add like terms: } & x^2 + 7x + 12 \\
\end{array}
$$

Procedure. **To multiply two polynomials, first arrange them in descending or ascending powers of a common variable (if there is one). Then use the distributive property: multiply each term of one polynomial by each term of the other polynomial. Finally, combine like terms.**

Multiplication can be checked by interchanging the two polynomials and multiplying again. The product should remain the same.

Model Problems

In 1 and 2, multiply the polynomials.

1. $(3x - 4)(4x + 5)$

Solution

$$
\begin{array}{ll}
3x \;-\; 4 & \\
4x \;+\; 5 & \\
\hline
12x^2 - 16x & \text{partial product} \\
 + 15x - 20 & \text{partial product} \\
\hline
12x^2 - x - 20 & \text{product} \\
\end{array}
$$

Answer: $12x^2 - x - 20$

(The checks are left to the student.)

2. $(x^2 + 3xy + 9y^2)(x - 3y)$

Solution

$$
\begin{array}{l}
x^2 + 3xy \;+ 9y^2 \\
x \;- 3y \\
\hline
x^3 + 3x^2y + 9xy^2 \\
 - 3x^2y - 9xy^2 - 27y^3 \\
\hline
x^3 + 0 + 0 - 27y^3 \\
\end{array}
$$

Answer: $x^3 - 27y^3$

EXERCISES

In 1–39, multiply.

1. $(a + 2)(a + 3)$
2. $(d - 6)(d - 5)$
3. $(c + 8)(c - 6)$
4. $(x - 7)(x + 2)$
5. $(6 + y)(5 + y)$
6. $(8 - e)(6 - e)$
7. $(12 - r)(6 + r)$
8. $(x + 5)(x - 5)$
9. $(y + 7)(y - 7)$
10. $(a - \frac{1}{2})(a + \frac{1}{2})$
11. $(2x + 1)(x - 6)$
12. $(c - 5)(2c - 4)$
13. $(2a + 9)(3a + 1)$
14. $(3x - 4)(4x + 3)$
15. $(2x + 3)(2x - 3)$
16. $(6z - \frac{1}{3})(6z + \frac{1}{3})$
17. $(3d + 8)(3d - 8)$
18. $(x + y)(x + y)$
19. $(a - b)(a - b)$
20. $(a + b)(a - b)$
21. $(x - 4y)(x + 4y)$
22. $(5y + 12x)(7x - 2y)$
23. $(5k + 2m)(3r + 4s)$
24. $(3x + 4y)(3x - 4y)$
25. $(6a - 5b)(6a + 5b)$
26. $(r^2 + 5)(r^2 - 2)$
27. $(x^2 - y^2)(x^2 + y^2)$
28. $(x^2 + 3x + 5)(x + 2)$
29. $(2c^2 - 3c - 1)(2c + 1)$
30. $(3 - 2d - d^2)(5 - 2d)$
31. $(4a^2 - 3ab - 2b^2)(2a - 5b)$
32. $(x^3 - 3x^2 + 2x - 4)(3x - 1)$
33. $(2x + 1)(3x - 4)(x + 3)$
34. $(x^2 - 4x + 1)(x^2 + 5x - 2)$
35. $(x + 4)(x + 4)(x + 4)$
36. $(a + 5)^3$
37. $(5 + x^2 - 2x)(2x - 3)$
38. $(5x - 4 + 2x^2)(3 + 4x)$
39. $(3b^2 - 2c^2 - bc)(3b - 2c)$

In 40–45, simplify the expression.

40. $(x + 7)(x - 2) - x^2$
41. $2(3x + 1)(2x - 3) + 14x$
42. $8x^2 - (4x + 3)(2x - 1)$
43. $(x + 4)(x + 3) - (x - 2)(x - 5)$
44. $(y + 4)^2 - (y - 3)^2$
45. $(x + y)^2 + x(x + 3y)$

In 46 and 47, use symbols of grouping to write an algebraic expression which represents the answer. Then simplify the expression.

46. The length of a rectangle is $2x - 5$ and its width is $x + 7$. Express the area of the rectangle.

47. A plane travels at a rate represented by $(x + 100)$ kilometers per hour. Represent the distance it can travel in $(2x + 3)$ hours.

9. Dividing Powers of the Same Base

FINDING THE QUOTIENT OF POWERS

We know that division and multiplication can be viewed as inverse operations.

Since $x^2 \cdot x^3 = x^5$, then $x^5 \div x^3 = x^2$.

Since $y^5 \cdot y^4 = y^9$, then $y^9 \div y^4 = y^5$.

Since $c^4 \cdot c = c^5$, then $c^5 \div c = c^4$. (Remember that c means c^1.)

Observe that the exponent in each quotient is the difference between the exponent of the dividend and the exponent of the divisor.

In general, when $x \neq 0$ and a and b are positive integers with $a > b$:

$$x^a \div x^b = x^{a-b}$$

Procedure. In dividing powers of the same base, find the exponent of the quotient by subtracting the exponent of the divisor from the exponent of the dividend. The base of the power which is the quotient is the same as the base of the dividend and the base of the divisor.

We know that any nonzero number divided by itself is 1. Therefore, $x \div x = 1$ and $y^3 \div y^3 = 1$.

In general, when $x \neq 0$ and a is a positive integer:

$$x^a \div x^a = 1$$

Model Problems

In 1–5, simplify by performing the indicated division.

1. $x^9 \div x^5 = x^{9-5} = x^4$ 2. $y^5 \div y = y^{5-1} = y^4$ 3. $c^5 \div c^5 = 1$
4. $10^5 \div 10^3 = 10^{5-3} = 10^2$ 5. $y^{6b} \div y^{4b} = y^{6b-4b} = y^{2b}$

ANOTHER LOOK AT DIVIDING POWERS OF THE SAME BASE

We know from our experience in arithmetic that $7 \cdot \dfrac{2}{3} = \dfrac{7 \cdot 2}{3}$ and that $\dfrac{3}{4} \cdot \dfrac{1}{2} = \dfrac{3 \cdot 1}{4 \cdot 2}$.

In general, if a, b, x, and y are signed numbers with $b \neq 0$ and $y \neq 0$, then:

$$\frac{a}{b} \cdot \frac{x}{y} = \frac{a \cdot x}{b \cdot y}$$

Now let us study another explanation for $\dfrac{x^5}{x^3} = x^2$:

Step	Reason
1. Since $x^5 = x^3 \cdot x^2$, then $\dfrac{x^5}{x^3} = \dfrac{x^3 \cdot x^2}{x^3}$	1. Substitution principle
2. $\qquad\qquad\qquad = \left(\dfrac{x^3}{x^3}\right) \cdot x^2$	2. Meaning of multiplication

3.	$= 1 \cdot x^2$	3. Any nonzero number divided by itself is 1.
4.	$= x^2$	4. Multiplication property of 1

We can use a similar approach to solve model problems 1–5 above.

1. $\dfrac{x^9}{x^5} = \dfrac{x^5 \cdot x^4}{x^5} = \dfrac{x^5}{x^5} \cdot x^4 = 1 \cdot x^4 = x^4$

2. $\dfrac{y^5}{y} = \dfrac{y}{y} \cdot y^4 = 1 \cdot y^4 = y^4$

3. $\dfrac{c^5}{c^5} = 1$

4. $\dfrac{10^5}{10^3} = \dfrac{10^3}{10^3} \cdot 10^2 = 1 \cdot 10^2 = 10^2$

5. $\dfrac{y^{6b}}{y^{4b}} = \dfrac{y^{4b}}{y^{4b}} \cdot y^{2b} = 1 \cdot y^{2b} = y^{2b}$

FINDING A POWER OF A QUOTIENT

We know that $\left(\dfrac{x}{y}\right)^2 = \dfrac{x}{y} \cdot \dfrac{x}{y} = \dfrac{x^2}{y^2}$. Hence, $\left(\dfrac{x}{y}\right)^2 = \dfrac{x^2}{y^2}$. We also know that $\left(\dfrac{x}{y}\right)^3 = \dfrac{x}{y} \cdot \dfrac{x}{y} \cdot \dfrac{x}{y} = \dfrac{x^3}{y^3}$. Hence, $\left(\dfrac{x}{y}\right)^3 = \dfrac{x^3}{y^3}$.

In general, when x and y are signed numbers ($y \neq 0$), and a is a positive integer, then:

$$\left(\frac{x}{y}\right)^a = \frac{x^a}{y^a}$$

EXERCISES

In 1–16, divide.

1. $x^8 \div x^2$ 2. $a^{10} \div a^5$ 3. $b^7 \div b^3$ 4. $c^5 \div c^4$

5. $d^7 \div d^7$ 6. $\dfrac{e^9}{e^3}$ 7. $\dfrac{m^{12}}{m^4}$ 8. $\dfrac{n^{10}}{n^9}$

9. $\dfrac{r^6}{r^6}$ 10. $x^8 \div x$ 11. $z^{10} \div z$ 12. $t^5 \div t$

13. $2^5 \div 2^2$ 14. $10^6 \div 10^4$ 15. $3^4 \div 3^2$ 16. $5^3 \div 5$

In 17–21, divide. (The exponents in each exercise are positive integers.)

17. $x^{5a} \div x^{2a}$ **18.** $y^{10b} \div y^{2b}$ **19.** $r^c \div r^d$ **20.** $s^x \div s^2$ **21.** $a^b \div a^b$

In 22–26, simplify the expression.

22. $\dfrac{2^3 \cdot 2^4}{2^2}$ **23.** $\dfrac{5^8}{5^4 \cdot 5}$ **24.** $\dfrac{10^2 \cdot 10^3}{10^4}$ **25.** $\dfrac{10^6}{10^2 \cdot 10^4}$ **26.** $\dfrac{10^8 \cdot 10^2}{(10^5)^2}$

In 27–30, state whether the sentence is true or false.

27. $2^5 \div 2^3 = 2^2$ **28.** $5^6 \div 5^2 = 5^4$
29. $2^9 \div 2^3 = 2^3$ **30.** $3^8 \div 3^4 = 1^4$

10. Dividing a Monomial by a Monomial

We know that division and multiplication can be viewed as inverse operations.

Since $(-5x^2)(+4x^4) = -20x^6$, then $(-20x^6) \div (+4x^4) = -5x^2$. Observe that -20 divided by $+4$ equals -5 and that x^6 divided by x^4 equals x^2.

Since $(+7a^2 b^3)(-3a^3 b) = -21a^5 b^4$, then $\dfrac{-21a^5 b^4}{-3a^3 b} = +7a^2 b^3$. Observe that $(-21) \div (-3) = +7$, that $a^5 \div a^3 = a^2$, and that $b^4 \div b = b^3$.

Procedure. To divide monomials:

1. **Divide their numerical coefficients.**
2. **Divide variable factors that are powers having the same base.**
3. **Multiply the quotients previously obtained.**

Model Problems

In 1–4, divide:

1. $(+24a^5) \div (+3a^2) = +8a^3$

2. $(-15x^6 y^5) \div (-3x^3 y^2) = +5x^3 y^3$

3. $\dfrac{-18x^3 y^2}{+6x^2 y} = -3xy$

4. $\dfrac{+20a^3 c^4 d^2}{-5a^3 c^3} = -4cd^2$

ANOTHER LOOK AT DIVIDING A MONOMIAL BY A MONOMIAL

Now let us examine another method that may be used to do the preceding model problems.

1. $\dfrac{+24a^5}{+3a^2} = \dfrac{+24}{+3} \cdot \dfrac{a^5}{a^2} = +8a^3$

2. $\dfrac{-15x^6y^5}{-3x^3y^2} = \dfrac{-15}{-3} \cdot \dfrac{x^6}{x^3} \cdot \dfrac{y^5}{y^2} = +5x^3y^3$

3. $\dfrac{-18x^3y^2}{+6x^2y} = \dfrac{-18}{+6} \cdot \dfrac{x^3}{x^2} \cdot \dfrac{y^2}{y} = -3xy$

4. $\dfrac{+20a^3c^4d^2}{-5a^3c^3} = \dfrac{+20}{-5} \cdot \dfrac{a^3}{a^3} \cdot \dfrac{c^4}{c^3} \cdot d^2 = (-4) \cdot 1 \cdot c \cdot d^2 = -4cd^2$

EXERCISES

In 1–25, divide.

1. $18x$ by 2
2. $14x^2y^2$ by -7
3. $-35x^3$ by $+7x^2$
4. $-12ab$ by $+6a$
5. $-22c^2d$ by $-2c^2$
6. $24a^2b^2$ by $-8b^2$
7. $36a^4b^3$ by $9a^2b^2$
8. $15c^4d$ by $-5c^3d$
9. $-28c^2d$ by $7cd$
10. $(+8cd) \div (-4c)$
11. $(-14xy^3) \div (-7xy^3)$
12. $(-6a^3b^4) \div (+2a^2b^2)$
13. $(+18m^3n^2) \div (+6m^2n^2)$

14. $\dfrac{5x^2y^3}{-5y^3}$ 15. $\dfrac{-49c^4b^3}{7c^2b^2}$ 16. $\dfrac{-24x^2y}{-3xy}$ 17. $\dfrac{21r^2s^2}{-7rs^2}$

18. $\dfrac{-27xyz}{9xz}$ 19. $\dfrac{-57a^{10}b^8}{+3a^4b^2}$ 20. $\dfrac{-63x^9y^2z^3}{+7x^3y}$ 21. $\dfrac{-9.5r^{12}s^{10}t^5}{.5rst^5}$

22. $\dfrac{8(a+b)^5}{2(a+b)^2}$ 23. $\dfrac{15(x+y)^3}{3(x+y)^2}$ 24. $\dfrac{15(c-d)}{5(c-d)}$ 25. $\dfrac{18(x-3y)^3}{3(x-3y)^2}$

26. If $3y$ pens cost $12y^3$ dollars, represent the cost of a pen.
27. If the area of a rectangle is $35x^4$ and the length is $7x^2$, represent the width.

11. Dividing a Polynomial by a Monomial

Since division is the inverse operation of multiplication, if $(x+y)2 = 2x + 2y$, then $\dfrac{2x+2y}{2} = x + y$.

We can obtain the same result by using the multiplicative inverse and the distributive property:

$$\frac{2x+2y}{2} = \tfrac{1}{2}(2x+2y) = \tfrac{1}{2}(2x) + \tfrac{1}{2}(2y) = x + y$$

Observe that the quotient $x + y$ can be obtained by dividing each term of $2x + 2y$ by 2. Thus, $\dfrac{2x + 2y}{2} = \dfrac{2x}{2} + \dfrac{2y}{2} = x + y$.

In general, for all numbers a, x, and y $(a \neq 0)$:

$$\frac{ax + ay}{a} = \frac{ax}{a} + \frac{ay}{a} = x + y$$

Usually, the middle step $\dfrac{ax}{a} + \dfrac{ay}{a}$ is done mentally.

Procedure.   To divide a polynomial by a monomial, divide each term of the polynomial by the monomial.

Note that the monomial divisor is distributed over the terms of the polynomial.

Model Problems

In 1 and 2, divide:

1. $(8a^5 - 6a^4) \div 2a^2 = 4a^3 - 3a^2$

2. $\dfrac{24x^3y^4 - 18x^2y^2 - 6xy}{-6xy} = -4x^2y^3 + 3xy + 1$

EXERCISES

In 1–24, divide.

1. $(10x + 20y) \div 5$

2. $(xr - yr) \div r$

3. $(tr - r) \div r$

4. $\dfrac{12a - 6b}{-2}$

5. $\dfrac{8c^2 - 12d^2}{-4}$

6. $\dfrac{m^2 + 8m}{m}$

7. $\dfrac{p + prt}{p}$

8. $\dfrac{2e^2 - 5e}{e}$

9. $\dfrac{18d^3 + 12d^2}{6d}$

10. $\dfrac{-20x^2 + 15x}{-5x}$

11. $\dfrac{18r^5 + 12r^3}{6r^2}$

12. $\dfrac{16t^5 - 8t^4}{4t^2}$

13. $\dfrac{9y^9 - 6y^6}{-3y^3}$

14. $\dfrac{-15x^6 + 10x^4}{-5x^2}$

15. $\dfrac{3ab^2 - 4a^2b}{ab}$

16. $\dfrac{2\pi r^2 + 2\pi rh}{2\pi r}$

17. $\dfrac{-6a^2b - 12ab^2}{-2ab}$

18. $\dfrac{36a^4b^2 - 18a^2b^2}{-18a^2b^2}$

19. $\dfrac{-5y^5 + 15y - 25}{-5}$

20. $\dfrac{-2a^2 - 3a + 1}{-1}$

21. $\dfrac{1.6a^6x^2 - .8a^5y^2 + 1.2a^4z^2}{.4a^2}$

22. $\dfrac{2.4y^5 + 1.2y^4 - .6y^3}{-.6y^3}$

23. $\dfrac{15r^4s^4 + 20r^3s^3 - 5r^2s^2}{-5r^2s^2}$

24. $\dfrac{x^3y^3 - x^2y^2 + xy}{xy}$

25. If $px + py$ represents the cost of p suits, represent in simplest form the cost of 1 suit.

26. The area of a rectangle is $75r^2 + 15r$. Represent in simplest form its width if its length is:
    a. 5   b. 3   c. r d. $15r$

27. If $60x^2 + 20x$ represents the distance in kilometers traveled by a man, represent in simplest form the number of kilometers per hour he travels if the number of hours he travels is:
    a. 5   b. 20   c. x d. $10x$ e. $20x$

12. Dividing a Polynomial by a Polynomial

To divide one polynomial by another, we use a procedure similar to the one used when dividing one number of arithmetic by another. When we divide 736 by 32, we discover through repeated subtractions how many times 32 is contained in 736. Likewise, when we divide $x^2 + 6x + 8$ by $x + 2$, we discover through repeated subtractions how many times $x + 2$ is contained in $x^2 + 6x + 8$.

See how dividing $x^2 + 6x + 8$ by $x + 2$ follows the same pattern as dividing 736 by 32:

How to Proceed	*Solution 1*	*Solution 2*
1. Write the usual division form.	$32\overline{)736}$	$x + 2\overline{)x^2 + 6x + 8}$
2. Divide the left number of the dividend by the left number of the divisor to obtain the first number of the quotient.	$\dfrac{2}{32\overline{)736}}$	$\dfrac{x}{x + 2\overline{)x^2 + 6x + 8}}$
3. Multiply the whole divisor by the first number of the quotient.	$\begin{array}{r} 2 \\ 32\overline{)736} \\ 64 \end{array}$	$\begin{array}{r} x \\ x + 2\overline{)x^2 + 6x + 8} \\ x^2 + 2x \end{array}$
4. Subtract this product from the dividend and bring down the next number of the dividend to obtain the new dividend.	$\begin{array}{r} 2 \\ 32\overline{)736} \\ 64 \\ \overline{96} \end{array}$	$\begin{array}{r} x \\ x + 2\overline{)x^2 + 6x + 8} \\ x^2 + 2x \\ \overline{4x + 8} \end{array}$

5. Divide the left number of the new dividend by the left number of the divisor to obtain the next number of the quotient.

$$\begin{array}{r} 23 \\ 32\overline{)736} \\ 64 \\ \hline 96 \end{array}$$

$$\begin{array}{r} x + 4 \\ x+2\overline{)x^2 + 6x + 8} \\ x^2 + 2x \\ \hline 4x + 8 \end{array}$$

6. Repeat steps 3 and 4, multiplying the whole divisor by the second number of the quotient. Subtract the result from the new dividend. The last remainder is 0.

$$\begin{array}{r} 23 \\ 32\overline{)736} \\ 64 \\ \hline 96 \\ 96 \\ \hline \end{array}$$

$$\begin{array}{r} x + 4 \\ x+2\overline{)x^2 + 6x + 8} \\ x^2 + 2x \\ \hline 4x + 8 \\ 4x + 8 \\ \hline \end{array}$$

Ans. 23   *Ans.* $x + 4$

Note: When the dividend is not exactly divisible by the divisor, the last remainder will not be zero. We know that, in arithmetic, the division process is stopped when the remainder is less than the divisor. In algebra, the division process is stopped when the remainder is zero, or when the degree of the remainder is less than the degree of the divisor.

To check the division, test the relationship quotient $\times$ divisor + remainder = dividend as shown at the right.

$$\begin{array}{ll} 23 & x + 4 \\ 32 & x + 2 \\ \hline 46 & x^2 + 4x \\ 69 & + 2x + 8 \\ \hline 736 & x^2 + 6x + 8 \end{array}$$

ARRANGING TERMS IN DIVISION

Division becomes more convenient if the terms of both the divisor and the dividend are arranged in descending powers of one variable.

For example, if $3x - 1 + x^3 - 3x^2$ is to be divided by $x - 1$, write:

$$x - 1\overline{)x^3 - 3x^2 + 3x - 1}$$

MISSING POWERS IN DIVISION

If $x^3 + 8$ is to be divided by $x + 2$, note that the terms containing x^2 and x are missing in the dividend. In order to arrange the terms of the dividend in descending powers of x when we set down our division form, we use a zero as the coefficient of each missing term in the dividend because $x^3 + 8$ can also be considered as $x^3 + 0x^2 + 0x + 8$. We write:

$$x + 2\overline{)x^3 + 0x^2 + 0x + 8}$$

CHECKING DIVISION

Division may be checked by using the relationship:

quotient × divisor + remainder = dividend

Procedure. To divide a polynomial by a polynomial:

1. Arrange the terms of both divisor and dividend according to descending powers of one variable.
2. Divide the first term of the dividend by the first term of the divisor to obtain the first term of the quotient.
3. Multiply the whole divisor by the first term of the quotient.
4. Subtract this product from the dividend to obtain the new dividend.
5. Repeat steps 2 to 4 until the remainder is 0 or until the degree of the remainder polynomial is less than the degree of the divisor polynomial.
6. If the remainder is not 0, express the quotient as follows:

$$\frac{\text{dividend}}{\text{divisor}} = \text{quotient} + \frac{\text{remainder}}{\text{divisor}}$$

Model Problems

1. Divide $5s + 6s^2 - 15$ by $2s + 3$. Check.

   Solution:

   Arrange terms of dividend in descending powers of s.

   $$\begin{array}{r} 3s - 2 \\ 2s+3\overline{)6s^2 + 5s - 15} \\ \underline{6s^2 + 9s} \\ -4s - 15 \\ \underline{-4s - 6} \\ -9 \end{array}$$

   Answer: $3s - 2 + \dfrac{-9}{2s+3}$

   Check:

   $$\begin{array}{lr} 2s + 3 & \text{divisor} \\ 3s - 2 & \text{quotient} \\ \hline 6s^2 + 9s & \\ -4s - 6 & \\ \hline 6s^2 + 5s - 6 & \\ -9 & \text{remainder} \\ \hline 6s^2 + 5s - 15 & \text{dividend} \end{array}$$

2. Divide $3x^3 - 5y^3 + 18xy^2 - 14x^2y$ by $3x - 5y$.

   Solution:

   Arrange terms in descending powers of x.

$$\begin{array}{r}
x^2 - 3xy + y^2 \\
3x - 5y{\overline{\smash{\big)}\,3x^3 - 14x^2y + 18xy^2 - 5y^3}} \\
\underline{3x^3 - 5x^2y} \\
-9x^2y + 18xy^2 \\
\underline{-9x^2y + 15xy^2} \\
3xy^2 - 5y^3 \\
\underline{3xy^2 - 5y^3}
\end{array}$$

Answer: $x^2 - 3xy + y^2$

3. Divide $x^3 + 8$ by $x + 2$.

Solution:

Use zeros as the coefficients of the missing terms.

$$\begin{array}{r}
x^2 - 2x + 4 \\
x + 2{\overline{\smash{\big)}\,x^3 + 0x^2 + 0x + 8}} \\
\underline{x^3 + 2x^2} \\
-2x^2 + 0x \\
\underline{-2x^2 - 4x} \\
4x + 8 \\
\underline{4x + 8}
\end{array}$$

Answer: $x^2 - 2x + 4$

EXERCISES

In 1–34, divide and check.

1. $b^2 + 5b + 6$ by $b + 3$
2. $c^2 - 8c + 7$ by $c - 1$
3. $r^2 + 2r - 15$ by $r + 5$
4. $t^2 - 7t - 60$ by $t - 12$
5. $x^2 - 15x - 54$ by $x + 3$
6. $y^2 + 22y + 85$ by $y + 17$
7. $66 + 17x + x^2$ by $6 + x$
8. $30 - t - t^2$ by $5 - t$
9. $3t^2 - 8t + 4$ by $3t - 2$
10. $21a^2 - 10a + 1$ by $3a - 1$
11. $15x^2 - 19x - 56$ by $5x + 7$
12. $16y^2 - 46y + 15$ by $8y - 3$
13. $2x^2 - xy - 6y^2$ by $x - 2y$
14. $21x^2 - 72xy - 165y^2$ by $3x - 15y$
15. $45x^2 + 69xy - 10y^2$ by $3x + 5y$
16. $40x^2 + 11xy - 63y^2$ by $8x - 9y$
17. $56x^2 - 15 - 11x$ by $7x + 3$
18. $15 + 4a^2 - 16a$ by $2a - 3$
19. $a^2 - 8b^2 + 7ab$ by $a + 8b$
20. $cd + c^2 - 30d^2$ by $c - 5d$
21. $15ab + 9b^2 + 6a^2$ by $2a + 3b$
22. $5cd - 3d^2 + 2c^2$ by $2c - d$
23. $x^2 - 64$ by $x - 8$
24. $y^2 - 100$ by $y + 10$
25. $4m^2 - 49n^2$ by $2m + 7n$
26. $64a^2 - 81b^2$ by $8a - 9b$
27. $x^3 - 8x^2 + 17x - 10$ by $x - 5$
28. $6y^3 + y^2 - 28y - 30$ by $2y - 5$

29. $6b^3 - 8b^2 - 17b - 6$ by $3b + 2$ **30.** $2c^3 - 4c - c^2 + 3$ by $2c + 3$
31. $6y^3 + 11y^2 - 1$ by $3y + 1$ **32.** $d^3 - 64$ by $d - 4$
33. $8x^3 + 27$ by $2x + 3$ **34.** $a^3 - 8b^3$ by $a - 2b$

In 35–48, find the quotient and the remainder. Check the answer.

35. $(x^2 - 9x + 7) \div (x - 2)$ **36.** $(4x^2 + 6x + 9) \div (2x - 5)$
37. $(3x^2 + 9x - 4) \div (3x + 3)$ **38.** $(12x^2 - 9 + 24x) \div (6x - 3)$
39. $(c^3 - 8c^2 - 6c + 9) \div (c - 2)$
40. $(3c^3 + 14c^2 + 4c - 4) \div (c + 4)$
41. $(2 - 8a + 2a^3 - 5a^2) \div (2a + 3)$
42. $(6y^3 - 10 + 11y^2) \div (3y + 1)$
43. $(10x^2 - 3xy + 9y^2) \div (2x + y)$
44. $(6a^2 + 5ab - 4b^2) \div (3a - 2b)$
45. $(a^2 - 28b^2 + 3ab) \div (a - 6b)$
46. $(10x^2 - 5y^2 + 38xy) \div (2x + 8y)$
47. $(x^2 + 25) \div (x + 5)$ **48.** $(x^3 - 27) \div (x + 3)$

In 49–54, divide and check.

49. $\dfrac{x^3 + 2x^2 - 2x - 12}{x^2 + 4x + 6}$ **50.** $\dfrac{6r^3 - 30r + 14r^2 + 12}{2r^2 + 6r - 6}$

51. $\dfrac{2x^3 - x^2 - 4x + 3}{x^2 + 1 - 2x}$ **52.** $\dfrac{y^4 - 6y^2 + 8}{y^2 - 4}$

53. $\dfrac{4a^4 - 4a^2 b^2 - 15b^4}{2a^2 + 3b^2}$ **54.** $\dfrac{4x^4 + 1}{2x^2 + 2x + 1}$

55. One factor of $x^2 - 8x - 9$ is $x + 1$. Find the other factor.
56. One factor of $3y^2 + 8y + 4$ is $3y + 2$. Find the other factor.
57. Is $x - 2$ a factor of $x^3 - 2x^2 + 4x - 6$? Why?

13. Nonpositive Integral Exponents

Up to this point an exponent has meaning when it is a positive integer. For example, x^3 means use x as a factor 3 times, that is, $x^3 = x \cdot x \cdot x$. We have become familiar with the following laws of exponents.

For any numbers x and y and any positive integers, a, b, and c,

1. $x^a \cdot x^b = x^{a+b}$ **2.** $x^a \div x^b = x^{a-b}$ $(x \neq 0, a > b)$

3. $(x^a)^b = x^{a \cdot b}$ **4.** $(x^a \cdot y^b)^c = x^{ac} \cdot y^{bc}$ **5.** $\left(\dfrac{x}{y}\right)^a = \dfrac{x^a}{y^a}$ $(y \neq 0)$

Now, we will see that nonpositive integers such as 0, -1, and -2 can also be used as exponents. We will define powers having zero and negative integral exponents in such a way that the properties that were valid for positive integral exponents will also be valid for nonpositive integral exponents. Hence, these properties will be valid for all integral exponents.

THE ZERO EXPONENT

We know that $\frac{x^3}{x^3} = 1 (x \neq 0)$. If we wish $\frac{x^3}{x^3} = x^{3-3}$, that is, $\frac{x^3}{x^3} = x^0$, to be a true meaningful statement, then we must say that $x^0 = 1$, since both x^0 and 1 are each equal to $\frac{x^3}{x^3}$. This leads us to make the following definition.

$$x^0 = 1 \text{ if } x \text{ is a number such that } x \neq 0$$

It can be shown that all the laws of exponents remain valid when x^0 is defined as 1.

The definition $x^0 = 1$ ($x \neq 0$) permits us to say that the zero power of any number, except zero, equals 1. Thus, $4^0 = 1$, $(-4)^0 = 1$, $(4x)^0 = 1$, $(-4x)^0 = 1$, $(x + 4)^0 = 1$. Observe that $(4x)^0 = 1$. However, $4x^0 = 4$, because $4x^0 = 4 \cdot (x^0) = 4 \cdot (1) = 4$. Also, $(x + 4)^0 = 1$. However, $x + 4^0 = x + 1$. In this book, whenever we write x^0, it is assumed that $x \neq 0$.

THE NEGATIVE INTEGRAL EXPONENT

We know that $\frac{x^3}{x^5} = \frac{1}{x^2}$. If we wish $\frac{x^3}{x^5} = x^{3-5}$, that is, $\frac{x^3}{x^5} = x^{-2}$, to be a true meaningful statement, then we must say that $x^{-2} = \frac{1}{x^2}$, since x^{-2} and $\frac{1}{x^2}$ are each equal to $\frac{x^3}{x^5}$. This leads us to make the following definition:

$$x^{-n} = \frac{1}{x^n} \text{ if } x \text{ is a number such that } x \neq 0$$

Now, we can say that for all integral values of a and b,

$$\frac{x^a}{x^b} = x^{a-b} \ (x \neq 0)$$

It can be shown that all the laws of exponents remain valid if x^{-n} is defined as $\frac{1}{x^n}$.

The definition $x^{-n} = \dfrac{1}{x^n}$ $(x \neq 0)$ permits us to say that a power of any nonzero number having a negative exponent equals the reciprocal of the corresponding positive power of the same number. Thus, $r^{-8} = \dfrac{1}{r^8}$, $10^{-4} = \dfrac{1}{10^4}$, $a^{-b} = \dfrac{1}{a^b}$, and $(y + 6)^{-1} = \dfrac{1}{(y + 6)}$.

Observe that in each of the previous examples, as is true in general, when the exponents of the same base are additive inverses of each other, the powers themselves are multiplicative inverses of each other.

Consider the powers x^n and x^{-n}. Since $x^n \cdot x^{-n} = x^{n+(-n)}$, $x^n \cdot x^{-n} = x^0$ or $x^n \cdot x^{-n} = 1$. Therefore, x^n is the reciprocal of x^{-n}. This can be symbolized as follows:

$$x^n = \frac{1}{x^{-n}}.$$

See how we can make use of this relationship in dealing with fractions having factors involving negative exponents.

$$\frac{x}{ya^{-3}} = \frac{x}{y} \cdot \frac{1}{a^{-3}} = \frac{x}{y} \cdot a^3 = \frac{xa^3}{y}.$$

Hence, $\dfrac{x}{ya^{-3}} = \dfrac{xa^3}{y}$.

$$\frac{c^2 d^{-4}}{rs^{-5}} = \frac{c^2 d^{-4}}{r} \cdot \frac{1}{s^{-5}} = \frac{c^2 d^{-4}}{r} \cdot s^5 = \frac{c^2 s^5}{r} \cdot d^{-4} = \frac{c^2 s^5}{r} \cdot \frac{1}{d^4} = \frac{c^2 s^5}{rd^4}.$$

Hence, $\dfrac{c^2 d^{-4}}{rs^{-5}} = \dfrac{c^2 s^5}{rd^4}$.

These examples illustrate the general principle that any power which is a factor of the numerator of a fraction may be transferred to become a factor of the denominator, or vice versa, provided that the sign of the exponent is changed. For example,

$$\frac{8x^3}{15y^{-2}} = \frac{8x^3 y^2}{15}, \quad \frac{5ab^{-3}}{7c^{-2}d^4} = \frac{5ac^2}{7b^3 d^4}, \quad \text{and} \quad \frac{2m^3}{7n^2} = \frac{2n^{-2}}{7m^{-3}}.$$

Model Problems

1. Find the value of:

$7(3)^0 + (10)^{-2}$

2. Find the value of:

$3(10)^2 + 7(10)^1 + 6(10)^0 + 2(10)^{-1} + 9(10)^{-2}$

Solution	*Solution*
$7(1) + \dfrac{1}{(10)^2}$	$3(100) + 7(10) + 6(1) + 2\left(\dfrac{1}{10^1}\right) + 9\left(\dfrac{1}{10^2}\right)$
$7 + \dfrac{1}{100}$	$300 + 70 \quad + 6 + \dfrac{2}{10} + \dfrac{9}{100}$
$7\dfrac{1}{100}$ or 7.01 *Ans.*	$300 + 70 + 6 + .2 + .09$
	376.29 *Ans.*

3. Find the value of:

$(-2)^{-3} - (6 + 3)^0$

   Solution

   $\dfrac{1}{(-2)^3} - (9)^0$

   $-\dfrac{1}{8} - 1$

   $-1\dfrac{1}{8}$ *Ans.*

4. Find the value of:

$8y^0 - 100(y^{-2})$ if $y = 5$.

   Solution

   $8(5)^0 - 100(5^{-2})$

   $8(1) \ - 100\left(\dfrac{1}{5^2}\right)$

   $8 - 100\left(\dfrac{1}{25}\right)$

   $8 - 4$

   4 *Ans.*

5. Express $(2 \times 10^5)(3 \times 10^{-2})$ as the product of a number between 1 and 10 and an integral power of 10.

   Solution:

   $$(2 \times 10^5)(3 \times 10^{-2}) = (2 \times 3)(10^5 \times 10^{-2})$$
   $$= 6 \times 10^3 \ \ \textit{Ans.}$$

EXERCISES

In 1–16, transform the expression into an equivalent expression involving only positive exponents.

1. m^{-6} 2. r^{-3} 3. $5x^{-5}$ 4. $9b^{-7}$
5. $c^{-3}d^2$ 6. $8y^3x^{-1}$ 7. $(2t)^{-3}$ 8. $(21w)^{-5}$

9. $\dfrac{1}{g^{-2}}$ 10. $\dfrac{1}{z^{-5}}$ 11. $\dfrac{7}{a^{-1}}$ 12. $\dfrac{15}{b^{-6}}$

13. $\dfrac{m^{-3}}{n^{-2}}$ 14. $\dfrac{s^4}{t^{-2}}$ 15. $\dfrac{y^{-4}x}{wz^{-2}}$ 16. $\dfrac{8c^{-5}}{3d^3}$

In 17–20, transform the fraction into an equivalent expression without a denominator.

17. $\dfrac{r^3}{s^2}$ 18. $\dfrac{7xy^4}{d^5}$ 19. $\dfrac{s^5}{t^{-1}}$ 20. $\dfrac{5cd^2}{a^2b}$

In 21–38, find the value of the expression.

21. 10^0 22. m^0 23. $(7x)^0$ 24. $(m + 2n)^0$
25. $5x^0$ 26. $-8r^0$ 27. $(3)^{-2}$ 28. 2^{-4}
29. $(-6)^{-1}$ 30. $(-1)^{-5}$ 31. $3(10)^{-3}$ 32. $7(10)^{-1}$
33. $5^0 + 6^{-2}$ 34. $9x^0 - (8x)^0$ 35. $3^{-2} + (7 - 1)^0$
36. $(-1)^{-3} - (8 + 1)^0$ 37. $(10)^2 + (10)^1 + (10)^0 + (10)^{-1}$
38. $2(10)^2 + 6(10)^1 + 8(10)^0 + 9(10)^{-1} + 7(10)^{-2}$
39. Find the value of $3x^0 + 2x^{-1}$ if $x = 4$.
40. Find the value of $x^2 + (5x)^0 + 40x^{-3}$ when $x = -2$.
41. Find the value of $4x^2 + 3x + 2x^0 + 7x^{-1} + 9x^{-2}$ when $x = 10$.
42. Find the value of $y \cdot 10^n$ when:
     a. $y = 5.7, n = 5$ b. $y = 1.65, n = 9$
     c. $y = 3.2, n = -3$ d. $y = 8.23, n = -7$

In 43–86, use the laws of exponents to simplify the expression.

43. $y^7 \cdot y^{-3}$ 44. $d^{-1} \cdot d^5$ 45. $x \cdot x^{-5}$ 46. $m^{-7} \cdot m^{-2}$
47. $a^0 \cdot a^3$ 48. $2^5 \cdot 2^{-3}$ 49. $3^{-6} \cdot 3^6$ 50. $10^{-2} \cdot 10$
51. $x^4y^3 \cdot x^{-3}$ 52. $c^{-2} \cdot c^{-3}d^{-4}$ 53. $r^2s^{-4} \cdot r^{-4}s^5$
54. $x^3y^{-2} \cdot x^{-3}y^2$ 55. $m^2 \div m^7$ 56. $t^{-6} \div t^2$
57. $x^{-4} \div x$ 58. $c^4 \div c^{-2}$ 59. $2^3 \div 2^6$
60. $2^{-3} \div 2^{-5}$ 61. $10^{-4} \div 10^3$ 62. $10^{-3} \div 10^{-5}$
63. $(x^3)^4$ 64. $(a^{-4})^3$ 65. $(d^4)^{-5}$
66. $(t^{-2})^{-4}$ 67. $(4^{-1})^2$ 68. $(2^5)^{-1}$
69. $(10^{-2})^3$ 70. $(10^{-1})^{-5}$ 71. $(a^3y^{-1})^2$
72. $(x^0y^3)^{-4}$ 73. $(c^{-2}d^{-1})^3$ 74. $(2x^{-3})^4$
75. $y^5 \cdot y^0 \cdot y^{-2}$ 76. $a^{-1} \cdot a^{-3} \cdot a^5$ 77. $m^3 \cdot m^{-5} \cdot m^2$

78. $(n^2 \cdot m^{-8}) \div n^{-6}$ 79. $\dfrac{2^8 \cdot 2^{-5} \cdot 2^0}{2^2}$ 80. $\dfrac{5^{-3} \cdot 5^{-6}}{5^3 \cdot 5^0 \cdot 5^{-2}}$

81. $\dfrac{10^4 \cdot 10^{-2} \cdot 10^0}{10^{-1} \cdot 10^{-4}}$ 82. $\dfrac{10^5 \cdot 10^{-3} \cdot 10^{-7}}{10^{-3} \cdot 10^0 \cdot 10^{-2}}$ 83. $5^4 \cdot 25$

84. $2^{-5} \cdot 8$ 85. $3^7 \div 27$ 86. $100 \div 10^{-4}$

In 87–98, express the numerical expression as the product of a number between 1 and 10 and an integral power of 10.

87. $(2 \times 10^{-2})(4^0 \times 10^6)$

88. $(1.1 \times 10^4)(3.0 \times 10^{-9})$

89. $(1.9 \times 10^{-3})(3.7 \times 10^{-4})$

90. $(4 \times 10^3) \div (2 \times 10^6)$

91. $(6 \times 10^{-3}) \div (3 \times 10^5)$

92. $(8.4 \times 10^{34}) \div (4.2 \times 10^{-17})$

93. $\dfrac{(7 \times 10^5)(3.6 \times 10^9)}{4.2 \times 10^4}$

94. $\dfrac{8.4 \times 10^{-5}}{(2.1 \times 10^3)(2 \times 10^8)}$

95. $\dfrac{(2.00 \times 10^{11})(3.75 \times 10^{-4})}{2.5 \times 10^{-2}}$

96. $\dfrac{5.6 \times 10^{12}}{(1.4 \times 10^{-3})(2 \times 10^5)}$

97. $\dfrac{(3 \times 10^7)(6.8 \times 10^5)}{(1.7 \times 10^{-4})(6 \times 10^8)}$

98. $\dfrac{(2.25 \times 10^{12})(9 \times 10^{-8})}{(3 \times 10^{15})(1.5 \times 10^7)}$

14. Scientific Notation

A positive number is written in *scientific notation* when it is expressed as the product of two factors such that the first factor is a number between 1 and 10 and the second factor is an integral power of 10.

For example, the approximate number of seconds in a century, 3,150,000,000, may be expressed in scientific notation as 3.15×10^9; the approximate number of centimeters in the diameter of the smallest visible particle, .00005, may be expressed in scientific notation as 5×10^{-5}.

Scientific notation can be used effectively in the following ways.

1. To express very large numbers and very small numbers by means of a compact numeral.
2. To simplify calculations by using the laws of exponents.
3. To help approximate easily the results of a calculation, as is illustrated in model problem 2.

Procedure. To express a number in scientific notation:

1. **Express the number as a decimal if it is not already expressed as a decimal.**
2. **Place a caret ($\wedge$) immediately to the right of the first nonzero digit of the number.**
3. **Count the number of digits (moving to the left or to the right) between the caret and the decimal point in the number.**
4. **Replace the caret by a decimal point. The result will be a number between 1 and 10. Write this number as the first factor of the scientific notation for the given number.**

5. Use the number counted in step 3 to write the second factor of the scientific notation of the given number. If the count was to the right, write the second factor as 10 with an exponent which is the number counted in step 3. If the count was to the left, write the second factor as 10 with an exponent which is the negative of the number counted in step 3.

In the following examples, the arrow indicates the direction of counting.

	Given Number	=	$\left(\begin{array}{c}\text{Factor between}\\\text{1 and 10}\end{array}\right)$	X	(Power of 10)
1.	$1_\wedge 86000.$ $\xrightarrow{\hspace{1cm}}$	=	1.86	X	10^5
2.	$.0001_\wedge 86$ $\xleftarrow{\hspace{0.5cm}}$	=	1.86	X	10^{-4}
3.	1.86 $\wedge$	=	1.86	X	10^0

Model Problems

1. Write in scientific notation:

a. 6,270,000,000   b. .0000000703

How to Proceed	Solution	Solution
1. Place the caret.	$6_\wedge 270000000.$	$.00000007_\wedge 03$
2. Count the digits between the caret and the decimal point.	$6_\wedge 270000000.$ $\xrightarrow{\hspace{1cm}}$ 9 digits	$.00000007_\wedge 03$ $\xleftarrow{\hspace{1cm}}$ 8 digits
3. Replace the caret with a decimal point and write the first factor.	6.27	7.03
4. Write the second factor. Use a positive power of 10 when the count is to the right, as in part (a); a negative power of 10 when the count is to the left, as in part (b).	10^9	10^{-8}
5. Write the product of the two factors.	6.27×10^9 *Ans.*	7.03×10^{-8} *Ans.*

2. Find an approximate value of 2,990,000,000 $\times$ .0000102.

Solution:

$$2,990,000,000 \times .0000102 = (2.99 \times 10^9)\,(1.02 \times 10^{-5})$$
$$\approx (3 \times 10^9)\,(1 \times 10^{-5})$$
$$\approx (3 \times 1)\,(10^9 \times 10^{-5})$$
$$\approx 3 \times 10^4, \text{ or } 30,000 \quad \textit{Ans.}$$

3. Express 1.73×10^{-4} in ordinary decimal notation.

Solution:

$$10^{-4} = \frac{1}{10^4} = \frac{1}{10,000}; \text{ therefore, } 1.73 \times 10^{-4} = 1.73\,\frac{1}{10,000}$$
$$= .000173 \quad \textit{Ans.}$$

Note: To multiply a decimal by 10^{-4}, we can simply move the decimal point 4 places to the left. Think of the exponent -4 as "4 to the left." To multiply a decimal by 10^{+4}, we can simply move the decimal point 4 places to the right. Think of the exponent $+4$ as "4 to the right." In general, to multiply a decimal by 10^n, move the decimal point n places to the right when n is a positive integer; move the decimal point n places to the left when n is a negative integer.

EXERCISES

In 1–9, express the number as a power of 10.

1. 100,000

2. 10,000,000

3. 1,000,000,000

4. .001

5. .000001

6. .00000001

7. $\dfrac{1}{10,000}$

8. $\dfrac{1}{1,000,000}$

9. $\dfrac{1}{1,000,000,000}$

In 10–21, write the number in scientific notation.

10. 340

11. 340,000

12. .00034

13. 6,000,000

14. .000006

15. 519,000,000

16. .0000185

17. 12,500,000,000,000

18. .000000000789

19. $\dfrac{3}{10,000}$

20. $\dfrac{3}{1,000,000}$

21. $\dfrac{3}{1,000,000,000}$

In 22–27, write the number as an integer or in ordinary decimal notation.

22. 8.4×10^5

23. 8.4×10^{-5}

24. 5.75×10^8

25. 5.75×10^{-8}

26. 2.164×10^{-10}

27. 9.9999×10^3

In 28–37, calculate the result applying the laws of exponents. Represent the result (a) in scientific notation, (b) as an integer or as a decimal.

28. $(2 \times 10^4)(3 \times 10^{-5})$

29. $(2.25 \times 10^{11})(4 \times 10^4)$

30. $(6 \times 10^{23}) \div (1.5 \times 10^{18})$

31. $(9.3 \times 10^{-8}) \div (3.1 \times 10^{-12})$

32. $(1.5 \times 10^3)^2$

33. $(2.5 \times 10^{-4})^2$

34. $\dfrac{(1.2 \times 10^5)(2.5 \times 10^3)}{(1.25 \times 10^6)}$

35. $\dfrac{(8.4 \times 10^{-1})(1.7 \times 10^{-8})}{(4.2 \times 10^{-3})}$

36. $\dfrac{(6.8 \times 10^4)(5 \times 10^{-6})}{(4 \times 10^7)(1.7 \times 10^{-2})}$

37. $\dfrac{(7 \times 10^{-8})(2.25 \times 10^{11})}{(1.5 \times 10^7)(3 \times 10^{14})}$

In 38–43, find the value of n.

38. $n = 9 \times 10^5$

39. $n = 1.76 \times 10^{-5}$

40. $700,000 = 7 \times 10^n$

41. $.00000125 = 1.25 \times 10^n$

42. $892,000 = n \times 10^5$

43. $.00000064 = n \times 10^{-7}$

In 44–48, express the number in scientific notation.

44. The acceleration due to gravity is approximately 981 centimeters per second per second.

45. The wavelength of blue light is approximately .000000485 meter.

46. The mass of a hydrogen atom is approximately .000000000000000000000000167 gram.

47. The velocity of light in a vacuum is approximately 30,000,000,000 centimeters per second.

48. A light-year, the distance light travels in one year, is approximately 9,500,000,000,000 kilometers.

In 49–52, express the number as an integer or in ordinary decimal notation.

49. The distance between our solar system and Alpha Centauri, the nearest known star, is approximately 4.0×10^{13} kilometers.

50. The density of dry air is approximately 1.3×10^{-3} gram per centimeter.

51. The mass of the earth is approximately 5.9×10^{24} kilograms.

52. Planck's constant is approximately 6.63×10^{-27} erg second.

Chapter 7

First-Degree Equations and

Inequalities in One Variable

1. Understanding the Meaning of Solving an Equation

An *equation* is a sentence which uses the symbol = to state that two algebraic expressions are equal. For example, $x + 3 = 9$ is an equation in which $x + 3$ is called the *left side*, or *left member*, and 9 is called the *right side*, or *right member*.

An equation may be a true sentence such as $5 + 2 = 7$ or a false sentence such as $6 - 3 = 4$. An equation may also be an open sentence such as $x + 3 = 9$. We cannot determine whether this sentence is true or false until the value of the variable is known.

Consider the equation $x + 3 = 9$. When x is replaced by an element of {signed numbers}, the sentence may become either a true sentence or a false sentence. Only when x is replaced by 6 does $x + 3 = 9$ become a true sentence: $6 + 3 = 9$. The number 6, which satisfies the equation $x + 3 = 9$, is called a *root*, or a *solution*, of the equation. The set consisting of all the solutions of an equation is called its *solution set*, or *truth set*.

The solution set of an equation is a subset of the replacement set (the domain) of the variable. This subset consists of the elements of the replacement set which make the open sentence true. Therefore, if the replacement set of x is {signed numbers}, then the solution set of $x + 3 = 9$ is {6}. Observe that {6} is a subset of {signed numbers}.

Notice that what we learned about open sentences and truth sets (pages 40 and 41) is true for algebraic equations.

To *solve an equation* means to find its solution set.

If only some elements of the domain satisfy an equation, the equation is called a *conditional equation*, or simply an "equation." Therefore, $x + 3 = 9$ is a conditional equation.

If every element of the domain satisfies an equation, the equation is called an *identity*. Thus, $5 + x = x + 5$ is an identity when the domain of x is {signed numbers} because every element of the domain makes the sentence true.

Procedure. To verify, or check, whether a number is a root of an equation:

1. Replace the variable in the equation by the number.
2. Perform the indicated operations to determine whether the resulting statement is true.

Model Problems

1. Is 7 a root of the equation $5x - 10 = 25$?

How to Proceed	Solution
1. Write the equation.	$5x - 10 = 25$
2. Replace the variable x by 7.	$5 \times 7 - 10 \overset{?}{=} 25$
3. Do the multiplication.	$35 - 10 \overset{?}{=} 25$
4. Do the subtraction. A true statement results.	$25 = 25$ (true)

Answer: Yes

2. Is -4 a root of the equation $3x + 9 = 27$?

How to Proceed	Solution
1. Write the equation.	$3x + 9 = 27$
2. Replace the variable x by -4.	$3 \times (-4) + 9 \overset{?}{=} 27$
3. Do the multiplication.	$-12 + 9 \overset{?}{=} 27$
4. Do the addition. A false statement results.	$-3 = 27$ (false)

Answer: No

EXERCISES

In 1–12, "guess" a value (a signed number) which can replace the variable and make the resulting equation a true statement.

1. $4x = 20$ 2. $36 = 9r$ 3. $\frac{1}{2}x = 7$
4. $8 = \frac{1}{2}d$ 5. $x + 7 = 13$ 6. $18 = 5 - c$
7. $r - 4 = 1.2$ 8. $15 = m - 4$ 9. $2x + 1 = 19$

10. $3y + 8 = 17$ 11. $2x - 3 = 17$ 12. $-4m - 10 = 50$

In 13–21, tell whether the number in the parentheses is a root of the given equation.

13. $5x = 50$ (10)   14. $\frac{1}{2}x = 18$ (36)   15. $\frac{1}{3}y = -12$ (+4)
16. $x + 5 = -11$ (6)   17. $y - 8 = 14$ (22)   18. $-x - 5 = 13$ (8)
19. $m - 4\frac{1}{2} = 9$ ($4\frac{1}{2}$)   20. $2x + 7 = -21$ (−14)   21. $19 = 4x - 1$ (5)

In 22–30, using the domain $\{-5, -4, -3, -2, -1, 0, 1, 2, 3, 4, 5\}$, find the solution set of the equation. If the equation has no roots, indicate the solution set as the empty set, $\emptyset$.

22. $x + 5 = 7$ 23. $y - 3 = 4$ 24. $-2x + 1 = 9$
25. $6 = 3x - 6$ 26. $\frac{1}{2}x + 4 = 50$ 27. $4 - 2x = -2$

28. $\dfrac{x + 8}{4} = 3$ 29. $3x - 2 = -17$ 30. $\dfrac{-x + 1}{2} = -2$

In 31–36, using the domain $\{-3, -2, -1, 0, 1, 2, 3\}$, tell whether the equation is a conditional equation or an identity.

31. $x + 3 = 3 + x$ 32. $x + 3 = 5$ 33. $y + 3 + 4 = 7 + y$
34. $5a = a \times 5$ 35. $5a = -15$ 36. $5 \times 2 \times a = a \times 2 \times 5$

2. Postulates of Equality

In mathematics, any statement we accept as being true without proof is called an **assumption**, an **axiom**, or a **postulate**.

At this point we will study several postulates of equality. These postulates will be used to solve equations in a systematic manner.

POSTULATE 1: THE REFLEXIVE PROPERTY OF EQUALITY

The **reflexive property of equality** states that any number is equal to itself. For example, $5 = 5$, or $-7 = -7$.

In general, for every number a we assume:

$$a = a$$

POSTULATE 2: THE SYMMETRIC PROPERTY OF EQUALITY

The **symmetric property of equality** states that an equality may be reversed. For example, if $4 + 3 = 5 + 2$, then $5 + 2 = 4 + 3$.

In general, for every number a and every number b we assume:

$$\text{if } a = b, \quad \text{then } b = a$$

POSTULATE 3: THE TRANSITIVE PROPERTY OF EQUALITY

The *transitive property of equality* states that if one number is equal to a second number and if the second number is equal to a third number, then the first number is equal to the third number. For example, if $5 + 4 = 6 + 3$, and $6 + 3 = 7 + 2$, then $5 + 4 = 7 + 2$.

In general, for every number a, every number b, and every number c, we assume:

$$\text{if } a = b, \text{ and } b = c, \text{ then } a = c$$

The transitive property of equality is useful in the following ways:

If (1) $a = b$ and (2) $b = c$, the transitive property of equality makes it possible for us to replace b in (2) by a and to obtain $a = c$. Also, we may replace b in (1) by c and obtain $a = c$.

Finally, the transitive property of equality allows us to state that two numbers are equal if each of them is equal to a third number.

POSTULATE 4: THE ADDITION PROPERTY OF EQUALITY

The *addition property of equality* states that if the same number is added to each of two equal numbers, the sums are equal.

For example,

$$\text{if } 500 + 200 = 700, \text{ then } 500 + 200 + 100 = 700 + 100$$

In general, for all numbers a, b, and c, we assume:

$$\text{if } a = b, \text{ then } a + c = b + c$$

Therefore, we can say: If the same number is added to both members of an equality, the equality is retained. Study the following examples:

In Arithmetic	*In Algebra*	
if $8 = 8$	if $x - 2 = 8$	
then $8 + 2 = 8 + 2$	then $x - 2 + 2 = 8 + 2$	A_2 (Add 2 to both
and $10 = 10$	and $x = 10$	members of the previous equation.)

POSTULATE 5: THE SUBTRACTION PROPERTY OF EQUALITY

The *subtraction property of equality* states that if the same number is subtracted from each of two equal numbers, the differences are equal.

For example,

$$\text{if } 50 + 25 = 75, \text{ then } 50 + 25 - 25 = 75 - 25$$

In general, for all numbers a, b, and c, we assume:

$$\text{if } a = b, \quad \text{then } a - c = b - c$$

Therefore, we can say: If the same number is subtracted from both members of an equality, the equality is retained. Study the following examples:

In Arithmetic	In Algebra	
if $8 = 8$	if $x + 3 = 8$	
then $8 - 3 = 8 - 3$	then $x + 3 - 3 = 8 - 3$	S_3 (Subtract 3 from
and $5 = 5$	and $x = 5$	both members of the previous equation.)

POSTULATE 6: THE MULTIPLICATION PROPERTY OF EQUALITY

The *multiplication property of equality* states that if each of two equal numbers is multiplied by the same number, the products are equal.

For example,

$$\text{if } 10 = \frac{20}{2}, \text{ then } 2 \times 10 = 2 \times \frac{20}{2}$$

In general, for all numbers a, b, and c, we assume:

$$\text{if } a = b, \quad \text{then } ac = bc$$

Therefore, we can say: If both members of an equality are multiplied by the same number, the equality is retained. Study the following examples:

In Arithmetic	In Algebra	
if $8 = 8$	if $\dfrac{x}{4} = 8$	
then $4 \times 8 = 4 \times 8$	then $4 \times \dfrac{x}{4} = 4 \times 8$	M_4 (Multiply both members of the previous
and $32 = 32$	and $x = 32$	equation by 4.)

POSTULATE 7: THE DIVISION PROPERTY OF EQUALITY

The *division property of equality* states that if each of two equal numbers is divided by the same nonzero number, the quotients are equal.

For example,

$$\text{if } 30 = 6 \times 5, \text{ then } \frac{30}{6} = \frac{6 \times 5}{6}$$

In general, for all numbers a, b, and c ($c \neq 0$), we assume:

$$\text{if } a = b, \quad \text{then } \frac{a}{c} = \frac{b}{c}$$

Therefore, we can say: If both members of an equality are divided by the same nonzero number, the equality is retained. Study the following examples:

In Arithmetic	*In Algebra*		
if $8 = 8$	if $4w = 8$		
then $\frac{8}{4} = \frac{8}{4}$	then $\frac{4w}{4} = \frac{8}{4}$	D_4	(Divide both members of the previous equation by 4.)
and $2 = 2$	and $w = 2$		

EXERCISES

In 1–10, name the property of equality which the sentence illustrates.

1. $5 + 2 = 5 + 2$
2. If $6 + 2 = 5 + 3$, and $5 + 3 = 7 + 1$, then $6 + 2 = 7 + 1$.
3. If $4 + 3 = 6 + 1$, then $6 + 1 = 4 + 3$.
4. $x + y = x + y$
5. If $x = y$, then $y = x$.
6. If $m + n = r + s$, and $r + s = x + y$, then $m + n = x + y$.
7. If $y + 7 = 10$, then $y + 7 - 7 = 10 - 7$.
8. If $\frac{z}{8} = 3$, then $8 \times \left(\frac{z}{8}\right) = 8 \times 3$.
9. If $5x = -10$, then $\frac{5x}{5} = \frac{-10}{5}$.
10. If $w - 2 = -6$, then $w - 2 + 2 = -6 + 2$.

In 11–16, name the property of equality which is illustrated in each part.

11. If $10 + 8 = 18$ and $8 + 10 = 18$, then:
    a. $18 = 8 + 10$ b. $10 + 8 = 8 + 10$
12. If $(-2) \times (-3) = 6$ and $3 \times 2 = 6$, then:
    a. $6 = 3 \times 2$ b. $(-2) \times (-3) = 3 \times 2$
13. If $(2 + 3) + 4 = 9$ and $2 + (3 + 4) = 9$, then:
    a. $9 = 2 + (3 + 4)$ b. $(2 + 3) + 4 = 2 + (3 + 4)$
14. If $(2 \times 3) \times 4 = 24$ and $2 \times (3 \times 4) = 24$, then:
    a. $24 = 2 \times (3 \times 4)$ b. $(2 \times 3) \times 4 = 2 \times (3 \times 4)$
15. If $3 \times (4 + 1) = 15$, and $3 \times 4 + 3 \times 1 = 15$, then:
    a. $15 = 3 \times 4 + 3 \times 1$ b. $3 \times (4 + 1) = 3 \times 4 + 3 \times 1$
16. If $5 \times (3 + 1) = 5 \times 4$, and $5 \times 4 = 20$, and also $20 = 15 + 5$, then:
    a. $5 \times (3 + 1) = 20$ b. $5 \times (3 + 1) = 15 + 5$

3. Solving Equations by Using Addition or Subtraction Postulates

We have seen that when we are dealing with a simple equation where the domain of the variable has a small number of elements, we can find the solution set by "guessing" or by replacing the variable with the elements of the domain. When the equation is complicated, these methods are not effective. Therefore, we will now develop systematic procedures for solving equations. Unless we state otherwise, it is to be assumed that the domain of all variables in an equation is to be the set of signed numbers.

We have seen that:

$$\text{if } x - 2 = 8,$$
$$\text{then } x - 2 + 2 = 8 + 2, \quad A_2$$
$$\text{and } x = 10$$

In the first equation, $x - 2 = 8$, let us use the substitution principle and replace x with 10.

$$x - 2 = 8$$
$$10 - 2 \overset{?}{=} 8$$
$$8 = 8$$

We see that replacing x with 10 results in a true sentence.

If we replace x with 10 in the second equation, $x - 2 + 2 = 8 + 2$, we likewise obtain a true sentence. In fact, the number 10 is the only number that can replace x in each of the equations and make the resulting sentence true. Therefore, 10 is the root and $\{10\}$ is the solution set of each of these equations. Equations that have the same solution set are called *equivalent equations*. Notice that when the addition property is applied to an equation, we obtain an equivalent equation.

It is also true that when the subtraction property is applied to an equation, we obtain an equivalent equation. For example, the application of the subtraction property to the equation $x + 3 = 8$ results in the equivalent equations $x + 3 - 3 = 8 - 3$ and $x = 5$. All three equations have the same solution set $\{5\}$.

When we solve an equation, we transform it into a simpler equivalent equation that reveals the value which can replace the variable and make the resulting sentence true (the truth value of the variable). Now we will use the addition property and the subtraction property of equality in solving equations.

Model Problems

---

1. Solve and check: $x - 5 = 4$

Solution

$$x - 5 = 4$$
$$x - 5 + 5 = 4 + 5 \quad \text{A}_5$$
$$x = 9$$

Check

$$x - 5 \stackrel{}{=} 4$$
$$9 - 5 \stackrel{?}{=} 4$$
$$4 = 4$$

(Notice that when the variable x is replaced by 9, the resulting sentence is true.)

Answer: $x = 9$, or solution set is $\{9\}$.

2. Solve and check: $-.8 = .3 + t$

Solution

$$-.8 = .3 + t$$
$$-.8 = t + .3 \quad \text{(commutative property)}$$
$$-.8 - .3 = t + .3 - .3 \quad \text{S}_{.3}$$
$$-1.1 = t$$

Check

$$-.8 \stackrel{}{=} .3 + t$$
$$-.8 \stackrel{?}{=} .3 + (-1.1)$$
$$-.8 = -.8 \text{ (true)}$$

Answer: $t = -1.1$, or solution set is $\{-1.1\}$.

Procedure. To solve an equation in which a variable and a constant are related by the operation of addition or subtraction:

    1. Use the inverse operation, subtracting or adding (as the case may be) the constant to both members of the equation. Perform the indicated operation(s) to obtain an equivalent equation in which only the variable itself is one member of the equation.

2. Check by determining that when the value obtained for the variable replaces it in the given equation, the resulting statement is true.

It is possible to solve equations similar to model problems 1 and 2, for example, $x - 4 = 7$ and $x + 3\frac{2}{3} = 3$, using only the addition property of equality. Remember that the sum of a number and its additive inverse (opposite) is 0; that is, $a + (-a) = 0$. The following model problems illustrate how the additive inverse is used in solving equations.

Model Problems

1. Solve and check: $x - 4 = 7$

How to Proceed	Solution	Check
To transform $x - 4$ to x, add $+4$, the additive inverse (opposite) of -4, to both members of the equation.	$x - 4 = 7$ $x - 4 + (+4) = 7 + (+4)$ $x + 0 = 11$ $x = 11$	$x - 4 \overset{?}{=} 7$ $11 - 4 \overset{?}{=} 7$ $7 = 7$ (true)

Answer: $x = 11$, or solution set is $\{11\}$.

2. Solve and check: $x + 3\frac{2}{3} = 3$

How to Proceed	Solution	Check
To eliminate $+3\frac{2}{3}$, add its additive inverse (opposite), $-3\frac{2}{3}$, to both members of the equation.	$x + 3\frac{2}{3} = 3$ $x + 3\frac{2}{3} + (-3\frac{2}{3}) = 3 + (-3\frac{2}{3})$ $x + 0 = -\frac{2}{3}$ $x = -\frac{2}{3}$	$x + 3\frac{2}{3} = 3$ $(-\frac{2}{3}) + 3\frac{2}{3} \overset{?}{=} 3$ $3 = 3$ (true)

Answer: $x = -\frac{2}{3}$, or solution set is $\{-\frac{2}{3}\}$.

EXERCISES

In 1–20, solve for the variable and check.

1. $x - 5 = 13$ 2. $y + 8 = 12$ 3. $17 = t - 9$ 4. $36 = c + 20$
5. $x + 6 = 4$ 6. $x - 5 = -9$ 7. $n + 7 = 4$ 8. $3 = y + 12$
9. $5 + r = -9$ 10. $-5 = -7 + c$ 11. $-4 = d - 8$ 12. $s + 12 = 8$

13. $x + .9 = .5$ **14.** $w - 1.6 = .3$ **15.** $.6 + y = .2$ **16.** $-.3 = s + .7$
17. $n + 3\frac{1}{2} = 2$ **18.** $x - 2\frac{1}{3} = -5$ **19.** $-\frac{1}{2} = n - 1\frac{3}{4}$ **20.** $3\frac{1}{4} = y + 6\frac{1}{2}$
21. If $g + 9 = 11$, find the value of $7g$.
22. If $t - .5 = 2.5$, find the value of $t + 7$.
23. If $22 = y + 8$, find the value of $\frac{1}{2}y$.
24. If $c - 1\frac{1}{4} = 2\frac{1}{2}$, find the value of $8c - 2$.
25. If $1.8 + b = 2.7$, find the value of $\frac{1}{3}b - .3$.

In 26–31, determine the element of the set if $x \in \{$ signed numbers$\}$.

26. $\{x \mid x - 8 = 12\}$ **27.** $\{x \mid x + 3 = 10\}$ **28.** $\{x \mid x - 3 = -6\}$
29. $\{x \mid x + 7 = 2\}$ **30.** $\{x \mid 9 = x + 15\}$ **31.** $\{x \mid 10 = x + 10\}$

4. Solving Equations by Using Division or Multiplication Postulates

We have seen that when the addition or subtraction property of equality is applied to an equation, we obtain an equivalent equation. It is also true that when the division property of equality is applied to an equation, we obtain an equivalent equation. For example, the application of the division property to the equation $2x = 4$ results in the equivalent equations $\frac{2x}{2} = \frac{4}{2}$ and $x = 2$. All three equations have the same solution set $\{2\}$. It is important to remember that when we apply the division property of equality, we divide both members of an equation by the same *nonzero* number. Division by zero is impossible.

One might now anticipate that the application of the multiplication property of equality to an equation always gives an equivalent equation. This is true, *with one important exception*. We may not multiply both members of an equation by zero to obtain an equivalent equation. The solution set of the equation $x = 2$ is $\{2\}$. If we multiply both members of this equation by zero, we obtain the equation $0 \cdot x = 0 \cdot 2$ or $0 \cdot x = 0$. The new equation $0 \cdot x = 0$ is not equivalent to the original equation $x = 2$, because the two equations do not have the same solution set. The number 1 is a member of the solution set of $0 \cdot x = 0$, but not a member of the solution set of $x = 2$. If we multiply both members of an equation by the same nonzero number, then we always obtain an equivalent equation. For example, if we multiply both members of $x = 2$ by 3, we obtain the equivalent equations $3x = 3 \cdot 2$ and $3x = 6$. We will now use the division property and the multiplication property of equality in solving equations.

Model Problems

Solve and check.

1. $22 = 4x$ **2.** $.3x = 9$ **3.** $\dfrac{n}{3} = 12$

Solution   *Solution*   *Solution*

$22 = 4x$ $.3x = 9$ $\dfrac{n}{3} = 12$

$\dfrac{22}{4} = \dfrac{4x}{4}$ D_4 $\dfrac{.3x}{.3} = \dfrac{9}{.3}$ $D_{.3}$ $\left[\,.3\overline{)9.0}^{30.}\,\right]$ $3 \times \dfrac{n}{3} = 3 \times 12$ M_3

$5\tfrac{1}{2} = x$ $x = 30$ $n = 36$

Check   *Check*   *Check*

$22 = 4x$ $.3x = 9$ $\dfrac{n}{3} = 12$

$22 \overset{?}{=} 4(5\tfrac{1}{2})$ $.3(30) \overset{?}{=} 9$ $\dfrac{36}{3} \overset{?}{=} 12$

$22 = 22$ (true) $9 = 9$ (true) $12 = 12$ (true)

Answer: $x = 5\tfrac{1}{2}$, or   *Answer:* $x = 30$, or   *Answer:* $n = 36$, or
solution set is $\{5\tfrac{1}{2}\}$.   solution set is $\{30\}$.   solution set is $\{36\}$.

Procedure. To solve an equation in which a variable and a nonzero constant are related by the operation of division or multiplication:

1. Use the inverse operation, multiplying or dividing (as the case may be) both members of the equation by the constant. Perform the indicated operation(s) to obtain an equivalent equation in which only the variable itself is one member of the equation.
2. Check by determining that when the value obtained for the variable replaces it in the given equation, the resulting statement is true.

It is possible to solve equations similar to model problems 1, 2, and 3, for example, $5x = -20$, $-\dfrac{2}{3}y = 18$, and $\dfrac{x}{3} = -2$, using only the multiplication property of equality. Remember that the product of a nonzero number and its multiplicative inverse (reciprocal) is 1; that is, $a \cdot \dfrac{1}{a} = 1 \, (a \neq 0)$. The following model problems illustrate how the multiplicative inverse is used in solving equations.

Model Problems

1. Solve and check: $5x = -20$.

How to Proceed	*Solution*	*Check*

To transform $5x$ to x, multiply both members of the equation by $\frac{1}{5}$, the multiplicative inverse (reciprocal) of the coefficient 5.

$$5x = -20$$
$$\tfrac{1}{5}(5x) = \tfrac{1}{5}(-20)$$
$$1 \cdot x = -4$$
$$x = -4$$

$$5x = -20$$
$$5(-4) \overset{?}{=} -20$$
$$-20 = -20$$
(true)

Answer: $x = -4$, or solution set is $\{-4\}$.

2. Solve and check: $-\frac{2}{3}y = 18$.

How to Proceed	*Solution*	*Check*

To transform $-\frac{2}{3}y$ to y, multiply both members of the equation by $-\frac{3}{2}$, the multiplicative inverse (reciprocal) of the coefficient $-\frac{2}{3}$.

$$-\tfrac{2}{3}y = 18$$
$$(-\tfrac{3}{2})(-\tfrac{2}{3}y) = (-\tfrac{3}{2})(18)$$
$$1 \cdot y = -27$$
$$y = -27$$

$$-\tfrac{2}{3}y = 18$$
$$(-\tfrac{2}{3})(-27) \overset{?}{=} 18$$
$$18 = 18$$
(true)

Answer: $y = -27$, or solution set is $\{-27\}$.

3. Solve and check: $\frac{x}{3} = -2$.

How to Proceed	*Solution*	*Check*

In order to transform $\frac{x}{3}$, or $\frac{1}{3}x$, to x, multiply both members of the equation by 3, the multiplicative inverse (reciprocal) of $\frac{1}{3}$.

$$\frac{x}{3} = -2$$
$$3\left(\frac{x}{3}\right) = 3(-2)$$
$$1 \cdot x = -6$$
$$x = -6$$

$$\frac{x}{3} = -2$$
$$\frac{-6}{3} \overset{?}{=} -2$$
$$-2 = -2$$
(true)

Answer: $x = -6$, or solution set is $\{-6\}$.

EXERCISES

In 1–30, find the solution set of the sentence and check.

1. $3m = 15$
2. $9t = 36$
3. $15x = -45$
4. $23z = -46$
5. $-77 = 11k$
6. $4x = 9$
7. $-5 = 2y$
8. $9a = -6$
9. $-13a = 65$
10. $-8k = 8.8$
11. $-5m = -35$
12. $2x = -\frac{1}{9}$
13. $-x = 18$
14. $\frac{1}{4}y = 2$
15. $\frac{1}{3}z = 6$
16. $\frac{1}{2}c = -8$

17. $-20 = \frac{2}{5}d$ **18.** $\frac{5}{8}x = -10$ **19.** $12 = -\frac{2}{3}x$ **20.** $-\frac{3}{4}x = 36$

21. $\frac{1}{3}x = -1.8$ **22.** $\frac{3}{5}y = \frac{6}{8}$ **23.** $\frac{12}{9} = \frac{-4}{3}c$ **24.** $-\frac{3}{2}x = 1\frac{1}{2}$

25. $\frac{-25}{9} = 8\frac{1}{3}t$ **26.** $\frac{x}{2} = 12$ **27.** $\frac{y}{3} = -15$ **28.** $\frac{m}{-4} = -2\frac{1}{2}$

29. $\frac{c}{9} = -\frac{2}{3}$ **30.** $\frac{2x}{3} = \frac{4}{9}$

31. If $9x = 36$, find the value of $2x$.

32. If $2x = 64$, find the vlue of $\frac{1}{4}x$.

33. If $\frac{t}{2} = 12$, find the value of $5t$.

34. If $\frac{2}{3}y = 16$, find the value of $3y + 7$.

35. If $.08y = .96$, find the value of $\frac{1}{2}y - 3$.

In 36–41, determine the element of the set if $x \in \{$ signed numbers $\}$.

36. $\{x \mid 4x = 28\}$ **37.** $\{x \mid -3x = 15\}$ **38.** $\{x \mid \frac{1}{5}x = 25\}$

39. $\left\{x \mid \frac{x}{5} = -20\right\}$ **40.** $\{x \mid -\frac{4}{5}x = 40\}$ **41.** $\{x \mid .4x = -1\}$

5. Writing Verbal Sentences as Equations

In algebra, many verbal problems involving number relations are solved by using equations. Therefore, we must be able to express verbal sentences as equations. In Chapter 1 on page 17, we saw how the symbols of mathematics were used to express number relationships; in Chapter 3 on pages 45–47, we saw how verbal phrases were translated into algebraic language. Study the following examples to see how verbal sentences may be expressed as equations:

Verbal Sentence	*Equation*
Four times a number s equals 20.	$4s = 20$
A number y increased by 6 equals 8.	$y + 6 = 8$
A number x decreased by 3 equals -5.	$x - 3 = -5$
A number n divided by 2 equals 4.	$\frac{n}{2} = 4$

Procedure. To write a verbal sentence as an equation, choose a letter to represent the variable. Then use this letter to express the verbal sentence as an equation.

Model Problem

Write the following sentence as an equation: "5 times a number, decreased by 7, equals −12."

Solution: Let x represent the number.

5 times a number decreased by 7 equals −12.

$$5x \qquad - \qquad 7 \ = \ -12$$

Answer: $5x - 7 = -12$.

EXERCISES

In 1–9, write a verbal sentence which gives a meaning of the equation.

1. $8x = 56$ **2.** $x + 7 = 12$ **3.** $s - 5 = 15$

4. $12 = -x - 3$ **5.** $\frac{x}{4} = .8$ **6.** $2c + 4 = 12$

7. $-5y - .7 = 28$ **8.** $\frac{3}{4}c - 8 = -4$ **9.** $\frac{1}{2}c + \frac{1}{2} = 0$

In 10–17, select the equation which represents, in terms of the given variable, the numerical relationship expressed in the sentence.

10. 3 times Harold's height is 108 inches. Let h = Harold's height.
     a. $h + 3 = 108$ b. $3h = 108$ c. $h - 3 = 108$ d. $\frac{1}{3}h = 108$

11. $\frac{1}{2}$ of Mary's weight is 60 pounds. Let w = Mary's weight.
     a. $\frac{1}{2}w = 60$ b. $2w = 60$ c. $w - 2 = 60$ d. $w + 2 = 60$

12. A number increased by 7 equals 28. Let n = the number.
     a. $7n = 28$ b. $n + 7 = 28$ c. $n - 7 = 28$ d. $\frac{1}{7}n = 28$

13. A number decreased by 5 equals 15. Let x = the number.
     a. $x + 5 = 15$ b. $5x = 15$ c. $\frac{1}{5}x = 15$ d. $x - 5 = 15$

14. If 7 is subtracted from a number, the result is 8. Let x = the number.
     a. $7 - x = 8$ b. $x - 7 = 8$ c. $8 - x = 7$ d. $x - 8 = 7$

15. Jim bought \$6 worth of steaks that cost \$2 each. Let s = the number of steaks Jim bought.
     a. $s + 2 = 6$ b. $s - 2 = 6$ c. $2s = 6$ d. $\frac{1}{2}s = 6$

16. Tom, who is 18 years old, is $\frac{1}{3}$ as old as his father. Let f = the father's age.
     a. $3f = 18$ b. $f + 3 = 18$ c. $\frac{1}{3}f = 18$ d. $f - 3 = 18$

17. A movie star bought 15 suits and now has 75 suits. Let s = the number of suits the movie star had originally.
     a. $s + 15 = 75$ b. $s - 15 = 75$ c. $15s = 75$ d. $\frac{s}{15} = 75$

In 18–30, write the sentence as an equation. Use n to represent the number.

18. The product of 7 and a number equals -70.
19. 4 less than a number equals 32.
20. Twice a number, increased by -7, equals 27.
21. Twice a number, decreased by 5, equals 25.
22. The sum of 3 times a number and 7 is 22.
23. When 9 is subtracted from 5 times a number, the result is 31.
24. The sum of 100 and a number is equal to three times that number.
25. If 3 times a number is increased by 12, the result is the same as when twice the number is increased by -24.
26. If 8 times a number is decreased by 20, the result is the same as when 3 times the number is increased by 80.
27. The sum of a number and twice that number equals -45.
28. 3 times a number decreased by $\frac{1}{2}$ of that number equals 40.
29. The sum of $\frac{1}{2}$ of a number and 8 is the same as the difference between the number and 4.
30. Match the items in column A with those in column B.

Column A	*Column B*
1. 8 times a number is -32.	$a.\ 3 - 2n = -1$
2. A number divided by 5 is 35.	$b.\ n + 8 = 32$
3. A number increased by 8 is 32.	$c.\ n - \frac{1}{6}n = 70$
4. The product of 5 and a number is 35.	$d.\ 4n + 6 = 30$
5. 4 times a number increased by 6 is 30.	$e.\ 5n = 35$
6. $\frac{1}{4}$ of a number decreased by 6 is 30.	$f.\ n + 6n = 70$
7. When 3 is subtracted from twice a number, the result is 1.	$g.\ 8n = -32$
	$h.\ 2n - 3 = 1$
8. One number is 6 times another and their sum is 70.	$i.\ \dfrac{n}{5} = 35$
9. When twice a number is subtracted from 3, the result is -1.	$j.\ \frac{1}{4}n - 6 = 30$
10. One number is $\frac{1}{6}$ of another, and their difference is 70.	

6. Solving Problems by Using Variables and Equations

Now we are ready to solve some verbal problems algebraically.

Procedure. To solve a verbal problem by using an equation involving one variable:

1. **Read the problem carefully until you understand it.**

2. Determine what is given in the problem and what is to be found.
3. Select a variable that can be used in representing every number that the problem requires you to find.
4. Write an equation which symbolizes the information and relationships stated in the problem.
5. Find the root, or solution set, of the equation.
6. Check the answer by testing it in the word statement of the original problem to see that it satisfies all the required conditions.

Model Problems

1. When a number is decreased by 7, the result is -9. Find the number.

How to Proceed	Solution
1. Represent the number by a variable.	Let x = the number.
2. Write the word statement as an equation.	$x - 7 = -9$
3. Solve the equation. A_7 (mentally)	$x = -2$
4. Check in the original problem.	Is -2 decreased by 7 equal to -9? Yes.

Answer: The number is -2.

2. Bill is 10 years older than Sam. If Bill is 28 years old, how old is Sam?

How to Proceed	Solution
1. Represent Sam's age by a variable.	Let x = Sam's age.
2. Represent Bill's age using the same variable.	Then $x + 10$ = Bill's age.
3. Write the word statement as an equation.	$x + 10 = 28$ (Bill is 28 years old.)
4. Solve the equation. S_{10} or A_{-10} (mentally)	$x = 18$
5. Check in the original problem.	Sam is 18 years old and Bill is 28 years old. Is Bill 10 years older than Sam? Yes.

Answer: Sam is 18 years old.

3. When a number is multiplied by .2, the result is -10. Find the number.

How to Proceed	Solution
1. Represent the number by a variable.	Let y = the number

2. Write the word statement as an equation.

$.2y = -10$

3. Solve the equation. $D_{.2}$

$$\frac{.2y}{.2} = \frac{-10}{.2}$$

$$y = -50$$

4. Check in the original problem.

Is -50 multiplied by .2 equal to -10? Yes.

Answer: The number is -50.

4. Ned traveled $\frac{1}{4}$ the distance that Ben traveled. If Ned traveled 12 kilometers, how far did Ben travel?

How to Proceed	*Solution*
1. Represent by a variable the distance Ben traveled.	Let d = distance Ben traveled.
2. Using the same variable, represent the distance Ned traveled.	Then $\frac{1}{4}d$ = distance Ned traveled.
3. Write the word statement as an equation.	$\frac{1}{4}d = 12$ (Ned traveled 12 kilometers.)
4. Solve the equation. M_4 (mentally)	$d = 48$
5. Check in the original problem.	Ben traveled 48 kilometers and Ned traveled 12 kilometers. Did Ned travel $\frac{1}{4}$ the distance that Ben traveled? Yes.

Answer: Ben traveled 48 kilometers.

EXERCISES

In 1–35, solve the problem using a variable and an equation.

1. A number decreased by 20 equals 36. Find the number.
2. If 7 is subtracted from a number, the result is 46. Find the number.
3. What number increased by 25 equals 40?
4. If 18 is added to a number, the result is 32. Find the number.
5. Ten less than a number is 42. Find the number.
6. The sum of 42 and a number is 96. Find the number.
7. Seven times a number is 63. Find the number.
8. Negative five times a number is 50. Find the number.
9. When a number is doubled, the result is 36. Find the number.
10. A number divided by 5 equals -17. Find the number.
11. A number divided by 4 is $3\frac{1}{2}$. Find the number.
12. One-half of a number is -12. Find the number.

13. Three-fifths of a number is 30. Find the number.
14. A number multiplied by .3 is 6. Find the number.
15. Four-hundredths of a number is 16. Find the number.
16. 4% of a number is 8. Find the number.
17. 15% of a number is 4.5. Find the number.
18. One-eighth of a number is $4\frac{1}{2}$. Find the number.
19. $33\frac{1}{3}$% of a number is $3\frac{2}{3}$. Find the number.
20. After Henry spent $3.25, he had $8.75 left. How much money did he have originally?
21. After the price of a car rose $225, it was sold for $2670. What was the original price?
22. After Ben lost 10 kilograms, he weighed $90\frac{3}{4}$ kilograms. Find Ben's original weight.
23. After $2\frac{1}{2}$ feet were cut from a piece of lumber, $9\frac{1}{2}$ feet were left. What was the original length of the piece of lumber?
24. After a car increased its rate of speed by 24 kilometers per hour, it was traveling 76 kilometers per hour. What was its original rate of speed?
25. Bill traveled 5 times as far as Harold. Bill traveled 150 kilometers. How far did Harold travel?
26. A man saved 25% of his paycheck. If he saved $50, how much was his paycheck?
27. Baseballs cost $2.75 each. How many baseballs can be bought for $13.75?
28. The width of a rectangle is $\frac{1}{5}$ of its length. If the width of the rectangle is 6 feet, what is its length?
29. The width of a rectangle is 8 feet less than its length. If the width is 9.5 feet, find the length of the rectangle.
30. This year a college admitted 2125 freshmen, which was 78 fewer than the number admitted in the previous year. How many freshmen were admitted in the previous year?
31. After Marie had gained $7\frac{1}{2}$ pounds, she weighed 127 pounds. What was Marie's original weight?
32. A dealer sold an electric broiler for $39.98. This amount was $12.50 more than the broiler cost him. How much did the broiler cost the dealer?
33. Find Ted's weight if $\frac{3}{4}$ of his weight is 60 kilograms.
34. On a trip, Stanley traveled 75% of the total distance by plane. If he traveled 2400 kilometers by plane, what was the total distance he traveled?
35. Pearl bought a coat at a "40% off" sale. If she saved $24, what was the original price of the coat?

7. Solving Equations by Combining Like Terms

Procedure. To solve an equation in which like terms appear in either member of the equation:

1. Use the distributive property of multiplication to combine the like terms.
2. Solve the resulting equation.

Model Problems

1. Solve and check: $6x + 3x = 36$

How to Proceed	Solution	Check
1. Write the equation.	$6x + 3x = 36$	$6x + 3x = 36$
2. Use the distributive property to combine like terms.	$(6 + 3)x = 36$ $9x = 36$	$6 \times 4 + 3 \times 4 \overset{?}{=} 36$ $24 + 12 \overset{?}{=} 36$
3. D_9 or $M_{\frac{1}{9}}$	$x = 4$	$36 = 36$ (true)

Answer: $x = 4$, or solution set is $\{4\}$.

2. The larger of two numbers is 4 times the smaller. If the sum of the two numbers is 55, find the numbers.

How to Proceed	Solution
1. Represent the smaller number by a letter.	Let $x =$ the smaller number.
2. Represent "the larger of two numbers is 4 times the smaller."	Then $4x =$ the larger number.
3. Write as an equation "the sum of the two numbers is 55."	$x + 4x = 55$
4. Solve the equation. First, combine like terms. Then, D_5 or $M_{\frac{1}{5}}$.	$5x = 55$ $x = 11$
5. Find the larger number.	$4x = 44$

Check: Is the larger number 4 times the smaller? $44 \overset{?}{=} 4 \times 11$. Yes.
Is the sum of the two numbers 55? $11 + 44 \overset{?}{=} 55$. Yes.

Answer: The smaller number is 11 and the larger number is 44.

EXERCISES

In 1–12, solve and check the equation.

1. $2a + 2a = 50$ 2. $8x + x = 72$ 3. $144 = 9b + 3b$
4. $12x - 4x = 108$ 5. $18 = 7x - x$ 6. $3\frac{1}{2}c + 2\frac{1}{2}c = 54$
7. $-3.6d - 2.4d = 24$ 8. $8x + 3x + 4x = 60$ 9. $7y + 4y - y = 70$
10. $39 = 8c + 6c - c$ 11. $\frac{1}{4}x + \frac{1}{2}x = 18$ 12. $\frac{2}{3}x - \frac{1}{3}x = 17$

In 13–21, use an algebraic equation to solve the problem.

13. The larger of two numbers is twice the smaller. If the sum of the two numbers is 96, find the numbers.
14. One number is 5 times another. If their difference is 96, find the numbers.
15. A number is $\frac{1}{2}$ of another number. Find the numbers if their difference is 28.
16. A number is $\frac{2}{3}$ of another number. The sum of the two numbers is 50. Find the numbers.
17. Bob and Dan earned a total of $24 shoveling snow. If Bob earned 3 times as much as Dan, how much did each earn?
18. Lily spent 4 times as much as her sister Sue. If the women spent $24, how much did each spend?
19. Carl and Richard earned $32.50 chopping wood. If they agreed that Carl should get 1.5 times as much as Richard gets, how much did each man receive?
20. A house and a lot are worth $30,000. If the house is worth 6.5 times as much as the lot, find how much each is worth.
21. Sam's height is $\frac{7}{8}$ of Larry's height. If the difference between their heights is 24 centimeters, find the height of each man.

8. Solving Equations by Using Several Operations

In the equation $2x + 3 = 15$, two operations are indicated in the left member: *multiplication* and *addition*. To solve this equation we can use either the inverse operations *division* and *subtraction*, or the *multiplicative inverse* and the *additive inverse*. When the solution of an equation requires the use of both the additive and the multiplicative inverses, either inverse may be used first. However, the solution is usually easier when the additive inverse is used first.

Model Problems

1. Solve and check: $2x + 3 = 15$

   Solution: To solve $2x + 3 = 15$, we first eliminate 3 from the left member of the equation by using either of the following two methods:

Method 1	*Method 2*
Subtract 3 from both members of the equation, S_3.	Add -3, the additive inverse of $+3$, to both members of the equation, A_{-3}.

   $$\begin{array}{ll} 2x + 3 = 15 & \\ 2x + 3 - 3 = 15 - 3 & S_3 \\ 2x = 12 & \\ x = 6 & D_2 \end{array} \qquad \begin{array}{ll} 2x + 3 = 15 & \\ 2x + 3 + (-3) = 15 + (-3) & A_{-3} \\ 2x = 12 & \\ x = 6 & M_{\frac{1}{2}} \end{array}$$

   $$\begin{aligned} \textit{Check:} \quad 2x + 3 &= 15 \\ 2 \times 6 + 3 &\overset{?}{=} 15 \\ 12 + 3 &\overset{?}{=} 15 \\ 15 &= 15 \quad \text{(true)} \end{aligned}$$

   Answer: $x = 6$, or solution set is $\{6\}$.

2. Solve and check: $2x + 3x + 4 = -6$

How to Proceed	*Solution*
1. Write the equation.	$2x + 3x + 4 = -6$
2. Combine like terms.	$5x + 4 = -6$
3. Add -4, the additive inverse of $+4$.	$5x + 4 + (-4) = -6 + (-4) \quad (A_{-4})$ $5x = -10$
4. Multiply by $\frac{1}{5}$, the multiplicative inverse of 5.	$\frac{1}{5}(5x) = \frac{1}{5}(-10) \quad (M_{\frac{1}{5}})$ $x = -2$

   $$\begin{aligned} \textit{Check:} \quad 2x + 3x + 4 &= -6 \\ 2(-2) + 3(-2) + 4 &\overset{?}{=} -6 \\ (-4) + (-6) + 4 &\overset{?}{=} -6 \\ -6 &= -6 \quad \text{(true)} \end{aligned}$$

   Answer: $x = -2$, or solution set is $\{-2\}$.

   [*Note:* In step 3, if we had subtracted 4 from both members of the equation, we would have obtained the same result, $5x = -10$. Also, in step 4, if we had divided both members of the equation by 5, we would have obtained the same result, $x = -2$.]

3. Solve and check: $\frac{3}{4}x - 4 = 17$

How to Proceed	Solution	Check
1. Write the equation.	$\frac{3}{4}x - 4 = 17$	$\frac{3}{4}x - 4 = 17$
2. Add +4, the additive inverse of -4.	$\frac{3}{4}x - 4 + (+4) = 17 + (+4)$ (A_4) $\frac{3}{4}x = 21$	$\frac{3}{4}(28) - 4 \overset{?}{=} 17$ $21 - 4 \overset{?}{=} 17$
3. Multiply by $\frac{4}{3}$, the multiplicative inverse of $\frac{3}{4}$.	$\frac{4}{3}\left(\frac{3}{4}x\right) = \frac{4}{3}(21)$ $\left(M_{\frac{4}{3}}\right)$ $x = 28$	$17 = 17$ (true)

Answer: $x = 28$, or solution set is $\{28\}$.

4. If 4 times a number is increased by 7, the result is 43. Find the number.

How to Proceed	Solution
1. Represent the number by a letter.	Let x = the number.
2. Write the word statement as an equation.	$4x + 7 = 43$
3. Solve the equation.	$4x = 36$ S_7 (mentally) $x = 9$ D_4

Check: Does 4 × 9, increased by 7, give a result of 43? Yes.

Answer: The number is 9.

EXERCISES

In 1–33, solve the equation and check.

1. $3x + 4 = 16$	**2.** $5x - 9 = 16$	**3.** $35 = 21y - 7$
4. $2c + 1 = -31$	**5.** $5t - 2 = -32$	**6.** $2y + 18 = 8$
7. $2x + 9 = 37$	**8.** $5x + 15 = 0$	**9.** $4x + 2 = -34$
10. $-42 = 5x + 28$	**11.** $-5x + 9 = 14$	**12.** $-34 = 2 - 6t$
13. $13 = 8x - 7$	**14.** $4y + 8 = 2$	**15.** $-32 = 24y - 20$
16. $\frac{1}{2}z + 6 = 15$	**17.** $9 = \frac{1}{3}c + 11$	**18.** $\frac{1}{5}y - 3 = -4$
19. $\frac{2}{3}m + 7 = 29$	**20.** $\frac{3}{4}a + 14 = 8$	**21.** $\frac{2}{5}r - 9 = -19$
22. $\frac{3}{2}x - 14 = 16$	**23.** $\frac{9}{5}c + 32 = -4$	**24.** $-25 = \frac{7}{3}r - 11$
25. $-5.4 = 2.6 + 2x$	**26.** $1\frac{1}{4} - 4x = 17\frac{1}{4}$	**27.** $9x - 5x + 9 = 1$
28. $26 = 3y + 2y - 9$	**29.** $6x - x + 12 = 52$	
30. $95 = 8c - 3c + 15$	**31.** $5x + 2x - 17 = 53$	
32. $2y - 8y + 29 = 5$	**33.** $8x - 21 - 5x = -15$	

In 34–39, determine the element of the set if $x \in \{$ signed numbers$\}$.

34. $\{x \mid 2x + 3 = 11\}$
35. $\{x \mid 5x + 30 = 10\}$
36. $\{x \mid 15 = 6x - 15\}$
37. $\{x \mid \frac{2}{3}x - 12 = 60\}$
38. $\{x \mid -19 = \frac{2}{3}x + 17\}$
39. $\{x \mid 5x - 9x + 5 = -11\}$

In 40–47, use an algebraic equation to solve the problem.

40. The sum of 8 times a number and 5 is 37. Find the number.
41. If 12 times a number is diminished by 6, the result is 90. Find the number.
42. When 12 is subtracted from 3 times a number, the result is 24. Find the number.
43. If 9 is added to one-half of a number, the result is 29. Find the number.
44. If $\frac{2}{3}$ of a number is decreased by 4, the result is 56. Find the number.
45. The sum of $\frac{3}{5}$ of a number and 2.3 is 14.6. Find the number.
46. The number of sophomore men registered in a college is 235 more than the number of sophomore women registered. If 885 students are registered in the sophomore class, find the number of sophomore men and the number of sophomore women.
47. Jeff and Frank worked 89 hours. If Jeff worked 1 hour more than 3 times the number of hours Frank worked, find the number of hours worked by each.

9. Solving Equations Which Have the Variable in Both Members

A variable represents a number; as we know, any number may be added to or subtracted from both members of an equation without changing the solution set. Therefore, the same variable (or the same multiple of the same variable) may be added to or subtracted from both members of an equation without changing the solution set.

To solve $8x = 30 + 5x$, we first eliminate $5x$ from the right member of the equation as follows: Add $-5x$, the additive inverse of $+5x$, to both members of the equation, A_{-5x}.

$$8x = 30 + 5x$$
$$8x + (-5x) = 30 + 5x + (-5x)$$
$$3x = 30$$
$$x = 10$$

Answer: $x = 10$, or solution set is $\{10\}$.

(The check is left to the student.)

Procedure. To solve an equation which has the variable in both members, transform it into an equivalent equation in which the variable appears only in one member. Then solve this equation.

Model Problems

1. Solve and check: $7x = 63 - 2x$

How to Proceed	Solution	Check
1. Write the equation.	$7x = 63 - 2x$	$7x = 63 - 2x$
		$7(7) \stackrel{?}{=} 63 - 2(7)$
2. A_{+2x}	$7x + (+2x) = 63 - 2x + (+2x)$	$49 \stackrel{?}{=} 63 - 14$
3. Collect like terms.	$9x = 63$	$49 = 49$ (true)
4. D_9 or $M_{\frac{1}{9}}$	$x = 7$	

Answer: $x = 7$, or solution set is $\{7\}$.

2. Solve and check: $5t - 12 = 8t + 24$

How to Proceed	Solution
1. Write the equation.	$5t - 12 = 8t + 24$
2. A_{+12}	$5t - 12 + (+12) = 8t + 24 + (+12)$
3. Collect like terms.	$5t = 8t + 36$
4. A_{-8t}	$5t + (-8t) = 8t + 36 + (-8t)$
5. Collect like terms.	$-3t = 36$
6. D_{-3} or $M_{-\frac{1}{3}}$	$t = -12$

Answer: $t = -12$, or solution set is $\{-12\}$. The check is left to the student.

3. If 5 times a number is decreased by 13, the result is equal to twice the number increased by 11. Find the number.

Solution:

Let $x =$ the number.
Then $5x - 13 = 5$ times the number decreased by 13.
And $2x + 11 =$ twice the number increased by 11.

$$5x - 13 = 2x + 11$$
$$5x - 2x - 13 = 2x - 2x + 11 \qquad S_{2x} \text{ or } A_{-2x}$$
$$3x - 13 = 11$$
$$3x - 13 + 13 = 11 + 13 \qquad A_{13}$$
$$3x = 24$$
$$x = 8 \qquad D_3 \text{ or } M_{\frac{1}{3}}$$

Check

Show that 8 satisfies the original question:
$$5 \times 8 - 13 = 27$$
$$2 \times 8 + 11 = 27$$

Answer: The number is 8.

EXERCISES

In 1–45, solve the equation and check.

1. $7x = 10 + 2x$ 2. $9x = 44 - 2x$ 3. $8c = 6 - c$
4. $5c = 28 + c$ 5. $9x = 3x - 54$ 6. $2d = 36 + 5d$
7. $6\frac{1}{2}c = 7 - \frac{1}{2}c$ 8. $2\frac{1}{4}y = 1\frac{1}{4}y - 8$ 9. $.8m = .2m + 24$
10. $8y = 90 - 2y$ 11. $3 - y = 8y$ 12. $2.3x + 36 = .3x$
13. $2\frac{3}{4}x + 24 = 3x$ 14. $12 - 1\frac{1}{2}x = 2\frac{1}{2}x$ 15. $81 - \frac{3}{4}x = 1\frac{1}{2}x$
16. $x = 9x - 72$ 17. $.5m - 30 = 1.1m$ 18. $4\frac{1}{4}c = 9\frac{3}{4}c + 44$
19. $7r + 10 = 3r + 50$ 20. $4y + 20 = 5y + 9$
21. $8s + 56 = 14s + 26$ 22. $6b + 11 = 2b + 47$
23. $x + 4 = 9x + 4$ 24. $9x - 3 = 2x + 46$
25. $2z + 1 = 10z - 1$ 26. $c + 20 = 55 - 4c$
27. $\frac{2}{5}d + 36 = -\frac{3}{5}d - 54$ 28. $-4d - 37 = 7d + 18$
29. $2\frac{1}{2}m - 1 = 6\frac{1}{2}m + 1$ 30. $4x - 3 = 47 - x$
31. $5c - 13 = 43 - 2c$ 32. $\frac{2}{3}t - 11 = 64 - 4\frac{1}{3}t$
33. $11y - 8 = 22 - y$ 34. $10x - 21 = 2x - 5$
35. $18 - .4n = 6 - 1.6n$ 36. $7x - 4 = 5x - x + 35$
37. $8a - .15 - 6a = .85 - 3a$ 38. $5d + 9 - 4d = 51 - 5d$
39. $\frac{5}{3}x - \frac{2}{3}x + 13 = \frac{x}{6} + 3$ 40. $8\frac{1}{4}c + 1 = 7\frac{3}{4}c - 14 - 2c$
41. $9c - 2c + 8 = 4c + 38$ 42. $12x - 5 = 8x - x + 50$
43. $6d - 12 - d = 9d + 53 + d$ 44. $3m - 5m - 12 = 7m - 88 - 5$
45. $5 - 3z - 18 = z - 1 + 8z$

46. Eight times a number equals 35 more than the number. Find the number.
47. Six times a number equals 3 times the number, increased by 24. Find the number.
48. If a number is multiplied by 7, the result is the same as when 25 is subtracted from twice the number. Find the number.
49. If twice a number is subtracted from 132, the result equals 4 times the number. Find the number.
50. If 2 is added to 5 times a number, the result is the same as when 15 is added to twice the number. Find the number.
51. If 4 times a number is increased by 10, the result is the same as when 50 is diminished by 4 times the number. Find the number.
52. If 3 times a number is increased by 12, the result is the same as when -79 is decreased by 10 times the number. Find the number.
53. If 6 times a number is increased by 3, the result is equal to 9 times the number increased by 27. Find the number.
54. Seven times a number exceeds 150 by the same amount that 3 times the number exceeds 250. Find the number.

10. Solving Equations Containing Parentheses

Procedure. To solve an equation containing parentheses, transform it into an equation which does not contain parentheses. Do this by performing the indicated operation on the numbers and variables contained within the parentheses. Then solve the transformed equation.

Model Problems

1. Solve and check: $8x + (2x - 3) = 2$

   [*Note:* $8x + (2x - 3)$ means add $8x$ and $(2x - 3)$.]

How to Proceed	*Solution*
1. Write the equation.	$8x + (2x - 3) = 2$
2. Perform the addition.	$8x + 2x - 3 = 2$
3. Collect like terms	$10x - 3 = 2$
4. A_{+3}	$10x - 3 + (+3) = 2 + (+3)$
5. Collect like terms.	$10x = 5$
6. D_{10} or $M_{\frac{1}{10}}$	$x = \frac{1}{2}$

   Check

   $$8x + (2x - 3) = 2$$
   $$8 \times \tfrac{1}{2} + (2 \times \tfrac{1}{2} - 3) \overset{?}{=} 2$$
   $$8 \times \tfrac{1}{2} + (1 - 3) \overset{?}{=} 2$$
   $$4 + (-2) \overset{?}{=} 2$$
   $$2 = 2 \quad \text{(true)}$$

   Answer: $x = \frac{1}{2}$, or solution set is $\{\frac{1}{2}\}$.

2. Solve and check: $9t - (2t - 4) = 25$.

   [*Note:* $9t - (2t - 4)$ means from $9t$ subtract $(2t - 4)$.]

How to Proceed	*Solution*	*Check*
1. Write the equation.	$9t - (2t - 4) = 25$	$9t - (2t - 4) = 25$
		$9 \cdot 3 - (2 \cdot 3 - 4) \overset{?}{=} 25$
2. To subtract $(2t - 4)$, add its additive inverse $(-2t + 4)$.	$9t + (-2t + 4) = 25$	$9 \cdot 3 - (6 - 4) \overset{?}{=} 25$
	$9t - 2t + 4 = 25$	$27 - (2) \overset{?}{=} 25$
		$25 = 25$
3. Collect like terms.	$7t + 4 = 25$	(true)

4. A_{-4} or S_4 $\qquad\qquad\qquad 7t + 4 + (-4) = 25 + (-4)$

5. Collect like $\qquad\qquad\qquad\qquad\qquad 7t = 21$
   terms.

6. D_7 or $M_{\frac{1}{7}}$ $\qquad\qquad\qquad\qquad\qquad\quad t = 3$

Answer: $t = 3$, or solution set is $\{3\}$.

3. Solve and check: $27x - 3(x - 6) = 6$.

> [*Note:* Since $3(x - 6)$ means that 3 and $(x - 6)$ are to be multiplied, we will use the distributive property of multiplication.]

How to Proceed	*Solution*
1. Write the equation.	$27x - 3(x - 6) = 6$
2. Use the distributive property.	$27x - 3x + 18 = 6$
3. Collect like terms.	$24x + 18 = 6$
4. A_{-18}	$24x + 18 + (-18) = 6 + (-18)$
5. Collect like terms.	$24x = -12$
6. D_{24} or $M_{\frac{1}{24}}$	$x = -\frac{1}{2}$

Check

$$27x - 3(x - 6) = 6$$
$$27\left(-\tfrac{1}{2}\right) - 3\left(-\tfrac{1}{2} - 6\right) \stackrel{?}{=} 6$$
$$27\left(-\tfrac{1}{2}\right) - 3\left(-\tfrac{13}{2}\right) \stackrel{?}{=} 6$$
$$-\tfrac{27}{2} + \tfrac{39}{2} \stackrel{?}{=} 6$$
$$\tfrac{12}{2} \stackrel{?}{=} 6$$
$$6 = 6 \quad \text{(true)}$$

Answer: $x = -\frac{1}{2}$, or solution set is $\{-\frac{1}{2}\}$.

EXERCISES

In 1–39, solve and check the equation.

1. $x + (x - 6) = 20$
2. $x - (12 - x) = 38$
3. $5y + (2y - 7) = 63$
4. $10y - (5y + 2) = -42$
5. $(-15x + 7) - 12 = 4$
6. $(14 - 3c) + 7c = 94$
7. $7x - (4x - 39) = 0$
8. $5(x + 2) = 20$
9. $3(y - 9) = 30$
10. $-7(a + 3) = 28$
11. $8(2c - 1) = 56$
12. $\frac{1}{2}(10 - 3d) = 80$
13. $6(3c - 1) = -42$
14. $7(x + 3) = 5(x + 4)$
15. $3(a - 5) = 2(2a + 1)$
16. $5(3c - 2) + 8 = 43$
17. $41 + (3x + 4) = 8x$
18. $-6(2s + 3) - 2s = 38$

19. $8w - (3w + 6) = 19$
20. $4(y + 3) + 3y = 16$
21. $10z - (3z - 11) = 17$
22. $3z = 18 + (5z - 10)$
23. $15a - 2(a + 6) = 14$
24. $\frac{8}{5}b - \frac{4}{5}(b - 2) = 4\frac{4}{5}$
25. $5m - 2(m - 5) = 17$
26. $8t = 23 + 3(2t - 5)$
27. $4 + 2(5v + 3) = 13\frac{1}{3}v$
28. $3a + (2a - 5) = 13 - 2(a + 2)$
29. $2(t - 3) - 17 = 13 - 3(t + 2)$
30. $2(b + 1) - 3b = 3(3 + 2b)$
31. $2 - 7(d - 1) = 3(d - 2) - 5(d + 3)$
32. $4(y - 3) - 6(y + 1) = 4(3y + 4) - 2(8 + 6y)$
33. $6(2x + 1) - 3(4x - 3) - (6x + 10) = -(4x - 3) + 3$
34. $(x + 4)(x + 1) = x^2 + 59$
35. $x(x + 1) = (x - 6)(x + 4)$
36. $(y + 3)(y + 2) = y(y + 7)$
37. $(y - 5)(y - 1) - y^2 = -13$
38. $(a + 5)(a - 2) = (a + 1)^2$
39. $(4 - r)(6 + r) = 40 - (r^2 - 4r - 18)$

In 40–45, determine the element of the set if $x \in \{\text{ signed numbers}\}$.

40. $\{x \mid 5x - (3x + 2) = 18\}$
41. $\{x \mid 5 + 3(x - 1) = -34\}$
42. $\{x \mid 6x - 4(2x - 6) = .1\}$
43. $\{x \mid 5(x + 2) - 3(2x + 1) = 11\}$
44. $\{x \mid (x - 1)^2 + (x + 2)^2 - 2x^2 = 1\}$
45. $\{x \mid 2x(x + 2) - 4x \left(\dfrac{x}{2} + 3\right) = 8\}$

46. The larger of two numbers is 5 more than the smaller. The smaller number plus twice the larger equals 100. Find the numbers.
47. One number is 2 smaller than another. If 4 times the larger is subtracted from 5 times the smaller, the result is 10. Find the numbers.
48. Mrs. Powers travels 12 kilometers less each day in going to and from her job than Mrs. Clay does. The difference between the distance Mrs. Clay travels in 6 days and the distance that Mrs. Powers travels in 5 days is 96 kilometers. How far does each one travel each day?

11. Solving Equations Involving Absolute Values

Since $|+8| = 8$ and $|-8| = 8$, both $+8$ and -8 can replace x in the equation $|x| = 8$ and make the resulting sentence true. Therefore, $x = +8$ and $x = -8$ are solutions of $|x| = 8$, and the solution set is $\{+8, -8\}$.

If we apply the definition of absolute value, the two equations $x = 8$ and $x = -8$ together are equivalent to the equation $|x| = 8$.

Recall that, in general, $|x| = x$ when $x > 0$, $|x| = -x$ when $x < 0$, and $|x| = 0$ when $x = 0$.

Procedure.   To solve an equation involving the absolute value symbol, first write two equations that do not contain the absolute value symbol and which together are equivalent to the given equation. Then solve the resulting equations.

Model Problems

1. Solve and check: $|5x| = 20$

   [*Note:* $5x = 20$ and $5x = -20$ together are equivalent to $|5x| = 20$.]

Solution	*Check*

   $5x = 20$
   $x = 4$ D_5 or $M_{\frac{1}{5}}$

   For $x = 4$: $|5x| \overset{?}{=} 20$
   $|5(4)| \overset{?}{=} 20$
   $|20| = 20$ (true)

Solution	*Check*

   $5x = -20$
   $x = -4$ D_5 or $M_{\frac{1}{5}}$

   For $x = -4$: $|5x| \overset{?}{=} 20$
   $|5(-4)| \overset{?}{=} 20$
   $|-20| = 20$ (true)

   Answer: $x = 4$ and $x = -4$, or solution set is $\{4, -4\}$.

2. Solve and check: $4|x| = 24$

Solution	*Check*	*Check*

   $4|x| = 24$
   $\frac{1}{4} \cdot 4|x| = \frac{1}{4} \cdot 24$ $M_{\frac{1}{4}}$
   $|x| = 6$
   $x = 6$ and $x = -6$

   For $x = 6$: $4|x| \overset{?}{=} 24$
   $4|6| \overset{?}{=} 24$
   $4 \cdot 6 \overset{?}{=} 24$
   $24 = 24$
   (true)

   For $x = -6$: $4|x| \overset{?}{=} 24$
   $4|-6| \overset{?}{=} 24$
   $4 \cdot 6 \overset{?}{=} 24$
   $24 = 24$
   (true)

   Answer: $x = 6$ and $x = -6$, or solution set is $\{6, -6\}$.

3. Solve and check: $|2x - 3| = 13$

   [*Note:* $2x - 3 = 13$ and $2x - 3 = -13$ together are equivalent to $|2x - 3| = 13$.]

Solution	*Check*

   $2x - 3 = 13$
   $2x - 3 + (+3) = 13 + (+3)$
   $2x = 16$
   $x = 8$

   For $x = 8$: $|2x - 3| \overset{?}{=} 13$
   $|2(8) - 3| \overset{?}{=} 13$
   $|16 - 3| \overset{?}{=} 13$
   $13 = 13$ (true)

Solution	*Check*

$$2x - 3 = -13$$
$$2x - 3 + (+3) = -13 + (+3)$$
$$2x = -10$$
$$x = -5$$

For $x = -5$: $|2x - 3| \overset{?}{=} 13$

$$|2(-5) - 3| \overset{?}{=} 13$$
$$|-10 - 3| \overset{?}{=} 13$$
$$13 = 13 \quad \text{(true)}$$

Answer: $x = 8$ and $x = -5$, or solution set is $\{8, -5\}$.

4. Solve and check: $\left| \dfrac{4x + 8}{3} \right| = 12$

$$\left[Note: \frac{4x + 8}{3} = 12 \text{ and } \frac{4x + 8}{3} = -12 \text{ together are equivalent to} \right.$$

$$\left. \left| \frac{4x + 8}{3} \right| = 12. \right]$$

Solution	*Check*

$$\frac{4x + 8}{3} = 12$$

$$3 \left(\frac{4x + 8}{3} \right) = 3(12)$$

$$4x + 8 = 36$$
$$4x + 8 + (-8) = 36 + (-8)$$
$$4x = 28$$
$$x = 7$$

For $x = 7$: $\left| \dfrac{4x + 8}{3} \right| = 12$

$$\left| \frac{4(7) + 8}{3} \right| \overset{?}{=} 12$$

$$\left| \frac{28 + 8}{3} \right| \overset{?}{=} 12$$

$$\left| \frac{36}{3} \right| \overset{?}{=} 12$$

$$|12| = 12 \quad \text{(true)}$$

Solution	*Check*

$$\frac{4x + 8}{3} = -12$$

$$3 \left(\frac{4x + 8}{3} \right) = 3(-12)$$

$$4x + 8 = -36$$
$$4x + 8 + (-8) = -36 + (-8)$$
$$4x = -44$$
$$x = -11$$

For $x = -11$: $\left| \dfrac{4x + 8}{3} \right| = 12$

$$\left| \frac{4(-11) + 8}{3} \right| \overset{?}{=} 12$$

$$\left| \frac{-44 + 8}{3} \right| \overset{?}{=} 12$$

$$\left| \frac{-36}{3} \right| \overset{?}{=} 12$$

$$|-12| = 12 \quad \text{(true)}$$

Answer: $x = 7$ and $x = -11$, or solution set is $\{7, -11\}$.

EXERCISES

In 1–8, write two equations that do not contain the absolute value symbol and which together are equivalent to the given equation.

1. $|y| = 7$ **2.** $|3x| = 15$ **3.** $|t + 6| = 8$ **4.** $|m - 4| = 7$

5. $|3c + 8| = 29$ **6.** $|6 - 2x| = 2$ **7.** $\left|\dfrac{2c}{3}\right| = 6$ **8.** $\left|\dfrac{5c + 1}{4}\right| = 9$

In 9–28, find the solution set of the equation.

9. $|x| = 14$ **10.** $|c| = 10.2$ **11.** $|3r| = 36$
12. $2|m| = 32$ **13.** $|x + 8| = 17\frac{1}{2}$ **14.** $|r - 6| = 5$
15. $\frac{1}{2}|y + 1| = 8$ **16.** $4|4 - y| = 16$ **17.** $|2x + 1| = 12$
18. $|7 + 5y| = 32$ **19.** $|4c - 1| = 35$ **20.** $2|2t - 1| = 9$

21. $\left|\dfrac{x}{2}\right| = 10$ **22.** $4\left|\dfrac{y}{5}\right| = 20$ **23.** $\dfrac{1}{2}\left|\dfrac{t}{3}\right| = 8$

24. $-\left|\dfrac{2x}{3}\right| = -6$ **25.** $\left|\dfrac{2x + 3}{3}\right| = 3$ **26.** $\left|\dfrac{5m - 1}{6}\right| = 4$

27. $\left|\dfrac{2(x + 3)}{9}\right| = 2$ **28.** $\left|\dfrac{3(3x - 5)}{2}\right| = 15$

In 29–34, determine the element(s) of the set if $x \in \{$ signed numbers$\}$.

29. $\{x \mid |x + 1| = 2\}$ **30.** $\{x \mid |-x - 1| = 2\}$
31. $\{x \mid |3x - 2| = 3\}$ **32.** $\{x \mid |-3x + 2| = 3\}$

33. $\left\{x \left| \left|\dfrac{2x + 1}{2}\right| = \dfrac{5}{2}\right.\right\}$ **34.** $\{x \mid |2x| = 0\}$

35. Determine the set $\{x \mid |x| = -1\}$.

12. Solving Equations Containing More Than One Variable

An equation may contain more than one variable. Examples of such equations are $ax = b$, $x + c = d$, and $y - r = z$.

To solve such an equation for one of its variables means to express this particular variable in terms of the other variables. In order to plan the steps in the solution, it may be helpful to compare the equation with a similar equation that contains only the variable being solved for. For example, in solving $bx - c = d$ for x, compare it with $2x - 5 = 19$. The same operations are used in solving both equations.

We know that if a is a number, subtracting a is equivalent to adding $(-a)$. Therefore, henceforth we will use the notation S_a (subtract a) and A_{-a} interchangeably. We know also that if a is a nonzero number, then dividing by a is the same as multiplying by $\frac{1}{a}$. In the future, we will use the notations D_a (divide by a) and $M_{\frac{1}{a}}$ $\left(\text{multiply by } \frac{1}{a}\right)$ interchangeably.

Model Problems

1. Solve for x: $ax = b$ $(a \neq 0)$

Solution

Compare with $2x = 7$.
$$2x = 7 \qquad\qquad ax = b$$
$$\frac{2x}{2} = \frac{7}{2} \quad D_2 \qquad \frac{ax}{a} = \frac{b}{a} \quad D_a$$
$$x = \frac{7}{2} \quad Answer \qquad x = \frac{b}{a} \quad Ans.$$

Check
$$ax = b$$
$$a\left(\frac{b}{a}\right) \overset{?}{=} b$$
$$b = b \quad \text{(true)}$$

2. Solve for x: $x + a = b$

Solution

Compare with $x + 5 = 9$.
$$x + a = b$$
$$x + a + (-a) = b + (-a) \quad A_{-a}$$
$$x = b - a \qquad Ans.$$

Check
$$x + a \overset{?}{=} b$$
$$b - a + a \overset{?}{=} b$$
$$b = b \quad \text{(true)}$$

3. Solve for x: $2ax = 10a^2 - 3ax$ $(a \neq 0)$

How to Proceed

1. Write the equation.
2. A_{+3ax}
3. Collect like terms.
4. D_{5a}
5. Simplify.

Solution

Compare with $2x = 10 - 3x$.
$$2ax = 10a^2 - 3ax$$
$$2ax + (+3ax) = 10a^2 - 3ax + (+3ax)$$
$$5ax = 10a^2$$
$$\frac{5ax}{5a} = \frac{10a^2}{5a}$$
$$x = 2a \quad Ans.$$

Check

$$2ax \overset{?}{=} 10a^2 - 3ax$$
$$2a(2a) \overset{?}{=} 10a^2 - 3a(2a)$$
$$4a^2 \overset{?}{=} 10a^2 - 6a^2$$
$$4a^2 = 4a^2 \quad \text{(true)}$$

EXERCISES

In 1–22, solve for x or y and check. Whenever it is necessary to use the multiplicative inverse of a variable, assume that the variable does not represent 0.

1. $5x = b$
2. $sx = 8$
3. $ry = s$
4. $x + 5 = r$
5. $x + a = 7$
6. $y + c = d$
7. $x - 2 = r$
8. $y - a = 7$
9. $x - c = d$
10. $4x - 5c = 3c$
11. $bx = 9b^2$
12. $cx + c^2 = 5c^2 - 3cx$
13. $bx - 5 = c$
14. $a = by + 6$
15. $ry + s = t$
16. $abx - d = 5d$
17. $rsx - rs^2 = 0$
18. $m^2x - 3m^2 = 12m^2$
19. $9x - 24a = 6a + 4x$
20. $5y + 2b = y + 6b$
21. $8ax - 7a^2 = 19a^2 - 5ax$
22. $5by - 3b^2 = 2by + 6b^2$

13. Properties of Inequalities

THE ORDER PROPERTY OF NUMBER

If two signed numbers x and y are graphed on a number line, one and only one of the following situations happens:

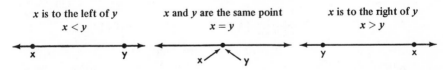

x is to the left of y	x and y are the same point	x is to the right of y
$x < y$	$x = y$	$x > y$

These graphs illustrate the ***order property of number*** (the law of trichotomy):

If x and y are two signed numbers, then one and only one of the following sentences is true:

$$x < y \qquad\qquad x = y \qquad\qquad x > y$$

THE TRANSITIVE PROPERTY OF INEQUALITIES

From the graph at the right, we see that if x lies to the left of y, or $x < y$, and if y lies to the left of z, or $y < z$, then x lies to the left of z, or $x < z$. Likewise, if z lies to the right of y, or $z > y$, and if y lies to the right of x, or $y > x$, then z lies to the right of x, or $z > x$.

This graph illustrates the *transitive property of inequalities:*

If x, y, and z are signed numbers, then:

if $x < y$ and $y < z$, then $x < z$

if $z > y$ and $y > x$, then $z > x$

THE ADDITION PROPERTY OF INEQUALITIES

If 3 is added to both members of the inequality $9 > 2$, which is a true sentence, then $9 + (3) > 2 + (3)$, or $12 > 5$, is also a true sentence. Observe that $2 < 9$ is a true sentence and that $2 + (-3) < 9 + (-3)$, or $-1 < 6$, is also a true sentence.

These examples illustrate the *addition property of inequalities:*

If x, y, and z are signed numbers, then:

if $x > y$, then $x + z > y + z$

if $x < y$, then $x + z < y + z$

Since subtracting a signed number from both members of an inequality means adding its additive inverse to both members of the inequality, we can say:

When the same number is added to or subtracted from both members of an inequality, the order of the inequality remains unchanged.

THE MULTIPLICATION PROPERTY OF INEQUALITIES

If we multiply both members of the inequality $5 > 3$, which is a true sentence, by 7, then $7 \times 5 > 7 \times 3$, or $35 > 21$, is also a true sentence. Observe that $-2 < 4$ is a true sentence and that $5(-2) < 5(4)$, or $-10 < 20$, is also a true sentence. Notice that when both members of an inequality are multiplied by the same positive number, the order of the inequality remains unchanged.

Now if we multiply both members of the inequality $5 > 3$ by -7, then $(-7)(5) > (-7)(3)$, or $-35 > -21$, is a false sentence. However, if we reverse the order in the resulting inequality $-35 > -21$, changing $>$ to $<$, we will have $-35 < -21$, a true sentence. Likewise, $-2 < 4$ is a true sentence, but $(-5)(-2) < (-5)(4)$, or $10 < -20$, is a false sentence.

However, if we reverse the order in the resulting inequality $10 < -20$ and write $10 > -20$, we have a true sentence.

These examples illustrate the *multiplication property of inequalities:*

If x, y, and z are signed numbers, then:

if $x > y$, then $xz > yz$ when z is positive $(z > 0)$

if $x < y$, then $xz < yz$ when z is positive $(z > 0)$

if $x > y$, then $xz < yz$ when z is negative $(z < 0)$

if $x < y$, then $xz > yz$ when z is negative $(z < 0)$

Since dividing both members of an inequality by a nonzero signed number is the same as multiplying by the reciprocal, or multiplicative inverse, of the number, we can say:

When both members of an inequality are multiplied or divided by a positive number, the order of the inequality remains unchanged; when both members are multiplied or divided by a negative number, the order of the inequality is reversed.

EXERCISES

In 1–24, replace the question mark with the symbol $>$ or the symbol $<$ so that the resulting sentence will be true.

1. Since $8 > 2, 8 + 1 ? 2 + 1.$
2. Since $-6 < 2, -6 + (-4) ? 2 + (-4).$
3. Since $9 > 5, 9 - 2 ? 5 - 2.$
4. Since $-2 > -8, -2 - (-4) ? -8 - (-4).$
5. Since $7 > 3, 5(7) ? 5(3).$
6. Since $-4 < 1, (-2)(-4) ? (-2)(1).$
7. Since $-8 < 4, (-8) \div (4) ? (4) \div (4).$
8. Since $9 > 6, (9) \div (-3) ? (6) \div (-3).$
9. If $5 > x$, then $5 + 7 ? x + 7.$
10. If $y < 6\frac{1}{4}$, then $y - 2 ? 6\frac{1}{4} - 2.$
11. If $20 > r$, then $4(20) ? 4(r).$
12. If $t < 1.21$, then $t \div 1.1 ? 1.21 \div 1.1.$
13. If $x > 8$, then $-2x ? (-2)(8).$
14. If $y < 8$, then $y \div (-4) ? 8 \div (-4).$
15. If $x + 2 > 7$, then $x + 2 + (-2) ? 7 + (-2)$ or $x ? 5.$
16. If $y - 3 < 12$, then $y - 3 + 3 ? 12 + 3$, or $y ? 15.$
17. If $2x > 8$, then $\dfrac{2x}{2} ? \dfrac{8}{2}$, or $x ? 4.$
18. If $\frac{1}{3}y < 4$, then $3 \times \frac{1}{3}y ? 3 \times 4$, or $y ? 12.$

19. If $-3x < 36$, then $\dfrac{-3x}{-3}$? $\dfrac{36}{-3}$, or x ? -12.

20. If $-2x > 6$, then $(-\frac{1}{2})(-2x)$? $(-\frac{1}{2})(6)$, or x ? -3.

21. If $x < 5$ and $5 < y$, then x ? y.

22. If $m > -7$ and $-7 > a$, then m ? a.

23. If $x < 10$ and $z > 10$, then x ? z.

24. If $a > b$ and $c < b$, then a ? c.

25. The following sequence of statements proves that if x is any non-zero signed number $(x \neq 0)$, then x^2 is a positive number, that is, $x^2 > 0$. Supply the reasons for each step.

1. Since $x \neq 0$, then $x > 0$ or $x < 0$.
2. If $x > 0$, then $x \cdot x > x \cdot 0$.
3. Thus, if $x > 0$, then $x^2 > 0$.
4. If $x < 0$, then $x \cdot x > x \cdot 0$.
5. Thus, if $x < 0$, then $x^2 > 0$.

26. Use the multiplication property of -1 to construct a sequence of true statements (together with their reasons) which shows that:

a. If x is positive, then $-x$ is negative.

b. If x is negative, then $-x$ is positive.

14. Finding the Solution Sets of Inequalities Containing One Variable

Let us find the solution set of the inequality $2x > 8$, when x is a member of the set of signed numbers. To do this, we must find the set of all numbers each of which can replace x in the sentence $2x > 8$ and result in a true sentence.

$$2x > 8$$

If $x = 1$, then $2(1) > 8$, or $2 > 8$, is a false sentence.

If $x = 2\frac{1}{2}$, then $2(2\frac{1}{2}) > 8$, or $5 > 8$, is a false sentence.

If $x = 3\frac{3}{4}$, then $2(3\frac{3}{4}) > 8$, or $7\frac{1}{2} > 8$, is a false sentence.

If $x = 4$, then $2(4) > 8$, or $8 > 8$, is a false sentence.

If $x = 4.1$, then $2(4.1) > 8$, or $8.2 > 8$, is a *true* sentence.

If $x = 5$, then $2(5) > 8$, or $10 > 8$, is a *true* sentence.

Notice that if x is replaced by any number greater than 4, the resulting sentence is true. Therefore, the solution set of $2x > 8$ is the set of all signed numbers greater than 4, written {all signed numbers greater than 4}. The solution set can also be described by the symbol

$\{x \mid x > 4\}$, which is read "the set of all x such that x is greater than 4."

Observe that every member of the solution set of $x > 4$ is also a member of the solution set of $2x > 8$. Therefore, we call $2x > 8$ and $x > 4$ *equivalent inequalities*.

The inequality $2x > 8$ is called a *conditional inequality* because it is true for at least one but not all the elements of the replacement set (which was the set of signed numbers). Other examples of conditional inequalities are $x + 5 > 7$ and $2x - 1 < 9$.

If $x \in \{\text{signed numbers}\}$, the inequality $x + 5 > x$ is true for every element of the replacement set. Such an inequality is called an *absolute inequality*, or an *unconditional inequality*. Other examples of absolute inequalities are $2x + 9 > 2x$ and $x - 7 < x$.

To find the solution set of an inequality, we will solve the inequality using methods similar to those used in solving an equation. We will use the properties of inequalities to transform the given inequality into a simpler equivalent inequality whose solution set is evident. Study the following model problems to learn how this is done.

Model Problems

In 1–6, the domain of the variable is the set of signed numbers.

1. Find and graph the solution set of the inequality $x - 4 > 1$.

How to Proceed	Solution
1. Write the inequality.	$x - 4 > 1$
2. Add 4 to both members, and use the addition property of inequalities.	$x - 4 + 4 > 1 + 4$ $x > 5$

Answer: The solution set is {all signed numbers greater than 5}, or $\{x \mid x > 5\}$.

The graph of the solution set is shown below. Note that 5 is not included in the graph.

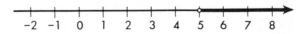

2. Find and graph the solution set of the inequality $x + 1 \leq 4$. (Remember that $x + 1 \leq 4$ means $x + 1 < 4$ or $x + 1 = 4$.)

How to Proceed	Solution	Check
1. Write the inequality.	$x + 1 \leq 4$	If $x = 3$, then $x + 1 = 4$.

2. Subtract 1 from both $x + 1 - 1 \leq 4 - 1$ If $x < 3$, then $x + 1 < 4$.
   members, and use the $x \leq 3$
   subtraction property
   of inequalities.

Answer: The solution set is {all signed numbers less than or equal to 3}, or
$\{x \mid x \leq 3\}$.

The graph of the solution set is
shown at the right. Note that 3 is
included in the graph.

$$-3 \quad -2 \quad -1 \quad 0 \quad 1 \quad 2 \quad 3 \quad 4$$

3. Find and graph the solution set of the inequality $\frac{1}{4}y \geq 1$.

How to Proceed	*Solution*
1. Write the inequality.	$\frac{1}{4}y \geq 1$
2. Multiply both members by 4, the multiplicative inverse of $\frac{1}{4}$. Use the inequality property of multiplying by a positive number.	$4 \cdot \frac{1}{4}y \geq 4 \cdot 1$ $y \geq 4$ The check is left to the student.

Answer: The solution set is {all signed numbers greater than or equal to 4},
or $\{y \mid y \geq 4\}$.

The graph of the solution
set is shown at the right. Note
that 4 is included in the graph.

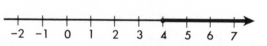
$$-2 \quad -1 \quad 0 \quad 1 \quad 2 \quad 3 \quad 4 \quad 5 \quad 6 \quad 7$$

4. Find and graph the solution set of the inequality $-15z < 10$.

How to Proceed	*Solution*
1. Write the inequality.	$-15z < 10$
2. Divide both members by -15. Use the inequality property of division by a negative number. Remember to reverse the order of the inequality.	$\frac{-15z}{-15} > \frac{10}{-15}$ $z > -\frac{2}{3}$ The check is left to the student.

Answer: The solution set is {all signed numbers greater than $-\frac{2}{3}$}, or
$\{z \mid z > -\frac{2}{3}\}$.

The graph of the solution set is shown at the
right. Note that $-\frac{2}{3}$ is not included in the graph.

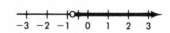
$$-3 \quad -2 \quad -1 \quad 0 \quad 1 \quad 2 \quad 3$$

5. Find and graph the solution set of the inequality $5x + 4 \leq 11 - 2x$.

How to Proceed	*Solution*
1. Write the inequality.	$5x + 4 \leq 11 - 2x$

2. Add $2x$ to each member, and use the addition property of inequalities.

$$5x + 4 + 2x \le 11 - 2x + 2x$$
$$7x + 4 \le 11$$

3. Subtract 4 from both members, and use the subtraction property of inequalities.

$$7x + 4 - 4 \le 11 - 4$$
$$7x \le 7$$

4. Divide both members by 7, and use the property of dividing by a positive number.

$$\frac{7x}{7} \le \frac{7}{7}$$
$$x \le 1$$

The check is left to the student.

Answer: The solution set is {all signed numbers less than or equal to 1}, or $\{x \mid x \le 1\}$.

The graph of the solution set is shown at the right. Note that 1 is included in the graph.

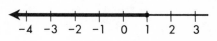

6. Find and graph the solution set of the inequality $2(2x - 8) - 8x \le 0$.

How to Proceed	*Solution*
1. Write the inequality.	$2(2x - 8) - 8x \le 0$
2. Use the distributive property.	$4x - 16 - 8x \le 0$
3. Collect like terms.	$-4x - 16 \le 0$
4. Add 16 to both members, and use the addition property of inequalities.	$-4x - 16 + 16 \le 0 + 16$ $-4x \le 16$
5. Divide both members by -4, and use the property of division by a negative number.	$\frac{-4x}{-4} \ge \frac{16}{-4}$ $x \ge -4$

The check is left to the student.

Answer: The solution set is {all signed numbers greater than or equal to -4}, or $\{x \mid x \ge -4\}$.

The graph of the solution set is shown at the right. Note that -4 is included in the graph.

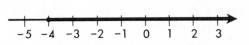

EXERCISES

In 1–57, find and graph the solution set of the inequality. Use the set of signed numbers as the domain of the variable.

1. $x - 2 > 4$
2. $z - 6 < 4$
3. $y - \frac{1}{2} > 2$
4. $x - 1.5 < 3.5$
5. $5\frac{3}{4} > w - 1\frac{1}{4}$
6. $x + 5 > 12$

7. $d + \frac{1}{4} > 3$

8. $m + .1 < 2.1$

9. $-3\frac{1}{2} > c + \frac{1}{2}$

10. $y + 3 \leq 8$

11. $25 \leq d + 22$

12. $3t > 6$

13. $4s > -8$

14. $2x \leq 12$

15. $15 \leq 3y$

16. $-24 > 6r$

17. $-10 \leq 4h$

18. $-3x > 21$

19. $-6y < 24$

20. $-10x > -20$

21. $-12x \geq 30$

22. $\frac{1}{3}x > 2$

23. $\frac{1}{2}y < -3$

24. $-\frac{2}{3}z \geq 6$

25. $\frac{x}{2} > 1$

26. $\frac{y}{3} \leq -1$

27. $\frac{1}{2} \leq \frac{z}{4}$

28. $1.5x > 6$

29. $-.4y \leq 4$

30. $-10 \geq 2.5z$

31. $2x - 1 > 5$

32. $3y - 6 \geq 12$

33. $5x - 1 > -31$

34. $2x - 3 < 12$

35. $-5 \leq 3y - 2$

36. $2y + 7 < 17$

37. $6c + 1 > -11$

38. $4d + 3 \leq 17$

39. $8h + 5 \geq -23$

40. $5x + 3x - 4 > 4$

41. $8y - 3y + 1 \leq 29$

42. $6x + 2 - 8x < 14$

43. $3x + 1 > 2x + 7$

44. $7y - 4 < 6 + 2y$

45. $4 - 3x \geq 16 + x$

46. $2x - 1 > 4 - \frac{1}{2}x$

47. $2c + 5 \geq 14 + 2\frac{1}{3}c$

48. $\frac{x}{3} - 1 \leq \frac{x}{2} + 3$

49. $4(x - 1) > 16$

50. $8x < 5(2x + 4)$

51. $12\left(\frac{1}{4} + \frac{x}{3}\right) > 15$

52. $8m - 2(2m + 3) \geq 0$

53. $12r - (8r - 20) > 12$

54. $3y - 6 \leq 3(7 + 2y)$

55. $5x \leq 10 + 2(3x - 4)$

56. $-3(4x - 8) > 2(3 + 2x)$

57. $4 - 5(y - 2) \leq -2(-9 + 2y)$

In 58–63, state whether the inequality is a conditional inequality or an absolute inequality. Use the set of signed numbers as the domain of the variable.

58. $x + 8 > x$

59. $x + 8 > 8$

60. $5x - 4 < 21$

61. $7x + x + 10 > 8x$

62. $2x + 3x < 4x + 1$

63. $6x + 3x - 1 < 8x + x$

64. Six times a number is less than 72. What numbers satisfy this condition?

65. A number increased by 10 is greater than 50. What numbers satisfy this condition?

66. A number decreased by 15 is less than 35. What numbers satisfy this condition?

67. Twice a number, increased by 6, is less than 48. What numbers satisfy this condition?

68. Five times a number, decreased by 24, is greater than 3 times the number. What numbers satisfy this condition?

In 69–71, use the set of signed numbers as the domain of the variable.

69. Determine the set $\{x \mid x + 5 < x\}$. Give a reason for your answer.

70. Determine the set $\{x \mid x^2 < 0\}$. Give a reason for your answer.

71. Find and graph the solution set of the inequality $x^2 > 0$.

Chapter 8

Solving Problems by Using First-Degree

Open Sentences in One Variable

We have already studied methods of solving some numerical problems that are stated in words. Now, we will study in greater detail the solution of numerical problems that come from areas such as business, science, and geometry. We will first translate the verbal relationships into open sentences involving one variable; then we will solve these open sentences.

1. Number Problems

EXERCISES

In 1–10, represent in terms of x:

1. twice the number represented by x increased by 8.
2. three times the number represented by x decreased by 12.
3. twelve decreased by 3 times the number represented by x.
4. four times the number which is 3 more than x.
5. five times the number which is 3 less than $2x$.
6. three times the number which exceeds x by 5.
7. twice the number which exceeds $3x$ by 4.
8. twice the sum of the number represented by x and 5.
9. ten times the number obtained when twice x is decreased by 10.
10. six times the number which is 4 less than one-third of x.
11. If the smaller of two numbers is represented by x, represent the larger when their sum is:
    a. 10   b. 25   c. 36   d. 50   e. 100   f. 3000
12. If the sum of two numbers is represented by S, and the smaller number is represented by x, represent the larger in terms of S and x.

13. If the larger of two numbers is represented by l, represent the smaller when their sum is:

    a. 5   b. 12   c. 20   d. 40   e. 75   f. 1000

14. If the sum of two numbers is represented by S, and the larger number is represented by l, represent the smaller in terms of S and l.

SOLVING NUMBER PROBLEMS

Model Problems ─────────────────────────────────

1. The larger of two numbers is twice the smaller. If the larger is decreased by 10, the result is 5 more than the smaller. Find the numbers.

How to Proceed	*Solution*
1. Represent the smaller number by a variable and all the other described numbers in terms of the same variable.	Let x = the smaller number. Then $2x$ = the larger number. Then $2x - 10$ = the larger decreased by 10. Then $x + 5$ = 5 more than the smaller.
2. Write an open sentence which symbolizes the relationships stated in the problem.	$2x - 10 = x + 5$
3. Solve the open sentence.	$2x - 10 + 10 = x + 5 + 10$ $2x = x + 15$ $2x + (-x) = x + 15 + (-x)$ $x = 15$ $2x = 30$
4. Check the answers in the original problem.	The larger decreased by $10 = 30 - 10 = 20$. 5 more than the smaller $= 15 + 5 = 20$. The results are the same, 20.

Answer: The smaller number is 15; the larger number is 30.

2. Separate 38 into two parts such that 3 times the smaller is 16 less than twice the larger.

Solution:

Let s = the smaller number.

Then $38 - s$ = the larger number.

Then $3s$ = 3 times the smaller number.

Then $2(38 - s) - 16$ = 16 less than twice the larger number.

$$3s = 2(38 - s) - 16$$
$$3s = 76 - 2s - 16$$
$$3s = 60 - 2s$$
$$3s + 2s = 60 - 2s + 2s$$
$$5s = 60$$
$$s = 12$$
$$38 - s = 26$$

Check: 3 times the smaller = $3(12) = 36$. 16 less than twice the larger = $2(26) - 16 = 36$. The results are the same, 36.

Answer: The smaller number is 12; the larger number is 26.

3. The larger of two numbers is 4 times the smaller. If the larger number exceeds the smaller number by 15, find the number.

Solution:

Let s = the smaller number.
Then $4s$ = the larger number.

> [*Note:* "The larger number exceeds the smaller by 15" has the following meanings. We will use the first.
> 1. The larger equals 15 more than the smaller, written $4s = s + 15$.
> 2. The larger decreased by 15 equals the smaller, written $4s - 15 = s$.
> 3. The larger decreased by the smaller equals 15, written $4s - s = 15$.]

$$4s = s + 15$$
$$4s + (-s) = s + 15 + (-s)$$
$$3s = 15$$
$$s = 5$$
$$4s = 20$$

Check: The larger number, 20, is 4 times the smaller number, 5. The larger number, 20, exceeds the smaller number, 5, by 15.

Answer: The larger number is 20; the smaller number is 5.

EXERCISES

1. If 6 times a number is decreased by 6, the result is the same as when 3 times the number is increased by 12. Find the number.
2. If 5 times a number is increased by 50, the result is the same as when 200 is decreased by the number. Find the number.

3. If 50 is decreased by 4 times a certain number, the result is 15 more than the number. Find the number.
4. If 3 times a number is increased by 22, the result is 14 less than 7 times the number. Find the number.
5. If 14 is added to a certain number and the sum is multiplied by 2, the result is equal to 8 times the number decreased by 14. Find the number.
6. The larger of two numbers is 5 less than twice the smaller. If their sum is 70, find the numbers.
7. The difference between two numbers is 24. Find the numbers if their sum is 88.
8. Separate 160 into two parts such that the larger will be 3 times the smaller.
9. Separate 45 into two parts such that 5 times the smaller is 6 less than twice the larger.
10. The larger of two numbers is 1 more than 3 times the smaller. The difference between 8 times the smaller and 2 times the larger is 10. Find the numbers.
11. The smaller of two numbers is 12 less than the larger. Four times the larger exceeds 3 times the smaller by 90. Find the numbers.
12. Separate 150 into two parts such that 4 times the larger exceeds 5 times the smaller by 60.
13. If 3 times a number is increased by 9, the result will be 6 times the excess of the number over 2. Find the number.
14. Find a number which exceeds 10 by as much as twice the number exceeds 38.
15. Find a number which is as much larger than 35 as 2 times the number is smaller than 190.
16. The second of three numbers is 2 more than the first. The third number is twice the first. The sum of the first and third exceeds the second by 2. Find the three numbers.
17. The second of three numbers is 1 less than the first. The third number is 5 less than twice the second. If the third number exceeds the first number by 12, find the three numbers.

2. Consecutive Integer Problems

PREPARING TO SOLVE CONSECUTIVE INTEGER PROBLEMS

Recall that the set of integers is $\{\ldots, -3, -2, -1, 0, 1, 2, 3, \ldots\}$. That is, an integer is a number which is either a whole number or the additive inverse of a whole number.

An *even integer* is an integer which is twice some integer. For example, 0, 6, and −10 are even integers.

An *odd integer* is an integer which is not an even integer. For example, 7 and −5 are odd integers.

Consecutive integers are integers which follow one another in order. To obtain a set of consecutive integers, we start with any integer and count by ones. Each number in the set is 1 more than the previous number in the set. Each of the following is a set of consecutive integers:

$$\{5, 6, 7, 8\}$$
$$\{-5, -4, -3, -2\}$$
$$\{x, x + 1, x + 2, x + 3\} \quad x \in \{\text{integers}\}$$

Consecutive even integers are even integers which follow one another in order. To obtain a set of consecutive even integers, we can start with any even integer and count by twos. Each number in the set is 2 more than the previous number in the set. Each of the following is a set of consecutive even integers:

$$\{2, 4, 6, 8\}$$
$$\{-12, -10, -8, -6\}$$
$$\{x, x + 2, x + 4, x + 6\} \quad x \in \{\text{even integers}\}$$

Consecutive odd integers are odd integers which follow one another in order. To obtain a set of consecutive odd integers, we start with any odd integer and count by twos. Each number in the set is 2 more than the previous number in the set. Each of the following is a set of consecutive odd integers:

$$\{3, 5, 7, 9\}$$
$$\{-5, -3, -1, 1\}$$
$$\{x, x + 2, x + 4, x + 6\} \quad x \in \{\text{odd integers}\}$$

Keep In Mind

1. Consecutive integers differ by 1.
2. Consecutive even integers and also consecutive odd integers differ by 2.

EXERCISES

1. Write four consecutive integers beginning with each of the following integers (y is an integer):

   a. 15   b. 31   c. −10   d. −2   e. y f. $2y + 1$ g. $3y - 2$

2. Write four consecutive even integers beginning with each of the following integers (y is an even integer):
   a. 8   **b.** 26   **c.** -20 **d.** -4 **e.** y **f.** $2y$ **g.** $2y - 6$
3. Write four consecutive odd integers beginning with each of the following integers (y is an odd integer):
   a. 9   **b.** 35   **c.** -15 **d.** -3 **e.** y **f.** $2y + 1$ **g.** $2y - 1$
4. If $2x - 3$ is an odd integer, write the following two even integers.
5. If $2x + 6$ is an even integer, write the following two odd integers.

In 6–12, give the replacement set each of whose elements can replace x and make the resulting sentence true.

6. $x + 1$ represents an even integer.
7. $x + 1$ represents an odd integer.
8. $2x$ represents an even integer.
9. x and $x + 2$ represent two consecutive even integers.
10. x and $x + 2$ represent two consecutive odd integers.
11. $2x$ and $2x + 2$ represent two consecutive even integers.
12. $2x - 1$ and $2x + 1$ represent two consecutive odd integers.

In 13–15, answer **(a)** odd or **(b)** even so that the resulting sentence is true.

13. The sum of an even number of consecutive odd integers is an _____ integer.
14. The sum of an odd number of consecutive odd integers is an _____ integer.
15. The sum of any number of consecutive even integers is an _____ integer.

SOLVING CONSECUTIVE INTEGER PROBLEMS

Model Problems

1. Find two consecutive integers whose sum is 95.

   Solution:

   Let n = the first integer.
   Then $n + 1$ = the second integer.
   Then $2n + 1$ = the sum of the two integers.

   The sum of the two integers is 95.

   $$2n + 1 = 95$$
   $$2n + 1 - 1 = 95 - 1$$
   $$2n = 94$$
   $$n = 47, n + 1 = 48$$

Check: The sum of the consecutive integers, 47 and 48, is 95.

Answer: 47 and 48

2. Find three consecutive even integers such that 4 times the first decreased by the second is 12 more than twice the third.

Solution:

Let n = the first even integer.
Then $n + 2$ = the second even integer.
Then $n + 4$ = the third even integer.

4 times the first decreased by the second is 12 more than twice the third.

$$4n - (n + 2) = 2(n + 4) + 12$$
$$4n - n - 2 = 2n + 8 + 12$$
$$3n - 2 = 2n + 20$$
$$3n - 2 + 2 = 2n + 20 + 2$$
$$3n = 2n + 22$$
$$3n + (-2n) = 2n + 22 + (-2n)$$
$$n = 22$$
$$n + 2 = 24, \ n + 4 = 28$$

Check: Show that 22, 24, and 28 satisfy the conditions in the given problem.

Answer: 22, 24, 28

EXERCISES

1. Find two consecutive integers whose sum is:
   a. 61   b. 35   c. 91   d. 125   e. −17   f. −81
2. Find three consecutive integers whose sum is:
   a. 18   b. 48   c. 99   d. 303   e. −12   f. −57
3. Find four consecutive integers whose sum is 234.
4. Find two consecutive even integers whose sum is:
   a. 22   b. 38   c. 146   d. 206   e. −10   f. −34
5. Find three consecutive odd integers whose sum is:
   a. 33   b. 45   c. 159   d. 615   e. −27   f. −105
6. Find four consecutive even integers whose sum is 60.
7. Find three consecutive integers such that the sum of the first and third is 40.
8. Find four consecutive integers such that the sum of the second and fourth is 132.

9. Find three consecutive integers such that twice the smallest is 12 more than the largest.

10. Find three consecutive even integers such that the sum of the smallest and twice the second is 20 more than the third.

11. Find two consecutive integers such that 4 times the larger exceeds 3 times the smaller by 23.

12. Find four consecutive odd integers such that the sum of the first three exceeds the fourth by 18.

13. Find three consecutive even integers such that twice the sum of the second and third exceeds 3 times the first by 34.

14. Find three consecutive integers such that the sum of the second and third exceeds $\frac{1}{2}$ of the first by 33.

15. Is it possible to find three consecutive even integers whose sum is 40?

16. Is it possible to find three consecutive odd integers whose sum is 59?

17. How many sets of three consecutive integers are there in which the sum of the three integers does not equal three times the middle integer?

3. Motion Problems

PREPARING TO SOLVE MOTION PROBLEMS

If a car travels at the rate of 50 miles per hour, in 2 hours it travels 2(50), or 100 miles. In this case, the three quantities that are related are:

1. **distance** traveled, 100 miles
2. rate of speed, or **rate**, 50 miles per hour (mph)
3. **time** traveled, 2 hours

The relation involving the distance, D, the rate, R, and the time, T, may be expressed in the following ways:

$$D = RT \qquad T = \frac{D}{R} \qquad R = \frac{D}{T}$$

In our work, *rate* will represent either of the following:

1. The *uniform rate of speed*, which represents a rate of speed that remains constant (does not change) throughout a trip. Thus, if a car is traveling at a uniform rate of 50 miles per hour (mph) on a 2-hour trip, the car is constantly traveling 50 miles per hour (mph) during the entire trip.

2. The *average rate of speed*, which represents the total distance traveled divided by the total time traveled. Thus, a car that travels 120 miles in 3 hours is traveling at an average rate of $120 \div 3$, or 40 miles per hour (mph).

[*Note:* If the distance traveled is measured in kilometers (km) and the time is measured in hours (h), then the rate is measured in kilometers per hour (km/h). Thus, a car that travels 300 kilometers (km) in 3 hours (h) is traveling at an average rate of $300 \div 3$, or 100 kilometers per hour (km/h).]

When any two of the three quantities, rate, time, and distance, have been represented, the third can be represented in terms of those two by using one of the three formulas previously stated. For example:

The distance traveled in 5 hours at an average rate of 40 mph equals $5(40) = 200$ miles. $(D = RT)$

The distance traveled in 7 hours at an average rate of $(x + 10)$ km/h equals $7(x + 10)$ kilometers. $(D = RT)$

The time required to travel 160 kilometers at an average rate of 80 km/h is $\dfrac{160}{80} = 2$ hours. $\left(T = \dfrac{D}{R}\right)$

The time required to travel 200 miles at an average rate of $(x + 20)$ mph is $\dfrac{200}{x + 20}$ hours. $\left(T = \dfrac{D}{R}\right)$

The average rate of speed at which one travels when 60 miles are covered in 2 hours is $\dfrac{60}{2} = 30$ mph. $\left(R = \dfrac{D}{T}\right)$

The average rate of speed at which one travels when 100 kilometers are covered in x hours is $\dfrac{100}{x}$ km/h. $\left(R = \dfrac{D}{T}\right)$

Keep In Mind

$$D = RT \qquad T = \frac{D}{R} \qquad R = \frac{D}{T}$$

EXERCISES

1. If a car is traveling 80 km/h, represent how far it will go in:

   a. 5 hr.   b. 3 hr. 30 min.   c. x hr.   d. $(2x + 1)$ hr.   e. $(10 - x)$ hr.

2. A train traveled 300 miles. Represent how long the trip took if the train was traveling at a rate of:

   a. 50 mph   b. 70 mph   c. x mph   d. $(x + 10)$ mph   e. $(x - 5)$ mph

3. A plane flew 4000 kilometers. Represent how fast it was flying if it flew for:

   a. 4 hr.   b. 6 hr. 40 min.   c. x hr.   d. $(x + 40)$ hr.   e. $(x - 50)$ hr.

4. Find the average rate for the entire trip if a car travels:

   a. 1 hour at 40 mph and 1 hour at 50 mph
   b. 1 hour at 30 mph, 1 hour at 40 mph, and 1 hour at 50 mph
   c. 1 hour at 30 mph and 2 hours at 36 mph
   d. 2 hours at 40 mph and 3 hours at 50 mph

5. Two cars started from the same point and traveled for x hours in opposite directions at rates of 60 km/h and 80 km/h, respectively.

   a. Represent in terms of x the distance traveled by the slow car.
   b. Represent in terms of x the distance traveled by the fast car.
   c. Represent how far apart the two cars were at the end of x hours.
   d. Write an open sentence indicating that the two cars were 140 kilometers apart at the end of x hours.

6. Jack and Harry started on bicycles at the same time from two different places on a straight road and traveled toward each other. Jack traveled 8 mph and Harry traveled 10 mph. They met in x hours.

   a. Represent in terms of x the distance Jack traveled.
   b. Represent in terms of x the distance Harry traveled.
   c. Represent in terms of x the total distance they traveled.
   d. Write an open sentence indicating that Jack and Harry were originally 27 miles apart.

7. Mr. Sands left his home by car, traveling on a certain road at the rate of 40 mph. One hour later, Mrs. Sands left home and started after him on the same road, traveling at the rate of 50 mph. Mrs. Sands overtook her husband in x hours.

   a. Represent in terms of x the number of hours Mr. Sands traveled.
   b. Represent in terms of x the distance Mr. Sands traveled.
   c. Represent in terms of x the distance Mrs. Sands traveled.
   d. Write an open sentence which represents the relationship between the distances traveled by Mr. Sands and Mrs. Sands.

8. Saul left his home and walked a distance of x kilometers at the rate of 5 km/h. He then retraced his steps, walking home at the rate of 4 km/h.

   a. Represent in terms of x the time Saul spent walking out.

b. Represent in terms of x the time Saul spent walking back.
c. Represent in terms of x the total time Saul spent on the trip.
d. Write an open sentence indicating that the total time Saul spent on the trip was 4 hours.

9. Represent the missing quantities in the following tables:

	Rate	Time	Distance
a.	40	x	?
b.	40	?	x
c.	?	2	x

	Rate	Time	Distance
d.	50	$x + 2$	?
e.	?	$x + 1$	150
f.	$x + 10$	?	200

SOLVING MOTION PROBLEMS

In solving motion problems, it is helpful to draw a diagram. The facts in the problem may be organized by using verbal sentences or by using a table.

Model Problems

1. Two planes start from the same point at the same time and travel in opposite directions. The slow plane travels at 280 mph, and the fast plane travels at 350 mph. In how many hours will the planes be 2520 miles apart?

   Solution: Since both planes start at the same time, they will *travel* the same number of hours.

   Let h = the number of hours traveled by each plane.
   Then $280h$ = the distance traveled by the slow plane.
   And $350h$ = the distance traveled by the fast plane.

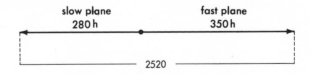

   The total distance traveled is 2520 miles.

   Check

   $$280h + 350h = 2520$$
   $$630h = 2520$$
   $$h = 4$$

   $280(4) = 1120$
   $350(4) = \underline{1400}$
   Total $= 2520$

   Answer: 4 hours

The following tabular arrangement may also be used:

Let h = the number of hours traveled by each plane.

First fill in the rate and time for each plane. Then represent the distance for each plane.

	(mph) Rate	(hr.) Time	(mi.) Distance
Slow plane	280	h	$280h$
Fast plane	350	h	$350h$

The total distance traveled is 2520 miles.

$$280h + 350h = 2520$$

Complete the solution as before.

2. A passenger train and a freight train start at the same time from stations which are 405 miles apart and travel toward each other. The rate of the passenger train is twice the rate of the freight train. In 3 hours, the trains pass each other. Find the rate of each train.

Solution:

Let r = the rate of the freight train.

Then $2r$ = the rate of the passenger train.

And $3r$ = the distance traveled by the freight train.

And $3(2r)$ = the distance traveled by the passenger train.

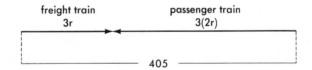

The total distance traveled was 405 miles.

$$3r + 3(2r) = 405$$
$$3r + 6r = 405$$
$$9r = 405$$
$$r = 45$$
$$2r = 90$$

Check

$$3(45) = 135$$
$$3(90) = \underline{270}$$
$$\text{Total} = 405$$

Answer: The rate of the freight train was 45 mph. The rate of the passenger train was 90 mph.

The following table may also be used:

Let r = the rate of the freight train.
Then $2r$ = the rate of the passenger train.

First fill in the time and rate for each train. Then represent the distance for each train.

	(mph) Rate	(hr.) Time	(mi.) Distance
Freight train	r	3	$3r$
Passenger train	$2r$	3	$3(2r)$

The total distance traveled was 405 miles.

$$3r + 3(2r) = 405$$

Complete the solution as before.

3. Two trains started at the same time from stations which were 600 kilometers apart and traveled toward each other. The rate of the fast train exceeded the rate of the slow train by 20 km/h. At the end of 2 hours, the trains were 200 kilometers apart. Find the rate of each train.

Solution:

Let r = the rate of the slow train.
Then $r + 20$ = the rate of the fast train.

First fill in the time and rate for each train. Then represent the distance for each train.

	(km/h) Rate	(h) Time	(km) Distance
Slow train	r	2	$2r$
Fast train	$r + 20$	2	$2(r + 20)$

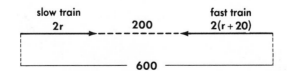

The total distance between the stations was 600 kilometers.

$$2r + 200 + 2(r + 20) = 600$$
$$2r + 200 + 2r + 40 = 600$$
$$4r + 240 = 600$$

Check

$$4r = 600 - 240$$
$$4r = 360$$
$$r = 90$$
$$r + 20 = 110$$

$$2(90) = 180$$
$$2(110) = \underline{220}$$
$$\text{Total} = \overline{400}$$
$$600 - 400 = 200$$

Answer: The rate of the slow train was 90 km/h. The rate of the fast train was 110 km/h.

4. Martin left his home by car, traveling on a certain road at the rate of 50 km/h. Two hours later, his brother William left the home and started after him on the same road, traveling at the rate of 70 km/h. In how many hours did William overtake Martin?

Solution: Since Martin started 2 hours earlier than William, he traveled 2 hours longer than William.

Let h = the number of hours William traveled.
Then $h + 2$ = the number of hours Martin traveled.

First fill in the rate and time for each brother. Then represent the distance for each brother.

	(km/h) Rate	(h) Time	(km) Distance
Martin	50	$h + 2$	$50(h + 2)$
William	70	h	$70h$

The distance traveled by William is the same as the distance traveled by Martin.

Check

$$70h = 50(h + 2)$$
$$70h = 50h + 100$$
$$70h + (-50h) = 50h + 100 + (-50h)$$
$$20h = 100$$
$$h = 5$$

$$5 + 2 = 7$$
$$7(50) = 350$$
$$5(70) = 350$$

Both brothers travel the same distance.

Answer: William overtook Martin in 5 hours.

5. How far can a woman drive out into the country at the average rate of 60 mph and return over the same road at the average rate of 45 mph if she travels a total of 7 hours?

Solution: *Method* 1

Let h = the number of hours she spent driving out.
Then $7 - h$ = the number of hours she spent driving back.

First fill in the rate and time for each trip. Then represent the distance for each trip.

	(mph) Rate	(hr.) Time	(mi.) Distance
Trip out	60	h	$60h$
Trip back	45	$7 - h$	$45(7 - h)$

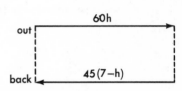

The distance out is the same as the distance back.

$$60h = 45(7 - h)$$
$$60h = 315 - 45h$$
$$60h + 45h = 315 - 45h + 45h$$
$$105h = 315$$
$$h = 3$$
$$60h = 180$$

Check

$7 - 3 = 4$
$3(60) = 180$
$4(45) = 180$
The distances are the same.

Answer: The woman can travel 180 miles out into the country.

Method 2

Since the woman drives out to a certain point and returns over the same road to her starting point, the distance traveled going out is the same as the distance traveled coming back.

Let d = the number of miles she can travel out into the country.

First fill in the rate and distance for each trip. Then represent the time for each trip.

	(mph) Rate	(hr.) Time	(mi.) Distance
Trip out	60	$\dfrac{d}{60}$	d
Trip back	45	$\dfrac{d}{45}$	d

Total time spent in traveling is 7 hours.

$$\frac{d}{60} + \frac{d}{45} = 7$$

Check

$$180\left(\frac{d}{60} + \frac{d}{45}\right) = 180(7)$$

$$\frac{180}{60} = 3$$

$$180\left(\frac{d}{60}\right) + 180\left(\frac{d}{45}\right) = 180(7)$$

$$\frac{180}{45} = 4$$

$$3d + 4d = 1260 \qquad 3 + 4 = 7$$

$$7d = 1260$$

$$d = 180$$

Answer: The woman can travel 180 miles out into the country.

EXERCISES

1. A destroyer traveling 40 mph and a battleship traveling 30 mph left the same naval base at the same time and sailed in opposite directions. In how many hours were the ships 350 miles apart?

2. At 7 A.M. two freight trains started from the same station. One traveled east at the rate of 75 km/h, and the other traveled west at the rate of 85 km/h. At what time were the trains 560 kilometers apart?

3. One plane departed from New York, and at the same time another plane departed from Mexico City. They flew toward each other at rates of 650 mph and 550 mph. If New York and Mexico City are 3000 miles apart, in how many hours did the planes pass each other?

4. Two trains are 680 kilometers apart. At 10 A.M. they start traveling toward each other at average rates of 75 and 95 kilometers per hour. At what time will they pass each other?

5. Saratoga and New York are 180 miles apart. One car left Saratoga for New York, averaging 50 mph. At the same time, another car left New York for Saratoga, averaging 40 mph. How far from Saratoga did the cars pass each other?

6. Two planes started at the same time from the same airport and flew in opposite directions. One flew 90 kilometers per hour faster than the other. In 5 hours, they were 4200 kilometers apart. Find the rate of each plane.

7. Two planes left at the same time from two airports which are 6600 kilometers apart and flew toward each other. In 5 hours, they

passed each other. The rate of the fast plane was twice the rate of the slow plane. Find the rate of each plane.

8. At 7:00 A.M. two cars started from the same place, one traveling east and the other traveling west. At 10:30 A.M. they were 406 miles apart. If the rate of the fast car exceeded the rate of the slow car by 6 mph, find the rate of each car.

9. A salesman made a trip of 375 miles by bus and train. He traveled 3 hours by bus and 4 hours by train. If the train averaged 15 mph more than the bus, find the rate of each.

10. A motorist made a trip of 420 miles in 8 hours. Before noon she averaged 55 mph, and after noon she averaged 50 mph. At what time did she begin her trip and when did she end it?

11. At 3 P.M. two ships started sailing toward each other, from ports which were 390 kilometers apart, at average rates of 27 and 34 kilometers per hour, respectively. At what time were the ships 85 kilometers apart?

12. A destroyer traveling 60 km/h and a battleship traveling 50 km/h leave the same base at the same time and sail in the same direction. In how many hours will they be 100 kilometers apart?

13. At 6:00 A.M. two planes started from the same airport and flew west. One plane averaged 260 mph, and the other plane averaged 300 mph. At what time were the planes 140 miles apart?

14. A ship left a port and sailed east at the rate of 30 kilometers per hour. One hour later, a second ship left the same port at the rate of 40 kilometers per hour, also traveling east. In how many hours did the second ship overtake the first ship?

15. Mrs. Stone started from home on a trip, planning to average 48 mph. How fast must her son Carl plan to travel in order to overtake her in 3 hours if Carl starts 30 minutes after his mother?

16. A cargo plane left an airport at noon and flew toward New York at the average rate of 300 mph. At 2 P.M. a jet plane left the same airport for New York and flew the same route as the cargo plane at the average rate of 500 mph. How many miles did the jet plane fly before it overtook the cargo plane?

17. Mr. Fields walked 6 hours on a trip out into the country and back. He walked out at the rate of 6 kilometers per hour and walked back at the rate of 3 kilometers per hour. How far out into the country did he go?

18. A flyer on reconnaissance duty spent $4\frac{1}{2}$ hours on a mission. He flew out from his base with the wind at the rate of 500 mph and returned to his base over the same route, flying against the wind, at the rate of 400 mph. How many miles did he fly out before he turned back?

19. A pilot plans to make a flight lasting 3 hours and 45 minutes. How far can he fly from his base at the rate of 600 kilometers per hour and return over the same route at the rate of 400 kilometers per hour?

20. Mrs. West drove her car from her home to Chicago at the rate of 40 mph and returned at the rate of 45 mph. If her time going exceeded her time returning by 30 minutes, find her time going and her time returning.

4. Coin Problems

PREPARING TO SOLVE COIN PROBLEMS

In solving problems dealing with coins of different denominations—for example, nickels, dimes, and quarters—it is often helpful to represent the values of the coins in the same unit of money. In the following examples, the unit of money is cents:

The value of 3 nickels in cents is 3(5), or 15 cents.
The value of d dimes in cents is $d(10)$, or $10d$ cents.
The value of q quarters in cents is $q(25)$, or $25q$ cents.

Keep In Mind _____

Number of coins X Value of each = Total value of the
coin in cents   coins in cents

EXERCISES

1. Represent the value of each of the following numbers of nickels in cents:

   a. 6   **b.** 10   **c.** x **d.** $3x$ **e.** $x + 3$ **f.** $2x - 1$

2. Represent the value of each of the following numbers of dimes in cents:

   a. 3   **b.** 8   **c.** y **d.** $2y$ **e.** $y + 2$ **f.** $3x - 2$

3. Represent the value of each of the following numbers of quarters in cents:

   a. 6   **b.** 13   **c.** q **d.** $5q$ **e.** $q + 5$ **f.** $2q - 3$

4. Represent the value of each of the following numbers of dollars in cents:

    a. 4   b. 15   c. D d. $4D$ e. $D+4$ f. $3D-4$

5. State the value of each of the following in cents:

    a. $4.00 b. $13.00 c. $5.50 d. $8.75 e. $19.25 f. $7.28

6. Represent the value of each of the following in cents:

    a. 8 pennies and 6 nickels   b. 8 nickels and 7 dimes
    c. 13 nickels and 7 quarters   d. 3 dollars and 5 half-dollars
    e. x pennies and $2x$ nickels   f. n nickels and $(2n-1)$ dimes
    g. q quarters and $(n+5)$ dimes h. x dollars and $(3x-2)$ dimes
    i. x nickels and $(15-x)$ dimes j. y dimes and $(20-y)$ quarters
    k. x pennies, $3x$ dimes, and $(x+3)$ quarters
    l. y nickels, $(2y+1)$ quarters, and $(2y-3)$ dollars

SOLVING COIN PROBLEMS

When solving coin problems, the facts in the problem may be organized by using verbal sentences or by using a table.

Model Problems

1. A box contains a collection of nickels, dimes, and quarters which amounts to $3.20. There are 3 times as many quarters as nickels, and 5 more dimes than nickels. How many coins of each kind are in the box?

Solution:

    Let n = the number of nickels.
   Then $3n$ = the number of quarters.
  And $n + 5$ = the number of dimes.
    Then $5n$ = the value of nickels in cents.
  And $25(3n)$ = the value of the quarters in cents.
  And $10(n + 5)$ = the value of the dimes in cents.

The total value of all the coins is 320 cents.

$5n + 25(3n) + 10(n + 5) = 320$	*Check*
$5n + 75n + 10n + 50 = 320$	
$90n + 50 = 320$	9 is 3 times 3
$90n + 50 + (-50) = 320 + (-50)$	8 is 5 more than 3
$90n = 270$	Value of 3 nickels = $ .15
$n = 3$	Value of 9 quarters = 2.25
$3n = 9$	Value of 8 dimes = .80
$n + 5 = 8$	Total value = $3.20

Answer: There are 3 nickels, 9 quarters, and 8 dimes in the box.

The following tabular arrangement may also be used. Let $n =$ the number of nickels.

Kind of coin	Number of coins	Value of each coin in cents	Total value in cents
Nickel	n	5	$5n$
Quarter	$3n$	25	$25(3n)$
Dime	$n + 5$	10	$10(n + 5)$

The total value of all the coins is 320 cents.

$$5n + 25(3n) + 10(n + 5) = 320$$

Complete the solution as before.

2. A purse contains $1.35 in nickels and dimes. In all there are 15 coins. How many coins of each kind are in the purse?

Solution:

Let $d =$ the number of dimes.
Then $15 - d =$ the number of nickels.

Kind of coin	Number of coins	Value of each coin in cents	Total value in cents
Dime	d	10	$10d$
Nickel	$15 - d$	5	$5(15 - d)$

The total value of all the coins is 135 cents.

$$10d + 5(15 - d) = 135$$
$$10d + 75 - 5d = 135$$
$$5d + 75 = 135$$
$$5d + 75 + (-75) = 135 + (-75)$$
$$5d = 60$$
$$d = 12$$
$$15 - d = 3$$

Check

$12 + 3 = 15$

Value of 12 dimes =	$1.20
Value of 3 nickels	.15
Total value	$1.35

Answer: There are 12 dimes and 3 nickels in the purse.

EXERCISES

1. Bill has 4 times as many quarters as dimes. In all he has $2.20. How many coins of each denomination does he have?
2. Paul has twice as many dimes as pennies and 3 times as many nickels as pennies. In all he has $1.80. How many coins of each denomination does he have?
3. Sam has $2.05 in quarters and dimes. He has 4 more quarters than dimes. Find the number he has of each denomination.
4. Bess has $2.80 in quarters and dimes. The number of dimes is 7 less than the number of quarters. Find the number she has of each denomination.
5. Marie has $5.05 in quarters and dimes. The number of quarters exceeds twice the number of dimes by 1. Find the number she has of each denomination.
6. Mr. Boyce deposited $170 in his bank. The number of $5 bills was 3 times the number of $10 bills, and the number of $1 bills was 30 more than the number of $5 bills. How many bills of each denomination did he deposit?
7. Mildred bought 2-cent stamps, 10-cent stamps, and 13-cent stamps for $17.50. The number of 2-cent stamps exceeded the number of 13-cent stamps by 50. The number of 10-cent stamps was 10 less than twice the number of 13-cent stamps. How many of each kind did she buy?
8. A purse containing $3.20 in quarters and dimes has, in all, 20 coins. Find the number of each kind of coin.
9. Stone bought 80 stamps for $6.40. Some were 2-cent stamps and some were 10-cent stamps. How many of each kind did he buy?
10. Mrs. Perkins cashed a 185-dollar check in her bank. She received 1-dollar bills, 5-dollar bills, and 10-dollar bills. In this order, the numbers of the three types of bills she received were three consecutive integers. How many bills of each denomination did she receive?
11. Roger has $3.10 consisting of quarters, dimes, and nickels. He has twice as many quarters as dimes and 3 more dimes than nickels. Find the number of each kind of coin.
12. Selma paid a bill of $2.70 with quarters, dimes, and pennies. She used 5 fewer quarters than dimes and 4 fewer quarters than pennies. How many coins of each kind did she use to pay the bill?
13. Is it possible to have $4.50 in dimes and quarters and have twice as many quarters as dimes?
14. Is it possible to spend $3.00 for 100 stamps consisting of 2-cent stamps and 5-cent stamps?

5. Percent and Percentage Problems

You have learned that **percent** means *per hundred* or *hundredths*. For example, 13% is $\frac{13}{100}$ or .13. Likewise, 6% is $\frac{6}{100}$ or .06; 100% is $\frac{100}{100}$ or 1; 150% = $\frac{150}{100}$ or 1.50.

Problems dealing with interest, discounts, commissions, and taxes frequently involve percents. For example, to find the amount of tax when $60 is taxed at a rate of 5%, we multiply $60 by 5%, .05 × 60, and get $3 as the result. In this case, the three quantities related are:

1. the sum of money being taxed, the **base**, which is $60
2. the rate of tax, the **rate**, which is 5% or .05
3. the amount of tax, the **percentage**, which is $3

The relation involving base, b, rate, r, and percentage, p, may be expressed as follows:

$$p = rb$$

Model Problems

1. If 25% of a number is 80, find the number.

Solution:

Method 1	*Method* 2
Let n = the number.	Let n = the number.
$p = rb \quad [p = 80,$	$p = rb \quad [p = 80,$
$\qquad\qquad r = 25\% = .25]$	$\qquad\qquad r = 25\% = \frac{25}{100} = \frac{1}{4}]$
$80 = .25n$	$80 = \frac{1}{4}n$
$\dfrac{80}{.25} = \dfrac{.25n}{.25} \quad D_{.25}$	$4(80) = 4(\frac{1}{4}n) \quad M_4$
$320 = n$	$320 = n$

Check: 25% of 320 is 80.

Answer: The number is 320.

2. Of the 560 students registered in a course, 476 passed the course. What percent of the registered students passed the course?

Solution: Let $\dfrac{x}{100}$ = the percent of the registered students who passed the course.

<table>
<tr><td align="center">Method 1</td><td align="center">Method 2</td></tr>
</table>

Method 1

$p = br$ $[p = 476, b = 560]$

$$476 = 560\left(\dfrac{x}{100}\right)$$

$47600 = 560x$ M_{100}

$\dfrac{47600}{560} = \dfrac{560x}{560}$ D_{560}

$85 = x$

$\dfrac{x}{100} = \dfrac{85}{100} = 85\%$

Method 2

$p = br$ $[p = 476, b = 560]$

$$476 = 560\left(\dfrac{x}{100}\right)$$

$476 = \dfrac{560}{100}x$

$\dfrac{100}{560}(476) = \dfrac{100}{560}\left(\dfrac{560}{100}x\right)$ $M_{\frac{100}{560}}$

$85 = x$

$\dfrac{x}{100} = \dfrac{85}{100} = 85\%$

Check: 85% of 560 is 476.

Answer: 85% of the students registered passed the course.

3. A dealer sold a radio for $39.20, which was 40% above its cost to him. Find the cost of the radio to the dealer.

Solution:

Method 1

Let x = the cost of the radio to the dealer.
Since the dealer sold the radio 40% above its cost to him, he sold it for 100% + 40%, or 140% of the original cost.

$p = br$ $[p = \$39.20, r = 140\% = 1.40]$

$39.20 = 1.40x$

$\dfrac{39.20}{1.40} = \dfrac{1.40x}{1.40}$ $D_{1.40}$

$28 = x$

Check: 40% of $28 is $11.20. $28 + $11.20 = $39.20

Answer: The dealer paid $28 for the radio.

Method 2

Let x = the cost of the radio to the dealer.
$.40x$ = the amount of the dealer's markup.

Cost of the radio to the dealer plus the markup equals the selling price.

$$x + .40x = 39.20$$
$$1.40x = 39.20$$
$$\frac{1.40x}{1.40} = \frac{39.20}{1.40} \quad D_{1.40}$$
$$x = 28$$

Answer: The dealer paid $28 for the radio.

EXERCISES

In 1–12, use the formula $p = br$ to find the indicated percentage.

1. 2% of 36
2. 29% of 92
3. 60% of 56
4. 100% of 7.5
5. 2.5% of 400
6. $4\frac{1}{2}$% of 200
7. $12\frac{1}{2}$% of 128
8. $33\frac{1}{3}$% of 72
9. $\frac{1}{4}$% of 2400
10. 150% of 18
11. 105% of 50
12. $166\frac{2}{3}$% of 99

In 13–22, use the formula $p = br$ to find the number.

13. 20 is 10% of what number?
14. 64 is 80% of what number?
15. 75% of what number is 3.6?
16. 6% of what number is 10.8?
17. 72 is 100% of what number?
18. 125% of what number is 45?
19. $37\frac{1}{2}$% of what number is 60?
20. $66\frac{2}{3}$% of what number is 54?
21. 3% of what number is 1.86?
22. $1\frac{1}{2}$% of what number is 240?

In 23–32, use the formula $p = br$ to find the rate.

23. 6 is what percent of 12?
24. 9 is what percent of 30?
25. What percent of 10 is 6?
26. What percent of 35 is 28?
27. 5 is what percent of 15?
28. What percent of 80 is 30?
29. 22 is what percent of 22?
30. 18 is what percent of 12?
31. 2 is what percent of 400?
32. 3 is what percent of 3000?

33. The price of a new car is $3450. Klein made a down payment of 15% of the price of the car when be bought it. How much was his down payment?
34. How much salt is in 30 grams of a solution of salt and water which is 10% salt?
35. In a factory, 54,650 parts were made. When these were tested, 4% were found to be defective. How many parts were good?
36. Sixty students participate in a certain activity. If this is 12% of the student body, how many students are there in the school?
37. Louise bought a coat at a "20% off" sale and saved $12. What was the original price of the coat?
38. A businessman is required to collect a 5% sales tax. One day he collected $281 in taxes. Find the total amount of sales he made that day.

39. Helen took a 2% discount on a bill. She paid the balance with a check for $76.44. What was the original amount of the bill?
40. After the price of a pound of meat was increased 10%, the new price was 99 cents. What was the price of a pound of meat before the increase?
41. It is estimated that in 10 years the population of Keysport will increase 75% and will then be 2800. Find the present population of Keysport.
42. After Sims lost 15% of his investment, he had $2550 left. How much did he invest originally?
43. A salesperson sold a vacuum cleaner for $110 and received a commission of $8.80. What was the rate of commission?
44. A man bought a car for $3600. At the end of a year, the value of the car had decreased $720. By what percent had the car decreased in value?
45. Mr. Brown's salary increased from $175 per week to $188 per week. Find the percent of increase in his salary.
46. During a sale, the price of a dress was decreased from $48 to $32. What was the percent of the decrease in price?

6. Mixture Problems

PREPARING TO SOLVE MIXTURE PROBLEMS

Many problems deal with the mixing of ingredients which have different costs. In solving these problems, it is helpful to express the total value of each ingredient in the same unit of money, such as cents. For example:

The value of 3 pounds of coffee worth 95 cents a pound is 3(95), or 285 cents.

The value of x pounds of candy worth 80 cents a pound is $x(80)$, or $80x$ cents.

The value of $(20-x)$ pounds of nuts worth $1.25 a pound is $(20-x)125$ or $125(20-x)$ cents.

Keep In Mind _____

Number of units X Price per unit = Total value of
of the same kind   all the units

EXERCISES

1. A certain kind of candy is worth 95 cents a pound. Represent the total value of:
   - a. 2 lb.
   - b. 10 lb.
   - c. x lb.
   - d. $2x$ lb.
   - e. $(x + 5)$ lb.
   - f. $(20 - x)$ lb.

2. A certain kind of nut is worth $3.50 a kilogram (kg). Represent the total value of:
   - a. 2 kg
   - b. 5 kg
   - c. x kg
   - d. $3x$ kg
   - e. $(x + 2)$ kg
   - f. $(30 - x)$ kg

3. Represent the total value of each of the following mixtures in cents:
   - a. 10 pounds of candy worth 85 cents a pound and 30 pounds of candy worth 75 cents a pound.
   - b. x kg of coffee worth $2.50 a kilogram and $(x + 2)$ kilograms of coffee worth $3.00 a kilogram.
   - c. x quarts of 75-cent oil and $(50 - x)$ quarts of 65-cent oil.
   - d. 40 kg of nuts worth $3.50 a kilogram and x kg of nuts worth $2.50 a kilogram.

SOLVING MIXTURE PROBLEMS

Model Problems ⎯⎯⎯⎯⎯⎯⎯⎯⎯⎯⎯⎯⎯⎯⎯⎯⎯⎯⎯⎯⎯⎯⎯

1. A coffee dealer wishes to mix coffee worth $1.20 per pound with coffee worth 90 cents per pound in order to produce 30 pounds of coffee that can be sold at $1.00 per pound. How many pounds of each type should the dealer use?

Solution:

Let n = the number of pounds of the $1.20 coffee.
Then $30 - n$ = the number of pounds of the 90-cent coffee.
$120n$ = the value of the $1.20 coffee in cents.
$90(30 - n)$ = the value of the 90-cent coffee in cents.
$100(30)$ = the value of the mixture in cents.

The total value of the $1.20 coffee and the 90-cent coffee equals the value of the mixture.

$$120n + 90(30 - n) = 100(30)$$
$$120n + 2700 - 90n = 3000$$
$$30n + 2700 = 3000$$
$$30n + 2700 - 2700 = 3000 - 2700$$
$$30n = 300$$
$$n = 10$$
$$30 - n = 20$$

Check:

20 + 10 = 30
Value of 20 lb. at 90 cents per lb. = $18.00
Value of 10 lb. at $1.20 per lb.   = 12.00
Total value   = $30.00
Value of 30 lb. at $1.00 per lb.   = $30.00

Answer: 20 lb. of the 90-cent coffee; 10 lb. of the $1.20 coffee

The following tabular arrangement may also be used:

Let n = the number of pounds of the $1.20 coffee.
Then $30 - n$ = the number of pounds of the 90-cent coffee.

Kind of coffee	Number of pounds	Price per pound in cents	Total value in cents
$1.20	n	120	$120n$
90-cent	$30 - n$	90	$90(30 - n)$
Mixture	30	100	$100(30)$

*The total value of the $1.20 coffee and the 90-cent coffee
equals the value of the mixture.*

$$120n + 90(30 - n) = 100(30)$$

Complete the solution as before.

2. How many kilograms of candy worth $3.60 per kilogram must be mixed with 70 kilograms of candy worth $2.40 per kilogram to produce a mixture which can be sold for $2.90 per kilogram?

Solution:

Let n = the required number of kilograms worth $3.60 per kilogram.

Kind of candy	Number of kilograms	Price per kilogram in cents	Total value in cents
$3.60	n	360	$360n$
$2.40	70	240	$70(240)$
Mixture	$n + 70$	290	$290(n + 70)$

*The total value of the $3.60 candy and the $2.40 candy
equals the value of the mixture.*

$$360n + 70(240) = 290(n + 70)$$
$$360n + 16,800 = 290n + 20,300$$
$$360n + 16,800 + (-290n) = 290n + 20,300 + (-290n)$$
$$70n + 16,800 = 20,300$$
$$70n + 16,800 + (-16,800) = 20,300 + (-16,800)$$
$$70n = 3500$$
$$n = 50$$

Check: Value of 50 kilograms at $3.60 per kilogram   = $180.00
Value of 70 kilograms at $2.40 per kilogram   = $168.00
Total value   = $348.00
Value of 120 kilograms at $2.90 per kilogram = $348.00

Answer: 50 kilograms of the candy worth $3.60 per kilogram are required.

EXERCISES

1. A grocer mixed nuts worth 90 cents a pound with nuts worth 75 cents a pound. How many pounds of each did he use to make a mixture of 30 pounds to sell at 85 cents a pound?

2. If almonds sell for $3.60 per kilogram and walnuts sell for $2.50 per kilogram, how many kilograms of each must be used to make 22 kilograms of a mixture of these nuts to sell at $3.00 per kilogram?

3. A dealer has some hard candy worth 70 cents a pound and some worth 95 cents a pound. He wishes to make a mixture of 100 pounds that will be worth 80 cents a pound. How many pounds of each kind should he use?

4. A dealer wishes to produce 300 liters of oil worth 75 cents a liter by mixing oil worth 70 cents a liter with oil worth 95 cents a liter. How many liters of each kind of oil should he use?

5. A dealer has tea worth $1.20 a pound and tea worth $1.90 a pound. How many pounds of each kind must he use to make 70 pounds that can be sold for $1.50 a pound?

6. A florist sold roses at $7.50 per dozen and carnations at $4.50 per dozen. In all, he sold 14 dozen and his total receipts were $90.00. How many dozens of each kind did he sell?

7. At a college football game, faculty members paid $6.00 each for admission and students paid $3.50 each. There were 8500 more students attending the game than faculty members. The total receipts for the game were $31,365.00.

   a. Find the number of students and the number of faculty members who attended the game.

 b. If the college has 425 faculty members, find the percentage of faculty members who attended the game.

  8. Is it possible for 150 people to pay $150 to attend a performance if adults pay $1.25 and children pay 60 cents for admission?

  9. How many pounds of nuts worth $1.40 per pound must be mixed with 12 pounds of nuts worth $1.00 per pound to produce a mixture which can be sold for $1.30 per pound?

10. How many pounds of tea worth $1.80 a pound must be mixed with 15 pounds of tea worth $1.10 a pound to produce a mixture worth $1.50 a pound?

11. How many kilograms of seed worth $2.20 per kilogram must be mixed with 75 kilograms of seed worth $3.00 per kilogram to produce a mixture worth $2.50 per kilogram?

7. Percent Mixture Problems

PREPARING TO SOLVE PERCENT MIXTURE PROBLEMS

The percent mixture problem is a type of mixture problem that involves percents. For example:

The amount of pure salt in 25 ounces of a 20% solution of salt and water is .20(25), or 5 ounces.

The amount of butterfat in x pounds of milk testing 4% butterfat is .04(x), or .04x pounds.

The amount of pure acid in $(100 - x)$ grams of a 25% solution of acid in water is .25$(100 - x)$ grams.

Keep In Mind _____

The number of units of a solution (mixture) which contains a given pure substance X the percent of the solution (mixture) which is that pure substance = the amount of that pure substance in the solution (mixture).

EXERCISES

1. A solution is 40% pure acid. Represent the number of pounds of pure acid in this solution if it weighs:

 a. 100 lb.   **b.** 60 lb.   **c.** 12 lb.   **d.** x lb.   **e.** $(x - 2)$ lb.

2. Represent the total amount of pure acid in a solution if the solution contains x grams of acid which is 50% pure acid and $.25(100 - x)$ grams of acid which is 30% pure acid.

3. A solution which is 20% pure iodine weighs 60 ounces.
   a. Find the number of ounces of pure iodine in the solution.
   b. If x ounces of pure iodine is added to this solution, represent (1) the amount of pure iodine in the resulting solution and (2) the number of ounces in the resulting solution.

4. 120 grams of a solution of salt and water contains 25% pure salt.
   a. Find the number of grams of pure salt in the solution.
   b. If x grams of water is evaporated from the solution, represent the number of grams in the resulting solution.
   c. If the resulting solution is 30% pure salt, represent in terms of x the number of grams of salt in the resulting solution.

SOLVING PERCENT MIXTURE PROBLEMS

Model Problem

How much pure acid must be added to 15 grams of an acid solution which is 40% acid in order to produce a solution which is 50% acid?

Solution:

The number of grams of pure acid in the given mixture is $.40(15) = 6$.

Let n = the number of grams of pure acid to be added.
Then $6 + n$ = the number of grams of pure acid in the new mixture.
Also $15 + n$ = the total contents of the new mixture.

The number of grams of pure acid in the new mixture is 50% of the total contents of the new mixture.

$$6 + n = .50(15 + n)$$
$$6 + n = 7.50 + .50n$$
$$600 + 100n = 750 + 50n \qquad M_{100}$$
$$600 + 100n + (-50n) = 750 + 50n + (-50n)$$
$$600 + 50n = 750$$
$$600 + 50n + (-600) = 750 + (-600)$$
$$50n = 150$$
$$n = 3$$

Check

40% of $15 = .40(15) = 6$
$6 + 3 = 9$
50% of $(15 + 3) = .50(18) = 9$

Answer: 3 grams of pure acid must be added.

The following tabular arrangement may also be used:
Let n = the number of grams of pure acid to be added.

Kind of solution	Number of grams	Part pure acid	Number of grams of pure acid
Original solution	15	.40	6
Pure acid to be added	n	1.00	n
New mixture	$15 + n$	.50	$.50(15 + n)$

The total amount of pure acid in the original solution and in the pure acid added is equal to the amount of pure acid in the new mixture.

$$6 + n = .50(15 + n)$$

Complete the solution as before.

EXERCISES

1. A chemist has one solution which is 30% pure acid and another solution which is 60% pure acid. How many grams of each solution must be used to produce 60 grams of a solution which is 50% pure acid?

2. A farmer has some cream which is 24% butterfat and some cream which is 18% butterfat. How many pounds of each must he use to produce 90 pounds of cream which is 22% butterfat?

3. How many kilograms of a solution which is 75% pure acid must be mixed with 16 kilograms of a solution which is 30% pure acid to produce a solution which is 55% pure acid?

4. How much salt must be added to 80 kilograms of a 5% salt solution to make a 24% salt solution?

5. A chemist has 40 grams of a solution of iodine and alcohol which is 15% iodine. How much pure iodine must he add to make a solution which is 20% iodine?

6. Seventy pounds of an alloy contains 6 pounds of pure silver. How many pounds of pure silver must be added to make an alloy which is 20% pure silver?

7. A solution of iodine and alcohol contains 3 grams of iodine and 21 grams of alcohol. How much pure iodine must be added to produce a solution which is 25% iodine?

8. A solution of alcohol and water which is 20% alcohol weighs 60 pounds. How much water must be added to make a solution which is 5% alcohol?

9. In a tank there are 100 kilograms of a solution of acid and water which is 20% acid. How much water must be evaporated to produce a solution which is 50% acid?

10. A solution contains 8 pounds of acid and 32 pounds of water. How many pounds of water must be evaporated to produce a solution which will be 40% acid?

11. How much water must be added to 30 grams of a solution of salt in water which contains 20% salt so that the resulting solution will be 15% salt?

8. Investment Problems

PREPARING TO SOLVE INVESTMENT PROBLEMS

A woman invested $500 at 6%. Her annual income was 6% of $500, which equals .06 ($500), or $30. In finding the annual income, we make use of the **annual interest formula** $i = pr$. In this formula, p represents the **principal**, or amount invested, $500; r represents the **annual rate of interest**, 6%; and i represents the **annual income**, $30.

Keep In Mind_____

Principal in dollars X Annual rate of income = Annual income in dollars

EXERCISES

1. Represent the annual income when the annual rate is 5% and the amount invested is:
   a. $600 b. $2500 c. $x d. $3x e. $(x + 500) f. $(5000 − x)

2. Represent the annual income when the annual rate is $4\frac{1}{2}$% and the principal invested is:
   a. $800 b. $3000 c. $x d. $8x e. $(2x + 400) f. $(4000 − x)

3. Represent the total annual income from each of the following:
   a. $4000 invested at 5% and $6500 invested at 9%
   b. $3500 invested at $5\frac{1}{2}$% and $4200 invested at $7\frac{1}{2}$%
   c. $8000 invested at 6% and $x invested at 8%

    d. $x invested at 5% and $4x invested at 6%
    e. $x invested at 6% and $(x + 2000)$ invested at 7%
    f. $x invested at 5% and $(8000 - x)$ invested at 10%

4. Mr. Walker invested $x at 5%. He also invested $500 more than this sum at 6%.

    a. Represent the amount he invested at 6%.
    b. Represent the annual income from the 5% investment.
    c. Represent the annual income from the 6% investment.
    d. Represent the total annual income from both investments.
    e. Write an open sentence indicating that Mr. Walker's total annual income was $195.

5. Mr. Collins invested a portion of $9000 at 5% and the remainder at 10%. Let x represent the amount he invested at 5%.

    a. Represent the amount he invested at 10%.
    b. Represent the annual income from the 5% investment.
    c. Represent the annual income from the 10% investment.
    d. Write an open sentence indicating that the annual incomes from both investments were the same.

SOLVING INVESTMENT PROBLEMS

Model Problems

1. Mrs. Parsons invested a sum of money at 6% and a second sum, $500 more than the first, at 8%. Her total annual income was $180. How much did she invest at each rate?

Solution:

       Let p = the number of dollars invested at 6%.
   Then $p + 500$ = the number of dollars invested at 8%.
         $.06p$ = the annual income from the 6% investment.
 $.08(p + 500)$ = the annual income from the 8% investment.

The total annual income was $180.

$$.06p + .08(p + 500) = 180$$
$$.06p + .08p + 40 = 180$$
$$.14p + 40 = 180$$
$$.14p + 40 - 40 = 180 - 40$$
$$.14p = 140$$
$$p = 1000$$
$$p + 500 = 1500$$

Check

$1000 + $500 = $1500
$.06($1000) = $60
$.08($1500) = \underline{$120}$
Total   = $180

Answer: $1000 was invested at 6%; $1500 was invested at 8%.

The following tabular arrangement may also be used:

Let p = the number of dollars invested at 6%.

Then $p + 500$ = the number of dollars invested at 8%.

Investment	Principal in dollars	Annual rate of income	Annual income in dollars
6% investment	p	.06	$.06p$
8% investment	$p + 500$	.08	$.08(p + 500)$

The total annual income was $180.

$$.06p + .08(p + 500) = 180$$

Complete the solution as before.

2. Mr. Harvey invested a part of $1000 at 5% and the remainder at 6%. The annual income from the 5% investment exceeded the annual income from the 6% investment by $39. Find the amount he invested at each rate.

Solution:

Let p = the amount invested at 5%.

Then $1000 - p$ = the amount invested at 6%.

Investment	Principal in dollars	Annual rate of income	Annual income in dollars
5% investment	p	.05	$.05p$
6% investment	$1000 - p$	.06	$.06(1000 - p)$

*The annual income from the 5% investment exceeded
the annual income from the 6% investment by $39.*

$$.05p = .06(1000 - p) + 39$$
$$.05p = 60 - .06p + 39$$
$$.05p = 99 - .06p$$
$$.05p + .06p = 99 - .06p + .06p$$
$$.11p = 99$$
$$p = 900$$
$$1000 - p = 100$$

Check

$900 + $100 = $1000

$.05($900) = $45

$.06($100) = $6

$45 exceeds $6 by $39.

Answer: $900 was invested at 5%; $100 was invested at 6%.

EXERCISES

1. Mr. Sawyer invested a sum of money at 8%. He invested twice as much at 5%. The total annual income from these investments was $180. Find the amount he invested at each rate.
2. Mr. Traynor invested a sum of money at 5%. He invested a second sum, $250 more than the first sum, at 6%. If the total annual income from these investments was $59, how much did he invest at each rate?
3. Mr. Wayne invested a sum of money at 11%. He invested a second sum, $150 less than the first sum, at 6%. The total annual income was $76. Find the amount invested at each rate.
4. Mr. Fox invested a sum of money at 6%. He invested a second sum, $2000 less than this sum, at 5%. He invested a third sum, which was $3000 less than the first sum, at $7\frac{1}{2}$%. His total annual income was $304. Find the amount he invested at each rate.
5. Mrs. Ryan invested a sum of money at 6%. She invested a second sum, which exceeded twice the first sum by $1000, at 10%. Her total annual income was $620. Find the amount she invested at each rate.
6. Mr. Joyce invested $25,000, part at 4% and the remainder at 9%. The total income he received at the end of the year was $1950. How much did he invest at each rate?
7. Mr. Carlson has invested $7500 in two parts, one part at 6% and the other at 10%. Find the amount invested at each rate if the total yearly income is $590.
8. Mr. Daniels had a sum of money to invest. He invested $\frac{1}{2}$ of the sum at 5%, $\frac{1}{3}$ of the sum at 6%, and the remainder at 8%. His total annual income was $350. What was the total sum that Daniels invested?
9. Mrs. Mack invested a sum of money at 6%. She invested $600 less than this sum at 10%. If the annual incomes from both investments were the same, find the amount invested at each rate.
10. Mr. Doyle invested $7500 in two business enterprises. At the end of a year, he made a profit of $130. This resulted from a 5% profit on his investment in one enterprise and a 2% loss on his investment in the other enterprise. Find the amount he invested in each enterprise.
11. Mr. Lamb has invested $18,000 in two parts. One part is invested at 8% and the other at 10%. The annual income from the 10% investment is $360 more than the annual income from the 8% investment. Find the amount invested at each rate.
12. Mrs. Jewel bought two bonds for $15,000. One bond pays 6% interest and the other pays 8% interest. The annual interest from

the 6% bond is $500 less than the annual interest from the 8% bond. Find the cost of each bond.

13. Mr. Crawford has invested $6000 at 5%. How much additional money must he invest at 8% so that his total annual income will be 6% of his total investment?

14. Mr. Walker has $2000 invested at 7% and $5000 invested at 4%. How much additional money must he invest at 10% to make his total annual income 6% of his total investment?

9. Age Problems

PREPARING TO SOLVE AGE PROBLEMS

If Ken is 20 years old now, 5 years ago Ken was $20 - 5$, or 15 years old; 5 years from now Ken will be $20 + 5$, or 25 years old.

Keep In Mind

1. To represent a past age, subtract from the present age.

2. To represent a future age, add to the present age.

EXERCISES

1. Chuck is x years old now. Represent his age 10 years from now.
2. Marion is y years old now. Represent her age 8 years ago.
3. Marilyn is $5y$ years old now. Represent her age 4 years ago.
4. Sue is $(2x - 3)$ years old now. Represent her age 8 years from now.
5. Robert is $(30 - x)$ years old now. Represent his age 7 years ago.
6. A man is x years old now. Represent his age y years from now.
7. A woman is x years old now. Represent her age y years ago.
8. Six years ago, Paul's age was $2x$. Represent his age 3 years from now.
9. Two years from now, Martin's age will be $3x + 5$. Represent his age 4 years ago.
10. Ted is 7 years younger than his brother, whose age is $5x + 1$. Represent Ted's age 3 years from now.
11. Gloria is three times as old as Marie, whose age is x.
    a. Represent each girl's age 6 years from now.
    b. Represent each girl's age 3 years ago.

SOLVING AGE PROBLEMS

Model Problems _____

1. Bill is 3 times as old as his nephew Peter. Six years from now, Bill will be twice as old as Peter will be then. Find the present age of both Bill and Peter.

Solution:

      Let x = Peter's present age.
    Then $3x$ = Bill's present age.
  Then $x + 6$ = Peter's age 6 years from now.
Then $3x + 6$ = Bill's age 6 years from now.

Six years from now, Bill will be twice as old as Peter will be then.

$$3x + 6 = 2(x + 6)$$
$$3x + 6 = 2x + 12$$

Check

$$3x + 6 + (-6) = 2x + 12 + (-6)$$
$$3x = 2x + 6$$

$$18 = 3(6)$$
$$6 + 6 = 12$$
$$3x + (-2x) = 2x + 6 + (-2x)$$
$$18 + 6 = 24$$
$$x = 6$$
$$24 = 2(12)$$
$$3x = 18$$

Answer: Peter's age is 6 years. Bill's age is 18 years.

The following tabular arrangement may also be used:

Let x = Peter's present age.
Then $3x$ = Bill's present age.

Person	Present age in years	Future age, 6 years from now
Peter	x	$x + 6$
Bill	$3x$	$3x + 6$

Six years from now, Bill will be twice as old as Peter will be then.

$$3x + 6 = 2(x + 6)$$

Complete the solution as before.

2. Helen is now 20 years old and Arlene is 10 years old. How many years ago was Helen three times as old as Arlene was then?

Solution:

Let $x =$ the required number of years ago.

Person	Present age in years	Past age, x years ago
Helen	20	$20 - x$
Arlene	10	$10 - x$

Helen was three times as old as Arlene was then.

$$20 - x = 3(10 - x)$$
$$20 - x = 30 - 3x$$
$$20 - x + (+3x) = 30 - 3x + (+3x)$$
$$20 + 2x = 30$$
$$20 + 2x + (-20) = 30 + (-20)$$
$$2x = 10$$
$$x = 5$$

Check

$20 - 5 = 15$
$10 - 5 = 5$
$15 = 3(5)$

Answer: 5 years ago

EXERCISES

1. A man is now 6 times as old as his son. In 6 years, the father will be three times as old as the son will be then. Find their present ages.
2. Marie is $\frac{1}{9}$ as old as her mother. In 3 years, she will be $\frac{1}{5}$ as old as her mother will be then. Find their present ages.
3. A father is now 24 years older than his son. In 8 years, the father will be twice as old as his son will be then. Find their present ages.
4. Marion is twice as old as Judy. Three years ago, Marion was 3 times as old as Judy was then. Find the age of each girl now.
5. A father is 3 times as old as his son. Fifteen years ago, the father was 9 times as old as his son was then. Find their present ages.
6. Robert is $\frac{1}{2}$ as old as his father. Twelve years ago, Robert was $\frac{1}{3}$ as old as his father was then. Find their present ages.
7. Josephine is 22 years old and Ruth is 10 years old. In how many years will Josephine be twice as old as Ruth will be then?

8. A man is 40 years old and his son is 8 years old. In how many years will the man be 3 times as old as his son will be then?

9. Mr. Atkins is 33 years old and Mr. Speyer is 27 years old. How many years ago was Mr. Atkins $1\frac{1}{2}$ times as old as Mr. Speyer was then?

10. The sum of a man's age and his daughter's age is 50 years. Eight years from now, the man will be twice as old as his daughter will be then. Find the present age of each.

11. Mrs. Sanford is 3 times as old as Mrs. Fox. Eight years from now, Mrs. Sanford's age will exceed twice Mrs. Fox's age at that time by 14 years. Find the present age of each.

12. Mrs. Watson was 25 years old when her daughter Rose was born. Now Mrs. Watson's age exceeds 4 times Rose's age by 10 years. Find their ages now.

13. The sum of Wilbur's age and Fred's age is 20 years. Wilbur's age 1 year from now will be 9 times Fred's age 1 year ago. Find the present age of each.

14. Mark is 10 years younger than Larry. Larry's age 8 years from now will exceed twice Mark's age 3 years ago by 4 years. How old is each now?

10. Perimeter Problems

PREPARING TO SOLVE PERIMETER PROBLEMS

Keep In Mind

> The perimeter of a geometric plane figure is the sum of the measures of all its sides.

EXERCISES

1. Represent the perimeter of each of the following figures:

(a)   (b)   (c)   (d)

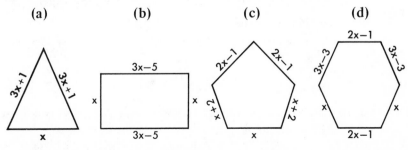

2. Represent the length and the perimeter of a rectangle whose width is represented by x and whose length:
   a. is twice its width
   b. is 4 more than its width
   c. is 5 less than twice its width
   d. is 3 more than twice its width
   e. is 4 times its width diminished by 1
   f. exceeds 3 times its width by 6

SOLVING PERIMETER PROBLEMS

In solving problems dealing with the perimeters of geometric plane figures, it is helpful to draw the figures.

Model Problem

The perimeter of a rectangular garden is 40 meters. The length is 2 meters more than 5 times the width. Find the dimensions of the rectangle.

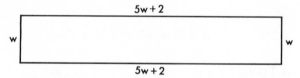

Solution:

Let w = the width of the rectangle.
Then $5w + 2$ = the length of the rectangle.

The sum of the measures of all its sides is 40.

$w + 5w + 2 + w + 5w + 2 = 40$
$12w + 4 = 40$
$12w + 4 - 4 = 40 - 4$ *Check*
$12w = 36$ $3 + 17 + 3 + 17 = 40$
$w = 3$ $17 \overset{?}{=} 5(3) + 2$
$5w + 2 = 17$ $17 = 17$ (true)

Answer: The width is 3 meters; the length is 17 meters.

EXERCISES

1. In a triangle whose perimeter is 144 centimeters, two sides are of equal length. If the length of each of these sides is 4 times the length of the third side, find the length of each side of the triangle.

2. The length of the second side of a triangle is 3 times the length of the first side. The length of the third side of the triangle is $2\frac{1}{2}$ times the length of the first side. If the perimeter of the triangle is 65 feet, find the length of each side.

3. The length of a rectangle is 3 times its width. The perimeter of the rectangle is 24 meters. Find the dimensions of the rectangle.

4. The length of a rectangle is $2\frac{1}{2}$ times its width. The perimeter of the rectangle is 84 centimeters. Find the dimensions of the rectangle.

5. The length of a rectangle is 25% more than its width. The perimeter is 72 inches. Find the length and the width.

6. The lengths of the sides of a triangle are represented by three consecutive even integers. If the perimeter of the triangle is 30 meters, find the lengths of its sides.

7. The perimeter of a triangle is 40 centimeters. The length of the second side exceeds twice the length of the first side by 4 centimeters, and the length of the third side is 8 centimeters less than the length of the second side. Find the length of each side of the triangle.

8. The length of a rectangle is 5 centimeters more than its width. The perimeter is 66 centimeters. Find the dimensions of the rectangle.

9. The length of a rectangle exceeds the width by 5 inches. The perimeter of the rectangle is 168 inches. Find the dimensions of the rectangle.

10. The perimeter of a rectangular parking lot is 146 meters. Find its dimensions if the length is 7 meters less than 4 times the width.

11. The perimeter of a rectangular tennis court is 228 feet. If the length of the court exceeds twice its width by 6 feet, find its dimensions.

12. The length of a rectangle is twice the width. If the length is increased by 4 inches and the width is decreased by 1 inch, a new rectangle is formed whose perimeter is 198 inches. Find the dimensions of the original rectangle.

13. The length of a rectangle exceeds 3 times its width by 1 inch. If the length of the rectangle is decreased by 3 inches and the width is doubled, a new rectangle is formed whose perimeter is 46 inches. Find the dimensions of the original rectangle.

14. If the length of one side of a square is increased by 4 centimeters and the length of an adjacent side is multiplied by 4, the perimeter of the resulting rectangle is 3 times the perimeter of the square. Find the length of a side of the original square.

15. The length of a rectangle exceeds its width by 4 feet. If the width is doubled and the length is reduced by 2 feet, a new rectangle is formed whose perimeter is 8 feet more than the perimeter of the original rectangle. Find the dimensions of the original rectangle.

16. The length of each side of a hexagon (a polygon that has six sides) is 4 centimeters less than the length of a side of a square. The perimeter of the hexagon is equal to the perimeter of the square. Find the length of a side of the hexagon and the length of a side of the square.

17. The length of each side of a pentagon (a polygon having five sides) is 80% of the length of each side of a square. What percent of the perimeter of the pentagon is the perimeter of the square?

11. Area Problems

PREPARING TO SOLVE AREA PROBLEMS

Keep In Mind _____

Area of a rectangle = Length X Width

Area of a triangle = $\frac{1}{2}$ X (measure of the base) X (measure of the height)

EXERCISES

1. Represent the area of a rectangle whose length and width are represented by:
   a. $l = 7, w = x$ b. $l = 5, w = x + 2$ c. $l = 10, w = 2x - 3$
   d. $l = x, w = x - 1$ e. $l = x + 5, w = x$ f. $l = x + 3, w = x + 2$

2. Represent the area of a triangle the measures of whose base and height are represented by:
   a. $b = 8, h = y$ b. $b = y - 2, h = 3$ c. $b = 3y + 4, h = 11$
   d. $b = y, h = y - 2$ e. $b = y + 4, h = 2y$ f. $b = y + 6, h = 9y - 7$

3. The length of a rectangle is 10 more than its width, x. Represent the area of the rectangle.

4. The measure of the base of a triangle is 8 less than twice the measure of its height, x. Represent the area of the triangle.

5. The length of a rectangle exceeds 3 times its width, x, by 2. Represent the area of the rectangle.

6. The measure of the base of a triangle exceeds half the measure of the height, x, by 11. Represent the area of the triangle.

7. The length of a rectangle is 2 centimeters more than its width, x. If the length of the rectangle is increased by 6 centimeters and the width is decreased by 3 centimeters, a new rectangle is formed.
   a. Represent the dimensions of the original rectangle.

b. Represent the dimensions of the new rectangle.
c. Represent the area of the original rectangle.
d. Represent the area of the new rectangle.
e. Write an open sentence indicating that the areas of the new and original rectangles are equal.
f. Write an open sentence indicating that the area of the new rectangle is 6 square centimeters more than the area of the original rectangle.

SOLVING AREA PROBLEMS

In solving problems dealing with areas of geometric figures, it is helpful to draw the figures.

Model Problems

1. The length of a rectangle exceeds its width by 7 centimeters. If the length of the rectangle is decreased by 2 centimeters and the width is increased by 3 centimeters, a new rectangle is formed whose area is 20 square centimeters more than the area of the original rectangle. Find the dimensions of the original rectangle.

Solution: Let w = the width of the original rectangle.
Then $w + 7$ = the length of the original rectangle.

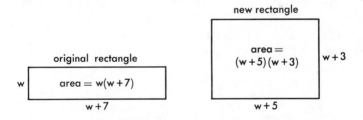

Figure	Length in centimeters	Width in centimeters	Area in square centimeters
Original rectangle	$w + 7$	w	$w(w + 7)$
New rectangle	$w + 5$	$w + 3$	$(w + 5)(w + 3)$

The area of the new rectangle is 20 square centimeters more than the area of the old rectangle.

$$(w + 5)(w + 3) = w(w + 7) + 20$$
$$w^2 + 8w + 15 = w^2 + 7w + 20$$
$$w^2 + 8w + 15 + (-w^2) + (-7w) = w^2 + 7w + 20 + (-w^2) + (-7w)$$
$$w + 15 = 20$$
$$w + 15 + (-15) = 20 + (-15)$$
$$w = 5$$
$$w + 7 = 12$$

Check: In the old rectangle, $l = 12$, $w = 5$, and area $= 12(5) = 60$.
In the new rectangle, $l = 10$, $w = 8$, and area $= 10(8) = 80$.
80 is 20 more than 60.

Answer: The length of the rectangle is 12 centimeters; the width is 5
centimeters.

2. In a triangle the base and the height (altitude) have equal measures. The
measure of the base of a second triangle exceeds the measure of the base
of the first triangle by 12 feet. The measure of the height of the second
triangle is 4 feet less than the measure of the height of the first triangle. If
the two triangles are equal in area, find the measures of the base and the
height of each triangle.

Solution:

Let $b =$ the measure of the base of the first triangle.
Then $b =$ the measure of the height of the first triangle.

First Triangle   *Second Triangle*

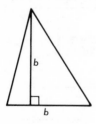   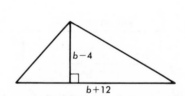

Area $= \frac{1}{2}b \cdot b$ Area $= \frac{1}{2}(b + 12)(b - 4)$

Figure	Base in feet	Height in feet	Area in square feet
First triangle	b	b	$\frac{1}{2}b \cdot b$
Second triangle	$b + 12$	$b - 4$	$\frac{1}{2}(b + 12)(b - 4)$

The areas of the two triangles are equal.

$$\tfrac{1}{2}b \cdot b = \tfrac{1}{2}(b + 12)(b - 4)$$
$$2 \cdot \tfrac{1}{2}b \cdot b = 2 \cdot \tfrac{1}{2}(b + 12)(b - 4)$$
$$b \cdot b = (b + 12)(b - 4)$$
$$b^2 = b^2 + 8b - 48$$
$$b^2 - b^2 = b^2 - b^2 + 8b - 48$$
$$0 = 8b - 48$$
$$8b = 48$$
$$b = 6$$
$$b + 12 = 18$$
$$b - 4 = 2$$

Check: In the first triangle, $b = 6$ and $h = 6$. Area $= \tfrac{1}{2}(6)(6) = 18$
In the second triangle, $b = 18$ and $h = 2$. Area $= \tfrac{1}{2}(18)(2) = 18$
The areas of the two triangles are equal.

Answer: The base and the height of the first triangle measure 6 feet each.
The base and the height of the second triangle measure, respectively,
18 feet and 2 feet.

EXERCISES

1. The length of a rectangle is 8 centimeters more than its width. If the length is increased by 4 centimeters and the width is decreased by 1 centimeter, the area is unchanged. Find the dimensions of the rectangle.
2. The length of a rectangle exceeds 3 times the width by 1 foot. If the length is decreased by 5 feet and the width is increased by 2 feet, the area is unchanged. Find the dimensions of the rectangle.
3. If the length of one side of a square is increased by 3 inches and the length of the adjacent side is decreased by 2 inches, a rectangle is formed whose area is equal to the area of the square. Find the length of a side of the square.
4. If the length of one side of a square is increased by 3 meters and the length of the adjacent side is decreased by 4 meters, a rectangle is formed whose area is 19 square meters less than the area of the square. Find the length of a side of the original square.
5. The width of a rectangle is 2 inches less than its length. If the width is increased by 4 inches and the length is decreased by 2 inches, the area is increased by 8 square inches. Find the measurements of the rectangle.
6. The length of a rectangle is 3 meters more than its width. The length of a side of a square is equal to the length of the rectangle.

The area of the square exceeds the area of the rectangle by 24 square meters. Find the dimensions of the rectangle.

7. The base of a triangle measures 5 feet less than twice the measure of its altitude. If the measure of the base is increased by 9 feet and the measure of the altitude is increased by 12 feet, the area will be increased by 156 square feet. Find the measures of the base and the altitude of the triangle.

8. The measure of the base of one triangle exceeds the measure of the height by 15 feet. The measure of the base of a second triangle is 46 feet longer than the measure of the base of the first triangle. The height of the second triangle measures 67 feet less than the base of the second triangle. If the area of the first triangle is 3 square feet more than the area of the second triangle, find the measures of the base and the height of each triangle.

9. The area of a triangle is 50% of the area of a rectangle. The length of the rectangle is 18 meters more than the measure of the altitude of the triangle. The altitude of the triangle measures 14 meters more than the base of the triangle. The base of the triangle measures 6 meters more than the width of the rectangle. Find the measures of the length and the width of the rectangle.

12. Lever Problems

A *lever* is a bar which can rotate about a fixed point called the *fulcrum*. A seesaw is an example of a lever.

Let a weight w_1 be placed on one arm of the lever at a distance d_1 from the fulcrum; let a weight w_2 be placed on the other arm of the lever at a distance d_2 from the fulcrum. In physics, it is shown that when a lever is in balance, the following relationship, called the *law of the lever*, is true:

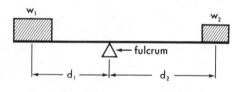

$$w_1 \times d_1 = w_2 \times d_2$$

Model Problems

1. Sid, who weighs 75 kilograms, sits 2 meters from the fulcrum of a seesaw. Marie just balances him when she is sitting 3 meters from the fulcrum. Find Marie's weight.

Solution:

Let x = Marie's weight in kilograms.

$w_1 \times d_1 = w_2 \times d_2$ [the law of the lever]

$w_1 = 75, d_1 = 2, w_2 = x, d_2 = 3$

$w_1 \times d_1 = w_2 \times d_2$

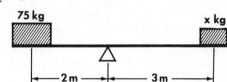

$(75)(2) = (x)(3)$

$150 = 3x$

$50 = x$

Check: Does $75 \times 2 = 50 \times 3$? Yes.

Answer: Marie weighs 50 kilograms.

2. A plank 14 feet long is to be used as a seesaw by Harry and Ted. Harry weighs 120 pounds and Ted weighs 90 pounds. If the boys are to balance each other, how far from the fulcrum must each sit?

Solution:

Let x = Harry's distance from the fulcrum.

Then $14 - x$ = Ted's distance from the fulcrum.

$w_1 \times d_1 = w_2 \times d_2$ [the law of the lever]

$w_1 = 120, d_1 = x, w_2 = 90, d_2 = 14 - x$

$w_1 \times d_1 = w_2 \times d_2$

$120x = 90(14 - x)$

$120x = 1260 - 90x$

$120x + 90x = 1260$ A_{90x}

$210x = 1260$

$x = 6$

$14 - x = 8$

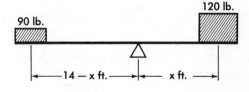

Check: Does $120 \times 6 = 90 \times 8$? Yes.

Answer: Harry sits 6 feet from the fulcrum; Ted sits 8 feet from the fulcrum.

EXERCISES

1. Sue, who weighs 148 pounds, sits 6 feet from the fulcrum of a seesaw and balances Lillian, who is sitting 8 feet from the fulcrum. Find Lillian's weight.

2. Robert weighs 90 kilograms; Gene weighs 60 kilograms. How far from the fulcrum of a seesaw must Robert sit to balance Gene, who is sitting 3 meters from the fulcrum?

3. The figure shows how a crowbar 2 meters long is used to lift a rock which weighs 120 kilograms. The fulcrum is placed 0.5 meters from the rock. What weight must be applied to the upper end of the crowbar to lift the rock?

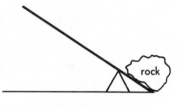

4. Marvin can exert a force of 180 pounds. How heavy a rock can he lift if he uses a crowbar which is 5 feet long and places the fulcrum so that it is 6 inches from the rock?

5. Fred, who weighs 100 pounds, and Jack, who weighs 140 pounds, use a 12-foot plank as a seesaw. Where should the fulcrum be placed if the boys are to balance each other?

6. Bill wished to carry two bundles, one weighing 60 pounds and the other weighing 40 pounds. He put one of them at each end of a bar 5 feet long and placed the bar on his shoulder. If he balanced the weights, where did he place the fulcrum (his shoulder)?

7. Ronald, who can exert a force of 100 kilograms, wishes to raise an object which weighs 300 kilograms using a 2-meter bar as a fulcrum. Where should he place the fulcrum?

13. Miscellaneous Problems

In solving the problems in this group, use the procedure described on pages 165–166.

Model Problem

Mr. Podell left an estate of $90,000 to his wife, son, and daughter. The wife received $10,000 less than 6 times the son's share. The daughter received $20,000 more than the son's share. How much did each receive?

How to Proceed	Solution
1. Represent one unknown number by a variable and all the other described numbers in terms of the same variable.	Let x = the son's share. Then $6x - 10,000$ = the wife's share. Then $x + 20,000$ = the daughter's share. *The total of all three shares is $90,000.*

2. Write an open sentence which symbolizes the relationships stated in the problem.

$$x + 6x - 10,000 + x + 20,000 = 90,000$$

3. Solve the open sentence.

$$8x + 10,000 = 90,000$$
$$8x = 80,000$$
$$x = 10,000$$
$$6x - 10,000 = 50,000$$
$$x + 20,000 = 30,000$$

4. Check the answers in the original problem.

Son received $10,000
Wife received
  6($10,000) − $10,000 . . . . . . $50,000
Daughter received
  $10,000 + $20,000 . . . . $30,000
Total estate $90,000

Answer: The son received $10,000; the daughter received $30,000; the wife received $50,000.

EXERCISES

1. In an algebra class of 36 students, there are 8 fewer women than men. How many men and how many women are in the class?
2. Four sections of a city salvaged 214 tons of tin cans. Section B collected 3 times as many tons as section A; section C collected 2 tons less than 5 times as many tons as section A; and section D collected 7 tons more than twice as many tons as section A. Find the number of tons collected in each section.
3. John gathered 3 times as many kilograms of walnuts as James. Tom gathered 5 kilograms more than James. In all they gathered 15 kilograms. Find the number of kilograms gathered by each.
4. Mrs. James and Mrs. Frank bought the same number of $25 E bonds over a period of years. Mrs. James still has all the bonds she bought. Mrs. Frank has kept $\frac{2}{3}$ of the number of bonds she bought. Together they now have 75 bonds. How many bonds did each woman purchase?
5. The distance between two villages, L and M, is 8 kilometers less than the distance from M to a third village, S. One-half the distance between M and S is 6 kilometers less than the distance between L and M. Find the number of kilometers from L to M.
6. Mrs. Jones bought 36 meters of material that she used to make curtains. She used $\frac{3}{4}$ as much in the dining room as in the living room

and $\frac{1}{2}$ as much in the kitchen as in the living room. How many meters did she use in each room?

7. Mr. Dwyer bought a house on which he made improvements. The cost of the house and the cost of the improvements amounted to $46,200. The house cost $1200 more than 6 times the cost of the interior improvements. The exterior improvements cost half as much as the interior improvements. Find the cost of the house, the cost of the interior improvements, and the cost of the exterior improvements.

8. In basketball, a foul basket counts 1 point and a field basket counts 2 points. A team scored 109 points in a game, making 26 more field baskets than foul baskets. How many baskets of each kind did the team make?

9. At a sale, the price of a fur coat was reduced 20%. Mrs. Pearson bought the coat for $360. What was the original price of the coat?

10. Mr. Slater, a jeweler, bought a ring for $150. For how much must he sell it so that his margin will be 40% of the selling price?

11. A dealer bought a coat for $37.50. For how much must he sell it so that the margin will be 25% of the selling price?

12. Mr. Calvin sold a lot for $2400. If his profit was 50% of the cost of the lot, find the cost of the lot. (Assume there were no expenses other than the cost of the lot.)

14. Solving Verbal Problems by Using Inequalities

Model Problems

1. Hank is 5 years older than his brother Bob. The sum of their ages is less than 53 years. Find, in years, the greatest possible age of each brother.

Solution:

Let x = Bob's age.
Then $x + 5$ = Hank's age.

The sum of the two ages is less than 53 years.

$$x + x + 5 < 53$$
$$2x + 5 < 53$$
$$2x < 48$$
$$x < 24$$
$$x + 5 < 29$$

Since Bob's age must be less than 24 years, his greatest possible age, in years, is 23 years. Since Hank's age must be less than 29 years, his greatest possible age, in years, is 28 years.

Answer: Bob's greatest possible age is 23 years.
         Hank's greatest possible age is 28 years.

2. In a college, the number of women is 50 more than twice the number of men. If the college has at most 650 students, find the greatest possible number of men and the greatest possible number of women in the college.

   Solution: If the college has at most 650 students, then the sum of the number of men and the number of women is either 650 or less than 650.

   Let x = the number of men.
   Then $2x + 50$ = the number of women.

   The number of men plus the number of women is 650 or less than 650.

$$x + 2x + 50 \leq 650$$
$$3x + 50 \leq 650$$
$$3x \leq 600$$
$$x \leq 200 \quad \text{(There are at most 200 men.)}$$
$$2x + 50 \leq 450 \quad \text{(There are at most 450 women.)}$$

   Answer: There are at most 200 men and at most 450 women in the college. (The check is left to the reader.)

3. A purse contains twice as many nickels as quarters. The value of all the coins is at least $7.00; find the smallest possible number of coins in the purse.

   Solution: If the value of all the coins is at least $7.00, then the value of the nickels plus the value of the quarters is either 700 cents or more than 700 cents.

   Let x = the number of quarters.
   Then $2x$ = the number of nickels.
   Then $25x$ = the value of the quarters in cents.
   Then $10x$ = the value of the nickels in cents.

   The value of the nickels plus the value of the quarters is 700 cents or more than 700 cents.

$$10x + 25x \geq 700$$
$$35x \geq 700$$
$$x \geq 20 \quad \text{(There are at least 20 quarters.)}$$
$$2x \geq 40 \quad \text{(There are at least 40 nickels.)}$$

   Answer: There are at least 60 coins in the purse. (The check is left to the reader.)

EXERCISES

1. 6 more than 2 times a certain number is less than the number increased by 20. Find the numbers that satisfy this condition.
2. If 19 more than a number is divided by 4, the result is greater than the original number decreased by 2. Find the numbers that satisfy this condition.
3. Carol weighs 3 times as much as Sue. The sum of their weights is less than 80 kilograms. Find, in kilograms, the greatest possible weight of each girl.
4. Clara's age is 10 years less than 4 times Muriel's age. If the sum of their ages is greater than 25 years, find, in years, the least possible age of each.
5. Mr. Burke had a sum of money in a bank. After he deposited an additional sum of $100, he had at least $550 in the bank. At least how much money did Mr. Burke have in the bank originally?
6. A club agreed to buy at least 250 tickets for a theater party. If it agreed to buy 80 fewer orchestra tickets than balcony tickets, what was the least number of balcony tickets it could buy?
7. Mrs. Scott decided to spend no more than $120 for a coat and a dress. If the price of the coat was $20 more than 3 times the price of the dress, find the highest possible price of the dress.
8. The number of nickels in a bank is 1 less than twice the number of dimes. If the total value of the coins in the bank is at least $4.35, find the smallest possible number of coins in the bank.
9. Bill received grades of 87, 92, 88, and 86 on four mathematics tests. Find the least grade that he must receive on a fifth test in order to have an average of at least 90 on the five tests.
10. The length of a rectangle is 10 centimeters less than 3 times its width. If the perimeter of the rectangle is at most 1.8 meters, find the maximum length of the rectangle.
11. The cashier in a movie box office sold 200 more adult admission tickets at $2.00 each than children's admission tickets at $.75 each. What is the minimum number of tickets in each price group that the cashier had to sell for the total receipts to be at least $620?
12. Mr. Drake wishes to save at least $1500 in 12 months. If he saved $300 during the first 4 months, what is the minimum average amount that he must save in each of the remaining 8 months?
13. Two consecutive even integers are such that their sum is more than 98 decreased by twice the larger. Find the smallest possible values for the integers.
14. Three consecutive integers are such that the sum of the two smaller integers is less than 32 decreased by half of the largest integer. Find the largest possible values for the integers.

Chapter 9

Special Products and Factoring

1. Understanding the Meaning of Factoring

When two integers are multiplied, the result is called their *product*. The integers being multiplied are called the *factors* of the product. Since $3 \times 5 = 15$, then 3 and 5 are factors of the product 15. Since $3 \times 5 = 15$, then $15 \div 3 = 5$ and $15 \div 5 = 3$.

This illustrates that over the set of integers:

1. A factor of an integer is an exact divisor of the integer. In general, if an integer f is a factor of an integer n, then $n \div f$ represents an integer.
2. When the product of two integers is divided by one of its factors, the quotient is the other factor.

Factoring a number is the process of finding those numbers whose product is the given number. When we factor an integer, we will deal with integral factors only. For example, although $\frac{1}{3} \times 18 = 6$, we will not say that $\frac{1}{3}$ is a factor of 6.

If an integer greater than 1 has no factors other than itself and 1, it is called a *prime number*. Thus, the members of the set $\{2, 3, 5, 7, 11, 13, 17, \ldots\}$ are prime numbers.

Every integer greater than 1 is either a prime number or can be expressed as a product of prime factors. Although the factors may be written in any order, there

$$21 = 3 \times 7$$
$$20 = 2 \cdot 2 \cdot 5 \text{ or } 2^2 \cdot 5$$

is one and only one combination of prime factors whose product is a given integer. Study the examples at the right. Note that a prime factor may appear in the product more than once.

$180 = 2 \cdot 90$
$180 = 2 \cdot 2 \cdot 45$
$180 = 2 \cdot 2 \cdot 3 \cdot 15$
$180 = 2 \cdot 2 \cdot 3 \cdot 3 \cdot 5$ or
$180 = 2^2 \cdot 3^2 \cdot 5$

To express an integer, for example 180, as a product of primes, we test in order the primes 2, 3, 5, and so on, until all factors are prime numbers. The smallest prime factor of 180 is 2. Then $180 \div 2 = 90$. Therefore, $180 = 2 \cdot 90$. The smallest prime factor of 90 is 2. Then $90 \div 2 = 45$. Therefore, $180 = 2 \cdot 2 \cdot 45$. The smallest prime factor of 45 is 3. Then $45 \div 3 = 15$. Therefore, $180 = 2 \cdot 2 \cdot 3 \cdot 15$. The smallest prime factor of 15 is 3. Then $15 \div 3 = 5$. Therefore, $180 = 2 \cdot 2 \cdot 3 \cdot 3 \cdot 5$ or $180 = 2^2 \cdot 3^2 \cdot 5$.

Expressing each of two integers as the product of prime factors makes it possible to discover the greatest integer which is a factor of both of them. We call this factor their *greatest common factor,* or *greatest common divisor*.

Let us find the greatest common factor of 180 and 54.

$180 = 2 \cdot 2 \cdot 3 \cdot 3 \cdot 5$ or $2^2 \cdot 3^2 \cdot 5$ $54 = 2 \cdot 3 \cdot 3 \cdot 3$ or $2 \cdot 3^3$

We see that the greatest number of times that 2 appears as a factor in both 180 and 54 is once; the greatest number of times that 3 appears as a factor in 180 and 54 is twice. No other prime number appears as a factor in both 180 and 54. Therefore, the greatest common factor of 180 and 54 is $2 \cdot 3 \cdot 3$, or $2 \cdot 3^2$, or 18.

The *greatest common factor* of two or more monomials is the product of the greatest common factor of their numerical coefficients and the highest power of every variable that is a factor of each monomial. For example, the greatest common factor of $24a^3 b^2$ and $18a^2 b$ is $6a^2 b$, because it is the product of 6, the greatest common factor of the numerical coefficients 24 and 18, and a^2 and b, the highest power of each variable that is a factor of each monomial.

When we are factoring algebraic expressions, we will agree that:

1. **Numerical coefficients need not be factored.**
2. **Powers of variables need not be represented as the product of several equal factors. For example, $6a^2 b$ need not be written $2 \cdot 3 \cdot a \cdot a \cdot b$.**

Model Problems

1. Express 700 as a product of prime factors.

   Solution:

   $$700 = 2 \cdot 350$$

$700 = 2 \cdot 2 \cdot 175$
$700 = 2 \cdot 2 \cdot 5 \cdot 35$
$700 = 2 \cdot 2 \cdot 5 \cdot 5 \cdot 7$ or $2^2 \cdot 5^2 \cdot 7$ *Answer*

2. Find the greatest common factor of the monomials $60r^2s^4$ and $36rs^2t$.

Solution:

$60r^2s^4 = 2 \cdot 2 \cdot 3 \cdot 5 \cdot r \cdot r \cdot s \cdot s \cdot s \cdot s$ or $2^2 \cdot 3 \cdot 5 \cdot r^2 \cdot s^4$
$36rs^2t = 2 \cdot 2 \cdot 3 \cdot 3 \cdot r \cdot s \cdot s \cdot t$ or $2^2 \cdot 3^2 \cdot r \cdot s^2 \cdot t$

The greatest common factor is $2 \cdot 2 \cdot 3 \cdot r \cdot s \cdot s$ or $2^2 \cdot 3 \cdot r \cdot s^2$ or $12rs^2$.
Answer

EXERCISES

In 1–4, write all the prime numbers between the given numbers.

1. 1 and 10   2. 10 and 20   3. 20 and 30   4. 30 and 40

In 5–14, express the integer as a product of prime numbers.

5. 35   6. 18   7. 108   8. 77   9. 128
10. 400   11. 202   12. 129   13. 590   14. 316

In 15–20, write all the positive integral factors of the number.

15. 26   16. 50   17. 36   18. 88   19. 100   20. 242
21. The product of two integers is 144. Find the second factor if the first factor is:
     a. 2   b. 8   c. 18   d. 36   e. 48
22. The product of two monomials is $36x^3y^4$. Find the second factor if the first factor is:
     a. $3x^2y^3$ b. $6x^3y^2$ c. $12xy^2$ d. $-9x^3y$ e. $18x^3y^2$

In 23–30, find the greatest common factor of the given integers.

23. 10; 15   24. 12; 28   25. 14; 35; 70   26. 18; 24; 36
27. 75; 50   28. 72; 108   29. 144; 200   30. 96; 156; 175

In 31–39, find the greatest common factor of the given monomials.

31. $4x; 4y$ 32. $6; 12a$ 33. $4r; 6r^2; 18n^3$
34. $8xy; 6xz$ 35. $10x^2; 15xy^2; 25x^2y^2$
36. $7c^3d^3; -14c^2d$ 37. $36xy^2z; -27xy^2z^2$
38. $50m^3n^2; 75m^3n$ 39. $24ab^2c^3; 18ac^2$
40. Find the greatest common factor of:
     a. $12(x + y)$ and $18(x + y)$ b. $20(r - s), 12(r - s)$, and $8(r - s)$

2. Factoring Polynomials Whose Terms Have a Common Monomial Factor

Factoring a polynomial over a designated set of numbers means to express it as a product of polynomials whose coefficients are members of that set of numbers. Later, when we factor a polynomial, if no set of numbers is designated, it is to be understood that the polynomial is to be factored over the set of integers. There will be a limited number of exceptions, such as in the case of $\frac{1}{2}hx + \frac{1}{2}hy$, $.01a^2 - .36b^2$ and $\pi x^2 + \pi y^2$, where we will factor over a different set of numbers in which the numerical coefficients are elements. In this chapter we will also assume that all literal exponents represent positive integers.

For polynomials it is true that:

1. **A factor of a polynomial is an exact divisor of the polynomial.**
2. **When the product of two polynomials is divided by one of its factors, the quotient is the other factor.**

For example, since 3 and $x + 2$ are factors of $3x + 6$, because $3x + 6 = 3(x + 2)$, then:
1. Both 3 and $x + 2$ are exact divisors of $3x + 6$.
2. When $3x + 6$ is divided by the factor 3, the quotient, which is $x + 2$, is the other factor; when $3x + 6$ is divided by the factor $x + 2$, the quotient, which is 3, is the other factor.

Every polynomial P with integer coefficients always has the following four factors: $1, -1$, P (the polynomial itself), and $-P$ (the negative of the polynomial). If these are the only factors (with integer coefficients) of a polynomial having integer coefficients, we say that the polynomial is a *prime polynomial.* Notice that the polynomial $2x + 3y$ is prime over the integers, but it can be factored in infinitely many ways into the product of two polynomials with signed number coefficients. For example, since $2x + 3y = 2(x + \frac{3}{2}y)$, here the polynomial 2 and the polynomial $x + \frac{3}{2}y$ are the factors of $2x + 3y$; and since $2x + 3y = -\frac{1}{2}(-4x - 6y)$, here the polynomial $-\frac{1}{2}$ and the polynomial $-4x - 6y$ are the factors of $2x + 3y$.

Since the distributive property states that $2(x + y) = 2x + 2y$, we know that $2x + 2y = 2(x + y)$. Thus, we have used the distributive property to factor the polynomial $2x + 2y$. Notice that the monomial 2 is a factor of each term of the polynomial $2x + 2y$. Therefore, 2 is called a *common monomial factor* of the polynomial $2x + 2y$.

When we factor a polynomial, we look first for the **greatest common monomial factor,** that is, the greatest monomial which is a factor of each term of the polynomial.

For example, to factor $4r^3s^2 + 8r^2s^3$, we first find the greatest common factor, which is $4r^2s^2$. Then, we divide $4r^3s^2 + 8r^2s^3$ by $4r^2s^2$ and obtain the quotient $r + 2s$, which is the other factor of $4r^3s^2 + 8r^2s^3$. Therefore, $4r^3s^2 + 8r^2s^3 = 4r^2s^2 (r + 2s)$.

Procedure. **To factor a polynomial whose terms have a common monomial factor:**

1. **Find the greatest monomial that is a factor of each term of the polynomial.**
2. **Divide the polynomial by the monomial factor. The quotient is the other factor.**
3. **Express the polynomial as the indicated product of the two factors.**
4. **Check by multiplying the factors to obtain the original polynomial.**

Model Problems

1. Write in factored form: $5x^3 + 15x^2$

   Solution:

   1. $5x^2$ is the greatest common factor of $5x^3$ and $15x^2$.
   2. To find the other factor, divide $5x^3 + 15x^2$ by $5x^2$.

   $$(5x^3 + 15x^2) \div 5x^2 = x + 3$$

   3. $5x^3 + 15x^2 = 5x^2 (x + 3)$ *Ans.*

2. Factor $\frac{1}{2}na + \frac{1}{2}nl$ over the set of rational numbers.

   Solution:

   1. $\frac{1}{2}n$ is the greatest common factor of $\frac{1}{2}na$ and $\frac{1}{2}nl$.
   2. To find the other factor, divide $\frac{1}{2}na + \frac{1}{2}nl$ by $\frac{1}{2}n$.

   $$(\tfrac{1}{2}na + \tfrac{1}{2}nl) \div \tfrac{1}{2}n = a + l$$

   3. $\frac{1}{2}na + \frac{1}{2}nl = \frac{1}{2}n (a + l)$ *Ans.*

3. Factor the polynomial: $6c^3d - 12c^2d^2 + 3cd$

   Solution:

   1. $3cd$ is the greatest common factor of $6c^3d$, $12c^2d^2$, and $3cd$.
   2. To find the other factor, divide $6c^3d - 12c^2d^2 + 3cd$ by $3cd$.

   $$(6c^3d - 12c^2d^2 + 3cd) \div 3cd = 2c^2 - 4cd + 1$$

   3. $6c^3d - 12c^2d^2 + 3cd = 3cd(2c^2 - 4cd + 1)$ *Ans.*

4. Factor the polynomial: $x^{n+2} - 7x^n$ (n is a positive integer).

   Solution:

   1. x^n is the greatest common factor of $x^{n+2} - 7x^n$.
   2. To find the other factor, divide $x^{n+2} - 7x^n$ by x^n.

   $$(x^{n+2} - 7x^n) \div x^n = x^2 - 7$$

   3. $x^{n+2} - 7x^n = x^n(x^2 - 7)$ *Ans.*

5. Use factoring to evaluate $87 \times 64 + 87 \times 36$.

   Solution: $87 \times 64 + 87 \times 36 = 87(64 + 36) = 87(100) = 8700$ *Ans.*

EXERCISES

In 1–49, factor the polynomial.

1. $2a + 2b$	2. $6R - 6r$	3. $bx + by$
4. $sr - st$	5. $4x + 8y$	6. $3m - 6n$
7. $15c - 10d$	8. $8x + 16$	9. $8x - 12$
10. $7y - 7$	11. $8 - 4y$	12. $y^2 - 3y$
13. $2x^2 + 5x$	14. $3x^2 - 6x$	15. $32x + x^2$
16. $rs^2 - 2r$	17. $ax - 5ab$	18. $3y^4 + 3y^2$
19. $10x - 15x^3$	20. $p + prt$	21. $\frac{1}{2}hb + \frac{1}{2}hc$
22. $\pi r^2 + \pi R^2$	23. $\pi r^2 + 2\pi rh$	24. $4x^2 + 4y^2$
25. $3a^2 - 9$	26. $3ab^2 - 6a^2b$	27. $10xy - 15x^2y^2$
28. $21r^3s^2 - 14r^2s$	29. $3x^2 - 6x - 30$	30. $ay - 4aw - 12a$

31. $c^3 - c^2 + 2c$ 32. $\frac{1}{4}ma + \frac{1}{4}mb + \frac{1}{4}mc$

33. $9ab^2 - 6ab - 3a$ 34. $15x^3y^3z^3 - 5xyz$

35. $8a^4b^2c^3 + 12a^2b^2c^2$ 36. $28m^4n^3 - 70m^2n^4$

37. $x^{5n} + x^n$ 38. $y^{2n} - 3y^n$ 39. $w^{3n} - w^nz$

40. $x^{n+1} - x$ 41. $y^{2a+1} - y^{2a}$ 42. $aby^r - ay^r$

43. $x^{n+2} + x^{n+1} + x^n$ 44. $y^{2n+2} + y^{2n+1} - y^{2n}$

45. $x^{2n+1} + x^{n+1} + 5x$ 46. $a(x + y) + b(x + y)$

47. $c(m - n) + d(m - n)$ 48. $r(y + z) - s(y + z)$

49. $c(t - s) - d(t - s)$

In 50–55, use factoring to simplify the computation involved in evaluating the number expression.

50. $35 \times 49 + 35 \times 51$ 51. $85 \times 19 + 15 \times 19$

52. $63 \times 87 - 63 \times 77$ 53. $\frac{1}{2} \times 153 + \frac{1}{2} \times 47$

54. $\frac{22}{7} \times 1600 - \frac{22}{7} \times 900$ 55. $\frac{1}{2} \times 7 \times 6.3 + \frac{1}{2} \times 7 \times 1.7$

3. Squaring a Monomial

To square a monomial means to use that monomial as a factor two times. For example:

$(3x)^2 = (3x)(3x) = (3)(3)(x)(x) = (3)^2(x)^2$ or $9x^2$

$(-6b^4)^2 = (-6b^4)(-6b^4) = (-6)(-6)(b^4)(b^4) = (-6)^2(b^4)^2$ or $36b^8$

$(4c^2d^3)^2 = (4c^2d^3)(4c^2d^3) = (4)(4)(c^2)(c^2)(d^3)(d^3)$
$$= (4)^2(c^2)^2(d^3)^2 \text{ or } 16c^4d^6$$

Notice that when a product which has several factors is squared, the operation of squaring is distributed over each factor of the product.

In general, when a and b are signed numbers and m and n are positive integers:

$$(a^m b^n)^2 = a^{2m} b^{2n}$$

Observe that in the case we are discussing, when a monomial is a square, its numerical coefficient is a square and the exponent of each variable is an even number. This is the case with each of the previous results: $9x^2$, $36b^8$, $16c^4d^6$, $a^{2m}b^{2n}$.

Model Problems

In each of the following, square the monomial mentally.

1. $(3a^3)^2 = 9a^6$ 2. $(\frac{2}{5}ab)^2 = \frac{4}{25}a^2b^2$
3. $(-7xy^2)^2 = 49x^2y^4$ 4. $(x^{2a}y^b)^2 = x^{4a}y^{2b}$

EXERCISES

In 1–24, square the monomial in the parentheses mentally.

1. $(a^2)^2$ 2. $(b^3)^2$ 3. $(-d^5)^2$ 4. $(2rs)^2$
5. $(m^2n^2)^2$ 6. $(-x^3y^2)^2$ 7. $(-5y^4)^2$ 8. $(9ab)^2$
9. $(10x^2y^2)^2$ 10. $(-15r^2s^4)^2$ 11. $(\frac{3}{4}a)^2$ 12. $(\frac{5}{7}xy)^2$

13. $(-\frac{7}{8}a^2b^2)^2$ 14. $(-\frac{9}{10}rs^2)^2$ 15. $\left(\frac{x}{6}\right)^2$ 16. $\left(-\frac{4x^2}{5}\right)^2$

17. $(.8x)^2$ 18. $(.5y^2)^2$ 19. $(.1xy)^2$ 20. $(-.6a^2b)^2$
21. $(x^a)^2$ 22. $(y^{3b})^2$ 23. $(c^x d^{2y})^2$ 24. $(m^{4a}n^{3b})^2$

25. Represent the area of a square each of whose sides is represented by:
    a. $4x$ b. $10y$ c. $\frac{2}{3}x$ d. $1.5x$
26. From a square piece of paper the length of each of whose sides is represented by $10x$, a square is cut the length of each of whose sides is represented by $9x$. Represent the area of the region that is left.

4. Multiplying the Sum and Difference of Two Terms

Suppose we multiply the sum of two terms by the difference of the same two terms. Study each of the following examples to see why the product contains two terms, not three:

```
a   + 4          a   + b          3x² + 5y
a   - 4          a   - b          3x² - 5y
a² + 4a          a² + ab          9x⁴ + 15x²y
    - 4a - 16        - ab - b²         - 15x²y - 25y²
a²      - 16     a²      - b²     9x⁴          - 25y²
```

These examples illustrate the following procedure, which will enable us to find the products mentally:

Procedure. To multiply the sum of two terms by the difference of the same two terms:

1. **Square the first term.**
2. **From this result subtract the square of the second term.**

Keep In Mind _____

$$(a+b)(a-b) = a^2 - b^2$$

Model Problems _____

In 1-4, find the product mentally.

Problem	Think	Write

1. $(y+7)(y-7)$ $= (y)^2 - (7)^2$ $= y^2 - 49$ *Ans.*

2. $(3a+4b)(3a-4b)$ $= (3a)^2 - (4b)^2$ $= 9a^2 - 16b^2$ *Ans.*

3. $(x^3 - \frac{1}{5}y^2)(x^3 + \frac{1}{5}y^2) = (x^3)^2 - (\frac{1}{5}y^2)^2 = x^6 - \frac{1}{25}y^4$ *Ans.*

4. $(x^n + 4)(x^n - 4)$ $\qquad = (x^n)^2 - (4)^2$ $\qquad = x^{2n} - 16$ *Ans.*

5. In the expression 33×27, first express the factors as the sum and difference of the same two numbers; then multiply mentally.

  Solution: $33 \times 27 = (30 + 3)(30 - 3) = (30)^2 - (3)^2 = 900 - 9 = 891$

EXERCISES

In 1–22, find the product mentally.

1. $(x + 8)(x - 8)$
2. $(n - 9)(n + 9)$
3. $(10 + a)(10 - a)$
4. $(c + d)(c - d)$
5. $(3x + 1)(3x - 1)$
6. $(20x - 9)(20x + 9)$
7. $(5r - 7s)(5r + 7s)$
8. $(3 - 5y^2)(3 + 5y^2)$
9. $(a + \frac{1}{2})(a - \frac{1}{2})$
10. $(\frac{3}{4}c - d)(\frac{3}{4}c + d)$
11. $(r + .5)(r - .5)$
12. $(ab + 8)(ab - 8)$
13. $(r^3 - 2s^4)(r^3 + 2s^4)$
14. $(5c^2 d^3 + 7e^5)(5c^2 d^3 - 7e^5)$
15. $(a + 5)(a - 5)(a^2 + 25)$
16. $(x - 3)(x + 3)(x^2 + 9)$
17. $(a + b)(a - b)(a^2 + b^2)$
18. $(m^2 + n^2)(m^2 - n^2)(m^4 + n^4)$
19. $(x^a + 10)(x^a - 10)$
20. $(x^a - y^a)(x^a + y^a)$
21. $(a^n + b^{2n})(a^n - b^{2n})$
22. $(4x^{2b} - 3y^{3a})(4x^{2b} + 3y^{3a})$

In 23–30, first express the factors as the sum and difference of the same two numbers; then multiply mentally.

23. 22×18
24. 39×41
25. 53×47
26. 66×74
27. 38×42
28. 55×65
29. 88×92
30. 94×106

5. Factoring the Difference of Two Squares

An expression of the form $a^2 - b^2$ is called a **difference of two squares**. Factoring an expression which is the difference of two squares is the reverse of multiplying the sum of two terms by the difference of the same two terms. Since the product of $a + b$ and $a - b$ is $a^2 - b^2$, the factors of $a^2 - b^2$ are $a + b$ and $a - b$. Therefore:

$$a^2 - b^2 = (a + b)(a - b)$$

Remember that for a monomial to be a square (the case we have discussed), its numerical coefficient must be a square and the exponent of each of its variables must be an even number.

Procedure. To factor a binomial which is a difference of two squares:

1. **Express each of its terms as the square of a monomial.**
2. **Apply the rule $a^2 - b^2 = (a + b)(a - b)$.**

Model Problems

1. Factor $r^2 - 9$ over the set of integers.

   Solution: $r^2 - 9 = (r)^2 - (3)^2$
   $r^2 - 9 = (r + 3)(r - 3)$ *Ans.*

2. Factor $25x^2 - \frac{1}{49}y^2$ over the set of rational numbers.

   Solution: $25x^2 - \frac{1}{49}y^2 = (5x)^2 - (\frac{1}{7}y)^2$
   $25x^2 - \frac{1}{49}y^2 = (5x + \frac{1}{7}y)(5x - \frac{1}{7}y)$ *Ans.*

3. Factor $.04 - c^6d^4$ over the set of rational numbers.

   Solution: $.04 - c^6d^4 = (.2)^2 - (c^3d^2)^2$
   $.04 - c^6d^4 = (.2 + c^3d^2)(.2 - c^3d^2)$ *Ans.*

In 4–6, factor the polynomial mentally.

Problem	Think	Write
4. $x^2y^2 - 81$ $= (xy)^2 - (9)^2$		$= (xy + 9)(xy - 9)$ *Ans.*
5. $49a^4b^6 - 100c^8 = (7a^2b^3)^2 - (10c^4)^2$		$= (7a^2b^3 + 10c^4)(7a^2b^3 - 10c^4)$
		Ans.
6. $x^{6n} - 25$ $= (x^{3n})^2 - (5)^2$		$= (x^{3n} + 5)(x^{3n} - 5)$ *Ans.*

EXERCISES

In 1–9, if possible, express the binomial as the difference of the squares of monomials; if not possible, tell why.

1. $y^2 - 64$ 2. $4r^2 - b^2$ 3. $r^2 + s^2$
4. $t^2 - 7$ 5. $9n^2 - 16m^2$ 6. $c^2 - .09d^2$
7. $p^2 - \frac{9}{25}q^2$ 8. $16a^4 - 25b^6$ 9. $x^4 - y^9$

In 10–42, factor the binomial.

10. $a^2 - 4$ 11. $c^2 - 100$ 12. $t^2 - 81$
13. $144 - c^2$ 14. $121 - m^2$ 15. $16a^2 - b^2$
16. $25m^2 - n^2$ 17. $x^4 - 64$ 18. $25 - s^4$
19. $100x^2 - 81y^2$ 20. $64e^2 - 9f^2$ 21. $r^2s^2 - 144$
22. $w^2 - \frac{1}{64}$ 23. $s^2 - \frac{1}{100}$ 24. $\frac{1}{81} - t^2$

25. $49x^2 - \frac{1}{9}$ 26. $\frac{4}{25} - \frac{49d^2}{81}$ 27. $\frac{1}{9}r^2 - \frac{64s^2}{121}$

28. $y^2 - 1.44$ 29. $.04 - 49r^2$ 30. $81n^2 - .01$
31. $64a^2b^2 - c^2d^2$ 32. $81m^2n^2 - 49x^2y^2$ 33. $25x^6 - 121y^{10}$

34. $x^4y^8 - 144a^6b^{10}$ **35.** $(a + b)^2 - c^2$ **36.** $25 - (m + n)^2$
37. $y^{2n} - 100$ **38.** $49 - x^{2n}$ **39.** $x^{4n} - y^{2n}$
40. $a^{4n} - 64$ **41.** $4x^{2n} - 25y^{2n}$ **42.** $y^{6a} - 144x^{2a}$

6. Finding the Product of Two Binomials

Let us learn how to find the product of two binomials of the form $ax + b$ and $cx + d$ mentally.

Study carefully the multiplication of the two binomials $2x - 3$ and $4x + 5$ shown at the right, which makes use of the distributive property.

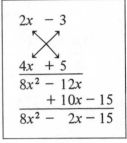

Note:

1. $8x^2$, the first term in the product, is equal to the product of $2x$ and $4x$, the first terms in the binomials.
2. -15, the last term in the product, is equal to the product of -3 and $+5$, the last terms in the binomials.
3. $-2x$, the middle term, is obtained by multiplying the first term of each binomial by the second term of the other and adding these products: $(-12x) + (+10x) = -2x$.

If we arrange the two multipliers horizontally, we can find the middle term by adding the product of the two inner terms of the binomials and the product of the two outer terms of the binomials.

$$\overset{\displaystyle -12x}{\overbrace{(2x - 3)\,(4x + 5)}} \qquad \text{Think:}\ (-12x) + (+10x) = -2x$$
$$\underset{\displaystyle +10x}{\underbrace{}}$$

Procedure. To find the product of two binomials of the form $ax + b$ and $cx + d$:

1. **Multiply the first terms of the binomials.**
2. **Multiply the first term of each binomial by the last term of the other binomial and add these products.**
3. **Multiply the last terms of the binomials.**
4. **Add the results obtained in steps 1, 2, and 3.**

Using this procedure, we would have, in general:

$$(ax + b)\,(cx + d) = acx^2 + (adx + bcx) + bd, \text{ or}$$
$$(ax + b)\,(cx + d) = acx^2 + (ad + bc)\,x + bd.$$

The previous result can also be obtained in the following manner:

$$\boxed{(ax + b)}\ (cx + d) = \boxed{(ax + b)}\ \cdot cx + \boxed{(ax + b)}\ \cdot d$$

$$= acx^2 + bcx + adx + bd$$
$$= acx^2 + (bc + ad)\,x + bd$$
$$= acx^2 + (ad + bc)\,x + bd$$

Model Problems

1. Multiply: $(x - 5)\,(x - 7)$.

   Solution: *Think:*

   $-5x$ 1. $(x)\,(x) = x^2$

   $(x - 5)\,(x - 7)$ 2. $(-5x) + (-7x) = -12x$

   $-7x$ 3. $(-5)\,(-7) = +35$

   Write: $(x - 5)\,(x - 7) = x^2 - 12x + 35$ *Ans.*

2. Multiply: $(3y - 8)\,(4y + 3)$.

   Solution: *Think:*

   $-32y$ 1. $(3y)\,(4y) = 12y^2$

   $(3y - 8)\,(4y + 3)$ 2. $(-32y) + (+9y) = -23y$

   $+9y$ 3. $(-8)\,(+3) = -24$

   Write: $(3y - 8)\,(4y + 3) = 12y^2 - 23y - 24$ *Ans.*

3. Multiply: $(5x + 2y)\,(5x + 2y)$.

   Solution: *Think:*

   $+10xy$ 1. $(5x)\,(5x) = 25x^2$

   $(5x + 2y)\,(5x + 2y)$ 2. $(+10xy) + (+10xy) = +20xy$

   $+10xy$ 3. $(+2y)\,(+2y) = +4y^2$

   Write: $(5x + 2y)\,(5x + 2y) = 25x^2 + 20xy + 4y^2$ *Ans.*

EXERCISES

In 1–30, multiply the binomials mentally.

1. $(x + 5)(x + 3)$ 2. $(6 + d)(3 + d)$ 3. $(1 + m)(9 + m)$
4. $(y + 8)(y + 8)$ 5. $(x - 10)(x - 5)$ 6. $(8 - c)(3 - c)$
7. $(z - 4)(z - 4)$ 8. $(1 - t)(1 - t)$ 9. $(x + 7)(x - 2)$
10. $(y + 11)(y - 4)$ 11. $(m - 15)(m + 2)$ 12. $(n - 20)(n + 3)$
13. $(5 - t)(9 + t)$ 14. $(3x + 2)(x + 5)$ 15. $(c - 5)(3c - 3)$
16. $(m - 6)(3m + 2)$ 17. $(-7m + 5)(m - 4)$ 18. $(7x + 3)(2x - 1)$
19. $(5z - 3)(2z - 5)$ 20. $(3t^2 - 2)(4t^2 + 7)$
21. $(-5y - 4)(-5y - 4)$ 22. $(3x + y)(4x + 2y)$
23. $(2c + 3d)(5c - 2d)$ 24. $(4a - 3b)(3a + b)$
25. $(5a + 7b)(5a + 7b)$ 26. $(-3r - 4s)(-3r - 4s)$
27. $(x^n + 4)(x^n - 2)$ 28. $(r^a - 6)(2r^a + 1)$
29. $(y^{2a} - 3)(y^{2a} - 7)$ 30. $(m^{3n} + 3)(2m^{3n} - 9)$
31. Represent the area of a rectangle whose length and width are represented by:
    a. $(x + 5)$ and $(x + 4)$ b. $(2x + 3)$ and $(x - 1)$
32. Represent the area of a square each of whose sides is represented by:
    a. $(x + 6)$ b. $(x - 2)$ c. $(2x + 1)$ d. $(3x - 2)$

7. Factoring Trinomials of the Form $ax^2 + bx + c$

We have learned that $(x + 3)(x + 5) = x^2 + 8x + 15$. Therefore, the factors of $x^2 + 8x + 15$ are $(x + 3)$ and $(x + 5)$. Factoring a trinomial of the form $ax^2 + bx + c$ is the reverse of multiplying binomials of the form $(dx + e)$ and $(fx + g)$. When we factor a trinomial of this form, we list the possible pairs of factors and test them out one by one until we find the correct result.

For example, let us factor $x^2 + 7x + 10$.

1. Since the product of the first terms of the binomials must be x^2, each first term must be x. We write:

$$x^2 + 7x + 10 = (x\quad)(x\quad)$$

2. Since the product of the last terms of the binomials must be $+10$, these last terms must be either both positive or both negative. The pairs of integers whose product is $+10$ are $(+10)$ and $(+1)$, $(+5)$ and $(+2)$, (-10) and (-1), and (-5) and (-2).

3. From the results obtained in steps 1 and 2, we see that the possible pairs of factors are:

$$(x + 10)(x + 1) \qquad (x - 10)(x - 1)$$
$$(x + 5)(x + 2) \qquad (x - 5)(x - 2)$$

4. Now, we test each pair of factors. For example,

$+10x$

$(x + 10)(x + 1)$ is not correct because the middle term, $(+10x) + (+1x)$, is $+11x$, not $+7x$.

$(x + 10)(x + 1)$

$+1x$

$+5x$

$(x + 5)(x + 2)$ is correct because the middle term, $(+5x) + (+2x)$, is $+7x$.

$(x + 5)(x + 2)$

$+2x$

None of the remaining pairs of factors is correct.
5. Therefore, $x^2 + 7x + 10 = (x + 5)(x + 2)$. *Ans.*

Procedure. To factor a trinomial of the form $ax^2 + bx + c$, we must find two binomials which have the following properties:

1. **The product of the first terms of both binomials must be equal to the first term in the trinomial (ax^2).**
2. **The product of the last terms of both binomials must be equal to the last term of the trinomial (c).**
3. **When the first term of each binomial is multiplied by the second term of the other and the sum of these products is found, this result must be equal to the middle term of the trinomial (bx).**

Model Problems

1. Factor: $c^2 + 5c - 6$

   Solution:

   1. The product of the first terms of the binomials must be c^2. Therefore, each first term must be c. We write:

      $$c^2 + 5c - 6 = (c \quad)(c \quad)$$

   2. Since the product of the last terms of the binomials must be -6, one of these last terms must be positive, the other negative. The pairs of integers whose product is -6 are $(+1)$ and (-6), (-1) and $(+6)$, $(+3)$ and (-2), (-3) and $(+2)$.
   3. The possible factors are:

      $(c + 1)(c - 6)$ $(c + 3)(c - 2)$
      $(c - 1)(c + 6)$ $(c - 3)(c + 2)$

4. When we find the middle term of each of the trinomial products, we find that only $(c-1)(c+6)$ yields a middle term of $+5c$.

5. $c^2 + 5c - 6 = (c-1)(c+6)$ *Ans.*

2. Factor: $2x^2 - 7x - 15$

Solution:

1. Since the product of the first terms of the binomials must be $2x^2$, one of these terms must be $2x$, the other x. We write:

$$2x^2 - 7x - 15 = (2x \quad)(x \quad)$$

2. Since the product of the last terms of the binomials must be -15, one of these last terms must be positive, the other negative. The pairs of integers whose product is -15 are $(+1)$ and (-15), (-1) and $(+15)$, $(+3)$ and (-5), (-3) and $(+5)$.

3. The possible pairs of factors are:

$(2x + 1)(x - 15)$	$(2x - 1)(x + 15)$
$(2x + 15)(x - 1)$	$(2x - 15)(x + 1)$
$(2x + 3)(x - 5)$	$(2x - 3)(x + 5)$
$(2x + 5)(x - 3)$	$(2x - 5)(x + 3)$

4. When we find the middle term of each of the trinomial products, we find that only $(2x + 3)(x - 5)$ yields a middle term of $-7x$.

5. $2x^2 - 7x - 15 = (2x + 3)(x - 5)$ *Ans.*

3. Factor: $y^4 + 3y^2 + 2$

Solution:

1. The trinomial $y^4 + 3y^2 + 2$ can be expressed in the form $ax^2 + bx + c$ if we write it as $(y^2)^2 + 3(y^2) + 2$.

2. The possible pairs of factors are:

$$(y^2 + 2)(y^2 + 1) \qquad (y^2 - 2)(y^2 - 1)$$

3. Only the product $(y^2 + 2)(y^2 + 1)$ yields a middle term $+3y^2$.

4. $y^4 + 3y^2 + 2 = (y^2 + 2)(y^2 + 1)$ *Ans.*

Keep In Mind

In factoring a trinomial of the form $ax^2 + bx + c$:

1. If the last term, the constant c, is positive, the last terms of the binomial factors must be either both positive or both negative.

2. If the last term, the constant c, is negative, one of the last terms in the binomial factors must be positive, the other negative.

EXERCISES

In 1–72, factor the trinomial.

1. $a^2 + 3a + 2$ 2. $c^2 + 6c + 5$ 3. $x^2 + 8x + 7$
4. $r^2 + 12r + 11$ 5. $t^2 + 7t + 10$ 6. $x^2 + 9x + 18$
7. $x^2 + 12x + 27$ 8. $z^2 + 13z + 40$ 9. $a^2 + 11a + 18$
10. $b^2 + 13b + 30$ 11. $16 + 17c + c^2$ 12. $x^2 + 2x + 1$
13. $z^2 + 10z + 25$ 14. $a^2 - 8a + 7$ 15. $x^2 - 12x + 11$
16. $a^2 - 6a + 5$ 17. $x^2 - 11x + 10$ 18. $y^2 - 6y + 8$
19. $r^2 - 11r + 18$ 20. $a^2 - 9a + 8$ 21. $15 - 8y + y^2$
22. $x^2 - 10x + 24$ 23. $y^2 - 13y + 36$ 24. $t^2 - 17t + 72$
25. $x^2 - 16x + 48$ 26. $y^2 - 16y + 64$ 27. $z^2 - 20z + 100$
28. $x^2 - x - 2$ 29. $x^2 - 3x - 4$ 30. $y^2 + 4y - 5$
31. $z^2 - 12z - 13$ 32. $a^2 - 3a - 10$ 33. $b^2 - 2b - 8$
34. $r^2 + 4r - 21$ 35. $t^2 + t - 6$ 36. $y^2 - 5y - 24$
37. $z^2 + 9z - 36$ 38. $m^2 - 6m - 27$ 39. $x^2 + 3x - 40$
40. $x^2 + 11x - 60$ 41. $x^2 - 2x - 80$ 42. $2x^2 + 5x + 2$
43. $3x^2 + 10x + 3$ 44. $2x^2 + 11x + 5$ 45. $2x^2 + 11x + 12$
46. $3x^2 + 10x + 8$ 47. $2y^2 - 3y + 1$ 48. $14 - 13y + 3y^2$
49. $3x^2 - 5x - 2$ 50. $2x^2 + x - 6$ 51. $5x^2 - 3x - 8$
52. $3x^2 - 5x - 12$ 53. $4x^2 - 12x + 5$ 54. $6x^2 + 5x - 6$
55. $6x^2 + 5x - 4$ 56. $10a^2 - 9a + 2$ 57. $10x^2 + 49x - 5$
58. $18y^2 - 23y - 6$ 59. $x^2 + 3xy + 2y^2$ 60. $c^2 + 4cd - 5d^2$
61. $3a^2 - 7ab + 2b^2$ 62. $5m^2 + 3mn - 2n^2$ 63. $4x^2 - 5xy - 6y^2$
64. $x^4 - 10x^2 + 21$ 65. $a^6 - 3a^3 - 28$ 66. $15 + 2x^2 - x^4$
67. $x^{2a} + 5x^a + 4$ 68. $y^{2n} - 8y^n + 7$ 69. $x^{2b} - 2x^b - 15$
70. $r^{2n} + 6r^n - 16$ 71. $3x^{2a} - 11x^a + 6$ 72. $2x^{2a} - 3x^a - 20$

8. Squaring a Binomial

Now we will consider the squaring of a binomial, which is a special case of the multiplication of two binomials.

We know that $(x + y)^2$ means $(x + y)(x + y)$. Hence, $(x + y)^2 = x^2 + 2xy + y^2$. The polynomial $x^2 + 2xy + y^2$, which is the result of squaring a binomial, is called a **perfect square trinomial**.

Observe that in the perfect square trinomial, $x^2 + 2xy + y^2$, the first term x^2 and the last term y^2 are the respective squares of x, the first term of the binomial $x + y$, and y the second term. Observe also that $2xy$, the middle term of $x^2 + 2xy + y^2$, is twice the product of x and y, the two terms of the binomial $x + y$.

This characteristic form of a perfect square trinomial enables us to square a binomial mentally using the following procedure:

Procedure. To square a binomial:

1. Square the first term of the binomial.
2. Double the product of the two terms of the binomial.
3. Square the second term of the binomial.
4. Add the three terms obtained in steps 1, 2, and 3.

Keep In Mind

$$(x + y)^2 = x^2 + 2xy + y^2$$
$$(x - y)^2 = x^2 - 2xy + y^2$$

Model Problems

In 1-5, find the square of the binomial mentally.

Problem	Think	Write
1. $(x + 6)^2$	$= (x)^2 + 2(x)(6) + (6)^2$	$= x^2 + 12x + 36$
2. $(y - 3)^2$	$= (y)^2 + 2(y)(-3) + (-3)^2$	$= y^2 - 6y + 9$
3. $(3x + 1)^2$	$= (3x)^2 + 2(3x)(1) + (1)^2$	$= 9x^2 + 6x + 1$
4. $(5x - \frac{1}{3}y)^2$	$= (5x)^2 + 2(5x)(-\frac{1}{3}y) + (-\frac{1}{3}y)^2$	$= 25x^2 - \frac{10}{3}xy + \frac{1}{9}y^2$
5. $(x^n + 7)^2$	$= (x^n)^2 + 2(x^n)(7) + (7)^2$	$= x^{2n} + 14x^n + 49$

6. Find the value of $(101)^2$ using the procedure for squaring a binomial.

Solution:

$$(101)^2 = (100 + 1)^2$$
$$= (100)^2 + 2(100)(1) + (1)^2$$
$$= 10,000 + 200 + 1$$
$$= 10,201 \qquad 10,201 \quad Ans.$$

EXERCISES

In 1-24, find the square of the binomial in the parentheses mentally.

1. $(x + 9)^2$ 2. $(y + \frac{1}{3})^2$ 3. $(a - 6)^2$ 4. $(c - 8)^2$
5. $(2x + 1)^2$ 6. $(3y + 2)^2$ 7. $(4x - 3)^2$ 8. $(9a - \frac{1}{2})^2$
9. $(a + b)^2$ 10. $(c - b)^2$ 11. $(2x + 5y)^2$ 12. $(4a - 5b)^2$

13. $(2x^2 + 1)^2$ **14.** $(6c^2 - \frac{1}{5})^2$ **15.** $(5m^2 - 3n)^2$ **16.** $(8s^2 - 7t^3)^2$
17. $(a^x + 5)^2$ **18.** $(c^n + d^m)^2$ **19.** $(x^{2a} + 10)^2$ **20.** $(b^{2x} - c^{3y})^2$
21. $(30 + 2)^2$ **22.** $(50 - 1)^2$ **23.** $(70 + 1)^2$ **24.** $(100 - 1)^2$

In 25-34, use the procedure for squaring a binomial to find the value of the numerical expression.

25. $(21)^2$ **26.** $(19)^2$ **27.** $(32)^2$ **28.** $(28)^2$ **29.** $(53)^2$
30. $(68)^2$ **31.** $(1\frac{1}{2})^2$ **32.** $(85)^2$ **33.** $(8\frac{2}{3})^2$ **34.** $(99)^2$

9. Factoring Perfect Square Trinomials

A perfect square trinomial can be factored by the same method as that used in factoring the general quadratic trinomial. However, the perfect square trinomial can be factored by a special method that will now be illustrated. When a trinomial is arranged in descending order according to one of the variables, and its first and third terms are perfect squares, it is wise to check the second term to discover whether or not the trinomial is a perfect square trinomial. If it is a perfect square trinomial, the special method can be used.

Model Problems

1. Factor $16x^2 + 24xy + 9y^2$

   Solution:

   The first term $16x^2$ is the square of $4x$ or $-4x$.
   The third term $9y^2$ is the square of $3y$ or $-3y$.
   The second term $+24xy$ is twice the product of $4x$ and $3y$ or $-4x$ and $-3y$.
   Hence, $16x^2 + 24xy + 9y^2$ is a perfect square trinomial.
   Therefore, $16x^2 + 24xy + 9y^2 = (4x + 3y)^2$ or $(-4x - 3y)^2$.

2. Factor $100a^2 - 140a + 49$

   Solution:

   The first term $100a^2$ is the square of $10a$ or $-10a$.
   The third term 49 is the square of 7 or -7.
   The second term $-140a$ is twice the product of $10a$ and -7 or $-10a$ and 7.
   Hence, $100a^2 - 140a + 49$ is a perfect square trinomial.
   Therefore, $100a^2 - 140a + 49 = (10a - 7)^2$ or $(-10a + 7)^2$.

EXERCISES

In 1–12, determine whether the polynomial is a perfect square trinomial.

1. $m^2 + 6m + 9$
2. $x^2 - 2x + 1$
3. $4x^2 + 20x + 25$
4. $y^2 - 5y + 25$
5. $49 + 14c + c^2$
6. $a^2 - 4 + 4a$
7. $4x^2 + 9y^2 + 12xy$
8. $r^2 - 9rs + 81s^2$
9. $w^2 - 6wz - 9z^2$
10. $81x^2 + 4y^2 - 36xy$
11. $x^2 - y^2$
12. $d^2 + 100$

In 13–33, factor the polynomial, if possible.

13. $x^2 + 4x + 4$
14. $y^2 - 2y + 1$
15. $a^2 - 14a + 49$
16. $x^2 - 5x + 25$
17. $4x^2 - 4x + 1$
18. $9c^2 + 6c + 1$
19. $36x^2 + 14x + 1$
20. $9x^2 - 12xy + 4y^2$
21. $16m^2 + 49n^2 - 56mn$
22. $9a^2 + 6ab + 4b^2$
23. $100x^2 - 140xy + 49y^2$
24. $y^4 + 20y^2 + 100$
25. $64x^4 + 48x^2y + 9y^2$
26. $r^4 - 18r^2s^3 + 81s^6$
27. $y^{10m} + 4y^{5m} + 4$
28. $(x + 2)^2 + 12(x + 2) + 36$
29. $(a - 1)^2 - 14(a - 1) + 49$
30. $(a + b)^2 + 16(a + b) + 64$
31. $4 - 20(r - s) + 25(r - s)^2$
32. $(x + y)^2 + 20r(x + y) + 100r^2$
33. $4(c + d)^2 + 12a(c + d) + 9a^2$

In 34–39: (a) Insert the proper middle term which will make the resulting trinomial a perfect square; (b) express the resulting trinomial as the square of a binomial.

34. $x^2 + ? + 9$
35. $25r^2 - ? + 1$
36. $16a^2 + ? + 9$
37. $49x^2 + ? + 16y^2$
38. $36a^2 - ? + 25b^2$
39. $121c^2 + ? + 100d^2$

10. Factoring by Grouping

Polynomials with four terms can sometimes be factored by using the associative property of addition to group the terms in such a way that the previously developed methods of factoring can be used to factor the resulting groups of terms.

For example, the polynomial $x^2 + 9x + xy + 9y$ can be factored if we group the first two terms, group the last two terms, factor each group separately, and then factor the resulting expression in the following manner:

$$
\begin{aligned}
x^2 + 9x + xy + 9y &= (x^2 + 9x) + (xy + 9y) \\
&= x(x + 9) + y(x + 9) \\
&= (x + 9)(x + y)
\end{aligned}
$$

The polynomial $x^2 + 6x + 9 - y^2$ can be factored if we group the first three terms which form a perfect square trinomial, express the trinomial as the square of a binomial, and then factor the resulting expression as the difference of two squares in the following manner:

$$\begin{aligned} x^2 + 6x + 9 - y^2 &= (x^2 + 6x + 9) - y^2 \\ &= (x + 3)^2 - y^2 \\ &= [(x + 3) + y] \, [(x + 3) - y] \\ &= (x + 3 + y)(x + 3 - y) \end{aligned}$$

Keep In Mind

When factoring a polynomial of four terms, try grouping two terms and two terms, or three terms and one term, and then apply the usual methods of factoring to these groups.

Model Problems

1. Factor: $rx + ry - sx - sy$.

   Solution: $\begin{aligned} rx + ry - sx - sy &= (rx + ry) + (-sx - sy) \\ &= r(x + y) + (-s)(x + y) \\ &= (x + y)(r - s) \quad Ans. \end{aligned}$

   Note: Since $x + y$ was a factor of the first group, $rx + ry$, we factor $-sx - sy$ as $(-s)(x + y)$ in order that $x + y$ should also be a factor of the second group $-sx - sy$.

2. Factor: $a^2 - b^2 + 8b - 16$.

   Solution: $\begin{aligned} a^2 - b^2 + 8b - 16 &= a^2 + (-b^2 + 8b - 16) \\ &= a^2 - (b^2 - 8b + 16) \\ &= a^2 - (b - 4)^2 \\ &= [a + (b - 4)] \, [a - (b - 4)] \\ &= (a + b - 4)(a - b + 4) \quad Ans. \end{aligned}$

EXERCISES

In 1–20, factor the polynomial.

1. $y^2 + 5y + yw + 5w$
2. $x^2 - 5x + 2xy - 10y$
3. $c^2 + 4c + cd + 4d$
4. $y^2 - 5y - 2y + 10$
5. $ax + ay + bx + by$
6. $cm - cn + dm - dn$

7. $ar - as - br + bs$
9. $y^2 - 4y + 4 - z^2$
11. $4x^2 - 20xy + 25y^2 - w^2$
13. $a^2 - b^2 + 20b - 100$
15. $49r^2 - s^2 - 14s - 49$
17. $mx^{2a} + my^{2b} - nx^{2a} - ny^{2b}$
19. $x^{2a} - y^{2b} + 14y^b - 49$

8. $tc + sc - td - sd$
10. $25a^2 - 10a + 1 - b^2$
12. $c^2 - d^2 - 6c + 9$
14. $x^2 - 4y^2 + 20y - 25$
16. $4m^2 - 9n^2 - 6n - 1$
18. $rs^2 - bt^3 - rt^3 + bs^2$
20. $c^{2x} - 81 - d^{2y} + 18d^y$

11. Factoring Completely

The polynomials $x^2 + 4$ and $x^2 + x + 1$ cannot be factored over the set of polynomials with integral coefficients. We say that these polynomials are *prime over this set of polynomials.*

To factor a polynomial completely means to find the *prime factors* of the polynomial over a designated set of numbers. Therefore, whenever we factor a polynomial, we will continue the process of factoring until all factors other than monomial factors are prime factors over the designated set of numbers.

Procedure. To factor a polynomial completely, use the following steps:

1. **Look for the greatest common factor of its terms. If there is a common factor other than 1, factor the given polynomial. Then examine each factor.**
2. **If one of these factors is a binomial, see if it is a difference of two squares. If it is, factor it as such.**
3. **If one of these factors is a trinomial, see if it can be factored. If it can, find its binomial factors.**
4. **Write the answer as the product of all the factors. Make certain that in the answer all factors other than monomial factors are prime factors.**

Model Problems

1. Factor completely: $5x^2 - 45$

How to Proceed	Solution
1. Find the greatest common factor.	$5x^2 - 45 = 5(x^2 - 9)$

2. Factor the difference of two squares. $5x^2 - 45 = 5(x + 3)(x - 3)$ *Ans.*

2. Factor completely: $3x^2 - 6x - 24$

How to Proceed	Solution
1. Find the grestest common factor.	$3x^2 - 6x - 24 = 3(x^2 - 2x - 8)$
2. Factor the trinomial.	$3x^2 - 6x - 24 = 3(x - 4)(x + 2)$ *Ans.*

3. Factor completely: $x^4 - 16$

How to Proceed	Solution
1. Factor the difference of two squares.	$x^4 - 16 = (x^2 + 4)(x^2 - 4)$
2. Factor the difference of two squares.	$x^4 - 16 = (x^2 + 4)(x + 2)(x - 2)$ *Ans.*

4. Factor completely: $9x^{n+2} - x^n$

How to Proceed	Solution
1. Find the greatest common factor.	$9x^{n+2} - x^n = x^n(9x^2 - 1)$
2. Factor the difference of two squares.	$9x^{n+2} - x^n = x^n(3x + 1)(3x - 1)$ *Ans.*

EXERCISES

In 1–37, factor the polynomial completely.

1. $2a^2 - 2b^2$
2. $6x^2 - 6y^2$
3. $ax^2 - ay^2$
4. $st^2 - s$
5. $2x^2 - 32$
6. $3x^2 - 27y^2$
7. $18m^2 - 8$
8. $12a^2 - 27b^2$
9. $63c^2 - 7$
10. $y^3 - 25y$
11. $4a^3 - ab^2$
12. $9db^2 - d$
13. $4a^2 - 36$
14. $y^4 - 81$
15. $\pi R^2 - \pi r^2$
16. $100x^2 - 36y^2$
17. $ax^2 + 3ax + 2a$
18. $3x^2 + 6x + 3$
19. $4r^2 - 4r - 48$
20. $x^3 + 7x^2 + 10x$
21. $2ax^2 - 2ax - 12a$
22. $abx^2 - ab$
23. $z^6 - z^2$
24. $16x^2 - x^2y^4$
25. $x^4 + x^2 - 2$
26. $a^4 - 10a^2 + 9$
27. $y^4 - 13y^2 + 36$
28. $5x^{2a} - 20$
29. $y^{3a+2} - y^{3a}$
30. $cx^{2+2b} - cx^2$
31. $2x^{2a} - 4x^a + 2$
32. $6a^{2n} - 24a^n + 24$
33. $x^{n+2} + 3x^{n+1} - 18x^n$
34. $ax^2 + bx^2 - ay^2 - by^2$
35. $x^2m - x^2n - 4m + 4n$
36. $ax^2 - 10ax + 25a - ay^2$
37. $12c^2 - 3d^2 + 12de - 12e^2$

Chapter 10

Operations With Fractions

1. The Meaning of an Algebraic Fraction

A fraction is a symbol which indicates the quotient of two numbers (remember that division by zero is not possible). For example, the arithmetic fraction $\frac{3}{4}$ indicates the quotient of 3 and 4. Keep in mind that the symbol $\frac{3}{4}$ is a numeral representing an arithmetic number. In our work, the word *fraction* will be used to mean either the numeral or the number. The context will determine which meaning is intended.

An *algebraic fraction* is a quotient of polynomials. An algebraic fraction is sometimes called a *rational expression*. Examples of algebraic fractions are: $\dfrac{2}{5}, \dfrac{x}{2}, \dfrac{2}{x}, \dfrac{a}{b}, \dfrac{4c}{3d}, \dfrac{x+5}{x-2}, \dfrac{x^2+4x+3}{x+1}$.

The fraction $\dfrac{a}{b}$ means that the number represented by a, the numerator, is to be divided by the number represented by b, the denominator. Since division by zero is not possible, the value of the denominator, b, may not be zero. In all our work with fractions, we will assume that the denominator is not zero.

Model Problem ————————————————————————

Find the value of x for which $\dfrac{12}{x-9}$ has no meaning.

Solution: $\dfrac{12}{x-9}$ is not defined when the denominator $x-9$ is equal to 0.

Let $x-9=0$. Then $x=9$. *Answer:* 9

EXERCISES

In 1–6, represent the symbol as a fraction and give the value or values of the variable, if any, for which the fraction has no meaning.

1. $x \div 7$ **2.** $(x + 6) \div x^2$

3. $15 \div (y - 3)$ **4.** $(x + 4) \div (2x - 6)$

5. $(5y + 3) \div (3y + 1)$ **6.** $(x - 5) \div (x^2 - 25)$

In 7–14, find the value or values of the variable for which the fraction is not defined.

7. $\dfrac{2}{x}$ **8.** $\dfrac{-5}{6x}$ **9.** $\dfrac{12}{y^2}$ **10.** $\dfrac{x}{x - 8}$

11. $\dfrac{y + 5}{y + 2}$ **12.** $\dfrac{x^2 - 9}{2x - 1}$ **13.** $\dfrac{2y + 3}{4y + 2}$ **14.** $\dfrac{4x - 5}{x^2 - 9}$

In 15–22, represent the answer to the problem as a fraction.

15. If string beans cost 39 cents a pound, represent the number of pounds that can be bought for y cents.

16. If x pencils cost y cents, represent the cost of one pencil.

17. If $(x + 1)$ dresses cost $(4x + 9)$ dollars, represent the cost of one dress.

18. If a car travels m miles in 4 hours, represent the number of miles it travels in 1 hour.

19. If a man walks at the rate of r kilometers per hour, represent the number of hours that he will require to travel d kilometers.

20. In a college there are m men and w women. What fractional part of the students are women?

21. Sam can mow a lawn in 90 minutes. What part of the lawn can he mow in x minutes?

22. Harold can paint a fence in h hours. What part of the fence can he paint in 4 hours?

2. Reducing Fractions to Lowest Terms

A fraction is said to be ***reduced to lowest terms*** when its numerator and denominator have no common factor other than 1 or -1.

The fractions $\dfrac{5}{10}$ and $\dfrac{1a}{2a}$ each become the fraction $\dfrac{1}{2}$ when reduced to lowest terms. Let us use the multiplication property of 1 to show that $\dfrac{5}{10}$ names the same number as $\dfrac{1}{2}$ and that $\dfrac{1a}{2a}$ also names the same number as $\frac{1}{2}$. Remember that any nonzero number divided by itself equals 1.

$$\frac{5}{10} = \frac{1 \cdot 5}{2 \cdot 5} = \frac{1}{2} \cdot \frac{5}{5} = \frac{1}{2} \cdot 1 = \frac{1}{2} \quad and \quad \frac{1a}{2a} = \frac{1 \cdot a}{2 \cdot a} = \frac{1}{2} \cdot \frac{a}{a} = \frac{1}{2} \cdot 1 = \frac{1}{2}$$

These examples illustrate the ***division property of a fraction:*** If the numerator and the denominator of a fraction are divided by the same nonzero number, the resulting fraction is equivalent to the original fraction.

In general, for any numbers x, y, and a, where $y \neq 0$ and $a \neq 0$:

$$\frac{x}{y} = \frac{x \div a}{y \div a}$$

Note the following examples of the division property of fractions:

$$\frac{15}{20} = \frac{15 \div 5}{20 \div 5} = \frac{3}{4}$$

$$\frac{4x}{5x} = \frac{4x \div x}{5x \div x} = \frac{4}{5}$$

$$\frac{cy}{dy} = \frac{cy \div y}{dy \div y} = \frac{c}{d}$$

$$\frac{2(x + 5)}{3(x + 5)} = \frac{2(x + 5) \div (x + 5)}{3(x + 5) \div (x + 5)} = \frac{2}{3}$$

When reducing a fraction, the division of the numerator and the denominator by a common factor may be indicated by a ***cancellation***. For example, we may write:

$$\frac{2(x + 5)}{3(x + 5)} = \frac{2\overset{1}{\cancel{(x + 5)}}}{3\underset{1}{\cancel{(x + 5)}}} = \frac{2}{3}$$

Procedure: To reduce a fraction to its lowest terms:

Method 1

1. Factor both its numerator and its denominator.
2. Examine the factors and determine the greatest common factor of the numerator and the denominator.
3. Express the given fraction as the product of two fractions, one of which has as its numerator and its denominator the greatest common factor determined in step 2.
4. Use the multiplication property of 1.

Method 2

1. Factor both its numerator and its denominator.
2. Divide both the numerator and the denominator by their greatest common factor.

Model Problems

1. Reduce $\dfrac{8x^3y^2}{12x^2y^4}$ to lowest terms.

Solution:

Method 1

$$\frac{8x^3y^2}{12x^2y^4} = \frac{2x}{3y^2} \cdot \frac{4x^2y^2}{4x^2y^2}$$

$$= \frac{2x}{3y^2} \cdot 1$$

$$= \frac{2x}{3y^2} \quad Ans.$$

Method 2

$$\frac{8x^3y^2}{12x^2y^4} = \frac{4x^2y^2 \cdot 2x}{4x^2y^2 \cdot 3y^2}$$

$$= \frac{4x^2y^2 \cdot 2x \div 4x^2y^2}{4x^2y^2 \cdot 3y^2 \div 4x^2y^2}$$

$$= \frac{2x}{3y^2} \quad Ans.$$

2. Reduce $\dfrac{(x-4)^2}{x^2 - 5x + 4}$ to lowest terms.

Solution:

Method 1

$$\frac{(x-4)^2}{x^2 - 5x + 4} = \frac{(x-4)(x-4)}{(x-1)(x-4)}$$

$$= \frac{(x-4)}{(x-1)} \cdot 1$$

$$= \frac{x-4}{x-1} \quad Ans.$$

Method 2

$$\frac{(x-4)^2}{x^2 - 5x + 4} = \frac{(x-4)(x-4)}{(x-1)(x-4)}$$

$$= \frac{(x-4)\overset{1}{\cancel{(x-4)}}}{(x-1)\underset{1}{\cancel{(x-4)}}}$$

$$= \frac{x-4}{x-1} \quad Ans.$$

3. Reduce $\dfrac{2-x}{4x-8}$ to lowest terms.

Solution:

$$\frac{2-x}{4x-8} = \frac{-x+2}{4x-8} = \frac{-1(x-2)}{4(x-2)} = \frac{-1}{4} \cdot \frac{(x-2)}{(x-2)} = -\frac{1}{4} \cdot 1 = -\frac{1}{4} \quad Ans.$$

WRONG METHODS OF REDUCING FRACTIONS

Students sometimes make mistakes in reducing fractions because they carelessly "cross off" or "cancel" the same quantity in some part of the numerator and in some part of the denominator. Remember that a fraction may be reduced by *dividing* the numerator and the denominator by a common factor. Thus, $\dfrac{\cancel{3}x}{\cancel{3}+y} = \dfrac{x}{y}$ is wrong, because 3 is not a factor of the denominator, $3 + y$.

When the same number is subtracted from both terms of a fraction, the resulting fraction is not always equivalent to the original fraction. For example, $\dfrac{4}{5}$ does not equal $\dfrac{4-2}{5-2}$, or $\dfrac{2}{3}$. Also, $\dfrac{x+\cancel{2}}{y+\cancel{2}} = \dfrac{x}{y}$ is wrong, because the numerator and the denominator were not *divided* by a factor 2; since 2 was *subtracted* from the numerator and from the denominator, the result is not always an equivalent fraction.

Similarly, when the same number is added to both terms of a fraction, the resulting fraction is not always equivalent to the original fraction. For example, $\dfrac{5}{6}$ does not equal $\dfrac{5+4}{6+4}$, or $\dfrac{9}{10}$. $\dfrac{x-\cancel{4}}{y-\cancel{4}} = \dfrac{x}{y}$ is wrong because the numerator and the denominator were not *divided* by a factor 4; since 4 was *added* to the numerator and to the denominator, the result is not always an equivalent fraction.

Keep In Mind

The word *cancellation* may be used in reducing fractions if it means dividing both the numerator and the denominator of a fraction by the same factor.

EXERCISES

In 1–47, reduce the fraction to lowest terms.

1. $\dfrac{4}{12}$

2. $\dfrac{27}{36}$

3. $\dfrac{24c}{36d}$

4. $\dfrac{3m^2}{5m^2}$

5. $\dfrac{ab}{cb}$

6. $\dfrac{3ay^2}{6by^2}$

7. $\dfrac{4xyz}{7xyz}$

8. $\dfrac{15x^3}{5x}$

9. $\dfrac{5x^2}{25x^3}$

10. $\dfrac{8xy^2}{24x^2y}$

11. $\dfrac{36a^4y^2}{48ay^3}$

12. $\dfrac{64a^2b^2c^2}{24ab^2c^2}$

13. $\dfrac{+12a^2b}{-8ac}$ 14. $\dfrac{-20x^2y^2}{-90xy^2}$ 15. $\dfrac{-32a^3b^3}{+48a^3b^3}$ 16. $\dfrac{+5xy}{+45x^2y^2}$

17. $\dfrac{5(x+2)}{7(x+2)}$ 18. $\dfrac{15(y-3)}{20(y-3)}$ 19. $\dfrac{m(a+b)}{n(a+b)}$ 20. $\dfrac{6x^2(r-2s)}{3x(r-2s)}$

21. $\dfrac{2x(a+b)}{8x^2}$ 22. $\dfrac{9a-18}{4a-8}$ 23. $\dfrac{6(x+2y)}{9x+18y}$ 24. $\dfrac{(x+4)^2}{x+4}$

25. $\dfrac{ab+ac}{db+dc}$ 26. $\dfrac{(x+y)^2}{x^2-y^2}$ 27. $\dfrac{x^2-4}{(x-2)^2}$ 28. $\dfrac{9y-18}{3y^2-12}$

29. $\dfrac{75-12x^2}{15-6x}$ 30. $\dfrac{5a^2-20}{(a-2)^2}$ 31. $\dfrac{1-x}{x-1}$ 32. $\dfrac{2s-2r}{s^2-r^2}$

33. $\dfrac{x^2-y^2}{3y-3x}$ 34. $\dfrac{6y-12y^2}{9y}$ 35. $\dfrac{x}{x^2+x}$ 36. $\dfrac{3m}{6m-9m^2}$

37. $\dfrac{x^2-3x}{x^2-4x+3}$ 38. $\dfrac{a^2-a-6}{a^2-9}$ 39. $\dfrac{2x^2-50}{x^2+8x+15}$

40. $\dfrac{r^2-4r-5}{r^2-2r-15}$ 41. $\dfrac{48+8x-x^2}{x^2+x-12}$ 42. $\dfrac{2x^2-7x+3}{(x-3)^2}$

43. $\dfrac{3x^2-15x+18}{x^2-x-6}$ 44. $\dfrac{x^2-7xy+12y^2}{x^2+xy-20y^2}$ 45. $\dfrac{18c^2-32d^2}{6c^2-cd-12d^2}$

46. $\dfrac{x^2-4xy+4y^2}{x^2-5xy+6y^2}$ 47. $\dfrac{10x^2-8xy-2y^2}{ax-ay+bx-by}$

In 48–53, tell whether the solution is correct. State the reason for your answer.

48. $\dfrac{a+\cancel{7}}{b+\cancel{7}} = \dfrac{a}{b}$ 49. $\dfrac{c-\cancel{d}}{d-\cancel{d}} = \dfrac{c}{d}$ 50. $\dfrac{\overset{1}{\cancel{b}}\overset{1}{\cancel{(x+2)}}}{2\underset{1}{\cancel{b}}\underset{1}{\cancel{(x+2)}}} = \dfrac{1}{2}$

51. $\dfrac{\overset{1}{\cancel{d}}}{3\underset{1}{\cancel{d}}+e} = \dfrac{1}{3+e}$ 52. $\dfrac{3\overset{1}{\cancel{x+y}}}{\underset{1}{\cancel{x+y}}} = 3$ 53. $\dfrac{\overset{x}{\cancel{x^2}}+\overset{y}{\cancel{y^2}}}{\underset{1}{\cancel{x}}+\underset{1}{\cancel{y}}} = \dfrac{x+y}{2}$

3. Multiplying Fractions

The product of two fractions is the fraction with the following properties:
1. The product's numerator is the product of the numerators of the given fractions.
2. The product's denominator is the product of the denominators of the given fractions.

In general, for any numbers a, b, x, and y, when $b \neq 0$ and $y \neq 0$:

$$\frac{a}{b} \cdot \frac{x}{y} = \frac{ax}{by}$$

We can find the product of $\frac{7}{27}$ and $\frac{9}{4}$ in lowest terms by using either one of the following two methods:

Method 1   *Method 2*

$$\frac{7}{27} \cdot \frac{9}{4} = \frac{7 \cdot 9}{27 \cdot 4} = \frac{63}{108} = \frac{7 \cdot \overset{1}{\cancel{9}}}{12 \cdot \underset{1}{\cancel{9}}} = \frac{7}{12} \qquad \frac{7}{27} \cdot \frac{9}{4} = \frac{7 \cdot \overset{1}{\cancel{9}}}{\underset{3}{\cancel{27}} \cdot 4} = \frac{7}{12}$$

Notice that method 2 requires less computation than method 1 since the reduced form of the product was obtained by dividing the numerator and the denominator by a common factor *before* the product was found. This method may be called the ***cancellation method***.

When we multiply algebraic fractions, the product has the same properties as when we multiply arithmetic fractions.

Thus, to multiply $\dfrac{5x^2}{7y}$ by $\dfrac{14y^2}{15x^3}$, we may use either one of the following two methods:

Method 1

$$\frac{5x^2}{7y} \cdot \frac{14y^2}{15x^3} = \frac{5x^2 \cdot 14y^2}{7y \cdot 15x^3} = \frac{70x^2y^2}{105x^3y} = \frac{2y}{3x} \cdot \frac{35x^2y}{35x^2y} = \frac{2y}{3x} \cdot 1 = \frac{2y}{3x}$$

Method 2 (the cancellation method)

$$\frac{5x^2}{7y} \cdot \frac{14y^2}{15x^3} = \frac{\overset{1}{\cancel{5x^2}}}{\underset{1}{\cancel{7y}}} \cdot \frac{\overset{2y}{\cancel{14y^2}}}{\underset{3x}{\cancel{15x^3}}} = \frac{2y}{3x}$$

Procedure. To find the product of two fractions:

1. **Factor, when possible, the numerators and the denominators of the fractions.**

2. **Divide both the numerator and the denominator by common factors.**
3. **Multiply the remaining factors of the numerators to find the numerator of the product.**
4. **Multiply the remaining factors of the denominators to find the denominator of the product.**

Model Problem

Multiply and express the product in reduced form: $\dfrac{a^2 - b^2}{10x^3} \cdot \dfrac{5x^2}{2a + 2b}$

How to Proceed   *Solution*

1. Factor the numerators and $\dfrac{a^2 - b^2}{10x^3} \cdot \dfrac{5x^2}{2a + 2b} = \dfrac{(a + b)(a - b)}{10x^3} \cdot \dfrac{5x^2}{2(a + b)}$
   the denominators.

2. Divide the numerators and $= \dfrac{\overset{1}{\cancel{(a+b)}}(a - b)}{\underset{2x}{\cancel{10x^3}}} \cdot \dfrac{\overset{1}{\cancel{5x^2}}}{2\cancel{(a+b)}}$
   the denominators by the
   common factors, $5x^2$ and
   $(a + b)$.

3. Multiply the remaining nu- $= \dfrac{a - b}{4x}$ *Ans.*
   merators and then multi-
   ply the remaining denominators.

Keep In Mind

Any integer or polynomial may be expressed as a fraction whose denominator is 1. For example:

$$5 = \frac{5}{1} \qquad 3x^2 = \frac{3x^2}{1} \qquad 5y - 6 = \frac{5y - 6}{1}$$

EXERCISES

In 1–40, find the product in lowest terms.

1. $\dfrac{3}{5} \times \dfrac{7}{8}$ 2. $\dfrac{8}{12} \times \dfrac{30}{36}$ 3. $\dfrac{3}{8} \times 32$ 4. $40 \times \dfrac{b}{8}$

5. $\dfrac{5}{d} \times d^2$ 6. $cd \times \dfrac{5}{c}$ 7. $\dfrac{x^2}{36} \times 20$ 8. $6y^2 \times \dfrac{4}{3y}$

9. $mn \times \dfrac{8}{m^2 n^2}$ 10. $\dfrac{3c}{4d} \cdot \dfrac{5r}{3s}$ 11. $\dfrac{24x}{35y} \cdot \dfrac{14y}{8x}$ 12. $\dfrac{ab}{c} \cdot \dfrac{c}{a}$

13. $\dfrac{12x}{5y} \cdot \dfrac{15y^2}{36x^2}$ 14. $\dfrac{m^2}{8} \cdot \dfrac{32}{3m}$ 15. $\dfrac{6r^2}{5s^2} \cdot \dfrac{10rs}{6r^3}$ 16. $\dfrac{24a^3 b^2}{7c^3} \cdot \dfrac{21c^2}{12ab}$

17. $\dfrac{7}{x^2 - 4} \cdot \dfrac{2x + 4}{21}$ 18. $\dfrac{3a + 9}{15a} \cdot \dfrac{a^2}{a^2 - 9}$

19. $\dfrac{5x - 5y}{x^2 y} \cdot \dfrac{xy^2}{x^2 - y^2}$ 20. $\dfrac{x^2 - 9}{5c^5} \cdot \dfrac{10c^4}{x - 3}$

21. $\dfrac{(a + 3)^2}{x^2} \cdot \dfrac{4x^2}{4a + 12}$ 22. $\dfrac{a(a - b)^2}{4b} \cdot \dfrac{4b}{a(a^2 - b^2)}$

23. $\dfrac{(a - 2)^2}{4b} \cdot \dfrac{16b^3}{4 - a^2}$ 24. $\dfrac{a^2 - 7a - 8}{2a + 2} \cdot \dfrac{5}{a - 8}$

25. $\dfrac{y^2 - 2y - 3}{2c^3} \cdot \dfrac{4c^2}{2y + 2}$ 26. $\dfrac{4a - 6}{4a + 8} \cdot \dfrac{6a + 12}{5a - 15}$

27. $\dfrac{x^2 - 25}{4x^2 - 9} \cdot \dfrac{2x + 3}{x - 5}$ 28. $\dfrac{y^2 - 81}{(y + 9)^2} \cdot \dfrac{10y + 90}{5y - 45}$

29. $\dfrac{x + 2d}{5x^2 - 20d^2} \cdot \dfrac{25x - 50d}{25x}$ 30. $\dfrac{(x - 4)^2}{2x^2 - 32} \cdot \dfrac{4x + 16}{20x}$

31. $\dfrac{x^2 - 3x - 18}{x - 6} \cdot \dfrac{16b^3}{4 - a^2}$ 32. $\dfrac{a - b}{a + b} \cdot \dfrac{a^2 - b^2}{a^2 - 2ab + b^2}$

33. $\dfrac{y^2 - 3y - 10}{y^2 + 3y + 2} \cdot \dfrac{y^2 + 8y + 7}{y^2 - 6y + 5}$ 34. $\dfrac{a^2 + 8a + 12}{a^2 - 8a + 16} \cdot \dfrac{20 - a - a^2}{a^2 + 11a + 30}$

35. $\dfrac{x^2 - x - 2}{6x^2 - 13x + 6} \cdot \dfrac{10x^2 - 11x - 6}{6x - 3x^2}$

36. $\dfrac{(a + 7)^2 - b^2}{a^2 - ab + 7a} \cdot \dfrac{a - b - 7}{(a - b)^2 - 49}$ 37. $\dfrac{a - b}{c - a} \cdot \dfrac{a - c}{c - b} \cdot \dfrac{c - b}{b - a}$

38. $\dfrac{x^4 - 81}{2x^2 + 18} \cdot \dfrac{x^2 + 6x + 9}{9 - x^2}$

39. $\dfrac{2x - 2}{30x^2} \cdot \dfrac{9x^2 + 27x}{x^2 - 9} \cdot \dfrac{x^2 + 2x - 15}{x^2 + 4x - 5}$

40. $\dfrac{c^2 + 6cd + 9d^2}{c^2 - 4d^2} \cdot \dfrac{15c + 30d}{3c^2 + 9cd} \cdot \dfrac{c^2 - cd - 2d^2}{c^2 + 2cd - 3d^2}$

4. Dividing Fractions

We know that the operation of division may be defined by means of the multiplicative inverse, the reciprocal. A quotient can be expressed as the product of the dividend and the reciprocal of the divisor. Thus, $8 \div 5 = 8 \cdot \frac{1}{5} = \frac{8}{5}$ and $\frac{8}{7} \div \frac{5}{3} = \frac{8}{7} \cdot \frac{3}{5} = \frac{24}{35}$.

In general, for any numbers a, b, c, and d, when $b \neq 0$, $c \neq 0$, and $d \neq 0$:

$$\frac{a}{b} \div \frac{c}{d} = \frac{a}{b} \cdot \frac{d}{c} = \frac{ad}{bc}$$

Procedure. **To divide by an algebraic fraction, multiply the dividend by the reciprocal of the divisor.**

Keep In Mind

The reciprocal of $\frac{1}{n}$ is n; the reciprocal of $\frac{a}{b}$ is $\frac{b}{a}$; the reciprocal of $\frac{a+b}{c+d}$ is $\frac{c+d}{a+b}$. In each example, the product of the two expressions is 1.

Model Problems

1. Divide: $\dfrac{16c^3}{21d^2} \div \dfrac{24c^4}{14d^3}$

How to Proceed   *Solution*

Multiply the dividend by the reciprocal of the divisor.

$$\frac{16c^3}{21d^2} \div \frac{24c^4}{14d^3} = \frac{\overset{2}{\cancel{16c^3}}}{\underset{3}{\cancel{21d^2}}} \cdot \frac{\overset{2d}{\cancel{14d^3}}}{\underset{3c}{\cancel{24c^4}}} = \frac{4d}{9c} \quad Ans.$$

2. Divide: $\dfrac{8x^2}{x^2-25} \div \dfrac{4x}{3x+15}$

How to Proceed   *Solution*

1. Multiply the dividend by the reciprocal of the divisor.

$$\frac{8x^2}{x^2-25} \div \frac{4x}{3x+15}$$

$$= \frac{8x^2}{x^2-25} \cdot \frac{3x+15}{4x}$$

2. Factor the numerators and the denominators. Divide by the common factors.

$$= \frac{\overset{2x}{\cancel{8x^2}}}{(\cancel{x+5})(x-5)} \cdot \frac{\overset{1}{3(\cancel{x+5})}}{\underset{1}{\cancel{4x}}}$$

3. Multiply the remaining numerators and then the remaining denominators.

$$= \frac{6x}{x-5} \quad Ans.$$

EXERCISES

In 1–26, perform the indicated operations and express the result in lowest terms.

1. $\dfrac{7}{10} \div \dfrac{21}{5}$

2. $8 \div \dfrac{1}{2}$

3. $\dfrac{x}{9} \div \dfrac{x}{3}$

4. $\dfrac{3x}{5y} \div \dfrac{21x}{20y}$

5. $\dfrac{7ab^2}{10cd} \div \dfrac{14b^3}{5c^2d^3}$

6. $\dfrac{8x^2}{3y^2} \div \dfrac{4x}{6y^3}$

7. $8rs \div \dfrac{24r}{s}$

8. $\dfrac{6a^2b^2}{8c} \div 3ab$

9. $\dfrac{y^2 - 25}{18} \div \dfrac{y-5}{27}$

10. $\dfrac{3x - 3y}{xy^2} \div \dfrac{x^2 - y^2}{x^2 y}$

11. $\dfrac{x^2 - 36}{7y^3} \div \dfrac{x-6}{14y^4}$

12. $\dfrac{b}{a^2 - 49} \div \dfrac{4b^3}{2a + 14}$

13. $\dfrac{(m+1)^2}{n^2} \div \dfrac{6m+6}{9n^2}$

14. $\dfrac{8r^4}{(s-7)^2} \div \dfrac{20r}{s^2 - 49}$

15. $\dfrac{y^2 - 3y - 10}{8y^2} \div \dfrac{2y - 10}{16y^2}$

16. $\dfrac{y^2 - 49}{(y+7)^2} \div \dfrac{21 - 3y}{2y + 14}$

17. $\dfrac{(x-2)^2}{4x^2 - 16} \div \dfrac{21x}{3x+6}$

18. $\dfrac{x^2 - 2xy - 8y^2}{x^2 - 16y^2} \div \dfrac{5x + 10y}{3x + 12y}$

19. $(y^2 - 9) \div \dfrac{y^2 + 8y + 15}{2y + 10}$

20. $\dfrac{x^2 - 4x + 4}{3x - 6} \div (x - 2)$

21. $\dfrac{6x^2 - 5x - 4}{2x^2 - x - 1} \div \dfrac{12x^2 - 7x - 12}{4x^2 - x - 3}$

22. $\dfrac{3x - y}{3y - x} \div \dfrac{6x^2 - 17xy - 3y^2}{3xy + y^2 - 18x^2}$

23. $\dfrac{x-1}{x+1} \cdot \dfrac{2x+2}{x+2} \div \dfrac{4x-4}{x+2}$

24. $\dfrac{x+y}{x^2 + y^2} \cdot \dfrac{x}{x-y} \div \dfrac{(x+y)^2}{x^4 - y^4}$

25. $\dfrac{4x^2 - xy - 5y^2}{2x^2 - xy - 3y^2} \div \dfrac{16x^2 - 25y^2}{4x^2 - 12xy + 9y^2} \div \dfrac{2x^2 + xy - 6y^2}{4x^2 + xy - 5y^2}$

5. Adding or Subtracting Fractions Which Have the Same Denominator

We know that the sum of two arithmetic fractions which have the same denominator is a fraction whose numerator is the sum of the numerators and whose denominator is the common denominator of the given fractions. We use the same rule to add algebraic fractions which have the same nonzero denominator. Thus:

Arithmetic fractions   *Algebraic fractions*

$$\frac{5}{7} + \frac{1}{7} = \frac{5+1}{7} = \frac{6}{7}$$ $$\frac{a}{c} + \frac{b}{c} = \frac{a+b}{c}$$ $$\frac{a}{x-y} + \frac{b}{x-y} = \frac{a+b}{x-y}$$

$$\frac{5}{7} - \frac{1}{7} = \frac{5-1}{7} = \frac{4}{7}$$ $$\frac{a}{c} - \frac{b}{c} = \frac{a-b}{c}$$ $$\frac{a}{x-y} - \frac{b}{x-y} = \frac{a-b}{x-y}$$

Note: The relationships $\frac{a}{c} + \frac{b}{c} = \frac{a+b}{c}$ and $\frac{a}{c} - \frac{b}{c} = \frac{a-b}{c}$ are discussed in exercises 30 and 31 on page 278.

Procedure. To add (or subtract) fractions which have the same denominator:

1. Write a fraction whose numerator is the sum (or difference) of the numerators and whose denominator is the common denominator of the given fractions.
2. Reduce the resulting fraction to lowest terms.

Model Problems

Add or subtract as indicated. Reduce answers to lowest terms.

1. $\dfrac{5}{4x} + \dfrac{9}{4x} - \dfrac{8}{4x}$

Solution

$$\frac{5}{4x} + \frac{9}{4x} - \frac{8}{4x}$$

$$= \frac{5+9-8}{4x}$$

$$= \frac{6}{4x}$$

2. $\dfrac{4x+7}{x-3} - \dfrac{2x-5}{x-3}$

Solution

$$\frac{4x+7}{x-3} - \frac{2x-5}{x-3}$$

$$= \frac{(4x+7)-(2x-5)}{x-3}$$

$$= \frac{4x+7-2x+5}{x-3}$$

$$= \frac{3}{2x} \quad Ans.$$

$$= \frac{2x + 12}{x - 3} \quad Ans.$$

[*Note:* In model problem 2, since the fraction bar is a symbol of grouping, we place in parentheses numerators which have more than one term.]

Keep In Mind

When we add or subtract fractions, we are combining the fractions.

EXERCISES

In 1–29, add or subtract (combine) the fractions as indicated. Reduce answers to lowest terms.

1. $\dfrac{1}{8} + \dfrac{4}{8}$

2. $\dfrac{6}{12} - \dfrac{1}{12}$

3. $\dfrac{9}{16} - \dfrac{6}{16} + \dfrac{5}{16}$

4. $\dfrac{7}{3b} - \dfrac{2}{3b}$

5. $\dfrac{11}{4c} + \dfrac{5}{4c} - \dfrac{6}{4c}$

6. $\dfrac{3x}{4} + \dfrac{2x}{4}$

7. $\dfrac{x}{2} - \dfrac{y}{2} + \dfrac{z}{2}$

8. $\dfrac{5r}{t} - \dfrac{2s}{t}$

9. $\dfrac{a}{n} + \dfrac{b}{n} - \dfrac{2c}{n}$

10. $\dfrac{11b}{3y} - \dfrac{4b}{3y}$

11. $\dfrac{19c}{12d} + \dfrac{9c}{12d}$

12. $\dfrac{6}{10c} + \dfrac{9}{10c} - \dfrac{3}{10c}$

13. $\dfrac{5}{x + 2} + \dfrac{3}{x + 2}$

14. $\dfrac{r}{y - 2} + \dfrac{x}{y - 2}$

15. $\dfrac{y}{y^2 - 4} - \dfrac{2}{y^2 - 4}$

16. $\dfrac{4x + 12}{16x} + \dfrac{8x + 4}{16x}$

17. $\dfrac{6x - 9}{6} - \dfrac{4x - 8}{6}$

18. $\dfrac{12a - 15}{12a} - \dfrac{9a - 6}{12a}$

19. $\dfrac{6y - 4}{4y + 3} + \dfrac{7 - 2y}{4y + 3}$

20. $\dfrac{9d + 6}{2d + 1} - \dfrac{7d + 5}{2d + 1}$

21. $\dfrac{6x - 5}{x^2 - 1} - \dfrac{5x - 6}{x^2 - 1}$

22. $\dfrac{a^2 + 3ab}{a + b} + \dfrac{b^2 - ab}{a + b}$

23. $\dfrac{x^2 - 2xy}{x - 2y} - \dfrac{xy - 2y^2}{x - 2y}$

24. $\dfrac{8x - 8}{6x - 5} - \dfrac{2x - 7}{6x - 5} + \dfrac{6x - 9}{6x - 5}$

25. $\dfrac{a + 4b}{a^2 - b^2} + \dfrac{4a - 7b}{a^2 - b^2} - \dfrac{3a - b}{a^2 - b^2}$

26. $\dfrac{x}{(x + y)(x - y)} - \dfrac{y}{(x + y)(x - y)}$

27. $\dfrac{5a + b}{(2a + 3b)(a - b)} - \dfrac{a - 5b}{(2a + 3b)(a - b)}$

28. $\dfrac{r^2 + 4r}{r^2 - r - 6} + \dfrac{8 - r^2}{r^2 - r - 6}$

29. $\dfrac{4m^2 + 7m}{2m^2 + 5m + 2} - \dfrac{1 + 7m}{2m^2 + 5m + 2}$

30. The following sequence of steps can be used to show that $\dfrac{a}{c} + \dfrac{b}{c} = \dfrac{a + b}{c}$. Give a reason to justify each step.

1. $\dfrac{a}{c} = a \cdot \dfrac{1}{c}$ Also $\dfrac{b}{c} = b \cdot \dfrac{1}{c}$

2. $\dfrac{a}{c} + \dfrac{b}{c} = a \cdot \dfrac{1}{c} + b \cdot \dfrac{1}{c}$

3. $\dfrac{a}{c} + \dfrac{b}{c} = (a + b) \cdot \dfrac{1}{c}$

4. $\dfrac{a}{c} + \dfrac{b}{c} = \dfrac{a + b}{c}$

31. Prepare a sequence of steps which could be used to prove that $\dfrac{a}{c} - \dfrac{b}{c} = \dfrac{a - b}{c}$. Give a reason to justify each step.

6. Adding or Subtracting Fractions Which Have Different Denominators

Each of the fractions $\dfrac{2}{8}$, $\dfrac{3}{12}$, and $\dfrac{1a}{4a}$ is equivalent to the fraction $\dfrac{1}{4}$ since each one names the fraction $\dfrac{1}{4}$. Let us use the multiplication property of 1 to show that this statement is true $\left(\text{remember that } \dfrac{a}{a} = 1 \text{ when } a \neq 0\right)$:

$$\frac{1}{4} = \frac{1}{4} \cdot 1 = \frac{1}{4} \cdot \frac{2}{2} = \frac{2}{8}$$

$$\frac{1}{4} = \frac{1}{4} \cdot 1 = \frac{1}{4} \cdot \frac{3}{3} = \frac{3}{12}$$

$$\frac{1}{4} = \frac{1}{4} \cdot 1 = \frac{1}{4} \cdot \frac{a}{a} = \frac{1a}{4a}$$

These examples illustrate the ***multiplication property of a fraction:*** If the numerator and the denominator of a fraction are multiplied by the same nonzero number, the resulting fraction is equivalent to the original fraction.

To add $\frac{11}{24}$ and $\frac{7}{36}$, we first transform the fractions to equivalent fractions which have a common denominator. Any integer which has both 24 and 36 as factors could become a common denominator. To simplify our work, we will use the ***lowest common denominator*** (L.C.D.), which can be found in the following manner:

1. Express each denominator as a product of prime factors.

   $$24 = 2 \cdot 2 \cdot 2 \cdot 3 = 2^3 \cdot 3 \qquad 36 = 2 \cdot 2 \cdot 3 \cdot 3 = 2^2 \cdot 3^2$$

2. Write the product of the highest power of each of the different prime factors of the denominators.

   $$\text{L.C.D.} = 2^3 \cdot 3^2 = 8 \cdot 9 = 72$$

To find the integer by which to multiply the numerator and the denominator of $\frac{11}{24}$ to transform it into an equivalent fraction whose denominator is the L.C.D., 72, we divide 72 by the denominator 24. The result is 3. Then, $\dfrac{11}{24} = \dfrac{11 \cdot 3}{24 \cdot 3} = \dfrac{33}{72}$.

To find the integer by which to multiply the numerator and the denominator of $\frac{7}{36}$ to transform it into an equivalent fraction whose denominator is the L.C.D., 72, we divide 72 by 36. The result is 2. Then, $\dfrac{7}{36} = \dfrac{7 \cdot 2}{36 \cdot 2} = \dfrac{14}{72}$.

Now we add $\dfrac{33}{72}$ and $\dfrac{14}{72}$ and obtain $\dfrac{47}{72}$ as the result.

The entire solution may be written as follows:

$$\frac{11}{24} + \frac{7}{36} = \frac{11 \cdot 3}{24 \cdot 3} + \frac{7 \cdot 2}{36 \cdot 2} = \frac{33}{72} + \frac{14}{72} = \frac{33 + 14}{72} = \frac{47}{72} \quad Ans.$$

Algebraic fractions are added in the same manner as arithmetic fractions.

Procedure. **To add (or subtract) fractions which have different denominators:**

1. **Factor each denominator in order to find the lowest common denominator, L.C.D.**
2. **Transform each fraction to an equivalent fraction by multiplying its numerator and its denominator by the quotient that is obtained when the L.C.D. is divided by the denominator of the fraction.**

3. Write a fraction whose numerator is the sum (or difference) of the numerators of the new fractions and whose denominator is the L.C.D.

4. Reduce the resulting fraction to lowest terms.

Note: It is also possible to add or subtract fractions by making use of the following relationships which are discussed in exercises 106 and 107 on page 284.

$$\frac{a}{b} + \frac{c}{d} = \frac{ad + bc}{bd} \quad and \quad \frac{a}{b} - \frac{c}{d} = \frac{ad - bc}{bd}$$

For example, $\dfrac{11}{24} + \dfrac{7}{36} = \dfrac{(11)(36) + 24(7)}{(24)(36)} = \dfrac{396 + 168}{864} = \dfrac{564}{864} = \dfrac{47}{72}$

$$\frac{11}{24} - \frac{7}{36} = \frac{11(36) - (24)(7)}{(24)(36)} = \frac{396 - 168}{864} = \frac{228}{864} = \frac{19}{72}$$

Model Problems

1. Combine: $\dfrac{3x}{2} + \dfrac{7x}{4} - \dfrac{x}{6}$

Solution

$2 = 2 \cdot 1; 4 = 2 \cdot 2 = 2^2;$
  $6 = 2 \cdot 3$
L.C.D. $= 2^2 \cdot 3 = 12$
$12 \div 2 = 6; 12 \div 4 = 3;$
  $12 \div 6 = 2$

$\dfrac{3x}{2} + \dfrac{7x}{4} - \dfrac{x}{6}$

$= \dfrac{3x(6)}{2(6)} + \dfrac{7x(3)}{4(3)} - \dfrac{x(2)}{6(2)}$

$= \dfrac{18x}{12} + \dfrac{21x}{12} - \dfrac{2x}{12}$

$= \dfrac{18x + 21x - 2x}{12}$

$= \dfrac{37x}{12}$ *Ans.*

2. Subtract: $\dfrac{5}{a^2 b} - \dfrac{2}{ab^2}$

Solution

$a^2 b = a^2 \cdot b; ab^2 = a \cdot b^2$
L.C.D. $= a^2 \cdot b^2 = a^2 b^2$
$a^2 b^2 \div a^2 b = b;$
  $a^2 b^2 \div ab^2 = a$

$\dfrac{5}{a^2 b} - \dfrac{2}{ab^2}$

$= \dfrac{5(b)}{a^2 b(b)} - \dfrac{2(a)}{ab^2 (a)}$

$= \dfrac{5b}{a^2 b^2} - \dfrac{2a}{a^2 b^2}$

$= \dfrac{5b - 2a}{a^2 b^2}$ *Ans.*

3. Subtract: $\dfrac{2x+5}{3} - \dfrac{x-2}{4}$

Solution

$3 = 3 \cdot 1; \ 4 = 2 \cdot 2 = 2^2$
L.C.D. $= 3 \cdot 2^2 = 12$
$12 \div 3 = 4; \ 12 \div 4 = 3$

$$\dfrac{2x+5}{3} - \dfrac{x-2}{4}$$

$$= \dfrac{4(2x+5)}{4(3)} - \dfrac{3(x-2)}{3(4)}$$

$$= \dfrac{8x+20}{12} - \dfrac{3x-6}{12}$$

$$= \dfrac{(8x+20)-(3x-6)}{12}$$

$$= \dfrac{8x+20-3x+6}{12}$$

$$= \dfrac{5x+26}{12} \quad Ans.$$

4. Add: $\dfrac{2a-5}{18a} + \dfrac{3a+2}{15a}$

Solution

$18a = 2 \cdot 3^2 \cdot a; \ 15a = 3 \cdot 5 \cdot a$
L.C.D. $= 2 \cdot 3^2 \cdot 5 \cdot a = 90a$
$90a \div 18a = 5; \ 90a \div 15a = 6$

$$\dfrac{2a-5}{18a} + \dfrac{3a+2}{15a}$$

$$= \dfrac{5(2a-5)}{5(18a)} + \dfrac{6(3a+2)}{6(15a)}$$

$$= \dfrac{10a-25}{90a} + \dfrac{18a+12}{90a}$$

$$= \dfrac{(10a-25)+(18a+12)}{90a}$$

$$= \dfrac{10a-25+18a+12}{90a}$$

$$= \dfrac{28a-13}{90a} \quad Ans.$$

5. Add: $\dfrac{5}{3x-15} + \dfrac{2}{5x-25}$

Solution

$3x-15 = 3(x-5)$
$5x-25 = 5(x-5)$
L.C.D. $= 15(x-5)$

$$\dfrac{5}{3x-15} + \dfrac{2}{5x-25}$$

$$= \dfrac{5}{3(x-5)} + \dfrac{2}{5(x-5)}$$

$[15(x-5) \div 3(x-5) = 5;$
$\ 15(x-5) \div 5(x-5) = 3]$

$$= \dfrac{5 \cdot 5}{5 \cdot 3(x-5)} + \dfrac{3 \cdot 2}{3 \cdot 5(x-5)}$$

$$= \dfrac{25}{15(x-5)} + \dfrac{6}{15(x-5)}$$

$$= \dfrac{25+6}{15(x-5)}$$

6. Subtract: $\dfrac{5x}{x^2-4} - \dfrac{-3}{2-x}$

Solution

$$\dfrac{5x}{x^2-4} - \dfrac{-3}{2-x} = \dfrac{5x}{x^2-4} - \dfrac{3}{x-2}$$

$x^2 - 4 = (x-2)(x+2)$
$x - 2 = 1 \cdot (x-2)$
L.C.D. $= (x-2)(x+2)$

$$\dfrac{5x}{x^2-4} - \dfrac{3}{x-2}$$

$$= \dfrac{5x}{(x-2)(x+2)} - \dfrac{3}{(x-2)}$$

$[(x-2)(x+2) \div (x-2) = (x+2)]$

$$= \dfrac{5x}{(x-2)(x+2)} - \dfrac{3(x+2)}{(x-2)(x+2)}$$

$$= \dfrac{5x-(3x+6)}{(x-2)(x+2)}$$

$$= \frac{31}{15(x - 5)} \text{ or}$$

$$\frac{31}{15x - 75} \text{ Ans.}$$

$$= \frac{5x - 3x - 6}{(x - 2)(x + 2)}$$

$$= \frac{2x - 6}{(x - 2)(x + 2)} \text{ or}$$

$$\frac{2x - 6}{x^2 - 4} \text{ Ans.}$$

EXERCISES

In 1–16, find the lowest common denominator for two fractions whose denominators are:

1. $10; 5$ 2. $8; 12$ 3. $6a; 2a$ 4. $3; x$ 5. $r; s$
6. $15a; 6b$ 7. $xy; yz$ 8. $m^2 n; mn^2$ 9. $12x^2; 18y^2$ 10. $6c^2 d^2; 10cd$
11. $x + 3; x - 3$ 12. $4(c + 1); 6(c + 1)$ 13. $3c + 9; 4c + 12$
14. $x; x + 5$ 15. $x^2 - 1; 3x + 3$ 16. $3x - 4; 4 - 3x$

In 17–33, transform the given fractions into equivalent fractions that have the L.C.D. as their denominators.

17. $\dfrac{3}{5}; \dfrac{4}{3}$

18. $\dfrac{5}{8}; \dfrac{9}{20}$

19. $\dfrac{5y}{3}; \dfrac{7y}{6}$

20. $\dfrac{3x}{12}; \dfrac{7x}{90}$

21. $\dfrac{5y}{3c}; \dfrac{7y}{6c}$

22. $\dfrac{8}{x^2}; \dfrac{2}{x}$

23. $\dfrac{a}{cd}; \dfrac{m}{bc}$

24. $\dfrac{7}{4c^2}; \dfrac{5}{18d^2}$

25. $\dfrac{a - 6}{2}; \dfrac{2a + 5}{4}$

26. $\dfrac{3c + 1}{18d}; \dfrac{5c - 3}{24d}$

27. $\dfrac{5x - 4}{20y}; \dfrac{3x + 7}{72y}$

28. $\dfrac{1}{x + 2}; \dfrac{3}{x - 2}$

29. $\dfrac{5m - 1}{3(m - 2)}; \dfrac{8}{2(m - 2)}$

30. $\dfrac{2t - 1}{8t - 8}; \dfrac{4t + 1}{6t - 6}$

31. $\dfrac{4}{y}; \dfrac{y - 1}{y + 2}$

32. $\dfrac{6x + 1}{x^2 - 9}; \dfrac{-3}{x - 3}$

33. $\dfrac{7}{1 - 3a}; \dfrac{2}{3a - 1}$

In 34–105, add or subtract (combine) the fractions as indicated. Reduce answers to lowest terms.

34. $\dfrac{5}{6} + \dfrac{1}{12}$

35. $\dfrac{7}{8} - \dfrac{1}{4}$

36. $\dfrac{5}{4} + \dfrac{3}{2} - \dfrac{1}{3}$

37. $\dfrac{3x}{10} + \dfrac{7x}{5}$

38. $\dfrac{10y}{7} - \dfrac{3y}{4}$

39. $\dfrac{8x}{5} - \dfrac{3x}{4} + \dfrac{7x}{10}$

40. $\dfrac{5a}{6} - \dfrac{3a}{4}$

41. $\dfrac{7y}{8} + \dfrac{3y}{10} - \dfrac{y}{5}$

42. $\dfrac{a}{7} + \dfrac{b}{14}$

43. $\dfrac{c}{5} - \dfrac{2d}{3}$

44. $\dfrac{a}{3} + \dfrac{b}{4} - \dfrac{c}{5}$

45. $\dfrac{9}{4x} + \dfrac{3}{2x}$

46. $\dfrac{8}{5c} - \dfrac{1}{4c}$

47. $\dfrac{5x}{2d} + \dfrac{4x}{3d}$

48. $\dfrac{7x}{4y} - \dfrac{3x}{5y}$

49. $\dfrac{3r}{2s} - \dfrac{5r}{4s} - \dfrac{2r}{3s}$

50. $\dfrac{c}{a} - \dfrac{a}{b}$ 51. $\dfrac{1}{x} + \dfrac{1}{y} + \dfrac{1}{z}$ 52. $\dfrac{5}{y^2} - \dfrac{2}{y}$ 53. $\dfrac{x}{a^2 b} + \dfrac{y}{ab^2}$

54. $\dfrac{1}{xy} + \dfrac{1}{yz}$ 55. $\dfrac{2}{ab} - \dfrac{3}{bc}$ 56. $\dfrac{5}{rs} + \dfrac{9}{st}$ 57. $\dfrac{x}{3ab} - \dfrac{y}{2bc}$

58. $\dfrac{9}{ab} + \dfrac{2}{bc} - \dfrac{3}{ac}$ 59. $\dfrac{2}{y^3} - \dfrac{3}{y^2} + \dfrac{7}{y}$ 60. $\dfrac{1}{x^2} + \dfrac{3}{xy} - \dfrac{5}{y^2}$

61. $\dfrac{y-1}{2} - \dfrac{y-5}{8}$ 62. $\dfrac{m+9}{2} + \dfrac{m-3}{3}$ 63. $\dfrac{x+7}{3} - \dfrac{2x-3}{5}$

64. $\dfrac{3x-5}{4} + \dfrac{2x+3}{6}$ 65. $\dfrac{3y-4}{5} - \dfrac{y-2}{4}$ 66. $\dfrac{6a+b}{30} - \dfrac{2a-b}{10}$

67. $\dfrac{a-b}{4} - \dfrac{a+b}{6}$ 68. $\dfrac{9y-2}{12y} - \dfrac{4y+1}{6y}$ 69. $\dfrac{3x-4}{5x} - \dfrac{2x-3}{20x} + \dfrac{5x}{2}$

70. $\dfrac{3b+1}{5b} - \dfrac{4b-3}{4b}$ 71. $\dfrac{y-4}{4y^2} + \dfrac{3y-5}{3y}$ 72. $\dfrac{2x+3}{12x} - \dfrac{3x-6}{8x} - \dfrac{5}{x}$

73. $5 + \dfrac{8a-6}{4}$ 74. $\dfrac{3c-7}{4} - 2c$ 75. $6x - \dfrac{4x-9}{5}$

76. $\dfrac{3x+5}{3} + \dfrac{2-5x}{4} - \dfrac{x-8}{5}$ 77. $\dfrac{2x+3y}{6x} - \dfrac{4x-5y}{4x} - x$

78. $\dfrac{x+y}{x} - \dfrac{y-z}{y} - \dfrac{z-x}{z}$ 79. $\dfrac{6}{ab} + \dfrac{a-3}{a^2} - \dfrac{7+b}{b^2}$

80. $\dfrac{2}{3y} - \dfrac{4y-7}{6y^2} + \dfrac{3y-2y^2}{4y^3}$ 81. $\dfrac{4a+1}{6a^2 b} - \dfrac{3b-5}{4ab^2} - \dfrac{2b+1}{9ab}$

82. $\dfrac{5}{x-3} + \dfrac{7}{2x-6}$ 83. $\dfrac{10}{3x-6} + \dfrac{3}{2x-4}$ 84. $\dfrac{11x}{8x-8} - \dfrac{3x}{4x-4}$

85. $\dfrac{3}{2x-3y} + \dfrac{5}{3y-2x}$ 86. $\dfrac{3x-2}{2x+2} + \dfrac{4x-1}{3x+3}$ 87. $\dfrac{5x+2}{6x-3} - \dfrac{3x-5}{8x-4}$

88. $\dfrac{9}{y+4} - \dfrac{6}{y-4}$ 89. $\dfrac{7}{a+3} + \dfrac{4}{2-a}$ 90. $\dfrac{7}{x-2} + \dfrac{3}{x}$ 91. $\dfrac{9}{c+8} - \dfrac{2}{c}$

92. $\dfrac{2a+b}{a-b} + \dfrac{a}{b}$ 93. $\dfrac{5}{y^2-9} + \dfrac{3}{y-3}$ 94. $\dfrac{9}{a^2-b^2} + \dfrac{3}{b-a}$

95. $\dfrac{x}{x^2-36} - \dfrac{4}{3x+18}$ 96. $\dfrac{9}{a^2-ab} + \dfrac{3}{ab-b^2}$

97. $\dfrac{1}{y-3} + \dfrac{2}{y+4} + \dfrac{2}{3}$ 98. $\dfrac{1}{(x+2)^3} - \dfrac{1}{(x+2)^2} + \dfrac{1}{x+2}$

99. $\dfrac{7a}{(a-1)(a+3)} + \dfrac{2a-5}{(a+3)(a+2)}$ 100. $\dfrac{5}{r^2-4} - \dfrac{3}{r^2+3r-10}$

101. $\dfrac{x+2y}{3x+12y} - \dfrac{6x-y}{x^2+3xy-4y^2}$ 102. $\dfrac{2a+7}{a^2-2a-15} - \dfrac{3}{r^2+3r-10}$

103. $\dfrac{10x}{3x^2 + 8x - 3} - \dfrac{7x}{2x^2 + 5x - 3}$ **104.** $\dfrac{4}{a^2 - 4} + \dfrac{3}{2a - a^2} - \dfrac{2}{2a + a^2}$

105. $\dfrac{1}{9b^2 - 9b + 2} + \dfrac{10}{45b^2 - 5} - \dfrac{1}{9b^2 - 3b - 2}$

106. The following sequence of steps can be used to show that $\dfrac{a}{b} + \dfrac{c}{d} = \dfrac{ad + bc}{bd}$. Give a reason to justify each step.

1. $\dfrac{a}{b} = \dfrac{a}{b} \cdot 1$ also $\dfrac{c}{d} = 1 \cdot \dfrac{c}{d}$

2. $\quad = \dfrac{a}{b} \cdot \dfrac{d}{d}$ also $\quad = \dfrac{b}{b} \cdot \dfrac{c}{d}$

3. $\quad = \dfrac{ad}{bd}$ also $\quad = \dfrac{bc}{bd}$

4. $\dfrac{a}{b} + \dfrac{c}{d} = \dfrac{ad}{bd} + \dfrac{bc}{bd}$

5. $\dfrac{a}{b} + \dfrac{c}{d} = \dfrac{ad + bc}{bd}$

107. Prepare a sequence of steps which can be used to show that $\dfrac{a}{b} - \dfrac{c}{d} = \dfrac{ad - bc}{bd}$. Give a reason to justify each step.

7. Mixed Expressions

The mixed number $3\frac{1}{2}$, which means the sum of the integer 3 and the fraction $\frac{1}{2}$, can be expressed as a fraction. To do this, we express the integer 3 as the fraction $\frac{3}{1}$ and then add $\frac{3}{1}$ and $\frac{1}{2}$.

$$3\tfrac{1}{2} = \frac{3}{1} + \frac{1}{2} = \frac{3 \cdot 2}{1 \cdot 2} + \frac{1}{2} = \frac{6}{2} + \frac{1}{2} = \frac{6 + 1}{2} = \frac{7}{2}$$

The indicated sum or difference of a polynomial and a fraction is called a ***mixed expression***. For example, $y + \dfrac{5}{y}$ is a mixed expression. A mixed expression can be expressed as a fraction.

Procedure. To express a mixed expression as a fraction:

1. **Write the polynomial of the expression as a fraction whose denominator is 1.**
2. **Add the two fractions.**

Model Problems

In 1 and 2, express the mixed expression as a fraction.

1. $y + \dfrac{5}{y}$

2. $y + 1 - \dfrac{1}{y-1}$

Solution

$$y + \frac{5}{y} = \frac{y}{1} + \frac{5}{y}$$

$$= \frac{y \cdot y}{1 \cdot y} + \frac{5}{y}$$

$$= \frac{y^2}{y} + \frac{5}{y}$$

$$= \frac{y^2 + 5}{y} \quad \text{Ans.}$$

Solution

$$y + 1 - \frac{1}{y-1} = \frac{y+1}{1} - \frac{1}{y-1}$$

$$= \frac{(y+1)(y-1)}{1(y-1)} - \frac{1}{y-1}$$

$$= \frac{y^2 - 1}{y-1} - \frac{1}{y-1}$$

$$= \frac{y^2 - 1 - 1}{y-1}$$

$$= \frac{y^2 - 2}{y-1} \quad \text{Ans.}$$

EXERCISES

In 1–15, express the mixed expression as a fraction in its lowest terms.

1. $5\frac{2}{3}$

2. $9\frac{3}{4}$

3. $5 + \dfrac{1}{x}$

4. $9 - \dfrac{7}{s}$

5. $m + \dfrac{1}{m}$

6. $d - \dfrac{7}{5d}$

7. $7 + \dfrac{2a}{b+c}$

8. $t + \dfrac{1}{t+1}$

9. $s - \dfrac{1}{s-1}$

10. $5 - \dfrac{2x}{x+y}$

11. $\dfrac{c+2}{c-3} + 8$

12. $7 - \dfrac{x+y}{x-y}$

13. $a + 1 + \dfrac{1}{a+1}$

14. $x - 5 - \dfrac{x}{x+3}$

15. $\dfrac{2x-1}{x+2} + 2x - 3$

8. Multiplying and Dividing Mixed Expressions

Procedure. To multiply mixed expressions or to divide mixed expressions:

1. Express each mixed expression as a single fraction.
2. Perform the indicated multiplication or division.

Model Problems

1. Simplify $\left(\dfrac{a}{b} + 3\right)\left(\dfrac{a}{b} - 3\right)$

Solution

$$\left(\dfrac{a}{b} + 3\right)\left(\dfrac{a}{b} - 3\right)$$

$$= \left(\dfrac{a}{b} + \dfrac{3}{1}\right)\left(\dfrac{a}{b} - \dfrac{3}{1}\right)$$

$$= \left(\dfrac{a}{b} + \dfrac{3 \cdot b}{1 \cdot b}\right)\left(\dfrac{a}{b} - \dfrac{3 \cdot b}{1 \cdot b}\right)$$

$$= \dfrac{a + 3b}{b} \cdot \dfrac{a - 3b}{b}$$

$$= \dfrac{a^2 - 9b^2}{b^2} \quad Ans.$$

2. Simplify $\left(1 - \dfrac{2}{x}\right) \div \left(1 - \dfrac{4}{x^2}\right)$

Solution

$$\left(1 - \dfrac{2}{x}\right) \div \left(1 - \dfrac{4}{x^2}\right)$$

$$= \left(\dfrac{1}{1} - \dfrac{2}{x}\right) \div \left(\dfrac{1}{1} - \dfrac{4}{x^2}\right)$$

$$= \left(\dfrac{1 \cdot x}{1 \cdot x} - \dfrac{2}{x}\right) \div \left(\dfrac{1 \cdot x^2}{1 \cdot x^2} - \dfrac{4}{x^2}\right)$$

$$= \dfrac{x - 2}{x} \div \dfrac{x^2 - 4}{x^2}$$

$$= \dfrac{x - 2}{x} \cdot \dfrac{x^2}{x^2 - 4}$$

$$= \dfrac{\overset{1}{\cancel{(x-2)}}}{\underset{1}{x}} \cdot \dfrac{\overset{x}{\cancel{x^2}}}{(x + 2)\underset{1}{\cancel{(x-2)}}}$$

$$= \dfrac{x}{x + 2} \quad Ans.$$

EXERCISES

In 1–10, perform the indicated operations. Express the result in simplest form.

1. $\left(\dfrac{m}{n} + 4\right)\left(\dfrac{m}{n} - 4\right)$

2. $\left(\dfrac{x^2}{x^2 - y^2}\right)\left(1 + \dfrac{y}{x}\right)$

3. $\left(\dfrac{x^2}{y^2} - 9\right)\left(1 - \dfrac{x}{x + 3y}\right)$

4. $\left(\dfrac{a^2}{b} - b\right) \div \left(\dfrac{a}{b} - 1\right)$

5. $\left(7 + \dfrac{7}{3b}\right) \div \left(\dfrac{1}{9b} - b\right)$

6. $\left(\dfrac{25}{a} + a - 10\right) \div \left(a - 6 + \dfrac{5}{a}\right)$

7. $\left(\dfrac{2a}{b} - 2\right) \div \left(\dfrac{1}{a} - \dfrac{1}{b}\right)$

8. $\left(\dfrac{x^2}{4y^2} - \dfrac{c^2}{d^2}\right) \div \left(\dfrac{c}{d} - \dfrac{x}{2y}\right)$

9. $(a - 3) \div \left(1 - \dfrac{10}{a^2 + 1}\right)$

10. $\left(\dfrac{1}{y - 1} + 1\right) \cdot \left(y - 1 - \dfrac{y^2 - 1}{y}\right)$

9. Simplifying Complex Fractions

A complex fraction is a fraction that contains one or more fractions in the numerator or the denominator or in both the numerator and the denominator.

The following are examples of complex fractions:

$$\frac{\dfrac{1}{4}}{\dfrac{1}{5}} \qquad \frac{3x}{\dfrac{1}{x}} \qquad \frac{x + \dfrac{2}{x}}{5x} \qquad \frac{25 - \dfrac{1}{x^2}}{5 - \dfrac{1}{x}}$$

There are two basic methods for simplifying a complex fraction.

Method 1. Multiplying the numerator and the denominator of the complex fraction by the lowest common denominator (L.C.D.) of all the fractions that appear in the numerator and in the denominator.

Method 2. Expressing the numerator and the denominator of the complex fraction as single fractions, then dividing the numerator of the resulting fraction by its denominator.

Model Problems

Method 1

Simplify:

1. $\dfrac{2 + \dfrac{x}{y}}{2 - \dfrac{x}{y}}$ 2. $\dfrac{y - \dfrac{1}{3}}{y^2 - \dfrac{1}{9}}$

How to Proceed	*Solution*	*Solution*
1. Find the L.C.D. of all fractions that appear in the complex fraction.	L.C.D. for $\dfrac{x}{y}$ and $\dfrac{x}{y}$ is y.	L.C.D. for $\dfrac{1}{3}$ and $\dfrac{1}{9}$ is 9.
2. Multiply both the numerator and the denominator of the complex fraction by this L.C.D.	$\dfrac{2 + \dfrac{x}{y}}{2 - \dfrac{x}{y}}$	$\dfrac{y - \dfrac{1}{3}}{y^2 - \dfrac{1}{9}}$

$$= \frac{y\left(2+\dfrac{x}{y}\right)}{y\left(2-\dfrac{x}{y}\right)} \qquad\qquad = \frac{9\left(y-\dfrac{1}{3}\right)}{9\left(y^2-\dfrac{1}{9}\right)} = \frac{9y-3}{9y^2-1}$$

3. Use the distributive property and simplify the result.

$$= \frac{2y+x}{2y-x} \ \textit{Ans.} \qquad\qquad = \frac{3\,\overset{1}{\cancel{(3y-1)}}}{\underset{1}{\cancel{(3y-1)}}\,(3y+1)}$$

$$= \frac{3}{3y+1} \ \textit{Ans.}$$

Method 2

Simplify:

1. $\dfrac{2+\dfrac{x}{y}}{2-\dfrac{x}{y}}$ 2. $\dfrac{y-\dfrac{1}{3}}{y^2-\dfrac{1}{9}}$

How to Proceed *Solution* *Solution*

$$\dfrac{2+\dfrac{x}{y}}{2-\dfrac{x}{y}} \qquad\qquad \dfrac{y-\dfrac{1}{3}}{y^2-\dfrac{1}{9}}$$

1. Express both the numerator and the denominator of the complex fraction as single fractions.

$$= \dfrac{\dfrac{2y}{y}+\dfrac{x}{y}}{\dfrac{2y}{y}-\dfrac{x}{y}} \qquad\qquad = \dfrac{\dfrac{3y}{3}-\dfrac{1}{3}}{\dfrac{9y^2}{9}-\dfrac{1}{9}}$$

$$= \dfrac{\dfrac{2y+x}{y}}{\dfrac{2y-x}{y}} \qquad\qquad = \dfrac{\dfrac{3y-1}{3}}{\dfrac{9y^2-1}{9}}$$

2. Divide the numerator of the resulting fraction by its denominator.

$$= \left(\frac{2y+x}{y}\right) \div \left(\frac{2y-x}{y}\right) \qquad = \left(\frac{3y-1}{3}\right) \div \left(\frac{9y^2-1}{9}\right)$$

$$= \frac{(2y+x)}{\cancel{y}} \cdot \frac{\overset{1}{\cancel{y}}}{(2y-x)} \qquad = \frac{(3y-1)}{3} \cdot \frac{\overset{3}{\cancel{9}}}{(3y-1)(3y+1)}$$

$$= \frac{2y+x}{2y-x} \ \textit{Ans.} \qquad\qquad = \frac{3}{3y+1} \ \textit{Ans.}$$

EXERCISES

In 1–20, simplify the complex fraction.

1. $\dfrac{5-\frac{1}{3}}{12}$

2. $\dfrac{9-\frac{1}{4}}{15}$

3. $\dfrac{4+\frac{1}{6}}{1+\frac{2}{3}}$

4. $\dfrac{7-\frac{3}{4}}{4-\frac{1}{2}}$

5. $\dfrac{\dfrac{m^3}{n^2}}{\dfrac{m^5}{n}}$

6. $\dfrac{\dfrac{2ab}{c+2d}}{\dfrac{4bt}{c+2d}}$

7. $\dfrac{\dfrac{x-3y}{a}}{\dfrac{x^2-9y^2}{a^3}}$

8. $\dfrac{\frac{1}{3}+2a}{\frac{1}{9}-4a^2}$

9. $\dfrac{1-\dfrac{5}{c}}{1-\dfrac{25}{c^2}}$

10. $\dfrac{\dfrac{1}{rs}}{\dfrac{r}{s}-\dfrac{s}{r}}$

11. $\dfrac{\dfrac{1}{x^2}+\dfrac{1}{y^2}}{\dfrac{4}{xy}}$

12. $\dfrac{1-\dfrac{x}{x+4}}{\dfrac{x}{x+4}-1}$

13. $\dfrac{\dfrac{2}{a}-6}{a-9a}$

14. $\dfrac{\dfrac{b}{a}-1}{\dfrac{a}{b}-\dfrac{b}{a}}$

15. $\dfrac{1-\dfrac{7}{y}+\dfrac{10}{y^2}}{1-\dfrac{4}{y}-\dfrac{12}{y^2}}$

16. $\dfrac{\dfrac{6}{x^2-y^2}}{\dfrac{3}{x+y}-\dfrac{3}{x-y}}$

17. $\dfrac{\dfrac{1}{c}+\dfrac{1}{d}}{\dfrac{1}{c}+\dfrac{2}{c+d}}$

18. $\dfrac{\dfrac{x-y}{x}-\dfrac{x+y}{y}}{\dfrac{x-y}{y}+\dfrac{x+y}{x}}$

19. $\dfrac{\dfrac{(y+1)^2-4}{y^2+y-2}}{\dfrac{4}{y-1}-\dfrac{2}{y+2}}$

20. $\dfrac{\dfrac{a}{a-b}-\dfrac{b}{a+b}}{\dfrac{a}{a+b}-\dfrac{b}{b-a}}$

21. Simplify. $\dfrac{1}{1+\dfrac{1}{1+\frac{1}{2}}}$. $\left[\textit{Hint:}\ \text{First simplify the fraction } \dfrac{1}{1+\frac{1}{2}}.\right.$ $\left.\text{Then, simplify the resulting fraction.}\right]$

In 22–25, simplify the complex fraction.

22. $\dfrac{1+\dfrac{1}{3}}{1+\dfrac{1}{1+\frac{1}{3}}}$

23. $\dfrac{1+\dfrac{1}{y}}{1+\dfrac{1}{1+\frac{1}{y}}}$

24. $\dfrac{1}{x-\dfrac{1}{x+\frac{1}{x}}}$

25. $\dfrac{1}{y+\dfrac{1}{y}-\dfrac{1}{y}}$

In 26–29, find, in simplest form, the reciprocal of the given expression.

26. $\dfrac{x - \dfrac{1}{x}}{7 + \dfrac{7}{x}}$ 27. $\dfrac{x - \dfrac{1}{y}}{y - \dfrac{1}{x}}$ 28. $\dfrac{1 + \dfrac{1}{x}}{1 + \dfrac{1}{1 + \dfrac{1}{x}}}$ 29. $\dfrac{1}{x - \dfrac{1}{x + \dfrac{1}{x}}}$

10. Studying the Changes in the Value of a Fraction

If a variable appears in a fraction, the value of the fraction may change as the variable is replaced by different numbers.

The sequence of numbers $\frac{5}{10}, \frac{5}{9}, \frac{5}{8}, \frac{5}{7}$, and so on, illustrates:

Principle 1. If the numerator of a fraction has a fixed positive value and the denominator is positive and decreases, then the value of the fraction increases.

Thus, the value of $\dfrac{5}{x}$ increases as x decreases from 10 to 1.

The sequence of numbers $\frac{4}{3}, \frac{4}{4}, \frac{4}{5}, \frac{4}{6}$, and so on, illustrates:

Principle 2. If the numerator of a fraction has a fixed positive value and the denominator is positive and increases, then the value of the fraction decreases.

Thus, the value of $\dfrac{4}{x}$ decreases as x increases from 1 to 10.

The sequence of numbers $\frac{10}{3}, \frac{9}{3}, \frac{8}{3}, \frac{7}{3}$, and so on, illustrates:

Principle 3. If the denominator of a fraction has a fixed positive value and the numerator is positive and decreases, then the value of the fraction decreases.

Thus, the value of $\dfrac{x}{3}$ decreases as x decreases from 10 to 1.

The sequence of numbers $\frac{3}{9}, \frac{4}{9}, \frac{5}{9}, \frac{6}{9}$, and so on, illustrates:

Principle 4. If the denominator of a fraction has a fixed positive value and the numerator is positive and increases, then the value of the fraction increases.

Thus, the value of $\dfrac{x}{9}$ increases as x increases from 1 to 10.

Model Problem

If $y = \dfrac{5}{x + 2}$, does y increase or decrease as x decreases from 5 to 3?

Solution: In the equation $y = \dfrac{5}{x + 2}$, replace x by the values 5, 4, and 3.

As x decreases from 5 to 3, $x + 2$ decreases from 7 to 5.

We see by principle 1 that y increases.

Answer: y increases.

EXERCISES

1. If x is positive and $y = \dfrac{1}{x}$, does y increase or decrease as x increases?

2. If x is positive and $y = \dfrac{12}{x}$, does y increase or decrease as x decreases?

3. If $y = \dfrac{5}{2x}$ and x is positive, does y increase or decrease as x increases?

4. If $y = \dfrac{3x}{2}$ and x is positive, does y increase or decrease as x increases?

5. If $y = \dfrac{5x}{3}$ and x is positive, does y increase or decrease as x decreases?

6. If x is positive, does the value of the fraction $\dfrac{12}{x + 3}$ increase or decrease as x increases?

7. If x is positive and $y = \dfrac{2}{3x + 1}$, does y increase or decrease as x decreases?

8. If $y = \dfrac{4x + 3}{5}$ and x is positive, does y increase or decrease as x increases?

9. If $y = \dfrac{5x - 1}{2}$ and x is positive, does y increase or decrease as x decreases?

10. If $y = \dfrac{x^2 - 5}{10}$ and x is greater than 3 and increases, does y increase or decrease as x increases?

11. State whether the value of the fraction $\dfrac{x}{y}$ increases or decreases when:

   a. x is positive and increasing, and y is positive and decreasing
   b. x is positive and decreasing, and y is positive and increasing

12. $\dfrac{y}{z}$ and $\dfrac{z}{y}$ are fractions in which y and z are positive integers and y is less than z ($y < z$). Select the fraction which has the larger value.

13. Select the fraction which will have the least value if any pair of positive integers is substituted for x and y.

   a. $\dfrac{x}{y}$ b. $\dfrac{x + 2}{y}$ c. $\dfrac{x}{y - 2}$ d. $\dfrac{x + 2}{y - 2}$

14. Select the fraction which will have the greatest value if x and y are replaced by any pair of positive integers.

   a. $\dfrac{2x}{3y}$ b. $\dfrac{2x}{3y - 1}$ c. $\dfrac{2x + 1}{3y - 1}$ d. $\dfrac{2x + 1}{3y}$

   In 15–17, select the choice which correctly completes the statement.

15. If positive integers are substituted for x and y in the fractions $\dfrac{x}{y}$ and $\dfrac{x + 5}{y + 5}$, then the second fraction as compared with the first will be (a) always equal, (b) always greater, (c) always less, (d) sometimes greater and sometimes less.

16. If positive integers are substituted for r and s in the fractions $\dfrac{r}{s}$ and $\dfrac{r + 2}{s + 2}$, then the first fraction as compared to the second will be (a) always equal, (b) sometimes equal, (c) always greater, (d) always less.

17. If positive integers are substituted for a, b, and c in the fractions $\dfrac{a}{b}$ and $\dfrac{a + c}{b + c}$, then the first fraction as compared to the second will be (a) always less, (b) sometimes less and sometimes greater, (c) always greater, (d) always equal.

Chapter 11

First-Degree Equations and

Inequalities Involving Fractions

1. Solving Equations Containing Fractional Coefficients or Fractional Constants

Examples of equations that contain fractional coefficients or fractional constants are:

$$\frac{1}{4}x = \frac{5}{8}; \quad \frac{1}{2}x = 10 \text{ or } \frac{x}{2} = 10; \quad \frac{1}{3}x + 60 = \frac{5}{6}x \text{ or } \frac{x}{3} + 60 = \frac{5x}{6}$$

In solving such equations, we make use of the previously learned methods of solving equations.

Procedure. **To solve an equation that contains fractional coefficients or fractional constants: First transform it into a simpler equation which does not contain fractions (clear the equation of fractions). Do this by multiplying both of its members by the lowest common denominator, L.C.D., of all the fractional coefficients involved in the equation. Then solve the resulting equation by the usual methods.**

Note: In solving an equation or an inequality involving fractions, the lowest common denominator (L.C.D.) used as a multiplier is sometimes called the *lowest common multiple* or *least common multiple* (L.C.M.) of the denominators in the equation or inequality.

Model Problems

1. Solve and check: $\dfrac{3x}{4} = 20 + \dfrac{x}{4}$

How to Proceed

1. Write the equation.

2. Multiply by the L.C.D., 4.

Solution

$$\frac{3x}{4} = 20 + \frac{x}{4}$$

$$4\left(\frac{3x}{4}\right) = 4\left(20 + \frac{x}{4}\right)$$

3. Use the distributive property. $4\left(\dfrac{3x}{4}\right) = 4(20) + 4\left(\dfrac{x}{4}\right)$

4. Multiply. $3x = 80 + x$

5. S_x or A_{-x}. $3x + (-x) = 80 + x + (-x)$

6. Collect like terms. $2x = 80$

7. D_2 or $M_{\frac{1}{2}}$. $x = 40$

Check

$$\frac{3x}{4} = 20 + \frac{x}{4}$$

$$\frac{3(40)}{4} \overset{?}{=} 20 + \frac{40}{4}$$

$$\frac{120}{4} \overset{?}{=} 20 + 10$$

$$30 \overset{?}{=} 20 + 10$$

$$30 = 30 \quad \text{(true)}$$

Answer: $x = 40$, or solution set is $\{40\}$.

2. Solve: $\dfrac{2x + 7}{6} - \dfrac{2x - 9}{10} = 3$

How to Proceed   *Solution*

1. Write the equation. $\dfrac{2x + 7}{6} - \dfrac{2x - 9}{10} = 3$

2. Multiply by the L.C.D., 30. $30\left(\dfrac{2x + 7}{6} - \dfrac{2x - 9}{10}\right) = 30(3)$

3. Use the distributive property. $30\left(\dfrac{2x + 7}{6}\right) - 30\left(\dfrac{2x - 9}{10}\right) = 30(3)$

4. Multiply. $5(2x + 7) - 3(2x - 9) = 90$

5. Use the distributive property. $10x + 35 - 6x + 27 = 90$

6. Collect like terms. $4x + 62 = 90$

7. S_{62} or A_{-62}. $4x + 62 + (-62) = 90 + (-62)$

8. Collect like terms. $4x = 28$

9. D_4 or $M_{\frac{1}{4}}$. $x = 7$

Check by substituting 7 for x in the given equation.

Answer: $x = 7$, or solution set is $\{7\}$.

EXERCISES

In 1–37, solve and check.

1. $\dfrac{x}{7} = 3$

2. $\dfrac{t}{6} = 18$

3. $\dfrac{3x}{5} = 15$

4. $\dfrac{5n}{7} = 35$

5. $\dfrac{x+8}{4} = 6$

6. $\dfrac{m-2}{9} = 3$

7. $\dfrac{2r+6}{5} = -4$

8. $\dfrac{30-5y}{7} = 0$

9. $\dfrac{x}{5} = \dfrac{8}{10}$

10. $\dfrac{5x}{2} = \dfrac{15}{4}$

11. $\dfrac{y+2}{4} = \dfrac{5}{2}$

12. $\dfrac{m-5}{35} = \dfrac{5}{7}$

13. $\dfrac{2c+8}{28} = \dfrac{12}{7}$

14. $\dfrac{2x+1}{3} = \dfrac{6x-9}{5}$

15. $\dfrac{2m}{3} = \dfrac{3m+9}{4}$

16. $\dfrac{x}{5} + \dfrac{x}{3} = \dfrac{8}{15}$

17. $10 = \dfrac{x}{3} + \dfrac{x}{7}$

18. $\dfrac{r}{3} - \dfrac{r}{6} = 2$

19. $1 = \dfrac{3r}{4} - \dfrac{2r}{3}$

20. $\dfrac{3t}{4} - 6 = \dfrac{t}{12}$

21. $\dfrac{y}{4} = \dfrac{3y}{5} - 2\dfrac{1}{10}$

22. $\dfrac{a}{2} + \dfrac{a}{3} + \dfrac{a}{4} = 26$

23. $\dfrac{s}{3} + 7 = \dfrac{s}{5} - 3$

24. $\dfrac{3y}{2} - \dfrac{17}{3} = \dfrac{2y}{3} - \dfrac{3}{2}$

25. $\dfrac{7y}{12} - \dfrac{1}{4} = 2y - \dfrac{5}{3}$

26. $\dfrac{5c}{4} - \dfrac{1}{2} = \dfrac{2c}{3} + 6\dfrac{1}{2}$

27. $\dfrac{x}{3} - 2 = \dfrac{3x-30}{6}$

28. $\dfrac{t+1}{2} + \dfrac{2t-3}{3} = 10$

29. $\dfrac{y+2}{4} - \dfrac{y-3}{3} = \dfrac{1}{2}$

30. $\dfrac{7s+5}{8} - \dfrac{3s+15}{10} = 2$

31. $\dfrac{6v-3}{2} - \dfrac{v+2}{5} = \dfrac{37}{10}$

32. $\dfrac{2a-3}{5} - \dfrac{a-3}{3} = 2$

33. $\dfrac{5s-3}{4} - \dfrac{3s+5}{8} = 3$

34. $6 + \dfrac{x-2}{4} = \dfrac{x+3}{3}$

35. $\dfrac{3m+1}{4} = 2 - \dfrac{3-2m}{6}$

36. $\dfrac{5x-1}{9} + \dfrac{2x+4}{6} = \dfrac{3x-4}{3}$

37. $\dfrac{3c-4}{3} - \dfrac{2c+4}{6} = \dfrac{5c-1}{9}$

38. If one-half of a number is increased by 20, the result is 35. Find the number.

39. If two-thirds of a number is decreased by 30, the result is 10. Find the number.

40. If 5 is added to one-half of a number, the result is the same as when three-fifths of the number is decreased by 3. Find the number.

41. If 3 times a number is decreased by 9, the result is $1\frac{1}{2}$. Find the number.

42. If 3 more than 3 times a number is divided by 15, the result is the same as when 18 less than twice the number is divided by 6. Find the number.

2. Solving Equations Containing Decimals

Decimals (decimal fractions) are fractions whose denominators are 10, 100, 1000, and so on. For example:

$$.7 = \tfrac{7}{10} \qquad\qquad .21 = \tfrac{21}{100} \qquad\qquad .125 = \tfrac{125}{1000}$$

Procedure. To solve an equation containing decimals:

Method 1

Follow the same procedure that is used in solving equations containing whole numbers.

Method 2

In order to clear the equation of decimals, multiply both members of the equation by the largest denominator among the decimal fractions in the equation. Then solve the resulting equation.

Model Problem ———————————————————

Solve and check: $.05x + .04(500 - x) = 22$

Solution:

Method 1

$$.05x + .04(500 - x) = 22$$
$$.05x + 20 - .04x = 22$$
$$.01x + 20 = 22$$
$$.01x + 20 + (-20) = 22 + (-20)$$
$$.01x = 2$$
$$x = 200 \quad D_{.01}$$

Method 2

$$.05x + .04(500 - x) = 22$$
$$100[.05x + .04(500 - x)] = 100(22)$$
$$5x + 4(500 - x) = 2200$$
$$5x + 2000 - 4x = 2200$$
$$x + 2000 = 2200$$
$$x + 2000 + (-2000) = 2200 + (-2000)$$
$$x = 200$$

Check by substituting 200 for x in the given equation.

Answer: $x = 200$, or solution set is $\{200\}$.

EXERCISES

In 1–25, solve and check.

1. $3x = .9$
2. $.08 = 2z$
3. $.3m = -2.4$
4. $.04z = 6$
5. $.45c = 9$
6. $8.7 = 3w$
7. $.4t = .012$
8. $.09d = .018$
9. $.7x - .4 = 1$
10. $.03y - 1.2 = 8.7$
11. $2c + .5c = 50$
12. $.08y - .9 = .02y$
13. $1.5y - 1.69 = .2y$
14. $.08c = 1.5 + .07c$
15. $.8m + 2.6 = .2m + 9.8$
16. $.05x - .25 = .02x + .44$
17. $.13x - 1.4 = .08x + 7.6$
18. $.02(x + 5) = 8$
19. $.05(x - 8) = .07x$
20. $.06(x - 5) = .04(x + 8)$
21. $.04x + .03(2000 - x) = 75$
22. $.05x + 10 = .06(x + 50)$
23. $.08x = .03(x + 200) - 4$
24. $.07x + .04(9000 - x) = 450$
25. $.06x - .04(3500 - x) = 160$
26. Seven-hundredths of a number increased by 2.5 equals eight-hundredths of the number. Find the number.
27. If seventeen-hundredths of a number is decreased by 1.4, the result is the same as when twelve-hundredths of the number is increased by 7.6. Find the number.
28. 15% of a number decreased by 40 is equal to 7% of the number. Find the number.

3. Solving Inequalities Containing Fractional Coefficients

Procedure. To solve an inequality which contains fractional coefficients: First transform it into a simpler inequality which does not contain fractions (clear the inequality of fractions). Do this by multiplying

both its members by the lowest common denominator, L.C.D. (a positive number). Then solve the resulting inequality by the usual methods.

Model Problems

1. Solve: $\dfrac{x}{3} - \dfrac{x}{6} > 12$

Solution

$$\frac{x}{3} - \frac{x}{6} > 12$$

$$6\left(\frac{x}{3} - \frac{x}{6}\right) > 6(12)$$

$$6\left(\frac{x}{3}\right) - 6\left(\frac{x}{6}\right) > 72$$

$$2x - x > 72$$

$$x > 72$$

Answer: x > 72

2. Solve: $\dfrac{9y}{2} + \dfrac{8 - 12y}{7} \le 3$

Solution

$$\frac{9y}{2} + \frac{8 - 12y}{7} \le 3$$

$$14\left(\frac{9y}{2} + \frac{8 - 12y}{7}\right) \le 14(3)$$

$$14\left(\frac{9y}{2}\right) + 14\left(\frac{8 - 12y}{7}\right) \le 42$$

$$63y + 16 - 24y \le 42$$

$$39y \le 26$$

$$y \le \frac{2}{3}$$

Answer: $y \le \dfrac{2}{3}$

EXERCISES

In 1–20, solve the inequality.

1. $\frac{1}{4}x - \frac{1}{5}x > \frac{9}{20}$

2. $y - \frac{2}{3}y < 5$

3. $\frac{5}{6}c < \frac{1}{3}c + 3$

4. $\frac{x}{4} - \frac{x}{8} \le \frac{5}{8}$

5. $\frac{y}{6} \ge \frac{y}{12} + 1$

6. $\frac{y}{9} - \frac{y}{4} > \frac{5}{36}$

7. $\frac{t}{10} \le 4 + \frac{t}{5}$

8. $1 + \frac{2x}{3} \ge \frac{x}{2}$

9. $2.5x - 1.6x > 4$

10. $2y + 3 \ge .2y$

11. $\frac{3x + 1}{7} > 5$

12. $\frac{5y - 30}{7} \le 0$

13. $2d + \frac{1}{4} < \frac{7d}{12} + \frac{5}{3}$

14. $\frac{4c}{3} - \frac{7}{9} \ge \frac{c}{2} + \frac{7}{6}$

15. $\dfrac{2m}{3} \ge \dfrac{7-m}{4} + 1$

16. $\dfrac{3x-30}{6} < \dfrac{x}{3} - 2$

17. $\dfrac{6x-3}{2} > \dfrac{37}{10} + \dfrac{x+2}{5}$

18. $\dfrac{2y-3}{3} + \dfrac{y+1}{2} < 1$

19. $\dfrac{3r-3}{5} - \dfrac{r-\frac{1}{5}}{3} \le 2$

20. $\dfrac{3t-4}{3} \ge \dfrac{2t+4}{6} + \dfrac{5t-1}{9}$

4. Solving Fractional Equations

A fractional equation is an equation whose terms are rational expressions.

For example, $\dfrac{1}{3} + \dfrac{1}{x} = \dfrac{1}{2}$ and $\dfrac{6}{x} = \dfrac{7}{x+2}$ are called *fractional equations*.

To transform a fractional equation into an equivalent equation none of whose terms are rational expressions, we can multiply both members of the equation by the lowest common denominator (L.C.D.) of all the fractions involved in the equation. If we multiply by an expression which involves the variable, we will obtain an equivalent equation only when the variable does not represent a number which makes the value of the multiplier zero.

For example, to solve $\dfrac{x}{x-5} = \dfrac{5}{x-5}$, we would multiply both members of the equation by $x - 5$.

$$(x-5)\left(\dfrac{x}{x-5}\right) = (x-5)\left(\dfrac{5}{x-5}\right)$$

$$x = 5$$

Note that when $x = 5$, the value of the multiplier $x - 5$ is 0. Let us see whether 5 is a solution of the equation.

$$\dfrac{x}{x-5} = \dfrac{5}{x-5}$$

$$\dfrac{5}{5-5} \overset{?}{=} \dfrac{5}{5-5}$$

$$\dfrac{5}{0} \overset{?}{=} \dfrac{5}{0}$$

Since division by 0 is not defined, $\dfrac{5}{0}$ is meaningless. Hence, 5 is not a root of the given equation, although 5 is a root of the derived equation $x = 5$. Therefore, the given equation $\dfrac{x}{x-5} = \dfrac{5}{x-5}$ and the derived equation $x = 5$ are not equivalent equations.

A number which is a root of the derived equation but is not a root of the original equation, in this example the number 5, is called an **extraneous root**.

In fact, the equation $\dfrac{x}{x-5} = \dfrac{5}{x-5}$ has no roots. Hence, its solution set is the empty set, $\emptyset$.

Note that in solving the equation $\dfrac{x}{x-5} = \dfrac{5}{x-5}$, we multiplied both members of the equation by $x - 5$. If $x = 5$, then $x - 5 = 0$. Hence, in reality, we were multiplying both members of the equation by 0. This is the reason why the original equation and the derived equation were not equivalent equations.

Model Problems

1. Solve and check: $\dfrac{1}{3} + \dfrac{1}{x} = \dfrac{1}{2}$

   Solution: Multiply both members of the equation by the L.C.D., $6x$.

   $$\frac{1}{3} + \frac{1}{x} = \frac{1}{2}$$

   $$6x\left(\frac{1}{3} + \frac{1}{x}\right) = 6x\left(\frac{1}{2}\right) \quad \text{M}_{6x}$$

   $$6x\left(\frac{1}{3}\right) + 6x\left(\frac{1}{x}\right) = 6x\left(\frac{1}{2}\right)$$

   $$2x + 6 = 3x$$

   $$6 = x$$

   Check

   $$\frac{1}{3} + \frac{1}{x} = \frac{1}{2}$$

   $$\frac{1}{3} + \frac{1}{6} \overset{?}{=} \frac{1}{2}$$

   $$\frac{3}{6} \overset{?}{=} \frac{1}{2}$$

   $$\frac{1}{2} = \frac{1}{2} \quad \text{(true)}$$

   Answer: $x = 6$, or solution set is $\{6\}$.

2. Solve and check: $\dfrac{2}{3d} + \dfrac{1}{3} = \dfrac{11}{6d} - \dfrac{1}{4}$

Solution: Multiply both members of the equation by the L.C.D., 12*d*.

$$\frac{2}{3d} + \frac{1}{3} = \frac{11}{6d} - \frac{1}{4}$$

$$12d\left(\frac{2}{3d} + \frac{1}{3}\right) = 12d\left(\frac{11}{6d} - \frac{1}{4}\right) \quad M_{12d}$$

$$12d\left(\frac{2}{3d}\right) + 12d\left(\frac{1}{3}\right) = 12d\left(\frac{11}{6d}\right) - 12d\left(\frac{1}{4}\right)$$

$$8 + 4d = 22 - 3d$$

$$8 + 4d + (-8) = 22 - 3d + (-8)$$

$$4d = 14 - 3d$$

$$4d + (3d) = 14 - 3d + (3d)$$

$$7d = 14$$

$$d = 2$$

Check

$$\frac{2}{3d} + \frac{1}{3} = \frac{11}{6d} - \frac{1}{4}$$

$$\frac{2}{3(2)} + \frac{1}{3} \stackrel{?}{=} \frac{11}{6(2)} - \frac{1}{4}$$

$$\frac{2}{6} + \frac{1}{3} \stackrel{?}{=} \frac{11}{12} - \frac{1}{4}$$

$$\frac{4}{12} + \frac{4}{12} \stackrel{?}{=} \frac{11}{12} - \frac{3}{12}$$

$$\frac{8}{12} = \frac{8}{12} \quad \text{(true)}$$

Answer: $d = 2$, or solution set is $\{2\}$.

3. Solve and check: $\dfrac{3x - 5}{3x + 5} = \dfrac{1}{3}$

Solution: Multiply both members of the equation by the L.C.D., $3(3x + 5)$.

$$\frac{3x - 5}{3x + 5} = \frac{1}{3}$$

$$3(3x + 5)\left(\frac{3x - 5}{3x + 5}\right) = 3(3x + 5)\left(\frac{1}{3}\right) \quad M_{3\,(3x+5)}$$

$$3(3x - 5) = 1(3x + 5)$$

$$9x - 15 = 3x + 5$$

$$9x - 3x = 5 + 15$$

$$6x = 20$$

$$x = \frac{10}{3}$$

Check

$$\frac{3x - 5}{3x + 5} = \frac{1}{3}$$

$$\frac{3\left(\dfrac{10}{3}\right) - 5}{3\left(\dfrac{10}{3}\right) + 5} \stackrel{?}{=} \frac{1}{3}$$

$$\frac{10 - 5}{10 + 5} \stackrel{?}{=} \frac{1}{3}$$

$$\frac{1}{3} = \frac{1}{3} \quad \text{(true)}$$

Answer: $x = \dfrac{10}{3}$, or solution set is $\left\{\dfrac{10}{3}\right\}$.

Keep In Mind

When both members of an equation are multiplied by a variable expression which may represent zero, the resulting equation may not be equivalent to the given equation. Each solution, therefore, must be checked in the original equation.

EXERCISES

In 1–35, solve and check.

1. $\dfrac{10}{x} = 5$

2. $\dfrac{15}{y} = 3$

3. $\dfrac{6}{x} = 12$

4. $\dfrac{8}{b} = -2$

5. $\dfrac{3}{2x} = \dfrac{1}{2}$

6. $\dfrac{15}{4x} = \dfrac{1}{8}$

7. $\dfrac{7}{3y} = -\dfrac{1}{3}$

8. $\dfrac{4}{5y} = -\dfrac{1}{10}$

9. $\dfrac{10}{x} + \dfrac{8}{x} = 9$

10. $\dfrac{15}{y} - \dfrac{3}{y} = 4$

11. $\dfrac{7}{c} + \dfrac{1}{c} = 16$

12. $\dfrac{9}{2x} = \dfrac{7}{2x} + 2$

13. $\dfrac{30}{x} = 7 + \dfrac{18}{2x}$

14. $\dfrac{4}{c} - \dfrac{1}{2} = \dfrac{5}{12} - \dfrac{3}{2c}$

15. $\dfrac{y+9}{2y} + 3 = \dfrac{15}{y}$

16. $\dfrac{2+x}{6x} = \dfrac{3}{5x} + \dfrac{1}{30}$

17. $\dfrac{15}{a+1} = 3$

18. $\dfrac{12}{x-2} = 4$

19. $\dfrac{9}{2x+1} = 3$

20. $\dfrac{16}{1-3t} = 4$

21. $\dfrac{6}{3x-1} = \dfrac{3}{4}$

22. $\dfrac{5x}{x+1} = 4$

23. $\dfrac{3}{5-3a} = \dfrac{1}{2}$

24. $\dfrac{1-r}{1+r} = \dfrac{2}{3}$

25. $\dfrac{5}{a} = \dfrac{7}{a-4}$

26. $\dfrac{b+1}{b-3} = \dfrac{b-3}{b+1}$

27. $\dfrac{x-2}{x+1} = \dfrac{x+1}{x-2}$

28. $\dfrac{1}{d-1} = \dfrac{4}{d^2-1} - \dfrac{1}{d+1}$

29. $\dfrac{5}{x^2-4} - \dfrac{x+12}{x+2} + \dfrac{x-1}{x-2} = 0$

30. $\dfrac{y}{y+1} - \dfrac{1}{y} = 1$

31. $\dfrac{x-3}{x-1} - \dfrac{x-1}{x} = \dfrac{5}{x^2-x}$

32. $\dfrac{y+1}{y-5} - \dfrac{2}{y^2-3y-10} = \dfrac{y+3}{y+2}$

33. $\dfrac{7y-4}{1-y^2} = \dfrac{y-1}{y+1} - \dfrac{y+3}{y-1}$

34. $\dfrac{6}{3y+1} + \dfrac{2}{y-2} + \dfrac{2y+10}{3y^2-5y-2} = 0$

35. $\dfrac{5}{5a+3} - \dfrac{2}{2a-1} = \dfrac{4-6a}{10a^2+a-3}$

5. Solving More Difficult Equations Involving Several Variables

When we solve an equation involving several variables for one of those variables, we express this variable in terms of the other variables.

Procedure. To solve an equation which involves several variables for one of those variables:

1. **If the equation contains fractions, clear the fractions by multiplying both members of the equation by the L.C.D. of the denominators.**
2. **If the equation contains parentheses, use the distributive property to remove them.**
3. **Collect on one side of the equation all terms involving the variable for which we are solving. Collect all other terms on the other side.**
4. **Find the coefficient of this variable. If necessary, use the distributive property or factoring.**
5. **Divide both members of the equation by the coefficient found in step 4.**
6. **Simplify the answer if necessary.**

Model Problems _____

1. Solve for x and check: $cx + d^2 = c^2 + dx$

Solution

$$cx + d^2 = c^2 + dx$$
$$cx + d^2 - dx = c^2 + dx - dx$$
$$cx + d^2 - dx = c^2$$
$$cx + d^2 - dx - d^2 = c^2 - d^2$$
$$cx - dx = c^2 - d^2$$
$$x(c - d) = c^2 - d^2$$

$$\frac{x\cancel{(c-d)}}{\cancel{(c-d)}} = \frac{\cancel{(c-d)}\,(c+d)}{\cancel{(c-d)}}$$

$$x = c + d \quad Ans.$$

Check

$$cx + d^2 = c^2 + dx$$
$$c(c + d) + d^2 \overset{?}{=} c^2 + d(c + d)$$
$$c^2 + cd + d^2 = c^2 + cd + d^2 \quad (true)$$

2. Solve for y and check: $\dfrac{y}{b} + \dfrac{y}{a} = a + b$

Solution

$$\frac{y}{b} + \frac{y}{a} = a + b$$

$$ab\left(\frac{y}{b} + \frac{y}{a}\right) = ab(a + b) \quad \text{M}_{ab} \ (ab \text{ is the L.C.D.})$$

$$ab\left(\frac{y}{b}\right) + ab\left(\frac{y}{a}\right) = ab(a) + ab(b)$$

$$ay + by = a^2b + ab^2$$

$$y(a + b) = ab(a + b)$$

$$\frac{\overset{1}{y(a+b)}}{\underset{1}{(a+b)}} = \frac{\overset{1}{ab(a+b)}}{\underset{1}{(a+b)}}$$

$$y = ab \quad \text{Ans.}$$

Check

$$\frac{y}{a} + \frac{y}{b} = a + b$$

$$\frac{ab}{a} + \frac{ab}{b} \overset{?}{=} a + b$$

$$b + a \overset{?}{=} a + b$$

$$a + b = a + b \quad \text{(true)}$$

EXERCISES

In 1–36, solve for x or y and check.

1. $\dfrac{x}{5} = t$ **2.** $\dfrac{x}{c} = 8$ **3.** $\dfrac{x}{3a} = b$ **4.** $\dfrac{x}{ab} = c$

5. $\dfrac{x}{2} - c = d$ **6.** $2m = \dfrac{y}{5} + n$ **7.** $\dfrac{y}{2} - \dfrac{b}{3} = 0$ **8.** $\dfrac{x}{6} + \dfrac{c}{4} = 0$

9. $\dfrac{x}{a} = \dfrac{b}{c}$ **10.** $\dfrac{x}{n} = \dfrac{s}{n^2}$ **11.** $\dfrac{mx}{r} + c = d$ **12.** $t = s - \dfrac{nx}{d}$

13. $\dfrac{5}{x} = a$ **14.** $\dfrac{t}{y} - r = 0$ **15.** $\dfrac{2x + c}{3} = 9c$

16. $\dfrac{3y - 2a}{4} - 7a = 0$ **17.** $\dfrac{a + b}{x} = c$ **18.** $\dfrac{a}{b} = \dfrac{c + d}{x}$

19. $\dfrac{y}{4} + \dfrac{y}{6} = 5b$ **20.** $\dfrac{x}{3a} + \dfrac{x}{5a} = 8$ **21.** $\dfrac{y}{2a} - \dfrac{y}{3a} = 3a^2$

22. $\dfrac{8}{x} - \dfrac{7}{x} = e$ **23.** $\dfrac{r}{y} + s = \dfrac{t}{y}$ **24.** $\dfrac{c}{y} = \dfrac{d}{y} + h$

25. $ax + bx = 4a + 4b$ **26.** $ax - b = bx$

27. $cx - c^2 = dx - d^2$ **28.** $a(x + b) = 6ax - 9ab$

29. $8x = 2x - 4(x - 5c)$

30. $(x - a)(x - b) = x^2$

31. $\dfrac{1}{x} = \dfrac{1}{c} + \dfrac{1}{d}$

32. $\dfrac{x}{d} - \dfrac{x}{c} = c - d$

33. $\dfrac{1}{a} + \dfrac{1}{x} = \dfrac{1}{b} - \dfrac{1}{x}$

34. $x = \dfrac{a - x}{b}$

35. $\dfrac{x + s}{r} = \dfrac{r - x}{s}$

36. $\dfrac{y + m}{y + n} = \dfrac{y + n}{y + m}$

6. Solving Number Problems Involving Fractions

NUMBER PROBLEMS

Model Problems

1. The denominator of a fraction exceeds the numerator by 7. If 3 is subtracted from the numerator of the fraction and if the denominator is unchanged, the value of the resulting fraction becomes $\frac{1}{3}$. Find the original fraction.

Solution:

Let x = the numerator of the original fraction.
Then $x + 7$ = the denominator of the original fraction.

And $\dfrac{x}{x + 7}$ = the original fraction.

And $\dfrac{x - 3}{x + 7}$ = the new fraction.

The value of the new fraction is $\frac{1}{3}$.

$$\frac{x - 3}{x + 7} = \frac{1}{3}$$

$$3(x + 7)\left(\frac{x - 3}{x + 7}\right) = 3(x + 7)\left(\frac{1}{3}\right) \quad M_{3(x+7)}$$

$$3(x - 3) = 1(x + 7)$$
$$3x - 9 = x + 7$$
$$3x - x = 7 + 9$$
$$2x = 16$$
$$x = 8$$
$$x + 7 = 15$$

Check: The original fraction was $\dfrac{8}{15}$. The new fraction is $\dfrac{8 - 3}{15} = \dfrac{5}{15} = \dfrac{1}{3}$.

Answer: The original fraction was $\frac{8}{15}$.

2. The larger of two numbers is 2 less than 4 times the smaller. When the larger number is divided by the smaller number, the quotient is 3 and the remainder is 5. Find the numbers.

Solution:

Note: When 17 is divided by 3, the quotient is 5 and the remainder is 2. This may be written as follows: $\frac{17}{3} = 5 + \frac{2}{3}$. Similarly, "when D is divided by d, the quotient is Q and the remainder is R" may be written as:

$$\frac{D}{d} = Q + \frac{R}{d}.$$

Let $x =$ the smaller number. Then $4x - 2 =$ the larger number.

When the larger number is divided by the smaller,
the quotient is 3 and the remainder is 5.

$$\frac{4x - 2}{x} = 3 + \frac{5}{x}$$

$$x\left(\frac{4x - 2}{x}\right) = x\left(3 + \frac{5}{x}\right) \qquad M_x$$

$$4x - 2 = 3x + 5$$
$$4x - 3x = 5 + 2$$
$$x = 7$$
$$4x - 2 = 26$$

Check: The larger number, 26, is 2 less than 4 times the smaller number, 7. When 26 is divided by 7, the quotient is 3 and the remainder is 5.

Answer: The larger number is 26; the smaller number is 7.

EXERCISES

1. The larger of two numbers is 12 less than 5 times the smaller. If the smaller number is equal to one-third of the larger number, find the numbers.
2. Separate 150 into two parts such that one part is two-thirds of the other part.
3. One-third of the result obtained by adding 5 to a certain number is equal to one-half of the result obtained when 5 is subtracted from the number. Find the number.
4. The numerator of a fraction is 8 less than the denominator of the fraction. The value of the fraction is $\frac{3}{5}$. Find the fraction.

5. The denominator of a fraction is 30 more than the numerator of the fraction. If 10 is added to the numerator of the fraction and the denominator is unchanged, the value of the resulting fraction becomes $\frac{3}{5}$. Find the original fraction.

6. The numerator of a certain fraction is three times the denominator. If the numerator is decreased by 1 and the denominator is increased by 2, the value of the resulting fraction is $\frac{5}{2}$. Find the original fraction.

7. What number must be added to both the numerator and the denominator of the fraction $\frac{7}{19}$ to make the value of the resulting fraction $\frac{3}{4}$?

8. Separate 96 into two parts such that when the larger part is divided by the smaller part, the quotient is 7 and the remainder is zero.

9. The larger of two numbers is 25 more than the smaller. If the larger is divided by the smaller, the quotient is 5 and the remainder is 1. Find the numbers.

10. The larger of two numbers is 2 less than 7 times the smaller. If the larger is divided by the smaller, the quotient is 6 and the remainder is 5. Find the numbers.

11. When the reciprocal of a number is increased by $\frac{1}{4}$, the result is 3. Find the number.

12. One-half of the reciprocal of a number exceeds one-third of the reciprocal of the number by 2. Find the number.

7. Solving Average Problems Involving Fractions

PREPARING TO SOLVE AVERAGE PROBLEMS

Bill received grades of 80, 90, 70, and 80 on his four algebra tests. To find his average for these four tests, he added the four grades and divided by 4, giving $\dfrac{80 + 90 + 70 + 80}{4} = \dfrac{320}{4} = 80$. To find the average of several grades, we find the sum of all the grades and divide the sum by the number of grades.

EXERCISES

1. Mary received grades of 75, 85, and 89 on three exams. Find her average.

2. Harold received grades of 90, 70, 75, and x on four exams. Represent his average in terms of x.

3. Sarah received the grade x on each of two tests and the grade y on each of three tests. Represent her average for all the tests in terms of x and y.

4. Paul has an average of 75 for the 6 exams that he has taken. What is the sum of all his grades?

5. Eleanor has an average of $x + y$ for the five exams that she has taken. Represent in terms of x and y the sum of all her grades.

SOLVING AVERAGE PROBLEMS

Model Problem

A student has marks of 75 in English, 82 in psychology, and 90 in algebra. What mark must he obtain in economics to have an average of 85 for all four courses?

Solution: Let x = the student's grade in economics.
           The sum of the four grades divided by 4 is 85.

$$\frac{75 + 82 + 90 + x}{4} = 85$$

$$\frac{247 + x}{4} = 85$$

$$247 + x = 340 \quad M_4$$
$$x = 93 \quad S_{247}$$

Check

$$\frac{75 + 82 + 90 + 93}{4} \overset{?}{=} 85$$

$$\frac{340}{4} \overset{?}{=} 85$$

$$85 = 85 \quad \text{(true)}$$

Answer: The student must obtain a grade of 93 in economics.

EXERCISES

1. A student received the following grades in algebra: 72, 90, 70, 80. What must be his fifth grade if his average for the five tests is to be 80?

2. William has received 85 in each of three tests and 95 in a fourth test in physics. What grade must he receive in a fifth test in order to have an average of 90 for all five tests?

3. Sam, William, and Bob together weigh 340 pounds. How much does Ray weigh if the average of the weights of all four boys is 120 pounds?

4. The average of the weights of Sue, Mary, and Betty is 55 kilograms. How much does Agnes weigh if the average of the weights of the four girls is 60 kilograms?
5. The average of the heights of three men is 5 feet 10 inches. What is the height of a fourth man if the average of the heights of the four men is $5\frac{3}{4}$ feet?
6. The average of three consecutive even numbers is 20. Find the numbers.
7. The average of three numbers is 31. The second is 1 more than twice the first. The third is 4 less than 3 times the first. Find the numbers.
8. Laura has grades of 95, 70, and 85 in her history tests. On how many successive tests must she receive 100 in order to have an average of 90 for all her history tests?
9. Sue has taken 20 courses in college and has an average of 80. This semester she is taking 5 courses. What must her average for these 5 courses be in order to raise her average for all her course work to 82?

8. Solving Motion Problems Involving Fractions

Model Problems ────────────────────────────────

1. On a trip, a motorist traveled 100 kilometers before lunch and 300 kilometers after lunch. His average rate after lunch was twice his average rate before lunch. He spent 5 hours on the entire trip, not counting the time spent in eating lunch. Find his average rate on each part of the trip.

Solution:

Let r = the average rate before lunch in kilometers per hour.
Then $2r$ = the average rate after lunch in kilometers per hour.

	(km) Distance	(km/h) Rate	(hr.) Time
Before lunch	100	r	$\dfrac{100}{r}$
After lunch	300	$2r$	$\dfrac{300}{2r}$

$$\text{Time} = \frac{\text{Distance}}{\text{Rate}}$$

The total time spent in traveling was 5 hours.

$$\frac{100}{r} + \frac{300}{2r} = 5$$

$$2r\left(\frac{100}{r} + \frac{300}{2r}\right) = 2r(5) \quad M_{2r}$$

$$200 + 300 = 10r$$
$$500 = 10r$$
$$50 = r$$
$$100 = 2r$$

Check: Time spent in traveling before lunch was $\frac{100}{50} = 2$ hours. Time spent in traveling after lunch was $\frac{300}{100} = 3$ hours. Total time was $3 + 2$, or 5 hours.

Answer: The average rate before lunch was 50 kilometers per hour. The average rate after lunch was 100 kilometers per hour.

2. A boat can travel 20 mph in still water. It can travel 75 miles downstream in the same time that it requires to travel 45 miles upstream. Find the rate of the stream.

Solution:

Let $c =$ the rate of the stream in miles per hour.
Then $20 + c =$ the rate of the boat downstream in miles per hour.
And $20 - c =$ the rate of the boat upstream in miles per hour.

	(mi.) Distance	(mph) Rate	(hr.) Time
Downstream	75	$20 + c$	$\dfrac{75}{20 + c}$
Upstream	45	$20 - c$	$\dfrac{45}{20 - c}$

$$\text{Time} = \frac{\text{Distance}}{\text{Rate}}$$

The time spent traveling upstream is the same as the time spent traveling downstream.

$$\frac{45}{20 - c} = \frac{75}{20 + c}$$

Multiply by the L.C.D., $(20 - c)(20 + c)$.

$$(20 - c)(20 + c)\left(\frac{45}{20 - c}\right) = (20 - c)(20 + c)\left(\frac{75}{20 + c}\right)$$

$$45(20 + c) = 75(20 - c)$$
$$900 + 45c = 1500 - 75c$$
$$45c + 75c = 1500 - 900$$
$$120c = 600$$
$$c = 5$$

Check: Time spent traveling downstream is $\dfrac{75}{20 + 5} = \dfrac{75}{25}$, or 3 hours.

Time spent traveling upstream is $\dfrac{45}{20 - 5} = \dfrac{45}{15}$, or 3 hours also.

Answer: Rate of the stream is 5 mph.

EXERCISES

1. Mr. Stewart rode a distance of 12 miles out into the country on a bicycle and returned on foot. His rate on the bicycle was 4 times his rate on foot. He spent 5 hours on the entire trip. Find his rate of walking.

2. A man traveled a distance of 1000 kilometers by ship to an island. He returned by plane. The rate of the plane was 20 times the rate of the ship. He spent 42 hours on the trip. Find the rate of the ship and the rate of the plane.

3. Mr. James is traveling 160 mph slower than Mr. Kenton. Mr. James can travel 150 miles in the same time that Mr. Kenton can travel 220 miles. Find the rate at which each man is traveling.

4. The rate at which a jet plane is traveling exceeds by 100 mph twice the rate at which a propeller plane is traveling. The jet plane can fly 1800 miles in the same time that the propeller plane requires to fly 750 miles. Find the rate of each plane.

5. The rate of a passenger train is 60 kilometers per hour more than the rate of a freight train. It takes the passenger train one-half as much time to travel 240 kilometers as it does the freight train. Find the rate of each train.

6. A boat can travel 8 mph in still water. If it can travel 15 miles downstream in the same time that it can travel 9 miles upstream, what is the rate of the stream?

7. A plane can fly 320 mph in still air. Flying with the wind, the plane can fly 1400 miles in the same time that it can fly 1160 miles against the wind. Find the rate of the wind.

8. A light private plane can fly 180 kilometers per hour in still air. Flying with the wind, it can fly 960 kilometers in a certain time. Flying against the wind, it can fly only half of this distance in the same time. Find the rate of the wind.

9. Solving Work Problems Involving Fractions

PREPARING TO SOLVE WORK PROBLEMS

If Harry can paint a wall in 40 minutes, then in 1 minute he will complete $\frac{1}{40}$ of the job. The part of a job that can be completed in one unit of time is called the **rate of work**. Thus, $\frac{1}{40}$ is Harry's rate of work. In 2 minutes Harry will complete $2(\frac{1}{40})$ or $\frac{2}{40}$ of the job; in x minutes he will complete $x\left(\frac{1}{40}\right)$ or $\frac{x}{40}$ of the job. Therefore, we see that:

Rate of work × Time of work = Part of the work done

If Sam can paint the same wall in 60 minutes, then in 1 minute he will complete $\frac{1}{60}$ of the job; in two minutes he will complete $2(\frac{1}{60})$ or $\frac{2}{60}$ of the job; in x minutes he will complete $x\left(\frac{1}{60}\right)$ or $\frac{x}{60}$ of the job.

If Harry and Sam both start painting the wall at the same time, at the end of 1 minute, working together, they will finish $\frac{1}{40} + \frac{1}{60}$ or $\frac{5}{120}$ of the job. At the end of 2 minutes, they will finish $\frac{2}{40} + \frac{2}{60}$ or $\frac{10}{120}$ of the job. At the end of x minutes, they will finish $\frac{x}{40} + \frac{x}{60}$ or $\frac{5x}{120}$ of the job.

After Harry and Sam have worked for 24 minutes, Harry has finished $\frac{24}{40}$ or $\frac{72}{120}$ of the job and Sam has finished $\frac{24}{60}$ or $\frac{48}{120}$ of the job. Together they have finished $\frac{72}{120} + \frac{48}{120}$ or $\frac{120}{120}$ of the job, or the whole job. Notice that in order for Harry and Sam to complete the whole job, the sum of the fractional part of the job that Harry finished and the fractional part of the job that Sam finished must be a fraction whose value is 1.

EXERCISES

1. a. If Sid can mow a lawn in 80 minutes, what part of the lawn can he mow in (1) 1 minute? (2) x minutes?
   b. If Gene can mow the same lawn in 120 minutes, what part of the lawn can he mow in (1) 1 minute? (2) x minutes?
   c. Represent the part of the job that Sid and Gene, working together, can complete in x minutes.
   d. If Sid and Gene mowed the entire lawn in x minutes, what must be the value of the answer given in part c?
   e. Write an equation whose solution reveals the number of minutes that Sid and Gene, working together, would require to mow the entire lawn.

2. **a.** A large pipe can fill a tank in 2 hours. What part of the tank can the pipe fill in (1) 1 hour? (2) x hours?
   b. If a smaller pipe can fill the same tank in 3 hours, what part of the tank can this pipe fill in (1) 1 hour? (2) x hours?
   c. Represent the part of the tank that is filled in x minutes when both pipes are being used.
   d. Write an equation whose solution reveals the number of hours that both pipes, being used together, would require to fill the entire tank.

3. A tank can be filled in 4 hours by one pipe and emptied by another pipe in 6 hours. The tank is empty and the faucets of both pipes are opened.
   a. Represent the part of the tank that is filled in 1 hour.
   b. Represent the part of the tank that is filled in x hours.
   c. Write an equation whose solution reveals the number of hours required to fill the tank.

SOLVING WORK PROBLEMS

Model Problems

1. Sam can mow a lawn in 20 minutes. Bob can mow the same lawn in 30 minutes. If they work together, how long will it take them to complete the job?

   Solution:

   Let x = number of minutes required to complete the job when both boys work together.

   20 = number of minutes Sam needs to do the job alone.

   30 = number of minutes Bob needs to do the job alone.

   Then $\dfrac{1}{20}$ = part of the job finished by Sam in 1 minute (Sam's rate of work).

   And $\dfrac{1}{30}$ = part of the job finished by Bob in 1 minute (Bob's rate of work).

   Then $x\left(\dfrac{1}{20}\right)$ or $\dfrac{x}{20}$ = part of the job finished by Sam in x minutes.

   And $x\left(\dfrac{1}{30}\right)$ or $\dfrac{x}{30}$ = part of the job finished by Bob in x minutes.

   If the job is finished, the sum of the fractional part of the job finished by Sam and the fractional part finished by Bob must equal 1.

   $$\frac{x}{20} + \frac{x}{30} = 1$$

$$60\left(\frac{x}{20} + \frac{x}{30}\right) = 60(1)$$
$$3x + 2x = 60$$
$$5x = 60$$
$$x = 12$$

Check: In 12 minutes, Sam will mow $\frac{12}{20}$ or $\frac{36}{60}$ of the lawn.

In 12 minutes, Bob will mow $\frac{12}{30}$ or $\frac{24}{60}$ of the lawn.

In 12 minutes, Sam and Bob together will mow $\frac{36}{60} + \frac{24}{60} = \frac{60}{60}$, or the whole lawn.

Answer: 12 minutes

Alternate solution: Let x = number of minutes required to complete the job when both boys work together.

Worker	(part of job per min.) Rate of work	(min.) Time of work	(part of job) Work done
Sam	$\frac{1}{20}$	x	$\frac{x}{20}$
Bob	$\frac{1}{30}$	x	$\frac{x}{30}$

Rate of work X Time of work = Work done

If the job is finished, the sum of the fractional parts done by each must be 1.

$$\frac{x}{20} + \frac{x}{30} = 1$$

The remaining steps are the same as in the previous solution.

2. Mr. Cooper can paint a fence in 2 hours. His son Bill can paint the fence in 6 hours. Mr. Cooper painted alone for 1 hour and stopped working. How many hours would Bill require to finish the job?

Solution: Let x = number of hours required by Bill to finish the job.

Worker	(part of job per hr.) Rate of work	(hr.) Time of work	(part of job) Work done
Mr. Cooper	$\frac{1}{2}$	1	$\frac{1}{2}$
Bill	$\frac{1}{6}$	x	$\frac{x}{6}$

Rate of work $\times$ Time of work = Work done

If the job is finished, the sum of the fractional parts done by each must be 1.

$$\frac{1}{2} + \frac{x}{6} = 1$$

$$6\left(\frac{1}{2} + \frac{x}{6}\right) = 6(1)$$

$$3 + x = 6$$

$$x = 3$$

Check: In 1 hour, Mr. Cooper finished $\frac{1}{2}$ of the job.
In 3 hours, his son finished $\frac{3}{6}$ or $\frac{1}{2}$ of the job.
Therefore, Mr. Cooper and his son finished $\frac{1}{2} + \frac{1}{2}$, or the whole job.

Answer: 3 hours

3. The larger of two pipes can fill a tank twice as fast as the smaller. Together the two pipes require 20 minutes to fill the tank. Find the number of minutes required for the larger pipe, operating alone, to fill the tank.

Solution:

Let x = number of minutes required for the larger pipe, operating alone, to fill the tank.
Then $2x$ = number of minutes required for the smaller pipe, operating alone, to fill the tank.

Size of pipe	(part of job per min.) Rate of work	(min.) Time of work	(part of job) Work done
Larger pipe	$\dfrac{1}{x}$	20	$\dfrac{20}{x}$
Smaller pipe	$\dfrac{1}{2x}$	20	$\dfrac{20}{2x}$

Rate of work $\times$ Time of work = Work done

If the tank is filled, the sum of the fractional parts filled by each pipe must be 1.

$$\frac{20}{x} + \frac{20}{2x} = 1$$

$$2x\left(\frac{20}{x} + \frac{20}{2x}\right) = 2x(1)$$

$$40 + 20 = 2x$$
$$60 = 2x$$
$$30 = x$$

Answer: 30 minutes (The check is left to the student.)

EXERCISES

1. Mr. Ford can paint the fence around his house in 6 hours. His son needs 12 hours to do the job. How many hours would it take them to do the job if they worked together?
2. One printing press can print the weekly edition of the local newspaper in 12 hours. Another press can do the job in 18 hours. How long would it take both presses, working together, to do the job?
3. One pipe can fill a tank in 8 minutes, a second can fill it in 12 minutes, and a third can fill it in 24 minutes. If the tank is empty, how long will it take the three pipes, operating together, to fill it?
4. A farmer, working together with his son, needs 3 hours to plow a field. Working alone, the farmer can plow the field in 4 hours. How long would it take the son, working alone, to plow the field?
5. Mr. Downey can build a brick wall in 9 hours. His son Carl can build the same wall in 18 hours. Mr. Downey started to build the wall, worked for 3 hours, and then stopped working. How many hours would Carl require to complete the wall?
6. A farmer can plow a field with a tractor in 4 hours. He requires 12 hours to plow the same field with a team of horses. After working for 2 hours, the tractor broke down. How long will it take the farmer to complete the job with the team of horses?
7. An old machine requires 3 times as many hours to complete a job as a new machine. When both machines work together, they require 9 hours to complete a job. How many hours would it take the new machine, operating alone, to do the job?
8. A large pipe can fill a tank 4 times as rapidly as a small pipe. When both pipes are operating together, 4 hours are required to fill the tank. How many hours are required to fill the tank when the small pipe is operating alone?
9. An inlet pipe can fill a tank in 3 hours. An outlet pipe can empty the tank in 6 hours. If the tank is empty and both pipes are opened, how many hours will it take to fill the tank?
10. A bathtub can be filled by the hot water pipe in 20 minutes, and it can be filled by the cold water pipe in 10 minutes. It can be drained

in 12 minutes. If the tub is empty and the pipes and drain are opened, in how many hours will the bathtub be filled?

11. A printing press can print an edition of a newspaper in 4 hours. After the press has been at work for 1 hour, another press also starts to print the edition and, together, both presses require 1 more hour to finish the job. How long would it take the second press to print the entire edition alone?

12. Howard and Edward, working together, can complete a job in 12 hours. Edward requires 18 hours to do this job alone. Howard and Edward start the job. After they worked for 4 hours, Howard left the job. How many hours will Edward require to finish the job, working alone?

13. A new printing machine can do a job in 6 hours. An old machine can complete the same job in 16 hours. If 3 new machines and 4 old machines are used to do the job, how many hours will be required to finish it?

10. Solving Miscellaneous Problems Involving Fractions

EXERCISES

1. What number added to 8% of itself is 64.8?

2. Find a number such that $\frac{1}{4}$ of the number is 50 less than $\frac{2}{3}$ of the number.

3. The denominator of a fraction exceeds the numerator of the fraction by 25. The value of the fraction is $\frac{3}{8}$. Find the fraction.

4. What number must be subtracted from both the numerator and the denominator of $\frac{17}{25}$ so that the value of the resulting fraction will become $\frac{3}{7}$?

5. The denominator of a fraction is 3 times the numerator. If 8 is added to the numerator and 6 is subtracted from the denominator, the value of the resulting fraction is $\frac{8}{9}$. Find the original fraction.

6. A cash register contains nickels, dimes, and quarters. One-half of the coins are nickels, $\frac{1}{5}$ of the coins are dimes, and the rest are quarters. The total value of the coins is $6.00. Find the total number of coins in the cash register.

7. Mr. Ray invested $\frac{1}{3}$ of a sum of money at 6%, $\frac{1}{2}$ of the sum of money at 5%, and the remainder at 3%. His total annual income was $600. Find the sum he invested.

8. Mrs. Ives invested $\frac{2}{5}$ of a sum of money at 4%, $\frac{1}{3}$ of the sum at 5%, and the remainder at 3%. If her annual income was $1220, find the amount she invested.

9. Mr. Brink is 24 years older than his son, Stanley. Four years from now, Stanley will be $\frac{2}{5}$ of his father's age at that time. Find Mr. Brink's present age.

10. The width of a rectangle is $\frac{3}{5}$ of its length. If the perimeter of the rectangle is 192 feet, find its length and its width.

11. Find Alice's present age if $\frac{1}{6}$ of her present age is $\frac{1}{4}$ of her age 6 years ago.

12. The sum of two numbers is 44. If $\frac{1}{4}$ of the larger is subtracted from $\frac{1}{2}$ of the smaller, the result is 4. Find the numbers.

13. A farmer wishes to produce 100 liters of milk which will test 3.2% butterfat by mixing milk testing 3.8% butterfat with milk testing 2.8% butterfat. How many liters of each type of milk should he use?

14. A pharmacist has 20 ounces of a 30% Argyrol solution. How many ounces of a 40% Argyrol solution should he add to produce a 32% Argyrol solution?

15. How much water must be added to 40 grams of a 5% solution of salt in water so that the resulting solution will be 3% salt?

16. Mr. Reynolds drove a distance of 360 kilometers at a certain rate of speed. He covered the first 240 kilometers in 2 hours more time than was required for the rest of the trip. Find the rate of speed at which he was traveling.

17. A certain fraction is equivalent to $\frac{2}{5}$. If the numerator of this fraction is decreased by 4 and its denominator is increased by 14, the resulting fraction is equivalent to $\frac{1}{4}$. Find the numerator and denominator of the original fraction.

18. Mr. Blackstone drove from his city home to his country home, stopping for lunch on the way. Before lunch, he traveled 80 miles farther than he did after lunch. Before lunch, he averaged 40 mph; after lunch, he averaged 50 mph. His traveling time, not including the time spent for lunch, was $6\frac{1}{2}$ hours. Find the number of miles he drove before lunch and also after lunch.

19. In a purse which contains only nickels and dimes, the number of nickels is 2 less than twice the number of dimes. If the purse had contained $\frac{1}{2}$ as many dimes and $\frac{1}{3}$ as many nickels, the total value of the coins would have been 80 cents. How many coins of each denomination are in the purse?

Chapter 12

The Formula

1. Translating Verbal Sentences Into Formulas

A formula uses mathematical language to express the relationship between two or more variables. We will now learn how to translate verbal sentences into formulas.

Model Problems

1. Write a formula for each of the following relationships:

   a. The perimeter, P, of a square is equal to 4 times the length, s, of each side.

   Answer: $P = 4s$

   b. The cost, C, of a number of articles is the product of the number, n, of articles and the price, p, of each article.

   Answer: $C = np$

   c. The area, A, of a circle is equal to π times the square of the radius, r.

   Answer: $A = \pi r^2$

2. Write a formula which expresses the number, m, of months there are in y years, in terms of y.

   Solution: First discover the rule that states the relation between the variables m and y. Then write this rule as a formula.

   Since there are 12 months in a year, the number of months, m, in y years is equal to 12 times the number of years, y.

   Answer: $m = 12y$

EXERCISES

In 1–18, write a formula which expresses the relationship.

1. The total length, l, of 10 pieces of lumber, each f feet in length, is 10 times the length of each piece of lumber.
2. The selling price, s, of an article equals its cost, c, plus the margin, m.
3. The perimeter, p, of a rectangle is equal to the sum of twice its length, l, and twice its width, w.
4. The number, d, of diagonals that can be drawn from one vertex of a polygon to all other vertices is two less than the number, n, of sides of the polygon.
5. The average, M, of three numbers, a, b, c, is their sum divided by 3.
6. The area, A, of a triangle is equal to one-half the length, b, of the base multiplied by the length, h, of the altitude.
7. The area, A, of a square is equal to the square of the length, s, of a side.
8. The volume, V, of a cube is equal to the cube of the length, e, of an edge.
9. The surface, S, of a cube is equal to 6 times the square of the length, e, of an edge.
10. The surface, S, of a sphere is equal to the product of 4π and the square of the radius, r.
11. The Fahrenheit temperature, F, is $32°$ more than nine-fifths of the Celsius (centigrade) temperature, C.
12. The distance, d, which a body will fall from rest is one-half the product of the gravitational constant, g, and the square of the time, t.
13. The Celsius (centigrade) temperature, C, is equal to five-ninths of the difference between the Fahrenheit temperature, F, and 32.
14. To find the approximate number, n, of bushels in a bin, multiply the length, l, by the width, w, by the height, h, each expressed in feet, and divide this product by 1.25.
15. The dividend, D, equals the product of the divisor, d, and the quotient, Q, plus the remainder, R.
16. A worker's earnings during a week, E, are equal to his weekly salary, S, increased by $1\frac{1}{2}$ times his hourly rate of pay, P, times the number of hours he works overtime, H.
17. A sales tax, T, that must be paid when an article is purchased is equal to 8% of the value, V, of the article.
18. A salesman's weekly earnings, E, is equal to his weekly salary, S, increased by 2% of his total volume, V, of sales.

In 19–27, each required formula will express one of the variables in terms of the others.

19. Write the formula for the total number of seats, n, in the school auditorium, if it has two sections, each with r rows having s seats in each row.
20. Write a formula for the number, n, of students that may be seated in a room in which there are S single seats and T double seats.
21. Write a formula for the number, c, of centimeters in m meters.
22. Write a formula for the number, f, of feet in i inches.
23. Write a formula for the number, n, of days in w weeks and 5 days.
24. Write a formula for the surface area, A, of the four side walls of a room whose length is L, width W, and height H.
25. A group of n persons in an automobile crosses the Hudson River on a ferry. Write a formula for the total ferry charge, c, in cents, if the charge is 50 cents for the car and driver and t cents for each additional person.
26. Write a formula for the cost, c, in cents of a telephone conversation which lasts m minutes, m being greater than 3, if the charge for the first 3 minutes is x cents and the cost for each additional minute is y cents.
27. A gasoline dealer is allowed a profit of 2 cents a gallon for each gallon he sells. If he sells more than 25,000 gallons in a year, he is given an additional profit of 1 cent for every gallon over that number. Assuming that he always sells more than 25,000 gallons a year, express as a formula the number of dollars, D, in his yearly income in terms of the number, N, of gallons sold.

2. Evaluating the Subject of a Formula

The variable for which a formula is solved is called the **subject of the formula.** For example, P is the subject of $P = 4s$, the formula for the perimeter, P, of a square each of whose sides has a length represented by s.

As we have seen, $P = 4s$ is an open sentence. There are pairs of numbers which, when they replace s and P, result in a true sentence; and there are pairs of numbers which, when they replace s and P, result in a false sentence. For example, when $s = 3$ and $P = 12$, the resulting sentence $12 = 4 \times 3$ is true; when $s = 5$ and $P = 30$, the resulting sentence $30 = 4 \times 5$ is false.

The solution set of the open sentence $P = 4s$ has an infinite number of elements. Each element is a pair of numbers in which the second number, the value of P, is always 4 times the first number, the value of s. For example, the pairs of numbers $(1, 4)$, $(2, 8)$, and $(3, 12)$ are elements of the solution set of the formula $P = 4s$.

Since the side of a square and the perimeter of a square cannot be negative numbers or 0, the largest possible replacement set for s and also for P is {all positive numbers}. The domains of the variables in any formula are determined by the nature of the quantities they represent.

If the values of all the variables of a formula except the subject are known, we can compute its value; that is, we can evaluate the subject of the formula.

Procedure. To evaluate the subject of a formula, replace the other variables in the formula by their values. Then perform the indicated operations.

EVALUATING PERIMETER FORMULAS

Model Problems

1. If $P = 3s$, find P when $s = 5$.

   Solution

   $P = 3s$
   $P = 3(5)$ $[s = 5]$
   $P = 15$ *Ans.*

2. If $P = 2b + 2h$, find P when $b = 3$ and $h = 7$.

   Solution

   $P = 2b + 2h$
   $P = 2(3) + 2(7)$ $[b = 3, h = 7]$
   $P = 6 + 14$
   $P = 20$ *Ans.*

EXERCISES

1. The formula for the perimeter of a triangle is $P = a + b + c$. Find P when:
   a. $a = 12$ ft., $b = 8$ ft., $c = 6$ ft.
   b. $a = 4.5$ m, $b = 1.7$ m, $c = 3.8$ m
   c. $a = 7\frac{1}{2}$ ft., $b = 5\frac{3}{4}$ ft., $c = 6\frac{1}{2}$ ft.
   d. $a = 9$ ft., $b = 8$ ft., $c = 18$ in.

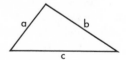

2. The formula for the perimeter of an equilateral triangle is $P = 3s$. Find P when s equals:
   a. 6 ft.   **b.** 12 cm   **c.** 4.8 m   **d.** $9\frac{1}{3}$ ft.   **e.** $8\frac{1}{2}$ in.

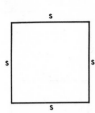

3. The formula for the perimeter of a square is $P = 4s$. Find P when s equals:
   a. 7 in.   **b.** 4 cm   **c.** 3.5 m   **d.** $8\frac{3}{4}$ in.   **e.** $5\frac{1}{8}$ in.

4. The formula for the perimeter of a rectangle is $P = 2b + 2h$. Find P when:
   a. $b = 20$ m, $h = 9$ m
   b. $b = 7.3$ m, $h = 6.9$ m
   c. $b = 5\frac{1}{2}$ in., $h = 5\frac{1}{4}$ in.
   d. $b = 5\frac{1}{3}$ ft., $h = 6\frac{1}{2}$ in.

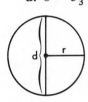

5. The formula for the circumference of a circle is $C = \pi d$. Find C when $\pi = \frac{22}{7}$ and d equals:
   a. 14 ft.   **b.** 7 m   **c.** 21 cm   **d.** 3 ft.   **e.** 10 in.

6. The formula for the circumference of a circle is $C = 2\pi r$. Find C when $\pi = 3.14$ and r equals:
   a. 10 ft.   **b.** 5 m   **c.** 40 cm   **d.** 13 ft.   **e.** 5.6 in.

EVALUATING AREA FORMULAS

Model Problems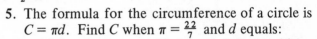

1. If $A = s^2$, find A when $s = 7$.

   Solution

   $A = s^2$

   $A = (7)^2$ $[s = 7]$

   $A = (7)(7)$

   $A = 49$ *Ans.*

2. If $A = \frac{1}{2}h(b + c)$, find A when $h = 3$, $b = 4$, and $c = 5$.

   Solution

   $A = \frac{1}{2}h(b + c)$

   $A = \frac{1}{2}(3)(4 + 5)$ $[h = 3, b = 4, c = 5]$

   $A = \frac{1}{2}(3)(9)$

   $A = \frac{1}{2}(27) = 13.5$ *Ans.*

Keep In Mind

Areas are measured in square units, such as square inches, abbreviated sq. in.; square feet, abbreviated sq. ft.; square centimeters, abbreviated cm^2; and square meters, abbreviated m^2.

EXERCISES (continued)

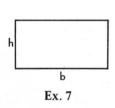

Ex. 7

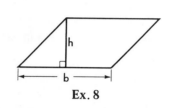

Ex. 8

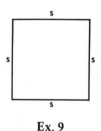

Ex. 9

7. The formula for the area of a rectangle is $A = bh$. Find A when:
    a. $b = 10$ cm, $h = 8$ cm
    b. $b = 7.5$ yd., $h = 3.4$ yd.
    c. $b = 1$ m, $h = 40$ cm
    d. $b = 4\frac{1}{3}$ yd., $h = 8$ ft.
8. The formula for the area of a parallelogram is $A = bh$. Find A when:
    a. $b = 11$ m, $h = 9$ m   b. $b = 3.5$ ft., $h = 6.4$ ft.
    c. $b = 1$ m, $h = 10$ cm   d. $b = 5\frac{1}{2}$ in., $h = 8\frac{1}{4}$ in.
9. The formula for the area of a square is $A = s^2$. Find A when s equals:
    a. 25 in.   b. 32 ft.   c. 9 cm   d. $2\frac{1}{2}$ ft.   e. 6.1 m

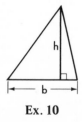

Ex. 10

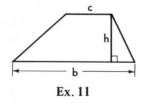

Ex. 11

Ex. 12

10. The formula for the area of a triangle is $A = \frac{1}{2}bh$. Find A when:
    a. $b = 10$ cm, $h = 6$ cm   b. $b = 1.2$ m, $h = 2$ m
    c. $b = 4\frac{1}{2}$ in., $h = 7\frac{3}{4}$ in.   d. $b = 3\frac{1}{2}$ ft., $h = 19$ in.

11. The formula for the area of a trapezoid is $A = \frac{1}{2}h(b + c)$. Find A when:
   a. $h = 8$ in., $b = 12$ in., $c = 5$ in.
   b. $h = 9$ in., $b = 14$ in., $c = 8$ in.
   c. $h = 5$ in., $b = 3\frac{1}{4}$ in., $c = \frac{3}{4}$ in.
   d. $h = 2$ m, $b = 1.8$ m, $c = 1.1$ m

12. The formula for the area of a circle is $A = \pi r^2$. Find A when $\pi = \frac{22}{7}$ and r equals:
   a. 7 ft.   b. 14 cm   c. 2.8 m   d. $3\frac{1}{2}$ yd.   e. 10 in.

EVALUATING FORMULAS FOR SURFACES OF SOLIDS

13. The formula for the surface area of a rectangular solid is $S = 2LW + 2HL + 2HW$. Find S when:
   a. $L = 6$ cm, $W = 5$ cm, $H = 3$ cm
   b. $L = 7$ in., $W = 6$ in., $H = 9$ in.
   c. $L = 4.5$ m, $W = 1.4$ m, $H = 2.6$ m
   d. $L = 3\frac{1}{2}$ in., $W = 4$ in., $H = 4\frac{1}{4}$ in.

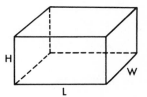

14. The formula for the surface area of a cube is $S = 6e^2$. Find S when e equals:
   a. 6 in.   b. 5 yd.   c. 9 cm
   d. $\frac{1}{4}$ ft.   e. 1.5 m

15. The formula for the surface area of a sphere is $S = 4\pi r^2$. Find S when:
   a. $\pi = \frac{22}{7}, r = 14$ cm
   b. $\pi = \frac{22}{7}, r = 3\frac{1}{2}$ ft.
   c. $\pi = 3.14, r = 10$ m
   d. $\pi = 3.14, r = 20$ in.

16. The formula for the surface area of a cylinder is $S = 2\pi r(r + h)$. Find S when:
   a. $\pi = \frac{22}{7}, r = 4$ in., $h = 3$ in.
   b. $\pi = \frac{22}{7}, r = 2$ ft., $h = 1\frac{1}{2}$ ft.
   c. $\pi = 3.14, r = 5$ cm, $h = 5$ cm
   d. $\pi = 3.14, r = 2.5$ m, $h = 7.5$ m

EVALUATING FORMULAS FOR VOLUMES OF SOLIDS

Keep In Mind

Volumes are measured in cubic units such as cubic inches, abbreviated cu. in.;
cubic feet, abbreviated cu. ft.; cubic centimeters, abbreviated cm^3; and cubic
meters, abbreviated m^3.

17. The formula for the volume of a rectangular solid is $V = LWH$. Find V when:
a. $L = 5$ ft., $W = 4$ ft., $H = 7$ ft.
b. $L = 8$ cm, $W = 7$ cm, $H = 5$ cm
c. $L = 8.5$ m, $W = 4.2$ m, $H = 6.0$ m
d. $L = 2\frac{1}{2}$ in., $W = 8$ in., $H = 5\frac{1}{4}$ in.

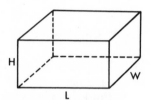

18. The formula for the volume of a cube is
$V = e^3$. Find V when e equals:
a. 2 in.   b. 3 m   c. 8 cm
d. $\frac{1}{3}$ ft.   e. 1.5 in.

19. The formula for the volume of a sphere is
$V = \frac{4}{3}\pi r^3$. Find V when:
a. $\pi = \frac{22}{7}, r = 7$ ft.
b. $\pi = \frac{22}{7}, r = 2\frac{1}{3}$ ft.
c. $\pi = 3.14, r = 10$ cm
d. $\pi = 3.14, r = 30$ in.

20. The formula for the volume of a cylinder
is $V = \pi r^2 h$. Find V when $\pi = \frac{22}{7}$ and:
a. $r = 21$ cm, $h = 10$ cm
b. $r = 35$ cm, $h = 12$ cm
c. $r = 1.4$ m, $h = 2$ m
d. $r = 1.4$ ft., $h = 8$ ft.
e. $r = 10$ in., $h = 2.1$ in.
f. $r = 9$ in., $h = 5.6$ in.

EVALUATING MISCELLANEOUS FORMULAS

Model Problems

1. If $F = \frac{9}{5}C + 32$, find F when $C = 40°$.

   Solution

   $F = \frac{9}{5}C + 32$

   $F = \frac{9}{5}(40) + 32$ $[C = 40]$

   $F = 9(8) + 32$

   $F = 72 + 32$

   $F = 104°$ *Ans.*

2. If $C = \frac{5}{9}(F - 32)$, find C when $F = -13°$.

   Solution

   $C = \frac{5}{9}(F - 32)$

   $C = \frac{5}{9}(-13 - 32)$ $[F = -13]$

   $C = \frac{5}{9}(-45)$

   $C = 5(-5)$

   $C = -25°$ *Ans.*

EXERCISES (continued)

21. If $E = \dfrac{360}{n}$, find E when:

   a. $n = 4$ b. $n = 6$ c. $n = 8$ d. $n = 10$ e. $n = 12$

22. If $I = prt$, find I when:
   a. $p = \$200, r = 8\%, t = 4$ yr.   b. $p = \$800, r = 9\%, t = 5$ yr.
   c. $p = \$640, r = 6\%, t = 2\frac{3}{4}$ yr.   d. $p = \$1200, r = 5\%, t = 3.5$ yr.

23. If $A = p + prt$, find A when:
   a. $p = \$600, r = 6\%, t = 2$ yr.   b. $p = \$4000, r = 10\%, t = 8$ yr.
   c. $p = \$1250, r = 4\%, t = 2\frac{1}{4}$ yr.   d. $p = \$3500, r = 8\%, t = 4.5$ yr.

24. If $S = \frac{1}{2}gt^2$, find S when $g = 32$ and t equals:
   a. 2   b. 3   c. 4   d. 6   e. 10   f. 1.5   g. $3\frac{1}{2}$ h. $1\frac{3}{4}$

25. If F represents a Fahrenheit temperature and C represents the equivalent Celsius temperature, $F = \frac{9}{5}C + 32$. Find F when:
   a. $C = 20°$ b. $C = 0°$ c. $C = 41°$ d. $C = -20°$ e. $C = -27°$

26. If C represents a Celsius temperature and F represents the equivalent Fahrenheit temperature, $C = \frac{5}{9}(F - 32)$. Find C when:
   a. $F = 50°$ b. $F = 32°$ c. $F = 40°$ d. $F = -22°$ e. $F = -7°$

27. The formula for the sum, S, of n numbers in arithmetic progression, where a is the first term and l is the last term, is given by

   $S = \dfrac{n}{2}(a + l)$. Find S when:

   a. $n = 20, a = 2, l = 40$ b. $n = 7, a = 1.3, l = 1.9$
   c. $n = 10, a = 18, l = -8$ d. $n = 9, a = -17, l = 1$

28. The lifting force on an airfoil is given by the formula $L = KAV^2$. Find L when:
   a. $K = .0025, A = 350, V = 100$ b. $K = .0027, A = 200, V = 150$

29. The horsepower required for flight is given by the formula $H = \dfrac{DV}{375}$. Find H when:

   a. $D = 187.5$ lb., $V = 200$ mph b. $D = 160$ lb., $V = 240$ mph

30. In the formula $L = a + (n - 1)d$, find the value of L when $a = 7$, $n = 13$, and $d = 3$.

31. In the formula $K = 2a - 5(n - 1)$, find the value of K when $a = 8$ and $n = 3$.

32. If $S = \dfrac{a}{1 - r}$, find S when $a = 8$ and $r = .5$.

33. If $S = \dfrac{rl - a}{r - 1}$, find S when $r = 3, l = 15$, and $a = 5$.

In 34–37: From the given domains, choose a replacement for each variable which will make the formula a true statement.

34. $C = 5n$ $C: \{3, 7, 15, 22\}$ $n: \{1, 2, 3, 4\}$
35. $A = e^2$ $A: \{10, 15, 20, 25\}$ $e: \{4, 5, 6, 7\}$
36. $A = bh$ $A: \{11, 13, 15, 17\}$ $b: \{3, 4, 5, 6\}$ $h: \{1, 2, 3, 4\}$
37. $C = \frac{5}{9}(F - 32)$ $C: \{5, 10, 15, 20\}$ $F: \{40, 50, 60, 70\}$

3. Evaluating a Formula by Solving an Equation

If the value of the subject of a formula and all its other variables but one are known, the value of the remaining variable can be computed.

Procedure. To find the value of a variable in a formula when the values of the other variables including the subject of the formula are given, substitute the given values in the formula. Then solve the resulting equation.

Model Problem

If $S = \dfrac{n}{2}(a + l)$, find a when $S = 40, n = 8$, and $l = 6$.

| *Solution* | *Check* |

$$S = \frac{n}{2}(a + l)$$ $$S = \frac{n}{2}(a + l)$$

$$40 = \frac{8}{2}(a + 6) \quad [S = 40, n = 8, l = 6] \qquad 40 \stackrel{?}{=} \frac{8}{2}(4 + 6)$$

$$40 = 4(a + 6) \qquad\qquad\qquad 40 \stackrel{?}{=} 4(10)$$
$$40 = 4a + 24 \qquad\qquad\qquad 40 = 40 \quad \text{(true)}$$
$$40 - 24 = 4a + 24 - 24$$
$$16 = 4a$$
$$4 = a \quad Ans.$$

EXERCISES

1. If $p = a + b + c$, find c when $p = 80, a = 20$, and $b = 25$.
2. If $A = lw$, find w when (a) $A = 80, l = 10$ (b) $A = 3.6, l = .9$.
3. If $A = \frac{1}{2}bh$, find h when (a) $A = 24, b = 8$ (b) $A = 12, b = 3$.
4. If $S = 2\pi rh$, find h when $S = 440, \pi = \frac{22}{7}, r = 5$.
5. If $V = lwh$, find w when $V = 72, l = \frac{3}{4}, h = 12$.
6. If $I = prt$, find t when $I = \$36, r = 6\%$, and $p = \$300$.
7. If $I = prt$, find p when $I = \$135, r = 9\%$, and $t = 3$ years.
8. If $I = prt$, find r when $I = \$160, p = \$1000, t = 2$ years.
9. If $p = 2a + b$, find a when $p = 18.6$ and $b = 5.8$.
10. If $F = \frac{9}{5}C + 32$, find C when (a) $F = 95°$ (b) $F = 68°$ (c) $F = 59°$.
11. If $A = p + prt$, find t when $A = \$600, p = \$500, r = 4\%$.
12. If $S = \frac{n}{2}(a + l)$, find a when $S = 42, n = 14, l = 2$.
13. If $C = \frac{5}{9}(F - 32)$, find F when (a) $C = 5°$ (b) $C = 10°$ (c) $C = 77°$.
14. If $A = \frac{1}{2}h(b + c)$, find h when $A = 24, b = 9, c = 3$.
15. If $A = \frac{1}{2}h(b + c)$, find b when $A = 50, h = 4, c = 11$.
16. If $A = \frac{1}{2}h(b + c)$, find c when $A = 54, h = 12, b = 5.5$.

4. Transforming Simple Formulas

A formula may be expressed in more than one form. Sometimes it is desirable to solve a formula for a variable different from the one for which it is solved. This is called *transforming* the formula, or *changing the subject* of the formula. For example, the formula $D = 40t$ can be transformed into the equivalent formula $\dfrac{D}{40} = t$. In the formula

$D = 40t$, D is expressed in terms of t; in the formula $t = \dfrac{D}{40}$, t is expressed in terms of D. If we know the value of D and wish to find the value of t, the computation is more convenient when we use the formula $t = \dfrac{D}{40}$. (See model problem 1 following Procedure.)

Procedure. To transform a formula so that it is solved for a particular variable, consider the formula as an equation with several variables and solve it for the indicated variable in terms of the others.

Model Problems

1. a. Solve the formula $D = 40t$ for t.
   b. Use the answer found in a to find the value of t when $D = 200$.

   Solution:

   a. $D = 40t$ b. $t = \dfrac{D}{40}$

   $\dfrac{D}{40} = \dfrac{40t}{40}$ D_{40} $t = \dfrac{200}{40}$ $[D = 200]$

   $\dfrac{D}{40} = t$ $t = 5$ *Ans.*

   $t = \dfrac{D}{40}$ *Ans.*

2. Solve the formula   3. Solve the formula $P = 2(L + W)$ for W.
   $V = \frac{1}{3}Bh$ for B.

   Solution   *Solution*

   $V = \frac{1}{3}Bh$ $P = 2(L + W)$
                                                  $P = 2L + 2W$ [distributive
   $3V = 3 \cdot \frac{1}{3}Bh$ M_3 property]
   $3V = Bh$ $P + (-2L) = 2L + 2W + (-2L)$ A_{-2L}
                                          $P - 2L = 2W$
   $\dfrac{3V}{h} = \dfrac{Bh}{h}$ D_h
                                          $\dfrac{P - 2L}{2} = \dfrac{2W}{2}$ D_2

$$\frac{3V}{h} = B$$

$$\frac{P - 2L}{2} = W$$

$$B = \frac{3V}{h} \quad Ans.$$

$$W = \frac{P - 2L}{2} \quad Ans.$$

EXERCISES

In 1–23, transform the given formula by solving for the indicated letter.

1. $A = 6h$ for h
2. $36 = bh$ for h
3. $D = rt$ for t
4. $A = bh$ for h
5. $V = lwh$ for h
6. $C = 2\pi r$ for r
7. $i = prt$ for p
8. $CN = 360$ for N
9. $400 = BH$ for B
10. $A = \frac{1}{2}bh$ for h
11. $A = \frac{1}{3}BH$ for H
12. $K = \frac{AP}{2}$ for A
13. $S = \frac{1}{2}gt^2$ for g
14. $E = \frac{1}{2}mv^2$ for m
15. $S = \pi \frac{R^2 A}{90}$ for A
16. $S = c + g$ for g
17. $l = c - s$ for c
18. $P = 2l + 2w$ for l
19. $F = \frac{9}{5}C + 32$ for C
20. $2S = n(a + l)$ for a
21. $A = \frac{h}{2}(b + c)$ for c
22. $T = m(g - b)$ for g
23. $E = I(R + r)$ for R
24. If $A = \frac{1}{2}rp$, express r in terms of A and p.
25. If $P = 2a + b + c$, express a in terms of the other variables.

In 26–30: (a) Transform the given formula by solving for the variable to be evaluated. (b) Substitute the given values (in the result obtained in part a) to find the value of this variable.

26. If $LWH = 144$, find W when $L = 3$ and $H = 6$.
27. If $A = \frac{1}{2}bh$, find h when $A = 15$ and $b = 5$.
28. If $F = \frac{9}{5}C + 32$, find C when $F = 95$.
29. If $P = 2L + 2W$, find L when $P = 64$ and $W = 13$.
30. If $S = \frac{n}{2}(a + l)$, find l when $S = 36$, $n = 4$, and $a = 5$.

31. The formula for finding the area of a rectangle is $A = bh$. Rewrite this formula if $b = 4h$.
32. The formula for the area of a triangle is $A = \frac{1}{2}bh$. Rewrite this formula if $h = 4b$.
33. The formula for the area of a trapezoid is $A = \frac{h}{2}(b + c)$. If $h = 3b$ and $c = 5b$, express A in terms of b.

5. Transforming More Difficult Formulas

Model Problems

1. a. Solve the formula $C = \frac{5}{9}(F - 32)$ for F in terms of C.
   b. Find F when $C = 10$.

   Solution:

   a. $\qquad C = \frac{5}{9}(F - 32)$ b. $F = \dfrac{9C + 160}{5}$ $[C = 10]$

   $\qquad 9 \times C = 9 \times \frac{5}{9}(F - 32)$ M_9 $F = \dfrac{9(10) + 160}{5}$

   $\qquad\qquad 9C = 5(F - 32)$ $F = \dfrac{90 + 160}{5}$
   $\qquad\qquad 9C = 5F - 160$

   $\qquad 9C + 160 = 5F$ A_{160}

   $\qquad \dfrac{9C + 160}{5} = F$ D_5 $F = \dfrac{250}{5}$

   $\qquad\qquad\qquad\qquad\qquad\qquad\qquad F = 50$ *Ans.*

   $\qquad F = \dfrac{9C + 160}{5}$ *Ans.*

2. Solve the formula $R = \dfrac{gs}{g + s}$ for s.

   Solution:

   $$R = \frac{gs}{g + s}$$

   $$R(g + s) = \frac{gs}{(\cancel{g + s})} \cdot \overset{1}{(\cancel{g + s})} \qquad M_{(g + s)}$$

   $$Rg + Rs = gs \qquad [\text{distributive property}]$$
   $$Rg = gs - Rs \qquad S_{Rs} \text{ or } A_{-Rs}$$
   $$Rg = s(g - R) \qquad [\text{factoring}]$$

   $$\frac{Rg}{(g - R)} = \frac{s(\cancel{g - R})}{(\cancel{g - R})} \qquad D_{(g - R)}$$

   $$\frac{Rg}{(g - R)} = s$$

   Answer: $s = \dfrac{Rg}{g - R}$

EXERCISES

In 1–18, solve the formula for the indicated variable.

1. $v = \dfrac{s}{t}$ for t

2. $F = \dfrac{mv^2}{gr}$ for m

3. $V^2 = \dfrac{L}{KA}$ for A

4. $H = \dfrac{3V}{\pi R^2}$ for V

5. $\dfrac{P}{N} = \dfrac{p}{n}$ for N

6. $F = 32 + \tfrac{9}{5}C$ for C

7. $\dfrac{D}{d} = q + \dfrac{r}{d}$ for d

8. $S = \dfrac{n}{2}(a + l)$ for a

9. $S = \dfrac{n}{2}(a + l)$ for n

10. $A = p + prt$ for p

11. $n = \dfrac{a - W}{6W}$ for W

12. $\dfrac{1}{f} = \dfrac{1}{p} + \dfrac{1}{q}$ for p

13. $I = \dfrac{E}{R + r}$ for r

14. $R = \dfrac{gs}{g + s}$ for g

15. $C = \dfrac{nE}{R + nr}$ for n

16. $\dfrac{1}{f} - \dfrac{1}{q} = \dfrac{1}{p}$ for q

17. $S = \dfrac{rl - a}{r - l}$ for r

18. $I = \dfrac{E}{r_1 + r_2}$ for r_2

19. If $S = \tfrac{1}{2}at^2$, express a in terms of S and t.

20. If $V = \dfrac{h}{6}(B + B' + 4m)$, express h in terms of V, B, B', and m.

In 21–27: **(a)** Transform the given formula into a formula which is solved for the variable to be evaluated. **(b)** Substitute the given values (in the result obtained in part a) to find the value of this variable.

21. If $\dfrac{P}{B} = r$, find B when $P = 80$ and $r = .04$.

22. If $A = \tfrac{1}{2}h(b + c)$, find h when $A = 48$, $b = 12$, and $c = 4$.

23. If $A = \dfrac{h}{2}(b + c)$, find c when $A = 36$, $h = 12$, and $b = 2$.

24. If $n = \dfrac{a - K}{5K}$, find K when $a = 33$ and $n = 2$.

25. If $\dfrac{1}{F} = \dfrac{1}{g} + \dfrac{1}{h}$, find F when $g = \tfrac{1}{2}$ and $h = \tfrac{2}{5}$.

26. If $S = \dfrac{n}{2}(a + l)$, express S in terms of a when $n = 3a$ and $l = 5a$.

27. If $A = \tfrac{1}{2}h(b + c)$, express A in terms of c when $h = 5c$ and $b = 9c$.

6. Using Formulas to Study Related Changes

The formula $P = 4s$ states the relationship between the length of a side of a square, s, and its perimeter, P. A change in the value of the variable s will bring about a change in the value of the variable P. A table of values prepared from the formula can help us study the effect that a change in one variable has on the other variable.

Model Problems

1. The formula for the perimeter of a square is $P = 4s$. If s increases, what change takes place in P?

   Solution: Assume a set of increasing values for s; for example, 3, 4, and 5. Use the formula to find the corresponding values for P. The table shows that the values for P increase.

   Answer: If s increases, then P increases.

s	P
3	12
4	16
5	20

2. The formula for the perimeter of a square is $P = 4s$. If s is doubled, what change takes place in P?

   Solution: Assume a set of values for s in which each number after the first is double the previous one; for example, 4, 8, 16. Find the corresponding values for P. The table shows that each value for P is double the previous value.

   Answer: If s is doubled, then P is doubled.

s	P
4	16
8	32
16	64

It is also possible to use algebraic representation to study the effect that a change in one variable in a formula has on the other variable.

Model Problems

1. If the length of a side of a square is doubled, what change takes place in its perimeter?

   Solution: The formula for the perimeter of a square is $P = 4s$. Since the length, s, of the side of the square is to be doubled, the length of a side of the new square can be represented by $2s$. The perimeter of the new square, P', can be found by substituting $2s$ for s in the formula $P = 4s$.

   $$P' = 4(2s)$$
   $$P' = 8s$$

   Since $8s$ is twice $4s$, then P' is twice P.

   Answer: The perimeter is doubled.

2. If the length, s, of a side of a square is multiplied by 2, what change takes place in its area?

   Solution: The formula for the area of a square is $A = s^2$. Represent the length of a side of the new square by $2s$. Find the area of the new square, A', by substituting $2s$ for s in the formula $A = s^2$.

   $$A' = (2s)^2$$
   $$A' = (2s)(2s)$$
   $$A' = 4s^2$$

   Since $4s^2$ is 4 times s^2, then A' is 4 times A.

   Answer: The area is multiplied by 4.

EXERCISES

In 1–9, prepare a table of values to help you complete each statement correctly. In the formula:

1. $p = 3s$, if s is positive and increases, then p ———.
2. $C = 5n$, if n is positive and decreases, then C ———.
3. $A = s^2$, if s is positive and increases, then A ———.
4. $S = 6e^2$, if e is positive and decreases, then S ———.
5. $a = \dfrac{360}{n}$, if n is positive and increases, then a ———.
6. $C = \dfrac{40}{n}$, if n is positive and is halved, then C is ———.

7. $A = 12 - 2b$, if b is positive and increases, then A ——.
8. $A = BH$, if B is positive and remains unchanged and H is positive and increases, then A ——.
9. $D = RT$, if T is positive and remains unchanged and R is positive and decreases, then D ——.

In 10–18, use algebraic representation to discover how to complete the statement correctly. In the formula:

10. $P = 6s$, if s is multiplied by 4, then P is ——.
11. $E = 60R$, if R is divided by 2, then E is ——.
12. $A = s^2$, if s is multiplied by 5, then A is ——.
13. $P = ns$, if n remains unchanged and s is multiplied by 6, then P is ——.
14. $A = lw$, if l remains unchanged and w is halved, then A is ——.
15. $A = \frac{1}{2}bh$, if h remains unchanged and b is doubled, then A is ——.
16. $I = prt$, if p and r are unchanged and t is multiplied by 3, then I is ——.
17. $D = RT$, if R is doubled and T is tripled, then D is ——.
18. $p = br$, if b is doubled and r is halved, then p is ——.
19. The formula for the perimeter of a square is $P = 4s$. If the length, s, of a side of the square is multiplied by 10, what change takes place in the perimeter, P?
20. The formula for the area of a square is $A = s^2$. If the length, s, of a side of the square is multiplied by 10, what change takes place in the area, A?
21. The formula for the volume of a cube is $V = e^3$. If the length, e, of an edge of the cube is multiplied by 10, what change takes place in the volume, V?
22. The formula for the area of a rectangle is $A = lw$. Find the change that takes place in the area, A, when:
    a. the length, l, is multiplied by 4 and the width, w, is multiplied by 3.
    b. the length, l, remains unchanged and the width, w, is multiplied by 4.
    c. the length, l, is multiplied by 3 and the width, w, is divided by 3.

7. More Algebraic Representation

If you have difficulty working with the variables in the following questions, it may be helpful to solve similar questions involving numbers.

Model Problem

If 5 pears cost c cents, represent the cost of n pears.

Solution: The cost of 5 pears is c cents. The cost of 1 pear is $\frac{1}{5}$ of c cents, or $\frac{c}{5}$ cents. The cost of n pears is n times the cost of 1 pear, or $n\left(\frac{c}{5}\right)$ cents.

Answer: $n\left(\frac{c}{5}\right)$ cents, or $\frac{nc}{5}$ cents

EXERCISES

1. A carton contains r cans of sardines. Represent the number of cans in t cartons.
2. One pound of apples costs 27 cents and one pound of peaches costs 49 cents. Represent the cost of r pounds of apples and w pounds of peaches.
3. Represent the cost of k kilograms of butter at f cents per kilogram and t kilograms of cheese at m cents per kilogram.
4. A woman earns d dollars a month and spends s dollars a month. Represent the number of dollars she will save in 3 years.
5. If 8 books cost m dollars, represent the cost of 1 book.
6. If t bats cost q dollars, represent the cost of 1 bat.
7. If 6 boxes of candy cost r dollars, represent the cost of z boxes of this candy.
8. If t tons of coal cost S dollars, represent the cost of g tons.
9. A basketball player in three games scored P, S, and T points. Represent his average score.
10. Represent the width of a rectangle whose area is K and whose length is L.
11. If a plane flies k kilometers in h hours, represent the average number of kilometers it flies in 1 hour.
12. If a car travels b miles in c hours, represent the number of hours required to travel d miles at the same rate of speed.

13. A team won W games and lost L games. What fractional part of all the games played did the team win? (There are no tie games.)
14. A college is comprised of m male students and f female students. What fractional part of the students is female?
15. In a junior college, there are x men students, y women students, and z professors. Represent the number of students in each professor's class if all classes have the same number of students.

8. Writing Formulas for Areas

Irregularly shaped geometric plane figures may be formed by combining polygons, circles, and parts of polygons and circles.

To find the area of an irregularly shaped figure, find the areas of the polygons and circles which comprise it. Then add or subtract the results as the shape of the irregular figure requires.

Model Problem _____

Write the formula for the area, A, of the shaded figure.

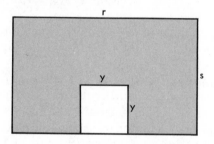

Solution:

Area of the shaded region = area of rectangle − area of square.
Area of rectangle = length × width = rs.
Area of square = length of side × length of side = $y \times y = y^2$.

Answer: Area of the shaded region = $rs - y^2$

EXERCISES

In 1-18, write the formula for the area, A, of the following shaded regions:

1.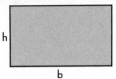

2.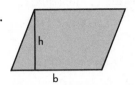

3.

4.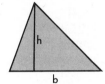

5.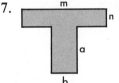

6.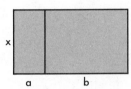

7.

8.

9.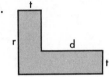

10.

11.

12.

13.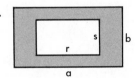

14.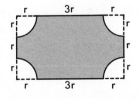

15.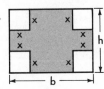

16.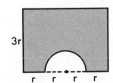

17.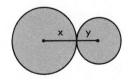

18.

19. The dimensions of a rectangle are p and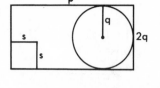
    $2q$. From it a circle of radius q and a
    square of side s are cut.
    a. Represent the area of the rectangle.
    b. Represent the area of the square.
    c. Represent the area of the circle.
    d. Represent the waste.
    e. If $p = 28$ in., $q = 7$ in., $s = 6$ in., and
       $\pi = \frac{22}{7}$, find the area of the waste.

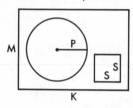

20. Using the diagram at the left:
    a. Represent the area of the rectangle.
    b. Represent the area of the circle.
    c. Represent the area of the square.
    d. If the circle and the square are cut
       from the rectangle, what represents
       the waste?
    e. If $K = 24$ cm, $M = 18$ cm, $P = 7$ cm,
       $S = 6$ cm, and $\pi = \frac{22}{7}$, find the area of
       the waste.

Chapter 13

Graphs of Linear Open Sentences

in Two Variables

1. Ordered Number Pairs and Points in a Plane

Let us begin by examining a system of locating points in a plane. We start with two signed number lines in the plane, called *coordinate axes*, drawn at right angles to each other. The horizontal line is called the x-*axis*. The vertical line is called the y-*axis*. Such a plane with coordinate axes is called a *coordinate plane*, or Cartesian plane. The point *O* at which the two axes intersect is called the *origin*.

The Cartesian plane is named after the seventeenth-century mathematician René Descartes, who, in 1637, made the wonderful discovery that algebraic relations between variables could be described by points and lines (straight or curved) in a plane.

The x-axis and the y-axis divide the set of points of the plane not on the axes into four regions called *quadrants*. These quadrants are numbered I, II, III, and IV in a counterclockwise order, as shown in the drawing.

Point *P* in the plane can be located by starting at the origin, moving 2 units to the right along the x-axis, then moving 3 units upward in a direction parallel to the y-axis.

Distances measured to the *right* of the y-axis, along the x-axis or along a line parallel to the x-axis, are considered to be *positive;* distances measured to the *left* of the y-axis are considered to be *negative*. Distances measured *upward* from the x-axis, along the y-axis or along a line parallel to the y-axis, are considered to be *positive;* distances measured *downward* from the x-axis are considered to be *negative*.

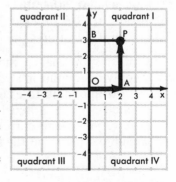

341

The distance of a point from the y-axis, measured either along the x-axis or along a line parallel to it, is called the *x-coordinate*, or *abscissa*. The distance of a point from the x-axis, measured either along the y-axis or along a line parallel to it, is called the *y-coordinate*, or *ordinate*. For example, consider point P previously discussed (page 341). The abscissa, BP, the distance from B to P, which can be read along the x-axis as OA, the distance from O to A, is $+2$, or 2; the ordinate, AP, which can be read along the y-axis as OB, is $+3$, or 3.

The two numbers associated with any particular point, the abscissa and ordinate of the point, are called the *coordinates* of the point. The coordinates of a point may be written as an ordered number pair in which the first number is always the abscissa and the second number is always the ordinate. Thus, the coordinates of point P in the graph below may be written $(2, 3)$. The point P is called the *graph of the ordered number pair (2, 3)*. In general, the coordinates of a point may be represented as (x, y).

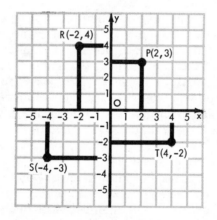

We must be careful not to interchange the numbers 2 and 3 in the number pair $(2, 3)$, because the resulting number pair $(3, 2)$ would be associated with a point different from point P. In fact, it is impossible to find a point other than P whose coordinates are $(2, 3)$. It is also impossible for an ordered pair other than $(2, 3)$ to represent point P. This example illustrates the following true statements:

1. Corresponding to each ordered number pair there is one, and only one, point in a coordinate plane.
2. Corresponding to each point in a coordinate plane there is one, and only one, ordered number pair. Therefore, we say that there is a one-to-one correspondence between the set of all ordered number pairs and the set of all points in a coordinate plane.

Two ordered pairs of numbers are equal when their first members are equal and when their second members are equal. For example, $(1, 3) = (\frac{5}{5}, \frac{9}{3})$ because $1 = \frac{5}{5}$ and $3 = \frac{9}{3}$. However, $(1, 3) \neq (1, 2)$, because the second members, 3 and 2, are unequal.

In general, for all real numbers, a, b, c, and d:

$$(a, b) = (c, d) \text{ if and only if } a = c \text{ and } b = d$$

In the preceding graph, point R in quadrant II is 2 units to the left of the y-axis; thus, the abscissa of point R is -2. Since point R is 4 units above the x-axis, its ordinate is 4. The coordinates of point R may be written $(-2, 4)$. Point R is the graph of the number pair $(-2, 4)$.

Similarly, the point described by $(-4, -3)$ is point S in quadrant III, and the point described by $(4, -2)$ is point T in quadrant IV. When we graph the point described by an ordered number pair, we are plotting the point.

Model Problem

Find the value of x and the value of y for which $(2x, 3y) = (10, 2y + 1)$.

Solution: The ordered pairs $(2x, 3y)$ and $(10, 2y + 1)$ are equal when their first members, $2x$ and 10, are equal. Their second members, $3y$ and $2y + 1$, must also be equal. Therefore, we solve the equations $2x = 10$ and $3y = 2y + 1$ as follows:

$$2x = 10 \qquad 3y = 2y + 1 \qquad\qquad Check$$
$$x = 5 \qquad 3y - 2y = 2y + 1 - 2y$$
$$y = 1$$

$$Check$$
$$(2x, 3y) \stackrel{?}{=} (10, 2y + 1)$$
$$(2 \times 5, 3 \times 1) \stackrel{?}{=} (10, 2 \times 1 + 1)$$
$$(10, 3) = (10, 3) \quad \text{(true)}$$

Answer: $x = 5$, $y = 1$

EXERCISES

1. Write as ordered number pairs the coordinates of points A, B, C, D, E, F, G, H, and O in the graph.

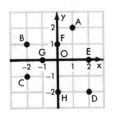

In 2–26, draw a pair of coordinate axes on a sheet of graph paper and graph the point associated with the ordered number pair.

2. $(5, 4)$ 3. $(-3, 2)$ 4. $(2, -6)$ 5. $(-4, -5)$
6. $(2\frac{1}{4}, -3\frac{3}{4})$ 7. $(1, 6)$ 8. $(-8, 5)$ 9. $(4, -4)$
10. $(-2, -7)$ 11. $(-1.5, -2.5)$ 12. $(5, 0)$ 13. $(-3, 0)$
14. $(8, 0)$ 15. $(-10, 0)$ 16. $(3\frac{1}{3}, 0)$ 17. $(0, 4)$
18. $(0, -6)$ 19. $(0, 1)$ 20. $(0, -4)$ 21. $(0, 0)$
22. $(|2|, |4|)$ 23. $(|-5|, |3|)$ 24. $(|1|, |-2|)$
25. $(|-3|, |-11|)$ 26. $(-5, |-2|)$

In 27–31, name the quadrant in which the graph of the point described appears.

27. $(5, 7)$ 28. $(-3, -2)$ 29. $(-7, 4)$ 30. $(1, -3)$ 31. $(|-2|, |-3|)$

32. Graph the following points: $A(5, 3), B(-5, 3), C(-5, -3), D(5, -3)$. Connect these points with straight lines in the order given. What kind of quadrilateral is $ABCD$?

33. Locate the points described by $(2, -3)$ and $(-3, 2)$. Join them with a straight line. At what point does the line intersect the y-axis?

34. Plot the points described by $x = 12, y = 5$; and $x = 4, y = -3$. What is the value of x where the line joining these two points crosses the x-axis?

35. Plot the points described by $(-1, 2)$ and $(3, -2)$. Join them with a straight line. Where does this line intersect the x-axis?

36. Plot the points described by $x = 4, y = 2$; and $x = -5, y = 5$. Draw the line joining these points. What is the y-value of the point on this line for which the x-value is 1?

37. Graph several points on the x-axis. What is the value of the ordinate for every point in the set of points on the x-axis?

38. Graph several points on the y-axis. What is the value of the abscissa for every point in the set of points on the y-axis?

39. What are the coordinates of the origin on the coordinate axes?

40. The coordinates of point P are (x, y). Name the set of numbers of which the abscissa must be a member, and the set of which the ordinate must be a member if the graph of P is not on the coordinate axes and is in:

a. quadrant I   b. quadrant II   c. quadrant III   d. quadrant IV

41. Name the quadrant in which the graph of point $P(x, y)$ lies when:

a. $x > 0$ and $y > 0$ b. $x > 0$ and $y < 0$
c. $x < 0$ and $y > 0$ d. $x < 0$ and $y < 0$

42. Name the quadrant in which the graph of the point $P(|x|, |y|)$ lies when:

a. $x > 0$ and $y > 0$ b. $x > 0$ and $y < 0$
c. $x < 0$ and $y > 0$ d. $x < 0$ and $y < 0$

In 43–49, find the value for x and the value for y for which the ordered pairs of numbers are equal.

43. $(x, 15)$ and $(10, y)$

44. $(2x, 21)$ and $(20, 7y)$

45. $(5x, 4y)$ and $(2x + 12, 3y + 6)$

46. $(3x - 1, y - 3)$ and $(x + 7, 4y + 12)$

47. $(\frac{1}{2}x, 6)$ and $(4, \frac{2}{3}y)$

48. $(\frac{1}{3}x, y + 20)$ and $(x - 12, \frac{1}{5}y - 5)$

49. State the relationship that must exist between x and y in order that $(x, y) = (y, x)$.

2. Finding Solution Sets of Open Sentences in Two Variables

There are some replacements for x and y that cause $y = 3x$ to become a true sentence. For example, if x is replaced by 1 and y by 3, the resulting sentence $3 = 3 \times 1$ is a true sentence. Therefore, the pair of numbers $x = 1$, $y = 3$ is said to *satisfy* the open sentence in two variables $y = 3x$. Such a pair of numbers is called a *root*, or *solution*, of $y = 3x$. We can write the solution $x = 1$, $y = 3$ as an ordered pair $(1, 3)$ if we agree that the first value in the pair always represents a value of the variable x and the second value always represents a value of the variable y.

On the other hand, some replacements for x and y cause $y = 3x$ to become a false sentence. For example, when x is replaced by 3 and y is replaced by 1, $y = 3x$ becomes $1 = 3 \times 3$, which is a false sentence. Therefore, the pair of numbers $x = 3$, $y = 1$, which may be written as the ordered pair $(3, 1)$, is not a solution of the sentence $y = 3x$.

The solutions of $y = 3x$, when the replacement set for x and for y is $\{1, 2, 3, 4, 5, 6, 7, 8, 9\}$, are the ordered pairs $(1, 3)$, $(2, 6)$, and $(3, 9)$. We call this set of ordered pairs $\{(1, 3), (2, 6), (3, 9)\}$ the *solution set* of the sentence $y = 3x$. The solution set of a sentence involving two variables is the set whose members are all the ordered pairs that are solutions of the sentence. If there are no ordered pairs which are solutions of the sentence, we say the solution set is the empty set, $\emptyset$.

If the replacement set is the set of signed numbers, there are many more members in the solution set of $y = 3x$ than when the replacement set was $\{1, 2, 3, \ldots, 9\}$. Some members of this new solution set are $(-2, -6)$, $(-1, -3)$, $(\frac{1}{3}, 1)$, $(\frac{2}{3}, 2)$, $(10, 30)$. It is impossible to list all the members of the solution set because there are an infinite number of them. In such a case, we can describe the solution set as $\{(x, y)| y = 3x\}$, which is read "the set of all ordered pairs (x, y) such that $y = 3x$."

The solution set of $y > 3x$, when the replacement set for x and for y is $\{1, 2, 3, 4, 5, 6, 7, 8, 9\}$, is the set of ordered pairs $\{(1, 4), (1, 5), (1, 6), (1, 7), (1, 8), (1, 9), (2, 7), (2, 8), (2, 9)\}$.

To verify that $(1, 9)$ is a solution of $y > 3x$, we replace x by 1 and y by 9. We obtain $9 > 3 \times 1$, which is a true sentence. All the other ordered pairs of the solution set can be verified in the same way.

If the replacement set is the set of signed numbers, there are many more members in the solution set of $y > 3x$ than when the replacement set was $\{1, 2, 3, \ldots, 9\}$. Some members of this new solution set are $(-2, -4)$, $(-1, -2)$, $(-1, 2)$, $(-\frac{1}{3}, 1)$, $(\frac{2}{3}, 3)$, $(5, 16)$. It is impossible to list all the members of the solution set because there are an infinite number of them. In such a case, we can describe the solution set as $\{(x, y)| y > 3x\}$, which is read "the set of all ordered pairs (x, y) such that $y > 3x$."

Model Problems

1. Find the solution set of $y - 2x = 4$ when the replacement set for x is $R = \{1, 2, 3, 4, 5\}$ and the replacement set for y is $S = \{6, 7, 8, 9, 10\}$.

How to Proceed	*Solution*

1. Transform the sentence into an equivalent sentence which has y alone as one member.

$$y - 2x = 4$$
$$y - 2x + 2x = 4 + 2x$$
$$y = 2x + 4$$

2. Replace x by each member of R, the replacement set for x. Then compute each of the corresponding y-values.

3. Determine whether or not each y-value computed in step 2 is a member of S, the replacement set for y. If the y-value belongs to S, then the ordered pair consisting of an x-value and its corresponding y-value is a solution of the sentence.

Answer: Solution set is
$\{(1, 6), (2, 8), (3, 10)\}$.

x	$2x + 4$	y
1	$2 \times 1 + 4$	6 is a member of S
2	$2 \times 2 + 4$	8 is a member of S
3	$2 \times 3 + 4$	10 is a member of S
4	$2 \times 4 + 4$	12 is not a member of S
5	$2 \times 5 + 4$	14 is not a member of S

2. Find the solution set of $y - 2x > 4$ when the replacement set for x is $R = \{1, 2, 3, 4, 5\}$ and the replacement set for y is $S = \{6, 7, 8, 9, 10\}$.

How to Proceed	*Solution*

1. Transform the sentence into an equivalent sentence which has y alone as one member.

$$y - 2x > 4$$
$$y - 2x + 2x > 4 + 2x$$
$$y > 2x + 4$$

2. Replace x by each member of R, the replacement set for x. Then compute the corresponding y-values.

3. If any y-values computed in step 2 are members of S (S is the replacement set for y), then each ordered pair consisting of an x-value and its corresponding y-value is a solution of the sentence.

x	$2x + 4$	$y > 2x + 4$	y
1	$2 \times 1 + 4$	$y > 6$	7, 8, 9, 10
2	$2 \times 2 + 4$	$y > 8$	9, 10
3	$2 \times 3 + 4$	$y > 10$	no values in S
4	$2 \times 4 + 4$	$y > 12$	no values in S
5	$2 \times 5 + 4$	$y > 14$	no values in S

Answer: Solution set is $\{(1, 7), (1, 8), (1, 9), (1, 10), (2, 9), (2, 10)\}$.

EXERCISES

In 1–10, find the missing member in each ordered pair if the second member of the pair is twice the first member.

1. $(3, ?)$ **2.** $(\frac{1}{2}, ?)$ **3.** $(0, ?)$ **4.** $(-2, ?)$ **5.** $(a, ?)$
6. $(?, 10)$ **7.** $(?, 11)$ **8.** $(?, 0)$ **9.** $(?, -8)$ **10.** $(?, a)$

In 11–20, find the missing member in each ordered pair if the first member of the pair is 4 more than the second member.

11. $(?, 5)$ **12.** $(?, \frac{1}{2})$ **13.** $(?, 0)$ **14.** $(?, -6)$ **15.** $(?, a)$
16. $(12, ?)$ **17.** $(9\frac{1}{4}, ?)$ **18.** $(0, ?)$ **19.** $(-8, ?)$ **20.** $(a, ?)$

In 21–28, state whether the given ordered pair of numbers is a solution of the sentence. The replacement set for x and for y is the set of whole numbers.

21. $y = 4x; (16, 4)$ **22.** $y = 3x + 1; (7, 22)$
23. $4x - 5y = 18; (7, 2)$ **24.** $3x - 2y = 0; (3, 2)$
25. $y < 2x + 3; (0, 2)$ **26.** $3y > 2x + 1; (4, 3)$
27. $2x + 3y \leq 9; (0, 3)$ **28.** $5x - 4y \geq 23; (4, 3)$

In 29–34, state whether the given ordered pair of numbers is a solution of the sentence. The replacement set for x and for y is the set of signed numbers.

29. $4x + 3y = 2; (\frac{1}{4}, \frac{1}{3})$ **30.** $3x = y + 4; (-7, -1)$
31. $x - 2y = 15; (1, -7)$ **32.** $y > 6x; (-1, -2)$
33. $y \geq 3 - 2x; (-1, 6)$ **34.** $5x - 2y \leq 19; (3, -2)$

In 35–40, find the solution set of the sentence.

35. $x + y = 4$ when the replacement set for x is $\{5, 7\}$ and the replacement set for y is $\{$natural numbers$\}$.

36. $y = 3x - 1$ when the replacement set for x is $\{-3, -1, 2\}$ and the replacement set for y is $\{$signed numbers$\}$.

37. $4x + y = 2$ when the replacement set for x is $\{5, 6, 7\}$ and the replacement set for y is $\{$positive numbers$\}$.

38. $y < 2x - 1$ when the replacement set for x is $\{5, 6\}$ and the replacement set for y is $\{8, 9, 10, 11\}$.

39. $x + y \geq 12$ when the replacement set for x is $\{-7, 10, 12\}$ and the replacement set for y is $\{-2, 2, 6, 10\}$.

40. $y - 3 \leq 2x$ when the replacement set for x is $\{-1, 0, 1, 2\}$ and the replacement set for y is $\{-1, 0, 1, 2\}$.

In 41–46, use set notation to describe the solution set when the replacement set for x and for y is the set of signed numbers.

41. $y = 6x$ **42.** $y = x + 9$ **43.** $3x + y = 11$
44. $y > 10x$ **45.** $y < 3x - 1$ **46.** $y - x \geq 4$

3. Graphing a Linear Equation in Two Variables by Means of Its Solutions

If we wish to find number pairs which satisfy the equation $x + y = 6$, we can replace one variable, for example x, by a convenient value. Then we can solve the resulting equation for the corresponding value of the other variable, y. If we let $x = 1$, then $1 + y = 6$ and $y = 5$. Thus, the ordered pair $(1, 5)$ is a solution of $x + y = 6$.

We can also transform the equation $x + y = 6$ into an equivalent equation in which y is expressed in terms of x. Then we can assign a value to x and find the corresponding value of y. For example:

$$x + y = 6$$
$$\text{Let } x = 1: \quad \begin{aligned} y &= 6 - x \\ y &= 6 - 1 \\ y &= 5 \end{aligned}$$

Thus, a solution of $x + y = 6$ is $(1, 5)$, the same result as before.

If the replacement set for both x and y is {signed numbers}, we can find an infinite number of ordered pairs that are solutions of $x + y = 6$. Some of these solutions are shown in the following table.

x	7	6	5	4	3	$2\frac{1}{2}$	2	1	$\frac{1}{2}$	0	-1
y	-1	0	1	2	3	$3\frac{1}{2}$	4	5	$5\frac{1}{2}$	6	7

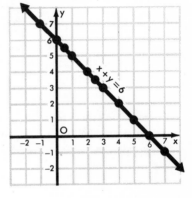

Let us plot the points associated with the ordered number pairs that are shown in the table. Notice that these points seem to lie on a straight line. In fact, if {signed numbers} is the replacement set for both x and y, then the following is true:

The graphs of all ordered pairs (x, y) which are solutions of $x + y = 6$ lie on this same line; the graphs of all ordered pairs which are not solutions of $x + y = 6$ do not lie on this line.

This line, which is the set of all those points and only those points whose coordinates satisfy the equation $x + y = 6$, is called the **graph** of $x + y = 6$. In other words, this line is the graph of $\{(x, y) \mid x + y = 6\}$.

A first-degree equation in two variables, such as $x + y = 6$, may be written in the form $Ax + By + C = 0$, where A, B, and C are signed numbers, with A and B not both zero. It can be proved that the graph of such an equation is a straight line. We therefore call such an equation a **linear equation**.

When we graph a linear equation, we may determine the straight line by plotting two points whose coordinates satisfy that equation. However, we should always plot a third point as a check on the first two. If the third point lies on the line determined by the first two points, we have probably made no error.

[*Note:* When we graph a linear equation, the replacement set of the variables is {signed numbers} unless otherwise indicated.]

Keep In Mind

1. Every ordered pair of numbers which satisfies an equation represents the coordinates of a point on the graph of the equation.
2. Every point on the graph of an equation has as its coordinates an ordered pair of numbers which satisfies the equation.

Model Problem

a. Write the following verbal sentence as an equation: "The sum of twice the abscissa of a point and the ordinate of that point is 4."
b. Graph the equation written in part a.

a. *Solution:* Let x = the abscissa of the point.
    Let y = the ordinate of the point.
    Then $2x + y = 4$ *Ans.*

b.   *How to Proceed*

Solution

$2x + y = 4$
$y = -2x + 4$

1. Transform the equation into an equivalent equation in which y is expressed in terms of x.

x	$-2x + 4$	y
0	$-2(0) + 4$	4
1	$-2(1) + 4$	2
2	$-2(2) + 4$	0

2. Determine three solutions of the equation by assuming values for x and computing the corresponding values for y.

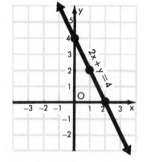

3. Plot the points associated with the three solutions found previously.
4. Draw a straight line through the points that were plotted.

   Note: This straight line is also the graph of

$$\{(x, y) \mid 2x + y = 4\}$$

EXERCISES

1. In each part, state whether the pair of values for x and y satisfies the equation $2x - y = 6$.
   a. $x = 0, y = 6$ b. $x = 2, y = 2$
   c. $x = 4, y = 2$ d. $x = 4, y = -2$

   In 2–4, plot the points that are associated with the ordered number pairs in the table and draw the line on which they seem to lie.

2.
x	0	1	2
y	0	4	8

3.
x	-1	0	1
y	-1	1	3

4.
x	-1	4	2
y	-6	9	3

In 5–13, solve the equation for y in terms of x.

5. $y - x = 5$ 6. $3x + y = -1$ 7. $4x - y = 6$
8. $2y = 6x$ 9. $6x + 3y = 0$ 10. $12x = \frac{3}{2}y$
11. $4x + 2y = 8$ 12. $6x - 3y = 5$ 13. $3x + 2y + 8 = 0$

In 14–16, find the missing values of the variable needed to complete the table. Plot the points described by the pairs of values in the completed table; then draw the line on which they seem to lie.

14. $y = 4x$ 15. $y = 3x + 1$ 16. $x + 2y = 3$

x	y
0	?
1	?
2	?

x	y
-1	?
0	?
1	?

x	y
-1	?
2	?
5	?

In 17–34, graph the equation.

17. $y = 2x$ 18. $y = -3x$ 19. $y = -x$
20. $x = 3y$ 21. $x = -y$ 22. $x = \frac{1}{2}y$
23. $y = x + 3$ 24. $y = 2x - 1$ 25. $y = -2x + 4$
26. $x + y = 8$ 27. $x - y = 5$ 28. $y - x = 0$
29. $2x + y = 10$ 30. $x + 3y = 12$ 31. $x - 2y = 0$
32. $y - 3x = -5$ 33. $3x - 2y = -6$ 34. $4x + 3y = -12$

In 35–40, graph the indicated set of points.

35. $\{(x, y)|y = 5x\}$ 36. $\{(x, y)|x = 2y\}$
37. $\{(x, y)|y = 3x + 1\}$ 38. $\{(x, y)|y + x = 4\}$
39. $\{(x, y)|2x + 3y = 6\}$ 40. $\{(x, y)|3x + 4y = 12\}$

In 41–44, state whether the point whose coordinates are given is on the graph of the given equation.

41. $x + y = 7; (4, 3)$ 42. $3x - 2y = 8; (2, 1)$
43. $4x + y = 10; (2, -2)$ 44. $2y = 3x - 5; (-1, -4)$

In 45–47, a point is to lie on the graph of each equation. Find its abscissa (x-value) if its ordinate (y-value) is the number indicated in the parentheses.

45. $x + y = 12; (5)$ 46. $2x - y = 8; (-2)$ 47. $3x + 2y = 24; (3)$

In 48–50, a point is to lie on the graph of each equation. Find its ordinate if its abscissa is the number indicated in the parentheses.

48. $x + 2y = 9; (3)$ 49. $4x - y = 7; (-1)$ 50. $2x + 3y = 5; (-2)$

In 51–53, find a value which can replace k so that the graph of the resulting equation will pass through the point whose coordinates are given.

51. $x + y = k; (2, 5)$ **52.** $x - y = k; (5, -3)$

53. $5y - 2x = k; (-2, -1)$

In 54–59: **a.** Write the verbal sentence as an equation.
b. Graph the equation.

54. The ordinate of a point is equal to the abscissa.

55. The ordinate of a point is twice the abscissa.

56. The ordinate of a point is 2 more than the abscissa.

57. The ordinate of a point is 4 less than 3 times the abscissa.

58. The sum of the ordinate and the abscissa of a point is 6.

59. Twice the ordinate of a point decreased by 3 times the abscissa is 6.

4. Graphing a Linear Equation in Two Variables by the Intercepts Method

The **x-intercept** of a line is the x-coordinate of the point at which the line intersects the x-axis. The graph of the equation $y = \frac{2}{3}x + 2$, shown in the figure, intersects the x-axis at $A(-3, 0)$. Therefore, the x-intercept of the graph of $y = \frac{2}{3}x + 2$ is −3. Notice that the value of y at point A must be zero, since A is on the x-axis.

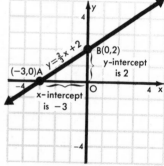

The **y-intercept** of a line is the y-coordinate of the point at which the line intersects the y-axis. The graph of $y = \frac{2}{3}x + 2$ intersects the y-axis at $B(0, 2)$. Therefore, the y-intercept of the graph of $y = \frac{2}{3}x + 2$ is 2. Notice that the value of x at point B must be 0, since B is on the y-axis.

In the following section we will see that a line need not have both an x-intercept and a y-intercept. Also, notice that the x-axis does not have a unique x-intercept and that the y-axis does not have a unique y-intercept.

FINDING THE INTERCEPTS OF A LINE

Procedure. To find the x-intercept of a line, substitute 0 for y in the equation of the line. Then solve the resulting equation for x.

To find the y-intercept of a line, substitute 0 for x in the equation of the line. Then solve the resulting equation for y.

Study the model problem to learn how to graph a linear equation by the intercepts method.

Model Problem

Find the x-intercept and the y-intercept of the line $2x - y = 4$. Then use these intercepts to graph the equation.

How to Proceed	Solution

1. Find the x-intercept by substituting 0 for y; find the y-intercept by substituting 0 for x.

x-intercept	*y-intercept*
$2x - y = 4$	$2x - y = 4$
$2x - 0 = 4$	$2(0) - y = 4$
$2x = 4$	$-y = 4$
$x = 2$	$y = -4$

2. On the x-axis, graph a point whose abscissa is the x-intercept. Since $x = 2$ when $y = 0$, the point is $(2, 0)$. On the y-axis, graph a point whose ordinate is the y-intercept. Since $y = -4$ when $x = 0$, the point is $(0, -4)$.

3. Draw a line through these points.

4. To check, find a third pair of values that satisfies the equation. The graph of this pair of values must be on the line.

Check

$$2x - y = 4$$
$$\text{Let } x = 1: 2(1) - y = 4$$
$$-y = 2$$
$$y = -2$$

The point $(1, -2)$ is on the graph of the line.

EXERCISES

In 1–6, find the x-intercept and the y-intercept of the line which is the graph of the equation.

1. $x + y = 8$
2. $x - 5y = 10$
3. $y = 4x + 12$
4. $y = 6x$
5. $4x - 3y = -12$
6. $5x + 3y = 8$

In 7–15, draw the graph of the equation by the intercepts method.

7. $x + y = 3$
8. $2x + y = 8$
9. $3x - y = 12$
10. $y = 2x + 8$
11. $y = -3x + 6$
12. $x = 4y - 12$
13. $2x + 3y = 6$
14. $5x - 4y = 20$
15. $3x - 6y = 9$

16. a. Find the x-intercept and the y-intercept for the graph of the equation $y = 3x$.
   b. Can you graph the equation $y = 3x$ by the intercepts method?
   c. Draw the graph of $y = 3x$ using another method.

5. Graphing Lines Parallel to the X-Axis or the Y-Axis

SYMBOLS FOR A LINE, A SEGMENT, AND A RAY

In future discussions, we will deal with lines, segments, and rays. We will now give the meanings of the symbols that we will use in such discussions.

In Figure 1, line PQ, the straight line that passes through points P and Q, extending infinitely in both directions, will be symbolized as $\overleftrightarrow{PQ}$. A line is named by placing a double arrow ($\longleftrightarrow$) over two capital letters which are the names of two points on the line.

Figure 1

In Figure 2, line segment PQ, or segment PQ which is the set of points consisting of P, Q, and all the points on $\overleftrightarrow{PQ}$ which lie between P and Q will be symbolized as $\overline{PQ}$. A line segment is named by placing a bar (——) over two capital letters which are the names of the end points of the segment.

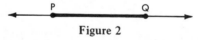

Figure 2

In Figure 3, point P separates the set of all points of $\overleftrightarrow{PQ}$, except the point P, into two sets of points, those on the same side of P as Q, and those on the other side of P. The set consisting of point P together with all points of $\overleftrightarrow{PQ}$ which are on the same side of P as Q is called ray PQ and is symbolized as $\overrightarrow{PQ}$. In $\overrightarrow{PQ}$, the first letter names the end point of the ray. $\overrightarrow{PQ}$ extends infinitely in only one direction. A ray is named by placing an arrow ($\longrightarrow$) over two capital letters. The first letter must be the letter which names the end point of the ray; the second letter may be the name of any other point on the ray.

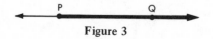

Figure 3

In Figure 2, the length of $\overline{PQ}$ is symbolized by PQ. PQ is a non-negative number which is the distance between P and Q. If P is different from Q, then P is positive. If P is the same as Q, then PQ is zero.

Note that $\overleftrightarrow{PQ}$ and $\overleftrightarrow{QP}$ name the same line; $\overline{PQ}$ and $\overline{QP}$ name the same segment; PQ and QP name the same number. However, $\overrightarrow{PQ}$ and $\overrightarrow{QP}$ do not name the same ray because they have different endpoints.

LINES PARALLEL TO THE X-AXIS

Study the graph. $\overleftrightarrow{AB}$, whose y-intercept is 2, is parallel to the x-axis. Notice that the y-value of each ordered pair associated with a point on $\overleftrightarrow{AB}$ equals 2. This is true no matter what the value of x is. Therefore, an equation of $\overleftrightarrow{AB}$ is written simply $y = 2$. Similarly, $y = -2$ represents an equation of a line ($\overleftrightarrow{CD}$) whose graph is parallel to the x-axis and whose y-intercept is -2.

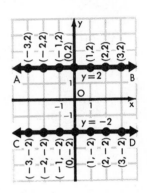

An equation for a line parallel to the x-axis, when its y-intercept is a, is $y = a$.

Note: $\overleftrightarrow{AB}$ is the graph of $\{(x, y)| y = 2\}$

$\overleftrightarrow{CD}$ is the graph of $\{(x, y)| y = -2\}$

Neither line has an x-intercept.

LINES PARALLEL TO THE Y-AXIS

Study the graph. $\overleftrightarrow{EF}$, whose x-intercept is 2, is parallel to the y-axis. Notice that the x-value of each ordered pair associated with a point of $\overleftrightarrow{EF}$ equals 2. This is true no matter what the value of y is. Therefore, an equation of $\overleftrightarrow{EF}$ is written simply $x = 2$. Similarly, $x = -2$ represents an equation of a line ($\overleftrightarrow{GH}$) whose graph is parallel to the y-axis and whose x-intercept is -2.

An equation for a line parallel to the y-axis, when its x-intercept is b, is $x = b$.

Note: $\overleftrightarrow{EF}$ is the graph of $\{(x, y) | x = 2\}$

$\quad\quad\overleftrightarrow{GH}$ is the graph of $\{(x, y) | x = -2\}$

Neither line has a y-intercept.

EXERCISES

In 1–10, draw the graph of the equation.

1. $x = 6$ 2. $x = \frac{2}{3}$ 3. $x = 0$ 4. $x = -3$ 5. $x = -5$
6. $y = 4$ 7. $y = 2\frac{1}{4}$ 8. $y = 0$ 9. $y = -4$ 10. $y = -7$

In 11–14, graph the indicated set of points.

11. $\{(x, y) | x = 3\}$ 12. $\{(x, y) | x = -\frac{3}{2}\}$ 13. $\{(x, y) | y = -4\}$
14. $\{(x, y) | y = 3\frac{1}{2}\}$

15. Write an equation of a line that is parallel to the x-axis and whose y-intercept is:

   a. 1   b. 5   c. -4 d. -8 e. -2.5

16. Write an equation of a line that is parallel to the y-axis and whose x-intercept is:

   a. 3   b. 10   c. $4\frac{1}{2}$ d. -6 e. -10

6. The Slope of a Line

MEANING OF THE SLOPE OF A LINE

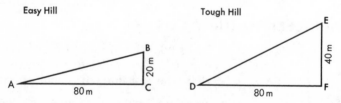

It is more difficult to hike up Tough Hill than it is to hike up Easy Hill. Tough Hill rises 40 m vertically over a horizontal distance of 80 m, whereas Easy Hill rises only 20 m vertically over the same horizontal distance of 80 m. Therefore, Tough Hill is steeper than Easy Hill. To compare the steepness of roads $\overline{AB}$ and $\overline{DE}$, the roads which lead up the two hills, we compare their *slopes*.

The slope of road $\overline{AB}$ is the ratio of the change in vertical distance, CB, to the change in horizontal distance, AC:

$$\text{slope of road } \overline{AB} = \frac{\text{change in vertical distance, } CB}{\text{change in horizontal distance, } AC} = \frac{20 \text{ m}}{80 \text{ m}} = \frac{1}{4}$$

Also:

$$\text{slope of road } \overline{DE} = \frac{\text{change in vertical distance, } FE}{\text{change in horizontal distance, } DF} = \frac{40 \text{ m}}{80 \text{ m}} = \frac{1}{2}$$

Since road $\overline{DE}$ rises $\frac{1}{2}$ m vertically for each 1 m of horizontal distance, whereas road $\overline{AB}$ rises only $\frac{1}{4}$ m vertically for each 1 m of horizontal distance, road $\overline{DE}$ is steeper than road $\overline{AB}$.

FINDING THE SLOPE OF A LINE

The slope of a line is equal to the slope of any line segment contained in the line.

Procedure. To find the slope of a line which is not parallel to the *y*-axis:

1. **Select any two points on the line.**
2. **Find the horizontal change, the change in *x*-values, in going from the point on the left to the point on the right.**
3. **Find the vertical change, the change in *y*-values, in going from the point on the left to the point on the right.**
4. **Divide the vertical change by the horizontal change.**

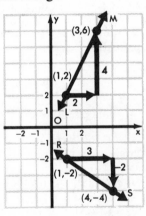

For example, in the figure:

$$\text{slope of } \overleftrightarrow{LM} = \frac{\text{vertical change}}{\text{horizontal change}} = \frac{4}{2} = 2$$

$$\text{slope of } \overleftrightarrow{RS} = \frac{\text{vertical change}}{\text{horizontal change}} = \frac{-2}{3} = -\frac{2}{3}$$

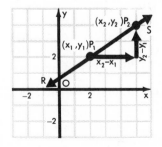

In general, the slope, m, of a line $\overleftrightarrow{RS}$ which passes through two points $P_1(x_1, y_1)$ and $P_2(x_2, y_2)$ when $x_1 \neq x_2$, is the ratio of the difference of the *y*-values of these points to the difference of the corresponding *x*-values. Thus:

$$\text{slope of a line} = \frac{\text{difference in } y\text{-values}}{\text{difference in } x\text{-values}}$$

$$\text{slope of } \overleftrightarrow{RS}, \text{ or } m = \frac{y_2 - y_1}{x_2 - x_1}$$

The expression "difference in x-values," $x_2 - x_1$, can be represented by Δx, read "delta x." Similarly, the "difference in y-values," $y_2 - y_1$, can be represented by Δy, read "delta y." Therefore, we write:

$$\text{slope of a line} = m = \frac{\Delta y}{\Delta x}$$

Observe that when we find the slope of a line passing through two points, it is immaterial which point is represented by (x_1, y_1) and which point is represented by (x_2, y_2). This is so because

$$\frac{y_2 - y_1}{x_2 - x_1} = \frac{-1}{-1} \cdot \frac{(y_2 - y_1)}{(x_2 - x_1)} = \frac{-y_2 + y_1}{-x_2 + x_1} = \frac{y_1 - y_2}{x_1 - x_2}$$

POSITIVE SLOPES

As a point moves along $\overleftrightarrow{AB}$ from left to right, for example, from C to D, the line is "rising." As the x-values increase, the y-values also increase. Between point C and point D, the change in y (Δy) is 1; the change in x (Δx) is 2. Since both Δy and Δx are positive, the slope of $\overleftrightarrow{AB}$ must be positive.

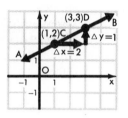

$$\text{slope} = m = \frac{\Delta y}{\Delta x} = \frac{1}{2}$$

This example illustrates:

Principle 1. As a point moves from left to right along a line that is "rising," y increases as x increases and the slope of the line is positive.

NEGATIVE SLOPES

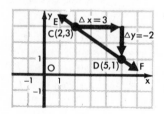

As a point moves along $\overleftrightarrow{EF}$ from left to right, for example, from C to D, the line is "falling." As the x-values increase, the y-values decrease. Between point C and point D, the change in y (Δy) is -2; the change in x (Δx) is 3. Since Δy is negative and Δx is positive, the slope of $\overleftrightarrow{EF}$ must be negative.

$$\text{slope} = m = \frac{\Delta y}{\Delta x} = \frac{-2}{3} = -\frac{2}{3}$$

This example illustrates:

Principle 2. As a point moves from left to right along a line that is "falling," y decreases as x increases and the slope of the line is negative.

ZERO SLOPE

$\overleftrightarrow{GH}$ is parallel to the x-axis. Consider a point moving along $\overleftrightarrow{GH}$ from left to right, for example, from C to D: As the x-values increase, the y-values are unchanged. Between point C and point D, the change in y (Δy) is 0, and the change in x (Δx) is 3. Since Δy is 0 and Δx is 3, the slope of $\overleftrightarrow{GH}$ must be 0.

$$\text{slope} = m = \frac{\Delta y}{\Delta x} = \frac{0}{3} = 0$$

The preceding example illustrates:

Principle 3. If a line is parallel to the x-axis, its slope is 0.

[*Note:* The slope of the x-axis itself is also 0.]

NO SLOPE

$\overleftrightarrow{LM}$ is parallel to the y-axis. Consider a point moving upward along $\overleftrightarrow{LM}$, for example, from C to D: The x-values are unchanged, but the y-values increase. Between point C and point D, the change in y (Δy) is 3 and the change in x (Δx) is 0. Since the slope of a line $= \dfrac{\Delta y}{\Delta x}$, and a nonzero number cannot be divided by 0, $\overleftrightarrow{LM}$ has no defined slope.

This example illustrates:

Principle 4. If a line is parallel to the y-axis, it has no defined slope.

[*Note:* The y-axis itself has no defined slope.]

Model Problems

1. Find the slope of the straight line which passes through the points $(-2, 4)$ and $(4, 2)$.

   Solution: Let the point $(-2, 4)$ be $P_1(x_1, y_1)$, and let the point $(4, 2)$ be $P_2(x_2, y_2)$. Then $x_1 = -2, y_1 = 4; x_2 = 4, y_2 = 2$.

   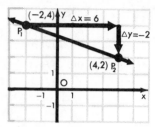

   $$\text{slope of } \overleftrightarrow{P_1P_2} = \frac{\Delta y}{\Delta x} = \frac{y_2 - y_1}{x_2 - x_1}$$

   $$= \frac{(2) - (4)}{(4) - (-2)}$$

   $$= \frac{2 - 4}{4 + 2}$$

   $$= \frac{-2}{6} = -\frac{1}{3}$$

   Answer: $-\frac{1}{3}$

2. Through the point $(2, -1)$, draw a line whose slope is $\frac{3}{2}$.

   | *How to Proceed* | *Solution* |

   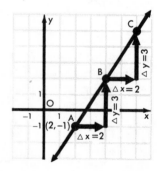

   1. Graph the point $A(2, -1)$.

   2. Since slope $= \dfrac{\Delta y}{\Delta x} \rightarrow \dfrac{3}{2}$, when x changes 2, then y changes 3.

   3. Start at point $A(2, -1)$ and move 2 units to the right and 3 units upward to locate point B. Start at B and repeat these movements to locate point C.

   4. Draw a straight line which passes through points $A, B,$ and C.

Keep In Mind

A fundamental property of a straight line which has a slope is that its slope is constant. Therefore, any two points on such a line may be used to compute the slope of the line.

EXERCISES

1. In **a–f**, state whether the line has a positive slope, a negative slope, a slope of zero, or no slope.

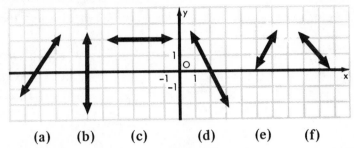

   (a)   (b)   (c)   (d)   (e)   (f)

2. In **a–f**, find the slope of the line; if the line has no slope, indicate that fact.

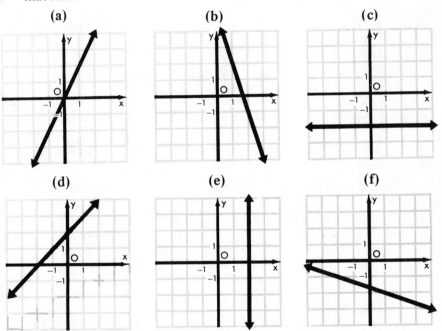

In 3–11, find the slope of the line which passes through the two points.

3. $(0, 0)$ and $(4, 4)$ 4. $(0, 0)$ and $(9, 3)$ 5. $(0, 0)$ and $(3, -6)$
6. $(5, 8)$ and $(4, 3)$ 7. $(-2, 4)$ and $(0, 2)$ 8. $(5, -2)$ and $(7, -8)$
9. $(4, 2)$ and $(8, 2)$ 10. $(-1, 3)$ and $(2, 3)$ 11. $(6, -1)$ and $(-2, -1)$
12. Find the value of y so that the slope of the line passing through the points $(2, y)$ and $(6, 10)$ will be:

    a. 1   **b.** 2   **c.** $\frac{1}{2}$ **d.** 0

In 13–16, use the definition of the slope of a line to determine whether the points lie on the same line (are *collinear*).

13. $(1, 3); (2, 5); (3, 7)$ **14.** $(-1, 5); (0, 2); (1, -1)$
15. $(2, 5); (4, 9); (6, 15)$ **16.** $(-4, -1); (0, 3); (2, 5)$

In 17–25, draw a line with the given slope, m, through the given point.

17. $(0, 0); m = 2$ **18.** $(1, 3); m = 3$ **19.** $(2, -5); m = 4$

20. $(4, 6); m = \frac{2}{3}$ **21.** $(-4, 5); m = \frac{1}{2}$ **22.** $(-3, -4); m = -2$

23. $(1, -5); m = -1$ **24.** $(2, 4); m = -\frac{3}{2}$ **25.** $(-2, 3); m = -\frac{1}{3}$

7. The Slope and *Y*-Intercept of a Line

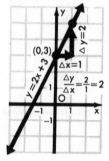

Figure 1

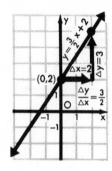

Figure 2

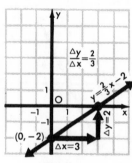

Figure 3

Each of the preceding figures shows the line which is the graph of the indicated equation. We can see that the slope of each line is the coefficient of the *x*-term in the equation and that the *y*-intercept of each line is the *constant* which follows the *x*-term in the equation.

	Equation	Slope $\left(\dfrac{\Delta y}{\Delta x}\right)$	*y*-intercept
In Figure 1:	$y = 2x + 3$	2	3
In Figure 2:	$y = \frac{3}{2}x + 2$	$\frac{3}{2}$	2
In Figure 3:	$y = \frac{2}{3}x - 2$	$\frac{2}{3}$	-2

These examples illustrate the following general principle:

If a linear equation is expressed in the form $y = mx + b$, then the slope of the line is m, the coefficient of x; the y-intercept is b, the constant term.

The following general principle is also true:

The equation of the straight line whose slope is m and whose y-intercept is b can be written $y = mx + b$.

Let us see why the principle holds. Since the y-intercept is b, the line must pass through the point $B(0, b)$, as indicated in the figure below. Let $P(x, y)$ be any other point on the line, with x different from 0. Since the slope of the line is m, it follows that:

$$m = \frac{\Delta y}{\Delta x}$$

$$m = \frac{y - b}{x - 0}$$

$$m = \frac{y - b}{x}$$

$$mx = y - b \qquad M_x$$

$$mx + b = y \qquad A_b$$

or $y = mx + b$

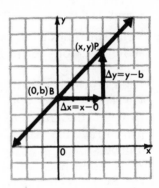

Model Problem

Find the slope and the y-intercept of the line which is the graph of $4x + 2y = 10$.

How to Proceed	Solution
1. Transform the equation into an equivalent equation of the form $y = mx + b$ by solving for y in terms of x.	$4x + 2y = 10$ $2y = -4x + 10$ $y = -2x + 5$
2. The coefficient of x is the slope.	slope $= -2$
3. The constant term is the y-intercept.	y-intercept $= 5$

Answer: slope $= -2$, y-intercept $= 5$

EXERCISES

In 1–15, find the slope and the y-intercept of the line which is the graph of the equation.

1. $y = 3x + 1$
2. $y = 2x$
3. $y = \frac{1}{2}x + 5$
4. $y = \frac{3}{4}x - \frac{1}{2}$
5. $y = -2x + 3$
6. $y = -x - 4$
7. $y = -2$
8. $y = -\frac{1}{2}x - 2$
9. $2x + y = 5$
10. $3y = 6x + 9$
11. $2y = 5x - 4$
12. $2x + 3y = 6$
13. $\frac{1}{2}x + \frac{3}{4} = \frac{1}{3}y$
14. $4x - 3y = 0$
15. $2y = 5(x + 1)$

In 16–24, write an equation of the line whose slope and y-intercept are respectively:

16. 2 and 7
17. -4 and 2
18. -1 and -3
19. -2 and 4
20. $\frac{2}{3}$ and 1
21. $\frac{3}{5}$ and -2
22. $\frac{1}{2}$ and 0
23. $-\frac{4}{3}$ and $-\frac{1}{3}$
24. $-\frac{3}{2}$ and 0

25. Write equations for three lines so that the slope of each line is 2.
26. Write equations for three lines so that the y-intercept of each line is -4.
27. What do the graphs of the lines described by the equations $y = 4x$, $y = 4x + 2$, and $y = 4x - 2$ all have in common?
28. How are the graphs of $y = mx + b$ affected when m is always replaced by the same number and b is replaced by different numbers?
29. What do the lines which are the graphs of the equations $y = 2x + 1$, $y = 3x + 1$, and $y = -4x + 1$ all have in common?
30. How are the graphs of $y = mx + b$ affected when b is always replaced by the same number and m is replaced by different numbers?
31. If two lines which have slopes are parallel, what is the relation of their slopes?
32. What will be true of two lines whose slopes are equal?

In 33–36, state whether the two lines are parallel.

33. $y = 3x + 2$, $y = 3x - 5$
34. $y = -2x - 6$, $y = 2x + 6$
35. $y = 4x - 8$, $y - 4x = 3$
36. $y = 2x$, $2y - 4x = 9$

8. Graphing a Linear Equation in Two Variables by the Slope-Intercept Method

The slope and the y-intercept of a line can be used to draw the graph of a linear equation.

Model Problem

Draw the graph of $2x + 3y = 9$ using the slope-intercept method.

How to Proceed	*Solution*

1. Transform the equation to the form $y = mx + b$.

$$2x + 3y = 9$$
$$3y = -2x + 9$$
$$y = \frac{-2}{3}x + 3$$

2. Find the slope of the line.

$$\text{slope} = \frac{-2}{3}$$

3. Find the y-intercept of the line.

$$y\text{-intercept} = 3$$

4. Graph a point A on the y-axis whose ordinate is the y-intercept.

5. Use the slope to find two more points on the line. Since slope $= \dfrac{\Delta y}{\Delta x} \to \dfrac{-2}{3}$,

when x changes 3, y changes -2. Start at point A and move 3 units to the right and 2 units down to locate point B. Start at point B and repeat this procedure to locate point C.

6. Draw the line which passes through the three points. Note that this straight line is also the graph of $\{(x,y) \mid 2x + 3y = 9\}$

EXERCISES

In 1–18, graph the equation using the slope and the y-intercept of each line (the slope-intercept method).

1. $y = 2x + 3$
2. $y = 2x - 5$
3. $y = x - 2$
4. $y = 3x - 2$
5. $y = 3x$
6. $y = -2x$
7. $y = \frac{2}{3}x + 2$
8. $y = \frac{1}{2}x - 1$
9. $y = \frac{1}{3}x$
10. $y = -\frac{4}{3}x + 5$
11. $y = -\frac{3}{4}x$
12. $y - 2x = 8$
13. $3x + y = 4$
14. $3y = 4x + 9$
15. $3x + 4y = 12$
16. $2x = 3y + 6$
17. $4x + 3y = 0$
18. $2x - 3y - 6 = 0$

In 19–24, graph the set of points using the slope-intercept method of graphing a line.

19. $\{(x, y) | y = 2x\}$　　　　　　　　　20. $\{(x, y) | y = 2x - 2\}$
21. $\{(x, y) | y = 5x\}$　　　　　　　　　22. $\{(x, y) | y = \frac{3}{2}x\}$
23. $\{(x, y) | 2y = 4x + 6\}$　　　　　　24. $\{(x, y) | 4x - y = 3\}$

9. Writing an Equation for a Line

Procedure. To write an equation for a line, determine its slope and its y-intercept. Then use the slope-intercept formula $y = mx + b$.

Model Problems

1. Write an equation of a line whose slope is 4 and which passes through the point (3, 5).

How to Proceed	Solution
1. In the equation of a line $y = mx + b$, replace m by the given slope, 4.	$y = mx + b$ $y = 4x + b$
2. Since the given point (3, 5) is on the line, its coordinates satisfy the equation $y = 4x + b$. Replace x by 3 and y by 5. Solve for b.	$5 = 4(3) + b$ $5 = 12 + b$ $-7 = b$
3. In $y = 4x + b$, replace b by -7.	$y = 4x - 7$

Answer: $y = 4x - 7$

2. Write an equation of a line which passes through the points (2, 5) and (4, 11).

How to Proceed	Solution
1. Find the slope of the line which passes through the two given points, (2, 5) and (4, 11).	Let P_1 be (2, 5). Let P_2 be (4, 11). $m = \dfrac{y_2 - y_1}{x_2 - x_1}$ $m = \dfrac{11 - 5}{4 - 2} = \dfrac{6}{2} = 3$
2. In $y = mx + b$, replace m by the slope, 3.	$y = mx + b$ $y = 3x + b$

3. Select one point which is on the line, for example (2, 5). Its coordinates must satisfy the equation $y = 3x + b$. Replace x by 2 and y by 5. Solve for b.

$$5 = 3(2) + b$$
$$5 = 6 + b$$
$$-1 = b$$

4. In $y = 3x + b$, replace b by -1.

$$y = 3x - 1$$

5. Check whether the coordinates of the second point (4, 11) satisfy the equation $y = 3x - 1$.

$$11 \overset{?}{=} 3(4) - 1$$
$$11 = 11 \quad \text{(true)}$$

Answer: $y = 3x - 1$

EXERCISES

In 1-9, write an equation of the line which has the given slope, m, and which passes through the given point.

1. $m = 2; (1, 4)$
2. $m = 2; (-3, 4)$
3. $m = -1; (0, -2)$
4. $m = -3; (-2, -1)$
5. $m = \frac{1}{2}; (4, 2)$
6. $m = \frac{2}{3}; (-6, 4)$
7. $m = \dfrac{-3}{4}; (0, 0)$
8. $m = \dfrac{-5}{3}; (-3, 0)$
9. $m = 0; (3, -6)$

In 10-18, write an equation of the line which passes through the given points.

10. $(1, 4); (3, 8)$
11. $(1, 0); (3, 6)$
12. $(3, 1); (9, 7)$
13. $(1, 2); (10, 14)$
14. $(0, -1); (6, 8)$
15. $(3, 6); (6, 0)$
16. $(-3, 11); (6, 5)$
17. $(-2, -5); (-1, -2)$
18. $(0, 0); (-3, 5)$

19. Write an equation of the line which is:
   a. parallel to the line $y = 2x - 4$ and whose y-intercept is 7.
   b. parallel to the line $y - 3x = 6$ and whose y-intercept is -2.
   c. parallel to the line $2x + 3y = 12$ and which passes through the origin.

20. Write an equation of the line which is:
   a. parallel to the line $y = 4x + 1$ and which passes through the point (2, 3).
   b. parallel to the line $y - 3x = 5$ and which passes through the point $(-1, 6)$.
   c. parallel to the line $2y - 6x = 9$ and which passes through the point $(-2, 1)$.
   d. parallel to the line $y = 4x + 3$ and which has the same y-intercept as the line $y = 5x - 3$.

10. Graphing Open Sentences Involving Absolute Values

Model Problems

1. Graph the equation $|x| = 3$.

   Solution:

   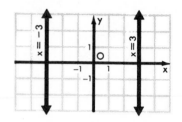

   1. The sentence $|x| = 3$ is equivalent to "$x = 3$ or $x = -3$."
   2. The graph of each of the equations $x = 3$ and $x = -3$ is a line parallel to the y-axis.
   3. The graph of $|x| = 3$ consists of two lines as shown in the figure.

2. Graph the equation $|y - 1| = 2$.

   Solution:

   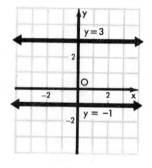

   1. The sentence $|y - 1| = 2$ is equivalent to:

      $y - 1 = 2$ OR $y - 1 = -2$

      $y = 3$ $y = -1$

   2. The graph of each of the equations $y = 3$ and $y = -1$ is a line parallel to the x-axis.
   3. The graph of $|y - 1| = 2$ consists of two lines as shown in the figure.

3. Graph the equation $y = |x|$.

   Discussion:

   We can find ordered number pairs which are solutions of $y = |x|$ by replacing x with signed numbers and finding the corresponding values of y. Notice that y will always be a non-negative number. For example, the ordered number pairs $(-3, 3)$, $(-2, 2)$, $(-1, 1)$, $(0, 0)$, $(1, 1)$, $(2, 2)$, and $(3, 3)$, among infinitely many others, are solutions of $y = |x|$. The graphs of these number pairs are shown in Figure 1. It is not possible to draw a straight line containing all these points. Yet it appears that the graph of $y = |x|$ may consist of parts of two straight lines. In the solution that follows, we will use the definition of absolute value to graph $y = |x|$.

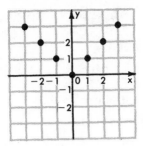

Figure 1

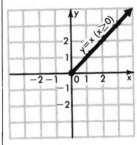

Figure 2

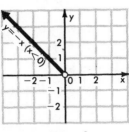

Figure 3

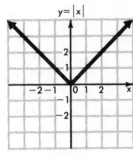

Figure 4

Solution:

1. The sentence $y = |x|$ is equivalent to
   $y = x$ if $x \geq 0$ or $y = -x$ if $x < 0$.
2. Graph the set of points whose coordinates satisfy the equation $y = x$
   whose x-coordinate is greater than or equal to zero and whose y-coordinate
   is non-negative. See Figure 2.
3. Graph the set of points whose coordinates satisfy the equation $y = -x$
   whose x-coordinate is less than zero and whose y-coordinate is non-
   negative. See Figure 3.
4. The graph of $y = |x|$ consists of the union of the two graphs found in
   steps 2 and 3. See Figure 4.

Note: The graph shown in Figure 4 is also the graph of $\{(x,y) \mid y = |x|\}$.

Keep In Mind

When graphing an open sentence involving absolute values, you may find it
helpful to plot several solutions first. Choose both positive and negative
values for the variable(s) within the absolute value signs.

EXERCISES

In 1–8, graph the equation.

1. $|x| = 1$ 2. $|x| = 4$ 3. $|y| = 2$
4. $|y| = 0$ 5. $|x - 1| = 4$ 6. $|x + 3| = 6$
7. $|y - 3| = 5$ 8. $|y + 2| = 3$

In 9–28, graph the open sentence.

9. $y = 3|x|$ 10. $y = \frac{1}{2}|x|$ 11. $y = -|x|$
12. $y = -3|x|$ 13. $x = |y|$ 14. $x = 2|y|$
15. $x = |-y|$ 16. $x = -2|y|$ 17. $y = |x| + 2$
18. $y = |x| - 3$ 19. $y = 2|x| + 1$ 20. $x = -|y| + 2$
21. $y = |x - 4|$ 22. $y = |x + 1|$ 23. $y = 2|x + 4|$
24. $x = |y + 2| - 3$ 25. $|x| = |y|$ 26. $|x| + |y| = 4$
27. $|x| + |y| = 6$ 28. $|x| - |y| = 6$

In 29–31, graph the indicated set.

29. $\{(x, y) \mid |x| = 4\}$ 30. $\{(x, y) \mid |y - 4| = 1\}$
31. $\{(x, y) \mid |y| = x\}$

11. Graphing an Inequality in Two Variables

The line which is the graph of the equation $y = 2x$ (Figure 1) is the set of all points for which the ordinate is equal to twice the abscissa. For example, at point $A(1, 2)$, the ordinate (2) is equal to twice the abscissa (1), $2 = 2 \times 1$. This line divides the set of points of the plane, not including the points of the line, into two regions called *half-planes*.

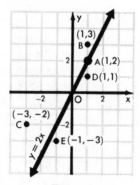

Figure 1

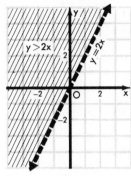

Figure 2

The half-plane above the line $y = 2x$ (Figure 1) is the set of all points for which the ordinate y is greater than twice the abscissa x. For example, at point $B(1, 3)$, the ordinate (3) is greater than twice the abscissa (1), $3 > 2 \times 1$, or $y > 2x$. The coordinates of point $C(-3, -2)$ also satisfy $y > 2x$ because $-2 > 2 \times (-3)$ is a true sentence. The graph of $y > 2x$ is the shaded half-plane above the line $y = 2x$ (Figure 2). Notice that the line is dashed to indicate that the line is not part of the graph. To graph $y \geq 2x$, we draw a solid line to indicate that the line $y = 2x$ is part of the graph.

The half-plane below the line $y = 2x$ (Figure 1) is the set of all points for which the ordinate y is less than twice the abscissa x. For example, at point $D(1, 1)$, the ordinate (1) is less than twice the abscissa (1), $1 < 2 \times 1$, or $y < 2x$. The coordinates of point $E(-1, -3)$ also satisfy $y < 2x$ because $-3 < 2 \times (-1)$ is a true sentence. The graph of $y < 2x$ is the shaded half-plane below the line $y = 2x$ (Figure 3). Notice that the line is dashed to indicate that the line is not part of the graph. To graph $y \leq 2x$, we draw a solid line to indicate that the line $y = 2x$ is part of the graph.

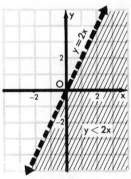

Figure 3

From the study of the graphs of $y = 2x$, $y > 2x$, and $y < 2x$, we see that the line which is the graph of $y = 2x$ acts as a *plane divider*. It divides the portion of the plane other than the line itself into two regions. The region "above" the line is the graph of $y > 2x$; the region "below" it is the graph of $y < 2x$.

In general, the graph of $y = mx + b$ is a line which divides the coordinate plane into three sets of points:

1. The set of points on the line. Each ordered number pair which describes a member of this set of points is a solution of $y = mx + b$. The line is the graph of the equation $y = mx + b$.
2. The set of points in the half-plane "above" the line. Each ordered number pair which describes a member of this set of points is a solution of $y > mx + b$. The half-plane is the graph of the inequality $y > mx + b$.

3. The set of points in the half-plane "below" the line. Each ordered number pair which describes a member of this set of points is a solution of $y < mx + b$. The half-plane is the graph of the inequality $y < mx + b$.

Keep In Mind

To graph $Ax + By + C > 0$ or $Ax + By + C < 0$, transform the inequality so that the left member is y alone: $y > rx + s$ or $y < rx + s$. This enables us first to graph the plane divider $y = rx + s$.

Model Problems

1. Graph the inequality $y - 2x \geq 2$.

How to Proceed	*Solution*
1. Transform the sentence into one having y as the left member.	$y - 2x \geq 2$ $y \geq 2x + 2$
2. Graph the resulting inequality by first graphing the plane divider, $y = 2x + 2$.	$y = 2x + 2$

x	−1	0	1
y	0	2	4

3. Shade the half-plane above the line. This region and the line are the required graph; the half-plane is the graph of $y - 2x > 2$, and the line is the graph of $y - 2x = 2$. Note that the line is drawn solid to show that it is part of the graph.

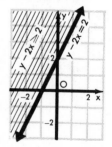

Note: The graph shown at the right is also the graph of $\{(x, y) \mid y - 2x \geq 2\}$.

2. Graph each of the following sentences in the coordinate plane:

   a. $x > 1$ b. $x \leq 1$ c. $y \geq 1$ d. $y < 1$

Solution

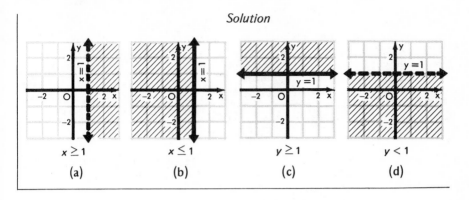

$x \geq 1$ $x \leq 1$ $y \geq 1$ $y < 1$

(a)   (b)   (c)   (d)

EXERCISES

In 1–9, transform the sentence into one whose left member is y.

1. $y - 2x > 0$ 2. $y + 3x \leq 0$ 3. $5x > 2y$
4. $y - x \geq 3$ 5. $2x + y \leq 0$ 6. $3x - y \geq 4$
7. $4y - 3x \leq 12$ 8. $3x + 2y > 6$ 9. $10 \geq 2x + 5y$

In 10–30, graph the sentence in the coordinate plane.

10. $x > 4$ 11. $x \leq -2$ 12. $y > 5$
13. $y \leq -3$ 14. $x \geq 6$ 15. $y \leq 0$
16. $y > 4x$ 17. $y < x - 2$ 18. $y \geq \frac{1}{2}x + 3$
19. $x + y < 4$ 20. $x + y \leq -3$ 21. $y - x \geq 5$
22. $x - y > 6$ 23. $x - y \leq -1$ 24. $y - 3x > 3$
25. $2x + y - 4 \leq 0$ 26. $y - x + 6 > 0$ 27. $2y - 6x > 0$
28. $3x + 4y \leq 0$ 29. $2x - 3y \geq 6$ 30. $10 \leq 5x - 2y$

In 31–33, graph the indicated set.

31. $\{(x, y) \mid y \leq 3x\}$ 32. $\{(x, y) \mid x + y \geq 4\}$
33. $\{(x, y) \mid x - 2y \leq 4\}$

In 34–39: a. Write the verbal sentence as an open sentence.
              b. Graph the open sentence in the coordinate plane.

34. The ordinate of a point is greater than the abscissa of that point.
35. The ordinate of a point is less than 4 times the abscissa of that point.
36. The ordinate of a point is equal to or greater than 3 more than the abscissa of that point.
37. The sum of the abscissa and the ordinate of a point is less than or equal to 5.
38. The ordinate of a point decreased by 3 times the abscissa of that point is greater than or equal to 2.
39. The sum of 3 times the abscissa of a point and twice the ordinate of that point is less than or equal to 12.

Chapter 14

Systems of Linear Open Sentences

in Two Variables

1. Graphic Solution of a System of Linear Equations in Two Variables

CONSISTENT EQUATIONS

We have learned that there are an infinite number of ordered number pairs in the solution set of the equation $x + y = 4$. In the coordinate plane pictured at the right, line L_1 is the graph of these ordered number pairs. In the same coordinate plane with the same set of axes, line L_2 is the graph of the infinite number of ordered number pairs in the solution set of the equation $x - y = 2$. The point of intersection of these two lines, $S(3, 1)$ is the only point these lines have in common. Therefore, the ordered number pair $(3, 1)$ is the *common solution* of the two equations $x + y = 4$ and $x - y = 2$. Hence, the solution set of this pair of equations is $\{(3, 1)\}$.

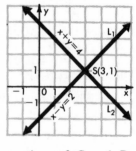

Recall that, given set C and set D, the intersection of C and D, $C \cap D$, is the set of elements that are common to C and D. If we represent the solution set of $x + y = 4$ by $C = \{(x, y) \mid x + y = 4\}$ and if we represent the solution set of $x - y = 2$ by $D = \{(x, y) \mid x - y = 2\}$, then the set of ordered number pairs common to both C and D, that is, $C \cap D = \{(3, 1)\}$.

A pair of linear equations such as $x + y = 4$ and $x - y = 2$, which impose on the variables x and y two conditions both of which must hold at the same time is called a *system of linear equations* in two variables, or a set of simultaneous linear equations. The solution of a system of two equations is the set of all ordered number pairs that satisfy both equations of the system. Each of these ordered pairs is called a solution of the system. The set of all solutions of the system is called the *solution set of the system*. Therefore, the solution set of the system $x + y = 4$ and $x - y = 2$ is $\{(3, 1)\}$.

When a pair of straight lines is graphed in the same coordinate plane on the same set of axes, one, and only one, of the following three possibilities can occur. The pair of lines will be the graph of:
1. two sets of ordered number pairs that have one ordered number pair in common,
2. two sets of ordered pairs that have no ordered number pairs in common, or
3. the same set of ordered number pairs.

If a system of linear equations such as $x + y = 4$ and $x - y = 2$ has one common solution, it is called a *system of consistent equations*. These equations are also called *independent equations*, because their solution sets are not identical. The graphs of two consistent linear equations are either two straight lines which have unequal slopes or two straight lines one of which has a slope and the other of which does not have a slope. These straight lines will intersect in one point.

INCONSISTENT EQUATIONS

Sometimes, when two linear equations are graphed in a coordinate plane using the same set of axes, the lines are parallel and do not intersect. This happens in the case of $x + y = 2$ and $x + y = 4$. There is no common solution for the system of equations $x + y = 2$ and $x + y = 4$. It is obvious that there can be no ordered number pair (x, y) such that the sum of those numbers, $x + y$, is both 2 and 4. Since the solution set of the system has no members, it is the empty set $\emptyset$.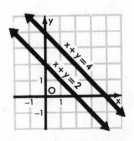

If a system of linear equations such as $x + y = 2$ and $x + y = 4$ has no common solution, it is called a *system of inconsistent equations*. The graphs of two inconsistent linear equations are straight lines which have equal slopes or straight lines that have no slopes. These straight lines will be parallel.

DEPENDENT EQUATIONS

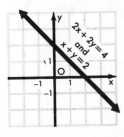

Sometimes, when two linear equations are graphed in a coordinate plane using the same set of axes, they turn out to be the same line; that is, they coincide. This happens in the case of $x + y = 2$ and $2x + 2y = 4$. Every one of the infinite number of solutions of $x + y = 2$ is also a solution of $2x + 2y = 4$. We see that $2x + 2y = 4$ and $x + y = 2$ are equivalent equations with identical solutions. Note that when both members of the equation $2x + 2y = 4$ are divided by 2, the result is $x + y = 2$.

If a system of two linear equations, for example $x + y = 2$ and $2x + 2y = 4$, is such that every solution of either one of the equations is also a solution of the other equation, it is called a *system of dependent equations*. The graphs of two dependent linear equations are the very same straight line.

Procedure. To solve a pair of linear equations graphically:

1. Graph one equation in a coordinate plane.
2. Graph the other equation in the same coordinate plane using the same set of coordinate axes.
3. Find the common solution which is the ordered number pair associated with the point of intersection of the two graphs.
4. Check the apparent solution by verifying that the ordered pair satisfies both equations.

Keep In Mind

The solution set of a system of two linear equations is the intersection of the solution sets of the individual equations.

Model Problem

Solve graphically and check: $2x + y = 8$
$y - x = 2$

Solution:

1. Graph $2x + y = 8$, or $y = -2x + 8$.

x	1	3	4
y	6	2	0

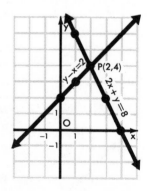

2. Graph $y - x = 2$, or $y = x + 2$.

x	0	1	2
y	2	3	4

3. Read the coordinates of the point of intersection P (2, 4).

4. *Check:* $(x = 2, y = 4)$

$$2x + y = 8 \qquad\qquad y - x = 2$$
$$2(2) + 4 \stackrel{?}{=} 8 \qquad\qquad 4 - 2 \stackrel{?}{=} 2$$
$$8 = 8 \quad \text{(true)} \qquad\qquad 2 = 2 \quad \text{(true)}$$

Answer: The common solution is $(2, 4)$. The solution set is $\{(2, 4)\}$.

Note: The same method of solution can be used to find the ordered number pair represented by $\{(x, y) \mid 2x + y = 8\} \cap \{(x, y) \mid y - x = 2\}$.

EXERCISES

In 1–15, solve the systems of equations graphically. Check.

1. $y = 2x$
$y = 3x - 3$

2. $y = -2x + 3$
$y = \frac{1}{2}x + 3$

3. $x + y = 4$
$x - y = 0$

4. $x + 2y = 7$
$y = 2x + 1$

5. $2x + y = -10$
$3x - 2y = -1$

6. $x + y = 3$
$2x - y = -9$

7. $y - 3x = 12$
$y = -3$

8. $3x + y = -9$
$x + 3y = -11$

9. $y = \frac{1}{3}x - 3$
$2x - y = 8$

10. $3x + y = 13$
$x + 6y = -7$

11. $x = 0$
$y = -5$

12. $2x = y + 9$
$6x + 3y = 15$

13. $x = 0$
$y = 0$

14. $y + 2x + 6 = 0$
$y = 2x$

15. $7x - 4y + 7 = 0$
$3x - 5y + 3 = 0$

In 16–21, graph both equations. Determine whether the system is consistent, inconsistent, or dependent.

16. $x + y = 1$
$x + y = 3$

17. $x + y = 5$
$2x + 2y = 10$

18. $y = 2x + 1$
$y = 3x + 3$

19. $2x - y = 1$
$2y = 4x - 2$

20. $y - 3x = 2$
$y = 3x - 2$

21. $x + 4y = 6$
$x = 2$

22. Are there any ordered number pairs which satisfy both equations $2x + y = 7$ and $2x = 5 - y$? Give your reasons.

23. Are there any ordered number pairs which satisfy the equation $y - x = 4$ but which do not satisfy the equation $2y = 8 + 2x$? Give your reasons.

In 24–27, find the intersection set, $R \cap S$ for set R and set S.

24. $R = \{-5, -3, -1, 0, 1, 3, 5\}$
$S = \{-3, -2, -1, 0, 1, 2, 3\}$

25. $R = \{(1, 1), (2, 4), (3, 9), (4, 16)\}$
$S = \{(1, 2), (2, 4), (3, 6), (4, 8)\}$

26. $R = \{(x, y) \mid y = 2x\}$
$S = \{(x, y) \mid y = x + 2\}$

27. $R = \{(x, y) \mid y = 2x + 4\}$
$S = \{(x, y) \mid x = y - 5\}$

28. Use the graphs of linear equations to find the ordered pair represented by:

a. $\{(x, y) \mid x + y = 7\} \cap \{(x, y) \mid x - y = 1\}$

   b. $\{(x,y) \mid y = x + 4\} \cap \{(x,y) \mid y = 2x + 5\}$

   c. $\{(x,y) \mid x + y + 2 = 0\} \cap \{(x,y) \mid x = y - 8\}$

29. a. Graph $\{(x,y) \mid 3x + y = 5\}$ and $\{(x,y) \mid 6x + 2y = 12\}$ using the same coordinate axes for both graphs.

   b. State the relation that exists between the lines that are the graphs of $3x + y = 5$ and $6x + 2y = 12$.

   c. State the solution set for the system $3x + y = 5$ and $6x + 2y = 12$.

2. Algebraic Solution of a System of Simultaneous Linear Equations by Using Addition or Subtraction

We will now learn algebraic methods for solving a system of linear equations in two variables. Solutions by these methods usually take less time and lead to more accurate results than the graphic method previously used.

Systems of equations that have the same solution set are called *equivalent systems*. For example, the following two systems are equivalent systems since they have the same solution set $\{(3, 1)\}$.

System A   *System B*

$x + y = 4$ $x = 3$

$x - y = 2$ $y = 1$

To solve a system of linear equations, such as system A, whose solution set is not obvious, we transform it into an equivalent system such as system B, whose solution set is obvious. To do this we make use of the properties of equality.

Model Problems

1. Solve the system of equations and check:
$$x + 3y = 13$$
$$x + y = 5$$

How to Proceed	*Solution*
1. The coefficients of the variable x are the same in both equations. Therefore, subtracting the members of equation [B] from the corresponding members of equation [A] will eliminate the variable x and will result in an equation which involves one variable, y.	$x + 3y = 13$ [A] $\underline{x + y = 5}$ [B] $2y = 8$

2. Solve the resulting equation for the variable, y. $y = 4$

3. Replace y by its value in any equation involving $x + y = 5$ [B]
   both variables. $x + 4 = 5$

4. Solve the resulting equation for the remaining $x = 1$
   variable, x.

5. *Check:* Substitute 1 for x and 4 for y in each of the given equations to
       verify that the resulting sentences are true.

$$x + 3y = 13 \qquad\qquad x + y = 5$$
$$1 + 3(4) \stackrel{?}{=} 13 \qquad\qquad 1 + 4 \stackrel{?}{=} 5$$
$$13 = 13 \ \ \text{(true)} \qquad\qquad 5 = 5 \ \ \text{(true)}$$

Answer: Since $x = 1$ and $y = 4$, the solution is $(1, 4)$, or the solution set is
$\{(1, 4)\}$.

2. Solve the system of equations and check: $5a + b = 13$
   $\qquad\qquad\qquad\qquad\qquad\qquad\qquad\qquad\qquad\quad 4a - 3b = 18$

How to Proceed	*Solution*

1. Multiply both members of equation [A] by 3. $5a + \ b = 13$ [A]
   This yields an equivalent equation [C] in $4a - 3b = 18$ [B]
   which the coefficient of b has the same abso- $\underline{15a + 3b = 39}$ [C]
   lute value as the coefficient of b in equation [B].

2. Add the corresponding members of equations $19a \qquad\quad = 57$
   [B] and [C] to eliminate the variable b.

3. Solve the resulting equation for the variable a. $a = 3$

4. Replace a by its value in any equation involving $5a + \ b = 13$ [A]
   both variables. $5(3) + \ b = 13$

5. Solve the resulting equation for the remaining $15 \ + \ b = 13$
   variable, b. $b = -2$

6. *Check:* Substitute 3 for a and -2 for b in each of the given equations to
       verify that the resulting sentences are true. This is left to the
       student.

Answer: Since $a = 3$ and $b = -2$, the solution is $(3, -2)$, or the solution set
is $\{(3, -2)\}$.

3. Solve the system of equations and check: $7x = 5 - 2y$
   $\qquad\qquad\qquad\qquad\qquad\qquad\qquad\qquad\qquad\quad 3y = 16 - 2x$

How to Proceed	*Solution*

1. Transform each of the given equations [A] $7x = \ 5 - 2y$ [A]
   and [B] into equivalent equations [C] and $3y = 16 - 2x$ [B]
   [D] in which the terms containing the vari- $7x + 2y = \ 5$ [C]
   ables appear on one side and the constant $2x + 3y = 16$ [D]
   appears on the other side.

2. To eliminate y, multiply both members of $21x + 6y = 15$ [E]
   equation [C] by 3; multiply both members $4x + 6y = 32$ [F]
   of equation [D] by 2. In the resulting
   equivalent equations [E] and [F], the absolute values of the coefficients of y are equal.
3. Subtract the members of equation [F] from $17x \qquad = -17$
   the corresponding members of equation [E]
   to eliminate the variable y.
4. Solve the resulting equation for the variable x. $x = -1$
5. Replace x by its value in any equation con- $3y = 16 - 2x$ [B]
   taining both variables. $3y = 16 - 2(-1)$
6. Solve the resulting equation for the remain- $3y = 16 + 2$
   ing variable, y. $3y = 18$
      $y = 6$

7. *Check:* Substitute -1 for x and 6 for y in each of the given equations to
   verify that the resulting sentences are true. This is left to the
   student.

Answer: Since $x = -1$ and $y = 6$, the solution is $(-1, 6)$, or the solution set
   is $\{(-1, 6)\}$.

Procedure. To solve a system of simultaneous linear equations in two variables by the method of elimination using addition or subtraction:

1. Transform each equation into an equivalent equation in which the variables appear on one side and the constant appears on the other side.
2. If necessary, multiply both members of each of the resulting equations by such numbers as will make the coefficients of one of the variables the same in absolute value.
3. If one of these coefficients is positive and the other negative, add the corresponding members of the two resulting equations. If these coefficients are either both positive or both negative, subtract the corresponding members of the resulting equations. Thus, one of the variables is eliminated.
4. Solve the resulting equation which has one variable for the value of that variable.
5. Substitute the value of the variable obtained in step 4 in any equation containing both variables. Solve the resulting equation for the remaining variable.
6. Check the common solution by substituting the values of the variables in each of the given equations to verify that the resulting sentences are true.

EXERCISES

In 1–39, solve each system of equations by eliminating one of the variables using addition or subtraction. Check.

1. $x + y = 12$
   $x - y = 4$

2. $r + s = -6$
   $r - s = -10$

3. $m + 2n = 14$
   $3n + m = 18$

4. $c - 2d = 14$
   $c + 3d = 9$

5. $s + r = 0$
   $r - s = 6$

6. $4r + 3s = 29$
   $2r - 3s = 1$

7. $8a + 5b = 9$
   $2a - 5b = -4$

8. $-2m + 4n = 13$
   $6m + 4n = 9$

9. $3a - b = 3$
   $a + 3b = 11$

10. $4x - y = 10$
    $2x + 3y = 12$

11. $5x + 4y = 27$
    $x - 2y = 11$

12. $2c - d = -1$
    $c + 3d = 17$

13. $3a - b = 13$
    $2a + 3b = 16$

14. $r - 3s = -11$
    $3r + s = 17$

15. $3x - y = 5$
    $5x - 2y = 8$

16. $3x + 4y = 26$
    $x - 3y = 0$

17. $3x + 7y = 22$
    $2x - 8y = 2$

18. $2x + 3y = 6$
    $3x + 5y = 15$

19. $3x + 7y = -2$
    $2x + 3y = -3$

20. $4a - 6b = 15$
    $6a - 4b = 10$

21. $x - 2y = 8$
    $2y = 3x - 16$

22. $3x + 4y = 16$
    $4x = 2y + 14$

23. $3a - 7 = 7b$
    $4a = 3b + 22$

24. $3x - 4y = 2$
    $x = 2(7 - y)$

25. $3x + 5(y + 2) = 1$
    $8y = -3x$

26. $\frac{1}{3}x + \frac{1}{4}y = 10$
    $\frac{1}{3}x - \frac{1}{2}y = 4$

27. $\frac{2}{3}x + \frac{3}{4}y = 2$
    $\frac{1}{6}x + \frac{1}{2}y = -2$

28. $\frac{1}{2}a + \frac{1}{3}b = 1$
    $\frac{3}{2}a - \frac{4}{3}b = -\frac{1}{2}$

29. $a - \frac{2}{3}b = 4$
    $\frac{3}{5}a + b = 15$

30. $2a + 3b = \frac{13}{6}$
    $a - \frac{1}{2}b = \frac{1}{12}$

31. $.04x + .06y = 26$
    $x + y = 500$

32. $.03x + .05y = 17$
    $x + y = 400$

33. $.03x = .06y + 9$
    $x + y = 600$

34. $x + 2y = 12$
    $\dfrac{x}{y} = 1 + \dfrac{6}{y}$

35. $x - 8y = -2$
    $\dfrac{3x}{2y} + 1 = \dfrac{10}{y}$

36. $2x + y = 23$
    $\dfrac{x - 6}{3y} = \dfrac{1}{5}$

37. $3d = 13 - 2c$
    $\dfrac{3c + d}{2} = 8$

38. $3x = 4y$
    $\dfrac{3x + 8}{5} = \dfrac{3y - 1}{2}$

39. $\dfrac{a}{3} + \dfrac{a + b}{6} = 3$
    $\dfrac{b}{3} - \dfrac{a - b}{2} = 6$

In 40–45, consider x and y as the variables of the system of equations. Solve the system by eliminating one of these variables using the method of addition or subtraction. Check.

40. $x + y = 13c$
    $x - y = 5c$

41. $5x + 3y = 14a$
    $2x + y = 6a$

42. $5x - 2y = 8t$
    $3x - 7y = -t$

43. $x + y = c$
    $x - y = d$

44. $3x + 8y = a$
    $5x + 10y = b$

45. $ax + by = c$
    $dx + ey = f$

3. Algebraic Solution of a System of Simultaneous Linear Equations by Using Substitution

Another algebraic method, called the ***substitution method***, can be used to eliminate one of the variables when solving a system of equations. When we use this method, we apply the substitution principle to transform one of the equations of the system into an equivalent equation that involves only one variable.

Model Problems

1. Solve the system of equations and check: $4x + 3y = 27$
   $$y = 2x - 1$$

How to Proceed	Solution
1. In equation [B], both y and $2x - 1$ name the same number when the values of the common solution replace x and y. Therefore, eliminate y in equation [A] by replacing y by $2x - 1$.	$4x + 3y = 27$ [A] $y = 2x - 1$ [B] $4x + 3(2x - 1) = 27$
2. Solve the resulting equation for x.	$4x + 6x - 3 = 27$ $10x = 30$ $x = 3$
3. Replace x by its value in any equation involving both variables.	$y = 2x - 1$ [B] $y = 2(3) - 1$
4. Solve the resulting equation for y.	$y = 6 - 1$ $y = 5$

5. *Check:* Substitute 3 for x and 5 for y in each of the given equations to verify that the resulting sentences are true.

$$4x + 3y = 27 \qquad\qquad y = 2x - 1$$
$$4(3) + 3(5) \overset{?}{=} 27 \qquad\qquad 5 \overset{?}{=} 2(3) - 1$$
$$12 + 15 \overset{?}{=} 27 \qquad\qquad 5 \overset{?}{=} 6 - 1$$
$$27 = 27 \ \ \text{(true)} \qquad\qquad 5 = 5 \ \ \text{(true)}$$

Answer: Since $x = 3$ and $y = 5$, the solution is $(3, 5)$, or the solution set is $\{(3, 5)\}$.

2. Solve the system of equations and check: $3x - 4y = 23$
   $$2x + 3y = 4$$

How to Proceed	Solution

1. Transform one of the equations [B] into an equivalent equation [C] in which one of the variables is expressed in terms of the other. In equation [B] solve for x in terms of y.

$$3x - 4y = 23 \quad \text{[A]}$$
$$2x + 3y = 4 \quad \text{[B]}$$
$$2x = 4 - 3y$$
$$x = \frac{4 - 3y}{2} \quad \text{[C]}$$

2. Eliminate x in equation [A] by replacing it with $\frac{4 - 3y}{2}$, the expression for x in equation [C].

$$3\left(\frac{4 - 3y}{2}\right) - 4y = 23$$

3. Solve the resulting equation for y.

$$3(4 - 3y) - 8y = 46 \quad M_2$$
$$12 - 9y - 8y = 46$$
$$-17y = 34$$
$$y = -2$$

4. Replace y by its value in any equation involving both variables.

$$x = \frac{4 - 3y}{2} \quad \text{[C]}$$
$$x = \frac{4 - 3(-2)}{2}$$

5. Solve the resulting equation for x.

$$x = \frac{4 + 6}{2}$$
$$x = 5$$

6. *Check:* Left to the student.

Answer: Since $x = 5$ and $y = -2$, the solution is $(5, -2)$, or the solution set is $\{(5, -2)\}$.

Procedure. To solve a system of simultaneous linear equations in two variables by the method of elimination using substitution:

1. Solve for one of the variables in terms of the other variable in one of the given equations.
2. Substitute this solution in the other equation; that is, replace the variable for which you solved with the expression to which it is equal. Thus, one of the variables is eliminated.
3. Solve the resulting equation, which has one variable, for the value of that variable.
4. Substitute the value of the variable obtained in step 3 in any equation containing both variables. Solve the resulting equation for the remaining variable.
5. Check the common solution by substituting the values of the variables in each of the given equations to verify that the resulting sentences are true.

EXERCISES

In 1–24, solve each system of equations by eliminating one of the variables by the substitution method. Check.

1. $y = x$
   $x + y = 14$

2. $x = y$
   $5x - 4y = -2$

3. $x = 4y$
   $2x + 3y = 22$

4. $r = -3s$
   $3r + 4s = -10$

5. $y = x + 1$
   $x + y = 9$

6. $x = 5 - y$
   $x - y = 1$

7. $y = x + 3$
   $3x + 2y = 26$

8. $y = 3x - 1$
   $7x + 2y = 37$

9. $a = 3b + 1$
   $5b - 2a = 1$

10. $a + b = 3$
    $3a - 2b = \frac{1}{2}$

11. $x + y = 0$
    $3x + 2y = 5$

12. $7x - 3y = 23$
    $x + 2y = 13$

13. $3x + 2y = 23$
    $x + 3y = 17$

14. $2x = 3y$
    $4x - 9y = -1$

15. $4y = -3x$
    $5x + 8y = 4$

16. $2x + 3y = 7$
    $4x - 5y = 25$

17. $7x + 3y = 3$
    $5x + 6y = 6$

18. $2a + 3b = 3$
    $3a + 4b = 3$

19. $y = 3x$
    $\frac{1}{3}x + \frac{1}{2}y = 11$

20. $t + u = 12$
    $t = \frac{1}{3}u$

21. $10t + u = 24$
    $t + u = \frac{1}{7}(10u + t)$

22. $x + y = 500$
    $y = 1.5x$

23. $x + y = 1000$
    $.06x = .04y$

24. $x + y = 300$
    $.25x + .75y = 195$

In 25–28, consider x and y as the variables of the system of equations. Solve the system using the method of substitution. Check.

25. $x + y = 18a$
    $x = y - 2a$

26. $x - y = 7b$
    $3x - 2y = 18b$

27. $x + y = r$
    $y = x + s$

28. $x + 5y = g$
    $x + y = h$

4. Solving Verbal Problems by Using Two Variables

We have previously learned how to solve word problems using one variable. Frequently, a problem can be solved more easily by using two variables rather than one variable. See how this is done in the solutions of the model problems that follow.

Procedure. To solve word problems by using a system of two equations involving two variables:

1. **Use two different variables to represent the different unknown quantities in the problem.**
2. **Translate two given relationships in the problem into a system of two equations.**
3. **Solve the system of equations to determine the answer(s) to the problem.**
4. **Check the answer(s) in the original word problem.**

Model Problems

1. The sum of two numbers is 10. Three times the larger decreased by twice the smaller is 15. Find the numbers.

How to Proceed	*Solution*
1. Represent the two different unknown quantities by two different variables.	1. Let x = the larger number. Let y = the smaller number.
2. Translate two given relationships in the problem into a system of two equations.	2. The sum of two numbers is 10. $$x + y = 10 \quad [A]$$ Three times the larger decreased by twice the smaller is 15. $$3x - 2y = 15 \quad [B]$$
3. Solve the system of equations. In equation [A], multiply both members by 2. Then add the members of the resulting equation to the corresponding members of equation [B].	$$\begin{aligned} x + y &= 10 \quad [A] \\ 3x - 2y &= 15 \quad [B] \\ 2x + 2y &= 20 \\ \hline 5x &= 35 \\ x &= 7 \\ x + y &= 10 \quad [A] \\ 7 + y &= 10 \\ y &= 3 \end{aligned}$$

Check: The sum of the larger number 7 and the smaller number 3 is 10. Three times the larger decreased by twice the smaller, $(3 \times 7) - (2 \times 3)$, equals $21 - 6$, or 15.

Answer: The larger number is 7; the smaller number is 3.

2. A boy deposited $6.50, consisting of dimes and quarters, in a bank. The number of quarters was 10 less than twice the number of dimes. How many coins of each kind did he deposit?

Solution:

Let d = the number of dimes.
Let q = the number of quarters.

Kind of coin	Number of coins	Value of each coin in cents	Total value in cents
Dime	d	10	$10d$
Quarter	q	25	$25q$

The total value of the coins was 650 cents.

$$10d + 25q = 650$$

The number of quarters was 10 less than twice the number of dimes.

$$q = 2d - 10$$

$10d + 25q = 650$	[A]
$q = 2d - 10$	[B]
$-2d + \quad q = -10$	[C]
$-10d + \ 5q = -50$	(In [C], M_5)
$\underline{10d + 25q = 650}$	[A]
$30q = 600$	
$q = 20$	
$q = 2d - 10$	[B]
$20 = 2d - 10$	
$30 = 2d$	
$15 = d$	

Check

Value of 15 dimes = \$1.50

Value of 20 quarters = \$5.00

Total value = \$6.50

The number of quarters, 20, is 10 less than twice 15, the number of dimes.

Answer: He deposited 15 dimes and 20 quarters.

3. A dealer wishes to obtain 50 pounds of mixed cookies to sell for \$1.00 per pound. If he mixes cookies worth \$1.20 per pound with cookies worth \$.70 per pound, find the number of pounds of each kind he should use.

Solution:

Let x = the number of pounds of the \$1.20 cookies to be used.
Let y = the number of pounds of the \$.70 cookies to be used.

Kind of cookie	Number of pounds	Price per pound in cents	Total value in cents
\$1.20 cookies	x	120	$120x$
\$.70 cookies	y	70	$70y$
Mixture	50	100	$100(50)$

The total number of pounds of cookies is 50.

$$x + y = 50$$

The total value of the \$1.20 cookies and \$.70 cookies is 100(50) cents.

$$120x + 70y = 100(50)$$

$$120x + 70y = 100(50) \ [A]$$
$$x + y = 50 \qquad [B]$$

$$70x + 70y = \quad 3500 \ (\text{In } [B], M_{70})$$
$$\underline{120x + 70y = \quad 5000} \ [A]$$
$$-50x \qquad = -1500$$
$$x = 30$$
$$x + y = 50 \qquad [B]$$
$$30 + y = 50$$
$$y = 20$$

Check

$$30 + 20 = 50$$

Value of 30 lb. at $1.20 per lb. = $36.00
Value of 20 lb. at $.70 per lb. $\;\;= \underline{\$14.00}$
Value of 50 lb. at $1.00 per lb. = $50.00

Answer: He should use 30 lb. of the $1.20 cookies and 20 lb. of the $.70 cookies.

4. The owner of a men's clothing store bought 6 shirts and 8 hats for $140. A week later, at the same prices, he bought 9 shirts and 6 hats for $132. Find the price of a shirt and the price of a hat.

Solution:

Let s = the price of a shirt in dollars.
Let h = the price of a hat in dollars.

6 shirts and 8 hats cost $140.

$$6s + 8h = 140 \ [A]$$

9 shirts and 6 hats cost $132.

$$9s + 6h = 132 \ [B]$$

1. In order to eliminate h, multiply both members of equation [B] by 4 and both members of equation [A] by 3.

$$36s + 24h = 528$$
$$\underline{18s + 24h = 420}$$
$$18s \qquad = 108$$
$$s = 6$$

2. In equation [A], substitute 6 for s.

$$36 + 8h = 140$$
$$8h = 104$$
$$h = 13$$

Check: 6 shirts and 8 hats cost $6($6) + 8($13) = $36 + $104 = $140.
9 shirts and 6 hats cost $9($6) + 6($13) = $54 + $78 = $132.

Answer: A shirt costs $6; a hat costs $13.

EXERCISES

In 1–21, solve the problem by using two variables.

Number Problems

1. The sum of two numbers is 104. The larger number is 1 less than twice the smaller number. Find the numbers.
2. The difference between two numbers is 34. The larger exceeds 3 times the smaller by 4. Find the numbers.
3. The sum of two numbers is 50. If twice the larger is subtracted from 4 times the smaller, the result is 8. Find the numbers.
4. If 5 times the smaller of two numbers is subtracted from twice the larger, the result is 16. If the larger is increased by 3 times the smaller, the result is 63. Find the numbers.

Coin Problems

5. Rae has $5.70 in quarters and dimes. The number of quarters is 6 more than the number of dimes. How many coins of each kind does Rae have?
6. A purse contains $7.60 in quarters and dimes. In all, there are 40 coins. How many coins of each kind are there?
7. A class contributed $6.10 in nickels and dimes to a welfare fund. In all, there were 80 coins. How many coins of each kind were there?
8. Mr. Charles cashed a $135 check in his bank. He received $5 bills and $10 bills. The number of $5 bills exceeded twice the number of $10 bills by 3. How many bills of each type did Mr. Charles receive?

Mixture Problems

9. A grocer mixed nuts worth $1.70 a pound with nuts worth $1.10 a pound. How many pounds of each kind did he use to make a mixture of 60 pounds to sell at $1.50 a pound?
10. A dealer has some candy worth $2.00 a kilogram and some worth $3.00 a kilogram. He wishes to make a mixture of 80 kilograms that he can sell for $2.20 a kilogram. How many kilograms of each kind should he use?
11. A dealer mixed some coffee worth 80 cents a pound with coffee worth 95 cents a pound to make a mixture to be sold for 85 cents a pound. If the number of pounds of 80-cent coffee was 10 more than the number of pounds of the 95-cent coffee, how many pounds of each kind did he use?
12. How many kilograms of seed worth $2.10 a kilogram must be mixed with 30 kilograms of seed worth $1.80 a kilogram in order to produce a mixture to sell for $2.00 a kilogram?

Investment Problems

13. Mrs. Morton invested $1400, part at 5% and the rest at 8%. Her total annual income from these investments was $100. Find the amount she invested at each rate.

14. Mr. Decker invested a certain amount of money in bonds yielding 3% a year and twice as much in bonds yielding 5% a year. If his total annual income from the two investments was $208, how much did he invest in each type of bond?

15. Mr. May invested $20,000, part at 4% and the rest at 6%. If the annual incomes from both investments were equal, find the amount he invested at each rate.

16. Mr. Burnside invested $8000 at 7%. How much additional money must he invest at 4% in order that his total annual income may equal 5% of his entire investment?

Business Problems

17. Six boxes of oranges and 5 boxes of grapefruits cost $142. At the same time and place, 3 boxes of oranges and 2 boxes of grapefruits cost $64. Find the cost of one box of each.

18. On one day, 4 plumbers and 5 helpers earned $325. On another day, working the same number of hours and at the same rate of pay, 5 plumbers and 6 helpers earned $400. How much does a plumber and how much does a helper earn each day?

19. A basketball manager bought 7 shirts and 4 pairs of shoes for $118. Another manager, who paid the same prices, paid $77 for 5 shirts and 2 pairs of shoes. Find the cost of a shirt and the cost of a pair of shoes.

20. A baseball manager bought 4 bats and 9 balls for $47.75. On another day, he bought 3 bats and 1 dozen balls at the same prices and paid $50.25. How much did he pay for each bat and each ball?

21. Mrs. Jones paid $18.70 for 4 kilograms of walnuts and 3 kilograms of pecans. At the same time Mrs. Kay paid $16.50 for 5 kilograms of walnuts and 1 kilogram of pecans. Find the price per kilogram of each kind of nut.

22. A merchant sells two types of lamps, model A and model B. He sold 4 lamps of model A and 5 lamps of model B and made a profit of $123 on the sale. He sold 6 lamps of model A and 3 lamps of model B to another customer and made a profit of $117 on this sale. How much profit did he make on each lamp of model A and how much profit did he make on each lamp of model B?

23. A manufacturer makes two types of electric toasters, model R and model S. He sold one customer 6 toasters of model R and 7 toasters of model S, making a profit of $51 on this sale. He sold another customer 4 toasters of model R and 3 toasters of model S,

making a profit of $29 on this sale. How much profit did he make on each toaster of model R, and how much profit did he make on each toaster of model S?

PREPARING TO SOLVE DIGIT PROBLEMS

In our decimal number system, every integer can be written by using only the symbols 0, 1, 2, 3, 4, 5, 6, 7, 8, 9. These ten number symbols are called *digits*.

In the integer 734, the digit 4 is in the units place, the digit 3 is in the tens place, and the digit 7 is in the hundreds place. Hence, we say that 734 means 7 hundreds plus 3 tens plus 4 ones. Therefore, $734 = 7(100) + 3(10) + 4(1)$. Similarly, 68 means 6 tens + 8 ones, or $6(10) + 8(1)$. In the number 68, we call 6 the tens digit and 8 the units digit. The value of the tens digit, 6, is 60. The value of the units digit, 8, is 8.

If we wish to represent a two-digit number whose tens digit is represented by t and whose units digit is represented by u, we write $t(10) + u(1)$, or more simply $10t + u$. Notice that we may not represent the two-digit number by tu, because tu means "t times u."

Keep In Mind

If t represents the tens digit and u represents the units digit of a two-digit number:

$10t + u$ represents the original number.

$10u + t$ represents the original number with its digits reversed.

$t + u$ represents the sum of the digits of the original number.

EXERCISES

In 1–5, give the value of each digit in each of the numbers.

1. 39   2. 625   3. 7803   4. 905   5. 25013

In 6–10, represent the number described.

6. The number whose tens digit is 9 and whose units digit is 1.
7. The number whose units digit is 7 and whose tens digit is 5.
8. The number obtained by reversing the digits of 38.
9. The number whose hundreds digit is represented by h, whose tens digit is represented by t, and whose units digit is represented by u.
10. The number obtained by reversing the digits of the number described in exercise 9.

SOLVING DIGIT PROBLEMS

Model Problem

In a two-digit number, the sum of the digits is 9. The number is 12 times the tens digit. Find the number.

Solution:

Using One Variable	*Using Two Variables*

Using One Variable

Let x = the tens digit.
Then $9 - x$ = the units digit.
And $10x + (9 - x)$ = the number.
The number is 12 times the tens digit.

$$10x + (9 - x) = 12x$$
$$10x + 9 - x = 12x$$
$$9 + 9x = 12x$$
$$9 = 3x \quad A_{-9x}$$
$$x = 3$$
$$9 - x = 6$$
$$10x + (9 - x) = 10(3) + 6 = 36$$

Using Two Variables

Let t = the tens digit.
Let u = the units digit.
$10t + u$ = the number.
The sum of the digits is 9.

$$t + u = 9 \quad [A]$$

The number is 12 times the tens digit.

$$10t + u = 12t \quad [B]$$
$$-2t + u = 0 \quad A_{-12t}$$
$$\underline{2t + 2u = 18 \quad (\text{In } [A], M_2)}$$
$$3u = 18$$
$$u = 6$$

In $[A]$, let $u = 6$.

$$t + 6 = 9$$
$$t = 3$$
$$10t + u = 10(3) + 6 = 36$$

Check: $3 + 6 = 9$ and $36 = 12(3)$.

Answer: The number is 36.

EXERCISES

1. In a two-digit number, the sum of the digits is 10 and the difference of the digits is 4. Find the number if the tens digit is greater than the units digit.
2. The tens digit of a two-digit number is 2 less than 4 times the units digit. The difference between the tens digit and the units digit is 4. Find the number.

3. The units digit of a two-digit number is 4 more than the tens digit. The number is 6 times the units digit. Find the number.
4. The tens digit of a two-digit number is 2 less than the units digit. The number is 4 times the sum of the digits. Find the number.
5. The tens digit of a two-digit number exceeds the units digit by 3. The number is 1 more than 8 times the sum of the digits. Find the number.
6. The units digit of a two-digit number is 11 less than twice the tens digit. The number is 6 less than 7 times the sum of the digits. Find the number.
7. The sum of the digits of a two-digit number is 11. If 45 is added to the number, the order of the digits is reversed. Find the number.
8. The tens digit of a two-digit number is 1 more than 4 times the units digit. If 63 is subtracted from the number, the order of the digits is reversed. Find the number.

PREPARING TO SOLVE MOTION PROBLEMS INVOLVING CURRENTS

Let us suppose that the motors of a boat supply enough power for the boat to travel at the rate of 20 mph in a body of still water, where there is no current. When the boat travels in a body of water where there is a current, the boat will move faster than 20 mph when it is traveling downstream with the current. It will move slower than 20 mph when it is traveling upstream against the current. For example, if the boat is traveling in a river flowing at the rate of 3 mph, the rate of the boat traveling downstream with the current will be $20 + 3$, or 23 mph. Its rate traveling upstream against the current will be $20 - 3$, or 17 mph.

The rate of speed of an airplane is similarly affected by an air current. Suppose the motors of a plane supply enough power for a plane to travel at the rate of 300 mph in still air, and there is a wind blowing at the rate of 20 mph. Flying with the wind, the plane will be traveling at the rate of $300 + 20$, or 320 mph. Flying against the wind, the plane will be traveling at the rate of $300 - 20$, or 280 mph.

Keep In Mind

If r = rate in still water or in still air,
and c = rate of the water current or air current,
then $r + c$ = rate traveling with the current
and $r - c$ = rate traveling against the current.

EXERCISES

1. A boy who can row 3 mph in still water is rowing in a stream which is flowing at the rate of 1 mph.
   a. Find his rate rowing downstream.
   b. Find his rate rowing upstream.
   c. How long would it take him to row 4 miles downstream?
   d. How long would it take him to return to his starting point rowing upstream?
   e. What is his total time going and returning?
2. A plane which can fly 400 kilometers per hour in still air is flying at a time when the wind is blowing at the rate of 40 kilometers per hour.
   a. Find the rate of the plane flying with the wind.
   b. Find the rate of the plane flying against the wind.
   c. How long would it take the plane to fly 990 kilometers with the wind?
   d. How long would it take the plane to return to its starting point flying against the wind?
   e. What is the total time going and returning?
3. A motorboat which can travel 35 mph in still water is traveling downstream at the rate of 38 mph. Find the rate of the stream.
4. A plane which was flying against a 40-km/h wind traveled 418 km in 1 hour. How far would the plane have traveled in 1 hour if there had been no wind?
5. If x mph represents the rate of a boat traveling in still water and y mph represents the rate of the current of a river in which it is traveling, find:
   a. the rate of the boat traveling downstream
   b. the rate of the boat traveling upstream
   c. the distance the boat would travel in 2 hours going downstream
   d. the distance the boat would travel in 3 hours going upstream

SOLVING MOTION PROBLEMS INVOLVING CURRENTS

Model Problem

A motorboat can travel 120 kilometers downstream in 3 hours. It requires 5 hours to make the return trip against the current. Find the rate of the boat in still water and the rate of the current.

Solution:

Let r = the rate of the boat in still water.
Let c = the rate of the current.

	(km/h) Rate	(hr.) Time	(km) Distance
Downstream	$r + c$	3	$3r + 3c$
Upstream	$r - c$	5	$5r - 5c$

The distance downstream is 120 kilometers.

$$3r + 3c = 120 \quad [A]$$

The distance upstream is 120 kilometers.

$$5r - 5c = 120 \quad [B]$$

1. In order to eliminate c in equation [A], multiply both members by 5; in equation [B], multiply both members by 3.

$$15r + 15c = 600$$
$$\underline{15r - 15c = 360}$$
$$30r \qquad = 960$$
$$r = 32$$

2. In equation [A], let $r = 32$.

$$3(32) + 3c = 120$$
$$96 + 3c = 120$$
$$3c = 24$$
$$c = 8$$

Check: Rate downstream = 32 + 8 or 40 kilometers per hour.
Rate upstream = 32 − 8 or 24 kilometers per hour.
Distance downstream = 3(40) = 120 kilometers.
Distance upstream = 5(24) = 120 kilometers.

Answer: The rate of the boat in still water is 32 kilometers per hour; the rate of the current is 8 kilometers per hour.

EXERCISES

In 1–7, solve each problem by using two variables.

1. Mr. Turner has a motorboat that can travel 14 mph in still water. He wishes to take a trip on a river whose current flows at the rate of 2 mph. If he has 7 hours at his disposal, how many hours should he spend on the first part of his trip going downstream before returning upstream to his starting point?

2. A plane which can fly 275 km/h in still air flies for 3 hours against a wind and for 2 hours with the same wind. The total distance it covers is 1315 km. Find the rate of the wind.

3. A plane flew for 4 hours against a 10-mph wind. It then flew for

3 hours with the same wind. In all, the plane flew 1390 miles. Find the rate of the plane in still air.

4. A boat is rowed downstream a distance of 24 kilometers in 2 hours. It is then rowed the same distance upstream in 6 hours. Find the rate of rowing in still water and the rate of the current.

5. A plane left an airport and flew with the wind for 4 hours, covering 2000 kilometers. It then returned over the same route to the airport against the same wind in 5 hours. Find the rate of the plane in still air and the speed of the wind.

6. In 3 hours, a plane flew 720 miles with a wind. It then flew $\frac{4}{9}$ of this distance against the same wind in 2 hours. Find the speed of the plane in still air and the speed of the wind.

7. A plane flew a distance of 1555 miles in 5 hours. During the first 3 hours of the flight, it flew with a wind a distance of 975 miles. During the remainder of the flight, the plane flew against a wind whose average speed was 5 mph less than what it had been during the first part of the flight. Find the rate of the plane in still air and the original speed of the wind.

Miscellaneous Problems

In 1–10, solve each problem by using two variables.

1. Tickets for a high school football game cost 50 cents each if purchased before the day of the game. They cost 75 cents each if bought at the gate on the day of the game. For a particular game, 600 tickets were sold and the receipts were $350. How many tickets were sold at the gate?

2. The perimeter of a rectangle is 28 centimeters. Three times the length increased by 4 times the width is 48 centimeters. Find the dimensions of the rectangle.

3. Paley hiked from his summer cabin to town at the rate of 3 miles per hour. He came back in a car which averaged 36 miles per hour. If the total time he traveled was $3\frac{1}{4}$ hours, find the amount of time he spent on each part of the trip.

4. Four years ago, Mike was 5 times as old as Daniel was then. Eight years from now, Mike will be twice as old as Daniel will be then. Find the age of each now.

5. A dealer has a solution which is 60% pure acid and another solution which is 35% pure acid. How many cubic centimeters of each solution should he use to make 100 cubic centimeters of a solution which is 50% pure acid?

6. If 3 is subtracted from the numerator of a certain fraction, the value becomes $\frac{2}{3}$. If 10 is added to the denominator of the original fraction, the value becomes $\frac{1}{2}$. Find the original fraction.

7. If 3 is added to both numerator and denominator of a fraction, the fraction becomes equal to $\frac{3}{4}$. When 5 is subtracted from both numerator and denominator of the original fraction, it becomes equal to $\frac{1}{4}$. Find the original fraction.

8. If the numerator of a fraction is decreased by 1 and the denominator is increased by 5, the value of the fraction becomes $\frac{1}{2}$. If the numerator of the original fraction is increased by 1 and the denominator of the original fraction is decreased by 6, the value of the resulting fraction becomes $\frac{4}{3}$. Find the original fraction.

9. The sum of the digits of a two-digit number is 6. If the number is divided by the sum of the digits, the quotient is 7. Find the number.

10. If a two-digit number is divided by the sum of the digits, the quotient is 4 and the remainder is 15. If the digits are reversed, the resulting number is 18 more than the original number. Find the original number.

5. Graphing Solution Sets of Systems of Inequalities

In order to find the solution set of a system of inequalities, we must find each of the ordered number pairs that satisfy all the open sentences of the system. We can do this by a graphic method similar to the method used in finding the solution set of a system of equations.

Model Problems ⎯⎯⎯⎯⎯⎯⎯⎯⎯⎯⎯⎯⎯⎯⎯⎯⎯⎯⎯⎯⎯⎯⎯⎯⎯⎯

1. Graph the solution set of the system: $x > 2$
$$y < -2$$

Solution:

1. Graph $x > 2$ by first graphing the plane divider $x = 2$. (In the figure, see the dashed line labeled A.) The half-plane to the right of this line is the graph of the solution set of $x > 2$.

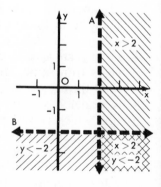

2. Using the same set of axes, graph $y < -2$
by first graphing the plane divider $y = -2$.
(In the figure, see the dashed line labeled B.)
The half-plane below this line is the graph of
the solution set of $y < -2$.

3. The solution set of the system $x > 2$ and
$y < -2$ consists of the intersection of the solution sets of $x > 2$ and
$y < -2$. Therefore, the crosshatched region, which is the intersection of
both graphs made in steps 1 and 2, is the graph of the solution set of the
system $x > 2$ and $y < -2$. All points in this region, and no others, satisfy
both sentences of the system. For example, the point $(4, -3)$, which lies
in the region, satisfies both sentences of the system because its x-value
$4 > 2$, and its y-value $-3 < -2$.

Note: The same solution could be used to plot the graph of
$\{(x, y) \mid x < 2 \text{ and } y < -2\}$ or $\{(x, y) \mid x > 2\} \cap \{(x, y) \mid y < -2\}$.

2. Graph the solution set of $3 < x < 5$.

Solution:

1. The sentence $3 < x < 5$ means $3 < x$
and $x < 5$. This may be written $x > 3$
and $x < 5$. Therefore, graph $x > 3$ by
first graphing the plane divider $x = 3$.
(In the figure, see the dashed line labeled A.) The half-plane to the right of
the line $x = 3$ is the graph of the solution set of $x > 3$.

2. Using the same set of axes, graph $x < 5$
by first graphing the plane divider
$x = 5$. (In the figure, see the dashed
line labeled B.) The half-plane to the
left of the line $x = 5$ is the graph of the solution set of $x < 5$.

3. The crosshatched region, which is the intersection of the graphs made in
steps 1 and 2, is the graph of the solution set of $x > 3$ and $x < 5$, or
$3 < x < 5$.

Note: The same solution could be used to plot the graph of
$\{(x, y) \mid 3 < x < 5\}$.

3. Graph the solution set of the system: $x + y \geq 4$
$\qquad\qquad\qquad\qquad\qquad\qquad\qquad y \leq 2x - 3$

Solution:

1. Graph $x + y \geq 4$ by first graphing the plane divider $x + y = 4$. (In the figure, see the solid line labeled R.) The line $x + y = 4$ and the half-plane above this line together form the graph of the solution set of $x + y \geq 4$.

2. Using the same set of axes, graph $y \leq 2x - 3$ by first graphing the plane divider $y = 2x - 3$. (In the figure, see the solid line labeled S.) The line $y = 2x - 3$ and the half-plane below this line together form the graph of the solution set of $y \leq 2x - 3$.

3. The crosshatched region, which is the intersection of both graphs made in steps 1 and 2, is the graph of the solution set of the system $x + y \geq 4$ and $y \leq 2x - 3$.

Note: The same solution could be used to graph the set $\{(x, y) \mid x + y \geq 4\} \cap \{(x, y) \mid y \leq 2x - 3\}$.

4. Graph the solution set of the system: $3x + 5y \geq 15$
$$y \leq x + 2$$
$$x \leq 3$$

Solution:

1. Graph $3x + 5y \geq 15$ by first graphing the plane divider $3x + 5y = 15$. (See line R.) The line $3x + 5y = 15$ and the half-plane above this line together form the graph of the solution set of $3x + 5y \geq 15$.

2. Using the same set of axes, graph $y \leq x + 2$ by first graphing the plane divider $y = x + 2$. (See line S.) The line $y = x + 2$ and the half-plane below this line together form the graph of the solution set of $y \leq x + 2$.

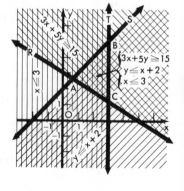

3. Using the same set of axes, graph $x \leq 3$ by first graphing the plane divider $x = 3$. (See line T.) The line $x = 3$ and the half-plane to the left of this line together form the graph of the solution set of $x \leq 3$.

4. The crosshatched region with all three types of hatching is the graph of the solution set of the system $3x + 5y \geq 15$, $y \leq x + 2$, $x \leq 3$. Notice that this region includes the interior of triangle ABC as well as all points on the line segments $\overline{AB}$, $\overline{BC}$, and $\overline{AC}$ which form the sides of the triangle.

Every point in this region is common to all three graphs made in steps 1, 2, and 3.

Note: The same solution could be used to graph
$\{(x,y) \mid 3x + 5y \geq 15\} \cap \{(x,y) \mid y \leq x + 2\} \cap \{(x,y) \mid x \leq 3\}$.

EXERCISES

In 1–21, graph the solution set of each system in a coordinate plane.

1. $x > 1$
   $y > -2$

2. $x \leq 2$
   $y \geq 3$

3. $x \geq 0$
   $y \geq 0$

4. $x < 0$
   $y > 0$

5. $y \geq x$
   $x < 2$

6. $y \leq x$
   $x \geq -1$

7. $y \geq 2x$
   $y > x + 3$

8. $y \leq 2x + 3$
   $y \geq -x$

9. $y - x \geq 5$
   $y - 2x \leq 7$

10. $x + y > 3$
    $x - y < 6$

11. $x - y \leq -2$
    $x + y \geq 2$

12. $2x + y > -4$
    $x - y \leq 1$

13. $2x + y \leq 6$
    $x + y - 2 > 0$

14. $2x + 3y \geq 6$
    $x + y - 4 \leq 0$

15. $5x - 3y - 2 \geq 0$
    $4x + 2y + 2 < 0$

16. $y \geq x$
    $x = 0$

17. $x + y \leq 3$
    $y - 2x = 0$

18. $y - 2x - 2 > 0$
    $x + y - 2 = 0$

19. $x \geq 0$
    $y \geq 0$
    $x + y \geq 4$

20. $x + 3y \leq 6$
    $2y \geq 2$
    $x \geq -2$

21. $y \geq x$
    $x + y - 3 \geq 0$
    $x - 4 \leq 0$

In 22–25, graph the solution set in a coordinate plane.

22. $1 < x < 4$

23. $-5 \leq x \leq -1$

24. $2 < y \leq 6$

25. $-2 \leq y \leq 3$

26. Graph the set $\{(x,y) \mid x - 1 < y < 2\}$.
27. Graph the set $\{(x,y) \mid y > 3x - 2\} \cap \{(x,y) \mid y < -2x + 3\}$.
28. Graph the set $\{(x,y) \mid 2x + y - 4 \geq 0\} \cap \{(x,y) \mid x = 3y + 5\}$.

Chapter 15

Ratio, Proportion, and Variation

1. Ratio

The ratio of one number to another is the quotient which represents the first number divided by the second. For example, if Mr. Cott is 50 years old and his daughter, Marion, is 10 years old, the ratio of Mr. Cott's age to Marion's age is $50 \div 10$, or $\frac{50}{10}$. The quotient is equivalent to $\frac{5}{1}$, or 5. To compare Mr. Cott's age to Marion's age, we say the ratio of Mr. Cott's age to his daughter's age is 5 to 1. We may also say Mr. Cott is 5 times as old as his daughter.

Another way to express the ratio $\frac{50}{10}$ is to use the ratio symbol "$:$" and write "$50:10$."

In general, the ratio of a to b can be expressed as $\frac{a}{b}$, $a \div b$, or $a:b$.

The numbers a and b are called the **terms** of the ratio.

A ratio is the quotient of two numbers in a definite order. The ratio of 5 to 1 is written $\frac{5}{1}$ or $5:1$, whereas the ratio of 1 to 5 is written $\frac{1}{5}$ or $1:5$. Therefore, a ratio may be considered as an ordered pair of numbers.

To find the ratio of two quantities, both quantities must be expressed in the same unit of measure before we find their quotient. For example, to compare a nickel with a penny, we first convert the nickel to 5 pennies and then find the ratio, which is $\frac{5}{1}$, or $5:1$. Therefore, a nickel is worth 5 times as much as a penny.

Since the ratio $\frac{5}{1}$ is a fraction, we can use the multiplication property of a fraction to find many equivalent ratios. For example:

$$\frac{5}{1} = \frac{5}{1} \cdot \frac{2}{2} = \frac{10}{2} \qquad \frac{5}{1} = \frac{5}{1} \cdot \frac{3}{3} = \frac{15}{3} \qquad \frac{5}{1} = \frac{5}{1} \cdot \frac{x}{x} = \frac{5x}{1x} \ (x \neq 0)$$

From the last example, we see that $5x$ and $1x$ represent two numbers whose ratio is $5:1$.

In general, if a, b, and x are numbers ($b \neq 0, x \neq 0$), ax and bx represent two numbers whose ratio is $a:b$ because:

$$\frac{a}{b} = \frac{a}{b} \cdot \frac{x}{x} = \frac{ax}{bx}$$

Also, since a ratio such as $\frac{24}{16}$ is a fraction, we can use the division property of a fraction to find equivalent ratios. For example:

$$\frac{24}{16} = \frac{24 \div 2}{16 \div 2} = \frac{12}{8} \qquad \frac{24}{16} = \frac{24 \div 4}{16 \div 4} = \frac{6}{4} \qquad \frac{24}{16} = \frac{24 \div 8}{16 \div 8} = \frac{3}{2}$$

A ratio is expressed in simplest form when both terms of the ratio are whole numbers and when no whole number other than 1 is a common divisor of these terms. Thus, to express the ratio $\frac{24}{16}$ in simplest form, we divide both terms by their greatest common divisor, 8. We obtain the ratio $\frac{3}{2}$ (as shown in the last example).

If Ted weighs 75 kilograms, May weighs 60 kilograms, and Sue weighs 45 kilograms, the ratio of Ted's weight to May's weight is 75:60 and the ratio of May's weight to Sue's weight is 60:45. We can write these two ratios in an abbreviated form as the continued ratio 75:60:45. We say that the ratio of the weights of Ted, May, and Sue is 75:60:45, or, in simplest form, 5:4:3.

In general, the ratio of the numbers a, b, and c ($b \neq 0$, $c \neq 0$) is $a:b:c$.

Model Problems

1. An oil tank has a capacity of 200 gallons. There are 50 gallons of oil in the tank. (a) Find the ratio of the number of gallons in the tank to the capacity of the tank. (b) What part of the tank is full?

   Solution:

   a. ratio $= \dfrac{\text{number of gallons of oil in the tank}}{\text{capacity of the tank}} = \dfrac{50}{200} = \dfrac{1}{4}$

   Answer: The ratio is 1 to 4.

   b. *Answer:* $\frac{1}{4}$ of the tank is full.

2. Compute the ratio of 1 minute to 45 seconds.

   Solution:

   First we express both quantities in the same unit of measure.

   $$1 \text{ minute} = 60 \text{ seconds}$$

   $$\text{ratio} = \frac{1 \text{ minute}}{45 \text{ seconds}} = \frac{60 \text{ seconds}}{45 \text{ seconds}} = \frac{60}{45} = \frac{4}{3}$$

   Answer: The ratio is 4 to 3.

3. Compute the ratio of 6.4 ounces to 1 pound.

Solution:

First we express both quantities in the same unit of measure.

$$1 \text{ pound} = 16 \text{ ounces}$$

$$\text{ratio} = \frac{6.4 \text{ ounces}}{1 \text{ pound}} = \frac{6.4 \text{ ounces}}{16 \text{ ounces}} = \frac{6.4}{16} = \frac{64}{160} = \frac{2}{5}$$

Answer: The ratio is $2:5$.

4. Phil's forearm is $1\frac{1}{2}$ feet long. In a photograph, his forearm is 1 inch long. What is the ratio of the actual length of Phil's forearm to the length of the forearm in the picture?

Solution:

$$\text{ratio} = \frac{\text{actual length of Phil's forearm}}{\text{length of forearm in picture}} = \frac{1\frac{1}{2} \text{ ft.}}{1 \text{ in.}} = \frac{18 \text{ in.}}{1 \text{ in.}} = \frac{18}{1}$$

Answer: $18:1$

5. Express the ratio $1\frac{3}{4}$ to $1\frac{1}{2}$ in simplest form.

Solution:

Method 1

$$\text{ratio} = 1\frac{3}{4}:1\frac{1}{2} = \frac{1\frac{3}{4}}{1\frac{1}{2}} = \frac{\frac{7}{4}}{\frac{3}{2}} = \frac{\frac{7}{4}}{\frac{3}{2}} \cdot \frac{4}{4} = \frac{\frac{7}{4} \cdot \frac{4}{1}}{\frac{3}{2} \cdot \frac{4}{1}} = \frac{7}{6} \quad Ans.$$

Method 2

$$\text{ratio} = 1\frac{3}{4}:1\frac{1}{2} = 1\frac{3}{4} \div 1\frac{1}{2} = \frac{7}{4} \div \frac{3}{2} = \frac{7}{4} \times \frac{2}{3} = \frac{14}{12} = \frac{7}{6} \quad Ans.$$

EXERCISES

1. Express each ratio as a fraction and also with a colon.
   a. 36 to 12   b. 48 to 24   c. 40 to 25   d. 2 to 3   e. 5 to 4
2. Express each ratio in simplest form.
   a. $\frac{8}{32}$ b. $\frac{36}{27}$ c. $\frac{36}{24}$ d. $20:10$ e. $48:20$
   f. $3x:2x$ g. $1y:4y$ h. $3c:5c$ i. $7x:7y$ j. $12s:4s^2$
3. The larger number is how many times the smaller number?
   a. 10, 5   b. 18, 6   c. 12, 8   d. 25, 10   e. 15, 25
4. If the ratio of two numbers is $4:1$, how many times the smaller number is the larger number?

5. What fractional part of the larger number is the smaller number?
   a. 8, 24   b. 7, 14   c. 50, 10   d. 12, 18   e. 36, 27
6. If the ratio of two numbers is 8 : 1, the smaller number is what fractional part of the larger number?
7. In each part, name the ratios that are equal.
   a. $\frac{2}{3}, \frac{6}{9}, \frac{10}{30}, \frac{28}{36}, \frac{50}{75}$ b. $10:8, 20:16, 15:13, 4:5, 50:40$
8. In each part, find the number which can replace the question mark and make the resulting statement true.

   a. $\dfrac{1}{2} = \dfrac{?}{24}$ b. $\dfrac{2}{3} = \dfrac{10}{?}$ c. $\dfrac{4}{5} = \dfrac{?}{100}$ d. $\dfrac{5}{8} = \dfrac{25}{?}$

9. Express each ratio in simplest form.
   a. $\frac{3}{4}$ to $\frac{1}{4}$ b. $1\frac{1}{8}$ to $\frac{3}{8}$ c. $1\frac{1}{6}:2\frac{5}{6}$ d. $\frac{3}{4}$ to $\frac{5}{8}$ e. $1\frac{2}{3}:2\frac{1}{2}$
   f. 1.2 to 2.4   g. .75 to .25   h. 1.2:4   i. 6:.25   j. .05 to .01
10. Express each ratio in simplest form.
   a. 45 min. to 15 min.   b. 12 oz. to 16 oz.   c. 40 ft. to 100 ft.
   d. 75 cents to 100 cents   e. 16 hrs. to 24 hrs.   f. 15 qt. to 20 qt.
   g. 100 mi. to 60 mi.   h. 50 gal. to 275 gal.   i. 15 hr. to 24 hr.
11. Express each ratio in simplest form.
   a. $1\frac{1}{2}$ hr. to $\frac{1}{2}$ hr.   b. $\frac{2}{3}$ yd. to $\frac{5}{6}$ yd.   c. 3 in. to $\frac{1}{2}$ in.
   d. 1 ft. to 1 in.   e. 1 yd. to 1 ft.   f. $\frac{1}{3}$ yd. to 6 in.
   g. 12 oz. to 3 lb.   h. 1 hr. to 15 min.   i. 12 hr. to 4 da.
   j. $6 to 50 cents   k. $\frac{2}{3}$ min. to 10 sec.   l. 2 mi. to 880 yd.
12. In class, there are 20 men and 10 women.
   a. What is the ratio of the number of men to the number of women?
   b. For one woman in the class, how many men are there?
   c. What is the ratio of the number of women to the number of men?
   d. What is the ratio of the number of men to the total number of students in the class?
   e. What is the ratio of the number of women to the total number of students in the class?
13. A student did 6 out of 10 problems correctly.
   a. What is the ratio of the number right to the number wrong?
   b. For every two answers that were wrong, how many answers were right?
14. The length of a rectangle is represented by $3x$ and its width by $2x$. Find the ratio of the width of the rectangle to its perimeter.
15. Represent in terms of x two numbers whose ratio is:
   a. 4 to 7   b. 5 to 3   c. 1 to 4   d. 3:5   e. 7:1
16. Represent in terms of x three numbers which have the continued ratio:
   a. 1 to 3 to 2   b. 7 to 3 to 1   c. 2:3:5   d. 1:5:4

2. Ratios in the Metric System

Previously we discussed the ratios of measures such as ounces, miles, yards, and gallons. These measures belong to our present United States system of measurement. Now we will discuss the ratios of measures in the metric system.

The following are some of the basic units in the metric system:

1. The unit of length is the *meter,* abbreviated m, 1 meter = 1.09 yards (approximately) or 1 meter = 39.37 inches (approximately).
2. The unit of weight, or mass is the *gram,* abbreviated g, 1 gram = .035 ounce (approximately).
3. The unit of liquid volume is the *liter,* abbreviated l, 1 liter = 1.06 liquid quarts (approximately).

In the metric system a prefix is used with a basic unit to indicate that the unit has been divided by a power of ten or multiplied by a power of ten. The following are some of the prefixes that are most frequently used:

1. *milli,* which is abbreviated m, means one-thousandth. Hence, 1 millimeter, abbreviated 1 mm, means 1/1000 of a meter; 1 milligram, abbreviated 1 mg, means 1/1000 of a gram; 1 milliliter, abbreviated 1 ml, means 1/1000 of a liter.
2. *centi,* which is abbreviated c, means one-hundredth. Hence, 1 centimeter, abbreviated 1 cm, means 1/100 of a meter; 1 centigram, abbreviated 1 cg, means 1/100 of a gram; 1 centiliter, abbreviated 1 cl, means 1/100 of a liter.
3. *kilo,* abbreviated k, means one thousand. Hence, 1 kilometer, abbreviated 1 km, means 1000 meters; 1 kilogram, abbreviated 1 kg, means 1000 grams; 1 kiloliter, abbreviated 1 kl, means 1000 liters.

Note: The milliliter and the cubic centimeter have almost the same volume. Therefore, one liter is equal to 1000 cubic centimeters, which may be written as 1000 cc or 1000 cm³. Some people prefer not to use the term kiloliter. Instead they use a cubic meter (m³), which is equal to a kiloliter.

Model Problems

1. Compute the ratio of 60 meters to 80 meters.

Solution:

$$\text{ratio} = \frac{60 \text{ meters}}{80 \text{ meters}} = \frac{60}{80} = \frac{3}{4}$$

Answer: The ratio is 3 to 4.

2. Compute the ratio of 500 grams to $1\frac{1}{2}$ kilograms.

Solution—Method 1:

Since 1 kilogram = 1000 grams, $1\frac{1}{2}$ kilograms = $1\frac{1}{2} \times 1000$ grams or 1500 grams.

$$\text{ratio} = \frac{500 \text{ grams}}{1\frac{1}{2} \text{ kilograms}} = \frac{500 \text{ grams}}{1500 \text{ grams}} = \frac{500}{1500} = \frac{1}{3}$$

Answer: The ratio is 1 to 3.

Solution—Method 2:

Since 1 gram = $\frac{1}{1000}$ of a kilogram, 500 grams = $500 \times \frac{1}{1000}$ of a kilogram, or $\frac{500}{1000}$ of a kilogram, or $\frac{1}{2}$ of a kilogram.

$$\text{ratio} = \frac{500 \text{ grams}}{1\frac{1}{2} \text{ kilograms}} = \frac{\frac{1}{2} \text{ kilogram}}{1\frac{1}{2} \text{ kilograms}} = \frac{\frac{1}{2}}{\frac{3}{2}}$$
$$= \frac{1}{2} \div \frac{3}{2} = \frac{1}{2} \times \frac{2}{3} = \frac{2}{6} = \frac{1}{3}$$

Answer: The ratio is 1 to 3.

Notice that when we find the ratio of two quantities that are expressed in different units, the ratio remains the same regardless of the common unit used in computing the ratio.

EXERCISES

1. Express each ratio in simplest form.
   a. 80 m to 16 m
   b. 75 g to 100 g
   c. 18 l to 60 l
   d. 36 cm to 72 cm
   e. 54 cg to 90 cg
   f. 75 cl to 35 cl
   g. 32 mm to 48 mm
   h. 90 mg to 72 mg
   i. 36 ml to 63 ml
   j. 150 km to 125 km
   k. 40 kg to 24 kg
   l. 54 kl to 81 kl
2. Express each ratio in simplest form.
   a. 25 cm to 1 m
   b. 300 gm to 1 kg
   c. 30 cl to 1 l
   d. 500 g to 2 kg
   e. 750 m to 3 km
   f. 250 ml to 1 l
   g. 25 cm to $1\frac{1}{4}$ m
   h. 50 mg to $1\frac{3}{4}$ g
   i. 35 cg to 50 g

3. Using a Ratio to Express a Rate

We have learned how to use a ratio to compare two quantities that are measured in the same unit. It is also possible to compare two quantities of different types. For example, if 120 students of algebra are registered in 4 classes, the ratio of the number of students registered to the number of classes in algebra is $\frac{120}{4}$, which is equal to 30. This tells us that the average number of students in an algebra class is 30. We say that there are on the average 30 students per class. Similarly, if a plane flies 1920 kilometers in 3 hours, the ratio of the distance traveled to the time that the plane was in flight is $\frac{1920}{3} = 640$. We say that the plane was flying at the rate of 640 kilometers per hour.

Model Problems

1. Clyde Champion scored 175 points in 7 basketball games. Express, in lowest terms, the ratio of the number of points Clyde scored to the number of games Clyde played.

   Solution:

   $$\text{ratio} = \frac{175}{7} = 25 \text{ points per game} \quad Ans.$$

2. There are 5 grams of salt in 100 cc of a solution of salt and water. Express, in lowest terms, the ratio of the number of grams of salt to the number of cc in the solution.

   Solution:

   $$\text{ratio} = \frac{5}{100} = .05 \text{ g per cc} \quad Ans.$$

3. At a picnic 375 hot dogs were eaten by 125 people. Express, in lowest terms, the ratio of the number of hot dogs eaten to the number of people at the picnic.

   Solution:

   $$\text{ratio} = \frac{375}{125} = 3 \text{ hot dogs per person} \quad Ans.$$

4. A motorist paid $4.80 for 8 gallons of gasoline. Express, in lowest terms, the ratio of the cost to the number of gallons purchased.

Solution:

$$\text{ratio} = \frac{4.80}{8} = .60 \text{ dollars per gallon, or 60 cents per gallon} \quad \textit{Ans.}$$

EXERCISES

In 1–10, express the ratio in lowest terms.

1. the ratio of 36 apples to 18 people
2. the ratio of 54 cents to 6 rolls
3. the ratio of 48 patients to 6 nurses
4. the ratio of $1.50 to 3 liters
5. the ratio of 96 cents to 16 grams
6. the ratio of 13.2 pounds to 6 kilograms
7. the ratio of 4.36 yards to 4 meters
8. the ratio of 6.75 ounces to 81 cents
9. the ratio of 3.5 ounces to 100 grams
10. the ratio of 241.65 miles to 4.5 hours

11. If there are 240 tennis balls in 80 cans, how many tennis balls are there in each can?
12. If an 11-ounce can of shaving cream costs 88 cents, what is the cost of each ounce of shaving cream in the can?
13. If, in traveling 31 miles, you travel 50 kilometers, how many miles are there in each kilometer?
14. A can of beans is marked 16 ounces net weight. The can is also marked 454 grams net weight. Find, correct to the nearest gram, the number of grams in 1 ounce.
15. If the volume of a bottle is 5 deciliters and the volume of the same bottle is 500 milliliters, how many milliliters are there in one deciliter?
16. In a supermarket the regular size of Cleanright cleanser contains 14 ounces and costs 23 cents. The giant size of Cleanright cleanser, which contains 20 ounces, costs 30 cents.
    a. Find, correct to the nearest tenth of a cent, the cost per ounce for the regular can.
    b. Find, correct to the nearest tenth of a cent, the cost per ounce for the giant can.
    c. Which is the better buy?

4. Solving Verbal Problems Involving Ratios

Model Problems

1. Tom and his helper Bill agreed to do a job for $120. They also agreed to share this money in the ratio 3:1. How much money did each receive?

   Solution:

   Let $3x$ = the number of dollars Tom received.
   Then $1x$ = the number of dollars Bill received.

   The total of the two amounts is $120.

$3x + 1x = 120$	*Check*
$4x = 120$	
$x = 30$	$90 + 30 = 120$
$3x = 90$	$90:30 = 3:1$

   Answer: Tom received $90 and Bill received $30.

2. Two positive numbers have the ratio 2:3. The larger is 30 more than $\frac{1}{2}$ of the smaller. Find the numbers.

   Solution:

   Let $2x$ = the smaller number.
   Then $3x$ = the larger number.

   The larger number is 30 more than $\frac{1}{2}$ of the smaller number.

$3x = \frac{1}{2}(2x) + 30$	*Check*
$3x = x + 30$	
$3x - x = x + 30 - x$	The ratio of 30 to 45 is 30:45
$2x = 30$	or 2:3. The larger number,
$x = 15$	45, is 30 more than 15,
$2x = 30$	which is $\frac{1}{2}$ of the smaller
$3x = 45$	number.

   Answer: The numbers are 30 and 45.

EXERCISES

1. Two positive numbers have the ratio 4:3. Their sum is 70. Find the numbers.
2. Two positive numbers have the ratio 7:5. Their difference is 12. Find the numbers.
3. Mr. Gray and Mr. Charles are business partners. They agree to share the business profits in the ratio 4:3. One year the profits amounted to $35,000. How much money did each partner receive?
4. An angle whose measure is 120° is divided into three parts in the ratio 2:3:7. Find the number of degrees in each part.
5. The perimeter of a triangle is 48 centimeters. The lengths of the sides are in the ratio 3:4:5. Find the length of each side.
6. The ratio of a father's age to his son's age is $\frac{7}{2}$. If the son's age is 10 years, how old is the father?
7. The weight of dried apples to the weight of the fresh apples from which they were dried is in the ratio of 2:5. How many kilograms of fresh apples are needed to produce 98 kilograms of dried apples?
8. The ratio of Charlotte's money to Gloria's money is 7:3. If Charlotte gives Gloria $20, the two then have equal amounts. Find the original amount that each one had.
9. Two positive numbers are in the ratio 4:3. One-half of the larger exceeds $\frac{1}{3}$ of the smaller by 5. Find the numbers.
10. Two positive numbers are in the ratio 4:15. If 25 is added to the smaller and the larger is diminished by 30, the resulting numbers are equal. Find the original numbers.
11. Two positive numbers are in the ratio 3:5. If 9 is added to their sum, the result is 41. Find the numbers.
12. A chemist wishes to make $12\frac{1}{2}$ liters of an acid solution by using water and acid in the ratio 3:2. How many liters of each should he use?
13. The numerator and the denominator of a fraction are in the ratio 3:7. If 2 is added to both the numerator and the denominator, the ratio becomes 1:2. Find the original fraction.
14. Two motorboats start at the same time from the same place and travel in opposite directions. The ratio of their rates of speed is 2:3. In 3 hours, they are 120 kilometers apart. Find the rate of each boat.
15. The ratio of Sue's age to Betty's age is 4:1. Twenty years from now, Sue will be twice as old as Betty will be then. Find their present ages.

5. Proportion

Since the ratio $\frac{4}{20}$ is equal to the ratio $\frac{1}{5}$, we may write $\frac{4}{20} = \frac{1}{5}$. The equation $\frac{4}{20} = \frac{1}{5}$ is called a **proportion**. A proportion is an equation which states that two ratios are equal.

Another way of writing the proportion $\frac{4}{20} = \frac{1}{5}$ is $4:20 = 1:5$. Both these equations are read "4 is to 20 as 1 is to 5."

The proportion $\frac{a}{b} = \frac{c}{d}$ $(b \neq 0, d \neq 0)$, or $a:b = c:d$, is read "a is to b as c is to d." There are four terms in this proportion, namely, a, b, c, and d. The first and fourth terms, a and d, are called the *extremes* of the proportion. The second and third terms are called the *means*.

Observe that in the proportion $4:20 = 1:5$, the product of the two means, 20×1, is equal to the product of the two extremes, 4×5, because each product is 20.

In the proportion $\frac{a}{b} = \frac{c}{d}$ we can also show that the product of the means is equal to the product of the extremes, $ad = bc$.

Since $\frac{a}{b} = \frac{c}{d}$ is an equation, we can multiply both members by the least common denominator, bd, as follows:

$$\frac{a}{b} = \frac{c}{d}$$

$$bd\left(\frac{a}{b}\right) = bd\left(\frac{c}{d}\right)$$

$$ad = bc$$

Therefore, we have shown that the following statement is always true:

In a proportion, the product of the means is equal to the product of the extremes.

It can be shown that if a sentence states that two ratios are equal and if the product of the first and fourth terms is equal to the product of the second and third terms, then the sentence is a true proportion.

It can also be shown that if a sentence states that two ratios are equal and if the product of the first and fourth terms does not equal the product of the second and third terms, then the sentence is not a true proportion.

Model Problems

1. Tell whether $\frac{4}{16} = \frac{5}{20}$ is a true proportion.

   Solution:

Method 1	*Method 2*

   Method 1

   $\frac{4}{16} = \frac{1}{4}$ and $\frac{5}{20} = \frac{1}{4}$

   Therefore, $\frac{4}{16}$ and $\frac{5}{20}$ are equal ratios and $\frac{4}{16} = \frac{5}{20}$ is a true proportion.

   Method 2

   In the equation $\frac{4}{16} = \frac{5}{20}$, the product of the second and third terms is 16×5, or 80. The product of the first and fourth terms, 4×20, is also 80. Therefore, $\frac{4}{16} = \frac{5}{20}$ is a true proportion.

   Answer: Yes

2. Solve for q in the proportion $25:q = 5:2$.

   Solution

   If $25:q = 5:2$ is a true proportion, then $5q = 25 \times 2$ (the product of the means is equal to the product of the extremes).

   $$5q = 25 \times 2$$
   $$5q = 50$$
   $$q = 10$$

   Answer: $q = 10$

   Check

   $25:q \overset{?}{=} 5:2$
   $25:10 \overset{?}{=} 5:2$
   $5:2 = 5:2$ (true)

3. Solve for x: $\dfrac{12}{x-2} = \dfrac{32}{x+8}$

   Solution

   $$\frac{12}{x-2} = \frac{32}{x+8}$$

   In a proportion, the product of the means is equal to the product of the extremes.

   $$32(x-2) = 12(x+8)$$
   $$32x - 64 = 12x + 96$$
   $$32x - 12x = 96 + 64$$
   $$20x = 160$$
   $$x = 8$$

   Answer: $x = 8$

   Check

   $$\frac{12}{x-2} = \frac{32}{x+8}$$
   $$\frac{12}{8-2} \overset{?}{=} \frac{32}{8+8}$$
   $$\frac{12}{6} \overset{?}{=} \frac{32}{16}$$
   $$2 = 2 \quad \text{(true)}$$

   Note that the proportion $\dfrac{12}{x-2} = \dfrac{32}{x+8}$ may also be written $12:x-2 = 32:x+8$.

EXERCISES

In 1–10, state whether the given ratios may form a true proportion.

1. $\frac{2}{3}, \frac{10}{5}$ 2. $\frac{3}{4}, \frac{30}{40}$ 3. $\frac{4}{5}, \frac{16}{25}$ 4. $\frac{2}{5}, \frac{5}{2}$ 5. $\frac{14}{18}, \frac{28}{36}$ 6. $\frac{12}{15}, \frac{36}{30}$

7. $\frac{5x}{9x}, \frac{10}{18}$ 8. $\frac{y}{3y}, \frac{4}{16}$ 9. $\frac{3x}{y}, \frac{6x}{2y}$ 10. $\frac{5a}{6b}, \frac{10b}{12a}$

In 11–14, use the given numbers to form a true proportion.

11. $1, 3, 30, 10$ 12. $2, 3, 18, 12$ 13. $15, 40, 8, 3$ 14. $24, 36, 9, 6$

In 15–22, find the number which can replace the question mark and make the result a true proportion.

15. $\frac{1}{2} = \frac{?}{8}$ 16. $\frac{3}{5} = \frac{18}{?}$ 17. $1:4 = 6:?$ 18. $4:6 = ?:42$

19. $\frac{4}{?} = \frac{12}{60}$ 20. $\frac{?}{9} = \frac{35}{63}$ 21. $?:60 = 6:10$ 22. $16:? = 12:9$

In 23–34, solve the equation.

23. $\frac{5}{4} = \frac{x}{12}$ 24. $\frac{90}{81} = \frac{10}{3x}$ 25. $\frac{5}{15} = \frac{x}{x+8}$

26. $\frac{x+10}{x} = \frac{18}{12}$ 27. $\frac{x}{12-x} = \frac{10}{30}$ 28. $5:x = 9:27$

29. $8:2x = 15:60$ 30. $\frac{5}{x+2} = \frac{4}{x}$ 31. $\frac{2x-1}{21} = \frac{3x-7}{15}$

32. $\frac{x}{x+4} = \frac{x+1}{x+6}$ 33. $\frac{x+1}{x-2} = \frac{x+3}{x-1}$ 34. $\frac{3x+1}{5x-7} = \frac{3x+6}{5x-3}$

In 35–37, solve for x in terms of the other variables.

35. $a:b = c:x$ 36. $2r:s = x:t$ 37. $2x:m = 4r:s$

6. Using Proportions to Convert Units of Measure

Proportions can be used to convert units of measure from one system to another, for example, to convert miles to kilometers, to convert grams to ounces, and so on. To convert units of measure, we will make use of the information contained in Tables I and II (see pages 415–416).

Let us convert 310 miles to kilometers. From Table II on page 416, we know that 1 kilometer = .62 mile. If we let x = the number of kilometers in 310 miles, we can write the following proportion which compares kilometers to miles: x kilometers is to 310 miles as 1 kilometer is to .62 mile. Hence, $\dfrac{x}{310} = \dfrac{1}{.62}$.

Since, in a proportion, the product of the means is equal to the product of the extremes,

$$.62x = (310)\,(1)$$
$$.62x = 310$$
$$x = \frac{310}{.62}$$
$$x = 500$$

Therefore, 310 miles is equivalent to 500 kilometers.

Note that the answer, 500 kilometers, is an approximate result, because .62 mile was an approximate measure. When we perform the computations in converting units, we will round approximate answers to three significant figures.

Model Problems

1. Convert 9 meters to feet.

   Solution:

   Let x = the number of feet in 9 meters.
   1 foot = .3 meter. See Table II on page 416. x feet is to 9 meters as 1 foot is to .3 meter.

   $$\frac{x}{9} = \frac{1}{.3}$$

   $.3x = (9)\,(1)$ [In a proportion, the product of the means is equal to the product of the extremes.]

   $.3x = 9$; hence, $x = \dfrac{9}{.3}$ or $x = 30$

   Answer: 9 meters is equivalent to 30.0 feet.

Note: We can also convert 9 meters to feet by multiplying 3.28 (the number of feet in 1 meter—see Table II) by 9, giving 29.52 feet, which can be rounded to 30 feet.

2. Convert 7 liters to quarts.

Solution:

Let x = the number of quarts in 7 liters.

1 quart = .95 liter. See Table II on page 416. x quarts is to 7 liters as 1 quart is to .95 liter.

$$\frac{x}{7} = \frac{1}{.95}$$

$.95x = (7)(1)$ [In a proportion, the product of the means is equal to the product of the extremes.]

$.95x = 7$; hence, $x = \dfrac{7}{.95}$ or $x = 7.37$

Answer: 7 liters is equivalent to 7.37 quarts.

Note: We can also convert 7 liters to quarts by multiplying 1.06 (the number of quarts in 1 liter—see Table II) by 7, giving 7.42 quarts. Observe that both 7.37 quarts and 7.42 quarts can be rounded to 7.4 quarts.

3. Convert $2\frac{1}{2}$ ounces to centigrams.

Solution: First we will convert $2\frac{1}{2}$ ounces to grams. Then, we will multiply the result by 100, because each gram is equivalent to 100 centigrams.

Let x = the number of grams in $2\frac{1}{2}$, or 2.5, ounces.

1 gram = .035 ounce. See Table II on page 416. x grams is to 2.5 ounces as 1 gram is to .035 ounce.

$$\frac{x}{2.5} = \frac{1}{.035}$$

$.035x = (2.5)(1)$ [In a proportion, the product of the means is equal to the product of the extremes.]

$.035x = 2.5$

$x = \dfrac{2.5}{.035}$

$x = 71.4$

There are 71.4 grams in $2\frac{1}{2}$ ounces.

71.4 grams = (71.4)(100) centigrams

71.4 grams = 7140 centigrams

Answer: $2\frac{1}{2}$ ounces is equivalent to 7140 centigrams.

EXERCISES

1. Convert 60 miles to kilometers.
2. Convert 45 kilometers to miles.
3. Convert 12 ounces to grams.
4. Convert 325 grams to ounces.
5. Convert 4 pounds to kilograms.
6. 7 kilograms equal how many pounds?
7. 5 quarts equal how many liters?
8. $5\frac{1}{2}$ ounces equal how many grams?
9. 17.4 feet equal how many meters?
10. 12 inches equal how many centimeters?
11. 3 quarts equal how many centiliters?
12. 8.4 ounces equal how many centigrams?
13. 750 grams equal how many ounces?
14. $30\frac{1}{2}$ kilometers equal how many miles?
15. 6.8 liters equal how many quarts?
16. 7.4 meters equal how many feet?
17. $4\frac{1}{2}$ kilograms equal how many pounds?
18. 6.5 feet equal how many centimeters?
19. $3\frac{1}{2}$ miles equal how many kilometers?
20. Convert 12.6 ounces to (a) grams, (b) centigrams, (c) kilograms.

Table I. The Metric System

Measures of Length

1 millimeter (mm) = .001 meter (m) or $\frac{1}{1000}$ meter (m)
1 centimeter (cm) = .01 meter (m) or $\frac{1}{100}$ meter (m)
1 decimeter (dm) = .1 meter (m) or $\frac{1}{10}$ meter (m)
1 dekameter (dkm) = 10 meters (m)
1 hectometer (hm) = 100 meters (m)
1 kilometer (km) = 1000 meters (m)

Measures of Weight or Mass

1 milligram (mg) = .001 gram (g) or $\frac{1}{1000}$ gram (g)
1 centigram (cg) = .01 gram (g) or $\frac{1}{100}$ gram (g)
1 decigram (dg) = .1 gram (g) or $\frac{1}{10}$ gram (g)
1 dekagram (dkg) = 10 grams (g)
1 hectogram (hg) = 100 grams (g)
1 kilogram (kg) = 1000 grams (g)

Measures of Volume

1 milliliter (ml) = .001 liter (l) or $\frac{1}{1000}$ liter (l)
1 centiliter (cl) = .01 liter (l) or $\frac{1}{100}$ liter (l)
1 deciliter (dl) = .1 liter (l) or $\frac{1}{10}$ liter (l)
1 dekaliter (dkl) = 10 liters (l)
1 hectoliter (hl) = 100 liters (l)
1 kiloliter (kl) = 1000 liters (l)

Table II. Metric–United States Equivalents

1 meter = 39.37 inches
1 meter = 3.28 feet
1 meter = 1.09 yards
1 centimeter = .39 inch
1 millimeter = .04 inch
1 kilometer = .62 mile
1 gram = .035 ounce
1 kilogram = 2.2 pounds
1 liter = 1.06 quarts

1 inch = 25.4 millimeters
1 foot = .3 meter
1 yard = .91 meter
1 mile = 1.61 kilometers
1 quart = .95 liter
1 ounce = 28.35 grams
1 pound = .45 kilogram

7. Solving Verbal Problems by Using Proportions

Model Problems

1. A man received $40 for working 8 hours. How much would he receive for working 14 hours at the same rate of pay?

   Solution: The ratio of the corresponding number of hours worked equals the ratio of the number of dollars earned.

   $$\frac{\text{number of hours worked on 1st job}}{\text{number of hours worked on 2d job}} = \frac{\text{number of dollars earned on 1st job}}{\text{number of dollars earned on 2d job}}$$

   Let d = the number of dollars he would receive.

   $$\frac{8}{14} = \frac{40}{d}$$

   In a proportion, the product of the means is equal to the product of the extremes.

   $$8d = 14 \times 40$$
   $$8d = 560$$
   $$d = 70$$

   Answer: $70

   Check

   $$\frac{8}{14} \overset{?}{=} \frac{40}{70}$$

   $$\frac{4}{7} = \frac{4}{7} \quad \text{(true)}$$

2. A board 12 feet long is cut into two pieces whose lengths are in the ratio 3:1. Find the length of each piece.

Solution:

Let x = the length of the longer piece.
Then $12 - x$ = the length of the shorter piece.

Then $\dfrac{x}{12 - x}$ = the ratio of the lengths of the two pieces.

The lengths of the two pieces are in the ratio 3:1.

$$\frac{x}{12 - x} = \frac{3}{1}$$

In a proportion, the product of the means is equal to the product of the extremes.

Check
$9 + 3 = 12$
$9:3 \overset{?}{=} 3:1$
$3:1 = 3:1$ (true)

$$1(x) = 3(12 - x)$$
$$x = 36 - 3x$$
$$x + 3x = 36 - 3x + 3x$$
$$4x = 36$$
$$x = 9$$
$$12 - x = 3$$

Answer: The lengths of the pieces are 9 feet and 3 feet.

Note: Previously, we have learned the following solution for the second model problem:

Let $3x$ = the length of the longer piece.
Then $1x$ = the length of the shorter piece.

The sum of the lengths of the two pieces is 12 feet.

$$3x + 1x = 12$$
$$4x = 12$$
$$x = 3$$
$$3x = 9$$

EXERCISES

Solve each of the following problems algebraically.

1. If 3 tickets to a show cost $13.20, find the cost of 7 tickets.
2. How much would you pay for 5 apples at the rate of $1.80 a dozen?
3. A 40-acre field yields 1200 bushels of wheat. At the same rate, what will a 75-acre field yield?
4. The weight of 20 meters of copper wire is .9 kilograms. Find the weight of 170 meters of the same wire.

5. A recipe calls for $1\frac{1}{2}$ cups of sugar for a 3-pound cake. How many cups of sugar should be used for a 5-pound cake?

6. The scale on a blueprint is 1 centimeter = 3 meters. If on the blueprint the length of a room is $2\frac{1}{2}$ centimeters, what is the actual length of the room?

7. A picture $3\frac{1}{4}$ inches long and $2\frac{1}{8}$ inches wide is to be enlarged so that its length will become $6\frac{1}{2}$ inches. What will be the width of the enlarged picture?

8. In a certain concrete mixture, the ratio of cement to sand is 1:4. How many bags of cement would be used with 100 bags of sand?

9. A team played 144 games. The ratio of the number of games won to the number of games lost was 3:1. Find the number of games the team won.

10. A board 3 meters long is to be cut into two pieces having the ratio 5:1. Find the length of each piece.

11. If a man can buy p pounds of candy for d dollars, represent the cost of n pounds of candy.

12. If a family consumes l liters of milk in d days, represent the amount of milk consumed in h days.

8. Direct Variation

If the length, s, of a side of a square is 1 centimeter, then the perimeter, p, of the square is 4 centimeters. Also, if s is 2 centimeters, p is 8 centimeters; if s is 3 centimeters, p is 12 centimeters. These pairs of values are shown in the table at the right.

s	1	2	3
p	4	8	12

In the table, observe that as s varies, p also varies. Let us find the value of the ratio $\dfrac{p}{s}$ for each pair of values in the table. If we represent the three values of s by s_1, s_2, and s_3 and the corresponding values of p by p_1, p_2, and p_3, then:

$$\frac{p_1}{s_1} = \frac{4}{1} \qquad\qquad \frac{p_2}{s_2} = \frac{8}{2} = \frac{4}{1} \qquad\qquad \frac{p_3}{s_3} = \frac{12}{3} = \frac{4}{1}.$$

Observe that the ratio $\dfrac{p}{s}$ is always the same, $\dfrac{4}{1}$. We say that the ratio $\dfrac{p}{s}$ is a *constant*.

Thus, in each case, $\dfrac{p}{s} = 4$. This result may be writ-

ten as $p = 4s$, which is the formula for the perimeter of a square. Such a relation is called a ***direct variation***.

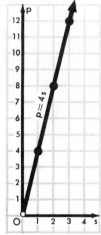

We know that the graph of $p = 4s$ is a straight line which passes through the origin $(0, 0)$ when both s and p are members of {signed numbers}. However, when s and p represent the length of a side and the perimeter of a square respectively, the graph of $p = 4s$ is a half-line, as is shown at the right, because both s and p must be positive numbers.

When two variables are related so that the ratio of the value of one variable to the corresponding value of the other variable is constant, we say that one variable ***varies directly*** as the other. We also say that one variable is ***directly proportional*** to the other. The constant ratio is called the ***constant of variation***. In the preceding example, the constant of variation is 4 $\left(\text{because } \dfrac{p}{s} = 4 \right)$.

In general, if y varies directly as x, the following ***principles of direct variation*** hold true:

Principle 1. The ratio $y:x$ is constant. $\dfrac{y}{x} = k$ or $y = kx$, where k ($k \neq 0$) is the constant of variation.

Principle 2. The ratio of y_1 and x_1, any pair of values for the variables, is equal to the ratio of y_2, and x_2, any other pair of values for the variables. Thus, $\dfrac{y_1}{x_1} = \dfrac{y_2}{x_2}$.

Principle 3. If x is *multiplied* by a number, y is *multiplied* by the same number. Thus, if x is multiplied by 2 (doubled), then y is also multiplied by 2 (doubled).

Principle 4. If x is *divided* by a nonzero number, y is *divided* by the same number. Thus, if x is divided by 2 (halved), y is also divided by 2 (halved).

Principle 5. The graph of $y = kx$ is a straight line whose slope is k and which passes through the origin.

Model Problems

1. Express the following relation as a formula: The salary a man earns, S, varies directly as the number of hours, n, which he works.

   Solution: The ratio of S to n must be constant. Let $k =$ the constant.

   Answer: $\dfrac{S}{n} = k$, or $S = kn$

2. If d varies directly as t and if $d = 60$ when $t = 2$, find the value of d when $t = 7$.

   Solution:

Method 1	*Method 2*
Since d varies directly as t,	Let $x =$ the unknown value of d.
$\qquad d = kt$	Since d varies directly as t,
If $d = 60$ when $t = 2$,	
$\qquad 60 = 2k$	$\dfrac{d_1}{t_1} = \dfrac{d_2}{t_2}$
$\qquad 30 = k$	$\dfrac{60}{2} = \dfrac{x}{7}$
In $d = kt$, replace k by 30.	$2x = 420$
Hence, $d = 30t$.	$x = 210$
If $t = 7$, then	
$\qquad d = 30(7)$	*Check*
$\qquad d = 210$	$\dfrac{60}{2} \overset{?}{=} \dfrac{210}{7}$
Answer: $d = 210$	$30 = 30$ (true)

Method 2 tables:

d	60	x
t	2	7

EXERCISES

In 1–6, tell whether one variable varies directly as the other. If it does, express the relation between the variables by means of a formula.

1.

p	3	6	9
s	1	2	3

2.

n	3	4	5
c	6	8	10

3.

x	4	5	6
y	6	8	10

4.

t	1	2	3
d	20	40	60

5.

x	2	3	4
y	-6	-9	-12

6.

x	1	2	3
y	1	4	9

In 7-9, one variable varies directly as the other. Find the missing numbers and write the formula which relates the variables.

7.

h	1	2	?
A	5	?	25

8.

h	4	8	?
S	6	?	15

9.

L	2	8	?
W	1	?	7

In 10-12, write the relation as a formula using k as the constant of variation.

10. The perimeter, P, of an equilateral triangle varies directly as the length, s, of a side.
11. The circumference, C, of a circle varies directly as the radius, r.
12. The resistance, R, of a copper wire varies directly as its length, l.

In 13-15, write the relation as a formula. Use k as the constant of variation.

13. The length, s, of the shadow of an object at a given time varies directly as the height, h, of the object.
14. If a car travels at a constant rate of speed, the distance covered, d, varies directly as the time, t, that it travels.
15. The income, I, of a man who works at a fixed hourly rate of pay is directly proportional to the number, n, of hours that he works.
16. $A = 12L$ is a formula for the area of any rectangle whose width is 12.

   a. Describe how A and L vary.
   b. How will the area of a rectangle whose length is 8 centimeters compare with the area of a rectangle whose length is 4 centimeters?
   c. If L is tripled, what change takes place in A?

In 17-20, state whether the relation between the variables is a direct variation. Give a reason for your answer.

17. $R + T = 80$ 18. $15T = D$ 19. $\dfrac{e}{i} = 20$ 20. $bh = 36$

21. The weight, w, of a pipe varies directly as its length, l.

   a. Write a formula relating w and l.
   b. If $w = 6$ when $l = 8$, find w when $l = 20$.
   c. If $w = 5$ when $l = 10$, find l when $w = 12.5$.

22. The circumference, c, of a circle varies directly as the length, d, of the diameter.

   a. Write a formula relating c and d.
   b. If $c = 44$ when $d = 14$, find c when $d = 21$.
   c. If $c = 6.28$ when $d = 2$, find d when $c = 62.8$.

23. Y varies directly as x. If $Y = 35$ when $x = -5$, find Y when $x = -20$.

24. A varies directly as h. $A = 48$ when $h = 4$. Find h when $A = 36$.

25. x varies directly as $y + 1$. If $y = 3$ when $x = 2$, find y when $x = 6$.

26. $R + 2$ varies directly as $2S - 3$. If $S = 4$ when $R = 3$, find S when $R = 9$.

27. The weight that can be lifted by an automobile jack varies directly as the downward force on the handle of the jack. If a force of 24 pounds will lift 2016 pounds, what weight can be lifted with a force of 36 pounds?

28. If the resistance is constant, then the voltage, E, of an electrical circuit varies directly with the amperage, I. If $E = 45$ volts when $I = 9$ amperes, find the amperage when $E = 220$ volts.

29. The force, f, required to stretch a spring varies directly as the elongation, e, of the spring. What force will be required to stretch a certain spring 6 centimeters when a force of 12 kilograms is required to stretch the spring 4 centimeters?

30. On a certain day, a sampling in a factory showed that for every 1000 couplings manufactured, 7 were defective. If 125,000 couplings were manufactured on that day, how many were defective?

31. If a train travels 360 kilometers in 4 hours, how far will it travel in 7 hours if it travels at the same rate of speed?

9. Inverse Variation

If the length, L, of a rectangle is 1 centimeter and its width, W, is 12 centimeters, its area is 12 square centimeters (cm^2). If L is 2 centimeters and W is 6 centimeters, the area is once again 12 square centimeters (cm^2). In the following table are listed some pairs of numbers, each pair representing the length and width of a rectangle whose area is 12 square centimeters (cm^2).

L	1	2	3	4	6	12
W	12	6	4	3	2	1

In the table, observe that as L varies, W also varies. Remember that L and W represent the dimensions of a rectangle whose area is 12 square centimeters (cm^2). Therefore, for each pair of numbers in the table, the product LW is always the same, 12. That is, the product LW is a constant:

$$L_1 W_1 = 1 \times 12 = 12 \quad L_2 W_2 = 2 \times 6 = 12 \quad L_3 W_3 = 3 \times 4 = 12$$
$$L_4 W_4 = 4 \times 3 = 12 \quad L_5 W_5 = 6 \times 2 = 12 \quad L_6 W_6 = 12 \times 1 = 12$$

Thus, in each case, $LW = 12$. Such a relation is called an **inverse variation.** The graph of $LW = 12$ is a curve, not a straight line, as shown on the right.

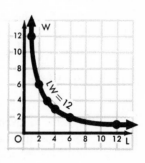

When two variables are related so that the product of the value of one variable and the corresponding value of the other variable is constant, we say that one variable **varies inversely** as the other. We also say that one variable is **inversely proportional** to the other. The constant product is called the **constant of variation.**

In the preceding table, which lists pairs of numbers that satisfy the equation $LW = 12$, notice that $\dfrac{L_1}{W_1}$ does not equal $\dfrac{L_2}{W_2}$. $\dfrac{L_1}{W_1}$ equals $\dfrac{1}{12}$, but $\dfrac{L_2}{W_2}$ equals $\dfrac{2}{6}$. However, notice that $\dfrac{L_1}{L_2}$, or $\dfrac{1}{2}$, does equal $\dfrac{W_2}{W_1}$, or $\dfrac{6}{12}$. That is, $\dfrac{L_1}{L_2} = \dfrac{W_2}{W_1}$.

In general, if y varies inversely as x, the following **principles of inverse variation** hold true:

Principle 1. The product of y and x is constant. $xy = k \ (k \neq 0)$, or $y = \dfrac{k}{x} \ (x \neq 0)$, where k is the constant of variation. We know that $y = \dfrac{k}{x}$ may be written $y = k \left(\dfrac{1}{x}\right)$. Therefore, when y varies inversely as x, we can also say that y varies directly as the reciprocal of x, or as the (multiplicative) inverse of x.

Principle 2. The product of x_1 and y_1, any pair of values for the variables, is equal to the product of x_2 and y_2, any other pair of values for the variables. Thus, $x_1 y_1 = x_2 y_2$. This relation may also be written as the proportion $\dfrac{x_1}{x_2} = \dfrac{y_2}{y_1}$.

Principle 3. If x is *multiplied* by a nonzero number, y is *divided* by the same number. Thus, if x is multiplied by 2, then y is divided by 2. (We can also say that y is multiplied by the reciprocal of 2, or $\frac{1}{2}$.)

Principle 4. If x is *divided* by a nonzero number, y is *multiplied* by the same number. Thus, if x is divided by 2, then y is multiplied by 2. (We can also say that y is divided by the reciprocal of 2, or $\frac{1}{2}$.)

Principle 5. The graph of $xy = k$ is a curve, not a straight line, since $xy = k$ is not a first-degree (linear) equation.

Model Problems

1. Express the following relation as a formula: The number, n, of articles of equal cost that can be bought with a fixed sum of money varies inversely as the cost of each article, c.

   Solution: The product of n and c must be constant. Let $k =$ the constant.

   Answer: $nc = k$

2. If y varies inversely as x and if $y = 5$ when $x = 8$, find y when $x = 4$.

   Solution:

Method 1	*Method* 2

   Method 1

   Since y varies inversely as x,
   $$xy = k$$
   If $y = 5$ when $x = 8$,
   $$(8)(5) = k$$
   $$40 = k$$
   Hence, $xy = 40$.
   If $x = 4$, then
   $$4y = 40$$
   $$y = 10$$

   Answer: $y = 10$

   Method 2

   Let $y_2 =$ the unknown value of y.
   Since y varies inversely as x,

   $$\frac{x_1}{x_2} = \frac{y_2}{y_1}$$

x	8	4
y	5	y_2

   $$\frac{8}{4} = \frac{y_2}{5}$$
   $$4y_2 = 40$$
   $$y_2 = 10$$

   Check
   $$8 \times 5 \overset{?}{=} 4 \times 10$$
   $$40 = 40 \quad \text{(true)}$$

EXERCISES

In 1–6, tell whether one variable varies inversely as the other. If it does, express the relation between the variables by means of a formula.

1.

n	2	4	6
c	18	9	6

2.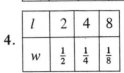

R	10	20	40
T	4	2	1

3.

x	1	2	3
y	8	7	6

4.

l	2	4	8
w	$\frac{1}{2}$	$\frac{1}{4}$	$\frac{1}{8}$

5.

x	3	6	9
y	-12	-6	-4

6.

C	12	24	36
D	6	3	2

In 7–9, one variable varies inversely as the other. Find the missing numbers and write the formula which relates the variables.

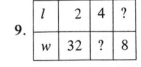

7.

w	2	?	6
d	12	8	?

8.

R	2	6	?
T	72	?	12

9.

l	2	4	?
w	32	?	8

In 10–13, write the relation as a formula using k as the constant of variation.

10. If the area of a rectangle is constant, the width, w, varies inversely as the length, l.
11. The time, t, required to travel a fixed distance varies inversely as the rate, r, of motion.
12. When a gas is kept at a constant temperature, its volume, V, varies inversely as the pressure, P.
13. The number, h, of hours required to complete a certain job varies inversely as the number, n, of persons doing the work, if all persons work at the same rate.
14. $RT = 400$ is the formula showing the relation between rate and time in traveling a distance of 400 kilometers.

   a. How do T and R vary?
   b. How will the time required to travel 400 kilometers when the rate is 100 kilometers per hour compare with the time required when the rate is 50 kilometers per hour?
   c. If the rate is doubled, what change takes place in the time?

15. $LW = 144$ is the formula showing the relation between the length and width of a rectangle whose area is 144 square meters.

   a. Describe how L and W vary.
   b. How will the length of a rectangle whose width is 6 compare with the length of a rectangle whose width is 12?
   c. If L is tripled, what change takes place in W?

In 16–19, state whether the relation between the variables is an inverse variation. Give a reason for your answer.

16. $N - C = 40$ 17. $NC = 40$ 18. $t = \dfrac{60}{r}$ 19. $h = 60b$

20. The number, d, of days necessary to finish a job varies inversely as the number, n, of men working, if all men are working at the same rate.

   a. Write a formula relating d and n.
   b. If $d = 2$ when $n = 12$, find d when $n = 6$.
   c. If $d = 4$ when $n = 9$, find n when $d = 3$.

21. The number, n, of times a wheel must turn to cover a given distance varies inversely as the radius, r, of the wheel.

   a. Write a formula relating n and r.
   b. If $n = 10$ when $r = 14$, find n when $r = 7$.
   c. If $n = 40$ when $r = 100$, find r when $n = 10$.

22. If x varies inversely as y and if $x = 8$ when $y = 9$, find x when $y = 18$.

23. If n varies inversely as c and if $n = 50$ when $c = 4$, find n when $c = 40$.

24. If y is inversely proportional to z and if $y = 6$ when $z = -4$, find y when $z = -3$.

25. If P varies inversely as r and if $P = 1000$ when $r = .06$, find r when $P = 3000$.

26. If x varies inversely as $y + 5$ and if $y = 1$ when $x = 2$, find y when $x = 1$.

27. If $M + 1$ varies inversely as $2N - 1$ and if $N = 13$ when $M = 3$, find N when $M = 24$.

28. Ten printing presses, all alike, can do a job in 3 hours. How many hours would it take 6 of these printing presses to do the same job?

Chapter 16

The Real Numbers

1. The Set of Rational Numbers

The numbers with which you are familiar consist of positive and negative integers, fractions, and zero. Examples of these numbers are 5, -3, $\frac{7}{4}$, $\frac{-5}{4}$, and 0. Each of these numbers can be expressed in the form $y = \frac{a}{b}$ where a and b are integers and $b \neq 0$. $\left(\text{Remember that 5 may be expressed as } \frac{5}{1}, -3 \text{ as } \frac{-3}{1}, \text{ and 0 as } \frac{0}{1}.\right)$ Numbers which can be expressed in this form are called *rational numbers*.

PROPERTIES OF THE SET OF RATIONAL NUMBERS

The set of rational numbers has all the addition and multiplication properties of the set of integers. This set also has additional properties.

Property 1. The set of rational numbers is closed under division by nonzero rational numbers as well as under addition, multiplication, and subtraction. When we divide one rational number by another nonzero rational number, we always get a unique rational number as the result. For example, -3 divided by 2 is $\frac{-3}{2}$; $\frac{5}{2}$ divided by $\frac{-4}{3}$ is $\frac{15}{-8}$ or $\frac{-15}{8}$.

Property 2. For every nonzero rational number, there is a unique corresponding number such that the product of these numbers is 1, the identity element of multiplication. For example, for the given number $\frac{2}{3}$, there is the unique corresponding number $\frac{3}{2}$ such that $\frac{2}{3} \times \frac{3}{2} = 1$.

Recall that the number $\frac{3}{2}$ is called the reciprocal, or multiplicative inverse, of $\frac{2}{3}$.

The set of rational numbers shares the following two properties with the set of integers.

Property 3. The set of rational numbers can be associated with points on a number line.

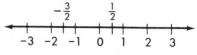

Property 4. The set of rational numbers is an ordered set. Given any two unequal rational numbers, we can tell which is the greater of the numbers. Study the following model problems to see how different methods may be used to order rational numbers.

Model Problems

1. Which is the greater of the numbers $\frac{1}{2}$ and -1?

   How to Proceed: Graph the numbers on a number line. Then determine which number is to the right. The number to the right is the greater number.

   Solution:

   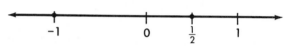

   We see that the number $\frac{1}{2}$ is to the right of the number -1.

   Answer: $\frac{1}{2} > -1$

2. In each part, determine which is the greater of the numbers:

   a. $\dfrac{5}{3}$ and $\dfrac{-5}{3}$ b. $\dfrac{1}{2}$ and $\dfrac{1}{3}$

   How to Proceed: Express the numbers as fractions which have the same positive denominator. Then compare the numerators of the resulting fractions.

   Solution:

   a. $\dfrac{5}{3} > \dfrac{-5}{3}$ because $5 > -5$. $\dfrac{5}{3} > \dfrac{-5}{3}$ *Ans.*

   b. $\dfrac{1}{2} = \dfrac{3}{6}$, and $\dfrac{1}{3} = \dfrac{2}{6}$. Since $\dfrac{3}{6} > \dfrac{2}{6}$, then $\dfrac{1}{2} > \dfrac{1}{3}$. $\dfrac{1}{2} > \dfrac{1}{3}$ *Ans.*

3. Which is the greater of the numbers $\frac{7}{9}$ and $\frac{8}{11}$?

   How to Proceed: Express the numbers as decimals and then compare the decimals. [See pages 429 and 430 for examples of expressing rational numbers as decimals.]

   Solution: By performing the indicated divisions:

   $\frac{7}{9} = .7777\ldots$ and $\frac{8}{11} = .7272\ldots$.
   Since $.7777\ldots > .7272\ldots$, then $\frac{7}{9} > \frac{8}{11}$. $\frac{7}{9} > \frac{8}{11}$ *Ans.*

The next property of the set of rational numbers is not shared by the set of integers.

Property 5. The set of rational numbers is everywhere dense. That is, given any two unequal rational numbers, it is always possible to find a rational number between them. The number midway between them, which is their average, is such a rational number.

Model Problem

Find a rational number between $\frac{1}{4}$ and $\frac{3}{4}$.

How to Proceed	Solution
1. Find the difference between $\frac{3}{4}$ and $\frac{1}{4}$.	$\frac{3}{4} - \frac{1}{4} = \frac{2}{4}$
2. Find half of the difference.	$\frac{1}{2} \cdot \frac{2}{4} = \frac{1}{4}$
3. Add the result to the smaller number.	$\frac{1}{4} + \frac{1}{4} = \frac{2}{4} = \frac{1}{2}$

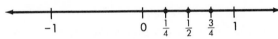

Answer: $\frac{1}{2}$ is a rational number between $\frac{1}{4}$ and $\frac{3}{4}$.

Note: We can also find a number midway between $\frac{1}{4}$ and $\frac{3}{4}$ by finding their average: $(\frac{1}{4} + \frac{3}{4}) \div 2 = (1) \div 2 = \frac{1}{2}$.

EXPRESSING A RATIONAL NUMBER AS A DECIMAL

To express as a decimal a rational number named as a fraction, we simply perform the indicated division.

Model Problem

Express as a decimal: a. $\frac{1}{2}$ b. $\frac{3}{4}$ c. $\frac{1}{16}$

Solution:

a. $\frac{1}{2} = 2\overline{)1.000000}$ $.500000$

b. $\frac{3}{4} = 4\overline{)3.000000}$ $.750000$

c. $\frac{1}{16} = 16\overline{)1.000000}$ $.062500$

In each of the examples $\frac{1}{2}$, $\frac{3}{4}$, and $\frac{1}{16}$, when we perform the division, we reach a point after which we continually obtain only zeros in the quotient. Decimals which result from such divisions, for example, .5, .75, and .0625, are called *terminating decimals*.

Not all rational numbers can be expressed as terminating decimals.

Model Problem

Express as a decimal: a. $\frac{1}{3}$ b. $\frac{2}{11}$ c. $\frac{1}{6}$

Solution:

a. $\frac{1}{3} = 3\overline{)1.000000}$ $.333333\ldots$

b. $\frac{2}{11} = 11\overline{)2.000000}$ $.181818\ldots$

c. $\frac{1}{6} = 6\overline{)1.000000}$ $.166666\ldots$

In each of the examples, $\frac{1}{3}$, $\frac{2}{11}$, and $\frac{1}{6}$, when we perform the division, we find, in the quotient, that the same group of digits is continually repeated in the same order. Decimals which keep repeating endlessly, such as $.333333\ldots$, $.181818\ldots$, and $.166666\ldots$, are known as *repeating decimals*, or *periodic decimals*.

A repeating decimal may be written in an abbreviated form by placing a bar ($^-$) over the group of digits that is to be continually repeated. For example:

$.333333\ldots = .\overline{3}$ $.181818\ldots = .\overline{18}$ $.166666\ldots = .1\overline{6}$

The six examples in the two preceding model problems illustrate the truth of the following statement:

Every rational number can be expressed as either a terminating decimal or a repeating decimal.

Note: The equalities $.5 = .5\overline{0}$ and $.75 = .75\overline{0}$ illustrate the fact that every terminating decimal can be expressed as a repeating decimal which, after a point, repeats with all zeros. Therefore, we may say:

Every rational number can be expressed as a repeating decimal.

Since every terminating decimal can be expressed as a repeating decimal, we will henceforth regard terminating decimals as repeating decimals.

EXPRESSING A DECIMAL AS A RATIONAL NUMBER

When we studied arithmetic, we learned how to express a terminating decimal as a rational number.

Model Problem

Express as a rational number: a. .3   b. .37   c. .139   d. .0777

Solution:

a. $.3 = \dfrac{3}{10}$ b. $.37 = \dfrac{37}{100}$ c. $.139 = \dfrac{139}{1000}$ d. $.0777 = \dfrac{777}{10,000}$

Study the following model problem to learn how to express any repeating decimal as a rational number.

Model Problem _____

Express as a rational number: a. .6666 ...   b. .4141 ...   c. .8̄3̄

Solution:

a. Let $N = .6666 \ldots$ [A]
   Multiply both members
   of [A] by 10.
   Then $10N = 6.6666 \ldots$ [B]
   Subtract [A] from [B].
   $10N = 6.6666 \ldots$ [B]
   $N = .6666 \ldots$ [A]
   ———————————
   $9N = 6$
   $N = \frac{6}{9} = \frac{2}{3}$

   Answer: $.6666 \ldots = \frac{2}{3}$

b. Let $N = .4141 \ldots$ [A]
   Multiply both members
   of [A] by 100.
   Then $100N = 41.4141 \ldots$ [B]
   Subtract [A] from [B].
   $100N = 41.4141 \ldots$ [B]
   $N = .4141 \ldots$ [A]
   ———————————
   $99N = 41$
   $N = \frac{41}{99}$

   Answer: $.4141 \ldots = \frac{41}{99}$

c. $.8\overline{3} = .8333 \ldots$
   Let $N = .8333 \ldots$ [A]
   Multiply both members of [A] by 10.
   Then $10N = 8.3333 \ldots$ [B]
   Subtract [A] from [B].
   $10N = 8.3333 \ldots$ [B]
   $N = .8333 \ldots$ [A]
   ———————————
   $9N = 7.5$

   $$N = \frac{7.5}{9} = \frac{75}{90} = \frac{5}{6}$$

   $$.8333 \ldots = \frac{5}{6}$$

   Answer: $.8\overline{3} = \frac{5}{6}$

The seven examples in the two preceding model problems illustrate the truth of the following statement:

Every repeating decimal represents a rational number.

EXERCISES

In 1–12, state which of the given numbers is the greater.

1. $\dfrac{5}{2}, \dfrac{7}{2}$ 2. $\dfrac{-9}{3}, \dfrac{-11}{3}$ 3. $\dfrac{5}{6}, -\dfrac{13}{6}$ 4. $-\dfrac{1}{5}, -5$

5. $\dfrac{5}{2}, \dfrac{7}{4}$ 6. $\dfrac{-10}{3}, \dfrac{-13}{6}$ 7. $\dfrac{13}{6}, \dfrac{15}{10}$ 8. $\dfrac{-5}{8}, \dfrac{-5}{12}$

9. $1.4, 1\frac{3}{5}$ 10. $-3.4, -3\frac{1}{3}$ 11. $.06, \dfrac{1}{6}$ 12. $\dfrac{-15}{11}, \dfrac{-11}{15}$

In 13–22, find a rational number midway between the given numbers.

13. $5, 6$ 14. $-4, -3$ 15. $-1, 0$ 16. $\frac{1}{4}, \frac{1}{2}$ 17. $\frac{1}{2}, \frac{7}{8}$

18. $\dfrac{-3}{4}, \dfrac{-2}{3}$ 19. $-2.1, -2.2$ 20. $2\frac{1}{2}, 2\frac{5}{8}$ 21. $-1\frac{1}{3}, -1\frac{1}{4}$ 22. $3.05, 3\frac{1}{10}$

In 23–32, write the rational number as a repeating decimal.

23. $\frac{5}{8}$ 24. $\frac{9}{4}$ 25. $-5\frac{1}{2}$ 26. $\frac{13}{8}$ 27. $-\frac{7}{12}$

28. $\frac{5}{3}$ 29. $\frac{7}{9}$ 30. $\dfrac{-7}{6}$ 31. $\frac{35}{99}$ 32. $\frac{11}{6}$

In 33–42, express the decimal as a fraction.

33. $.5$ 34. $.555\ldots$ 35. $-.\overline{2}$ 36. $.125\overline{0}$ 37. $.2525\ldots$
38. $.0\overline{7}$ 39. $3.666\ldots$ 40. $.\overline{579}$ 41. $1.5666\ldots$ 42. $-2.7\overline{23}$

2. The Set of Irrational Numbers

There are infinitely many decimals which are nonrepeating. An example of such a decimal is:

$$.03003000300003\ldots$$

Observe that, in this numeral, only the digits 0 and 3 appear. First we have a 3 preceded by one 0, then a 3 preceded by two 0's, then a 3 preceded by three 0's, and so on. Since it can be shown that this numeral does not represent a repeating decimal, it cannot represent a rational number.

A number represented by a nonrepeating (and hence nonterminating) decimal is called an *irrational number*. An irrational number cannot be expressed in the form $\dfrac{a}{b}$ where a and b are integers ($b \neq 0$).

Irrational numbers may be positive or negative. For example, $.030030003\ldots$ represents a positive irrational number; $-.030030003$ $\ldots$ represents a negative irrational number.

The set of irrational numbers is not closed under addition. For example, the numbers $a = .030030003\ldots$ and $-a = -.030030003\ldots$ are both irrational but their sum, $a + (-a) = 0$, is rational.

Also, the set of irrational numbers is not closed under multiplication because it can be shown that the reciprocal of an irrational number is irrational; and the product of a number and its reciprocal is 1, which is rational.

There are infinitely many irrational numbers. Among them is the number $\pi = 3.14159\ldots$; also among them is the number which represents the length of a diagonal of a square whose side is 1, a number which, we will later learn, is symbolized by $\sqrt{2}$.

It is interesting to note that the sum (also the difference) of a rational number and an irrational number is an irrational number. For example, $10 + \pi$ is an irrational number; also, $10 - \pi$ is an irrational number.

EXERCISES

In 1–3, tell how the numeral is formed. Then write the next five digits.

1. .272272227 ...   2. .656556555 ...   3. .95969798 ...
4. Write two numerals which represent irrational numbers.

In 5–12, tell whether the number is rational or irrational.

5. .36   6. .363636 ...   7. .363363336 ...   8. $-.\overline{945}$
9. $.8\overline{3}$ 10. .989889888 ...   11. .16171819 ...   12. 5.08

In 13–16: (a) Find a rational number between the given numbers. (b) Find an irrational number between the two numbers.

13. .7777 ... and .868686 ...
14. .151551555 ... and .161661666 ...
15. 3.6464 ... and $3.\overline{125}$
16. 2.343343334 ... and 2.414114111 ...

3. The Set of Real Numbers

The set of all rational numbers and all irrational numbers, taken together, is called the set of **real numbers**.

The union of the set of all rational numbers and the set of all irrational numbers is called the **set of real numbers**.

{real numbers} = {rational numbers} $\cup$ {irrational numbers}

PROPERTIES OF REAL NUMBERS

The following properties are assumed for the set of real numbers under the operations of addition and multiplication. They are used in operations with real numbers.

In the following eleven statements, a, b, and c represent any numbers which are members of the set of real numbers.

Property	*Symbolization*
1. Addition is closed.	1. $a + b = c$ (c is a unique number.)
2. Addition is commutative.	2. $a + b = b + a$
3. Addition is associative.	3. $(a + b) + c = a + (b + c)$
4. Zero is the additive identity.	4. $a + 0 = a$ and $0 + a = a$
5. Every number a has an additive inverse $-a$.	5. $a + (-a) = 0$
6. Multiplication is closed.	6. $ab = c$ (c is a unique number.)
7. Multiplication is commutative.	7. $ab = ba$
8. Multiplication is associative.	8. $(ab)c = a(bc)$
9. The number 1 is the multiplicative identity.	9. $a \times 1 = a$ and $1 \times a = a$
10. Every nonzero number a has a unique multiplicative inverse $\frac{1}{a}$.	10. $a \times \dfrac{1}{a} = 1$ $(a \neq 0)$
11. Multiplication is distributive over addition.	11. $a(b + c) = ab + ac$

[*Note:* Subtraction can be performed by means of addition. We assume that $a - b = a + (-b)$. Division can be performed by means of multiplication. We assume that $a \div b = a \times \dfrac{1}{b}$ $(b \neq 0)$.]

Note: Any set of numbers which satisfies properties 1–11 is called a *field*.

ORDERING REAL NUMBERS

When the set of real numbers is associated with the points on the number line, every real number, rational or irrational, corresponds to a unique point on the line; also, every point on the number line corresponds to a unique real number, rational or irrational.

Real numbers can be ordered by using a number line. The graph of the greater of two unequal real numbers is always to the right of the graph of the smaller number.

Given any two unequal real numbers, we can determine which is the larger by expressing each number as a decimal. Then we compare the resulting decimals.

Model Problem

Which is the greater of the two numbers $\frac{13}{99}$ and .131331333 . . . ?

Solution:

$$\frac{13}{99} = .131313 \ldots$$

Compare: .131331333 . . .
         .131313131 . . .

The first four digits of the two decimals are the same. However, the fifth digit in .131331333 . . . is 3, whereas the fifth digit in .131313 . . . is 1. Therefore, .131331333 . . . > .131313 . . . , and hence, .131331333 . . . > $\frac{13}{99}$.

Answer: .131331333 . . . > $\frac{13}{99}$

EXERCISES

In 1–6, determine which is the greater number.

1. 2 and 2.25   2. −5.7 and −5.9   3. .5353 and .5353 . . .
4. .7 and .$\overline{7}$ 5. −.$\overline{53}$ and −.$\overline{531}$ 6. .2121 . . . and .212112111 . . .

In 7–10, arrange the set of real numbers in order from smallest to largest:

7. $\{.3, .31, .333 \ldots , .313113111 \ldots\}$
8. $\{.\overline{25}, .20, .\overline{2}, .202002000 \ldots\}$
9. $\{\frac{2}{7}, .27, .\overline{27}, .272272227 \ldots\}$
10. $\{-\frac{3}{5}, -.\overline{61}, -.\overline{6}, -.60616263 \ldots\}$

11. Consider the set of positive integers, the set of negative integers, the set of odd integers, the set of even integers, the set of rational numbers, the set of irrational numbers, and the set of real numbers. Which sets are closed under **(a)** addition? **(b)** subtraction? **(c)** multiplication? **(d)** division?

12. Tell which of the following sets of numbers are everywhere dense:
    a. positive integers   b. negative integers   c. rational numbers
    d. irrational numbers   e. real numbers

13. Eleven properties of real numbers are listed on page 434. State which, if any, of these eleven properties do *not* hold for the set of integers $\{\ldots , -3, -2, -1, 0, 1, 2, 3, \ldots\}$.

14. The following chain of equations can be used to show that $x(yz) = (xz)y$ when x, y, and z are members of the set of real numbers. State the reason for each step from **(a)** through **(c)**.
    a. $x(yz) = x(zy)$ b. $x(zy) = (xz)y$ c. $x(yz) = (xz)y$

In 15–22, all variables represent members of the set of real numbers. Use the properties of real numbers to prove that the sentence is true. Justify each statement with a reason.

15. $(ab)c = a(cb)$

16. $(a + b) + c = c + (b + a)$

17. $a(b + c) = ab + ca$

18. $\dfrac{1}{n}(mn) = m \ (n \neq 0)$

19. $m + n + (-m) = n$

20. $\dfrac{1}{n}(m + n) = 1 + m \cdot \dfrac{1}{n} \ (n \neq 0)$

21. $-a + a(bc + 1) = cab$

22. $(a + b)(c + d) = ac + cb + bd + da$

In 23–28, all variables represent members of the set of real numbers.

23. If we assume that $\dfrac{1}{b} \cdot \dfrac{1}{d} = \dfrac{1}{bd}$, prove that $\dfrac{a}{b} \cdot \dfrac{c}{d} = \dfrac{ac}{bd} (b \neq 0, d \neq 0)$.

Justify each step with a reason. $\left[Hint: \dfrac{a}{b} = a \cdot \dfrac{1}{b} \right]$

24. Prove that $\dfrac{a}{b} + \dfrac{c}{b} = \dfrac{a + c}{b} \ (b \neq 0)$. Justify each step with a reason.

25. Prove that if $a + x = b + x$, then a = b. Justify each step with a reason.

26. Prove that $\dfrac{ax + ay}{a} = x + y \ (a \neq 0)$. Justify each step with a reason.

27. Prove that if a and b are real numbers and $ab = 0$, then either a or b (or both) is zero. [*Hint:* Assume that $a \neq 0$ and prove that b must then be zero.]

28. Prove that the set of rational numbers is a field.

4. Finding a Root of a Number

To *square* a number is to use it as a factor twice. For example, the square of 5 is 5 × 5 = 25, or $5^2 = 25$.

To *cube* a number is to use it as a factor three times. For example, the cube of 2 is 2 × 2 × 2 = 8, or $2^3 = 8$.

Finding a *square root* of a number is to find one of its two equal factors. For example, "a square root of 25," written $\sqrt{25}$, is 5 because 5 × 5 = 25, or $5^2 = 25$. In general, a number x is a square root of the number b, if and only if $x^2 = b$. Finding a square root of a number is the inverse operation of squaring the number.

Finding a cube root of a number is to find one of its three equal factors. For example, "a cube root of 8," written $\sqrt[3]{8}$, is 2 because

$2 \times 2 \times 2 = 8$, or $2^3 = 8$. In general, a number x is a cube root of the number b, if and only if $x^3 = b$. Finding a cube root of a number is the inverse operation of cubing a number.

Likewise, for any positive integer n: if $x^n = b$, then x is an nth root of b, written $\sqrt[n]{b}$.

To indicate a root of a number, a *radical sign*, $\sqrt{}$, is used. The symbol $\sqrt{25}$ is called a *radical*; 25, the number under the radical sign, is called the *radicand*. The number which indicates the root to be taken is called the *index* of the radical. In $\sqrt[3]{8}$, the index is 3; in $\sqrt[4]{16}$, the index is 4. When no index appears, a square root is indicated. For example, $\sqrt{25}$ indicates a square root of 25.

Since a square root of 25 is a number whose square is 25, we can write $(\sqrt{25})^2 = 25$.

In general, for every real non-negative number n:

$$(\sqrt{n})^2 = n$$

Since $(+5)(+5) = 25$ and $(-5)(-5) = 25$, both $+5$ and -5 are square roots of 25. This example illustrates the truth of the following statement:

Every positive number has two square roots which have the same absolute value, one root being a positive number, the other root being a negative number.

The positive square root of a number is called the ***principal square root***. To indicate that the principal square root of a number is to be found, a radical sign, $\sqrt{}$, is placed over the number. For example:

$$\sqrt{25} = 5 \qquad \sqrt{\tfrac{9}{16}} = \tfrac{3}{4} \qquad \sqrt{.49} = .7$$

To indicate that the negative square root of a number is to be found, we place a minus sign in front of the radical sign. For example:

$$-\sqrt{25} = -5 \qquad -\sqrt{\tfrac{9}{16}} = -\tfrac{3}{4} \qquad -\sqrt{.49} = -.7$$

To indicate that both square roots are to be found, we place a plus sign and a minus sign in front of the radical. For example:

$$\pm\sqrt{25} = \pm 5 \qquad \pm\sqrt{\tfrac{9}{16}} = \pm\tfrac{3}{4} \qquad \pm\sqrt{.49} = \pm.7$$

Observe that 0 is the only number whose square is 0. Thus, $\sqrt{0} = 0$.

Since the square of any real number is never negative, no negative number has a square root in the set of real numbers. For example, $\sqrt{-25}$ does not exist in the set of real numbers; there is no real number whose square is -25.

However, $\sqrt[3]{-8}$ does exist in the set of real numbers; Since $(-2)^3 = -8$, then $\sqrt[3]{-8} = -2$.

Model Problems

1. Find the principal square root of 64.

   Solution: Since $8 \times 8 = 64$, then $\sqrt{64} = 8$.   8 *Ans.*

2. Find the value of $\sqrt[3]{27}$.

   Solution: Since $3 \times 3 \times 3 = 27$, then $\sqrt[3]{27} = 3$.   3 *Ans.*

3. Find the value of $(\sqrt{13})^2$.

   Solution: Since $(\sqrt{n})^2 = n$, then $(\sqrt{13})^2 = 13$.   13 *Ans.*

4. Solve for x: $x^2 = 36$.

   Solution: If $x^2 = a$, then $x = \pm\sqrt{a}$ when a is a positive number.

$$x^2 = 36 \qquad Check: \quad x^2 = 36 \qquad\qquad x^2 = 36$$
$$x = \pm\sqrt{36} \qquad\qquad (+6)^2 \overset{?}{=} 36 \qquad\qquad (-6)^2 \overset{?}{=} 36$$
$$x = \pm 6 \qquad\qquad\qquad 36 = 36 \;\; (\text{true}) \qquad 36 = 36 \;\; (\text{true})$$

   Answer: $x = +6$ or $x = -6$; solution set is $\{+6, -6\}$.

EXERCISES

In 1–5, state the index and the radicand of the radical.

1. $\sqrt{36}$ 2. $\sqrt[3]{125}$ 3. $\sqrt[4]{81}$ 4. $\sqrt[5]{32}$ 5. $\sqrt[n]{1}$

In 6–15, find the principal square root of the number.

6. 81   7. 1   8. 121   9. 225   10. 900
11. $\frac{1}{9}$ 12. $\frac{4}{25}$ 13. .49   14. 1.44   15. .04

In 16–40, express the radical as integer(s), fraction(s), or decimal(s).

16. $\sqrt{16}$ 17. $\sqrt{81}$ 18. $\sqrt{121}$ 19. $-\sqrt{64}$ 20. $-\sqrt{144}$
21. $\sqrt{0}$ 22. $\pm\sqrt{100}$ 23. $\pm\sqrt{169}$ 24. $\sqrt{400}$ 25. $-\sqrt{625}$
26. $\sqrt{\frac{1}{4}}$ 27. $-\sqrt{\frac{9}{16}}$ 28. $\pm\sqrt{\frac{25}{81}}$ 29. $\sqrt{\frac{49}{100}}$ 30. $\pm\sqrt{\frac{144}{169}}$
31. $\sqrt{.64}$ 32. $-\sqrt{1.44}$ 33. $\pm\sqrt{.09}$ 34. $-\sqrt{.01}$ 35. $\pm\sqrt{.0004}$
36. $\sqrt[3]{1}$ 37. $\sqrt[4]{81}$ 38. $\sqrt[5]{32}$ 39. $\sqrt[3]{-8}$ 40. $-\sqrt[3]{-125}$

In 41–54, find the value of the expression.

41. $\sqrt{(8)^2}$ 42. $\sqrt{(\frac{1}{2})^2}$ 43. $\sqrt{(.7)^2}$ 44. $\sqrt{(-4)^2}$ 45. $\sqrt{(-5)^2}$
46. $(\sqrt{4})^2$ 47. $(\sqrt{36})^2$ 48. $(\sqrt{11})^2$ 49. $(\sqrt{39})^2$ 50. $(\sqrt{97})(\sqrt{97})$
51. $\sqrt{36} + \sqrt{49}$ 52. $\sqrt{100} - \sqrt{25}$
53. $(\sqrt{17})^2 + (\sqrt{7})(\sqrt{7})$ 54. $\sqrt{(-9)^2} - (\sqrt{83})^2$

In 55–66, solve for the variable when the replacement set is the set of real numbers.

55. $x^2 = 4$ **56.** $y^2 = 100$ **57.** $z^2 = \frac{4}{81}$ **58.** $x^2 = .49$
59. $x^2 - 16 = 0$ **60.** $y^2 - 36 = 0$ **61.** $2x^2 = 50$ **62.** $3x^2 - 75 = 0$
63. $x^3 = 8$ **64.** $x^3 = -1$ **65.** $2x^3 = 128$ **66.** $3x^4 = 48$

In 67–70, find the length of each side of a square which has the given area.

67. 36 sq. ft.   **68.** 196 sq. ft.   **69.** 1600 sq. ft.   **70.** 441 sq. ft.

5. Square Roots Which Are Irrational Numbers

Positive rational numbers such as 9 and $\frac{4}{49}$ (also the number 0) are called **perfect squares** because they are squares of rational numbers. For example, $\sqrt{9} = 3$, and 3 is a rational number; $\sqrt{\frac{4}{49}} = \frac{2}{7}$, and $\frac{2}{7}$ is a rational number; $\sqrt{0} = 0$, and 0 is a rational number. Similarly, if any non-negative rational number n is a perfect square, then $\sqrt{n}$ is a non-negative rational number.

Suppose n is a non-negative rational number which is not a perfect square, for example, 2. What kind of number is $\sqrt{n}$? What is the value of $\sqrt{2}$?

Since $1 \times 1 = 1$ and $2 \times 2 = 4$, then $\sqrt{2}$ must be a number between 1 and 2: $1 < \sqrt{2} < 2$.

Since $1.4 \times 1.4 = 1.96$ and $1.5 \times 1.5 = 2.25$, then $\sqrt{2}$ must be a number between 1.4 and 1.5: $1.4 < \sqrt{2} < 1.5$.

Since $1.41 \times 1.41 = 1.9881$ and $1.42 \times 1.42 = 2.0164$, then $\sqrt{2}$ must be a number between 1.41 and 1.42: $1.41 < \sqrt{2} < 1.42$.

Regardless of how far we continue this work, we will never reach a point where the number $\sqrt{2}$ is expressed as a terminating or a repeating decimal. Therefore, we call $\sqrt{2}$ an **irrational number.** We have been finding only approximations of $\sqrt{2}$; the value of $\sqrt{2}$ cannot be expressed as a rational number.

If a number cannot be expressed in the form $\frac{a}{b}$, where a and b are integers ($b \neq 0$), it is an irrational number.

It can be proved that if n is a positive number which is not a perfect square, then $\sqrt{n}$ is an irrational number. It can also be shown that if n is a positive integer which is not the square of an integer, then $\sqrt{n}$ is irrational. Examples of irrational numbers are $\sqrt{2}, \sqrt{3}, \sqrt{5}, \sqrt{7}$, and $\sqrt{8}$.

Even though the value of an irrational number can be only approximated, every square root which is an irrational number can be associated with a point on the real number line.

Although we cannot do so here, it can be shown that there are infinitely many irrational numbers which cannot be expressed as a root of a rational number. π is such a number.

Model Problems

1. Between which consecutive integers is $\sqrt{42}$?

    Solution: Since $6 \times 6 = 36$ and $7 \times 7 = 49$, then $\sqrt{42}$ is between 6 and 7

    Answer: $\sqrt{42}$ is between 6 and 7, or $6 < \sqrt{42} < 7$.

2. State whether $\sqrt{56}$ is a rational or an irrational number.

    Solution: Since 56 is a positive integer which is not the square of an integer, $\sqrt{56}$ is an irrational number.

    Answer: $\sqrt{56}$ is an irrational number.

EXERCISES

In 1–10, between which consecutive integers is each given number?

1. $\sqrt{5}$ 2. $\sqrt{13}$ 3. $\sqrt{40}$ 4. $-\sqrt{2}$ 5. $-\sqrt{14}$

6. $\sqrt{52}$ 7. $\sqrt{73}$ 8. $-\sqrt{125}$ 9. $\sqrt{143}$ 10. $-\sqrt{150}$

In 11–16, order the given numbers, starting with the smallest.

11. $2, \sqrt{3}, -1$ 12. $4, \sqrt{17}, 3$ 13. $-\sqrt{15}, -3, -4$

14. $0, \sqrt{7}, -\sqrt{7}$ 15. $5, \sqrt{21}, \sqrt{30}$ 16. $-\sqrt{11}, -\sqrt{23}, -\sqrt{19}$

In 17–26, state whether the number is rational or irrational.

17. $\sqrt{25}$ 18. $\sqrt{40}$ 19. $-\sqrt{36}$ 20. $-\sqrt{54}$ 21. $-\sqrt{150}$

22. $\sqrt{400}$ 23. $\sqrt{\frac{1}{2}}$ 24. $-\sqrt{\frac{4}{9}}$ 25. $\sqrt{.36}$ 26. $\sqrt{.1}$

6. Estimating Approximate Square Roots

To approximate the square root of a number which has only two or three digits, we can make an intelligent estimate and check by squaring the estimated value. This process can be continued until we have obtained the desired number of decimal places in our approximation.

Model Problem

Approximate $\sqrt{38}$ to (a) the *nearest integer* and (b) the *nearest tenth*.

Solution:

a. $\sqrt{38}$ is not an integer, because $6^2 = 36$ and $7^2 = 49$. Since 38 is between 36 and 49, $\sqrt{38}$ is between 6 and 7. Therefore, we test 6.5, the number midway between 6 and 7. Since $(6.5)^2 = 42.25$, and 38 is less than 42.25, then $\sqrt{38}$ is less than 6.5 and must be closer to 6 than to 7. Therefore, the value of $\sqrt{38}$, approximated to the nearest integer, is 6.

Answer: $\sqrt{38} \approx 6$

[*Note:* The symbol "$\approx$" means "is approximately equal to."]

b. Since we know from part a that $\sqrt{38}$ is a little greater than 6, we test 6.1. When we square 6.1, we get $(6.1)^2 = 37.21$, which is less than 38. We then test 6.2. When we square 6.2, we get $(6.2)^2 = 38.44$, which is greater than 38. Since $\sqrt{38}$ lies between 6.1 and 6.2, we test 6.15, the number midway between 6.1 and 6.2. Since $(6.15)^2 = 37.8225$, and 38 is greater than 37.8225, then $\sqrt{38}$ is greater than 6.15 and must be closer to 6.2 than to 6.1. Therefore, the value of $\sqrt{38}$, approximated to the nearest tenth, is 6.2.

Answer: $\sqrt{38} \approx 6.2$

EXERCISES

In 1–10, approximate the value of the expression to the *nearest integer*.

1. $\sqrt{5}$ 2. $\sqrt{19}$ 3. $\sqrt{22}$ 4. $\sqrt{34}$ 5. $-\sqrt{55}$

6. $\sqrt{93}$ 7. $\sqrt{105}$ 8. $-\sqrt{116}$ 9. $\sqrt{157}$ 10. $\sqrt{218}$

In 11–20, approximate the value of the expression to the *nearest tenth*.

11. $\sqrt{2}$ 12. $\sqrt{12}$ 13. $\sqrt{45}$ 14. $-\sqrt{67}$ 15. $-\sqrt{86}$

16. $\sqrt{106}$ 17. $\sqrt{125}$ 18. $-\sqrt{137}$ 19. $\sqrt{152}$ 20. $\sqrt{175}$

7. Using Division to Find Approximate Square Roots

Consider 144 and its square root, 12. $144 \div 12 = 12$ illustrates:

Principle 1. When a divisor of a number and the quotient are equal, the square root of the number is either the divisor or the quotient.

$144 \div 9 = 16$ and $144 \div 18 = 8$ illustrate:

Principle 2. When a divisor of a number and the quotient are unequal, the square root of the number lies between the divisor and the quotient.

The square root of a number may be approximated to any number of decimal places by applying the two preceding principles and using estimates, divisions, and averages.

Model Problem

Approximate $\sqrt{14}$ to the nearest (a) integer (b) tenth (c) hundredth (d) thousandth.

How to Proceed	*Solution*
1. Approximate the square root of the number 14 by estimation.	Since $3^2 = 9$ and $4^2 = 16$, then $\sqrt{14}$ lies between 3 and 4, closer to 4. Estimate $\sqrt{14} \approx 3.8$.

2. Divide the number 14 by the estimate, 3.8, finding the quotient to one more decimal place than there is in the divisor.

$$
\begin{array}{r}
3.68 \\
3.8_\wedge\overline{)14.0_\wedge00} \\
11\ 4 \\
\overline{26\ 0} \\
22\ 8 \\
\overline{3\ 20} \\
3\ 04 \\
\overline{16}
\end{array}
$$

[*Note:* The quotient is 3.68, not 3.8. This tells us that $\sqrt{14}$ is not 3.8, but lies between 3.68 and 3.8. Therefore, $3.68 < \sqrt{14} < 3.8$.]

3. Find the average of the divisor, 3.8, and the quotient, 3.68 (found in step 2).

$$\frac{3.8 + 3.68}{2} = \frac{7.48}{2} = 3.74$$

4. Divide the number 14 by the average, 3.74 (see step 3), finding the quotient to one more decimal place than there is in the divisor. Since $14 \div 3.74 \approx 3.743$, then $3.74 < \sqrt{14} < 3.743$.

$3.74\overline{)14.} \approx 3.743$
(The division is left to the student.)

5. Find the average of the divisor, 3.74, and the quotient, 3.743 (found in step 4).

$$\frac{3.74 + 3.743}{2} = \frac{7.483}{2} = 3.7415$$

[*Note:* This process may be continued to obtain as close an approximation as is desired.]

Since $\sqrt{14} \approx 3.7415$, we obtain the following approximations when we round off:

Answer: **a.** $\sqrt{14} \approx 4$ (nearest integer)
b. $\sqrt{14} \approx 3.7$ (nearest tenth)
c. $\sqrt{14} \approx 3.74$ (nearest hundredth)
d. $\sqrt{14} \approx 3.742$ (nearest thousandth)

EXERCISES

In 1–10, approximate each expression to the *nearest integer.*

1. $\sqrt{39}$ **2.** $\sqrt{80}$ **3.** $\sqrt{155}$ **4.** $-\sqrt{273}$ **5.** $\sqrt{2348}$
6. $\sqrt{4389}$ **7.** $\sqrt{1455}$ **8.** $-\sqrt{6258}$ **9.** $\sqrt{67.24}$ **10.** $\sqrt{134.56}$

In 11–20, approximate each expression to the *nearest tenth.*

11. $\sqrt{6}$ **12.** $\sqrt{11}$ **13.** $\sqrt{18}$ **14.** $\sqrt{21}$ **15.** $-\sqrt{34}$
16. $\sqrt{53}$ **17.** $\sqrt{90}$ **18.** $-\sqrt{108}$ **19.** $\sqrt{19.5}$ **20.** $\sqrt{41.7}$

In 21–30, approximate each expression to the *nearest hundredth.*

21. $\sqrt{7}$ **22.** $\sqrt{19}$ **23.** $\sqrt{28}$ **24.** $-\sqrt{61}$ **25.** $\sqrt{74}$
26. $\sqrt{106}$ **27.** $\sqrt{111}$ **28.** $-\sqrt{127}$ **29.** $\sqrt{23.5}$ **30.** $\sqrt{88.2}$

In 31–35, approximate each expression to the *nearest thousandth.*

31. $\sqrt{3}$ **32.** $\sqrt{15}$ **33.** $\sqrt{89}$ **34.** $-\sqrt{133}$ **35.** $\sqrt{29.2}$

36. How many digits are there in the integral part of the square root of every positive integer less than 100?

37. What is the smallest positive integer whose square root is **(a)** a two-digit integer? **(b)** a three-digit integer?

In 38–47, tell whether the number has a square root which is less than 10, greater than 10 but less than 100, or greater than 100 but less than 1000.

38. 49   **39.** 121   **40.** 8100   **41.** 14,400   **42.** 225,000
43. 87   **44.** 271   **45.** 4723   **46.** 18,625   **47.** 910,500

8. Using Another Method for Computing the Square Root of a Number

We will now illustrate still another method that can be used to compute the square root of a number to as many places as may be desired. The difficult reasoning which justifies the method will not be given here.

COMPUTING THE SQUARE ROOT OF A PERFECT SQUARE

Model Problems

1. Compute the positive square root of 1764.

How to Proceed	*Solution*
1. Starting at the decimal point and moving to the left, group the digits of the number in pairs of two digits. Place a decimal point directly above the decimal point in the number.	$\sqrt{\overline{17}\ \overline{64.}}$

2. Below the first group at the left, write the largest perfect square which is not more than that group. Write the square root of the perfect square above the first group.

$$\begin{array}{r} 4\quad. \\ \sqrt{\overline{17}\ \overline{64.}} \\ \underline{16} \end{array}$$

3. Subtract the perfect square from the first group and bring down and annex the next group to the remainder.

$$\begin{array}{r} 4\quad. \\ \sqrt{\overline{17}\ \overline{64.}} \\ \underline{16} \\ 1\ 64 \end{array}$$

4. Form a trial divisor by doubling (multiplying by 2) the part of the root already found in step 3 and annexing a 0.

$4 \times 2 = 8$
Trial divisor is 80.

$$\begin{array}{r} 4\quad. \\ \sqrt{\overline{17}\ \overline{64.}} \\ \underline{16} \\ 80\ \overline{|\ 1\ 64} \end{array}$$

5. Divide the remainder found in step 3 by the trial divisor found in step 4. Annex the quotient to the part of the root already found; also, add it to the trial divisor to form the complete divisor.

$164 \div 80 = 2+$
Complete divisor is
$80 + 2 = 82.$

$$\begin{array}{r} 4\quad 2. \\ \sqrt{\overline{17}\ \overline{64.}} \\ \underline{16} \\ 82\ \overline{|\ 1\ 64} \end{array}$$

6. Multiply the complete divisor by the last digit which was placed in the root, and subtract the product from the remainder found in step 3. The remainder is 0. The required root is 42.

$$2 \times 82 = 164$$

$$
\begin{array}{r}
4\ \ 2. \\
\sqrt{\overline{17}\ \overline{64}.} \\
16 \\
\end{array}
$$

$$
82\ \overline{\big|\ 1\ 64}
$$
$$
\ 1\ 64
$$

Check: Since $(42)^2 = 1764$, then $\sqrt{1764} = 42$.

Answer: $\sqrt{1764} = 42$

Note: When necessary, the procedure given in steps 4, 5, and 6 is repeated until the remainder is 0.

2. Compute: $\sqrt{552.25}$

Solution:

1. Starting at the decimal point, moving first to the left and then to the right, group the digits in pairs. The first group on the left may have one digit. If the last digit on the right has one digit, annex a 0 to form a two-digit group.
2. The largest perfect square not more than 5 is 4. Write 4 below 5. $\sqrt{4} = 2$. Write 2 above 5.
3. Subtract 4 from 5, obtaining 1. Bring down the next group, 52, and annex it to 1, forming 152.

$$
\begin{array}{r}
2\ \ \ 3.\ \ 5 \\
\sqrt{5\ \ \overline{52}.\overline{25}} \\
4 \\
\end{array}
$$

$$
43\ \overline{\big|\ 1\ 52}
$$
$$
\ 1\ 29
$$

$$
465\ \overline{\big|\ 23\ 25}
$$
$$
\ 23\ 25
$$

4. Find the first trial divisor by doubling 2 and annexing a 0: $2 \times 2 = 4$; the trial divisor is 40.
5. Divide the remainder, 152, by the trial divisor, 40. The quotient is 3. Therefore, the complete first divisor is $40 + 3$, or 43.
6. $3 \times 43 = 129$. Subtract: $152 - 129 = 23$. Bring down the next group, 25, and annex it to 23, forming 2325.
7. Find the second trial divisor by doubling 23 and annexing a 0: $2 \times 23 = 46$; the trial divisor is 460.
8. Divide the remainder, 2325, by the trial divisor, 460. The quotient is 5. Therefore, the complete divisor is $460 + 5$, or 465.
9. $5 \times 465 = 2325$. Subtract: $2325 - 2325 = 0$. The required root is 23.5.

Check: Since $(23.5)^2 = 552.25$, then $\sqrt{552.25} = 23.5$.

Answer: $\sqrt{552.25} = 23.5$

COMPUTING THE APPROXIMATE SQUARE ROOT OF A NUMBER

Model Problems

1. Find $\sqrt{42}$ correct to the *nearest tenth*.

Solution:

1. In order to approximate $\sqrt{42}$ correct to the nearest tenth, we carry the work to two decimal places and then round off the result to the nearest tenth.

2. Since we wish to carry the result to two decimal places, we annex to 42 (at the right of the decimal point) two groups, each containing two zeros. Since $42 = 42.0000$, then $\sqrt{42} = \sqrt{42.0000}$.

$$
\begin{array}{r|l}
 & 6 .\ 4\ \ 8 \\
 & \overline{\sqrt{42.00\ 00}} \\
 & 36 \\
\hline
124 & 6\ 00 \\
 & 4\ 96 \\
\hline
1288 & 1\ 04\ 00 \\
 & 1\ 03\ 04 \\
\hline
 & 96
\end{array}
$$

3. Perform the computation and round off the answer to the nearest tenth. Since $6.48 \approx 6.5$, the required root is 6.5.

Answer: $\sqrt{42} = 6.5$ to the nearest tenth

2. Find $\sqrt{65}$ correct to the *nearest hundredth*.

Solution:

1. In order to approximate $\sqrt{65}$ correct to the nearest hundredth, we carry the work to three decimal places and then round off the result to the nearest hundredth.

2. In order to carry the work in the result to three decimal places, we rename 65 as 65.000000 by annexing three groups, each containing two zeros, at the right of 65.

$$
\begin{array}{r|l}
 & 8 .\ 0\ \ 6\ \ 2 \\
 & \overline{\sqrt{65.00\ 00\ 00}} \\
 & 64 \\
\hline
160 & 1\ 00 \\
 & 0\ 00 \\
\hline
1606 & 1\ 00\ 00 \\
 & 96\ 36 \\
\hline
16122 & 3\ 64\ 00 \\
 & 3\ 22\ 44 \\
\hline
 & 41\ 56
\end{array}
$$

3. The first trial divisor is 160. Since $100 \div 160$ is less than 1, we say the quotient is 0. Therefore, the complete first divisor is $160 + 0 = 160$.

4. Complete the computation and round off the answer to the nearest hundredth. Since $8.062 \approx 8.06$, the required root is 8.06.

Answer: $\sqrt{65} = 8.06$ to the nearest hundredth

EXERCISES

In 1–12, find the square root.

1. $\sqrt{289}$ 2. $\sqrt{784}$ 3. $-\sqrt{1296}$ 4. $\sqrt{9801}$

5. $\sqrt{16,900}$ 6. $\sqrt{9.61}$ 7. $\sqrt{90.25}$ 8. $-\sqrt{56.25}$

9. $\sqrt{1.1025}$ 10. $\sqrt{16.1604}$ 11. $\sqrt{1.7689}$ 12. $\sqrt{.667489}$

In 13–22, find the square root correct to the *nearest tenth*.

13. $\sqrt{12}$ 14. $\sqrt{37}$ 15. $-\sqrt{58}$ 16. $\sqrt{79}$ 17. $\sqrt{200}$

18. $-\sqrt{416}$ 19. $\sqrt{18.25}$ 20. $\sqrt{205.78}$ 21. $-\sqrt{8.5}$ 22. $\sqrt{4.052}$

In 23–27, find the square root correct to the *nearest hundredth*.

23. $\sqrt{2}$ 24. $\sqrt{54}$ 25. $\sqrt{77}$ 26. $\sqrt{8.25}$ 27. $\sqrt{9.5}$

In 28–31, find the length of a side of a square whose area is the given measure. Round off your answers to the *nearest tenth of an inch*.

28. 8 sq. in.   29. 29 sq. in.   30. 96 sq. in.   31. 200 sq. in.

9. Using a Table to Find Squares and Square Roots

When computing the square or the square root of a number, much time can be saved by using a table of squares and square roots such as the one that appears on page 560.

Model Problems

1. Find the square of 58.

   Solution: In the table on page 560, in the column headed "No.," we find 58. We look to the right of 58 in the column headed "Square" and find 3,364.

   Answer: $(58)^2 = 3,364$

2. Approximate $\sqrt{48}$ (a) to the *nearest tenth* and (b) to the *nearest hundredth*.

   Solution: In the table on page 560, in the column headed "No.," we find 48. We look to the right of 48 in the column headed "Square Root" and find 6.928. Then we round off the decimal.

   Answer: (a) $\sqrt{48} = 6.9$ to the nearest tenth
   (b) $\sqrt{48} = 6.93$ to the nearest hundredth

3. Find $\sqrt{15,376}$.

  Solution: Since 15,376 is greater than 150, it does not appear in the column
    headed "No." In the column headed "Square," find 15,376. To its left,
    in the column headed "No.," appears 124. Since $(124)^2 = 15,376$, then
    $\sqrt{15,376} = 124$.

  Answer: $\sqrt{15,376} = 124$

4. Find $\sqrt{3,000}$ correct to the *nearest integer*.

  Solution: Since 3,000 is greater than 150, we look for
    3,000 in the column headed, "Square," but do not
    find it there. In that column, the number just smaller
    than 3,000 is 2,916, which is 54^2; and the number
    just larger than 3,000 is 3,025, which is 55^2. Since
    $(54.5)^2 = 2970.25$ and 3,000 is greater than
    2970.25, then the square root of 3,000 is greater
    than 54.5, or $54.5 < \sqrt{3,000} < 55$. We see that
    $\sqrt{3,000}$ is closer to 55 than to 54. Therefore, the
    square root of 3,000, to the nearest integer, is 55.

No.	Square
55	3,025
?	3,000
54	2,916

  Answer: $\sqrt{3,000} = 55$ to the nearest integer

EXERCISES

In 1–6, use the table on page 560 to find the square of the number.

1. 27 **2.** 68 **3.** 94 **4.** 119 **5.** 132 **6.** 147

In 7–21, use the table on page 560 to approximate the expression
to the *nearest tenth*.

7. $\sqrt{13}$ **8.** $\sqrt{53}$ **9.** $-\sqrt{63}$ **10.** $\sqrt{135}$ **11.** $-\sqrt{87}$
12. $\sqrt{5}$ **13.** $\sqrt{91}$ **14.** $\sqrt{85}$ **15.** $-\sqrt{111}$ **16.** $\sqrt{141}$
17. $2 + \sqrt{3}$ **18.** $9 - \sqrt{17}$ **19.** $\sqrt{55} + 7$ **20.** $\sqrt{120} - 4$ **21.** $-2 - \sqrt{13}$

In 22–31, use the table on page 560 to approximate the square root
to the *nearest hundredth*.

22. $\sqrt{8}$ **23.** $\sqrt{17}$ **24.** $\sqrt{29}$ **25.** $\sqrt{78}$ **26.** $-\sqrt{93}$
27. $-\sqrt{31}$ **28.** $\sqrt{103}$ **29.** $\sqrt{120}$ **30.** $\sqrt{138}$ **31.** $\sqrt{147}$

In 32–41, use the table on page 560 to express the square root as
an integer.

32. $\sqrt{961}$ **33.** $\sqrt{1,156}$ **34.** $\sqrt{4,356}$ **35.** $\sqrt{7,921}$ **36.** $\sqrt{9,409}$

37. $\sqrt{12,996}$ 38. $\sqrt{15,625}$ 39. $\sqrt{18,769}$ 40. $\sqrt{19,321}$ 41. $\sqrt{15,625}$

In 42–46, use the table on page 560 to approximate the square root to the *nearest integer*.

42. $\sqrt{170}$ 43. $\sqrt{1,865}$ 44. $\sqrt{5,420}$ 45. $-\sqrt{9,325}$ 46. $\sqrt{13,524}$

In 47–49, find c if $c = \sqrt{a^2 + b^2}$ and a and b have the given values. Use the table on page 560.

47. $a = 6, b = 8$ 48. $a = 5, b = 12$ 49. $a = 15, b = 36$

In 50–52, find b if $b = \sqrt{c^2 - a^2}$ and a and c have the given values. Use the table on page 560.

50. $c = 10, a = 6$ 51. $c = 26, a = 10$ 52. $c = 17, a = 8$

In 53–56, use the table on page 560 to find the value of $\sqrt{b^2 - 4ac}$ when:

53. $a = 5, b = 6, c = 1$ 54. $a = 2, b = 9, c = -5$
55. $a = 1, b = 2, c = -24$ 56. $a = 5, b = 0, c = -20$

In 57–59, approximate a to the *nearest tenth* if $a = \sqrt{c^2 - b^2}$ and b and c have the given values. Use the table on page 560.

57. $b = 5, c = 7$ 58. $b = 3, c = 6$ 59. $b = 8, c = 14$

In 60–61, approximate $\sqrt{b^2 - 4ac}$ to the *nearest tenth* when a, b, and c have the given values. Use the table on page 560.

60. $a = 1, b = 7, c = 2$ 61. $a = 3, b = -6, c = 1$

10. Finding the Principal Square Root of a Perfect Square Monomial or the Principal Cube Root of a Perfect Cube Monomial

Since we know that the principal square root of 49 is the positive number 7, we may write $\sqrt{49} = 7$. However, we do not know whether the principal square root of x^2 is $+x$ or $-x$ until we know whether x is a positive or a negative number. For example:

If $x = 5$, then $\sqrt{x^2} = \sqrt{(5)^2} = \sqrt{25} = 5 = x$.
If $x = -5$, then $\sqrt{x^2} = \sqrt{(-5)^2} = \sqrt{25} = 5 = -x$.

Therefore:

$\sqrt{x^2} = x$ if x is a positive number or zero. $(x \geq 0)$
$\sqrt{x^2} = -x$ if x is a negative number. $(x < 0)$

We could use an absolute value symbol to show that $\sqrt{x^2}$ is a non-negative number. If we write $\sqrt{x^2} = |x|$, then the result will be a positive number, the principal square root. In our work, however, we will not use absolute-value symbols. Rather, we will limit the domain of the variables which appear under the radical sign to non-negative numbers only. Therefore, we will write $\sqrt{x^2} = x$.

Since $(8y^2)(8y^2) = 64y^4$, then $\sqrt{64y^4} = 8y^2$. Observe that $8y^2$ is the product of two factors. The first factor 8 is $\sqrt{64}$ and the second factor y^2 is $\sqrt{y^4}$.

Procedure. To find the principal square root of a perfect square monomial which has more than one factor, write the indicated product of the square roots of its factors.

Note that we would find the principal cube root of a perfect cube monomial in a similar manner. Since $(3y^3)(3y^3)(3y^3)$, then $\sqrt[3]{27y^9} = 3y^3$. Observe that $3y^3$ is the product of two factors. The first factor, 3, is $\sqrt[3]{27}$, and the second factor, y^3, is $\sqrt[3]{y^9}$.

Keep In Mind

We limit the domain of the variables which appear under a radical sign to non-negative numbers only.

Model Problems

In 1–5, find the principal indicated root.

1. $\sqrt{25y^2}$ **2.** $\sqrt{16m^6}$ **3.** $\sqrt{\frac{4}{9}a^2b^4}$ **4.** $\sqrt{.81y^8}$ **5.** $\sqrt[3]{64y^6}$

Solution:

1. Since $(5y)(5y) = 25y^2$, then $\sqrt{25y^2} = 5y$. $5y$ *Ans.*
2. Since $(4m^3)(4m^3) = 16m^6$, then $\sqrt{16m^6} = 4m^3$. $4m^3$ *Ans.*
3. Since $(\frac{2}{3}ab^2)(\frac{2}{3}ab^2) = \frac{4}{9}a^2b^4$, then $\sqrt{\frac{4}{9}a^2b^4} = \frac{2}{3}ab^2$. $\frac{2}{3}ab^2$ *Ans.*
4. Since $(.9y^4)(.9y^4) = .81y^8$, then $\sqrt{.81y^8} = .9y^4$. $.9y^4$ *Ans.*
5. Since $(4y^2)(4y^2)(4y^2) = 64y^6$, then $\sqrt[3]{64y^6} = 4y^2$. $4y^2$ *Ans.*

EXERCISES

In 1–30, find the indicated root.

1. $\sqrt{9c^2}$ 2. $\sqrt{36y^4}$ 3. $\sqrt{64c^6}$ 4. $\sqrt{100x^{10}}$ 5. $\sqrt{81t^8}$

6. $\sqrt{c^2 d^2}$ 7. $\sqrt{x^4 y^2}$ 8. $\sqrt{r^8 s^6}$ 9. $\sqrt{x^{16} y^4}$ 10. $\sqrt{x^6 y^2 z^4}$

11. $\sqrt{4x^2 y^2}$ 12. $\sqrt{36a^6 b^4}$ 13. $\sqrt{144a^4 b^2}$ 14. $\sqrt{169x^4 y^2}$

15. $\sqrt{25r^8 s^{16} t^{12}}$ 16. $\sqrt{\frac{1}{4} y^2}$ 17. $\sqrt{\frac{25}{36} x^2 y^2}$ 18. $\sqrt{\frac{49}{9} a^4 b^2}$

19. $\sqrt{\frac{81}{121} a^6 b^2}$ 20. $\sqrt{\frac{64}{169} x^8 y^{10} z^{16}}$ 21. $\sqrt{.36m^2}$

22. $\sqrt{.49a^2 b^2}$ 23. $\sqrt{.04x^2 y^6}$ 24. $\sqrt{.01x^4 y^2}$

25. $\sqrt{1.21a^4 b^{16} c^{36}}$ 26. $\sqrt{6.25y^8 z^{18}}$ 27. $\sqrt[3]{125a^3}$

28. $\sqrt[3]{27x^{12}}$ 29. $\sqrt[3]{\frac{1}{8} a^6 b^9}$ 30. $\sqrt[3]{.064x^{12} y^{24}}$

11. Simplifying a Radical Whose Radicand Is a Product

Since $\sqrt{4 \cdot 9} = \sqrt{36} = 6$, and $\sqrt{4} \cdot \sqrt{9} = 2 \cdot 3 = 6$, then $\sqrt{4 \cdot 9} = \sqrt{4} \cdot \sqrt{9}$.

Since $\sqrt{16 \cdot 25} = \sqrt{400} = 20$, and $\sqrt{16} \cdot \sqrt{25} = 4 \cdot 5 = 20$, then $\sqrt{16 \cdot 25} = \sqrt{16} \cdot \sqrt{25}$.

These examples illustrate the following property of radicals:

The square root of a product of non-negative numbers is equal to the product of the square roots of the numbers.

In general, if a and b are non-negative numbers and n is a natural number, it can be proved that:

$$\sqrt[n]{a \cdot b} = \sqrt[n]{a} \cdot \sqrt[n]{b} \quad and \quad \sqrt[n]{a} \cdot \sqrt[n]{b} = \sqrt[n]{a \cdot b}$$

Hence, when $n = 2$ we have:

$$\sqrt{a \cdot b} = \sqrt{a} \cdot \sqrt{b} \quad and \quad \sqrt{a} \cdot \sqrt{b} = \sqrt{a \cdot b}$$

(See exercise 63 on page 454.) Also, when $n = 3$, we have:

$$\sqrt[3]{a \cdot b} = \sqrt[3]{a} \cdot \sqrt[3]{b} \quad and \quad \sqrt[3]{a} \cdot \sqrt[3]{b} = \sqrt[3]{a \cdot b}$$

These rules can at times be used to transform a radical into an equivalent radical. For example:

$$(1) \quad \sqrt{45} = \sqrt{9 \cdot 5} = \sqrt{9} \cdot \sqrt{5} = 3\sqrt{5}$$

Notice that we expressed 45 as the product of 9, the greatest perfect square factor of 45, and 5. Then we expressed $\sqrt{9}$ as 3.

$$(2) \quad \sqrt[3]{40} = \sqrt[3]{8 \cdot 5} = \sqrt[3]{8} \cdot \sqrt[3]{5} = 2\sqrt[3]{5}$$

Notice that we expressed 40 as the product of 8, the greatest perfect cube factor of 40, and 5. Then we expressed $\sqrt[3]{8}$ as 2.

When we expressed $\sqrt{45}$ as $3\sqrt{5}$, we simplified $\sqrt{45}$. When we expressed $\sqrt[3]{40}$ as $2\sqrt[3]{5}$, we simplified $\sqrt[3]{40}$.

A radical is said to be in simplest form when:

1. The radicand has no factor other than 1 whose indicated root can be taken exactly. Hence, $\sqrt{45}$ and $\sqrt[3]{40}$ are not in simplest form, whereas $3\sqrt{5}$ and $2\sqrt[3]{5}$ are in simplest form.

2. The radicand is not a fraction. Thus $\sqrt{\dfrac{7}{25}}$ is not in simplest form.

   Soon, we will learn how to transform $\sqrt{\dfrac{7}{25}}$ to $\dfrac{1}{5}\sqrt{7}$, which is in simplest form.

Procedure. To simplify a radical whose radicand is a product:

1. Find two factors of the radicand, one of which is the greatest perfect square factor of the radicand when simplifying a square root, or one of which is the greatest perfect cube factor of the radicand when simplifying a cube root.

2. Express the square root of the product as the product of the square roots of the factors; express the cube root of the product as the product of the cube roots of the factors.

3. Find the square root of the factor which is a perfect square when simplifying a square root radical; find the cube root of the factor which is a perfect cube when simplifying a cube root radical.

If we wish to find $\sqrt{200}$, correct to the nearest hundredth, by the use of the table on page 560, we can first simplify the radical as follows:

$$\sqrt{200} = \sqrt{100 \cdot 2} = \sqrt{100} \cdot \sqrt{2} = 10\sqrt{2} \approx 10(1.414) \approx 14.14$$

Note that 100 is the largest perfect square factor of 200.

Model Problems

In 1–6, simplify the expression.

1. $\sqrt{18}$ 2. $4\sqrt{50}$ 3. $-\sqrt{4y^3}$ 4. $\sqrt{75x^2y^3z^7}$ 5. $\frac{1}{2}\sqrt[3]{48}$ 6. $\sqrt[3]{8x^4}$

Solution:

1. $\sqrt{18} = \sqrt{9 \cdot 2} = \sqrt{9} \cdot \sqrt{2} = 3\sqrt{2}$ *Ans.*
2. $4\sqrt{50} = 4\sqrt{25 \cdot 2} = 4\sqrt{25} \cdot \sqrt{2} = 4 \cdot 5\sqrt{2} = 20\sqrt{2}$ *Ans.*
3. $-\sqrt{4y^3} = -\sqrt{4y^2 \cdot y} = -\sqrt{4y^2} \cdot \sqrt{y} = -2y\sqrt{y}$ *Ans.*
4. $\sqrt{75x^2y^3z^7} = \sqrt{25x^2y^2z^6 \cdot 3yz} = \sqrt{25x^2y^2z^6} \cdot \sqrt{3yz}$
   $$= 5xyz^3\sqrt{3yz} \text{ Ans.}$$
5. $\frac{1}{2}\sqrt[3]{48} = \frac{1}{2}\sqrt[3]{8 \cdot 6} = \frac{1}{2}\sqrt[3]{8} \cdot \sqrt[3]{6} = \frac{1}{2} \cdot 2\sqrt[3]{6} = \sqrt[3]{6}$ *Ans.*
6. $\sqrt[3]{8x^4} = \sqrt[3]{8x^3} \cdot \sqrt[3]{x} = 2x\sqrt[3]{x}$ *Ans.*

EXERCISES

In 1–48, simplify the expression.

1. $\sqrt{8}$
2. $\sqrt{12}$
3. $-\sqrt{24}$
4. $\sqrt{40}$
5. $-\sqrt{45}$
6. $\sqrt{54}$
7. $\sqrt{63}$
8. $-\sqrt{72}$
9. $\sqrt{98}$
10. $\sqrt{108}$
11. $-\sqrt{128}$
12. $\sqrt{162}$
13. $\sqrt{300}$
14. $-\sqrt{500}$
15. $3\sqrt{8}$
16. $4\sqrt{12}$
17. $-5\sqrt{24}$
18. $4\sqrt{90}$
19. $3\sqrt{200}$
20. $-6\sqrt{98}$
21. $\frac{1}{3}\sqrt{45}$
22. $\frac{1}{4}\sqrt{48}$
23. $\frac{1}{2}\sqrt{18}$
24. $\frac{3}{4}\sqrt{96}$
25. $\frac{2}{3}\sqrt{63}$
26. $\frac{3}{8}\sqrt{80}$
27. $-\frac{2}{5}\sqrt{125}$
28. $\sqrt{a^3}$
29. $2\sqrt{b^5}$
30. $3\sqrt{mn^2}$
31. $\sqrt{x^2y^3}$
32. $\sqrt{3x^3y}$
33. $-4\sqrt{2a^2b^3}$
34. $\sqrt{36r^2s}$
35. $5\sqrt{4x^3y^3}$
36. $\sqrt{27m^2}$
37. $\sqrt{20x^2y^3}$
38. $-7\sqrt{24a^3b^3}$
39. $\sqrt{4x^2y^4z^3}$
40. $\sqrt{12r^4s^3t^6}$
41. $5\sqrt{18y^3u^6z^8}$
42. $\frac{2}{3}\sqrt{72x^5y^4z^7}$
43. $\frac{3}{5}\sqrt{50r^3s^3t^3}$
44. $-\frac{4}{7}\sqrt{147x^2y^6z^{11}}$
45. $\sqrt[3]{24}$
46. $2\sqrt[3]{48x}$
47. $\sqrt[3]{7y^4}$
48. $\sqrt[3]{54x^3y^7}$

In 49–60, use the table on page 560 to approximate the expression to the *nearest tenth*.

49. $\sqrt{300}$
50. $\sqrt{180}$
51. $\sqrt{640}$
52. $\sqrt{405}$
53. $2\sqrt{288}$
54. $\frac{1}{3}\sqrt{252}$
55. $\frac{3}{4}\sqrt{176}$
56. $-\frac{2}{5}\sqrt{175}$
57. $3 + \sqrt{8}$
58. $7 - \sqrt{28}$
59. $-4 + \sqrt{200}$
60. $-5 - \sqrt{500}$

61. a. Does $\sqrt{9 + 16} = \sqrt{9} + \sqrt{16}$?
    b. Is finding a square root always distributive over addition?
    c. When does $\sqrt{a + b} = \sqrt{a} + \sqrt{b}$?

62. a. Does $\sqrt{25-9} = \sqrt{25} - \sqrt{9}$?
   b. Is finding a square root always distributive over subtraction?
   c. When does $\sqrt{a-b} = \sqrt{a} - \sqrt{b}$?
63. a. Use the properties of the set of real numbers to prove that $\sqrt{a \cdot b} = \sqrt{a} \cdot \sqrt{b}$ when a and b are non-negative. [*Hint:* Show $(\sqrt{a} \cdot \sqrt{b})^2 = ab$.]
   b. Is finding the square root of a product of two non-negative numbers always distributive over multiplication?
   c. Why is finding the nth root of the product of two non-negative numbers always distributive over multiplication?

12. Simplifying a Radical Whose Radicand Is a Fraction

Since $\sqrt{\dfrac{4}{9}} = \dfrac{2}{3}$ and $\dfrac{\sqrt{4}}{\sqrt{9}} = \dfrac{2}{3}$, then $\sqrt{\dfrac{4}{9}} = \dfrac{\sqrt{4}}{\sqrt{9}}$.

Since $\sqrt{\dfrac{16}{25}} = \dfrac{4}{5}$ and $\dfrac{\sqrt{16}}{\sqrt{25}} = \dfrac{4}{5}$, then $\sqrt{\dfrac{16}{25}} = \dfrac{\sqrt{16}}{\sqrt{25}}$.

These examples illustrate the following property of radicals:

The square root of a quotient of a non-negative number and a positive number is equal to the quotient of the square roots of the numbers.

In general if a is a non-negative number, b is a positive number, and n is a natural number, it can be proved that:

$$\sqrt[n]{\frac{a}{b}} = \frac{\sqrt[n]{a}}{\sqrt[n]{b}} \qquad and \qquad \frac{\sqrt[n]{a}}{\sqrt[n]{b}} = \sqrt[n]{\frac{a}{b}}$$

Hence, when $n = 2$, we have:

$$\sqrt{\frac{a}{b}} = \frac{\sqrt{a}}{\sqrt{b}} \qquad and \qquad \frac{\sqrt{a}}{\sqrt{b}} = \sqrt{\frac{a}{b}} \qquad \text{(See exercise 41 on page 456.)}$$

Also, when $n = 3$, we have:

$$\sqrt[3]{\frac{a}{b}} = \frac{\sqrt[3]{a}}{\sqrt[3]{b}} \qquad and \qquad \frac{\sqrt[3]{a}}{\sqrt[3]{b}} = \sqrt[3]{\frac{a}{b}}$$

For example:

$$\sqrt{\frac{81}{100}} = \frac{\sqrt{81}}{\sqrt{100}} = \frac{9}{10} \qquad and \qquad \sqrt[3]{\frac{27}{64}} = \frac{\sqrt[3]{27}}{\sqrt[3]{64}} = \frac{3}{4}$$

To simplify a square-root radical whose radicand is a fraction, we transform it and express it in terms of a radical whose radicand is not a fraction.

If we wish to find $\sqrt{\frac{1}{8}}$, correct to the nearest hundredth, by the use of the table on page 560, we first simplify the radical as follows:

$$\sqrt{\frac{1}{8}} = \sqrt{\frac{1}{8} \cdot \frac{2}{2}} = \sqrt{\frac{2}{16}} = \frac{\sqrt{2}}{\sqrt{16}} = \frac{\sqrt{2}}{4} \approx \frac{1.414}{4} \approx .353 \approx .35$$

Note that we multiply the radicand $\frac{1}{8}$ by $\frac{2}{2}$, which is another symbol for 1. We choose $\frac{2}{2}$ because it is the fraction whose numerator and denominator are the least number which makes the denominator of the product a perfect square.

Procedure. To simplify the square root or cube root of a quotient expressed as a fraction:

1. If the denominator of the radicand of a square-root radical is not a perfect square, multiply the radicand by 1 represented as a fraction whose numerator and denominator are the least number which makes the denominator of the product a perfect square; if the denominator of the radicand of a cube-root radical is not a perfect cube, multiply the radicand by 1 represented as a fraction whose numerator and denominator are the least number which makes the denominator of the product a perfect cube.
2. Express the indicated root of the resulting fraction as the indicated root of its numerator divided by the indicated root of its denominator.
3. Find the indicated root of the denominator and, if possible, simplify the result.

Model Problems

In 1-5, simplify the radical.

1. $\sqrt{\frac{3}{4}}$ 2. $6\sqrt{\frac{1}{3}}$ 3. $\sqrt{\frac{9}{5}}$ 4. $\sqrt{\frac{c}{d}}$ 5. $9\sqrt[3]{\frac{1}{3}}$

Solution:

1. $\sqrt{\dfrac{3}{4}} = \dfrac{\sqrt{3}}{\sqrt{4}} = \dfrac{\sqrt{3}}{2}$ or $\frac{1}{2}\sqrt{3}$ *Ans.*

2. $6\sqrt{\dfrac{1}{3}} = 6\sqrt{\dfrac{1}{3} \cdot \dfrac{3}{3}} = 6\sqrt{\dfrac{3}{9}} = \dfrac{6\sqrt{3}}{\sqrt{9}} = \dfrac{6\sqrt{3}}{3} = 2\sqrt{3}$ *Ans.*

3. $\sqrt{\dfrac{9}{5}} = \sqrt{\dfrac{9}{5} \cdot \dfrac{5}{5}} = \sqrt{\dfrac{45}{25}} = \dfrac{\sqrt{45}}{\sqrt{25}} = \dfrac{\sqrt{9} \cdot \sqrt{5}}{5} = \dfrac{3\sqrt{5}}{5}$ or $\frac{3}{5}\sqrt{5}$ *Ans.*

4. $\sqrt{\dfrac{c}{d}} = \sqrt{\dfrac{c}{d} \cdot \dfrac{d}{d}} = \sqrt{\dfrac{cd}{d^2}} = \dfrac{\sqrt{cd}}{\sqrt{d^2}} = \dfrac{\sqrt{cd}}{d}$ or $\dfrac{1}{d}\sqrt{cd}$ *Ans.*

5. $9\sqrt[3]{\dfrac{1}{3}} = 9\sqrt[3]{\dfrac{1}{3} \cdot \dfrac{9}{9}} = 9\sqrt[3]{\dfrac{9}{27}} = 9 \cdot \dfrac{\sqrt[3]{9}}{\sqrt[3]{27}} = 9 \cdot \dfrac{\sqrt[3]{9}}{3} = 3\sqrt[3]{9}$ *Ans.*

EXERCISES

In 1–32, simplify the radical.

1. $\sqrt{\dfrac{5}{9}}$ 2. $10\sqrt{\dfrac{24}{25}}$ 3. $\sqrt{\dfrac{1}{2}}$ 4. $12\sqrt{\dfrac{1}{6}}$ 5. $21\sqrt{\dfrac{1}{7}}$

6. $\sqrt{\dfrac{7}{5}}$ 7. $10\sqrt{\dfrac{3}{5}}$ 8. $\sqrt{\dfrac{12}{5}}$ 9. $4\sqrt{\dfrac{25}{2}}$ 10. $15\sqrt{\dfrac{16}{3}}$

11. $\sqrt{\dfrac{7}{12}}$ 12. $10\sqrt{\dfrac{25}{20}}$ 13. $\sqrt[3]{\dfrac{1}{2}}$ 14. $\sqrt[3]{\dfrac{5}{16}}$ 15. $6\sqrt[3]{\dfrac{4}{3}}$

16. $50\sqrt[3]{\dfrac{8}{25}}$ 17. $\sqrt{\dfrac{a}{3}}$ 18. $12\sqrt{\dfrac{c}{6}}$ 19. $8\sqrt{\dfrac{x^2}{2}}$ 20. $\sqrt{\dfrac{c}{d^2}}$

21. $\sqrt{\dfrac{1}{a}}$ 22. $\sqrt{\dfrac{m}{n}}$ 23. $\sqrt{\dfrac{A}{\pi}}$ 24. $\sqrt{\dfrac{2s}{g}}$ 25. $\sqrt{\dfrac{x^2}{y}}$

26. $\sqrt{\dfrac{7x}{5y}}$ 27. $\sqrt{\dfrac{9m}{8n}}$ 28. $\sqrt{\dfrac{25r^2}{12s^3}}$ 29. $\sqrt[3]{\dfrac{x}{9}}$ 30. $\sqrt[3]{\dfrac{x^2}{y}}$

31. $\sqrt[3]{\dfrac{8a^3}{b^2}}$ 32. $\sqrt[3]{\dfrac{27m^4}{8n^2}}$

In 33–40, use the table on page 560 to approximate the expression to the *nearest tenth*.

33. $\sqrt{\dfrac{7}{9}}$ 34. $\sqrt{\dfrac{17}{81}}$ 35. $\sqrt{\dfrac{1}{2}}$ 36. $15\sqrt{\dfrac{1}{3}}$

37. $8\sqrt{\dfrac{5}{8}}$ 38. $6\sqrt{\dfrac{7}{12}}$ 39. $\dfrac{5}{3}\sqrt{\dfrac{9}{50}}$ 40. $\dfrac{2}{5}\sqrt{\dfrac{25}{24}}$

41. a. Use the properties of the set of real numbers to prove that

$$\sqrt{\dfrac{a}{b}} = \dfrac{\sqrt{a}}{\sqrt{b}}$$ when a is non-negative and b is positive.

b. Is finding the square root of the quotient of a non-negative number and a positive number always distributive over division?

c. Why is finding the nth root of a quotient of a non-negative number and a positive number always distributive over division?

13. Adding and Subtracting Radicals

ADDING AND SUBTRACTING LIKE RADICALS

Like radicals are radicals which have the *same index* and the *same radicand*. For example, $3\sqrt{2}$ and $5\sqrt{2}$ are like radicals, as are $4\sqrt[3]{7}$ and $9\sqrt[3]{7}$. However, $3\sqrt{5}$ and $5\sqrt{2}$ are unlike radicals, as are $\sqrt[3]{2}$ and $\sqrt{2}$.

To add or subtract like radicals, we use the distributive property as follows:

$$7\sqrt{2} + 3\sqrt{2} = (7 + 3)\sqrt{2} = 10\sqrt{2}$$
$$5\sqrt[3]{3} - \sqrt[3]{3} = (5 - 1)\sqrt[3]{3} = 4\sqrt[3]{3}$$

Procedure. To add or subtract like radicals:

1. **Add or subtract the coefficients of the radicals.**
2. **Multiply the sum or difference obtained by the common radical.**

ADDING AND SUBTRACTING UNLIKE RADICALS

The sum of the unlike radicals $\sqrt{5}$ and $\sqrt{2}$ is indicated as $\sqrt{5} + \sqrt{2}$, which cannot be expressed as a single term. Similarly, the difference of $\sqrt[3]{5}$ and $\sqrt[3]{2}$ is indicated as $\sqrt[3]{5} - \sqrt[3]{2}$.

However, when it is possible to transform unlike radicals into equivalent radicals which are like radicals, the resulting like radicals can be added or subtracted. For example, it would appear that the sum of $2\sqrt{3}$ and $\sqrt{27}$ can be indicated only as $2\sqrt{3} + \sqrt{27}$ since $2\sqrt{3}$ and $\sqrt{27}$ are unlike radicals. However, since $\sqrt{27} = \sqrt{9 \cdot 3} = \sqrt{9} \cdot \sqrt{3} = 3\sqrt{3}$, we can express $2\sqrt{3} + \sqrt{27}$ as $2\sqrt{3} + 3\sqrt{3}$ and then add the like radicals:

$$2\sqrt{3} + \sqrt{27} = 2\sqrt{3} + 3\sqrt{3} = (2 + 3)\sqrt{3} = 5\sqrt{3}$$

Procedure. To combine certain unlike radicals which have the same index:

1. **Simplify each radical.**
2. **Combine like radicals by using the distributive property.**
3. **Indicate the sum or difference of the unlike radicals.**

Model Problems

1. Simplify: $8\sqrt{3} + 4\sqrt[3]{2} - \sqrt[3]{2} + \sqrt{3}$

   Solution: $8\sqrt{3} + 4\sqrt[3]{2} - \sqrt[3]{2} + \sqrt{3} = (8\sqrt{3} + \sqrt{3}) + (4\sqrt[3]{2} - \sqrt[3]{2})$
   $$= (8 + 1)\sqrt{3} + (4 - 1)\sqrt[3]{2}$$
   $$= 9\sqrt{3} + 3\sqrt[3]{2} \quad Ans.$$

2. Combine: $5\sqrt{3} + 4\sqrt{12} - 2\sqrt{75}$

   Solution: $5\sqrt{3} + 4\sqrt{12} - 2\sqrt{75} = 5\sqrt{3} + 4\sqrt{4 \cdot 3} - 2\sqrt{25 \cdot 3}$
   $$= 5\sqrt{3} + 4\sqrt{4} \cdot \sqrt{3} - 2\sqrt{25} \cdot \sqrt{3}$$
   $$= 5\sqrt{3} + 4 \cdot 2 \cdot \sqrt{3} - 2 \cdot 5 \cdot \sqrt{3}$$
   $$= 5\sqrt{3} + 8\sqrt{3} - 10\sqrt{3}$$
   $$= (5 + 8 - 10)\sqrt{3}$$
   $$= 3\sqrt{3} \quad Ans.$$

3. Combine: $6\sqrt{8x} - 4\sqrt{\frac{1}{2}x}$

   Solution: $6\sqrt{8x} - 4\sqrt{\frac{1}{2}x} = 6\sqrt{4 \cdot 2x} - 4\sqrt{\frac{1}{2}x \cdot \frac{2}{2}}$
   $$= 6\sqrt{4} \cdot \sqrt{2x} - 4 \cdot \frac{\sqrt{2x}}{\sqrt{4}}$$
   $$= 6 \cdot 2 \cdot \sqrt{2x} - \frac{4\sqrt{2x}}{2}$$
   $$= 12\sqrt{2x} - 2\sqrt{2x}$$
   $$= (12 - 2)\sqrt{2x}$$
   $$= 10\sqrt{2x} \quad Ans.$$

EXERCISES

In 1–35, combine the radicals.

1. $8\sqrt{2} + 7\sqrt{2}$

2. $5\sqrt[3]{3} + 2\sqrt[3]{3} + 8\sqrt[3]{3}$

3. $14\sqrt{6} - 2\sqrt{6}$

4. $4\sqrt{3} + 2\sqrt{3} - 6\sqrt{3}$

5. $4\sqrt[3]{7} - \sqrt[3]{7} - 5\sqrt[3]{7}$

6. $3\sqrt{5} + 6\sqrt{2} - 3\sqrt{2} + \sqrt{5}$

7. $7\sqrt{x} + 3\sqrt[3]{y} - \sqrt{x} - 3\sqrt[3]{y}$

8. $\sqrt{27} + \sqrt{75}$

9. $\sqrt{5} + \sqrt{45} + \sqrt{80}$

10. $\sqrt{72} - \sqrt{50}$

11. $\sqrt[3]{54} - \sqrt[3]{16}$

12. $3\sqrt{2} + 2\sqrt{32}$

13. $3\sqrt[3]{81} - 2\sqrt[3]{24}$

14. $5\sqrt{27} - \sqrt{108} + 2\sqrt{75}$

15. $5\sqrt{8} - 3\sqrt{18} + \sqrt{2}$

16. $3\sqrt{28} - 2\sqrt{63}$

17. $\sqrt{98} - 4\sqrt{8} + 3\sqrt{128}$

18. $\frac{1}{2}\sqrt{20} + \sqrt{45}$

19. $4\sqrt{18} - \frac{3}{4}\sqrt{32} - \frac{1}{2}\sqrt{8}$

20. $4\sqrt{3} + 6\sqrt{\frac{1}{3}}$

21. $4\sqrt{8} - \sqrt{\frac{1}{2}}$

22. $5\sqrt{\frac{3}{5}} + \sqrt{60} - \sqrt{15}$

23. $6\sqrt[3]{\frac{1}{9}} - 4\sqrt[3]{375}$

24. $\frac{1}{2}\sqrt{20} - \sqrt{\frac{1}{5}} + \frac{1}{5}\sqrt{80}$

25. $\sqrt{100b} - \sqrt{64b} + \sqrt{9b}$

26. $3\sqrt{3x} - \sqrt{12x}$

27. $5\sqrt{3y} - \sqrt{27x} + \sqrt{12y}$

28. $\sqrt{3a^2} + \sqrt{12a^2}$

29. $4\sqrt[3]{5y^3} - \sqrt[3]{40y^3}$

30. $4\sqrt{12r^2} + 2\sqrt{75r^2} - 3\sqrt{27r^2}$

31. $3\sqrt{2y^3} - \sqrt{8y^3}$

32. $5\sqrt{12a^3} - 2\sqrt{3a^3} + \sqrt{27a^3}$

33. $x\sqrt{8y} + 3\sqrt{2x^2y}$

34. $\sqrt[3]{2x^3} + 3\sqrt[3]{54x^3} - x\sqrt[3]{128}$

35. $\sqrt{3x^3} + 3\sqrt{12x^3} - x\sqrt{75}$

14. Multiplying Radicals Which Have the Same Index

MULTIPLYING MONOMIALS CONTAINING RADICALS

We have learned that $\sqrt[n]{a} \cdot \sqrt[n]{b} = \sqrt[n]{ab}$ when a and b are nonnegative numbers and n is a positive integer. For example:

$$\sqrt{3} \cdot \sqrt{7} = \sqrt{3 \cdot 7} = \sqrt{21} \quad \text{and} \quad \sqrt[3]{2} \cdot \sqrt[3]{5} = \sqrt[3]{2 \cdot 5} = \sqrt[3]{10}$$

To multiply $4\sqrt{2}$ by $5\sqrt{3}$, we use the commutative and associative properties of multiplication as follows:

$$(4\sqrt{2})(5\sqrt{3}) = (4)(5)(\sqrt{2})(\sqrt{3}) = (4 \cdot 5)(\sqrt{2 \cdot 3} = 20\sqrt{6})$$

Also, to multiply $3\sqrt[3]{2}$ by $4\sqrt[3]{3}$, we use the commutative and associative properties of multiplication as follows:

$$(3\sqrt[3]{2})(4\sqrt[3]{3}) = (3)(4)(\sqrt[3]{2})(\sqrt[3]{3}) = (3 \cdot 4)(\sqrt[3]{2 \cdot 3}) = 12\sqrt[3]{6}$$

In general, if a and b are non-negative numbers and n is a positive integer:

$$x\sqrt[n]{a} \cdot y\sqrt[n]{b} = xy\sqrt[n]{ab}$$

Procedure. To multiply two monomial radicals that have the same index:

1. **Multiply the coefficients to find the coefficient of the product.**
2. **Multiply the radicands to find the radicand of the product. Use the same index to write the product radical.**
3. **If possible, simplify the result.**

Model Problems

1. Multiply: $3\sqrt{6} \cdot 5\sqrt{2}$

   Solution: $3\sqrt{6} \cdot 5\sqrt{2} = 3 \cdot 5\sqrt{6 \cdot 2} = 15\sqrt{12}$
   $$= 15\sqrt{4} \cdot \sqrt{3} = 15 \cdot 2 \cdot \sqrt{3} = 30\sqrt{3} \quad Ans.$$

2. Find the value of $(2\sqrt{3})^2$.

   Solution: $(2\sqrt{3})^2 = 2\sqrt{3} \cdot 2\sqrt{3}$
   $$= 2 \cdot 2\sqrt{3 \cdot 3} = 4\sqrt{9} = 4 \cdot 3 = 12 \quad Ans.$$

3. Find the indicated product: $\sqrt[3]{9x^2} \cdot \sqrt[3]{6x}$

   Solution: $\sqrt[3]{9x^2} \cdot \sqrt[3]{6x} = \sqrt[3]{9x^2 \cdot 6x}$
   $$= \sqrt[3]{54x^3} = \sqrt[3]{27x^3 \cdot 2} = \sqrt[3]{27x^3} \cdot \sqrt[3]{2}$$
   $$= 3x\sqrt[3]{2} \quad Ans.$$

MULTIPLYING SUMS AND DIFFERENCES CONTAINING RADICALS

To find the product $\sqrt{3}(\sqrt{2} + \sqrt{5})$, we use the distributive property of multiplication as follows:

$$\sqrt{3}(\sqrt{2} + \sqrt{5}) = (\sqrt{3})(\sqrt{2}) + (\sqrt{3})(\sqrt{5}) = \sqrt{6} + \sqrt{15}$$

To find the product $(5 + \sqrt{2})(7 - \sqrt{2})$, we use the distributive property of multiplication and arrange the solution in the same way that was previously used in finding the product of two binomials.

$$
\begin{array}{r}
7 - \sqrt{2} \\
5 + \sqrt{2} \\
\hline
35 - 5\sqrt{2} \\
+ 7\sqrt{2} - \sqrt{4} \\
\hline
35 + 2\sqrt{2} - 2 = 33 + 2\sqrt{2}
\end{array}
$$

Model Problems

1. Find the product:
   $$2\sqrt{2}(\sqrt{6} + 3\sqrt{24})$$

   Solution:

   $$\sqrt{6} + 3\sqrt{24}$$

2. Perform the indicated operation:
   $$(2\sqrt{3} + 7)^2$$

   Solution:

   $$2\sqrt{3} + 7$$

$$\begin{array}{l} 2\sqrt{2} \\ \overline{2\sqrt{12} + 6\sqrt{48}} \\ = 2\sqrt{4} \cdot \sqrt{3} + 6\sqrt{16} \cdot \sqrt{3} \\ = 4\sqrt{3} + 24\sqrt{3} \\ = 28\sqrt{3} \quad Ans. \end{array}$$

$$\begin{array}{l} 2\sqrt{3} + 7 \\ \overline{4\sqrt{9} + 14\sqrt{3}} \\ + 14\sqrt{3} + 49 \\ \overline{ 12 + 28\sqrt{3} + 49} \\ = 61 + 28\sqrt{3} \quad Ans. \end{array}$$

Keep In Mind

The product of two radicals with the same index is equal to the root of the product of their radicands with the same index.

EXERCISES

In 1–51, multiply, or raise to the power, as indicated. Then simplify the result.

1. $\sqrt{5} \cdot \sqrt{5}$

2. $\sqrt{113} \cdot \sqrt{113}$

3. $\sqrt{a} \cdot \sqrt{a}$

4. $\sqrt{2x} \cdot \sqrt{2x}$

5. $\sqrt{12} \cdot \sqrt{3}$

6. $2\sqrt{18} \cdot 3\sqrt{8}$

7. $\sqrt{14} \cdot \sqrt{2}$

8. $\sqrt{60} \cdot \sqrt{5}$

9. $3\sqrt{6} \cdot \sqrt{3}$

10. $5\sqrt{8} \cdot 7\sqrt{3}$

11. $\frac{2}{3}\sqrt{24} \cdot 9\sqrt{3}$

12. $\frac{1}{3}\sqrt{18} \cdot 12\sqrt{3}$

13. $6\sqrt{\frac{1}{3}} \cdot 4\sqrt{12}$

14. $7\sqrt{56} \cdot 3\sqrt{\frac{1}{2}}$

15. $8\sqrt{225} \cdot 3\sqrt{\frac{1}{3}}$

16. $\sqrt[3]{3} \cdot \sqrt[3]{9}$

17. $4\sqrt[3]{25} \cdot 7\sqrt[3]{5}$

18. $6\sqrt[3]{4} \cdot 2\sqrt[3]{6}$

19. $(5\sqrt{x})(3\sqrt{x})$

20. $(-4\sqrt{a})(3\sqrt{a})$

21. $(-\frac{1}{2}\sqrt{y})(-6\sqrt{y})$

22. $(\sqrt{3})^2$

23. $(\sqrt[3]{5})^3$

24. $(\sqrt{y})^2$

25. $(\sqrt[3]{t})^3$

26. $(3\sqrt{6})^2$

27. $(\frac{1}{3}\sqrt[3]{3})^3$

28. $\sqrt{25x} \cdot \sqrt{4x}$

29. $\sqrt{27a} \cdot \sqrt{3a}$

30. $\sqrt{15x} \cdot \sqrt{3x}$

31. $\sqrt{9a} \cdot \sqrt{ab}$

32. $\sqrt{5x^2y} \cdot \sqrt{10y}$

33. $\sqrt{3a^2} \cdot \sqrt{18b^2}$

34. $(\sqrt{6z})^2$

35. $(3\sqrt{r})^2$

36. $(5\sqrt[3]{3m})^3$

37. $(\sqrt{2x+1})^2$

38. $(\sqrt{3x-2})^2$

39. $(\sqrt[3]{5x-3})^3$

40. $6(2\sqrt{5} - 3\sqrt{2} + 6)$

41. $\sqrt{5}(\sqrt{5} + \sqrt{11})$

42. $\sqrt{2}(\sqrt{8} - 2\sqrt{2} + 5)$

43. $2\sqrt{3}(3\sqrt{5} - 2\sqrt{20} - \sqrt{45})$

44. $(5 + \sqrt{2})(6 + \sqrt{2})$ **45.** $(3 + \sqrt{5})(7 - \sqrt{5})$

46. $(\sqrt{a} + \sqrt{b})(\sqrt{a} + \sqrt{b})$ **47.** $(\sqrt{a} - \sqrt{b})(\sqrt{a} + \sqrt{b})$

48. $(\sqrt{3} - 2)^2$ **49.** $(3 + \sqrt{7})^2$

50. $(3\sqrt{2} + 5)^2$ **51.** $(x - \sqrt{y})^2$

In 52–55, find the area of a square whose side measures:

52. $\sqrt{2}$ **53.** $2\sqrt{3}$ **54.** $6\sqrt{2}$ **55.** $5\sqrt{3}$

56. Find, in simplest radical form, the value of the expression $x^2 - 3x + 2$ when x is equal to:

     a. $\sqrt{2}$ b. $\sqrt{3}$ c. $\sqrt{5}$ d. $3\sqrt{2}$ e. $2\sqrt{3}$ f. $3 + \sqrt{2}$ g. $5 - \sqrt{3}$

57. Show, by substitution, that if $y = 3\sqrt{2}$, the expression $y^2 - 3y - 6$ has the value $3(4 - 3\sqrt{2})$.

58. Show, by substitution, that if $x = 1 + \sqrt{3}$, the expression $x^2 - 2x - 2$ has the value 0.

PRODUCTS INVOLVING IRRATIONAL NUMBERS

The product of the rational number 8 and the irrational number $\sqrt{2}$ is the irrational number $8\sqrt{2}$. This example illustrates the following principle which we will assume to be true.

The product of an irrational number and a nonzero rational number is an irrational number.

The product $\sqrt{7} \cdot \sqrt{3} = \sqrt{21}$ is an irrational number. Whereas the product $\sqrt{27} \cdot \sqrt{3} = 9$ is a rational number. Hence, we say:

The product of two irrational numbers is sometimes an irrational number and sometimes a rational number.

EXERCISES

In 1–4, state whether the product is an irrational number or a rational number.

1. $(5\sqrt{12})(4\sqrt{3})$ **2.** $8\sqrt{2}(3\sqrt{32} - 2\sqrt{18})$

3. $(5 + \sqrt{3})(9 - 2\sqrt{3})$ **4.** $(7 + 3\sqrt{2})(7 - 3\sqrt{2})$

15. Dividing Radicals Which Have the Same Index

We have learned that $\dfrac{\sqrt[n]{a}}{\sqrt[n]{b}} = \sqrt[n]{\dfrac{a}{b}}$ (when a is non-negative, b is positive, and n is a positive integer). For example:

$$\frac{\sqrt{72}}{\sqrt{8}} = \sqrt{\frac{72}{8}} = \sqrt{9} = 3 \quad and \quad \frac{\sqrt[3]{54}}{\sqrt[3]{2}} = \sqrt[3]{\frac{54}{2}} = \sqrt[3]{27} = 3$$

To divide $6\sqrt{10}$ by $3\sqrt{2}$, we use the property of fractions, $\dfrac{ac}{bd} = \dfrac{a}{b} \cdot \dfrac{c}{d}$. See how the division is performed:

$$\frac{6\sqrt{10}}{3\sqrt{2}} = \frac{6}{3} \cdot \frac{\sqrt{10}}{\sqrt{2}} = \frac{6}{3} \cdot \sqrt{\frac{10}{2}} = 2\sqrt{5}$$

In general, if a is non-negative, b is positive, n is a positive integer, and $y \neq 0$:

$$\frac{x\sqrt[n]{a}}{y\sqrt[n]{b}} = \frac{x}{y}\sqrt[n]{\frac{a}{b}}$$

Procedure. To divide two monomial radicals which have the same index:

1. **Divide the coefficients to find the coefficient of the quotient.**
2. **Divide the radicands to find the radicand of the quotient. Use the same index to write the quotient radical.**
3. **If possible, simplify the result.**

Model Problems

1. Divide: $8\sqrt{48} \div 4\sqrt{2}$

   Solution: $8\sqrt{48} \div 4\sqrt{2} = \frac{8}{4}\sqrt{\frac{48}{2}} = 2\sqrt{24} = 2\sqrt{4 \cdot 6} = 2 \cdot \sqrt{4} \cdot \sqrt{6}$
   $$= 2 \cdot 2 \cdot \sqrt{6} = 4\sqrt{6} \quad Ans.$$

2. Divide: $\sqrt[3]{6x^4} \div \sqrt[3]{2x}$

   Solution: $\sqrt[3]{6x^4} \div \sqrt[3]{2x} = \sqrt[3]{\frac{6x^4}{2x}} = \sqrt[3]{3x^3} = \sqrt[3]{x^3 \cdot 3} = \sqrt[3]{x^3} \cdot \sqrt[3]{3}$
   $$= x\sqrt[3]{3} \quad Ans.$$

3. Divide: $\dfrac{\sqrt{21}+\sqrt{35}}{\sqrt{7}}$

Solution: $\dfrac{\sqrt{21}+\sqrt{35}}{\sqrt{7}} = \dfrac{\sqrt{21}}{\sqrt{7}} + \dfrac{\sqrt{35}}{\sqrt{7}} = \sqrt{\dfrac{21}{7}} + \sqrt{\dfrac{35}{7}}$

$= \sqrt{3} + \sqrt{5}$ *Ans.*

Keep In Mind

The quotient of two radicals with the same index is equal to the root of the quotient of their radicands, using the same index.

EXERCISES

In 1–24, divide. Then simplify the quotient.

1. $\sqrt{72} \div \sqrt{2}$

2. $\sqrt{18} \div \sqrt{3}$

3. $8\sqrt{48} \div 2\sqrt{3}$

4. $\sqrt{150} \div \sqrt{3}$

5. $21\sqrt{40} \div \sqrt{5}$

6. $9\sqrt{6} \div 3\sqrt{6}$

7. $7\sqrt{3} \div 3\sqrt{3}$

8. $2\sqrt{2} \div 8\sqrt{2}$

9. $\sqrt[3]{24} \div \sqrt[3]{3}$

10. $\sqrt[3]{60} \div \sqrt[3]{15}$

11. $12\sqrt[3]{32} \div 4\sqrt[3]{2}$

12. $8\sqrt[3]{6} \div 2\sqrt[3]{6}$

13. $\sqrt{9y} \div \sqrt{y}$

14. $8\sqrt{3a} \div 2\sqrt{a}$

15. $5\sqrt[3]{54x^2} \div 15\sqrt[3]{2x^2}$

16. $\dfrac{20\sqrt{50}}{4\sqrt{2}}$

17. $\dfrac{25\sqrt{24}}{5\sqrt{2}}$

18. $\dfrac{3\sqrt[3]{32}}{6\sqrt[3]{2}}$

19. $\dfrac{\sqrt{y^3}}{\sqrt{y}}$

20. $\dfrac{6\sqrt{27a^5}}{2\sqrt{3a^3}}$

21. $\dfrac{2\sqrt[3]{81a^4b^2}}{6\sqrt[3]{3ab^2}}$

22. $\dfrac{\sqrt{27}+\sqrt{75}}{\sqrt{3}}$

23. $\dfrac{\sqrt{24}-\sqrt{6}}{\sqrt{2}}$

24. $\dfrac{20\sqrt{15}+15\sqrt{60}}{5\sqrt{3}}$

In 25–30, simplify the expression. Then approximate the result to the *nearest tenth.*

25. $\dfrac{\sqrt{8}+\sqrt{16}}{\sqrt{2}}$

26. $\dfrac{\sqrt{125}-\sqrt{10}}{\sqrt{5}}$

27. $\dfrac{6\sqrt{27}+12\sqrt{15}}{3\sqrt{3}}$

28. $\dfrac{4+\sqrt{8}}{2}$

29. $\dfrac{6-\sqrt{27}}{3}$

30. $\dfrac{-5-\sqrt{50}}{5}$

QUOTIENTS INVOLVING IRRATIONAL NUMBERS

The quotient of the irrational number $\sqrt{2}$ and the rational number 2 is the irrational number $\frac{\sqrt{2}}{2}$. Also, the quotient of the rational number 3 and the irrational number $\sqrt{3}$ is the irrational number $\frac{3}{\sqrt{3}}$. These examples illustrate the following principle which we will assume to be true.

A quotient involving an irrational number and a nonzero rational number is an irrational number.

The quotient $(\sqrt{48}) \div (\sqrt{3}) = \sqrt{16} = 4$ is a rational number. On the other hand, the quotient $(\sqrt{48}) \div (\sqrt{2}) = \sqrt{24}$ is an irrational number. Hence, we say:

The quotient of two irrational numbers is sometimes a rational number and sometimes an irrational number.

EXERCISES

In 1-4, state whether the quotient is an irrational number or a rational number.

1. $6\sqrt{162} \div 3\sqrt{2}$ 2. $6 \div \sqrt[3]{3}$ 3. $(15 + \sqrt{3}) \div 3$ 4. $\sqrt{54} \div \sqrt{3}$

16. Rationalizing an Irrational Radical Denominator

To find the approximate value of $\frac{1}{\sqrt{3}}$, we can use 1.732 as the approximate value of $\sqrt{3}$, and then divide 1 by 1.732. The result obtained is approximately .577, but the four-digit divisor makes this an inconvenient computation. To simplify the computation, we multiply $\frac{1}{\sqrt{3}}$ by 1 in the form of $\frac{\sqrt{3}}{\sqrt{3}}$. We obtain:

$$\frac{1}{\sqrt{3}} = \frac{1}{\sqrt{3}} \cdot \frac{\sqrt{3}}{\sqrt{3}} = \frac{\sqrt{3}}{3} \approx \frac{1.732}{3} \approx .577$$

We transformed the fraction $\frac{1}{\sqrt{3}}$, which has an irrational denominator, $\sqrt{3}$, into an equivalent fraction, $\frac{\sqrt{3}}{3}$, which has a rational denominator, 3. This process is called *rationalizing the denominator* of the fraction.

When a fraction has a radical which represents an irrational number in the denominator, it is not in simplest form. To simplify such a fraction, we rationalize the denominator.

Procedure. To rationalize an irrational radical denominator of a fraction, multiply the fraction by 1 represented as a fraction whose numerator and denominator are both the least radical that will make the denominator of the resulting fraction a rational number.

Model Problem

Rationalize the denominator of (a) $\dfrac{12}{\sqrt{2}}$ and (b) $\dfrac{4\sqrt[3]{5}}{5\sqrt[3]{3}}$

Solution:

a. $\dfrac{12}{\sqrt{2}} = \dfrac{12}{\sqrt{2}} \cdot \dfrac{\sqrt{2}}{\sqrt{2}} = \dfrac{12\sqrt{2}}{\sqrt{4}} = \dfrac{12\sqrt{2}}{2} = 6\sqrt{2}$ *Ans.*

b. $\dfrac{4\sqrt[3]{5}}{5\sqrt[3]{3}} = \dfrac{4\sqrt[3]{5}}{5\sqrt[3]{3}} \cdot \dfrac{\sqrt[3]{9}}{\sqrt[3]{9}} = \dfrac{4\sqrt[3]{45}}{5\sqrt[3]{27}} = \dfrac{4\sqrt[3]{45}}{5 \cdot 3} = \dfrac{4\sqrt[3]{45}}{15}$ *Ans.*

EXERCISES

In 1–25, rationalize the denominator and simplify the resulting fraction.

1. $\dfrac{1}{\sqrt{7}}$ 2. $\dfrac{1}{\sqrt{x}}$ 3. $\dfrac{5}{\sqrt{3}}$ 4. $\dfrac{9}{\sqrt{7}}$ 5. $\dfrac{8}{\sqrt{11}}$

6. $\dfrac{8}{\sqrt{2}}$ 7. $\dfrac{9}{\sqrt{3}}$ 8. $\dfrac{25}{\sqrt{5}}$ 9. $\dfrac{6}{\sqrt{6}}$ 10. $\dfrac{7}{\sqrt{7}}$

11. $\dfrac{12}{\sqrt{8}}$ 12. $\dfrac{6}{\sqrt{12}}$ 13. $\dfrac{36}{\sqrt{18}}$ 14. $\dfrac{25}{\sqrt{20}}$ 15. $\dfrac{30}{\sqrt{50}}$

16. $\dfrac{12}{2\sqrt{3}}$ 17. $\dfrac{18}{3\sqrt{2}}$ 18. $\dfrac{60}{3\sqrt{8}}$ 19. $\dfrac{\sqrt{6}}{\sqrt{5}}$ 20. $\dfrac{15\sqrt{3}}{\sqrt{5}}$

21. $\dfrac{9}{\sqrt[3]{9}}$ 22. $\dfrac{15}{\sqrt[3]{2}}$ 23. $\dfrac{6\sqrt[3]{3}}{\sqrt[3]{25}}$ 24. $\dfrac{7\sqrt[3]{15}}{\sqrt[3]{4}}$ 25. $\dfrac{5\sqrt[3]{2}}{7\sqrt[3]{3}}$

In 26–30, transform the fraction into an equivalent fraction which does not have a radical in the denominator.

26. $\dfrac{1}{\sqrt{y}}$ 27. $\dfrac{\sqrt{r}}{\sqrt{s}}$ 28. $\dfrac{a}{\sqrt[3]{b}}$ 29. $\dfrac{8}{\sqrt{2a}}$ 30. $\dfrac{\sqrt{2s}}{\sqrt{g}}$

In 31–34, rationalize the denominator and simplify the resulting fraction.

31. $\dfrac{\sqrt{8}+\sqrt{18}}{\sqrt{2}}$ 32. $\dfrac{\sqrt{7}-1}{\sqrt{7}}$ 33. $\dfrac{4\sqrt{3}+2}{\sqrt{3}}$ 34. $\dfrac{\sqrt{5}-\sqrt{7}}{\sqrt{5}}$

In 35–39, approximate the value of the fraction to the *nearest* *tenth*.

35. $\dfrac{12}{\sqrt{3}}$ 36. $\dfrac{4}{\sqrt{2}}$ 37. $\dfrac{8}{\sqrt{8}}$ 38. $\dfrac{5}{\sqrt{2}}$ 39. $\dfrac{\sqrt{2}-1}{\sqrt{2}}$

17. Rationalizing a Binomial Radical Denominator

The expressions $3+\sqrt{2}$ and $3-\sqrt{2}$ bear a special relationship to each other. They are called **conjugate binomial radicals.** Each binomial is the **conjugate** of the other. Other examples of conjugate binomial radicals are:

$$\sqrt{5}+\sqrt{7} \quad \text{and} \quad \sqrt{5}-\sqrt{7}$$
$$8\sqrt{3}+2\sqrt{13} \quad \text{and} \quad 8\sqrt{3}-2\sqrt{13}$$

In any pair of conjugate binomial radicals involving square roots, one of the binomials is a sum of two numbers and the other is the difference of the same two numbers.

In each of the following three examples we will find the product of two conjugate binomial radicals involving square roots.

1. $(3+\sqrt{2})(3-\sqrt{2})=9-4=5$, which is a rational number.
2. $(\sqrt{5}+\sqrt{7})(\sqrt{5}-\sqrt{7})=5-7=-2$, which is a rational number.
3. $(8\sqrt{3}+2\sqrt{13})(8\sqrt{3}-2\sqrt{13})=64\cdot3-4\cdot13=140$, which is a rational number.

In general, the following products are rational numbers:

$$(a+\sqrt{b})(a-\sqrt{b})=a^2-b \quad (a \text{ and } b \text{ are rational}, b \geq 0)$$
$$(\sqrt{a}+\sqrt{b})(\sqrt{a}-\sqrt{b})=a-b \quad (a \text{ and } b \text{ are rational}, a \geq 0,$$
$$b \geq 0)$$
$$(c\sqrt{a}+d\sqrt{b})(c\sqrt{a}-d\sqrt{b})=c^2a-d^2b \quad (a,b,c, \text{ and } d \text{ are rational},$$
$$a \geq 0, b \geq 0)$$

Hence, we say:

The product of two conjugate binomial radicals involving square roots is a rational number.

In each of the following model problems, we will make use of this fact to rationalize a binomial radical denominator involving square roots.

Model Problems

In 1 and 2, express the fraction as an equivalent fraction with a rational denominator.

$$1.\ \frac{10}{3+\sqrt{5}} \qquad\qquad 2.\ \frac{3\sqrt{3}-4}{2\sqrt{3}-3}$$

How to Proceed   *Solution*   *Solution*

1. Multiply the given fraction by 1 represented as a fraction whose numerator and denominator are each the conjugate of the denominator of the given fraction.

$$1.\ \frac{10}{3+\sqrt{5}}$$

$$=\frac{10}{3+\sqrt{5}}\cdot\frac{3-\sqrt{5}}{3-\sqrt{5}}$$

$$=\frac{10(3-\sqrt{5})}{9-5}$$

$$1.\ \frac{3\sqrt{3}-4}{2\sqrt{3}-3}$$

$$=\frac{3\sqrt{3}-4}{2\sqrt{3}-3}\cdot\frac{2\sqrt{3}+3}{2\sqrt{3}+3}$$

$$=\frac{18+\sqrt{3}-12}{12-9}$$

2. Simplify the resulting fraction.

$$2.\ =\frac{\overset{5}{\cancel{10}}(3-\sqrt{5})}{\underset{2}{\cancel{4}}}$$

$$=\frac{5(3-\sqrt{5})}{2}\ \textit{Ans.}$$

$$2.\ =\frac{6+\sqrt{3}}{3}\ \textit{Ans.}$$

EXERCISES

In 1–12, rationalize the denominator of the given fraction.

$$1.\ \frac{2}{4-\sqrt{3}} \qquad\qquad 2.\ \frac{3}{3-\sqrt{5}} \qquad\qquad 3.\ \frac{11}{\sqrt{2}-2}$$

4. $\dfrac{1}{\sqrt{6}-1}$ 5. $\dfrac{5}{3\sqrt{2}+2}$ 6. $\dfrac{2}{3\sqrt{5}-3}$

7. $\dfrac{\sqrt{3}+3}{\sqrt{3}-1}$ 8. $\dfrac{8+\sqrt{2}}{5-\sqrt{2}}$ 9. $\dfrac{4\sqrt{5}-3}{4\sqrt{5}+3}$

10. $\dfrac{3-4\sqrt{2}}{7+5\sqrt{2}}$ 11. $\dfrac{\sqrt{7}-\sqrt{5}}{\sqrt{7}+\sqrt{5}}$ 12. $\dfrac{2\sqrt{3}-3\sqrt{7}}{3\sqrt{7}+4\sqrt{3}}$

In 13-18, express the fraction as an equivalent fraction which has a rational denominator. In 16-18, a and b represent positive rational numbers.

13. $\dfrac{4}{1+\sqrt{2}}$ 14. $\dfrac{\sqrt{3}-5}{\sqrt{3}-1}$ 15. $\dfrac{2+\sqrt{3}}{2+\sqrt{5}}$

16. $\dfrac{1}{a+\sqrt{b}}\,(a\neq\sqrt{b})$ 17. $\dfrac{\sqrt{a}}{\sqrt{a}-\sqrt{b}}\,(a\neq b)$ 18. $\dfrac{a+\sqrt{b}}{a-\sqrt{b}}\,(a\neq\sqrt{b})$

18. Solving Radical Equations

A *radical equation* is an equation in which a variable appears in the radicand of a radical. For example, $\sqrt{x}=2$ and $\sqrt{2x-1}=3$ are radical equations.

The method used to solve such radical equations, in which the radical is the only term of one member of the equation, depends on the following principle:

If two numbers are equal, the squares of these numbers are equal.

For example, since $(4+3)=(6+1)$ because each numeral represents the number 7, then $(4+3)^2=(6+1)^2$ because both numerals represent the same number, 7^2, or 49.

In general, if $a=b$, then $a^2=b^2$.
Recall that if $\sqrt{a}=b$, then $(\sqrt{a})^2=b^2$.

Let us solve the radical equation $\sqrt{x}=2$ by squaring both members of the equation.

Solution	*Check*
$\sqrt{x}=2$	$\sqrt{x}=2$
$(\sqrt{x})^2=(2)^2$	$\sqrt{4}\overset{?}{=}2$
$x=4$	$2=2$ (true)

Since 4 can replace x in the original equation, 4 is a root of $\sqrt{x}=2$. The solution set is $\{4\}$.

Let us now consider the radical equation $\sqrt{x} = -2$.

| *Solution* | *Check* |

$$\sqrt{x} = -2$$
$$(\sqrt{x})^2 = (-2)^2$$
$$x = 4$$

$$\sqrt{x} = -2$$
$$\sqrt{4} \overset{?}{=} -2$$
$$2 = -2 \quad \text{(false)}$$

We see that 4 is not a root of $\sqrt{x} = -2$, although it is a root of the derived equation $x = 4$.

Let us see why this happened. If $a^2 = b^2$, it is not necessarily true that $a = b$. For example, $(-7)^2 = (+7)^2$, but $-7 \neq +7$. Therefore, when we square both members of an equation, the solution set of the derived equation may not be the same as the solution set of the original equation. That is, the derived equation and the original equation may not be equivalent equations.

It should come as no surprise to us that 4 is not a solution of $\sqrt{x} = -2$. Since $\sqrt{x}$ is non-negative, it cannot be equal to -2, which is negative. In fact, no real number can satisfy the equation $\sqrt{x} = -2$. Hence, the solution set of the equation $\sqrt{x} = -2$ is the empty set $\emptyset$.

Whenever we solve an equation by squaring both members, we must be very careful to check the roots of the derived equation in the given equation to see that these roots also satisfy the given equation.

Recall that if $\sqrt[3]{a} = b$, then $a = b^3$.

To solve the equation $\sqrt[3]{x-4} = 2$, we would cube both members of the equation.

| *Solution* | *Check* |

$$\sqrt[3]{x-4} = 2$$
$$(\sqrt[3]{x-4})^3 = (2)^3$$
$$x - 4 = 8$$
$$x = 12$$

$$\sqrt[3]{x-4} = 2$$
$$\sqrt[3]{12-4} \overset{?}{=} 2$$
$$\sqrt[3]{8} \overset{?}{=} 2$$
$$2 = 2 \quad \text{(true)}$$

Since 12 can replace x in the original equation, 12 is a root of $\sqrt[3]{x-4} = 2$. The solution set is $\{12\}$.

Procedure. To solve a radical equation:

1. **Isolate the radical in one member of the equation.**
2. **If the radical is a square root, square both members of the equation; if it is a cube root, cube both members of the equation; and so on.**
3. **Solve the derived equation.**
4. **Check the roots of the derived equation in the given equation.**

Model Problems

1. Solve and check: $\sqrt{2x-1} = 3$

How to Proceed	Solution	Check
Write the equation.	$\sqrt{2x-1} = 3$	$\sqrt{2x-1} = 3$
Square both members.	$(\sqrt{2x-1})^2 = (3)^2$	$\sqrt{(2)(5)-1} \overset{?}{=} 3$
Simplify.	$2x-1 = 9$	$\sqrt{10-1} \overset{?}{=} 3$
A_1	$2x = 10$	$\sqrt{9} \overset{?}{=} 3$
D_2	$x = 5$	$3 = 3$ (true)

Answer: $x = 5$, or solution set is $\{5\}$.

2. Solve and check: $3\sqrt[3]{x} + 1 = 10$

How to Proceed	Solution	Check
Write the equation.	$3\sqrt[3]{x} + 1 = 10$	$3\sqrt[3]{x} + 1 = 10$
S_1 to isolate the radical term.	$3\sqrt[3]{x} = 9$	$3\sqrt[3]{27} + 1 \overset{?}{=} 10$
Cube both members.	$(3\sqrt[3]{x})^3 = (9)^3$	$3(3) + 1 \overset{?}{=} 10$
Simplify.	$27x = 729$	$9 + 1 \overset{?}{=} 10$
D_{27}	$x = 27$	$10 = 10$ (true)

Answer: $x = 27$, or solution set is $\{27\}$.

3. Solve and check: $\sqrt{3x+4} - 3 = -7$

How to Proceed	Solution	Check
Write the equation.	$\sqrt{3x+4} - 3 = -7$	$\sqrt{3x+4} - 3 = -7$
A_3	$\sqrt{3x+4} = -4$	$\sqrt{(3)(4)+4} - 3 \overset{?}{=} -7$
Square.	$(\sqrt{3x+4})^2 = (-4)^2$	$\sqrt{12+4} - 3 \overset{?}{=} -7$
Simplify.	$3x+4 = 16$	$\sqrt{16} - 3 \overset{?}{=} -7$
S_4	$3x = 12$	$4 - 3 \overset{?}{=} -7$
D_3	$x = 4$	$1 = -7$ (false)

Since 4 does not satisfy the equation $\sqrt{3x+4} - 3 = -7$, it is not a root of that equation. The given equation has no root.

Answer: No root, or solution set is the empty set, $\emptyset$.

EXERCISES

In 1–36, solve and check the equation. If there is no root, write "no root."

1. $\sqrt{x} = 5$ 2. $\sqrt{y} = 8$ 3. $\sqrt{z} = -4$

4. $\sqrt{a} = 1.2$ 5. $\sqrt{b} = \frac{1}{4}$ 6. $\sqrt[3]{c} = 4$

7. $\sqrt{2x} = 8$ 8. $\sqrt{3y} = 4$ 9. $2\sqrt{x} = 6$

10. $4\sqrt{a} = 36$ 11. $2\sqrt{y} = 1$ 12. $3\sqrt[3]{m} = 6$

13. $5\sqrt{r} = -2$ 14. $\sqrt{\dfrac{x}{4}} = 6$ 15. $\sqrt{\dfrac{3z}{2}} = 6$

16. $3\sqrt{2x} = 12$ 17. $2\sqrt{5x} = 20$ 18. $4\sqrt{3x} = -9$

19. $\sqrt{b-1} = 8$ 20. $\sqrt{r+3} = 5$ 21. $\sqrt{3a+3} = 6$

22. $\sqrt{2b-4} = 10$ 23. $\sqrt{x+3} = 8$ 24. $\sqrt{m-6} = 2$

25. $\sqrt{2r+7} = 8$ 26. $3\sqrt[3]{x} - 2 = 10$ 27. $4\sqrt{y} + 1 = 8$

28. $\sqrt{2x+1} - 1 = 4$ 29. $\sqrt{5y-1} - 3 = 0$ 30. $5 + \sqrt{2x-4} = 1$

31. $\dfrac{10}{\sqrt{x}} = \sqrt{x}$ 32. $\dfrac{3}{\sqrt{y-5}} = \sqrt{y-5}$

33. $\sqrt{2x+1} = \dfrac{7}{\sqrt{2x+1}}$ 34. $\sqrt{3x-8} = \sqrt{x}$

35. $\sqrt{5y} = \sqrt{2y+6}$ 36. $\sqrt[3]{4z-3} = \sqrt[3]{3z+4}$

In 37–39, solve the equation for the indicated variable.

37. $s = \sqrt{A}$ for A 38. $R = \sqrt{\dfrac{A}{\pi}}$ for A 39. $e = \sqrt{\dfrac{s}{6}}$ for s

19. Rational Exponents

Until now, the exponent n of the power x^n has been limited to the set of integers. Now, we will see that a power can have as an exponent a rational number such as $\frac{1}{2}$ or $\frac{1}{3}$. If we wish $5^{\frac{1}{2}}$ to have a meaning which will preserve all the laws of exponents we have previously established, it should be true that $(5^{\frac{1}{2}})^2 = 5^{\frac{1}{2} \cdot 2} = 5^1 = 5$. Since $5^{\frac{1}{2}}$ must represent a number whose square is 5, this suggests that we define $5^{\frac{1}{2}}$ to be $\sqrt{5}$. Also, if it is to be true that $(5^{\frac{1}{3}})^3 = 5^{\frac{1}{3} \cdot 3} = 5^1 = 5$, then $5^{\frac{1}{3}}$ must represent a number whose cube is 5. This suggests that we define $5^{\frac{1}{3}}$ to be $\sqrt[3]{5}$.

In general, we define the symbol $x^{\frac{1}{n}}$ as follows:

$$x^{\frac{1}{n}} = \sqrt[n]{x} \text{ for all positive integers } n.$$

Hence, $x^{\frac{1}{2}} = \sqrt{x}$, the principal square root of x; $x^{\frac{1}{3}} = \sqrt[3]{x}$, the principal cube root of x; etc. For example, $25^{\frac{1}{2}} = \sqrt{25} = 5$; also $8^{\frac{1}{3}} = \sqrt[3]{8} = 2$.

Note: If n is even and x is negative, then $x^{\frac{1}{n}}$ is not defined in the set of real numbers. For example, $(-1)^{\frac{1}{2}}$ does not represent a real number because there is no real number whose square is -1.

Now, let us go one step further. If we wish $5^{\frac{2}{3}}$ to have a meaning which will preserve all the laws of exponents previously established, it should be true that $(5^{\frac{1}{3}})^2 = 5^{\frac{1}{3} \cdot 2} = 5^{\frac{2}{3}}$. This suggests that we define $5^{\frac{2}{3}}$ as $(5^{\frac{1}{3}})^2$. For similar reasons, we would define $5^{\frac{3}{2}}$ as $(5^{\frac{1}{2}})^3$.

In general, we define the symbol $x^{\frac{m}{n}}$ as follows:

$$x^{\frac{m}{n}} = (x^{\frac{1}{n}})^m \text{ for all positive integers } n \text{ and all integers } m.$$

For example:

$$4^{\frac{3}{2}} = (4^{\frac{1}{2}})^3 \quad = (\sqrt{4})^3 \quad = (2)^3 = 8$$
$$27^{\frac{2}{3}} = (27^{\frac{1}{3}})^2 \quad = (\sqrt[3]{27})^2 \quad = (3)^2 = 9$$
$$16^{-\frac{3}{4}} = (16^{\frac{1}{4}})^{-3} = (\sqrt[4]{16})^{-3} = 2^{-3} \quad = \frac{1}{2^3} = \frac{1}{8}$$

Observe that when a rational number, a fraction, serves as an exponent, both a root and a power are to be found. The denominator of the exponent indicates the root and the numerator represents the power.

We see, therefore, that any rational number may serve as an exponent. A rational number that serves as an exponent is called a ***rational exponent,*** or a ***fractional exponent.***

In all the situations with which we will deal, all the laws of exponents which held for integer exponents will hold for rational exponents also.

It is interesting to note that the order in which the operations of raising to a power and taking a root are performed has no effect on the result. For example, when we evaluated $4^{\frac{3}{2}}$, we first found the square root of 4 ($\sqrt{4} = 2$), then cubed the result ($2^3 = 8$), obtaining 8 as the value. If we now evaluate $4^{\frac{3}{2}}$ by first cubing 4 ($4^3 = 64$), then finding the square root of 64 ($\sqrt{64} = 8$), we again obtain 8 as the value. That is, $4^{\frac{3}{2}} = (4^{\frac{1}{2}})^3$; also $4^{\frac{3}{2}} = \sqrt{4^3}$. In general,

$$x^{\frac{m}{n}} = (x^{\frac{1}{n}})^m \text{ ; also } x^{\frac{m}{n}} = \sqrt[n]{x^m} \text{ for all positive integers } n \text{ and all integers } m.$$

Model Problems

1. Find the value of $4^{\frac{1}{2}} + 64^{\frac{1}{3}}$

Solution:

$4^{\frac{1}{2}} = \sqrt{4} = 2$

$64^{\frac{1}{3}} = \sqrt[3]{64} = 4$

$4^{\frac{1}{2}} + 64^{\frac{1}{3}} = 2 + 4$

$\qquad\qquad = 6$ *Ans.*

2. Find the value of $(27)^{-\frac{1}{3}} + \frac{1}{2}(16^{\frac{3}{2}})$

Solution:

$(27)^{-\frac{1}{3}} = (27^{\frac{1}{3}})^{-1} = \dfrac{1}{27^{\frac{1}{3}}} = \dfrac{1}{\sqrt[3]{27}} = \dfrac{1}{3}$

$16^{\frac{3}{2}} = (16^{\frac{1}{2}})^3 = (\sqrt{16})^3 = (4)^3 = 64$

$(27)^{-\frac{1}{3}} + \frac{1}{2}(16^{\frac{3}{2}}) = \frac{1}{3} + \frac{1}{2}(64)$

$\qquad\qquad\qquad = \frac{1}{3} + 32$

$\qquad\qquad\qquad = 32\frac{1}{3}$ *Ans.*

3. Simplify the expression $\left(\dfrac{8x^6}{y^{12}}\right)^{\frac{1}{3}}$.

Solution:

$\left(\dfrac{8x^6}{y^{12}}\right)^{\frac{1}{3}} = \sqrt[3]{\dfrac{8x^6}{y^{12}}}$

$\qquad = \dfrac{\sqrt[3]{8x^6}}{\sqrt[3]{y^{12}}}$

$\qquad = \dfrac{2x^3}{y^4}$ *Ans.*

EXERCISES

In 1–12, represent the expression by using a radical sign.

1. $3^{\frac{1}{2}}$ **2.** $2^{\frac{1}{3}}$ **3.** $a^{\frac{1}{4}}$ **4.** $(2y)^{\frac{1}{2}}$

5. $(-27)^{\frac{1}{3}}$ **6.** $(11b)^{\frac{1}{2}}$ **7.** $(49ab)^{\frac{1}{2}}$ **8.** $x^{\frac{2}{3}}$

9. $(2y)^{\frac{3}{4}}$ **10.** $a^{-\frac{1}{5}}$ **11.** $(27x)^{-\frac{4}{3}}$ **12.** $(2x^2y)^{-\frac{5}{4}}$

In 13–20, represent the radical by using a fractional exponent.

13. $\sqrt{3}$ **14.** $\sqrt[3]{27}$ **15.** $\sqrt[4]{x}$ **16.** $\sqrt[3]{3z}$

17. $\sqrt{\dfrac{1}{x^5}}$ **18.** $\sqrt[3]{b^4}$ **19.** $\sqrt[5]{x^3z^4}$ **20.** $\sqrt[3]{8y^2x}$

In 21–34, evaluate the expression.

21. $4^{\frac{1}{2}}$ **22.** $8^{\frac{1}{3}}$ **23.** $8^{\frac{2}{3}}$ **24.** $16^{\frac{5}{4}}$

25. $(4)^{-\frac{1}{2}}$ 26. $(8)^{-\frac{1}{3}}$ 27. $(125)^{-\frac{2}{3}}$ 28. $(16)^{-\frac{5}{4}}$

29. $16^{\frac{1}{2}} + 27^{\frac{1}{3}}$ 30. $125^{\frac{2}{3}} - 49^{\frac{1}{2}}$ 31. $(9)^{\frac{3}{2}} + (121)^{\frac{1}{2}} + (25)^{-\frac{1}{2}}$

32. $(64)^{\frac{1}{2}} \cdot (4)^{-\frac{3}{2}}$ 33. $(27)^{\frac{2}{3}} \cdot (3)^{-2}$ 34. $(81)^{-\frac{1}{2}} \cdot (27)^{\frac{1}{3}}$

35. Find the value of $3a^0 - 2a^{\frac{1}{2}}$ when $a = 4$.

36. Find the value of $3x^{\frac{3}{4}} - 2x^{-\frac{3}{2}}$ when $x = 16$.

37. Find the value of $2x^{-\frac{1}{3}} + 5x^{\frac{3}{2}}$ when $x = 64$.

In 38–45, simplify the expression. All literal exponents represent rational numbers.

38. $\left(\dfrac{x^2}{49}\right)^{\frac{1}{2}}$ 39. $\left(\dfrac{y^{3a}}{27}\right)^{\frac{1}{3}}$ 40. $\left(\dfrac{81z^{8b}}{y^4}\right)^{\frac{1}{4}}$ 41. $\left(\dfrac{c^4}{81}\right)^{\frac{3}{2}}$

42. $(x^{10})^{-\frac{1}{2}}$ 43. $\left(\dfrac{4y^6}{121}\right)^{-\frac{3}{2}}$ 44. $\left(\dfrac{x^4 \cdot y^6}{9z^2}\right)^{\frac{1}{2}}$ 45. $\left(\dfrac{c^{2a}}{4}\right)^{-\frac{1}{2}} \cdot \left(\dfrac{8c^{3b}}{d^6}\right)^{\frac{2}{3}}$

20. Applying the Laws of Exponents to Fractional Exponents

We have defined fractional exponents in such a way that they obey the same laws that integral exponents obey. Namely: if x and y are real numbers, $x \neq 0$, $y \neq 0$, and if a and b are rational numbers, then,

1. $x^a \cdot x^b = x^{a+b}$ 2. $(x^a)^b = x^{ab}$ 3. $\dfrac{x^a}{x^b} = x^{a-b}$

4. $(xy)^a = x^a y^a$ 5. $\left(\dfrac{x}{y}\right)^a = \dfrac{x^a}{y^a}$

Model Problems

In 1–6, simplify the expression.

1. $x^{\frac{1}{3}} \cdot x^{\frac{5}{3}}$ 2. $\left(x^{-8}\right)^{\frac{1}{2}}$ 3. $\dfrac{x^{\frac{3}{4}}}{x^{-\frac{1}{2}}}$

Solution

$x^{\frac{1}{3}} \cdot x^{\frac{5}{3}}$

$= x^{\frac{1}{3} + \frac{5}{3}}$

$= x^{\frac{6}{3}}$

$= x^2$ *Ans.*

Solution

$\left(x^{-8}\right)^{\frac{1}{2}}$

$= x^{(-8) \cdot \frac{1}{2}}$

$= x^{-\frac{8}{2}}$

$= x^{-4}$ or $\dfrac{1}{x^4}$ *Ans.*

Solution

$\dfrac{x^{\frac{3}{4}}}{x^{-\frac{1}{2}}}$

$= x^{\frac{3}{4} - (-\frac{1}{2})}$

$= x^{\frac{3}{4} + \frac{2}{4}}$

$= x^{\frac{5}{4}}$ *Ans.*

4. $(x^6 y^{-9})^{\frac{1}{3}}$

Solution

$(x^6 y^{-9})^{\frac{1}{3}}$

$= (x^6)^{\frac{1}{3}} (y^{-9})^{\frac{1}{3}}$

$= x^{6 \cdot \frac{1}{3}} y^{-9 \cdot \frac{1}{3}}$

$= x^2 y^{-3}$ *Ans.*

5. $\left(\dfrac{x^{\frac{1}{3}}}{y^{-\frac{5}{6}}}\right)^3$

Solution

$\left(\dfrac{x^{\frac{1}{3}}}{y^{-\frac{5}{6}}}\right)^3$

$= \dfrac{(x^{\frac{1}{3}})^3}{(y^{-\frac{5}{6}})^3}$

$= \dfrac{x^{\frac{1}{3} \cdot 3}}{y^{-\frac{5}{6} \cdot 3}}$

$= \dfrac{x}{y^{-\frac{5}{2}}}$ or $xy^{\frac{5}{2}}$ *Ans.*

6. $\left(\dfrac{10^{\frac{5}{3}} x^{-\frac{4}{3}}}{10^{\frac{1}{3}}}\right)^{-6}$

Solution

$\left(\dfrac{10^{\frac{5}{3}} x^{-\frac{4}{3}}}{10^{\frac{1}{3}}}\right)^{-6}$

$= (10^{\frac{5}{3} - \frac{1}{3}} x^{-\frac{4}{3}})^{-6}$

$= (10^{\frac{4}{3}})^{-6} (x^{-\frac{4}{3}})^{-6}$

$= 10^{-8} x^8$ or $\dfrac{x^8}{10^8}$ *Ans.*

7. Transform the radical $\sqrt[3]{x^2 y}$ to an equivalent radical whose index is 6.

Solution

Express $\sqrt[3]{x^2 y}$ in exponential form.

$\sqrt[3]{x^2 y} = (x^2 y)^{\frac{1}{3}} = (x^2 y)^{\frac{1}{3} \cdot \frac{2}{2}} = (x^2 y)^{\frac{2}{6}} = (x^2)^{\frac{2}{6}} (y)^{\frac{2}{6}} = x^{\frac{4}{6}} y^{\frac{2}{6}} = (x^4 y^2)^{\frac{1}{6}}$

$= \sqrt[6]{x^4 y^2}$ *Ans.*

8. Transform the radical $\sqrt[4]{16 x^4 y^6}$ to an equivalent radical which has the least possible index.

Solution

Express $\sqrt[4]{16 x^4 y^6}$ in exponential form.

$\sqrt[4]{16 x^4 y^6} = (2^4 x^4 y^6)^{\frac{1}{4}} = 2^{4 \cdot \frac{1}{4}} x^{4 \cdot \frac{1}{4}} y^{6 \cdot \frac{1}{4}} = 2xy^{\frac{3}{2}} = 2x\sqrt{y^3} = 2xy\sqrt{y}$

9. Multiply: $(\sqrt[3]{3x^2})(\sqrt{2x})$

Solution

Express radicals in exponential form.

$(\sqrt[3]{3x^2})(\sqrt{2x}) = (3x^2)^{\frac{1}{3}} (2x)^{\frac{1}{2}}$

$\qquad\qquad = (3x^2)^{\frac{2}{6}} (2x)^{\frac{3}{6}}$

$\qquad\qquad = (3^2 x^4 \cdot 2^3 x^3)^{\frac{1}{6}}$

$\qquad\qquad = \sqrt[6]{3^2 x^4 \cdot 2^3 x^3}$

$\qquad\qquad = \sqrt[6]{9 \cdot 8 \cdot x^7}$

$\qquad\qquad = x\sqrt[6]{72x}$ *Ans.*

Note that in this problem we found the product of two radicals which did not have the same index.

EXERCISES

In 1-20, simplify the expression. All literal exponents represent rational numbers.

1. $x^{\frac{1}{2}} \cdot x^{\frac{5}{2}}$ **2.** $y^{\frac{1}{2}} \cdot y^{-\frac{1}{4}}$ **3.** $10^{\frac{2}{3}} \cdot 10^{-\frac{1}{2}}$ **4.** $8^{-\frac{1}{3}} \cdot 8^{-\frac{5}{6}}$

5. $(x^6)^{\frac{1}{3}}$ **6.** $(x^{\frac{1}{2}})^{-4}$ **7.** $(x^{-\frac{2}{3}})^{-\frac{3}{2}}$ **8.** $(10^{\frac{1}{4}})^{\frac{3}{2}}$

9. $\dfrac{x^{\frac{3}{4}}}{x^{\frac{1}{2}}}$ **10.** $\dfrac{y^5}{y^{-\frac{2}{3}}}$ **11.** $\dfrac{y^{-\frac{5}{6}}}{y^{\frac{2}{3}}}$ **12.** $\dfrac{10^{-\frac{5}{8}}}{10^{-\frac{1}{2}}}$

13. $(x^4 y^{-6})^{\frac{1}{3}}$ **14.** $(x^{\frac{1}{4}} y^{-\frac{1}{2}})^6$ **15.** $(x^{\frac{1}{2}} y^{\frac{1}{3}})^{-6}$ **16.** $(2^{\frac{1}{2}} \cdot 3^{\frac{1}{4}})^{-2}$

17. $\left(\dfrac{x^{\frac{1}{2}}}{y^{\frac{3}{4}}}\right)^4$ **18.** $\left(\dfrac{x^{-\frac{2}{3}}}{y^{\frac{1}{2}}}\right)^6$ **19.** $\left(\dfrac{x^{\frac{5}{3}}}{y^{-\frac{1}{6}}}\right)^{12}$ **20.** $\left(\dfrac{x^{-\frac{3}{4}}}{x^{-\frac{5}{2}}}\right)^{-8}$

In 21-23, simplify the expression.

21. $\left(\dfrac{x^{\frac{2}{3}} y^{-\frac{1}{2}}}{z^{\frac{5}{6}}}\right)^6$ **22.** $\left(\dfrac{x^{-\frac{1}{4}} y^{-\frac{1}{2}}}{2^{\frac{3}{4}}}\right)^{-4}$ **23.** $\left(\dfrac{10^4 \cdot y^{-\frac{2}{3}}}{z^{\frac{5}{2}}}\right)^{\frac{1}{2}}$

In 24-28, transform the radical into an equivalent radical whose index is 12.

24. $\sqrt{x}$ **25.** $\sqrt{x^2 y^3}$ **26.** $\sqrt[3]{xy^2}$ **27.** $\sqrt[4]{x^3 y^2}$ **28.** $\sqrt[6]{2x^3 y^4}$

In 29-33, transform the radical into an equivalent radical which has the least possible index.

29. $\sqrt[4]{x^2}$ **30.** $\sqrt[4]{x^4 y^6}$ **31.** $\sqrt[4]{81 x^6 y^4}$

32. $\sqrt[6]{x^4 y^{12}}$ **33.** $\sqrt[6]{64 x^3 y^6}$

In 34-39, multiply the radicals.

34. $\sqrt{2} \cdot \sqrt[3]{3}$ **35.** $\sqrt[4]{2} \cdot \sqrt[3]{3}$ **36.** $\sqrt[4]{x^3} \cdot \sqrt[5]{x^2}$

37. $\sqrt[3]{9x^2} \cdot \sqrt{3x}$ **38.** $\sqrt[4]{8x^2} \cdot \sqrt[3]{2x^2}$ **39.** $\sqrt[3]{2xy^2} \cdot \sqrt{3x^3 y}$

Chapter 17

Quadratic Equations

1. The Standard Form of a Quadratic Equation

A *polynomial equation* is an equation which involves polynomials. When all terms of a polynomial equation in one variable are collected in one member of the equation and the other member is 0, we say the polynomial equation is in *standard form.* For example, the equation $x^2 - 3x - 10 = 0$ is in standard form.

The *degree of a polynomial equation* in standard form is the degree of the polynomial. For example, $x^2 - 3x - 10 = 0$ is an equation of the second degree. An equation of the second degree, such as $x^2 - 3x - 10 = 0$, is called a *quadratic equation.*

In general, the standard form of a quadratic equation in one variable is:

$$ax^2 + bx + c = 0$$

where a, b, and c are real numbers and $a \neq 0$.

Model Problems

1. In each part, tell whether the equation is a quadratic equation.

   a. $3x^2 - 5x + 2 = 0$ *Ans.* Yes   b. $x^3 + 2x^2 - 9 = 0$ *Ans.* No
   c. $x^2 - 4 = 0$ *Ans.* Yes   d. $2x - 4 = 0$ *Ans.* No

2. Transform the equation $x(x - 4) = 5$ into an equivalent quadratic equation which is in the standard form $ax^2 + bx + c = 0$.

   Solution

   $$x(x - 4) = 5$$
   $$x^2 - 4x = 5$$
   $$x^2 - 4x - 5 = 0 \quad Ans.$$

EXERCISES

In 1–9, state whether the equation is a quadratic equation.

1. $x^2 + 2x + 1 = 0$ **2.** $x^2 + 2x = 0$ **3.** $2x + 1 = 0$
4. $4 + x^2 = 7x$ **5.** $4x^3 + 7x^2 = 5$ **6.** $x^2 + 8 = x + x^2$

7. $\frac{1}{3}x^2 = \frac{1}{2}x$ **8.** $\dfrac{8}{x} = 5$ **9.** $x(x - 4) = 12$

In 10–18, transform the equation into an equivalent equation in the standard form $ax^2 + bx + c = 0$.

10. $x^2 + 9x = 10$ **11.** $2x^2 + 7x = 3x$ **12.** $x^2 = 3x - 8$
13. $4x + 3 = x^2$ **14.** $3x^2 = 27x$ **15.** $x(x - 3) = 10$

16. $x^2 = 5(x + 4)$ **17.** $\dfrac{x^2}{2} + 3 = \dfrac{x}{4}$ **18.** $x^2 = 6 - \dfrac{x}{2}$

2. Using Factoring to Solve a Quadratic Equation

Consider these products:

$$5 \times 0 = 0 \qquad \tfrac{1}{2} \times 0 = 0 \qquad (-2) \times 0 = 0$$

$$0 \times 7 = 0 \qquad 0 \times \tfrac{1}{3} = 0 \qquad 0 \times (-3) = 0$$

These examples illustrate the following principle, which we have called the *multiplication property of zero.*

The product of 0 and any real number is 0.

Consider the equation $ab = 0$: If $a = 5$, then $b = 0$; if $a = -4$, then $b = 0$; if $b = 3$, then $a = 0$; if $b = -\frac{1}{2}$, then $a = 0$.

These examples illustrate the following principle:

If the product of two real numbers is 0, then at least one of the numbers is 0.

In general, if a and b are real numbers, then:

$$ab = 0 \text{ if, and only if, } a = 0 \text{ or } b = 0$$

This principle will now be applied to solving quadratic equations.

Let us first solve the equation $(x - 2)(x - 1) = 0$. Since $(x - 2)$ $(x - 1) = 0$, then either $x - 2$ must be 0 or $x - 1$ must be 0. If $x - 2 = 0$, then $x = 2$. If $x - 1 = 0$, then $x = 1$.

Check

$$(x - 2)(x - 1) = 0$$
If $x = 2$, $(2 - 2)(2 - 1) \overset{?}{=} 0$
$$(0)(1) \overset{?}{=} 0$$
$$0 = 0 \text{ (true)}$$

$$(x - 2)(x - 1) = 0$$
If $x = 1$, $(1 - 2)(1 - 1) \overset{?}{=} 0$
$$(-1)(0) \overset{?}{=} 0$$
$$0 = 0 \text{ (true)}$$

Since both 2 and 1 satisfy the equation $(x - 2)(x - 1) = 0$, the solution set of this equation is $\{2, 1\}$. We may also say that the roots of the equation are 2 or 1.

Let us now solve the quadratic equation $x^2 - 3x + 2 = 0$. If we factor the left member of the equation, we get an equivalent equation, $(x - 2)(x - 1) = 0$. The solution set of this equation, as we have just seen, is $\{2, 1\}$. Therefore, the solution set of the given equation $x^2 - 3x + 2 = 0$ is also $\{2, 1\}$.

It can be shown that there are quadratic equations—for example, $x^2 + x + 1 = 0$—which do not have any real roots. We will not deal with such equations. All the quadratic equations with which we deal will have two real roots.

The two roots of a quadratic equation are not always different numbers. Sometimes the roots are the same number, as in the case of $x^2 - 2x + 1 = 0$, both of whose roots are 1. Such a root is called a *double root* and is written only once in the solution set.

Procedure. To solve a quadratic equation by using factoring:

1. **If necessary, transform the equation into standard form. Do this by removing parentheses, clearing fractions and combining like terms in the left member, and making the right member zero.**
2. **Factor the left member of the equation.**
3. **Set each factor containing the variable equal to zero.**
4. **Solve each of the resulting equations.**
5. **Check by substituting each value of the variable in the original equation.**

Model Problems

1. Solve and check: $x^2 - 7x = -10$

How to Proceed	*Solution*
	$x^2 - 7x = -10$
1. Transform into standard form.	$x^2 - 7x + 10 = 0$
2. Factor the left member.	$(x - 2)(x - 5) = 0$
3. Let each factor = 0.	$x - 2 = 0 \mid x - 5 = 0$
4. Solve each equation.	$x = 2 \mid x = 5$

Check

$$x^2 - 7x = -10$$
If $x = 2$, $(2)^2 - 7(2) \overset{?}{=} -10$
$$4 - 14 \overset{?}{=} -10$$
$$-10 = -10 \quad \text{(true)}$$

$$x^2 - 7x = -10$$
If $x = 5$, $(5)^2 - 7(5) \overset{?}{=} -10$
$$25 - 35 \overset{?}{=} -10$$
$$-10 = -10 \quad \text{(true)}$$

Answer: $x = 2$ or $x = 5$; the solution set is $\{2, 5\}$.

2. List the members of the following set: $\{x \mid 2x^2 = 3x\}$.

How to Proceed	*Solution*
	$2x^2 = 3x$
1. Transform into standard form.	$2x^2 - 3x = 0$
2. Factor the left member.	$x(2x - 3) = 0$
3. Let each factor = 0.	$x = 0 \mid 2x - 3 = 0$
4. Solve each equation.	$2x = 3$
	$x = \frac{3}{2}$

Check

$$2x^2 = 3x$$
If $x = 0$, $2(0)^2 \overset{?}{=} 3(0)$
$$2(0) \overset{?}{=} 0$$
$$0 = 0 \quad \text{(true)}$$

$$2x^2 = 3x$$
If $x = \frac{3}{2}$, $2(\frac{3}{2})^2 \overset{?}{=} 3(\frac{3}{2})$
$$2(\frac{9}{4}) \overset{?}{=} \frac{9}{2}$$
$$\frac{9}{2} = \frac{9}{2} \quad \text{(true)}$$

Answer: $\{0, \frac{3}{2}\}$.

3. Solve and check: $x(x - 6) = -9$.

How to Proceed	*Solution*
	$x(x - 6) = -9$
1. Use the distributive property.	$x^2 - 6x = -9$
2. Transform into standard form.	$x^2 - 6x + 9 = 0$
3. Factor the left member.	$(x - 3)(x - 3) = 0$
4. Let each factor = 0.	$x - 3 = 0 \mid x - 3 = 0$
5. Solve each equation.	$x = 3 \mid x = 3$

Check

$$x(x - 6) \overset{?}{=} -9$$
If $x = 3$, $3(3 - 6) \overset{?}{=} -9$
$$3(-3) \overset{?}{=} -9$$
$$-9 = -9 \quad \text{(true)}$$

Answer: $x = 3$; the solution set is $\{3\}$.

Keep In Mind _____

To solve a quadratic equation by using factoring, one member of the equation must be zero.

EXERCISES

In 1–57, solve and check the equations.

1. $x^2 - 3x + 2 = 0$
2. $y^2 - 7y + 6 = 0$
3. $x^2 - 8x + 16 = 0$
4. $r^2 - 12r + 35 = 0$
5. $c^2 + 6c + 5 = 0$
6. $x^2 + 2x + 1 = 0$
7. $y^2 + 11y + 24 = 0$
8. $x^2 - 4x - 5 = 0$
9. $x^2 - 2x - 35 = 0$
10. $q^2 + q - 72 = 0$
11. $x^2 + 2x - 15 = 0$
12. $r^2 - r - 72 = 0$
13. $x^2 - 49 = 0$
14. $m^2 - 64 = 0$
15. $2r^2 - 18 = 0$
16. $3x^2 - 12 = 0$
17. $d^2 - 2d = 0$
18. $m^2 - 5m = 0$
19. $x^2 + 3x = 0$
20. $z^2 + 8z = 0$
21. $2x^2 - 5x + 2 = 0$
22. $3x^2 - 10x + 3 = 0$
23. $2x^2 + x - 3 = 0$
24. $3x^2 - 8x + 4 = 0$
25. $2x^2 + x - 10 = 0$
26. $5x^2 + 11x + 2 = 0$
27. $x^2 - x = 6$
28. $y^2 - 4y = 12$
29. $y^2 - 3y = 28$
30. $2m^2 + 7m = -6$
31. $x^2 = 25$
32. $3x^2 = 12$
33. $y^2 = 6y$
34. $s^2 = -4s$
35. $y^2 = 8y + 20$
36. $z^2 = 15 - 2z$
37. $2x^2 - x = 15$
38. $30 + x = x^2$
39. $2y^2 = 7y - 3$
40. $x^2 + 3x - 4 = 50$
41. $x^2 - 8x + 28 = 3x$
42. $2x^2 + 7 = 5 - 5x$
43. $\frac{1}{3}x^2 + \frac{4}{3}x + 1 = 0$
44. $\frac{1}{2}x^2 + \frac{9}{2}x + 4 = 0$
45. $\frac{1}{2}x^2 - \frac{7}{6}x = 1$
46. $x(x - 2) = 35$
47. $y(y - 3) = 4$
48. $x(x + 3) = 40$
49. $\frac{x}{2} + 1 - \frac{12}{x} = 0$
50. $\frac{y}{3} + 1 = \frac{6}{y}$
51. $\frac{m}{3} + \frac{9}{m} = 4$
52. $\frac{16}{y} = \frac{y}{4}$
53. $x = \frac{40}{x - 3}$
54. $\frac{x}{3} = \frac{8}{x + 2}$
55. $\sqrt{2x^2 + x} = \sqrt{x^2 + 20}$
56. $x + 1 = \sqrt{5x + 5}$
57. $2x + \sqrt{x^2 - 16} = 7$

In 58–66, find the solution set of the equation.

58. $m^2 + 8m + 7 = 0$ **59.** $y^2 - 3y - 10 = 0$ **60.** $c^2 - 8c = -15$
61. $y^2 = 7y$ **62.** $c^2 = 12c - 36$ **63.** $5y^2 = 11y - 2$
64. $\sqrt{y^2 - 5} = 2$ **65.** $\sqrt{x^2 + 5x} = 6$ **66.** $\sqrt{13x + 22} + x = -4$

In 67–69, list the members of the set.

67. $\{x \mid x^2 - 5x - 6 = 0\}$ **68.** $\{x \mid 5x^2 + 4 = 12x\}$
69. $\{d \mid d(d - 8) = -15\}$

In 70–78, solve for x in terms of the other variable(s).

70. $x^2 - b^2 = 0$ **71.** $4x^2 = c^2$ **72.** $x^2 + ax = 0$
73. $x^2 = cx$ **74.** $rx^2 = sx$ **75.** $x^2 - 5bx + 6b^2 = 0$
76. $x^2 + 4ax = 21a^2$ **77.** $\dfrac{a}{x} = \dfrac{x}{a}$ **78.** $x = \dfrac{bx}{x + 3b}$

3. Solving Incomplete Quadratic Equations

A quadratic equation in which the first-degree term is missing is called an **incomplete quadratic equation**, or a **pure quadratic equation**. For example, $x^2 - 36 = 0$ (in general, $ax^2 + c = 0$ when $a \neq 0$) is an incomplete quadratic equation.

One method of solving $x^2 - 36 = 0$ is to factor the left member. We obtain $(x + 6)(x - 6) = 0$, from which we find that the solution set is $\{-6, 6\}$.

Another method which we may use to solve $x^2 - 36 = 0$ makes use of the following principle:

Every positive real number has two real square roots, each of which is the opposite of the other.

Solution

$$x^2 - 36 = 0$$
$$x^2 = 36$$
$$x = \sqrt{36} \text{ or } x = -\sqrt{36}$$
$$x = 6 \text{ or } x = -6$$

Check

$$x^2 - 36 = 0$$
$$\text{If } x = 6, (6)^2 - 36 \overset{?}{=} 0$$
$$36 - 36 \overset{?}{=} 0$$
$$0 = 0 \quad \text{(true)}$$

$$x^2 - 36 = 0$$
$$\text{If } x = -6, (-6)^2 - 36 \overset{?}{=} 0$$
$$36 - 36 \overset{?}{=} 0$$
$$0 = 0 \quad \text{(true)}$$

Answer: $x = 6$ or $x = -6$, which may be written $x = \pm 6$; the solution set is $\{6, -6\}$.

Procedure. To solve an incomplete quadratic equation:

1. Transform the equation into the form $x^2 = n$, where n is a non-negative real number.
2. Let $x = \sqrt{n}$ and let $x = -\sqrt{n}$.
3. Check the resulting values for x in the original equation.

Model Problems

1. Find the solution set of $7y^2 = 3y^2 + 36$.

    Solution

$$7y^2 = 3y^2 + 36$$
$$7y^2 - 3y^2 = 36$$
$$4y^2 = 36$$
$$y^2 = 9$$
$$y = \sqrt{9} = 3 \text{ or}$$
$$y = -\sqrt{9} = -3$$

Answer: The solution set is $\{3, -3\}$.

    Check

$$7y^2 = 3y^2 + 36$$
If $y = -3$, $7(-3)^2 \overset{?}{=} 3(-3)^2 + 36$
$$7(9) \overset{?}{=} 3(9) + 36$$
$$63 \overset{?}{=} 27 + 36$$
$$63 = 63 \quad (\text{true})$$
Similarly, check $y = +3$.

2. Solve and check: $4x^2 - 14 = 2x^2$

    Solution

$$4x^2 - 14 = 2x^2$$
$$4x^2 - 2x^2 - 14 = 0$$
$$2x^2 - 14 = 0$$
$$2x^2 = 14$$
$$x^2 = 7$$
$$x = \sqrt{7} \text{ or}$$
$$x = -\sqrt{7}$$

    Check

$$4x^2 - 14 = 2x^2$$
If $x = -\sqrt{7}$, $4(-\sqrt{7})^2 - 14 \overset{?}{=} 2(-\sqrt{7})^2$
$$4(7) - 14 \overset{?}{=} 2(7)$$
$$28 - 14 \overset{?}{=} 14$$
$$14 = 14 \quad (\text{true})$$
Similarly, check $x = \sqrt{7}$.

Answer: $x = \pm\sqrt{7}$, or the solution set is $\{\sqrt{7}, -\sqrt{7}\}$.

EXERCISES

In 1–21, solve and check the equation.

1. $x^2 = 4$
2. $\frac{1}{2}z^2 = 8$
3. $a^2 - 25 = 0$
4. $b^2 - .49 = 0$
5. $3k^2 = 147$
6. $27r^2 = 243$
7. $2x^2 - 8 = 0$
8. $3y^2 - 300 = 0$
9. $y^2 + 25 = 169$
10. $z^2 + .01 = .37$

11. $r^2 - 11 = 70$

12. $4x^2 + 5 = 21$

13. $2x^2 - 11 = 39$

14. $.05x^2 - 3 = 2$

15. $2x^2 + 3x^2 = 45$

16. $7x^2 = 4x^2 + .75$

17. $4y^2 - 13 = y^2 + 14$

18. $2z^2 + 7 = 10 - z^2$

19. $\dfrac{y^2}{3} = 12$

20. $\dfrac{x}{9} = \dfrac{4}{x}$

21. $\dfrac{4x}{25} = \dfrac{4}{x}$

In 22–39, solve for x in simplest radical form.

22. $x^2 = 3$

23. $x^2 = 20$

24. $x^2 = 27$

25. $2x^2 = 100$

26. $\frac{1}{2}x^2 = 6$

27. $4x^2 - 48 = 0$

28. $x^2 - 25 = 25$

29. $\frac{1}{3}x^2 - 3 = 3$

30. $3x^2 + 5 = 29$

31. $5x^2 - 40 = 100$

32. $3x^2 + 4x^2 = 35$

33. $8x^2 - 6x^2 = 54$

34. $9x^2 = 4x^2 + 100$

35. $3x^2 - 28 = 2x^2 + 33$

36. $3x^2 - 6 = 34 - 2x^2$

37. $\dfrac{x}{3} = \dfrac{5}{x}$

38. $\dfrac{x}{8} = \dfrac{4}{x}$

39. $\dfrac{2x}{9} = \dfrac{6}{x}$

In 40–42, list the numbers of the set.

40. $\{x \mid 3x^2 = 75\}$

41. $\{y \mid 6y^2 - 4y^2 = 98\}$

42. $\{x \mid 2x^2 = 20 - 3x^2\}$

In 43–57, find the positive value of x correct to the *nearest tenth*.

43. $x^2 = 7$

44. $x^2 = 24$

45. $\frac{1}{3}x^2 = 31$

46. $3x^2 = 45$

47. $4x^2 - 160 = 0$

48. $x^2 + 9 = 36$

49. $x^2 - 16 = 16$

50. $2x^2 + 7 = 67$

51. $5x^2 + 3x^2 = 320$

52. $7x^2 = x^2 + 198$

53. $5x^2 - 29 = x^2 + 11$

54. $x^2 - 42 = 82 - 3x^2$

55. $\dfrac{x}{5} = \dfrac{11}{x}$

56. $\dfrac{x}{9} = \dfrac{6}{x}$

57. $\dfrac{2x}{43} = \dfrac{8}{x}$

In 58–63, solve for x, expressing irrational answers in radical form.

58. $(x - 1)^2 = 4$

59. $(x + 2)^2 = 16$

60. $(x + 5)^2 = 23$

61. $\dfrac{4}{x - 1} = \dfrac{x - 1}{9}$

62. $\dfrac{x + 3}{2} = \dfrac{8}{x + 3}$

63. $\dfrac{x - 2}{3} = \dfrac{5}{x - 2}$

In 64–69, solve for x in terms of the other variable(s).

64. $x^2 = b^2$

65. $x^2 = 25a^2$

66. $9x^2 = r^2$

67. $4x^2 - a^2 = 0$

68. $x^2 + a^2 = c^2$

69. $x^2 + b^2 = c^2$

In 70–77, solve for the indicated variable in terms of the other variable(s).

70. Solve for S: $S^2 = A$

71. Solve for e: $S = 6e^2$

72. Solve for r: $A = \pi r^2$
74. Solve for I: $W = I^2 R$
76. Solve for t: $s = \frac{1}{2}gt^2$

73. Solve for r: $S = 4\pi r^2$
75. Solve for r: $V = \pi r^2 h$
77. Solve for v: $F = \dfrac{mv^2}{gr}$

4. Completing a Perfect Square Trinomial

At the right, we see that $(x + 3)^2 = x^2 + 6x + 9$. Since the expression $x^2 + 6x + 9$ represents $(x + 3)^2$, it is called a **perfect square trinomial**.

$$\begin{array}{r} x \;\; + 3 \\ x \;\; + 3 \\ \hline x^2 + 3x \\ + 3x + 9 \\ \hline x^2 + 6x + 9 \end{array}$$

Study the trinomial $x^2 + 6x + 9$ and the binomial $x + 3$. Notice that the constant 9 in the trinomial is equal to the square of the 3 in the binomial. Also, notice that the coefficient of x, which is 6 in the trinomial, is twice the 3 in the binomial. We will now use these facts to solve the following problem:

Find the number that must be added to $x^2 - 8x$ to make the resulting trinomial a perfect square. First we square $\frac{1}{2}$ of (-8), the coefficient of x. We see that $[\frac{1}{2}(-8)]^2 = (-4)^2 = 16$. Therefore, we must add 16 to $x^2 - 8x$ to obtain the perfect square trinomial $x^2 - 8x + 16$, which represents $(x - 4)^2$. This process is called *completing the square*.

Procedure. **To form a perfect square trinomial starting with a binomial of the form $x^2 + px$:** **Add to the binomial the square of one-half of p, the coefficient of the first degree term x.**

Model Problems

1. Find the value of k which will make the trinomial $x^2 + 14x + k$ a perfect square.

   Solution: $k = [\frac{1}{2}(14)]^2 = (7)^2 = 49$
   $x^2 + 14x + 49$ is a perfect square since $x^2 + 14x + 49 = (x + 7)^2$

   Answer: $k = 49$

2. Add a number to $x^2 + 10x$ which will complete the square. Also, express the resulting trinomial as the square of a binomial.

   Solution: $[\frac{1}{2}(10)]^2 = (5)^2 = 25$

   Answer: Add 25 to $x^2 + 10x$; $x^2 + 10x + 25 = (x + 5)^2$

3. Add a number to $x^2 - 3x$ which will complete the square. Also, express the resulting trinomial as the square of a binomial.

Solution: $[\frac{1}{2}(-3)]^2 = (-\frac{3}{2})^2 = \frac{9}{4}$

Answer: Add $\frac{9}{4}$ to $x^2 - 3x$; $x^2 - 3x + \frac{9}{4} = (x - \frac{3}{2})^2$

EXERCISES

In 1-3, find the value of k which will make the trinomial a perfect square.

1. $x^2 + 4x + k$ 2. $x^2 - 12x + k$ 3. $x^2 + 3x + k$

In 4-15, replace the question mark with a number which will complete the square. Also, express the resulting trinomial as the square of a binomial.

4. $x^2 - 4x + ?$ 5. $c^2 + 14c + ?$ 6. $x^2 - 18x + ?$
7. $r^2 + 5r + ?$ 8. $x^2 - 9x + ?$ 9. $x^2 - x + ?$
10. $x^2 + \frac{1}{2}x + ?$ 11. $y^2 - \frac{1}{3}y + ?$ 12. $x^2 - \frac{4}{5}x + ?$
13. $x^2 + (?)x + 9$ 14. $x^2 + (?)x + 25$ 15. $x^2 - (?)x + 64$

In 16-21, determine whether the trinomial is a perfect square.

16. $x^2 + 4x + 4$ 17. $x^2 - 14x + 49$ 18. $x^2 - 6x + 6$
19. $x^2 - 10x - 25$ 20. $x^2 - 3x + 2.25$ 21. $x^2 - x + 1$

In 22-27, factor the trinomial and determine whether it is a perfect square.

22. $x^2 - 2x + 1$ 23. $x^2 + 4x + 4$ 24. $x^2 + 6x - 16$
25. $x^2 + 12x + 36$ 26. $x^2 - 8x - 9$ 27. $x^2 - 16x + 64$

5. Solving Quadratic Equations by Completing the Square

We have learned that to solve the equation $x^2 = 16$, we use the property of square roots: $x = \sqrt{16} = 4$, or $x = -\sqrt{16} = -4$.

Similarly, to solve $(x - 1)^2 = 16$, we also use the property of square roots:

$$x - 1 = \sqrt{16} \ \text{ or } \ x - 1 = -\sqrt{16}$$
$$x - 1 = 4 \qquad\qquad x - 1 = -4$$
$$x = 5 \qquad\qquad\quad x = -3$$

Since both $x = 5$ and $x = -3$ satisfy the equation $(x - 1)^2 = 16$, the solution set of this equation is $\{5, -3\}$.

To solve $x^2 - 2x + 1 = 16$, we first represent $x^2 - 2x + 1$ as $(x - 1)^2$. Then we solve the equivalent equation $(x - 1)^2 = 16$ as before.

To solve $x^2 - 2x = 15$, we add a number to both members of the equation so that the left member, $x^2 - 2x$, becomes a perfect square trinomial. The number we add is the square of one-half the coefficient of x: $[\frac{1}{2}(-2)]^2 = (-1)^2 = 1$.

Thus, we have $x^2 - 2x + 1 = 15 + 1$, or $(x - 1)^2 = 16$. This resulting equation is solved as before.

When we solve a quadratic equation in this manner, we are solving it by the method of *completing the square*.

Procedure. To solve a quadratic equation by completing the square:

1. **Transform the equation to the form $x^2 + px = q$. Do this by collecting all terms containing the variable in the left member of the equation, the constant being in the right member. When the coefficient of x^2 is not 1, divide both members of the equation by that coefficient.**
2. **Complete the square by adding the square of one-half the coefficient of the first degree term to both members of the equation.**
3. **Express the resulting equation in the form $(x + d)^2 = n$. That is, write the square of a binomial equal to a positive number n.**
4. **Use the property of square roots to write $x + d = \sqrt{n}$ or $x + d = -\sqrt{n}$. Solve these equations.**
5. **Check the resulting values for x in the given equation.**

Model Problems

In 1-4, solve by completing the square. Give irrational answers in radical form.

1. $x^2 - 6x + 8 = 0$

   Solution

   $$x^2 - 6x + 8 = 0$$
   $$x^2 - 6x = -8$$
   $$[\tfrac{1}{2}(-6)]^2 = (-3)^2 = 9$$
   $$x^2 - 6x + 9 = -8 + 9$$
   $$(x - 3)^2 = 1$$

2. $2x^2 + 3x - 2 = 0$

   Solution

   $$2x^2 + 3x - 2 = 0$$
   $$2x^2 + 3x = 2$$
   $$x^2 + \tfrac{3}{2}x = 1 \quad D_2$$
   $$[\tfrac{1}{2}(\tfrac{3}{2})]^2 = (\tfrac{3}{4})^2 = \tfrac{9}{16}$$
   $$x^2 + \tfrac{3}{2}x + \tfrac{9}{16} = 1 + \tfrac{9}{16}$$

$x - 3 = \sqrt{1}$ | $x - 3 = -\sqrt{1}$

$x - 3 = 1$ | $x - 3 = -1$

$x = 4$ | $x = 2$

The check is left to the student.

Answer: The solution set is $\{4, 2\}$.

$(x + \frac{3}{4})^2 = \frac{25}{16}$

$x + \frac{3}{4} = \sqrt{\frac{25}{16}}$ | $x + \frac{3}{4} = -\sqrt{\frac{25}{16}}$

$x + \frac{3}{4} = \frac{5}{4}$ | $x + \frac{3}{4} = -\frac{5}{4}$

$x = \frac{5}{4} - \frac{3}{4}$ | $x = -\frac{5}{4} - \frac{3}{4}$

$x = \frac{2}{4} = \frac{1}{2}$ | $x = -\frac{8}{4} = -2$

The check is left to the student.

Answer: The solution set is $\{\frac{1}{2}, -2\}$.

3. $x^2 + 4 = 6x$

Solution

$$x^2 + 4 = 6x$$
$$x^2 - 6x + 4 = 0$$
$$x^2 - 6x = -4$$
$$[\tfrac{1}{2}(-6)]^2 = (-3)^2 = 9$$
$$x^2 - 6x + 9 = -4 + 9$$
$$(x - 3)^2 = 5$$

$x - 3 = \sqrt{5}$ | $x - 3 = -\sqrt{5}$

$x = 3 + \sqrt{5}$ | $x = 3 - \sqrt{5}$

The check is left to the student.

Answer: The solution set is $\{3 + \sqrt{5}, 3 - \sqrt{5}\}$.

We may also say that the roots are $x = 3 \pm \sqrt{5}$.

Note: If we wish to approximate the roots of this equation to the nearest tenth, we approximate $\sqrt{5}$ to two decimal places, $\sqrt{5} \approx 2.23$.

Then:

$3 + \sqrt{5} \approx 3 + 2.23 \approx 5.23 \approx 5.2$

$3 - \sqrt{5} \approx 3 - 2.23 \approx .77 \approx .8$

4. $3x^2 - 2x - 2 = 0$

Solution

$$3x^2 - 2x - 2 = 0$$
$$3x^2 - 2x = 2$$
$$x^2 - \tfrac{2}{3}x = \tfrac{2}{3} \quad D_3$$
$$[\tfrac{1}{2}(-\tfrac{2}{3})]^2 = (-\tfrac{1}{3})^2 = \tfrac{1}{9}$$
$$x^2 - \tfrac{2}{3}x + \tfrac{1}{9} = \tfrac{2}{3} + \tfrac{1}{9}$$
$$(x - \tfrac{1}{3})^2 = \tfrac{7}{9}$$

$x - \dfrac{1}{3} = \sqrt{\dfrac{7}{9}}$ | $x - \dfrac{1}{3} = -\sqrt{\dfrac{7}{9}}$

$x = \dfrac{1}{3} + \dfrac{\sqrt{7}}{3}$ | $x = \dfrac{1}{3} - \dfrac{\sqrt{7}}{3}$

$x = \dfrac{1 + \sqrt{7}}{3}$ | $x = \dfrac{1 - \sqrt{7}}{3}$

The check is left to the student.

Answer: The solution set is

$$\left\{ \frac{1 + \sqrt{7}}{3}, \frac{1 - \sqrt{7}}{3} \right\}.$$

We may also say that the roots are

$$x = \frac{1}{3} \pm \frac{\sqrt{7}}{3}, \text{ or } x = \frac{1 \pm \sqrt{7}}{3}.$$

EXERCISES

In 1–6, solve the equation by using the square root property.

1. $(x - 5)^2 = 7^2$ **2.** $(z + 3)^2 = 25$ **3.** $(b - 4)^2 = 100$
4. $(x - 2)^2 = (\frac{1}{2})^2$ **5.** $(y + 1)^2 = \frac{4}{9}$ **6.** $(x - 3)^2 = 6$

In 7–12, solve the equation by expressing the left member as the square of a binomial and then by using the square root property.

7. $x^2 - 2x + 1 = 4$ **8.** $z^2 + 4z + 4 = 49$ **9.** $y^2 - 10y + 25 = 50$
10. $x^2 - x + \frac{1}{4} = \frac{9}{4}$ **11.** $x^2 + 3x + \frac{9}{4} = \frac{49}{4}$ **12.** $x^2 + 5x + \frac{25}{4} = \frac{3}{4}$

In 13–33, solve the equation by completing the square. [Express irrational answers in simplest radical form.]

13. $x^2 + 2x = 8$ **14.** $z^2 - 4z = 21$ **15.** $x^2 - 4x + 3 = 0$
16. $x^2 = 6x + 40$ **17.** $y^2 - 5y - 14 = 0$ **18.** $z^2 = 6 - z$
19. $x^2 - 4x = -4$ **20.** $y^2 - 9 = 6y$ **21.** $2c^2 - 3c - 2 = 0$
22. $2x^2 + 7x + 3 = 0$ **23.** $3r^2 = 5r + 2$ **24.** $5y^2 + 9y - 2 = 0$
25. $x^2 + 2x = 1$ **26.** $x^2 - 4x + 2 = 0$ **27.** $x^2 + 3x - 5 = 0$
28. $m^2 - 1 = 4m$ **29.** $a^2 = 6a + 19$ **30.** $2x^2 - 4x = 1$
31. $3x^2 - 12x + 5 = 0$ **32.** $3x^2 - 2 = 6x$ **33.** $5x^2 = 3x + 1$

In 34–39, solve the equation by completing the square. [Approximate the answers correct to the *nearest tenth*.]

34. $x^2 - 6x + 9 = 7$ **35.** $x^2 + 4x + 4 = 3$ **36.** $x^2 - 2x = 4$
37. $x^2 = 8x + 2$ **38.** $2x^2 - 20x = 5$ **39.** $3x^2 - 4x - 2 = 0$

6. Solving Quadratic Equations by Formula

Since any quadratic equation can be solved by the method of completing the square, we can solve the general quadratic equation $ax^2 + bx + c = 0$ $(a \neq 0)$ for x in terms of $a, b,$ and c. Then the general roots may be used as formulas for finding the roots of any quadratic equation. Examine carefully the parallel solutions shown below to see how the same method is used in solving a particular quadratic equation and the general quadratic equation.

$$3x^2 + 5x + 1 = 0 \qquad\qquad ax^2 + bx + c = 0 \quad (a \neq 0)$$

$$3x^2 + 5x = -1 \qquad\qquad ax^2 + bx = -c$$

$$x^2 + \frac{5}{3}x = \frac{-1}{3} \qquad\qquad x^2 + \frac{b}{a}x = \frac{-c}{a}$$

$$\left[\frac{1}{2}\left(\frac{5}{3}\right)\right]^2 = \left(\frac{5}{6}\right)^2 = \frac{25}{36} \qquad\qquad \left[\frac{1}{2}\left(\frac{b}{a}\right)\right]^2 = \left(\frac{b}{2a}\right)^2 = \frac{b^2}{4a^2}$$

$$x^2 + \frac{5}{3}x + \frac{25}{36} = \frac{25}{36} - \frac{1}{3}$$

$$\left(x + \frac{5}{6}\right)^2 = \frac{25}{36} - \frac{12}{36}$$

$$\left(x + \frac{5}{6}\right)^2 = \frac{13}{36}$$

$$x + \frac{5}{6} = \pm\sqrt{\frac{13}{36}}$$

$$x = -\frac{5}{6} \pm \frac{\sqrt{13}}{6}$$

$$x = \frac{-5 \pm \sqrt{13}}{6}$$

$$x^2 + \frac{b}{a}x + \frac{b^2}{4a^2} = \frac{b^2}{4a^2} - \frac{c}{a}$$

$$\left(x + \frac{b}{2a}\right)^2 = \frac{b^2}{4a^2} - \frac{4ac}{4a^2}$$

$$\left(x + \frac{b}{2a}\right)^2 = \frac{b^2 - 4ac}{4a^2}$$

$$x + \frac{b}{2a} = \pm\sqrt{\frac{b^2 - 4ac}{4a^2}}$$

$$x = -\frac{b}{2a} \pm \frac{\sqrt{b^2 - 4ac}}{2a}$$

$$x = \frac{-b \pm \sqrt{b^2 - 4ac}}{2a}$$

The last step, $x = \dfrac{-b \pm \sqrt{b^2 - 4ac}}{2a}$, which is an abbreviated way of writing the solution $x = \dfrac{-b + \sqrt{b^2 - 4ac}}{2a}$ or $x = \dfrac{-b - \sqrt{b^2 - 4ac}}{2a}$, is called the **quadratic formula**. This formula may be used in solving any quadratic equation with which we will be dealing.

Procedure. To solve a quadratic equation by the quadratic formula:

1. **Transform the given equation into an equivalent equation in the standard form $ax^2 + bx + c = 0$. Do this by collecting all terms in the left member; the right member is zero.**

2. **Compare the resulting equation with the standard equation $ax^2 + bx + c = 0$ to determine the values of a, b, and c.**

3. **Substitute the values of a, b, and c in the quadratic formula:**

$$x = \frac{-b \pm \sqrt{b^2 - 4ac}}{2a}$$

4. **Perform the necessary arithmetic to find the values of x.**

Model Problems

1. Solve by using the quadratic formula: $2x^2 = 5 - 9x$

   Solution:

   Write the given equation: $2x^2 = 5 - 9x$

   $$2x^2 = 5 - 9x$$

   Transform the equation to standard form: $2x^2 + 9x - 5 = 0$

Compare with $ax^2 + bx + c = 0$: $a = 2, b = 9, c = -5$

The quadratic formula is $x = \dfrac{-b \pm \sqrt{b^2 - 4ac}}{2a}$.

Substituting: $\qquad x = \dfrac{-9 \pm \sqrt{(9)^2 - 4(2)(-5)}}{2(2)}$

$$x = \dfrac{-9 \pm \sqrt{81 + 40}}{4}$$

$$x = \dfrac{-9 \pm \sqrt{121}}{4}$$

$$x = \dfrac{-9 \pm 11}{4}$$

$$x = \dfrac{-9 + 11}{4} \qquad\qquad x = \dfrac{-9 - 11}{4}$$

$$x = \dfrac{2}{4} \qquad\qquad\qquad x = \dfrac{-20}{4}$$

$$x = \dfrac{1}{2} \qquad\qquad\qquad x = -5$$

Check

$$2x^2 = 5 - 9x$$
If $x = \tfrac{1}{2}$, $2(\tfrac{1}{2})^2 \overset{?}{=} 5 - 9(\tfrac{1}{2})$
$$\tfrac{2}{4} \overset{?}{=} 5 - 4\tfrac{1}{2}$$
$$\tfrac{1}{2} = \tfrac{1}{2} \quad \text{(true)}$$

$$2x^2 = 5 - 9x$$
If $x = -5$, $2(-5)^2 \overset{?}{=} 5 - 9(-5)$
$$2(25) \overset{?}{=} 5 + 45$$
$$50 = 50 \quad \text{(true)}$$

Answer: $x = \tfrac{1}{2}$ or $x = -5$; the solution set is $\{\tfrac{1}{2}, -5\}$.

2. Use the quadratic formula to approximate the roots of $2x^2 - 3x = 4$ correct to the *nearest tenth*.

Solution:

Write the given equation: $2x^2 - 3x = 4$

$$2x^2 - 3x = 4$$
Transform the equation to standard form: $2x^2 - 3x - 4 = 0$

Compare with $ax^2 + bx + c = 0$: $a = 2, b = -3, c = -4$

The quadratic
    formula is $x = \dfrac{-b \pm \sqrt{b^2 - 4ac}}{2a}$.

Substituting: $x = \dfrac{-(-3) \pm \sqrt{(-3)^2 - 4(2)(-4)}}{2(2)}$

$x = \dfrac{3 \pm \sqrt{9 + 32}}{4}$

$x = \dfrac{3 \pm \sqrt{41}}{4}$

$x \approx \dfrac{3 \pm 6.40}{4}$

$$
\begin{array}{r}
6.\ 4\ \ 0 \\
\sqrt{41.\overline{00}\ \overline{00}} \\
\hline
36 \\
\end{array}
$$

$$
\begin{array}{r|l}
124 & 5\ 00 \\
& 4\ 96 \\
\hline
1280 & 4\ 000 \\
& 0 \\
\hline
& 4\ 00 \\
\end{array}
$$

$x \approx \dfrac{3 + 6.40}{4}$ $\bigg|$ $x \approx \dfrac{3 - 6.40}{4}$

$x \approx \dfrac{9.40}{4} \approx 2.35$ $\bigg|$ $x \approx \dfrac{-3.40}{4} \approx -.85$

$x \approx 2.4$ $\bigg|$ $x \approx -.9$

Answer: $x \approx 2.4$ or $x \approx -.9$

EXERCISES

In 1–27, solve the equation by using the quadratic formula. [Express irrational roots in simplest radical form.]

1. $x^2 + 2x - 24 = 0$ 2. $x^2 - 9x + 20 = 0$ 3. $x^2 - 6x + 9 = 0$
4. $x^2 + 12 = 7x$ 5. $x^2 - 30 = x$ 6. $x^2 = 5x + 14$
7. $2x^2 - 5x + 2 = 0$ 8. $3x^2 - 10x + 3 = 0$ 9. $5x^2 = 3x + 2$
10. $x^2 - 8x = 0$ 11. $x^2 - 9 = 0$ 12. $4x^2 = 25$
13. $x^2 + 2x - 1 = 0$ 14. $y^2 - 2y - 2 = 0$ 15. $z^2 + 3z = 5$
16. $x^2 - 4x + 1 = 0$ 17. $x^2 + 5x = 2$ 18. $y^2 = 5y + 2$
19. $2x^2 - 3x - 1 = 0$ 20. $2x^2 + x - 4 = 0$ 21. $3x^2 - 2x - 3 = 0$

22. $2y^2 + y = 5$ 23. $\dfrac{y^2}{2} - \dfrac{1}{10} = \dfrac{y}{5}$ 24. $\dfrac{1}{3}x^2 = x - \dfrac{1}{6}$

25. $\dfrac{1}{4}x^2 - \dfrac{3}{2}x - 1 = 0$ 26. $1 + \dfrac{7}{x} + \dfrac{2}{x^2} = 0$ 27. $2x = 5 + \dfrac{4}{x}$

In 28–42, solve the equation by using the quadratic formula. [Approximate irrational roots correct to the *nearest tenth*.]

28. $x^2 + 3x - 3 = 0$ 29. $y^2 - 4y + 2 = 0$ 30. $2c^2 - 7c + 1 = 0$
31. $x^2 + 2x - 4 = 0$ 32. $3x^2 - 2x - 6 = 0$ 33. $2x^2 - 8x + 1 = 0$

34. $3x^2 + 5x - 1 = 0$ **35.** $2x^2 + 4x = 3$ **36.** $2x^2 - 10x = 9$

37. $2x^2 - 2x = 3$ **38.** $x^2 = 20x + 10$ **39.** $x^2 = 12 - 9x$

40. $x(x - 3) = -2$ **41.** $x(2x + 9) = 3$ **42.** $x = 4 + \dfrac{2}{x}$

7. Using the Theorem of Pythagoras

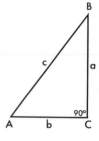

The figure represents a *right triangle*. Such a triangle contains one and only one right angle, an angle whose measure is 90°. In right triangle ABC, side $\overline{AB}$, which is opposite the right angle, is called the *hypotenuse*. The hypotenuse is the longest side of the triangle. The other two sides of the triangle, $\overline{AC}$ and $\overline{BC}$, form the right angle; they are called the *legs*, or *arms*, of the right triangle.

The following relation, known as the *theorem of Pythagoras*, is true for all right triangles:

In a right triangle, the square of the length of the hypotenuse is equal to the sum of the squares of the lengths of the other two sides.

In preceding right triangle ABC, if the length of the hypotenuse is represented by c and the lengths of the other two sides by a and b, then the theorem of Pythagoras can be represented by the following formula:

$$c^2 = a^2 + b^2$$

When the lengths of two sides of a right triangle are known, the theorem of Pythagoras can be used to find the length of the third side. It is also true that:

If the square of the length of the largest side of a triangle is equal to the sum of the squares of the lengths of the other two sides, then the triangle is a right triangle.

When the lengths of the three sides of a triangle are known, this relation can be used to discover whether the triangle is a right triangle.

Model Problems

1. Find the length of the hypotenuse of a right triangle in which the lengths of the other two sides are 5 inches and 12 inches.

   Solution: Let the length of the hypotenuse $= c$, the length of side $a = 5$, the length of side $b = 12$.

$c^2 = a^2 + b^2$ [theorem of Pythagoras]
$c^2 = 5^2 + 12^2$
$c^2 = 25 + 144$
$c^2 = 169$
$c = \sqrt{169} = 13$ or
$c = -\sqrt{169} = -13$ [Reject the negative value, because the length of the hypotenuse cannot be a negative number.]

Answer: 13 inches

2. The hypotenuse of a right triangle is 20 centimeters long and one leg is 16 centimeters long. Find the length of the other leg.

Solution: Let the length of the unknown leg $= a$, the length of the hypotenuse $c = 20$, the length of side $b = 16$.

$c^2 = a^2 + b^2$ [theorem of Pythagoras]
$20^2 = a^2 + 16^2$
$400 = a^2 + 256$
$144 = a^2$
$12 = a$ or
$-12 = a$ [Reject.]

Answer: 12 centimeters

3. Approximate, correct to the *nearest tenth of an inch*, the length of a side of a square whose diagonal is 10 inches.

Solution: In square QRST, angle QRS is a right angle. Therefore, triangle QRS is a right triangle. Let $x =$ the length of each side of the square.

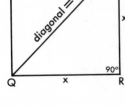

$a^2 + b^2 = c^2$ [$a = x, b = x, c = 10$]
$x^2 + x^2 = 10^2$
$2x^2 = 100$
$x^2 = 50$
$x = \pm \sqrt{50} \approx \pm 7.07$ [Use the table on
$x \approx 7.1$ page 560 or com-
                pute. Reject the negative value.]

Answer: The side of the square measures 7.1 inches.

4. Is a triangle whose sides measure 10 centimeters, 7 centimeters, and 4 centimeters a right triangle?

Solution: The square of 10, the length of the longest side, $= 10^2 = 100$.
The sum of the squares of the lengths of the other two sides $= 7^2 + 4^2 =$
$49 + 16 = 65$.

Answer: Since 100 does not equal 65, the triangle is not a right triangle.

EXERCISES

In 1–6, find the length of the third side of the right triangle the
length of whose hypotenuse is represented by c and the lengths of
whose other sides are represented by a and b.

1. $a = 3, b = 4$ **2.** $c = 13, a = 12$ **3.** $c = 17, b = 15$
4. $a = \sqrt{2}, b = \sqrt{2}$ **5.** $a = 4, b = 4\sqrt{3}$ **6.** $a = 5\sqrt{3}, c = 10$

In 7–12, express in simplest radical form the length of the third side
of the right triangle the length of whose hypotenuse is represented by c
and the lengths of whose other sides are represented by a and b.

7. $a = 2, b = 3$ **8.** $a = 3, b = 3$ **9.** $a = 4, c = 8$
10. $a = 7, b = 1$ **11.** $b = \sqrt{3}, c = \sqrt{15}$ **12.** $a = 4\sqrt{2}, c = 8$

In 13–18, approximate, correct to the *nearest tenth*, the length of
the third side of the right triangle the length of whose hypotenuse is
represented by c and the lengths of whose other sides are represented
by a and b.

13. $a = 5, b = 7$ **14.** $c = 15, a = 5$ **15.** $c = 23, a = 9$
16. $c = 12, b = 3$ **17.** $a = 7, b = 7$ **18.** $a = 5\sqrt{2}, c = 10$

In 19–22, find x and express irrational results in simplest radical
form.

19.   **20.**   **21.**   **22.**

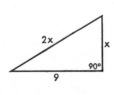
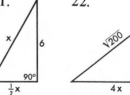

23. A ladder 39 feet long leans against a building and reaches the ledge
of a window. If the foot of the ladder is 15 feet from the foot of
the building, how high is the window ledge above the ground?

24. A man traveled 24 kilometers north and then 10 kilometers east. How far was he from his starting point?

25. Tom and Henry started from the same place. Tom traveled west at the rate of 60 kilometers per hour and Henry traveled south at the rate of 80 kilometers per hour. How far apart were they at the end of one hour?

In 26–29, find the length of a diagonal of a rectangle whose sides are the given measurements.

26. 8 inches and 15 inches   **27.** 15 centimeters and 20 centimeters

28. 10 feet and 24 feet   **29.** 10 meters and 24 meters

30. The diagonal of a rectangle measures 13 centimeters. One side is 12 centimeters long. Find the length of the other side.

31. Approximate, to the *nearest foot*, the diameter of the largest circular table top which can be taken through a rectangular doorway whose base measures 4 feet and whose height measures 7 feet.

32. Approximate, to the *nearest inch*, the length of the base of a rectangle whose diagonal measures 25 inches and whose altitude is 18 inches long.

In 33–37, approximate, to the *nearest tenth of an inch*, the length of a diagonal of a square whose side has the given measurement.

33. 2 inches   **34.** 4 inches   **35.** 5 inches   **36.** 6 inches   **37.** 7 inches

In 38–42, approximate, to the *nearest tenth of an inch*, the length of the side of a square whose diagonal has the given measurement.

38. 6 inches   **39.** 2 inches   **40.** 4 inches   **41.** 10 inches   **42.** 5 inches

In the figure, *ABC* is an equilateral triangle (it has 3 sides of equal length). $\overline{CD}$, which is drawn so that angle *CDB* is a right angle, is called the **altitude**. When altitude $\overline{CD}$ is drawn, it divides $\overline{AB}$ into two parts of equal length, *AD = DB*. In 43–47, approximate, to the *nearest tenth of a centimeter*, the length of the altitude of equilateral triangle *ABC* when each of its sides has the given measurement.

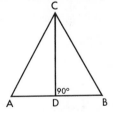

43. 4 cm   **44.** 6 cm   **45.** 8 cm   **46.** 10 cm   **47.** 5 cm

48. In the figure, *ABC* is a triangle in which sides $\overline{AC}$ and $\overline{CB}$ are of equal length, *AC = CB*. $\overline{CD}$, which is drawn so that angle *CDB* is a right angle, is called the **altitude drawn to the base of the triangle**. When altitude $\overline{CD}$ is drawn, it divides the base $\overline{AB}$ into two segments of equal measure, *AD = DB*. Each of the sides $\overline{AC}$ and $\overline{CB}$ measures 26 centimeters and the base of the triangle measures 20 centimeters.

    a. Find the length of the altitude drawn to the base.
    b. Find the area of triangle ABC.

49. In an isosceles triangle, the base measures 24 centimeters and the altitude drawn to the base measures 5 centimeters. Find the measure of each of the sides of the triangle that are of equal length.

50. A baseball diamond has the shape of a square 90 feet on each side. Approximate, to the *nearest tenth of a foot*, the distance from home plate to second base.

51. The length of the hypotenuse of a right triangle is 25 centimeters. One of the legs is 5 centimeters longer than the other. Find the length of each leg.

52. The ratio of the lengths of the two legs of a right triangle is 3:4. Find the length of each leg when the length of the hypotenuse measures:

    a. 10 cm   **b.** 20 cm   **c.** 25 cm   **d.** 100 cm

53. The ratio of the length of the hypotenuse of a right triangle to the length of one of its legs is 13:5. If the length of the other leg of the triangle is 24, find the length of the hypotenuse of the triangle.

54. The perimeter of a right triangle is 30 centimeters. If the hypotenuse measures 13 centimeters, find the length of each leg.

55. The length of a side of a square is represented by s and the length of a diagonal by d.

    a. Show that $d = s\sqrt{2}$.   **b.** Show that $s = \frac{1}{2}d\sqrt{2}$.

    In 56–59, tell whether the measurements can be the lengths of the sides of a right triangle.

56. 6 yards, 10 yards, 8 yards   **57.** 7 m, 4 m, 5 m
58. 12 cm, 16 cm, 20 cm   **59.** 10 feet, 15 feet, 20 feet

8. Locating Irrational Square Roots on a Number Line

    Consider a right triangle in which each leg measures 1. Using the theorem of Pythagoras, we discover that the hypotenuse of the right triangle measures $\sqrt{2}$.

$$c^2 = (1)^2 + (1)^2$$
$$c^2 = 2$$
$$c = \sqrt{2}$$

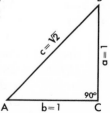

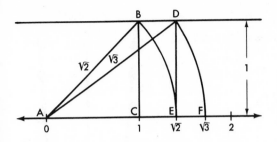

Let us associate the irrational number $\sqrt{2}$ with a point on a number line without using approximations. First we construct right triangle ACB using the length of the segment from 0 to 1 as the length of legs $\overline{AC}$ and $\overline{CB}$. Then with A as the center and a radius equal to AB (remember that the length of $\overline{AB}$ is $\sqrt{2}$), we construct an arc of a circle which intersects the number line at E. The coordinate of point E is $\sqrt{2}$.

To locate $\sqrt{3}$ on a number line, we first construct right triangle AED in which $AE = \sqrt{2}$ (which we constructed previously) and $ED = 1$. In this triangle, the length of hypotenuse $\overline{AD}$ is $\sqrt{3}$:

$$(AD)^2 = (\sqrt{2})^2 + (1)^2, (AD)^2 = 3, AD = \sqrt{3}$$

On the number line, we can now locate point F, whose coordinate is $\sqrt{3}$.

In a similar manner, we can locate $\sqrt{5}, \sqrt{6}$, and so on.

EXERCISES

In 1–10, without using approximations, locate on a number line the point associated with the given number.

1. $\sqrt{5}$ 2. $\sqrt{8}$ 3. $\sqrt{10}$ 4. $\sqrt{13}$ 5. $\sqrt{17}$
6. $\sqrt{18}$ 7. $\sqrt{20}$ 8. $\sqrt{32}$ 9. $\sqrt{6}$ 10. $\sqrt{7}$

9. Graphing a Quadratic Equation in Two Variables of the Form $y = ax^2 + bx + c$

We have learned that the graph of every first-degree equation in two variables is a straight line. For example, the graph of $x + y = 6$ is a straight line.

Let us graph the quadratic equation $y = 2x^2$. We will use integral values for x from $x = -3$ to $x = 3$ inclusive, that is, $-3 \leq x \leq 3$.

Solution: $y = 2x^2$

1. Develop the following table of values:

x	$2x^2$	$= y$
-3	$2(-3)^2$	18
-2	$2(-2)^2$	8
-1	$2(-1)^2$	2
0	$2(0)^2$	0
1	$2(1)^2$	2
2	$2(2)^2$	8
3	$2(3)^2$	18

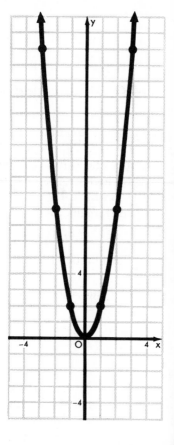

2. Plot the point associated with each ordered number pair (x, y): $(-3, 18)$, $(-2, 8)$, $(-1, 2)$, and so on.
3. Draw a smooth curve through the points. Notice that the graph of $y = 2x^2$ is a curve; it is not a straight line. This curve is called a ***parabola***.

   The graph of every quadratic equation of the form $y = ax^2 + bx + c$ (where a, b, and c are real numbers and $a \neq 0$) is a parabola.

EXERCISES

In 1–20, graph the quadratic equation. Use the integral values for x indicated in parentheses to prepare the necessary table of values.

1. $y = x^2$ $(-3 \leq x \leq 3)$
2. $5x^2 = y$ $(-2 \leq x \leq 2)$
3. $y = -x^2$ $(-3 \leq x \leq 3)$
4. $-4x^2 = y$ $(-2 \leq x \leq 2)$
5. $y = \frac{1}{2}x^2$ $(-4 \leq x \leq 4)$
6. $-\frac{1}{2}x^2 = y$ $(-2 \leq x \leq 2)$
7. $y = x^2 + 1$ $(-3 \leq x \leq 3)$
8. $y = x^2 - 4$ $(-3 \leq x \leq 3)$
9. $-x^2 + 4 = y$ $(-3 \leq x \leq 3)$
10. $-x^2 - 4 = y$ $(-3 \leq x \leq 3)$
11. $y = x^2 - 2x$ $(-1 \leq x \leq 3)$
12. $x^2 + 2x = y$ $(-3 \leq x \leq 1)$
13. $y = x^2 - 6x + 8$ $(0 \leq x \leq 6)$
14. $y = x^2 - 4x + 3$ $(-1 \leq x \leq 5)$
15. $x^2 - 2x - 3 = y$ $(-2 \leq x \leq 4)$
16. $x^2 - 2x + 1 = y$ $(-2 \leq x \leq 4)$
17. $y = x^2 - 3x + 2$ $(-1 \leq x \leq 4)$

18. $x^2 + x - 6 = y$ $(-4 \leq x \leq 3)$
19. $y = -x^2 + 6x - 8$ $(0 \leq x \leq 6)$
20. $-x^2 + 4x - 3 = y$ $(-1 \leq x \leq 5)$

10. Solving Quadratic Equations by Using Graphs

When we solve the equation $x^2 - 2x - 8 = 0$, we are finding the values of x for which $x^2 - 2x - 8$ equals 0.

Let us graph $x^2 - 2x - 8 = y$. We will use integral values for x from $x = -3$ to $x = 5$ inclusive. Both in the table that we develop and on the graph which we draw, we will find the values of x for which $x^2 - 2x - 8$ equals zero. These values of x are the roots of the equation $x^2 - 2x - 8 = 0$.

Solve graphically $x^2 - 2x - 8 = 0$.

Solution:

1. Let $x^2 - 2x - 8 = y$.
2. Develop the following table of values: $x^2 - 2x - 8 = y$

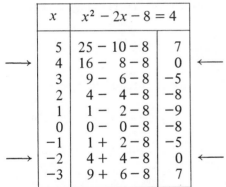

x	$x^2 - 2x - 8 = 4$	
5	$25 - 10 - 8$	7
4	$16 - 8 - 8$	0
3	$9 - 6 - 8$	-5
2	$4 - 4 - 8$	-8
1	$1 - 2 - 8$	-9
0	$0 - 0 - 8$	-8
-1	$1 + 2 - 8$	-5
-2	$4 + 4 - 8$	0
-3	$9 + 6 - 8$	7

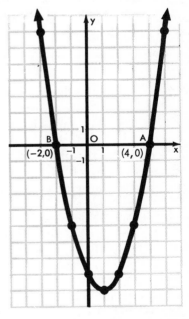

3. Plot the point associated with each ordered number pair (x, y): $(5, 7)$, $(4, 0)$, and so on. Draw a smooth curve through the points.
4. We are looking for values of x for which $x^2 - 2x - 8 = 0$. In the table, we see that when $x = 4$, $y = 0$ (that is, when $x = 4$, $x^2 - 2x - 8 = 0$).
   Also, when $x = -2$, $y = 0$ (that is, when $x = -2$, $x^2 - 2x - 8 = 0$). Therefore, 4 and -2 are the roots of $x^2 - 2x - 8 = 0$.
5. As we know, every point on the graph $y = x^2 - 2x - 8$ has an x-coordinate and a y-coordinate (x, y). Inspection reveals that the

y-coordinate has a value of 0 at $A(4, 0)$ and at $B(-2, 0)$. That is, y, or $x^2 - 2x - 8$, is equal to 0 at A, where $x = 4$, and at B, where $x = -2$. Therefore, 4 and -2 are roots of $x^2 - 2x - 8 = 0$.

6. Also, notice that the roots of $x^2 - 2x - 8 = 0$ (4 and -2) are the x-values of the two points at which the graph of $x^2 - 2x - 8 = y$ intersects the x-axis ($y = 0$).

Answer: $x = 4$ or $x = -2$; the solution set is $\{4, -2\}$.

Note: This graphic method of solving quadratic equations can also be used to approximate solutions, for example, to the nearest tenth, when they do not appear in the table.

Procedure. To solve a quadratic equation by using a graph:

1. **Transform the equation into an equivalent equation in standard form:** $ax^2 + bx + c = 0$ $(a \neq 0)$.
2. **Let** $ax^2 + bx + c = y$.
3. **Develop a table, choosing convenient values for** x**, and draw the graph of** $ax^2 + bx + c = y$.
4. **Read the** x**-values, or abscissas, of the points where the graph of** $ax^2 + bx + c = y$ **intersects the** x**-axis** ($y = 0$). **These** x**-values are the roots of the quadratic equation that is being solved.**

EXERCISES

1. a. Draw the graph of $x^2 - 4 = y$ using integral values of x from $x = -3$ to $x = 3$ inclusive.
   b. Use the graph made in answer to part **a** to solve the equation $x^2 - 4 = 0$.
2. a. Draw the graph of $x^2 - 6x + 8 = y$ using integral values of x from $x = 0$ to $x = 6$ inclusive.
   b. Use the graph made in answer to part **a** to solve the equation $x^2 - 6x + 8 = 0$.
3. a. Draw the graph of $x^2 - 3x = y$ using integral values of x from $x = -1$ to $x = 4$ inclusive.
   b. Use the graph made in answer to part **a** to solve the equation $x^2 - 3x = 0$.

In 4–12, use a graph to solve the equation.

4. $x^2 - 4x + 3 = 0$ 5. $x^2 + 2x - 8 = 0$ 6. $x^2 - 16 = 0$
7. $x^2 - 25 = 0$ 8. $x^2 - 2x = 0$ 9. $x^2 + 3x = 0$
10. $x^2 - x - 6 = 0$ 11. $x^2 - 2x = 8$ 12. $x^2 - 3 = 2x$

In 13–15, use a graph to solve the equation for x, correct to the nearest tenth.

13. $x^2 - 3x - 3 = 0$ 14. $x^2 - 2x - 5 = 0$ 15. $x^2 + 4x - 4 = 0$

11. Solving Verbal Problems by Using Quadratic Equations

The solutions of some verbal problems involve the solution of a quadratic equation. The most convenient method of solving the quadratic equation should be used.

NUMBER PROBLEMS

Model Problems

1. The product of two positive consecutive even integers is 80. Find the integers.

   Solution:

   Let x = the first positive even integer.
   Then $x + 2$ = the next consecutive positive even integer.

   The product of two positive consecutive even integers is 80.

   $$x(x + 2) = 80$$
   $$x^2 + 2x = 80$$
   $$x^2 + 2x - 80 = 0$$
   $$(x - 8)(x + 10) = 0$$

$x - 8 = 0$	$x + 10 = 0$
$x = 8$	$x = -10$ [Reject, because the integer
$x + 2 = 10$	must be positive.]

   Check: The product of the two positive consecutive even integers 8 and 10 is $(8)(10)$, or 80.

   Answer: The integers are 8 and 10.

2. The sum of two numbers is 8. The sum of the squares of the numbers is 34. Find the numbers.

   Solution:

   Let x = the first number.
   Then $8 - x$ = the second number.

   The sum of the squares of the numbers is 34.

   $$x^2 + (8 - x)^2 = 34$$
   $$x^2 + 64 - 16x + x^2 = 34 \qquad \text{Squaring } 8 - x$$
   $$2x^2 - 16x + 64 = 34 \qquad \text{Collecting like terms}$$
   $$2x^2 - 16x + 30 = 0 \qquad S_{34}$$

$$x^2 - 8x + 15 = 0 \qquad D_2$$
$$(x - 5)(x - 3) = 0 \qquad \text{Factoring}$$

$$x - 5 = 0 \mid x - 3 = 0$$
$$x = 5 \mid x = 3$$
$$8 - x = 3 \mid 8 - x = 5$$

Check: The sum of 5 and 3, $5 + 3 = 8$. The sum of $(5)^2$ and $(3)^2$, $25 + 9 = 34$.

Answer: The numbers are 5 and 3.

EXERCISES

1. The square of a number increased by 3 times the number is 28. Find the number.
2. When the square of a certain number is decreased by 9 times the number, the result is 36. Find the number.
3. The square of a number is equal to the sum of 21 and 4 times the number. Find the number.
4. Find two positive numbers whose ratio is $2 : 3$ and whose product is 600.
5. The larger of two positive numbers is 5 more than the smaller. The product of the numbers is 36. Find the numbers.
6. The balcony of a theater contains 240 seats. The number of seats in each row is 14 more than the number of rows. Find the number of rows.
7. The sum of two numbers is 9. Their product is 14. Find the numbers.
8. The product of two consecutive odd integers is 99. Find the integers.
9. Find two consecutive even integers such that the square of the smaller is 10 more than the larger.
10. Nine times a certain number is 5 less than twice the square of the number. Find the number.
11. If 5 times the square of a certain number is decreased by twice the number, the result is 16. Find the number.
12. The sum of the squares of two positive consecutive integers is 41. Find the integers.
13. Find three consecutive odd integers such that the square of the first increased by the product of the other two is 224.
14. The sum of two numbers is 12. The sum of their squares is 104. Find the numbers.
15. The difference between two numbers is 3. The sum of the squares of the numbers is 89. Find the numbers.

16. The sum of a number and its reciprocal is $\dfrac{-10}{3}$. Find the number.
17. The sum of a number and its reciprocal is $2\frac{1}{6}$. Find the number.
18. The sum of a number and its reciprocal is 4. Find the number.

GEOMETRIC PROBLEMS

Model Problem

The base of a rectangle measures 7 centimeters more than its height. If the area of the rectangle is 30 square centimeters, find the measure of its base and the measure of its height.

Solution:

Let x = the number of centimeters in the height of the rectangle.
Then $x + 7$ = the number of centimeters in the base of the rectangle.

$$\boxed{\text{area} = 30} \quad x$$
$$x+7$$

The area of the rectangle is 30.

$$x(x + 7) = 30 \quad [\text{area} = \text{length of the base} \times \text{length of the height}]$$
$$x^2 + 7x = 30$$
$$x^2 + 7x - 30 = 0$$
$$(x - 3)(x + 10) = 0$$

$$x - 3 = 0 \quad | \quad x + 10 = 0$$
$$x = 3 \quad | \quad x = -10 \quad [\text{Reject, because the height cannot be a negative}$$
$$x + 7 = 10 \quad | \qquad\qquad\quad \text{number.}]$$

Check: When the base of a rectangle measures 10 and its height measures 3, the area is 10×3, or 30. Also, the measure of the base, 10, is 7 more than the measure of the height, 3.

Answer: The height measures 3 centimeters; the base measures 10 centimeters.

EXERCISES

1. The length of a rectangle is 2 times its width. The area of the rectangle is 72 square centimeters. Find the dimensions of the rectangle.
2. The width of a rectangle is $\frac{1}{3}$ of its length. The area of the rectangle is 75 square yards. Find the dimensions of the rectangle.
3. The ratio of the measures of the base and height of a rectangle is 3:4. The area of the rectangle is 1200 square centimeters. Find the dimensions of the rectangle.

4. The length of a rectangular garden is 4 meters more than its width. The area of the garden is 60 square meters. Find the dimensions of the garden.

5. The perimeter of a rectangle is 20 inches and its area is 16 square inches. Find the dimensions of the rectangle.

6. Find the dimensions of a rectangle whose perimeter is 28 feet and whose area is 48 square feet.

7. If the measure of one side of a square is increased by 2 centimeters and the measure of an adjacent side is decreased by 2 centimeters, the area of the resulting rectangle is 32 square centimeters. Find the measure of one side of the square.

8. A rectangle is 6 feet long and 4 feet wide. If each dimension is increased by the same number of feet, a new rectangle is formed whose area is 39 square feet more than the area of the original rectangle. By how many feet was each dimension increased?

9. A rectangle is 8 feet long and 6 feet wide. If each dimension is increased by the same number of feet, a new rectangle is formed whose area exceeds the area of the original rectangle by 72 square feet. Find the dimensions of the new rectangle.

10. Joan's rectangular garden is 6 meters long and 4 meters wide. She wishes to double the area of her garden by increasing its length and width by the same amount. Find the number of meters by which each dimension must be increased.

11. A picture 6 inches by 12 inches is surrounded by a frame of uniform width. If the area of the frame is twice the area of the picture, find the width of the frame.

12. The length of the base of a parallelogram is twice the length of its altitude. The area of the parallelogram is 50 square centimeters. Find the length of its base and altitude. [*Remember:* Area of a parallelogram = length of base × length of altitude.]

13. The altitude of a triangle measures 5 centimeters less than its base. The area of the triangle is 42 square centimeters. Find the lengths of its base and altitude. [*Remember:* Area of triangle = $\frac{1}{2}$ length of base × length of altitude.]

14. A wire is stretched from the top of a 3-foot pole to the top of an 8-foot pole. Find the length of the wire if the poles are 12 feet apart.

15. A baseball diamond has the shape of a square 90 feet on each side. The pitcher's mound is 60.5 feet from home plate on the segment joining home plate and second base. Find the distance from the pitcher's mound to second base.

16. The measure of one leg of a right triangle exceeds the measure of the other leg by 2 meters. The hypotenuse of the triangle is 10 meters long. Find the measurements of the legs of the triangle.

17. The hypotenuse of a right triangle is 2 centimeters longer than one leg and 4 centimeters longer than the other leg. Find the length of each side of the triangle.

Miscellaneous Problems

18. The square of Clara's age 2 years from now is equal to 20 times her age 3 years ago. Find Clara's present age.

19. Harry and Saul start from the point of intersection of two straight roads which cross at right angles. Harry travels along one road at the rate of 10 km/h and Saul travels along the other road at the rate of 24 km/h. In how many hours will they be 52 kilometers apart?

20. Arthur and Ben start from the same point and travel at the rates of 30 mph and 40 mph along straight roads that are at right angles to each other. In how many hours will they be 100 miles apart?

21. Perry and Stuart started from the same point at the same time. Perry traveled south and Stuart traveled west. Perry traveled 3 km/h faster than Stuart. At the end of 2 hours, they were 30 kilometers apart. Find their rates.

22. Mrs. Perkins drove from her home to Boston, 40 miles away, at a certain rate of speed. She then returned home from Boston, traveling over the same road at an average rate of speed which was 30 mph faster than her rate going to Boston. She spent a total of 2 hours traveling. Find her rate of speed each way.

23. The rate of a motorboat in still water is 10 mph. The boat traveled 24 miles upstream and returned the same distance downstream. The round trip required 5 hours. Find the rate of the current.

24. Two cars made the same trip of 240 kilometers. One traveled 20 km/h faster than the other and took 1 hour less time to make the trip. Find the rate of each car.

25. Two cities are 150 miles apart. The time required to travel from one city to the other by train is 2 hours less than the time required by bus. The average rate of the bus is 20 mph less than the average rate of the train. Find the rate of the train.

26. If Sid and Ted work together, they can paint a fence in 4 hours. If each works alone, Sid needs 6 hours more than Ted to paint the fence. How many hours would each boy working alone need to complete the job?

27. Tom requires 3 hours less than Bill to mow a certain lawn. If the two boys work together, they can mow the lawn in 2 hours. How many hours would each boy working alone need to mow the lawn?

28. A number exceeds its reciprocal by $\frac{15}{4}$. Find the number.

29. The sum of two numbers is 7. The difference of their reciprocals is $\frac{1}{12}$. Find the numbers.

Chapter 18

Trigonometry of the Right Triangle

The word *trigonometry*, which comes from the Greek, means "measurement of triangles." In our study of trigonometry, we will develop relationships among the measures of the sides and angles of right triangles.

DIRECT AND INDIRECT MEASUREMENT

Many mathematical problems involve the measurement of the length of a segment. Sometimes, we can conveniently make a direct measurement of the length of a segment by applying the unit of measure to it. The number of times the unit of measure is contained in the segment represents the measure of the segment. For example, we may be able to measure the length of a side of a square with a yardstick.

In many situations, however, it is inconvenient or impossible to apply the unit of measure directly to the object being measured. For example, we cannot measure directly the height of a tall tree or building, the width of a river, or the distance to the sun. In such cases we resort to methods of indirect measurement.

When we use indirect measurement to discover the length of a line segment, for example, we first measure directly segments and angles which can be conveniently measured. We then compute the length of the segment we wish to measure by using a formula or mathematical relationship which relates the length of that segment with the measurements that were made directly. When we used the theorem of Pythagoras to compute the length of the hypotenuse of a right triangle when we knew the measures of the other two sides, we were using indirect measurement.

In our study of trigonometry of the right triangle, we will discover new relationships which will provide additional methods for measuring segments and angles indirectly. Engineers, surveyors, physicists, and astronomers frequently use these trigonometric methods in their work.

Before we begin our study of trigonometry we must first become familiar with some basic geometric information that we will need.

1. The Angle

In Chapter 13 we talked about lines, segments, and rays. Now we will study another geometric figure, the angle.

An *angle* is a set of points which is the union of two rays having the same endpoint.

In the illustration, rays $\overrightarrow{AB}$ and $\overrightarrow{AC}$, which form an angle, are called the *sides* of the angle. A, the endpoint of each ray, is called the *vertex* of the angle. The symbol for angle is $\angle$ (plural, ⅃s).

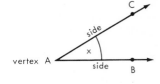

An angle, such as the one illustrated here, may be named in any of the following ways:

1. By a capital letter which names its vertex. For example, $\angle A$.
2. By a lower case letter or by a number placed inside the angle. For example, $\angle x$.
3. By three capital letters, one naming the vertex of the angle and the others naming points on the two sides of the angle. The letter at the vertex of the angle is always the middle letter. For example, $\angle BAC$ or $\angle CAB$.

In the figure at the right, we can think of $\angle TOS$ as having been formed by revolving ray $\overrightarrow{OT}$. If ray $\overrightarrow{OT}$ is revolved in a counterclockwise direction about vertex O, it will assume the position $\overrightarrow{OS}$, thus forming $\angle TOS$. $\overrightarrow{OT}$ is called the *initial side* of $\angle TOS$; $\overrightarrow{OS}$ is called the *terminal side*.

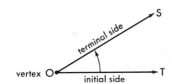

MEASURING ANGLES

To measure an angle means to determine the number of units of measure it contains. A common unit of measure of an angle is a degree, written as $1°$. A degree is $\frac{1}{360}$ of a complete revolution of a ray about a point. The *protractor* is an instrument used to measure angles. Study the protractor shown here.

The two scales on the protractor show divisions starting at $0°$ and going up to $180°$. One scale starts at $0°$ at the right and continues around to $180°$ at the left. The other scale starts at $0°$ at the left and continues around to $180°$ at the right. These

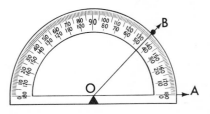

two scales make it convenient to measure an angle easily, regardless of its position.

To measure an angle, place the center of the protractor on the vertex of the angle. Place the upper part of the base of the protractor on one side of the angle. This side of the angle cuts across 0° on one scale. Notice that the other side of the angle also cuts across that scale. At the point at which the other side of the angle cuts across the scale, there is a reading that gives the measure of the angle. If the sides of the angle do not reach the scale, extend them until they do so.

In measuring angle AOB in the illustration, place the protractor so that side $\overrightarrow{OA}$ passes through the 0° reading on the inner scale. Side $\overrightarrow{OB}$ cuts across this scale at a point marked 45°. Therefore, angle AOB contains 45°. We will also say $m\angle AOB = 45°$, which is read "The measure of angle AOB is 45 degrees."

Note that when the angle being measured is less than one-quarter of a complete revolution, the reading on the scale must be less than 90°. When the angle being measured is greater than one-quarter of a complete revolution and less than one-half of a complete revolution, the reading on the scale must be greater than 90° and less than 180°.

TYPES OF ANGLES

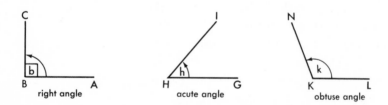

right angle   acute angle   obtuse angle

A right angle is an angle whose measure is 90°. $\angle ABC$ pictures a right angle. Hence, we can say that $m\angle ABC = 90°$, or $m\angle b = 90°$. It follows that *all right angles are equal in measure.* Note that symbol ⌐ at B is used to show that $\angle ABC$ is a right angle.

An acute angle is an angle whose measure is greater than 0° and less than 90°. $\angle GHI$ pictures an acute angle. Hence, $0° < m\angle h < 90°$.

An obtuse angle is an angle whose measure is greater than 90° and less than 180°. $\angle LKN$ pictures an obtuse angle. Hence, $90° < m\angle k < 180°$.

EXERCISES

1. Use a protractor to measure each of the following angles:

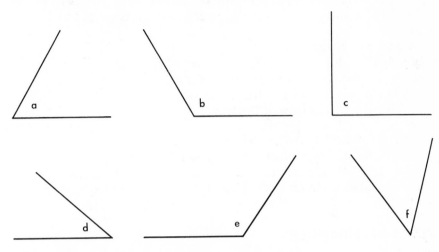

2. Use a protractor to draw an angle whose measure is:
   a. 30°   b. 80°   c. 90°   d. 65°   e. 48°   f. 24°
   g. 120°   h. 150°   i. 165°   j. 115°   k. 96°   l. 138°
3. What kind of angle is each angle of a rectangle?
4. In triangle *ABC*, what kind of angles do ∠*A*, ∠*B*, and ∠*C* appear to be?
5. In triangle *DEF*, what kinds of angles do ∠*D*, ∠*E*, and ∠*F* appear to be?
6. Order the measures of the following types of angles, naming the smallest angle first: right angle, obtuse angle, acute angle.

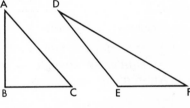

7. Using the figure shown:
   a. Name angle *x*, using three capital letters.
   b. Give the shorter name for angle *COB*.
   c. Name one acute angle.
   d. Name one obtuse angle.

8. Find the number of degrees in: (a) $\frac{1}{3}$ of a right angle   (b) $\frac{3}{5}$ of a right angle
9. Find the number of degrees through which the earth rotates in:
   a. 24 hours   b. 12 hours   c. 1 hour   d. 4 minutes

2. The Triangle

If three distinct points do not lie on the same straight line, the union of the three line segments determined by these points is called a *triangle*.

Consider triangle ABC ($\triangle ABC$). In triangle ABC, the points A, B, and C are the *vertices* of the triangle. Line segments $\overline{AB}$, $\overline{BC}$, and $\overline{CA}$ are the *sides* of the triangle. $\angle A$, $\angle B$, and $\angle C$ are the *angles* of the triangle.

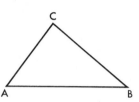

We say that side $\overline{AB}$ is included between $\angle A$ and $\angle B$, side $\overline{BC}$ is included between $\angle B$ and $\angle C$, and side $\overline{CA}$ is included between $\angle C$ and $\angle A$. We also say that $\angle A$ is included between sides $\overline{AB}$ and $\overline{AC}$, $\angle B$ is included between sides $\overline{BA}$ and $\overline{BC}$, and $\angle C$ is included between sides $\overline{CB}$ and $\overline{CA}$.

KINDS OF TRIANGLES

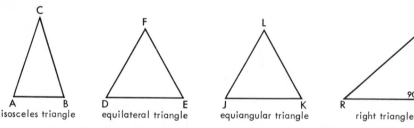

An *isosceles triangle* is a triangle that has two sides of equal length.

An *equilateral triangle* is a triangle that has three sides of equal length.

An *equiangular triangle* is a triangle that has three angles of equal measure.

A *right triangle* is a triangle that has one right angle.

Note: It can be shown that every equilateral triangle is equiangular and that every equiangular triangle is equilateral. That is, the set of all equilateral triangles is equal to the set of all equiangular triangles.

THE SUM OF THE MEASURES OF THE ANGLES OF A TRIANGLE

In each of the preceding triangles, when the three angles are measured and these measures are added, the sum is $180°$. All triangles, regardless of their size or shape, have the following property:

The sum of the measures of the angles of a triangle is $180°$.

Note: If the sum of the measures of three angles is not $180°$, these angles cannot be the angles of a triangle.

Model Problem

In triangle ABC, the measure of angle B is twice the measure of angle A, and the measure of angle C is three times the measure of angle A. Find the number of degrees in each angle of the triangle.

Solution:

Let x = the number of degrees in angle A.
Then $2x$ = the number of degrees in angle B.
Then $3x$ = the number of degrees in angle C.

The sum of the measures of the angles of a triangle is $180°$.

$$x + 2x + 3x = 180$$
$$6x = 180$$
$$x = 30$$
$$2x = 60$$
$$3x = 90$$

Check

$$60° = 2 \times 30°$$
$$90° = 3 \times 30°$$
$$30° + 60° + 90° = 180°$$

Answer: $m∠A = 30°, m∠B = 60°, m∠C = 90°$

EXERCISES

In 1–3, discover whether the three angles can be the three angles of a triangle.

1. $30°, 70°, 80°$
2. $70°, 80°, 90°$
3. $30°, 110°, 40°$

In 4–7, find the measure of the third angle of the triangle if the first two angles contain:

4. $60°, 40°$ 5. $100°, 20°$ 6. $55°, 85°$ 7. $24°, 82°$

8. **a.** Find the number of degrees in each angle of an equiangular triangle.
   b. Find the number of degrees in each angle of an equilateral triangle.

9. Can a triangle have: (a) two right angles? (b) two obtuse angles? (c) one right and one obtuse angle? Why?

10. What is the sum of the measures of the two acute angles of a right triangle?

11. If two angles in one triangle contain the same number of degrees as two angles in another triangle, what must be true of the third pair of angles in the two triangles? Why?

12. In a triangle, the measure of the second angle is 3 times the measure of the first angle, and the measure of the third angle is 5 times

the measure of the first angle. Find the number of degrees in each angle of the triangle.

13. In triangle RST, the measure of angle R is $\frac{1}{2}$ of the measure of angle S, and the measure of angle T is 3 times the measure of angle S. Find the measure of each angle of the triangle.

14. In a triangle, the measure of the second angle is 4 times the measure of the first angle. The measure of the third angle is equal to the sum of the measure of the first two angles. Find the number of degrees in each angle of the triangle.

15. In a triangle, the measure of the second angle is 30° more than the measure of the first angle, and the measure of the third angle is 45° more than the measure of the first angle. Find the number of degrees in each angle of the triangle.

16. In a triangle, the measure of the second angle exceeds twice the measure of the first angle by 5°. The measure of the third angle is 35° less than 3 times the measure of the first angle. Find the number of degrees in each angle of the triangle.

17. The measures of the two acute angles of a right triangle are in the ratio 8 : 1. Find the number of degrees in each acute angle.

In 18–21, find the number of degrees in each angle of a triangle if the measures of the three angles are in the ratio:

18. 2 : 3 : 4   **19.** 2 : 5 : 8   **20.** 2 : 2 : 5   **21.** 1 : 5 : 3

22. The measure of the second angle of a triangle is 20° less than the measure of the first angle. The measure of the third angle is $\frac{1}{2}$ the measure of the first angle. Find the measures of the three angles of the triangle.

3. Similar Triangles

Let us set up a correspondence between triangles ABC and DEF by pairing vertex A and vertex D, vertex B and vertex E, vertex C and vertex F. We call the angles whose vertices we have paired a pair of

corresponding angles. For example, $\angle A$ and $\angle D$, $\angle B$ and $\angle E$, $\angle C$ and $\angle F$ are pairs of corresponding angles. We call two sides whose endpoints have been paired in the correspondence that was set up between triangle ABC and triangle DEF a pair of *corresponding sides.* For example, $\overline{BC}$ and $\overline{EF}$, $\overline{AC}$ and $\overline{DF}$, $\overline{AB}$ and $\overline{DE}$ are each a pair of corresponding sides.

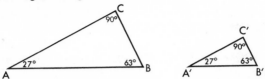

In triangles ABC and $A'B'C'$ shown above, note that $m\angle A = m\angle A'$ (each measures 27°); $m\angle B = m\angle B'$ (each measures 63°); and $m\angle C = m\angle C'$ (each measures 90°). Triangles such as triangle ABC and triangle $A'B'C'$ in which all pairs of corresponding angles are equal in measure are called **similar triangles**. Triangle ABC is similar to triangle $A'B'C'$, written $\triangle ABC \sim \triangle A'B'C'$. This example illustrates the following property of triangles:

Two triangles are similar if there is a correspondence between the vertices of the two triangles such that the measures of each pair of corresponding angles are equal.

Observe that when two triangles are similar, they have the same shape although they may not have the same size.

If we apply the property "the sum of the measures of the angles of a triangle is 180°," we can explain the following two properties of triangles:

Two triangles are similar if the measures of two pairs of corresponding angles are equal.

Two right triangles are similar if the measures of one pair of corresponding acute angles are equal.

In $\triangle ABC$ and $\triangle A'B'C'$ (see the preceding figure), if we measure $\overline{AB}$ and $\overline{A'B'}$, $\overline{BC}$ and $\overline{B'C'}$, $\overline{AC}$ and $\overline{A'C'}$, we find that the ratio of the measures of each pair of corresponding sides is $2:1$; that is, $\dfrac{AB}{A'B'} = \dfrac{2}{1}$, $\dfrac{BC}{B'C'} = \dfrac{2}{1}$, and $\dfrac{AC}{A'C'} = \dfrac{2}{1}$, or $\dfrac{AB}{A'B'} = \dfrac{BC}{B'C'} = \dfrac{AC}{A'C'}$. This example illustrates the following property of similar triangles:

If two triangles are similar, the ratio of the lengths of any pair of corresponding sides is equal to the ratio of the lengths of any other pair of corresponding sides.

Another way of expressing this property is:

The lengths of corresponding sides of similar triangles are in proportion.

A proportion involving two pairs of corresponding sides in two similar triangles may be written in more than one way. In the preceding figure, for example, the proportion $\dfrac{AB}{A'B'} = \dfrac{BC}{B'C'}$, which involves sides $\overline{AB}, \overline{A'B'}, \overline{BC}$, and $\overline{B'C'}$, may also be written $\dfrac{AB}{BC} = \dfrac{A'B'}{B'C'}$.

Model Problem

In triangle ABC, $m\angle A = 35°$, $m\angle B = 90°$. In triangle DEF, $m\angle F = 55°$,
$m\angle E = 90°$.

a. Is triangle ABC similar to
   triangle DEF? Why?
b. If $AB = 40$ cm, $BC = 28$ cm,
   and $DE = 60$ cm, find EF.

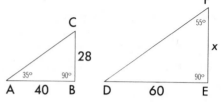

Solution:

a. The triangles will be similar if the measures of two angles in triangle ABC are
   equal to the measures of two angles in triangle DEF.
   1. $m\angle B = 90°$ and $m\angle E = 90°$. Therefore, $m\angle B = m\angle E$.
   2. In $\triangle ABC$, $m\angle A + m\angle B = 35° + 90° = 125°$.
      $m\angle C = 180° - 125° = 55°$.
   3. $m\angle C = 55°$ and $m\angle F = 55°$. Therefore, $m\angle C = m\angle F$.
   4. Therefore, $\triangle ABC$ is similar to $\triangle DEF$ because the measures of two pairs of
      corresponding angles are equal. *Ans.*
b. Since triangles ABC and DEF are similar, the lengths of their corresponding
   sides are in proportion.

   1. $\dfrac{EF}{BC} = \dfrac{DE}{AB}$ $AB = 40$ cm, $BC = 28$ cm, $DE = 60$ cm
                                       Let $x = EF$ in cm

   2. $\dfrac{x}{28} = \dfrac{60}{40}$

   3. $40x = (28)(60)$
   4. $40x = 1680$
   5. $x = 42$

   Answer: EF is 42 cm

EXERCISES

1. In triangle RST, $m\angle R = 90°$ and $m\angle S = 40°$. In triangle XYZ,
   $m\angle X = 40°$ and $m\angle Y = 50°$. Is triangle RST similar to triangle
   XYZ? Why?

   In 2–4, select the triangles that are similar and tell why they are
similar.

2.

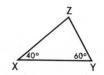

3.

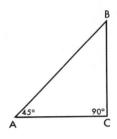
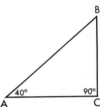
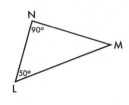

4.

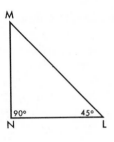

5. Are all equiangular triangles similar? Why?

6. In △*ABC* and △*RST*, *A* corresponds to *R*, *B* to *S*, and *C* to *T*. If △*ABC* ~ △*RST* and if *AB* = 9 in., *AC* = 6 in., and *RS* = 3 in., find *RT*.

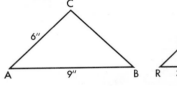

7. In the figure, *m∠A* = *m∠D* and *m∠C* = *m∠F*. If *AB* = 12, *AC* = 16, *BC* = 20, and *DE* = 6, find *DF* and *EF*.

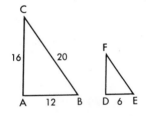

8. In the figure:
  a. Why is triangle *ABC* similar to triangle *A'B'C'*?
  b. Write the ratio of *BC* to *B'C'*.
  c. Write the ratio of *AC* to *A'C'*.
  d. Why are the ratios found in part **a** and part **b** equal?
  e. Find the value of *x*.
  f. Find the ratio of *BC* to *AC*.
  g. Find the ratio of *B'C'* to *A'C'*.
  h. What is true of the ratios found in part **f** and part **g**?

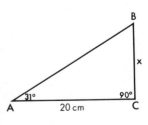
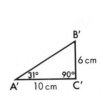

  i. Is the following statement true or false? Why? "If two triangles are similar, the ratio of the lengths of two sides of one triangle is equal to the ratio of the lengths of the corresponding sides of the other triangle."

9. In triangles LMN and DEF, $m\angle L = m\angle D$.

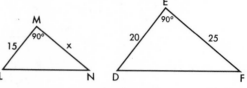

  a. Write the ratio of MN to ML.

  b. Write the ratio of EF to ED.

  c. Use the results found in part **a** and part **b** to write a proportion and tell why the proportion is true.

  d. Find the value of x.

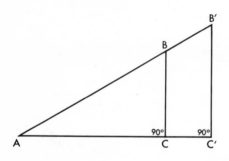

In 10–13, use the figure at the left.

10. If $BC = 3$ in., $AC = 4$ in., and $AC' = 8$ in., find $B'C'$.

11. If $AC = 5$ m, $BC = 2$ m, and $B'C' = 7$ m, find AC'.

12. If $B'C' = 12$ in., $AC = 6$ in., $CC' = 3$ in., find BC.

13. If $BC = 10$ cm and $AC = 8$ cm, find the ratio of $B'C'$ to AC'.

4. Using Similar Triangles in Indirect Measurement

Similar triangles may sometimes be used to discover by *indirect measurement* the measurements of line segments and angles which cannot be measured conveniently by direct measurement.

Model Problem

At the same time that a vertical flagpole casts a shadow 10 feet long, a nearby vertical pole that is 6 feet high casts a shadow 5 feet long. Find the height of the flagpole.

1. Since the sun is at a very great distance from the earth, the sun's rays, $\overleftrightarrow{AC}$ and $\overleftrightarrow{DF}$, are, for all practical purposes, parallel. Hence, it can be shown that $m\angle A = m\angle D$.

2. Since the poles are vertical, $\angle B$ and $\angle E$ are right angles. Hence, $m\angle B = m\angle E$.

3. Since two right triangles are similar if the measures of one pair of corresponding acute angles are equal, $\triangle DEF \sim \triangle ABC$.

4. $\dfrac{EF}{DE} = \dfrac{BC}{AB}$ [Let x = the length of the flagpole.]

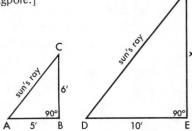

5. $\dfrac{x}{10} = \dfrac{6}{5}$

6. $5x = 60$

7. $x = 12$

Answer: The height of the flagpole is 12 feet.

EXERCISES

1. A vertical rod 8 ft. high casts a shadow 6 ft. long. At the same time,
   a nearby vertical tree casts a shadow 15 ft. long. Find the height of
   the tree.
2. A vertical tree casts a shadow 40 ft. long. At the same time, a
   nearby boy 5 ft. 6 in. tall casts a shadow 8 ft. long. Find the height
   of the tree.
3. In the figure, AB represents the
   width of a river. Angle B and angle
   D are right angles. $\overline{AE}$ and $\overline{BD}$ are
   line segments. $m\angle ACB = m\angle DCE$.
   $BC = 16$ m, $CD = 8$ m, and $DE = 4$ m.
   a. Is triangle ABC similar to tri-
      angle EDC? Why?
   b. Find AB, the width of the river.

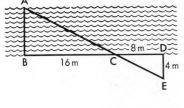

4. Using the figure in exercise 3, find AB, the width of the river, if
   $BC = 240$ ft., $CD = 80$ ft., and $DE = 25$ ft.
5. In the figure, $\overline{AD}$ and $\overline{CB}$ are line
   segments, $m\angle AEB = m\angle DEC$,   and
   $m\angle ABE = m\angle DCE$. Find AB, the distance across the pond, if:
   a. $CE = 40$ m, $EB = 120$ m, and $CD =$
      50 m
   b. $AE = 75$ m, $ED = 30$ m, and $CD =$
      36 m

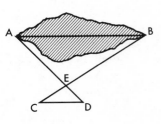

5. Trigonometry of the Right Triangle Involving the Tangent Ratio

In our study of the trigonometry of the right triangle, we will develop new relations from the properties of similar triangles. These relations will provide additional methods for measuring segments and angles indirectly.

Let us review some of the facts we learned about the right triangle (page 494).

In the figure, triangle ABC is a right triangle in which angle C is the right angle. $\overline{AB}$, the side opposite right angle C, is the hypotenuse of the right triangle; the length of $\overline{AB}$ is represented by c. The sides of the triangle which form the right angle, $\overline{BC}$ and $\overline{AC}$, are called the *legs* of the triangle. We call $\overline{BC}$ the leg opposite angle A; the length of $\overline{BC}$ is represented by a. We call $\overline{AC}$ the leg opposite angle B; the length of $\overline{AC}$ is represented by b. We may also call $\overline{AC}$ the leg adjacent to (next to) angle A. We may also call $\overline{BC}$ the leg adjacent to (next to) angle B.

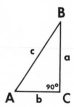

Each of the following triangles represents a right triangle in which there is a 31° angle. In each figure, the lengths of the leg opposite the 31° angle and the leg adjacent to the 31° angle are shown. In each triangle, let us find the ratio of the length of the leg opposite the 31° angle to the length of the leg adjacent to the 31° angle.

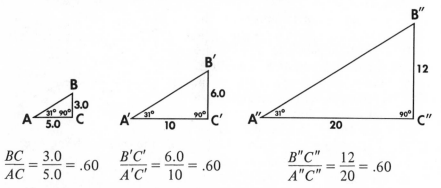

$$\frac{BC}{AC} = \frac{3.0}{5.0} = .60 \qquad \frac{B'C'}{A'C'} = \frac{6.0}{10} = .60 \qquad \frac{B''C''}{A''C''} = \frac{12}{20} = .60$$

Notice that in all three cases, the ratio is:

$$\frac{\text{length of the leg opposite the } 31° \text{ angle}}{\text{length of the leg adjacent to the } 31° \text{ angle}} = .60, \text{ a constant}$$

We might have expected that the three ratios $\dfrac{BC}{AC}, \dfrac{B'C'}{A'C'}$, and $\dfrac{B''C''}{A''C''}$

would be equal because the right triangles ABC, $A'B'C'$, and $A''B''C''$, each of which contains an angle of 31°, are similar, and the ratios of the lengths of corresponding sides in these similar triangles must be equal.

In fact, in all right triangles which contain an angle of 31°, the value of the ratio $\dfrac{\text{length of the leg opposite the 31° angle}}{\text{length of the leg adjacent to the 31° angle}}$ is constant (approximately .60), no matter what the size of the triangle.

What we have shown to be true for a 31° angle would be true for any other acute angle in a right triangle. In general, in every right triangle having an acute angle of a particular measure, the ratio of the length of the leg opposite the acute angle to the length of the leg adjacent to the acute angle is constant. This is true because every right triangle containing an acute angle of a particular measure is similar to every other right triangle containing an acute angle of the same measure. For acute angles of different measures the ratio is a different constant.

In the figure at the right, in which $\angle C$, $\angle C'$, and $\angle C''$ are right angles, we can see that $\triangle ABC \sim \triangle AB'C'$ and $\triangle ABC \sim \triangle AB''C''$. Hence, it follows that $\dfrac{BC}{AC} = \dfrac{B'C'}{AC'}$ and $\dfrac{B'C'}{AC'} = \dfrac{B''C''}{AC''}$.

That is:

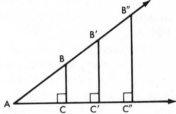

$$\frac{BC}{AC} = \frac{B'C'}{AC'} = \frac{B''C''}{AC''} = \text{a constant ratio for } \angle A.$$

This ratio is called the *tangent of the angle.*

The tangent of an acute angle of a right triangle is the ratio of the length of the leg opposite the acute angle to the length of the leg adjacent to the acute angle.

In right triangle ABC, with $m\angle C = 90°$, the tangent of angle A, abbreviated "tan A," is:

$$\tan A = \frac{\text{length of leg opposite } \angle A}{\text{length of leg adjacent to } \angle A} = \frac{a}{b}$$

THE TABLE OF TANGENTS

As the measure of angle A changes, the tangent ratio for angle A also changes. The tangent ratio for angle A depends upon the measure of angle A, not upon the size of the right triangle which contains angle

A. Mathematicians have constructed a table which contains approximations of tangent ratios for all acute angles whose measures are between 0° and 90°. This table, which is called a *table of trigonometric functions*, is found on page 561; tangent ratios are shown in the fourth column.

To find tan 28° from this table, for example, first look in the column headed Angle for the angle 28°. Then, in the fourth column headed Tangent on the same horizontal line as 28°, find the number .5317. Thus, tan 28° = .5317 to the *nearest ten-thousandth*.

> [*Note:* Although .5317 is an approximation of tan 28°, we wrote tan 28° = .5317 rather than tan 28° ≈ .5317. In our trigonometry work, we will use "=" rather than "≈" in order to simplify the symbolism in the computations. We will keep in mind that the trigonometric ratios in the tables are approximations.]

The table may also be used to find the measure of an angle when its tangent ratio is known. Thus, if tan x = 1.5399, we see from the table that $m\angle x$ must be 57°.

Sometimes the value of the tangent of an angle is not in the table. In such a case, we can approximate the value of the measure of the angle to the *nearest degree*. For example, suppose we wish to find $m\angle x$ when tan x = .5000. This value is not in the table of tangent ratios. In the table, we find the number which is just larger than .5000 and the number which is just smaller than .5000, and we then discover to which of these two ratios .5000 is closer.

Angle Measure   *Tangent*   *Difference*

Angle Measure	Tangent	Difference
27°	.5095	
x	.5000	.0095
26°	.4877	.0123

$$\begin{array}{rr} .5095 & .5000 \\ -.5000 & -.4877 \\ \hline .0095 & .0123 \end{array}$$

Since .0095 is less than .0123, .5000 is closer to .5095 than it is to .4877.

We then assume that the measure of angle x is closer to 27° than it is to 26°. We now know that the measure of angle x is 27° approximated to the nearest degree, and we write $m\angle x$ = 27°.

EXERCISES

In 1–4, name the hypotenuse, the leg opposite, and the leg adjacent to each acute angle of the right triangle.

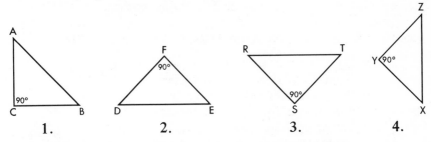

1.   **2.**   **3.**   **4.**

In 5–8, represent the tangent ratio for each acute angle.

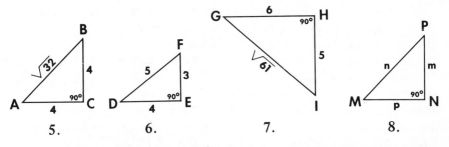

5.   **6.**   **7.**   **8.**

9. In triangle ABC, $m\angle C = 90°$, $AC = 6$, and $AB = 10$. Find $\tan A$.

10. In triangle RST, $m\angle T = 90°$, $RS = 13$, and $ST = 12$. Find $\tan S$.

In 11–15, use the table on page 561 to find:

11. $\tan 15°$ **12.** $\tan 32°$ **13.** $\tan 45°$ **14.** $\tan 74°$ **15.** $\tan 89°$

In 16–21, use the table on page 561 to find the measure of angle x if:

16. $\tan x = .1763$ **17.** $\tan x = .3443$ **18.** $\tan x = .8098$
19. $\tan x = 1.0000$ **20.** $\tan x = 2.3559$ **21.** $\tan x = 4.3315$

In 22–27, use the table on page 561 to find the measure of angle x to the *nearest degree* if:

22. $\tan x = .3285$ **23.** $\tan x = .7773$ **24.** $\tan x = 1.4000$
25. $\tan x = .2281$ **26.** $\tan x = 3.6231$ **27.** $\tan x = 2.3604$

28. a. Use the table on page 561 to discover whether $\tan 80°$ is twice $\tan 40°$.

   b. If the measure of an angle is doubled, is the tangent of the angle also doubled?

29. In triangle $ABC, m\angle C = 90°$, $AC = 5$, and $BC = 5$.
   a. Find $\tan A$.   **b.** Find the measure of angle A.
30. In triangle $RST, m\angle S = 90°$, $TS = 4$, and $RS = 3$.
   a. Find $\tan T$ to the *nearest ten-thousandth*.
   b. Find the measure of angle T to the *nearest degree*.

ANGLE OF ELEVATION AND ANGLE OF DEPRESSION

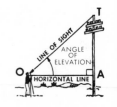

In the figure at the right, if a person using a
telescope or some similar instrument wishes to sight
the top of the telephone pole above him, he must
elevate the instrument from a horizontal position.
The line $\overleftrightarrow{OT}$ from the eye of the observer, O, to the
top of the pole, T, is called the ***line of sight***. The
angle determined by the horizontal line and the line
of sight, $\angle AOT$, is called the ***angle of elevation*** of the top of the pole,
T, from point O. (The horizontal line and the line of sight must be in
the same vertical plane.)

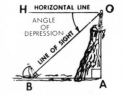

In the figure at the right, if a person using a
telescope or some similar instrument wishes to sight
the boat below him, he must depress the instrument
from a horizontal position.   The line $\overleftrightarrow{OB}$ from the
eye of the observer, O, to the boat, B, is the ***line of
sight***.   The angle determined by the horizontal line
and the line of sight, $\angle HOB$, is called the ***angle of depression*** of the
boat, B, from point O. (The horizontal line and the line of sight must
be in the same vertical plane.)

In the preceding figure, if we find the angle of elevation of O from
B, $\angle OBA$, and also find the angle of depression of B from O, $\angle HOB$,
we discover that both angles contain the same number of degrees. We
therefore say that the measure of the angle of elevation of O from B is
equal to the measure of the angle of depression of B from O.

USING THE TANGENT RATIO TO SOLVE PROBLEMS

Procedure. **To solve problems by use of the tangent ratio:**

1. **Make an approximate scale drawing which contains the line segments and angles given in the problem and those whose measures are to be found.**
2. **Select a right triangle in which either (a) the lengths of two legs are given (known) and the measure of an acute angle is to be found or (b) the length of one leg and the measure of an acute angle are given (known) and the length of the other leg is to be found.**

3. Write the formula for the tangent of the acute angle mentioned in step 2, and then substitute in the formula the values given in the problem.
4. Solve the resulting equation.

Model Problems

1. A ladder leaning against a building makes an angle whose measure is 75° with the ground. If the top of the ladder reaches a point 20 feet above the ground, find to the *nearest foot* the distance from the foot of the ladder to the foot of the building.

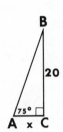

Solution: Since the segments mentioned in the problem are legs of a right triangle opposite (opp.) and adjacent (adj.) to one of its acute angles, use the tangent ratio.

Method 1	*Method* 2
1. $\tan A = \dfrac{\text{length of leg opp.}\angle A}{\text{length of leg adj. to }\angle A}$	Find $m\angle B$.
	1. $m\angle B = 180° - 90° - 75° = 15°$
2. $\tan A = \dfrac{BC}{AC}$	2. $\tan B = \dfrac{\text{length of leg opp.}\angle B}{\text{length of leg adj. to }\angle B}$
Let $x = AC$.	3. $\tan B = \dfrac{AC}{BC}$
3. $\tan 75° = \dfrac{20}{x}$	Let $x = AC$.
4. $3.7321 = \dfrac{20}{x}$	4. $\tan 15° = \dfrac{x}{20}$
5. $3.7321x = 20$ $\quad$ M$_x$	5. $.2679 = \dfrac{x}{20}$
6. $\quad x = \dfrac{20}{3.7321}$ D$_{3.7321}$	6. $x = 20(.2679)$ $\quad$ M$_{20}$
7. $\quad x = 5.3$	7. $x = 5.3580$

Answer: 5 feet

[*Note:* In method 1, since the unknown was the length of the leg adjacent to $\angle A$, the solution required the inconvenient long division $\dfrac{20}{3.7321}$. In method 2, however, when we used the other acute angle, $\angle B$, the unknown was the length of the leg opposite $\angle B$; and the solution required the convenient multiplication 20(.2679).]

2. Find to the *nearest degree* the measure of the angle of elevation of the sun when a vertical pole 6 meters high casts a shadow 8 meters long.

Solution: The angle of elevation of the sun is the same as $\angle A$, the angle of elevation of the top of the pole from A. Since the segments mentioned in the problem are legs of a right triangle opposite and adjacent to $\angle A$, use the tangent ratio.

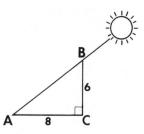

1. $\tan A = \dfrac{\text{length of leg opposite } \angle A}{\text{length of leg adjacent to } \angle A}$
2. $\tan A = \frac{6}{8}$ Express $\frac{6}{8}$ as the decimal .7500.
3. $\tan A = .7500$ In the table on page 561, $\tan 36° = .7265$ and
4. $A = 37°$ $\tan 37° = .7536$. Since .7500 is closer to .7536 than it is to .7265, $m\angle A$ is closer to 37°.

Answer: 37°

EXERCISES

In 1–8, find the length of the line segment marked x to the *nearest foot* or the measure of the angle marked x to the *nearest degree*.

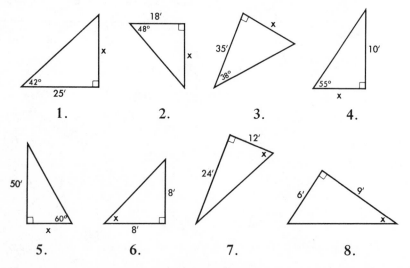

1.   **2.**   **3.**   **4.**

5.   **6.**   **7.**   **8.**

9. At a point on the ground 10 meters from the foot of a tree, the angle of elevation of the top of the tree measures 48°. Find the height of the tree to the *nearest meter*.

10. A boy visiting New York City views the Empire State Building from a point on the ground, A, which is 310 meters from the foot, C, of the building. The angle of elevation of the top, B, of the building as seen by the boy measures 53°. Find the height of the building to the *nearest meter*.

11. Find to the *nearest foot* the height of a vertical post if its shadow is 18 feet long when the angle of elevation of the sun measures 38°.

12. From the top of a lighthouse 50 meters high, the angle of depression of a boat out at sea measures 24°. Find to the *nearest meter* the distance from the boat to the foot of the lighthouse, the foot being at sea level.

13. Find the measure of the angle of elevation of the sun when a woman 5 feet high casts a shadow 5 feet long.

14. Find to the *nearest degree* the measure of the angle which the sun's rays make with the ground when a flagpole 8 meters high casts a shadow 6 meters long.

15. A ladder leans against a building. The top of the ladder reaches a point on the building which is 18 feet above the ground. The foot of the ladder is 7 feet from the building. Find to the *nearest degree* the measure of the angle which the ladder makes with the level ground.

16. When a yardstick held vertically casts a shadow 7 feet long on level ground, a flagpole nearby casts a shadow 140 feet long.

   a. Find the height of the flagpole to the *nearest foot*.
   b. Find the measure of the angle of elevation of the sun to the *nearest degree*.

6. Trigonometry of the Right Triangle Involving the Sine Ratio

Since the tangent ratio involves the lengths of two legs of a right triangle, it is not directly useful in solving problems in which the lengths of the hypotenuse and a leg, together with the measure of an acute angle, are involved. In such a case, ratios other than the tangent ratio can be more useful.

If we refer to the figure on page 521, we can see that since $\triangle ABC \sim \triangle AB'C'$ and $\triangle ABC \sim \triangle AB''C''$, it follows that $\dfrac{BC}{AB} = \dfrac{B'C'}{AB'}$ and $\dfrac{BC}{AB} = \dfrac{B''C''}{AB''}$; that is, $\dfrac{BC}{AB} = \dfrac{B'C'}{AB'} = \dfrac{B''C''}{AB''} =$ a constant ratio for $\angle A$.

This ratio is called the *sine of the angle*.

The sine of an acute angle of a right triangle is the ratio of the length of the leg opposite the acute angle to the length of the hypotenuse.

In right triangle ABC, with $m\angle C = 90°$, the sine of angle A, abbreviated "sin A," is:

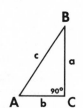

$$\sin A = \frac{\text{length of leg opposite } \angle A}{\text{length of hypotenuse}} = \frac{a}{c}$$

THE TABLE OF SINES

As the measure of angle A changes, the sine ratio for angle A also changes. The sine ratio for angle A depends upon the measure of angle A, not upon the size of the right triangle which contains angle A. The table containing approximations of sine ratios which mathematicians have constructed for all acute angles whose measures are between 0° and 90° is found on page 561; the sine ratio is shown in the second column.

If we use this table as we did when we studied the tangent ratio, we can obtain the following results:

1. sin 25° = .4226.
2. If sin x = .7660, $m\angle x = 50°$.
3. If sin x = .2500, we assume that $m\angle x = 14°$ to the *nearest degree* because .2500 is closer to .2419, which is sin 14°, than it is to .2588, which is sin 15°.

EXERCISES

In 1–4, represent the sine of each acute angle.

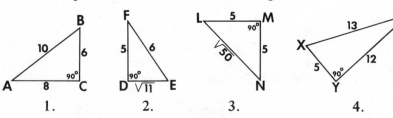

1.   2.   3.   4.

5. In triangle ABC, $m\angle C = 90°$, $AC = 4$, and $BC = 3$. Find sin A.
6. In triangle RST, $m\angle S = 90°$, $RS = 5$, and $ST = 12$. Find sin T.

In 7–11, use the table on page 561 to find:

7. sin 18°   8. sin 42°   9. sin 58°   10. sin 76°   11. sin 89°

In 12-14, use the table on page 561 to find the measure of angle *x* if:

12. sin *x* = .1908   **13.** sin *x* = .8387   **14.** sin *x* = .6561

In 15-17, use the table on page 561 to find the measure of angle *x* to the *nearest degree* if:

15. sin *x* = .1900   **16.** sin *x* = .8740   **17.** sin *x* = .1275

18. a. Use the table on page 561 to discover whether sin 50° is twice sin 25°.
    b. If the measure of an angle is doubled, is the sine of the angle also doubled?

19. In triangle *ABC*, *m∠C* = 90°, *BC* = 20, and *BA* = 40. **(a)** Find sin *A* to the *nearest ten-thousandth*. **(b)** Find the measure of angle *A*.

20. In triangle *ABC*, *m∠C* = 90°, *AC* = 5, and *BC* = 12. **(a)** Find sin *B* to the *nearest ten-thousandth*. **(b)** Find the measure of angle *B* to the *nearest degree*.

USING THE SINE RATIO TO SOLVE PROBLEMS

When the length of the hypotenuse, the length of a leg, and the measure of an acute angle of a right triangle are involved in a problem, with the measure of any two of these three parts given (known), the use of the sine ratio will help us to find the measure of the unknown third part. We proceed as we did when we were using the tangent ratio.

Model Problems

1. A boy who is flying a kite lets out 300 meters of string which makes an angle whose measure is 38° with the ground. Assuming that the string is straight, how high above the ground is the kite? [Give the answer correct to the *nearest meter*.]

Solution: Since the segments mentioned in the problem are the leg opposite the acute angle and the hypotenuse of the right triangle, use the sine ratio.

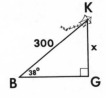

1. $\sin B = \dfrac{\text{length of leg opposite } \angle B}{\text{length of hypotenuse}}$

2. $\sin B = \dfrac{KG}{KB}$ Let *x* = *KG*.

3. $\sin 38° = \dfrac{x}{300}$ In the table on page 561, sin 38° = .6157.

4. $.6157 = \dfrac{x}{300}$

5. $x = 300(.6157)$ M_{300}
6. $x = 184.71$

Answer: 185 meters

2. A road is inclined 8° to the horizontal. Find to the *nearest hundred feet* the distance one must drive up this road to increase his altitude 1000 feet.

Solution: Since the segments mentioned in the problem are the leg opposite the acute angle and the hypotenuse of the right triangle, use the sine ratio.

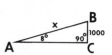

1. $\sin A = \dfrac{\text{length of leg opposite } \angle A}{\text{length of hypotenuse}}$

2. $\sin A = \dfrac{BC}{AB}$ Let $x = AB$.

3. $\sin 8° = \dfrac{1000}{x}$ In the table on page 561, sin 8° = .1392.

4. $.1392 = \dfrac{1000}{x}$

5. $.1392x = 1000$ M_x

6. $x = \dfrac{1000}{.1392}$ $D_{.1392}$

7. $x = 7184$

Answer: 7200 feet

3. A ladder 25 feet long leans against a building and reaches a point 23.5 feet above the ground. Find to the *nearest degree* the measure of the angle which the ladder makes with the ground.

Solution: Since the given segments are the hypotenuse and the leg opposite the acute angle to be found, use the sine ratio.

1. $\sin A = \dfrac{\text{length of leg opposite } \angle A}{\text{length of hypotenuse}}$

2. $\sin A = \dfrac{23.5}{25}$ Change $\dfrac{23.5}{25}$ to the decimal .9400.

3. $\sin A = .9400$

In the table on page 561, $\sin 70° = .9397$ and
$\sin 71° = .9455$. Since $.9400$ is closer to
$.9397$ than it is to $.9455$, $m \angle A$ is closer to
$70°$.

4. $m\angle A = 70°$

Answer: $70°$

EXERCISES

In 1–4, find the length of the line segment marked x to the *nearest foot* or the measure of the angle marked x to the *nearest degree*.

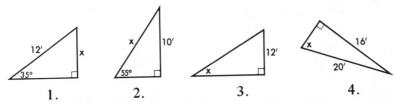

1.   2.   3.   4.

5. A wooden beam 24 feet long leans against a wall and makes an angle whose measure is $71°$ with the ground. Find to the *nearest foot* how high up the wall the beam reaches.

6. A straight road to the top of a hill is 2500 feet long and makes an angle whose measure is $12°$ with the horizontal. Find the height of the hill to the *nearest hundred feet*.

7. A straight road is inclined $10°$ to the horizontal. If a man drove a distance of 700 meters up the road, find to the *nearest hundred meters* his increase in altitude.

8. A ladder which leans against a building makes an angle whose measure is $75°$ with the ground and reaches a point on the building 20 feet above the ground. Find to the *nearest foot* the length of the ladder.

9. From an airplane flying at an altitude of 3000 feet, the measure of the angle of depression of an airport ground signal is $27°$. Find to the *nearest hundred feet* the distance between the airplane and the airport signal.

10. An airplane climbs at an angle which measures $11°$ with the ground. Find to the *nearest ten meters* the distance it has traveled when it has attained an altitude of 100 meters.

11. A 20-foot pole leaning against a wall reached a point 18 feet above the ground. Find to the *nearest degree* the measure of the angle which the pole makes with the ground.

12. In order to reach the top of a hill 250 feet high, one must travel 2000 feet up a straight road which leads to the top. Find to the *nearest degree* the number of degrees in the angle which the road makes with the horizontal.

7. Trigonometry of the Right Triangle Involving the Cosine Ratio

A third important ratio in a right triangle involves the length of the leg adjacent to one of the acute angles of the triangle and the length of the hypotenuse.

In the figure on page 521, we can see that since $\triangle ABC \sim \triangle A'B'C'$ and $\triangle ABC \sim \triangle AB''C''$, it follows that $\dfrac{AC}{AB} = \dfrac{AC'}{AB'}$ and $\dfrac{AC}{AB} = \dfrac{AC''}{AB''}$; that is:

$$\frac{AC}{AB} = \frac{AC'}{AB'} = \frac{AC''}{AB''} = \text{a constant ratio for } \angle A.$$

This ratio is called the ***cosine of the angle***.

The cosine of an acute angle of a right triangle is the ratio of the leg adjacent to the acute angle to the length of the hypotenuse.

In right triangle ABC, with $m\angle C = 90°$, the cosine of angle A, abbreviated "cos A," is:

$$\cos A = \frac{\text{length of leg adjacent to } \angle A}{\text{length of hypotenuse}} = \frac{b}{c}$$

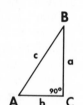

THE TABLE OF COSINES

As the measure of angle A changes, the cosine ratio for angle A also changes. The cosine ratio for angle A depends upon the measure of angle A, not upon the size of the right triangle which contains angle A. The table containing approximations of cosine ratios which mathematicians have constructed for all acute angles whose measures are between $0°$ and $90°$ is found on page 561; the cosine ratios are shown in the third column.

If we use this table as we did when we studied the tangent ratio, we can obtain the following results:

1. $\cos 55° = .5736$.
2. If $\cos x = .9063$, $m\angle x = 25°$.
3. If $\cos x = .3300$, we assume that $m\angle x = 71°$ to the *nearest degree* because .3300 is closer to .3256, which is cos 71°, than it is to .3420, which is cos 70°.

EXERCISES

In 1–4, represent the cosine of each acute angle.

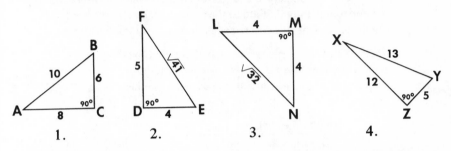

1.   2.   3.   4.

5. In triangle ABC, $m\angle C = 90°$, $AC = 4$, and $BC = 3$. Find $\cos A$.
6. In triangle RST, $m\angle S = 90°$, $RS = 5$, and $ST = 12$. Find $\cos T$.

In 7–11, use the table on page 561 to find the following:

7. $\cos 21°$ 8. $\cos 40°$ 9. $\cos 67°$ 10. $\cos 74°$ 11. $\cos 88°$

In 12–14, use the table on page 561 to find the measure of angle x if:

12. $\cos x = .9397$ 13. $\cos x = .3584$ 14. $\cos x = .0698$

In 15–17, use the table on page 561 to find the measure of angle x to the *nearest degree* if:

15. $\cos x = .9750$ 16. $\cos x = .5934$ 17. $\cos x = .2968$

18. a. Use the table on page 561 to discover whether $\cos 80°$ is twice $\cos 40°$.
   b. If the measure of an angle is doubled, is the cosine of the angle also doubled?
19. In triangle ABC, $m\angle C = 90°$, $AC = 40$, and $AB = 80$. (a) Find $\cos A$ to the *nearest ten-thousandth*. (b) Find the measure of angle A.

USING THE COSINE RATIO TO SOLVE PROBLEMS

When the leg adjacent to an acute angle in a right triangle and the hypotenuse of the right triangle are involved in a problem, the use of the cosine ratio will help us find the length of one of these sides when the length of the other side and the measure of the acute angle are given. We proceed as we did when we were using the tangent ratio or the sine ratio.

Model Problems

1. A plane took off from a field and rose at an angle whose measure was 8° with the horizontal ground. Find to the *nearest ten meters* the horizontal distance the plane had covered when it had flown 2000 meters.

   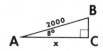

   Solution: Since the segments mentioned in the problem are the leg adjacent to an acute angle of the right triangle and the hypotenuse of the triangle, use the cosine ratio.

   1. $\cos A = \dfrac{\text{length of leg adjacent to } \angle A}{\text{length of hypotenuse}}$

   2. $\cos A = \dfrac{AC}{AB}$ Let $x = AC$.

   3. $\cos 8° = \dfrac{x}{2000}$ In the table on page 561, $\cos 8° = .9903$.

   4. $.9903 = \dfrac{x}{2000}$

   5. $x = 2000(.9903)$ M_{2000}
   6. $x = 1980.6$

   Answer: 1980 meters

2. A guy wire reaches from the top of a pole to a stake in the ground. The stake is 10 feet from the foot of the pole. The wire makes an angle which measures 65° with the ground. Find to the *nearest foot* the length of the wire.

   Solution: Since the segments mentioned in the problem are the leg adjacent to the acute angle and the hypotenuse of the right triangle, use the cosine ratio.

   1. $\cos S = \dfrac{\text{length of leg adjacent to } \angle S}{\text{length of hypotenuse}}$

   2. $\cos S = \dfrac{BS}{ST}$ Let $x = ST$.

   3. $\cos 65° = \dfrac{10}{x}$ In the table on page 561, $\cos 65° = .4226$.

   4. $.4226 = \dfrac{10}{x}$

   5. $.4226x = 10$ M_x

6. $x = \dfrac{10}{.4226}$ $\overline{D}_{.4226}$

7. $x = 23.6$

Answer: 24 feet

EXERCISES

In 1–4, find the length of the line segment marked x to the *nearest foot* or the measure of the angle marked x to the *nearest degree*.

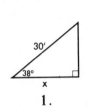

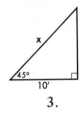
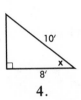

1.   2.   3.   4.

5. A 20-foot ladder leans against a building and makes an angle which measures 72° with the ground. Find to the *nearest foot* the distance between the foot of the ladder and the building.
6. A woman walked 800 meters along a straight road which is inclined 12° to the horizontal. Find to the *nearest meter* the horizontal distance traveled by the woman.
7. A guy wire attached to the top of a pole reaches a stake in the ground 20 feet from the foot of the pole and makes an angle whose measure is 58° with the ground. Find to the *nearest foot* the length of the guy wire.
8. An airplane rises at an angle whose measure is 14° with the ground. Find to the *nearest 10 feet* the distance it has flown when it has covered a horizontal distance of 1500 feet.
9. A boy is flying a kite. The kite string makes an angle which measures 43° with the ground. If the boy is standing 100 feet from a point on the ground directly below the kite, find to the *nearest foot* the length of the kite string.
10. A 9-meter steel girder is leaning against a wall. The foot of the girder is 6 meters from the wall. Find to the *nearest degree* the measure of the angle which the girder makes with the ground.
11. A plane took off from an airport. When the plane had flown 4000 feet in the direction in which it had taken off, it had covered a horizontal distance of 3900 feet. Find to the *nearest degree* the measure of the angle at which the plane rose from the ground.

12. A 10-meter ladder leaning against a wall reaches the wall at a point 9 meters from the ground. Find to the *nearest degree* the measure of the angle which the ladder makes with the wall.

8. Using All Three Trigonometric Ratios

When solving a problem by trigonometry, first make a drawing showing the parts whose measures are given and the part whose measure is to be found. Then use the proper ratio which relates the measure of the part that is to be found and the measures of the parts that are given.

Keep In Mind

$$\tan A = \frac{\text{length of leg opposite } \angle A}{\text{length of leg adjacent to } \angle A} = \frac{a}{b}$$

$$\sin A = \frac{\text{length of leg opposite } \angle A}{\text{length of hypotenuse}} = \frac{a}{c}$$

$$\cos A = \frac{\text{length of leg adjacent to } \angle A}{\text{length of hypotenuse}} = \frac{b}{c}$$

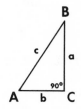

Model Problem

In isosceles triangle ABC, $AC = CB = 20$ cm, $m\angle A = m\angle B = 68°$. $\overline{CD}$ is perpendicular to $\overline{AB}$ ($\angle CDB$ is a right angle). $AD = DB$.

a. Find CD to the *nearest tenth of a centimeter*.
b. Find AB to the *nearest tenth of a centimeter*.

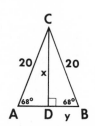

Solution:

a. 1. Let $x = CD$.
   2. In right $\triangle BDC$,
      $$\sin B = \frac{CD}{CB}$$

   3. $\sin 68° = \dfrac{x}{20}$

   4. $.9272 = \dfrac{x}{20}$

5. $x = 20(.9272)$
6. $x = 18.5440$
7. $x = 18.5$

Answer: CD = 18.5 centimeters

  b. We will find *DB* in right $\triangle BDC$ and double it to find *AB*.
    1. Let $y = DB$.
    2. In right triangle *BDC*,

$$\cos B = \frac{DB}{CB}$$

    3. $\cos 68° = \dfrac{y}{20}$

    4. $.3746 = \dfrac{y}{20}$

    5. $y = 20(.3746)$
    6. $y = 7.4920$
    7. $AB = 2y = 2(7.4920) = 14.9840$
    8. $AB = 15.0$

Answer: AB = 15.0 centimeters

EXERCISES

    Exercises 1–7 refer to right $\triangle ABC$. Name the ratio that can be used to find:

1. *a* when the measure of angle *A* and *c* are given.
2. *b* when the measure of angle *A* and *c* are given.
3. *c* when *a* and the measure of angle *A* are given.
4. *b* when *a* and the measure of angle *B* are given.
5. the measure of angle *A* when *a* and *b* are given.
6. the measure of angle *B* when *a* and *c* are given.
7. *a* when *b* and the measure of angle *A* are given.

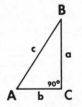

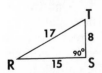

Exercises 8–13 refer to $\triangle RST$. In each exercise, give the value of the ratio as a fraction.

  8. $\sin R$ **9.** $\tan T$ **10.** $\sin T$
11. $\cos R$ **12.** $\cos T$ **13.** $\tan R$

    In 14–25, find the length of the line segment marked *x* to the *nearest foot* or the measure of the angle marked *x* to the *nearest degree*.

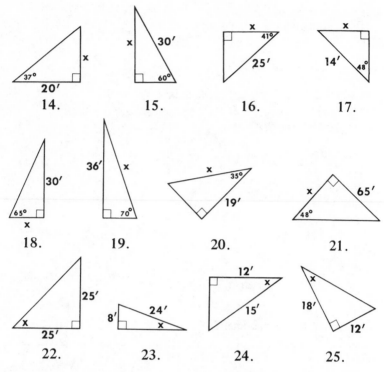

14.   15.   16.   17.

18.   19.   20.   21.

22.   23.   24.   25.

26. A monument stands on level ground. The angle of elevation of the top of the monument, taken at a point 175 meters from the foot of the monument, measures 32°. Find the height of the monument to the *nearest meter.*

27. A boy flying a kite lets out 150 feet of string that makes an angle measuring 64° with the ground. Assuming that the string is straight, find to the *nearest foot* how high the kite is above the ground.

28. A 25-foot guy wire attached to the top of a pole makes an angle which measures 62° with the ground. Find to the *nearest foot* the distance between the point where the guy wire meets the ground and the foot of the pole.

29. A woman walked 200 meters into a tunnel which slopes downward at an angle measuring 7° with the horizontal ground. Find to the *nearest ten meters* how far the woman was beneath the surface.

30. An airplane, *A*, is 1000 feet above the ground and directly over a church, *C*. The angle of elevation of the plane as seen by a woman at a point, *B*, on the ground some distance from the church measures 22°. Find to the *nearest foot:*

    a. how far the woman is from the church.
    b. how far the woman is from the plane.

31. An observer in a balloon 2000 feet above an airport finds that the angle of depression of a steamer out at sea measures 21°. Find to the *nearest hundred feet* the distance between the balloon and the steamer.

32. A plane takes off from a field and climbs at an angle measuring 12°. Find to the *nearest 100 feet* how far the plane must fly to be at an altitude of 1200 feet.

33. Find to the *nearest degree* the measure of the angle of elevation of the sun when a tree 8 meters high casts a shadow of 12 meters.

34. A 40-foot ladder is leaning against a building. The foot of the ladder is 32 feet from the building. Find to the *nearest degree* the measure of the angle which the ladder makes with the ground.

35. A railroad track slopes upward at an angle measuring 7° to the horizontal. Find to the *nearest ten feet* the vertical distance it rises in a horizontal distance of 1 mile (5280 feet).

36. A television tower is 50 meters high and an observer is 40 meters from the base of the tower. Find to the *nearest degree* the measure of the angle of elevation of the top of the tower from the point where the observer is standing.

37. The figure at the right represents a view of the roof of a wing of a house. $\overline{DB}$, the altitude of triangle ACD, measures 8 feet. Each of the rafters $\overline{AD}$ and $\overline{DC}$ measures 15 feet. Find to the *nearest degree* the measure of the angle that each rafter makes with $\overline{AC}$, the base of the triangle.

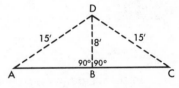

38. In isosceles triangle ABC, $\overline{AC}$ and $\overline{CB}$ each measure 15 inches. $m\angle A$ and $m\angle B$ are each 55°. $AD = DB$.

a. Find CD to the *nearest tenth of an inch*.

b. Find AD to the *nearest tenth of an inch*.

c. Find the area of triangle ABC to the *nearest square inch*.

39. In rectangle $ABCD$, diagonal $\overline{AC}$, which measures 20 inches in length, makes an angle measuring 35° with the base $\overline{AB}$.

a. Find AB to the *nearest tenth of an inch*.

b. Find BC to the *nearest tenth of an inch*.

c. Find the area of the rectangle to the *nearest square inch*.

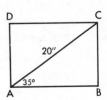

40. In a rectangle $ABCD$, $AB = 40$ centimeters and $BC = 30$ centimeters.

    a. Find to the *nearest degree* the measure of the angle which diagonal $\overline{AC}$ makes with side $\overline{AB}$.

    b. Find to the *nearest degree* the measure of the angle which diagonal $\overline{AC}$ makes with side $\overline{AD}$.

    c. What is a good way of checking the answers found in part **a** and part **b**?

41. $\overline{BC}$ is the base of triangle ABC, $BC = 1$ meter, $AB = 40$ centimeters, and $m\angle B = 62°$.

    a. Find the length of the altitude to base $\overline{BC}$ to the *nearest tenth of a centimeter*.

    b. Find the area of triangle ABC to the *nearest square centimeter*.

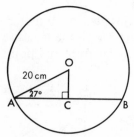

42. In the figure, $\overline{AB}$ is a chord in circle O. $\overline{OC}$ is perpendicular to $\overline{AB}$ at its midpoint C $(m\angle OCA = 90°, AC = CB)$. If radius OA measures 20 centimeters and $m\angle OAC = 27°$, find:

    a. OC to the *nearest centimeter*.

    b. AB to the *nearest centimeter*.

43. In the diagram, P represents a point 310 feet from the foot of a vertical cliff $\overline{BC}$. $\overline{AB}$ is a flagpole standing on the edge of the cliff. At P the angle of elevation of B measures $21°$; the angle of elevation of A measures $25°$. Find to the *nearest foot:*

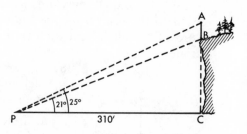

    a. the distance AC.

    b. the length of the flagpole $\overline{AB}$.

44. From the top of a lighthouse 30 meters above sea level, the angles of depression of two boats in line with the foot of the lighthouse are observed to measure $18°$ and $32°$ respectively. Find to the *nearest meter* the distance between the boats.

Chapter 19

Relations and Functions

1. Understanding the Meaning of a Relation

Consider the set of all squares, the lengths of whose sides are a whole number of inches less than 4. When we measure the length of a side, S, and the perimeter, P, we find for the squares in this set:

When $S = 1$ in., $P = 4$ in.
When $S = 2$ in., $P = 8$ in.
When $S = 3$ in., $P = 12$ in.

These results can be represented by the set of ordered number pairs $R = \{(1, 4), (2, 8), (3,12)\}$ in which the first element of each pair represents the number of inches in the length of a side of the square and the second element represents the number of inches in the perimeter of the square.

A set of ordered pairs is called a ***relation***.

In the figure, we see the graph of the relation $R = \{(1, 4), (2, 8), (3, 12)\}$, which consists of three points. These points are also the graph of the formula $P = 4S$ when S is a natural number less than 4.

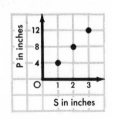

Thus, a relation may be described in one or more ways: (1) by a set of ordered pairs; (2) by a rule stated as a word sentence; (3) by a rule stated as a formula; (4) by a graph.

In a relation, the set of first members of the ordered pairs is called the ***domain of the relation***. The set of second elements of the ordered pairs in the relation is called the ***range*** or ***image of the relation***. For example, in the relation $\{(1, 4), (2, 8), (3, 12)\}$, the set of first elements $\{1, 2, 3\}$ is the *domain* of the relation; the set of second elements $\{4, 8, 12\}$ is the *range* of the relation.

Now consider the set of all squares, the lengths of whose sides are a positive number of inches. There are an infinite number of ordered pairs in the corresponding relation, some of which are $(4, 16), (10\frac{1}{2}, 42)$,

$(11.3, 45.2)$, $(\sqrt{2}, 4\sqrt{2})$, and so on. This relation is an infinite set of ordered pairs; it cannot be described by listing its elements. However, the relation can be described by the rule $P = 4S$, because this rule tells us how to assign a second number, P, to any first number, S, in every ordered pair of the relation. The domain, or the domain of definition, of this relation is the set of positive numbers, and the range is also the set of positive numbers. The graph of this relation is a half-line (a ray with its endpoint excluded), as shown in the following figure.

We can also use the set-builder notation to describe the relation we are discussing. We can write $\{(S, P) | P = 4S\}$, which is read "The set of all ordered pairs (S, P) such that P equals $4S$." (S and P are members of the set of positive numbers.)

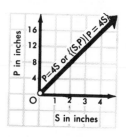

Let us consider the open sentence $y > x + 1$, with the replacement set for both x and y being $\{0, 1, 2, 3, 4\}$. The only ordered number pairs that satisfy $y > x + 1$ are $(0, 2)$, $(0, 3)$, $(0, 4)$, $(1, 3)$, $(1, 4)$, $(2, 4)$. These ordered number pairs are members of a relation. Since each ordered number pair of this relation must satisfy the rule $y > x + 1$, the relation is really the solution set for this rule. Notice that in a relation a member of the domain may be paired with more than one member of the range.

Suppose the sentence $y > x + 1$ has as the replacement set for both x and y the set of real numbers. There are now an infinite number of ordered number pairs in the solution set. This solution set, or relation, which is defined by the rule $y > x + 1$, can be represented in set notation as $\{(x, y) | y > x + 1\}$. (x and y are members of the set of real numbers.)

Model Problems

1. For the relation $\{(0, 0), (1, 1), (2, 4), (3, 9)\}$:
   a. Give the domain of the relation.
   b. Give the range of the relation.

   Solution:

   a. Since the domain of this relation is the set whose members are the first elements of the given ordered pairs, the domain of this relation is $\{0, 1, 2, 3\}$. *Ans.*
   b. Since the range of this relation is the set whose members are the second elements of the given ordered pairs, the range of this relation is $\{0, 1, 4, 9\}$. *Ans.*

2. If the replacement set for both x and y is $\{1, 2, 3, 4, 5\}$:

    a. List the set of all the ordered pairs in the relation described by the rule $y = 2x + 1$.

    b. State the domain of the relation.

    c. State the range of the relation.

    d. Graph the relation in the Cartesian plane.

Solution:

    a. The rule is $y = 2x + 1$.

        If $x = 1$, then $y = 2 \times 1 + 1$, or 3, which is a member of $\{1, 2, 3, 4, 5\}$.

        If $x = 2$, then $y = 2 \times 2 + 1$, or 5, which is a member of $\{1, 2, 3, 4, 5\}$.

        If $x = 3$, then $y = 2 \times 3 + 1$, or 7, which is not a member of $\{1, 2, 3, 4, 5\}$.

        If $x = 4$, then $y = 2 \times 4 + 1$, or 9, which is not a member of $\{1, 2, 3, 4, 5\}$.

        If $x = 5$, then $y = 2 \times 5 + 1$, or 11, which is not a member of $\{1, 2, 3, 4, 5\}$.

        Therefore, the relation is $\{(1, 3), (2, 5)\}$.   *Ans.*

    b. The domain is $\{1, 2\}$.   *Ans.*

    c. The range is $\{3, 5\}$.   *Ans.*

    d. The graph of the relation $\{(1, 3), (2, 5)\}$ is the set of two points whose coordinates are $(1, 3)$ and $(2, 5)$. Members of the domain are represented by points on the horizontal axis, the x-axis. Members of the range are represented by points on the vertical axis, the y-axis.

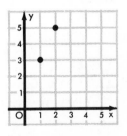

3. a. Write a rule for the relation $\{(1, 6),$ $(2, 12), (3, 18), (4, 24), (5, 30)\}$, which can also be arranged in tabular form as shown.

    b. Give the domain and range of the relation.

x	1	2	3	4	5
y	6	12	18	24	30

Solution:

    a. Let x represent a first element of each ordered pair; let y represent the second element. Note that the second number of each ordered pair, y, is 6 times the first number of the pair, x. For example, $6 = 6 \times 1$, $12 = 6 \times 2$, $18 = 6 \times 3$, and so on. Therefore, a rule for the relation is $y = 6x$.   *Ans.*

    b. The domain is $\{1, 2, 3, 4, 5\}$.   *Ans.*

    The range is $\{6, 12, 18, 24, 30\}$.   *Ans.*

EXERCISES

In 1-4: (a) Give the domain of the relation. (b) Give the range of the relation. (c) Graph the relation in the Cartesian plane.

1. $\{(1, 3), (2, 6), (3, 9), (4, 12)\}$
2. $\{(20, 15), (15, 10), (10, 5), (5, 0)\}$
3. $\{(2, -4), (3, -6), (4, -8), (5, -10)\}$
4. $\{(0, 3), (0, 0), (-1, -3), (-2, -8)\}$

In 5-13, using the replacement set $\{0, 1, 2, 3, 4, 5, 6\}$ for both x and y, list all the ordered pairs in the relation that is defined by the given rule.

5. $y = 2x$ 6. $y = 2x - 9$ 7. $y = \frac{1}{4}x + 2$
8. $x + y = 10$ 9. $2x - y = 8$ 10. $y = 2x^2$
11. $y = x^2 + 2$ 12. $y > 4x$ 13. $y > x^2$

In 14-23, using the set of rational numbers as the replacement set for both x and y:

a. Write an equation which describes the relation.
b. Use set notation to describe the relation.
c. Give four ordered pairs that are members of the relation.

14. y is 5 times x.   15. y is 1 more than twice x.
16. The sum of x and y is 8.   17. x decreased by y is 5.
18. Twice x increased by y is 8.   19. Three times y decreased by x is 6.
20. y is twice the square of x.   21. y is less than one-half of x.
22. y is greater than $3x + 1$.   23. y is less than $2x - 5$.

In 24-29: (a) Give the domain of the relation. (b) Give the range of the relation. (c) Graph the relation in the Cartesian plane. (d) State a rule which defines the relation.

24. $\{(0, 0), (1, 1), (2, 2), (3, 3)\}$
25. $\{(5, 10), (6, 12), (7, 14), (8, 16)\}$
26. $\{(-8, -2), (-4, -1), (0, 0), (4, 1)\}$
27. $\{(1, 0), (2, 2), (3, 4), (4, 6)\}$

28.

x	-1	0	1	2
y	5	4	3	2

29.

x	-4	-3	-2	-1
y	16	9	4	1

In 30-38, using the replacement set $\{-3, -2, -1, 0, 1, 2, 3\}$ for both x and y:

a. List the set of all the ordered pairs in the relation described by the rule.
b. State the domain of the relation.

c. State the range of the relation.

d. Graph the relation in the Cartesian plane.

30. $y = x$ **31.** $y = 3x$ **32.** $y = \frac{1}{2}x$

33. $y = 3x - 2$ **34.** $x + y = 3$ **35.** $x - y = 2$

36. $y = -x$ **37.** $y = x^2$ **38.** $y = |x|$

In 39–46, using the set of real numbers as the replacement sets for both x and y, graph the relation in the Cartesian plane.

39. $\{(x, y) \mid y = x\}$ **40.** $\{(x, y) \mid y = \frac{1}{2}x\}$

41. $\{(x, y) \mid y = 3x - 2\}$ **42.** $\{(x, y) \mid x + y = 3\}$

43. $\{(x, y) \mid y = -x\}$ **44.** $\{(x, y) \mid y = x^2\}$

45. $\{(x, y) \mid y = |x|\}$ **46.** $\{(x, y) \mid y = |x + 1|\}$

2. Understanding the Cartesian Products of Two Sets

Consider the set $A = \{1, 2\}$ and the set $B = \{1, 2, 3\}$. Using the members of these two sets, let us form in the following way a third set consisting of ordered number pairs such that the first number of each ordered pair is an element of set A and the second number is an element of set B. The members of this set are:

$$(1, 1) \quad (2, 1)$$
$$(1, 2) \quad (2, 2)$$
$$(1, 3) \quad (2, 3)$$

This third set $\{(1, 1), (1, 2), (1, 3), (2, 1), (2, 2), (2, 3)\}$ is called the *Cartesian product of A and B*, written $A \times B$ and read "*A* cross *B*." Using the set-builder notation, we can define the Cartesian product of set A and set B as follows:

$$A \times B = \{(x, y) \mid x \in A \text{ and } y \in B\}$$

Since $A \times B$ is a set of ordered number pairs, it is an example of a relation. The graph of the relation $A \times B$ is the graph of the set of all number pairs (x, y), with x belonging to A and y belonging to B. The figure, a *lattice of points*, shows the graph of $A \times B$, where $A = \{1, 2\}$ and $B = \{1, 2, 3\}$. Notice that the x-values are 1 and 2, the members of set A; the y-values are 1, 2, and 3, the members of set B.

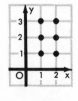

Consider the set of natural numbers less than 4, $U = \{1, 2, 3\}$. Let us form all ordered pairs of numbers which are members of U. They are:

$$(1, 1) \quad (2, 1) \quad (3, 1)$$
$$(1, 2) \quad (2, 2) \quad (3, 2)$$
$$(1, 3) \quad (2, 3) \quad (3, 3)$$

The set whose members are the ordered number pairs we have listed is called the *Cartesian set of U*, written $U \times U$ and read "U cross U." The graph of the relation $U \times U$, as is shown, is the graph of the set of all number pairs (x, y), with x belonging to U ($x \in U$) and y belonging to U ($y \in U$). Notice that the x-values are 1, 2, and 3, the members of set U; the y-values are 1, 2, and 3, the members of set U.

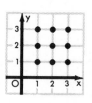

Suppose that the universal set U is the set of all real numbers from 1 to 3, including 1 and 3. Then the Cartesian set of U, the set $U \times U$, has an infinite number of ordered pairs, with the first and second member of each ordered pair belonging to the universal set U. The graph of the relation $U \times U$, as shown, is the graph of the set of all ordered number pairs (x, y) for which x and y are such that $1 \leq x \leq 3$ and $1 \leq y \leq 3$.

If the universal set U is the set of all real numbers, then the set $U \times U$ is the entire Cartesian plane.

Model Problem

If $A = \{-2, -1\}$ and $B = \{1, 2, 3\}$, (a) list the members of $A \times B$ and (b) graph the set $A \times B$.

Solution:

a. $\{(-2, 1), (-1, 1), (-2, 2), (-1, 2), (-2, 3), (-1, 3)\}$

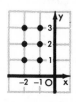

b. The graph of $A \times B$ is the graph of the set of the ordered pairs listed in answer to part a. Notice that the x-values are -2 and -1, the members of set A; the y-values are 1, 2, and 3, the members of set B.

EXERCISES

In 1–6: (a) List the members of the Cartesian product of the two given sets. (b) Graph the Cartesian product as a lattice of points.

1. $A = \{1, 2\}, B = \{2, 3, 4\}$
2. $A = \{1, 2, 3\}, B = \{1, 3\}$

3. $A = \{2, 4, 6\}, B = \{3, 5\}$
4. $A = \{2, 5\}, B = \{2, 3, 6\}$
5. $A = \{3, 5, 7\}, B = \{-3, -2\}$
6. $A = \{-1, 3\}, B = \{2, 3, 6, 8\}$

In 7-11: (a) List the members of the Cartesian set of the given set U. (b) Graph the Cartesian set of U.

7. $U = \{1\}$ 8. $U = \{1, 2\}$ 9. $U = \{1, 2, 3, 4\}$
10. $U = \{1, 2, 3, 4, 5\}$ 11. $U = \{1, 2, 3, 4, 5, 6\}$

In 12-18, graph the Cartesian set of U where U is the set of:

12. natural numbers greater than 2 and less than 5
13. integers greater than -2 and less than 4
14. integers greater than or equal to 2 and less than or equal to 6
15. integers greater than or equal to -1 and less than 3
16. real numbers greater than or equal to 1 and less than or equal to 6
17. real numbers greater than or equal to -2 and less than 2
18. real numbers greater than -3 and less than 3

19. If $A = \{1, 3\}$ and $B = \{2, 4\}$: (a) Find $A \times B$. (b) Find $B \times A$. (c) Is the set $A \times B$ the same as the set $B \times A$? Why?
20. If set A has n members and set B has m members, represent the number of members (a) in the set $A \times B$ and (b) in the set $B \times A$.
21. If the universal set U has r members, represent the number of members in the Cartesian set of U.

3. Understanding the Meaning of a Function

There is an important difference between the following two relations:

$$A = \{(-2, 2), (-1, 1), (0, 0), (1, 1), (2, 2)\}$$
$$B = \{ (0, 0), (1, 1), (1, -1), (2, 2), (2, -2)\}$$

In relation A, observe that every member of the domain $\{-2, -1, 0, 1, 2\}$ is paired with one and only one member of the range $\{0, 1, 2\}$. For example, the member of the domain, -2, is paired with a unique member of the range, 2.

In relation B, however, some members of the domain are paired with two members of the range. For example, the member, 1, of the domain is paired with two members, 1 and -1, of the range.

A relation such as set A is called a *function*.

A function is a relation (a set of ordered pairs) in which every member of the domain is paired with one and only one member of the range.

A relation such as set B is not a function. Thus, a function is a special kind of relation. Every function is a relation; however, not every relation is a function.

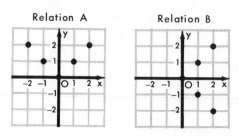

The graph of a relation can help us to determine whether or not that relation is a function.

The graphs of relation A and relation B are shown in the preceding figures. The first elements of the ordered pairs are associated with the horizontal axis, or x-axis; the second elements are associated with the vertical axis, or y-axis.

In the graph of relation A, notice that no vertical line passes through more than one point which is the graph of an ordered pair of the relation. That is, to every x-value, there corresponds one and only one y-value. Therefore, relation A is a function.

On the other hand, in the graph of relation B, notice that on the vertical line $x = 1$ there are two points which are graphs of ordered pairs of the relation. That is, to the x-value 1, there correspond two y-values, 1 and -1. Similarly, for the x-value 2, there correspond two y-values, 2 and -2. Therefore, relation B is not a function.

In our study of the graphs of relation A and relation B, we used the **vertical line test** for a function. If no vertical line intersects the graph of a relation in more than one point, the relation is a function. If any vertical line does intersect the graph of a relation in more than one point, the relation is not a function.

Model Problems

1. Determine whether the given relation is a function:
   a. $\{(-1, 4), (2, 4), (3, 4), (4, 4)\}$
   b. $\{(2, -1), (2, 0), (2, 1), (2, 2)\}$

Solution:

a. The first number of every ordered pair in the relation is associated with a unique second number. Therefore, the relation is a function.

b. In the ordered pair $(2, -1)$, the first number, 2, is associated with the second number, -1. In the ordered pair $(2, 0)$, the first number, 2, is associated with the second number, 0. In these two ordered pairs, the first number, 2, is associated with different second numbers. Therefore, the relation is not a function.

2. a. Graph the relation defined by the rule $y = 2x - 3$, or by $\{(x, y) | y = 2x - 3\}$ if $1 \leq x \leq 4$ and y is a real number.
b. State whether the relation is a function.
c. State the domain of the relation.
d. State the range of the relation.

Solution:

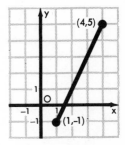

a. Graph the relation as shown. The endpoints $(1, -1)$ and $(4, 5)$ are part of the graph.

b. By the vertical line test, we see that the relation is a function.

c. The domain of the function is the set of x-values such that $1 \leq x \leq 4$, or $\{x | 1 \leq x \leq 4\}$.

d. The range of the function is the set of y-values such that $-1 \leq y \leq 5$, or $\{y | -1 \leq y \leq 5\}$.

3. For the relation whose graph is shown:
a. State the domain of the relation.
b. State the range of the relation.
c. State whether the relation is a function.

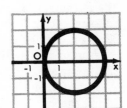

Solution:

a. The domain of the relation is the set of x-values such that $0 \leq x \leq 4$, or $\{x | 0 \leq x \leq 4\}$.

b. The range of the relation is the set of y-values such that $-2 \leq y \leq 2$, or $\{y | -2 \leq y \leq 2\}$.

c. By the vertical line test, we see that every x-value, other than $x = 0$ and $x = 4$, is paired with two different y-values. Therefore, the relation is not a function.

EXERCISES

In 1–8, state whether the relation is a function. Give the reason for your answer.

1. $\{(1, 3), (2, 6), (3, 9), (4, 12)\}$
2. $\{(4, 9), (5, 11), (6, 13), (7, 15)\}$
3. $\{(\frac{1}{4}, \frac{1}{2}), (\frac{1}{4}, -\frac{1}{2}), (49, 7), (49, -7)\}$
4. $\{(2, 5), (3, 10), (4, 17), (5, 26)\}$
5. $\{(-1, 3), (-2, 4), (-1, 2), (-2, 5)\}$
6. $\{(2, 1), (1, 2), (3, 4), (4, 3)\}$
7. $\{(2, 5), (3, 5), (4, 5), (5, 5)\}$
8. $\{(5, 2), (5, 3), (5, 4), (5, 5)\}$

In 9–20, x and y are members of the set of real numbers. (a) Graph the relation described by the rule. (b) From the graph, determine whether the relation is a function.

9. $y = 2x$, or $\{(x, y)| y = 2x\}$ 10. $y = x + 2$, or $\{(x, y)| y = x + 2\}$
11. $y > 2x$, or $\{(x, y)| y > 2x\}$ 12. $y < 2x$, or $\{(x, y)| y < 2x\}$
13. $x = -y$, or $\{(x, y)| x = -y\}$ 14. $y > -x$, or $\{(x, y)| y > -x\}$
15. $x = 3$, or $\{(x, y)| x = 3\}$ 16. $y = 3$, or $\{(x, y)| y = 3\}$
17. $y = 2x^2$, or $\{(x, y)| y = 2x^2\}$
18. $x = 2y^2$, or $\{(x, y)| x = 2y^2\}$
19. $y = |x|$, or $\{(x, y)| y = |x|\}$
20. $x = |y|$, or $\{(x, y)| x = |y|\}$

In 21–24, use a graph to determine the answer to the question. The variables are members of the set of real numbers.

21. Is the set of ordered pairs (s, p), each of whose members makes the sentence $p = 3s$ a true sentence, a function?
22. Is the set of ordered pairs (t, d), each of whose members makes the sentence $d = 40t$ a true sentence, a function?
23. Is the set of ordered pairs (x, y), each of whose members makes the sentence $y = -4$ a true sentence, a function?
24. Is the set of ordered pairs (x, y), each of whose members makes the sentence $x = -4$ a true sentence, a function?

In 25–32, x and y are members of the set of real numbers. In each exercise:

a. Graph the relation described by the rule.
b. State whether the relation is a function.
c. State the domain of the relation.
d. State the range of the relation.

25. $y = x$, or $\{(x, y)| y = x\}$ when $-3 \leq x \leq 3$.
26. $y = \frac{1}{2}x$, or $\{(x, y)| y = \frac{1}{2}x\}$ when $-2 < x \leq 4$.

27. $y = 3x + 1$, or $\{(x,y) \mid y = 3x + 1\}$ when $-1 < x \le 2$.
28. $y = 3$, or $\{(x,y) \mid y = 3\}$ when the replacement set for x is $\{x \mid x \ge 0\}$.
29. $\{(x,y) \mid x = 2\}$ when the replacement set for x is $\{x \mid x = 2\}$.
30. $y = |x|$, or $\{(x,y) \mid y = |x|\}$ when the replacement set for x is $\{x \mid -4 \le x \le 4\}$.
31. $x = |y|$, or $\{(x,y) \mid x = |y|\}$ when the replacement set for x is $\{x \mid -3 \le x \le 3\}$.
32. $x = y^2$, or $\{(x,y) \mid x = y^2\}$ when the replacement set for x is $\{x \mid 0 \le x \le 9\}$.

In 33–47, each figure is the graph of a relation. The first and second elements of each ordered pair of the relation are members of the set of real numbers. In each exercise:

a. State the domain of the relation.
b. State the range of the relation.
c. Tell whether the relation is a function.

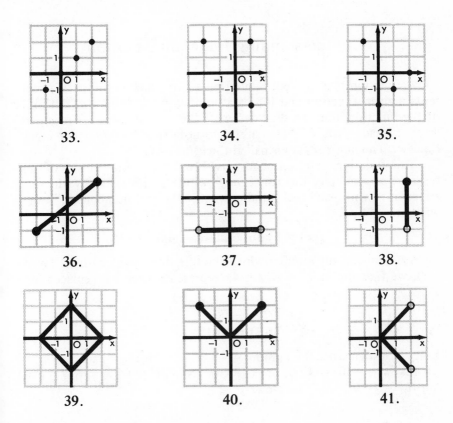

33.   34.   35.

36.   37.   38.

39.   40.   41.

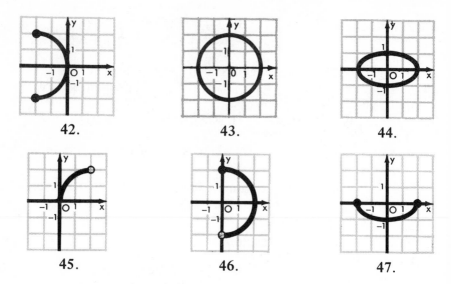

42.   43.   44.

45.   46.   47.

4. Understanding Function Notation

A function may be represented by a letter such as f or g. If f represents a given function and if x is a number in the domain of definition of the function, then we shall designate the number which f assigns to x as $f(x)$, read "f of x." Be careful to note that $f(x)$ *does not* mean f times x. The number $f(x)$ is called the *value of f at x*.

This function notation can be used to describe the pairings of numbers. For example, the function f, which is described by the word statement "with each real number x, pair the real number $4x$," can be written:

$$f(x) = 4x \text{ for each real number } x$$

Then $f(1)$ means the number which the function f pairs with 1. To find $f(1)$, we find the number which $4x$ represents when x is replaced by 1. Thus:

$$f(x) = 4x$$
$$f(1) = 4 \cdot 1 = 4$$

That is, f assigns to 1 the number 4.

Likewise, $f(0) = 4 \cdot 0$, or $f(0) = 0$. And $f(\frac{1}{4}) = 4 \times \frac{1}{4}$, or $f(\frac{1}{4}) = 1$, and $f(-\sqrt{3}) = 4(-\sqrt{3}) = -4\sqrt{3}$.

Model Problems

1. If g is the function defined by $g(x) = 5x + 3$ for each real number x, find:

   a. $g(-1)$ b. $g(|-1|)$ c. $g(2b)$ d. $g(r + 5)$

   Solution: It is given that $g(x) = 5x + 3$ for each real number x.

   a. $g(-1) = 5 \times (-1) + 3 = -5 + 3 = -2$

   $$g(-1) = -2 \quad Ans.$$

   b. Since $|-1| = 1$, $g(|-1|) = 5(1) + 3 = 5 + 3 = 8$

   $$g(|-1|) = 8 \quad Ans.$$

   c. $g(2b) = 5(2b) + 3 = 10b + 3$

   $$g(2b) = 10b + 3 \quad Ans.$$

   d. $g(r + 5) = 5(r + 5) + 3 = 5r + 25 + 3 = 5r + 28$

   $$g(r + 5) = 5r + 28 \quad Ans.$$

2. If h is the function defined by $h(x) = x^2 - 2$ for each real number x, find:

   a. $h(2)$ b. $h(-\frac{1}{2})$ c. $h(0)$ d. $h(b - 1)$

   Solution: It is given that $h(x) = x^2 - 2$.

   a. $h(2) = (2)^2 - 2 = 4 - 2 = 2$

   $$h(2) = 2 \quad Ans.$$

   b. $h(-\frac{1}{2}) = (-\frac{1}{2})^2 - 2 = \frac{1}{4} - 2 = -1\frac{3}{4}$

   $$h(-\tfrac{1}{2}) = -1\tfrac{3}{4} \quad Ans.$$

   c. $h(0) = (0)^2 - 2 = 0 - 2 = -2$

   $$h(0) = -2 \quad Ans.$$

   d. $h(b - 1) = (b - 1)^2 - 2 = b^2 - 2b + 1 - 2 = b^2 - 2b - 1$

   $$h(b - 1) = b^2 - 2b - 1 \quad Ans.$$

3. If f is the function defined by $f(x) = 2x + 3$ for each real number x, find the solution set of $f(x) = 9$.

   Solution: To find the solution set of $f(x) = 9$, we must find the number(s) which can replace x in the open phrase $2x + 3$ and give the result 9. That is, we must find the solution set of the open sentence $2x + 3 = 9$.

   Check

   $$2x + 3 = 9 \qquad f(x) = 2x + 3$$
   $$2x = 6 \qquad f(3) = 2(3) + 3$$
   $$x = 3 \qquad f(3) = 9 \quad (true)$$

   Answer: The solution set is $\{3\}$.

EXERCISES

In 1–12, the variable is a member of the set of real numbers. For the function defined, compute the value at $-2, -1, 0, 1, 2, |-3|, \frac{1}{3}, \frac{3}{2}, \sqrt{3}$.

1. $f(x) = 5x$ 2. $f(y) = 3y - 1$
3. $f(z) = -z + 2$ 4. $g(x) = x^2$
5. $h(x) = x^2 - 2x$ 6. $F(m) = 2m^2 - 4m + 3$
7. $s(x) = -4x^2$ 8. $f(r) = -r^2 + 8$
9. $t(a) = a^3 + 2a^2 - 5$ 10. $f(x) = |x|$
11. $g(y) = y^2 - |y|$ 12. $h(x) = x^2 + x - |x|$

13. For the function f defined by $f(x) = x^2 - 2x + 4$ for each real number x, find:

a. $f(5)$ b. $f(1)$ c. $f(\frac{3}{5})$ d. $f(0)$
e. $f(-2)$ f. $f(|-4|)$ g. $f(\sqrt{2})$ h. $2[f(3)]$
i. $f(b)$ j. $f(3a)$ k. $f(b + 3)$ l. $f(2b - 1)$

14. For the function F defined by $F(x) = x^2 - 2x$ for each real number x, find the real number represented by:

a. $F(2)$ b. $F(\frac{2}{3})$ c. $F(-3)$ d. $F(-\frac{1}{2})$
e. $-[F(-1)]$ f. $F(-2) + 3$ g. $-[F(|-2|)]$ h. $2[F(1)]$

15. If f is the function defined by $f(x) = 3x - 1$ for each real number x, find the solution set of each of the following sentences:

a. $f(x) = 2$ b. $f(x) = -4$ c. $f(x) = 8$
d. $f(x) = -10$ e. $f(x) = 0$ f. $f(x) = \frac{1}{2}$
g. $f(x) = -7$ h. $f(x) = |-20|$ i. $f(x) = 2x$
j. $f(x) > 2$ k. $f(x) > -4$ l. $f(x) \geq 0$

16. If f is the function defined by $f(x) = x^2 + 2x$ for each real number x, find the solution set of each of the following sentences:

a. $f(x) = 3$ b. $f(x) = 8$ c. $f(x) = 15$ d. $f(x) = 0$ e. $f(x) = 1$

In 17–22, determine the number(s) x for which the function is undefined.

17. $f(x) = \dfrac{1}{x}$ 18. $f(x) = \dfrac{1}{x - 1}$ 19. $f(x) = \dfrac{2}{x^2 - 1}$

20. $f(x) = \dfrac{3}{2x^2 - 3x - 2}$ 21. $f(x) = \dfrac{1}{|x + 2|}$

22. $f(x) = \dfrac{2}{|x| \cdot |x + 1|}$

5. Graphs of Linear Functions

We have learned that a function may be represented by means of a graph. The graph of the function defined by "$f(x) = x + 1$ for each real number x" is the graph of the solution set of the equation $y = x + 1$ where y equals $f(x)$. Since $y = x + 1$ is of the form $y = Ax + B$, it is a linear equation whose graph is a straight line as shown in Figure 1. Observe that the graph is endless, since the function is defined for the entire set of real numbers.

Figure 1   Figure 2   Figure 3

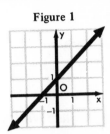 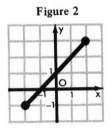 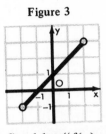

In Figure 2, we see the graph of the function defined by "$f(x) = x + 1$ for all x such that $-2 \leq x \leq 2$." Observe that this graph, which is the graph of $y = x + 1$ where $-2 \leq x \leq 2$, differs from the graph in Figure 1 in that it is not endless. The graph is a line segment whose endpoints are the points $(-2, -1)$ and $(2, 3)$.

In Figure 3, we see the graph of the function defined by "$f(x) = x + 1$ for all x such that $-2 < x < 2$." Observe that this graph, which is the graph of $y = x + 1$ where $-2 < x < 2$, differs from the graph in Figure 2 in that the points $(-2, -1)$ and $(2, 3)$ are not included in the graph.

The three functions which we have just discussed are three different functions because their domains of definition are different. However, all these functions are linear.

A function whose graph is a straight line or part of a straight line is called a *linear function*.

We must be careful not to make the mistake of thinking that every straight line in a Cartesian plane can be considered as the graph of some linear function. The equation of the line whose graph is shown at the right is $x = 3$, and we have learned that such a line does not represent a function. However, it is true that the graphs of all straight lines except those which are described by an equation of the form $x = c$ (for each real number c) are graphs of linear functions.

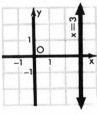

A linear function f can be defined by $f(x) = Ax + B$, where A and B are real numbers.

EXERCISES

1. $f(x) = Ax + B$ for each real number x. Draw the graph of $f(x)$
   when:

   a. $A = 2, B = 1$ b. $A = 1, B = -2$ c. $A = \frac{1}{2}, B = 0$

   d. $A = -3, B = 2$ e. $A = -1, B = -1$ f. $A = \frac{-3}{4}, B = 0$

   g. $A = 4, B = 0$ h. $A = 0, B = -3$ i. $A = 0, B = 0$

2. A line L passes through $(-3, -3)$ and $(2, 7)$.

   a. Draw the graph of line L.
   b. Describe the domain of the function whose graph consists of
      the points (x, y) of L such that:

   (1) $-3 \leq y \leq 7$ (2) $-3 \leq y \leq 3$ (3) $3 < y < 7$
   (4) $-3 < y < 7$

   In 3-10, x is a member of the set of real numbers. State whether
   the expression describes a linear function.

3. $x - 4$ 4. $-(x - 4)$ 5. $|x - 4|$ 6. $-|x - 4|$

7. $\dfrac{x - 4}{1}$ 8. $\dfrac{1}{x - 4}$ 9. $|x| - 4$ 10. $x^2 - 4$

11. If f is a function defined by $f(x) = x + 2$ for each real number x
    and if g is a function defined by $g(x) = 2x - 5$ for each real num-
    ber x:

    a. Represent $f(x) + g(x)$.
    b. Find: (1) $f(-2) + g(-2)$ (2) $f(0) + g(0)$ (3) $f(2) + g(2)$
    c. Draw the graph of $f(x) + g(x)$ for each real number x.
    d. Draw the graph of $f(x) + g(x)$ for each x such that $-2 \leq x \leq 2$.
    e. Find the solution set of each sentence:

    (1) $f(x) + g(x) = 0$ (2) $f(x) + g(x) = 12$
    (3) $f(x) + g(x) = -9$

6. Graphs of Quadratic Functions

A *quadratic function* f can be defined by $f(x) = Ax^2 + Bx + C$
where A, B, C are real numbers and $A \neq 0$.

If $A = 0$, the function is not a quadratic function. In this unit, we
shall assume that $A \neq 0$.

Each of the following formulas defines a quadratic function:

$$f(x) = 3x^2 \qquad g(y) = y^2 - 2y \qquad h(t) = t^2 + 2t - 15$$

If f is the function defined by $f(x) = 3x^2$ for each real number x, then let us calculate a few values of $f(x)$:

$$f(-2) = 3(-2)^2 = 12$$
$$f(-1) = 3(-1)^2 = 3$$
$$f(0) = 3(0)^2 = 0$$
$$f(1) = 3(1)^2 = 3$$
$$f(2) = 3(2)^2 = 12$$

Now let us graph the quadratic function defined by $f(x) = 3x^2$ for each integral value of x such that $-2 \leq x \leq 2$. We do this by graphing the solution set of the equation $y = 3x^2$. When we replace x by each of the elements of the domain, $-2, -1, 0, 1, 2$ (as we did previously), we find that the solution set consists of the ordered pairs $(-2, 12)$, $(-1, 3)$, $(0, 0)$, $(1, 3)$, $(2, 12)$. The set of points which represents the graphs of these ordered pairs is the graph of the given function, as shown in Figure 1.

Figure 1	Figure 2	Figure 3

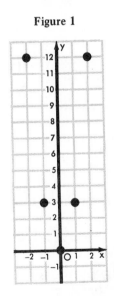 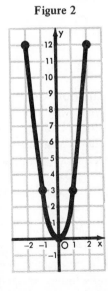 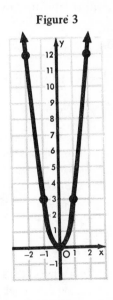

The graph of the quadratic function defined by $f(x) = 3x^2$ for each real number x such that $-2 \leq x \leq 2$ is the graph of an infinite set of ordered pairs (x, y) such that $y = 3x^2$ and $-2 \leq x \leq 2$. These points lie on a curved line, as shown in the graph in Figure 2. Notice that the endpoints $(-2, 12)$ and $(2, 12)$ are included in the graph.

The graph of the quadratic function defined by $f(x) = 3x^2$ for each real number x is the graph of an infinite set of ordered pairs (x, y) such that $y = 3x^2$ for each real number x. The graph is shown in Figure 3. Notice that the graph is an endless curve, not a straight line. As we have seen previously, this type of curve is called a *parabola*.

EXERCISES

1. For the quadratic function g defined by $g(t) = 2t^2 + 3t - 4$ for each real number t, find:

    a. $g(-2)$ **b.** $g(0)$ **c.** $g(3)$ **d.** $g(1.5)$ **e.** $g(\frac{3}{4})$
    f. $g(2)$ **g.** $g(r)$ **h.** $g(4s)$ **i.** $g(a + 1)$ **j.** $g(2a - 1)$
    k. $g(a^2)$ **l.** $g(2a)$ **m.** $2[g(a)]$ **n.** $g(a) + 2$ **o.** $g(a + 2)$

In 2–5, the domain of the function is the set of integers such that $-3 \le x \le 3$. Graph the function f which is defined by:

  2. $f(x) = 2x^2$ **3.** $f(x) = x^2 - 2$
  4. $f(x) = x^2 - 2x$ **5.** $f(x) = x^2 - 2x + 1$

In 6–17, x and y are members of the set of real numbers. Graph the function defined by the equation.

  6. $y = x^2$ **7.** $y = 2x^2$ **8.** $y = 3x^2$ **9.** $y = 4x^2$
10. $y = -x^2$ **11.** $y = -2x^2$ **12.** $y = -3x^2$ **13.** $y = -4x^2$

14. $y = \frac{1}{2}x^2$ **15.** $y = \frac{1}{4}x^2$ **16.** $y = \frac{-1}{2}x^2$ **17.** $y = \frac{-1}{4}x^2$

18. In exercises 6–17, the functions are described by equations of the form $y = Ax^2$. **(a)** In what way do the graphs of the functions in which A is a positive number differ from the graphs of the functions in which A is a negative number? **(b)** As $|A|$ increases and becomes very large, what change takes place in the graph of the function?

In 19–23, x and y are members of the set of real numbers. Graph the function defined by the equation:

19. $y = x^2 + 2$ **20.** $y = x^2 + 1$ **21.** $y = x^2$
22. $y = x^2 - 1$ **23.** $y = x^2 - 2$

24. In exercises 19–23, the functions are described by equations of the form $y = x^2 + C$. What change takes place in the graph of the function when C changes from a positive number to zero to a negative number?

In 25–27, the domain of the function is the set of real numbers. Graph the function f defined by:

25. $f(x) = x^2 - 2x - 3$ **26.** $f(x) = x^2 + 2x - 8$
27. $f(x) = -x^2 - 2x + 3$

28. f is the quadratic function defined by $f(x) = 2x^2 - 4x - 6$ for each
real number x. g is the quadratic function defined by $g(x) = -x^2 + 2x + 3$ for each real number x.

a. Find the solution set of the sentence $f(x) = 0$.
b. Draw the graph of $f(x)$.
c. Find the solution set of the sentence $g(x) = 0$.
d. Draw the graph of $g(x)$.
e. Find $f(x) + g(x)$.
f. Find $f(3) + g(3)$.
g. Find the solution set of the sentence $f(x) + g(x) = 0$.
h. Draw the graph of $f(x) + g(x)$.

Squares and Square Roots

No.	Square	Square Root	No.	Square	Square Root	No.	Square	Square Root
1	1	1.000	51	2,601	7.141	101	10,201	10.050
2	4	1.414	52	2,704	7.211	102	10,404	10.100
3	9	1.732	53	2,809	7.280	103	10,609	10.149
4	16	2.000	54	2,916	7.348	104	10,816	10.198
5	25	2.236	55	3,025	7.416	105	11,025	10.247
6	36	2.449	56	3,136	7.483	106	11,236	10.296
7	49	2.646	57	3,249	7.550	107	11,449	10.344
8	64	2.828	58	3,364	7.616	108	11,664	10.392
9	81	3.000	59	3,481	7.681	109	11,881	10.440
10	100	3.162	60	3,600	7.746	110	12,100	10.488
11	121	3.317	61	3,721	7.810	111	12,321	10.536
12	144	3.464	62	3,844	7.874	112	12,544	10.583
13	169	3.606	63	3,969	7.937	113	12,769	10.630
14	196	3.742	64	4,096	8.000	114	12,996	10.677
15	225	3.873	65	4,225	8.062	115	13,225	10.724
16	256	4.000	66	4,356	8.124	116	13,456	10.770
17	289	4.123	67	4,489	8.185	117	13,689	10.817
18	324	4.243	68	4,624	8.246	118	13,924	10.863
19	361	4.359	69	4,761	8.307	119	14,161	10.909
20	400	4.472	70	4,900	8.367	120	14,400	10.954
21	441	4.583	71	5,041	8.426	121	14,641	11.000
22	484	4.690	72	5,184	8.485	122	14,884	11.045
23	529	4.796	73	5,329	8.544	123	15,129	11.091
24	576	4.899	74	5,476	8.602	124	15,376	11.136
25	625	5.000	75	5,625	8.660	125	15,625	11.180
26	676	5.099	76	5,776	8.718	126	15,876	11.225
27	729	5.196	77	5,929	8.775	127	16,129	11.269
28	784	5.292	78	6,084	8.832	128	16,384	11.314
29	841	5.385	79	6,241	8.888	129	16,641	11.358
30	900	5.477	80	6,400	8.944	130	16,900	11.402
31	961	5.568	81	6,561	9.000	131	17,161	11.446
32	1,024	5.657	82	6,724	9.055	132	17,424	11.489
33	1,089	5.745	83	6,889	9.110	133	17,689	11.533
34	1,156	5.831	84	7,056	9.165	134	17,956	11.576
35	1,225	5.916	85	7,225	9.220	135	18,225	11.619
36	1,296	6.000	86	7,396	9.274	136	18,496	11.662
37	1,369	6.083	87	7,569	9.327	137	18,769	11.705
38	1,444	6.164	88	7,744	9.381	138	19,044	11.747
39	1,521	6.245	89	7,921	9.434	139	19,321	11.790
40	1,600	6.325	90	8,100	9.487	140	19,600	11.832
41	1,681	6.403	91	8,281	9.539	141	19,881	11.874
42	1,764	6.481	92	8,464	9.592	142	20,164	11.916
43	1,849	6.557	93	8,649	9.644	143	20,449	11.958
44	1,936	6.633	94	8,836	9.695	144	20,736	12.000
45	2,025	6.708	95	9,025	9.747	145	21,025	12.042
46	2,116	6.782	96	9,216	9.798	146	21,316	12.083
47	2,209	6.856	97	9,409	9.849	147	21,609	12.124
48	2,304	6.928	98	9,604	9.899	148	21,904	12.166
49	2,401	7.000	99	9,801	9.950	149	22,201	12.207
50	2,500	7.071	100	10,000	10.000	150	22,500	12.247

Values of the Trigonometric Functions

Angle	Sine	Cosine	Tangent	Angle	Sine	Cosine	Tangent
1°	.0175	.9998	.0175	46°	.7193	.6947	1.0355
2°	.0349	.9994	.0349	47°	.7314	.6820	1.0724
3°	.0523	.9986	.0524	48°	.7431	.6691	1.1106
4°	.0698	.9976	.0699	49°	.7547	.6561	1.1504
5°	.0872	.9962	.0875	50°	.7660	.6428	1.1918
6°	.1045	.9945	.1051	51°	.7771	.6293	1.2349
7°	.1219	.9925	.1228	52°	.7880	.6157	1.2799
8°	.1392	.9903	.1405	53°	.7986	.6018	1.3270
9°	.1564	.9877	.1584	54°	.8090	.5878	1.3764
10°	.1736	.9848	.1763	55°	.8192	.5736	1.4281
11°	.1908	.9816	.1944	56°	.8290	.5592	1.4826
12°	.2079	.9781	.2126	57°	.8387	.5446	1.5399
13°	.2250	.9744	.2309	58°	.8480	.5299	1.6003
14°	.2419	.9703	.2493	59°	.8572	.5150	1.6643
15°	.2588	.9659	.2679	60°	.8660	.5000	1.7321
16°	.2756	.9613	.2867	61°	.8746	.4848	1.8040
17°	.2924	.9563	.3057	62°	.8829	.4695	1.8807
18°	.3090	.9511	.3249	63°	.8910	.4540	1.9626
19°	.3256	.9455	.3443	64°	.8988	.4384	2.0503
20°	.3420	.9397	.3640	65°	.9063	.4226	2.1445
21°	.3584	.9336	.3839	66°	.9135	.4067	2.2460
22°	.3746	.9272	.4040	67°	.9205	.3907	2.3559
23°	.3907	.9205	.4245	68°	.9272	.3746	2.4751
24°	.4067	.9135	.4452	69°	.9336	.3584	2.6051
25°	.4226	.9063	.4663	70°	.9397	.3420	2.7475
26°	.4384	.8988	.4877	71°	.9455	.3256	2.9042
27°	.4540	.8910	.5095	72°	.9511	.3090	3.0777
28°	.4695	.8829	.5317	73°	.9563	.2924	3.2709
29°	.4848	.8746	.5543	74°	.9613	.2756	3.4874
30°	.5000	.8660	.5774	75°	.9659	.2588	3.7321
31°	.5150	.8572	.6009	76°	.9703	.2419	4.0108
32°	.5299	.8480	.6249	77°	.9744	.2250	4.3315
33°	.5446	.8387	.6494	78°	.9781	.2079	4.7046
34°	.5592	.8290	.6745	79°	.9816	.1908	5.1446
35°	.5736	.8192	.7002	80°	.9848	.1736	5.6713
36°	.5878	.8090	.7265	81°	.9877	.1564	6.3138
37°	.6018	.7986	.7536	82°	.9903	.1392	7.1154
38°	.6157	.7880	.7813	83°	.9925	.1219	8.1443
39°	.6293	.7771	.8098	84°	.9945	.1045	9.5144
40°	.6428	.7660	.8391	85°	.9962	.0872	11.4301
41°	.6561	.7547	.8693	86°	.9976	.0698	14.3007
42°	.6691	.7431	.9004	87°	.9986	.0523	19.0811
43°	.6820	.7314	.9325	88°	.9994	.0349	28.6363
44°	.6947	.7193	.9657	89°	.9998	.0175	57.2900
45°	.7071	.7071	1.0000	90°	1.0000	.0000	

ANSWERS

to Odd-Numbered Exercises

Chapter 1

---

1. Symbols and Numerals (*pages 2-3*)

1. object **3.** symbol **5.** symbol **7.** 4 **9.** 0 **11.** examples: **a.** 5 + 1
b. 100 ÷ 5 **c.** 10 × 10 **d.** 4 × ¼ **e.** 8 - 8 **f.** 3 ÷ 12 **13.** no **15.** no
17. yes **19.** no **21.** 80 ÷ 100 **23.** $\frac{4}{15} - \frac{1}{5}$ **25.** 76.25 **27.** 1 **29.** $4\frac{1}{2}$
31. 1.60 **33.** 5.00 **35.** 48.00

2. The Numbers of Arithmetic (*pages 5-6*)

1. 1 **3.** Add one to the number. **5.** examples: **a.** $\frac{8}{2}$ **b.** $\frac{9}{1}$ **c.** $\frac{36}{3}$ **d.** $\frac{100}{2}$
e. $\frac{0}{8}$ **7.** examples: **a.** $\frac{60}{100}$ **b.** $\frac{25}{100}$ **c.** $\frac{8}{10}$ **d.** $\frac{15}{10}$ **e.** $\frac{2750}{1000}$ **9. a.** 3, 5
b. 0, 3, 5 **c.** all **11.** true **13.** false **15.** true **17.** true **19.** true
21. true

3. The Number Line (*pages 9-10*)

1. T is $\frac{1}{2}$; E is $1\frac{1}{2}$; A is 2; R is $2\frac{1}{2}$; S is 3 **3.** R is $\frac{1}{4}$; E is $\frac{3}{4}$; A is $1\frac{1}{2}$; D is 2; Y is 3
7. examples: **a.** $\frac{5}{5}$ **b.** $\frac{1}{2}$ **c.** .75 **d.** $\frac{9}{6}$ **e.** $3\frac{3}{4}$ **9.** A, E, I, M **11.** A
13. a. 3, 4, 5 **b.** 4, 5, 6, 7 **c.** 2, 3, 4, 5, 6, 7, 8, 9 **d.** 13, 14, 15, 16
15. a. infinitely many **b.** example: $\frac{51}{1000}$ **17. a.** infinitely many
b. example: .24394 **19. a.** right **b.** larger **21. a.** right **b.** larger
23. a. right **b.** larger **25. a.** right **b.** larger **27. a.** left
b. smaller **29. a.** right **b.** larger

4. Comparing Numbers (*pages 10-11*)

1. true **3.** false **5.** true **7.** true **9.** false **11.** true **13.** 2 **15.** 0
17. $\frac{1}{4}$

Symbols of Inequality (*pages 11-12*)

1. true **3.** false **5.** true **7.** 12 + 3 < 20 **9.** 80 ÷ 4 > 6 + 3
11. 8 + 7 > 20 ÷ 5 **13.** The difference between 12 and 2 is less than the
product of 4 and 7. **15.** false **17.** true **19.** true **21.** false **23.** false
25. any number > 10 **27.** any number ≠ 2 **29.** 3.3 or any number < 3.3
31. +, -, × **33.** +, -, ÷ **35.** -, ÷

Ordering Numbers on a Number Line (*page 13*)

1. The graph of 1 is to the left of the graph of 7.
3. The graph of 0 is to the left of the graph of 6.
5. The graph of $2\frac{1}{2}$ is to the right of the graph of 1.5.
7. 4, 16   **9.** 2.5, 3.2   **11.** 2, 3, 9   **13.** $\frac{1}{4}, \frac{2}{3}, \frac{7}{8}$ **15.** $3\frac{1}{4}, 3\frac{1}{3}, 3.75$
17. $4\frac{1}{2} < 5\frac{1}{3} < 6\frac{1}{4}$ **19.** $4.5 < 4\frac{7}{8} < 5\frac{1}{4}$

5. Order of Operations (*page 14*)

1. a. The product of 3 and 7 is to be added to 5.   **b.** 26
3. a. The product of 6 and 2 is to be subtracted from 15.   **b.** 3
5. a. The quotient of 8 and 2 is to be added to 10.   **b.** 14
7. a. The quotient of 14 and 2 is to be subtracted from 26.   **b.** 19
9. a. The product of 9 and 2 is to be added to the product of 3 and 4.   **b.** 30
11. 29   **13.** 41   **15.** 26

6. Using Grouping Symbols (*page 16*)

1. a. The sum of 6 and 1 is to be added to 20. *Ans.* 27.   **b.** Add the three numbers 20, 6, and 1. *Ans.* 27.
3. a. Add the difference of 6 and 4 to 17. *Ans.* 19.   **b.** Add 6 to 17 and then subtract 4. *Ans.* 19.
5. a. Multiply the sum of 2 and 1 by 15. *Ans.* 45.   **b.** Multiply 15 by 2 and add 1. *Ans.* 31.
7. a. Divide the sum of 12 and 8 by 4. *Ans.* 5.   **b.** Divide 8 by 4 and add 12. *Ans.* 14.
9. $(10 + 8) - 5$ **11.** $8 \times (6 - 2)$ **13.** $(12 - 2) \times (3 + 4)$ **15.** 15   **17.** 50
19. 4   **21.** 18   **23.** 60   **25.** 3   **27.** 70   **29.** 104   **31.** 60   **33.** 29
35. 3

7. Expressing Verbal Phrases and Sentences by Using Mathematical Symbols (*pages 17–18*)

1. $5 + (6 \times 7)$ **3.** $(1 + 8) + 10$ **5.** $(4 \times 6) + 8 = 32$ **7.** $14 + 2(.4 + .6) = 16$
9. $16 - 14 > 1$ **11.** $(18 - 10) \div 5 \neq 9$ **13.** $(50 \times 10) + 2(8 + 15) < 1000$
15. $(.5 \times 300) + [.3(800 - 300)] = 300$ **17.** the sum of .5 and .3, decreased by .4   **19.** the sum of 15 and 5, decreased by the difference of 15 and 5
21. When the sum of 5 and 1 is subtracted from 20, the result is the product of 40 and .3.
23. Two times the sum of $6\frac{1}{2}$ and $\frac{5}{2}$ is not equal to 20.
25. When the difference between 5 and 1 is divided by the sum of 4 and 3, the result is less than 10 decreased by 9.

Chapter 2

1. The Meaning of a Set and Set Notation (*pages 21–22*)

1. example: {Ann, Susan, Mary} **3.** example: {saw, hammer, wrench}
5. example: {destroyer, battleship, aircraft carrier} **7.** yes **9.** no **11.** yes
13. yes **15.** {June, Tuesday, Easter} **17.** {violin, piano, drum} **19. a.**
{e|e is one of the first four even natural numbers} **b.** e **21.** true
23. true **25.** false **27.** true **29.** false **31.** {Truman, Eisenhower,
Kennedy, Johnson, Nixon, Ford} **33.** {m, i, s, o, u, r} **35.** {71, 73, 75, 77,
79} **37.** {1, 3, 9} **39.** {U.S. states beginning with the letter "a"}
41. {multiples of 3 between 0 and 20} **43.** true **45.** true **47.** {0, 2, 4, 6, 8}
49. a. A = {n|n is a natural number} **b.** 0 ∉ A **c.** 4 ∈ A
51. 7 ∉ {n|n is an even whole number} **53.** 19 ∉ {n|n is an even number less
than 20}

2. Kinds of Sets and Relations Between Sets (*page 24*)

1. {301, 303, 305, 307, 309} **3.** {4, 8, 12, . . . , 496} **5.** finite but non-
empty **7.** empty **9.** finite but non-empty **11.** infinite **13.** finite but
non-empty **15.** finite but non-empty **17.** infinite **19.** empty
21. infinite

Subsets and the Universal Set (*pages 25–26*)

1. False; 13 is not a member of {10, 11, 12}.
3. True; every element of {10, 20, 30} is a member of {30, 20, 10}.
5. False; athletes such as basketball players are not elements of {baseball
players in your college}.
7. True; every element of {10, 11, 12, 13} is a member of {13, 12, 11, 10}.
9. False; a is not an element of ϕ .
11. True; every element of A is an element of A .
13. improper **15.** proper **17.** ϕ, {5}, {6}, {5, 6} **19.** ϕ, {5}, {6},
{7}, {8}, {5, 6}, {5, 7}, {5, 8}, {6, 7}, {6, 8}, {7, 8}, {5, 6, 7}, {5, 6, 8},
{5, 7, 8}, {6, 7, 8}, {5, 6, 7, 8} **21.** ϕ, {w}, {x}, {y}, {z}, {w, x}, {w, y},
{w, z}, {x, y}, {x, z}, {y, z}, {w, x, y}, {w, x, z}, {w, y, z}, {x, y, z},
{w, x, y, z} **23.** example: x = {1, 2}, y = {1, 2, 3, 4} **25. a.** example:
$G = \{2, 4, 6\}; H = \{6, 4, 2\}$ **b.** $G = H$

Equal Sets (*pages 26–27*)

1. $A = B$ **3.** $E \neq F$ **5.** $K = L$ **7.** $R = S$ **9.** $T \neq V$

Equivalent Sets (*page 28*)

1. yes **3.** yes **5.** yes **7.** no **9.** no **11. a.** yes **b.** no **13. a.** yes
b. no **15.** example: {1, 3, 5, 7} and {2, 4, 6, 8, 10}

3. Picturing a Universal Set and Its Subsets (*page 29*)

1. a. {penny, nickel, dime, quarter, half-dollar, dollar}   **b.** {penny, nickel, dime}
3. a. example: $E = \{y \mid y$ is an even natural number between 10 and 20}

4. Intersection of Sets (*pages 31–32*)

1. {6, 7}   **3. a.** {13, 14, 15}   **5. a.** $U = \{1, 2, 3, 4, 5, \ldots, 19\}$,
$A = \{1, 2, 3, \ldots, 9\}, B = \{11, 12, 13, \ldots, 19\}$ **b.** none   **c.** ϕ **7.** $A = B$
9. Not disjoint; 5 is in the intersection.
11. Disjoint; there are no common elements.
13. a. There are some bass in the pond that weigh at least 5 pounds.   **b.** There are no bass in the pond that weigh at least 5 pounds.   **c.** All the fish in the pond that weigh at least 5 pounds are bass.   **d.** All the bass in the pond weigh at least 5 pounds.
15. ϕ **17.** ϕ **19.** A **21.** A **23.** D

5. Union of Sets (*pages 33–34*)

1. {0, 1, 2, 3, 4}   **3.** {0, 1, 2, 3, 4, 5, 6}   **5. a.** {a, e, i, o, u, r, s, t}
9. {2, 4, 5, 6, 7, 8, 9, 10, 11}   **11.** {4, 6}   **13.** A **15.** A **17.** C

6. The Complement of a Set (*pages 35–36*)

1. {3, 5, 7, 9, 11}   **3.** {1, 9}   **5.** ϕ **7.** {1, 2, 3, 4, 5, 7, 9}
9. {1, 2, 3, 4, 5, 7, 9}   **11.** {2, 4, 7, 9}   **13.** {the union of odd natural numbers less than 40 and all natural numbers greater than 40}   **15.** {the even natural numbers}   **17.** {natural numbers not divisible by 9}   **19.** false

7. De Morgan's Laws (*page 37*)

1. $(A \cup B)' = A' \cap B' = \{4, 5, 6, 7, 8, 9\} \cap \{1, 3, 5, 7, 9\} = \{5, 7, 9\}$;
$A \cup B = \{1, 2, 3, 4, 6, 8\}; (A \cup B)' = \{5, 7, 9\}$
3. $A' \cap B' = \{4, 5, 6, \ldots\} \cap \{1, 3, 5, \ldots\} = \{5, 7, 9, \ldots\}$;
$A \cup B = \{1, 2, 3, 4, 6, 8, \ldots\}; (A \cup B)' = \{5, 7, 9, \ldots\}$
5. $A' \cap B' = \phi \cap \phi = \phi; A \cup B = U; (A \cup B)' = \phi$
7. $A' \cap B' = U \cap U = U; A \cup B = \phi; (A \cup B)' = U$
9. $A' \cup B' = \{2, 4, 6, 7, 8, \ldots\} \cup \{1, 3, 5, 7, 9, 10, 11, \ldots\} = \{1, 2, 3, \ldots\}$;
$A \cap B = \phi; (A \cap B)' = U = \{1, 2, 3, \ldots\}$
11. $A' \cup B' = \{1, 3, 5, \ldots\} \cup \{2, 4, 6, \ldots\} = U = \{1, 2, 3, \ldots\}; A \cap B = \phi$;
$(A \cap B)' = U = \{1, 2, 3, \ldots\}$
13. $A' \cup B' = \phi \cup U = U; A \cap B = \phi; (A \cap B)' = U$

8. Graphing Sets of Numbers (*page 39*)

1. {B, D, F, H}   **3.** {L, M}   **5.** cannot be drawn   **7.** {C, E, G, I}
9. {D, G, J, M}   **11.** {D, F, H, J, L, N}   **13.** {A, B, C, D, E, F, G}
29. examples: **a.** {1, 3, 5}   **b.** {4, 8}   **c.** {8, 12}   **31. a.** {0, 1, 4, 6}
b. {0, 1, 3, 4, 5, 6, 8, 9, 10}

Chapter 3

1. Open Sentences and Truth Sets (*pages 42–43*)

1. no **3.** no **5.** yes **7.** yes **9.** she **11.** R **13.** y **15.** n **17.** h
19. 2 **21.** 2 **23.** 0, 1, 2 **25.** 0, 1, 2, 3 **27.** none **29.** none **31.** $\{2\}$
33. ϕ **35.** $\{4\frac{1}{2}\}$ **37.** ϕ **39.** $\{3\}$ **41.** $\{3\}$ **43.** ϕ **45.** ϕ **47.** $\{10\}$
49. $\{7, 8\}$ **51.** $\{2, 3, 4\}$ **53.** $\{0, 1, 2, 3\}$

2. Graphing the Truth Set of an Open Sentence Containing One Variable (*page 45*)

1. $\{3\}$ **3.** $\{0, 1, 2, 3, 4, 5\}$ **5.** $\{0\}$ **7.** $\{0, 1, 2, 3, 4, 5, 6, 7, 8\}$

4. Units of Measure in the United States System and the Metric System (*pages 49–50*)

1. $b + 8$ **3.** xy **5.** $12 + a$ **7.** $8 \div y$ **9.** $(2c)(3d)$ **11.** $c - d$ **13.** $\frac{1}{3}(z)$
15. $m + 4$ **17.** $5x + 2$ **19.** $\dfrac{36}{t + u}$ **21.** $xy - \frac{1}{2}(x + y)$ **23.** $n + 2$ **25.** $8 + n$
27. $n - 2$ **29.** $3n$ **31.** $4n + 3$ **33.** $30 + 4n$ **35.** $2n - 3$ **37.** $\frac{1}{3}(5n)$
39. $(m + 5)(4)$ **41.** x **43.** $5x$ **45.** $f + 2$ **47.** $2L + 2W$ **49.** $10W - 6L$
51. 3 times a number **53.** 3 less than a number **55.** 1 more than twice a
number **57.** the difference between 5 and a number **59.** a number divided
by 4
61. the difference of a number and 8, divided by 3
63. 2 times the sum of a number and 1
65. one-half the sum of 2 times a number and 1
67. the difference between x and 10; the difference between 10 and x
69. the difference between a and b; the difference between b and a
71. the quotient of x and 4; the quotient of 4 and x

5. Problems Involving Variables Represented by Letters (*pages 51–52*)

1. $39x$ **3.** $w - 50$ **5.** $c - d$ **7.** $b + x$ **9.** $x - b$ **11.** $20 - x$ **13.** $c + 25$
15. $L - 5$ **17.** $25q$ **19.** $5x + 10(25 - x)$ **21.** $5r$ **23.** $2r$ **25.** $\dfrac{m}{3}$
27. $\dfrac{c}{m}$

6. Understanding the Meaning of Some Vocabulary Used in Algebra (*pages 54–55*)

1. x, y **3.** $5, n$ **5.** $13, x, y, 13x, 13y, xy$ **7.** 8 **9.** $\frac{1}{2}$ **11.** 1.4 **13.** Base is
m; exponent is 2. **15.** Base is t; exponent is 1. **17.** Base is $5y$; exponent is 4.
19. m^3 **21.** 10^4 **23.** $4x^5$ **25.** $7r^3s^2$ **27.** $(6a)^3$ **29.** $5 \cdot x \cdot x \cdot x \cdot x$
31. $4 \cdot a \cdot a \cdot a \cdot a \cdot b \cdot b$ **33.** $3y \cdot 3y \cdot 3y \cdot 3y \cdot 3y$

8. Evaluating Algebraic Expressions Involving Addition, Subtraction, Multiplication, and Division (*page 56*)

1. 40   **3.** 1.5   **5.** 60   **7.** 6   **9.** 9   **11.** 30   **13.** 35   **15.** 25   **17.** $4\frac{2}{3}$

9. Evaluating Algebraic Expressions Involving Powers (*pages 57-58*)

1. 64   **3.** 81   **5.** 6   **7.** 48   **9.** 27,648   **11.** 100   **13.** 91   **15.** 48   **17.** 78
19. 8   **21.** 116   **23.** 28   **25.** 32   **27.** 11   **29.** 1024   **31.** 729   **33.** 729

10. Evaluating Expressions Containing Parentheses or Other Symbols of Grouping (*page 59*)

1. 26   **3.** 4   **5.** 28   **7.** 39   **9.** 36   **11.** 248   **13.** 192   **15.** 29   **17.** 488
19. 172   **21.** 644   **23.** 100   **25.** 6400   **27.** 6400   **29.** 4   **31.** 1   **33.** 1
35. 7   **37.** 1   **39.** 1   **41.** .092

Chapter 4

1. Understanding the Meaning of Closure Under an Operation (*page 62*)

1. yes   **3.** yes   **5.** yes   **7.** yes   **9.** a, c **11.** no   **13.** yes   **15.** no   **17.** no
19. yes   **21. a.** No; $1 + 1 = 2$.   **b.** No; $1 - 1 = 0$.   **c.** Yes; $1 \times 1 = 1$.   **d.** Yes;
$1 \div 1 = 1$.   **23. a.** No; $1 + 1 = 2$.   **b.** No; $0 - 1 \neq 0, 0 - 1 \neq 1$.   **c.** Yes;
$0 \times 1 = 0, 1 \times 1 = 1$.   **d.** No; $0 \div 0$ is not in set.   **25. a.** No; $4 + 6 = 10$.   **b.** No;
$2 - 2 = 0$.   **c.** No; $2 \times 4 = 8$.   **d.** No; $6 \div 2 = 3$.
27. a. No; the sum of two odd numbers is even.   **b.** No; $7 - 5 = 2$, which is not
odd.   **c.** Yes; the product of two odd numbers is an odd number.   **d.** No; $3 \div 5$
is not an odd number.
29. a. Yes; the sum of multiples of $\frac{1}{2}$ is a multiple of $\frac{1}{2}$.   **b.** No; $\frac{1}{2} - \frac{1}{2} = 0$.
c. No; $\frac{1}{2} \times \frac{1}{2} = \frac{1}{4}$.   **d.** No; $\frac{1}{2} \div 2 = \frac{1}{4}$.
31. a. No; $.1 + .1 = .2$.   **b.** No; $.1 - .1 = 0$.   **c.** Yes; the product of two powers
of .1 is a power of .1.   **d.** No; $.1 \div .1 = 1$.
32. examples: **a.** $\{0\}$ **b.** $\{0\}$ **c.** $\{0, 1\}$ **d.** $\{1\}$

2. Properties of Addition (*pages 64-65*)

Note: In this section, the following abbreviations are used: AA = associative
property of addition; CA = commutative property of addition; S = substitution principle.

1. CA **3.** AA **5.** CA **7. a.** 2   **b.** CA **9. a.** x **b.** CA **11.** $(275 + 125) +$
$83 = 483$ **13.** $(.79 + .21) + .63 = 1.63$ **15.** $(2\frac{3}{4} + 4\frac{1}{4}) + 1\frac{1}{3} = 8\frac{1}{3}$ **17. a.** CA
b. AA **c.** S **d.** S **19. a.** CA **b.** AA **c.** S
21. example: **a.** $(592 + 649) + 408 = (649 + 592) + 408$ $\quad CA$
$\qquad\qquad$ **b.** $\qquad\qquad\qquad = 649 + (592 + 408)$ $\quad AA$

23. example: **a.** $(10 + t) + 13 = (t + 10) + 13$ CA
              b. $= t + (10 + 13)$ AA
              c. $= t + 23$ S

3. Properties of Multiplication (*pages 67-68*)

Note: In this section, the following abbreviations are used: AA = associative property of addition; CA = commutative property of addition; AM = associative property of multiplication; CM = commutative property of multiplication; S = substitution principle.

1. CM **3.** CM **5.** AM **7. a.** z **b.** CM **9. a.** g **b.** CM **11.** $(50 \times 2) \times 93 = 9,300$ **13.** $(125 \times 8) \times 798 = 798,000$ **15.** $(2\frac{1}{2} \times 40) \times 49 = 4,900$ **17.** $(2.5 \times 4) \times 6.9 = 69$ **19.** $(125 \times 8) \times 7.66 = 7,660$ **21. a.** CM **b.** AM **c.** S **d.** S **23. a.** AM **b.** CM **c.** CM **d.** AM
25. a. example: *a.* $\frac{5}{9} \times (731 \times \frac{9}{5}) = \frac{5}{9} \times (\frac{9}{5} \times 731)$
                    b. $= (\frac{5}{9} \times \frac{9}{5}) \times 731$
                    c. $= 1 \times 731$
b. *a. CM* *b. AM* *c. S*
27. a. example: *a.* $dc \times 8 = 8 \times dc$
                    b. $= 8 \times cd$
b. *a. CM* *b. CM*
29. AM **31.** CM **33.** CM, AM, and S **35.** CA and CM

4. The Distributive Property (*page 70*)

1. yes **3.** No; $(7 + 9)5 = 7 \times 5 + 9 \times 5$. **5.** No; $2(y + 6) = 2y + 2 \times 6$. **7.** yes
9. yes **11.** yes **13.** yes **15.** $9 \times 7 + 9 \times 3$ **17.** $4p + 4q$
19. $(8 + 13)t = 21t$ **21.** $15(36 + 64) = 1500$ **23.** $(128 - 28)615 = 61,500$
25. $937(.8 + .2) = 937$ **27.** $50(8 + \frac{3}{5}) = 430$ **29.** $4m + 4n$ **31.** $8x + 24$
33. $21a - 3ab$ **35.** $2(p + q)$ **37.** $(12 - 4)y = 8y$ **39.** $2b(c + 2)$
41. a. Commutative property of addition **b.** Distributive property
c. Commutative property of multiplication

5. Combining Like Terms (*pages 72-73*)

1. a. $5(9) - 2(9) = 45 - 18 = 27, 3(9) = 27$
  b. $5(144) - 2(144) = 720 - 288 = 432, 3(144) = 432$
  c. $5(.04) - 2(.04) = .2 - .08 = .12, 3(.04) = .12$
  d. $5(\frac{1}{9}) - 2(\frac{1}{9}) = \frac{5}{9} - \frac{2}{9} = \frac{1}{3}, 3(\frac{1}{9}) = \frac{1}{3}$
  e. $5(0) - 2(0) = 0, 3(0) = 0$
3. $10x$ **5.** $11c$ **7.** $4.7y$ **9.** $14m$ **11.** $20\frac{1}{4}s$ **13.** $1\frac{1}{4}xy$ **15.** $P = 15x$
17. a. $P = 2x + 4x + 4x + 5x = 15x$ **b.** $P = 6m + 8m + 10m = 24m$
c. $P = 2.5a + 2.5a + 2a + 4a + 2a = 13a$ **d.** $P = 7\frac{1}{4}y + 4y + 8\frac{1}{2}y + 4y = 23\frac{3}{4}y$
19. $3a + m$ **21.** $10x + 2$ **23.** $5ab + 8ac$ **25.** $10c + 45 + 12c - 21 = 22c + 24$
27. $S = 9\frac{1}{4}a + 3\frac{1}{4}b$

6. Properties of Zero and One (*page 75*)

1. $10 \times 0 + 6 \times 1 = 10 \times 0 + 6$ Multiplication property of one
                  $= 0 + 6$ Multiplication property of zero
                  $= 6$ Substitution principle

3. $(0 + 6) + 1 \times 8 = (0 + 6) + 8$ Multiplication property of one
                  $= 6 + 8$ Addition property of zero
                  $= 14$ Substitution principle

5. $4 \times 1 - (0 + 2) = 4 \times 1 - 2$ Addition property of zero
                  $= 4 - 2$ Multiplication property of one
                  $= 2$ Substitution principle

7. $10x + x = 10x + 1x$ Multiplication property of one
        $= (10 + 1)x$ Distributive property
        $= 11x$ Substitution principle

9. $8y - y = 8y - 1y$ Multiplication property of one
       $= (8 - 1)y$ Distributive property
       $= 7y$ Substitution principle

11. $8x^2 - x^2 = 8x^2 - 1x^2$ Multiplication property of one
        $= (8 - 1)x^2$ Distributive property
        $= 7x^2$ Substitution principle

Chapter 5

1. Extending the Number Line (*pages 77–78*)

7. same   **9.** opposite   **11.** same   **13.** opposite   **15.** the sign   **17.** $^-10$
19. $^-10$ **21.** $^-8$ **23.** $^+8$ **25.** $^+5$ **27.** $^+7$ **29.** 0   **31.** $^-4$ **33.** $^-7$ **35.** $^-1\frac{1}{2}$
37. $^-2.5$ **39.** $^-9$ **41.** $^-5$

2. Using Signed Numbers to Represent Opposite Situations
(*pages 79–80*)

1. a drop in price   **3.** traveling east   **5.** a loss in weight   **7.** a loss of \$8
9. $40°$ south of the equator   **11.** 90 kilometers west   **13.** $^-12$ **15.** $^+1200$
17. $^-1\frac{1}{2}$ **19.** $^-25$ **21.** It is 1290 feet below sea level.   **23.** $^+13$ **25.** $^-12$
27. a. example: At 1 P.M. the temperature was $5°$ below zero.   **b.** $^+3$ **c.** $^-7$
d. 1 P.M. and 5 P.M.   **e.** 5 P.M. and 9 P.M.

3. Ordering Signed Numbers on a Number Line (*page 82*)

1. True because $^+5$ is to the right of $^+2$.   **3.** false   **5.** false   **7.** true   **9.** $^-4 < {}^+8$
11. $^-1\frac{1}{2} < {}^+1\frac{1}{2}$ **13.** $^-2 < 0 < {}^+8$ **15.** $^+7 > {}^-4$ **17.** $0 > {}^-1\frac{1}{2}$ **19.** $0 > {}^-1 > {}^-5$
21. $^+2$ **23.** $^+.6$ **25.** true   **27.** true   **29.** $\{^+1, {}^+2, {}^+3, {}^+4\}$
31. $\{0, {}^+1, {}^+2, {}^+3, {}^+4\}$ **33.** $\{0, {}^+1, {}^+2, {}^+3, {}^+4\}$ **35.** $\{^+1, {}^+2, {}^+3, {}^+4\}$
37. $\{0, {}^+1, {}^+2\}$ **39.** $\{0, {}^+1, {}^+2\}$

4. The Opposite of a Directed Number (*pages 84–85*)

1. -8 **3.** $-3\frac{1}{2}$ **5.** -19 **7.** 0 **9.** -7 **11.** -5 **13.** 10 **15.** -4
17. $\{-4, -3\}$ **19.** $\{-4, -3, -2, -1\}$ **21.** $\{-4, -3, -2, -1\}$ **23.** $\{4\}$
25. $\{-4, -3, -2, -1, 0, 1, 2\}$ **27.** $\{-3, -2, -1, 0, 1, 2, 3\}$ **41.** false **43.** false
45. false **47.** true

5. The Absolute Value of a Number (*pages 86–87*)

1. a. 3 b. -3 **2.** a. 5 b. $+5$ **3.** a. 18 b. -18 **4.** a. 13 b. $+13$
5. a. 20 b. $+20$ **6.** a. $1\frac{1}{2}$ b. $-1\frac{1}{2}$ **7.** a. $3\frac{3}{4}$ b. $+3\frac{3}{4}$ **8.** a. $1\frac{1}{2}$ b. $+1\frac{1}{2}$
9. a. 2.7 b. -2.7
11. true **13.** false **15.** false **17.** true **19.** 12 **21.** 10 **23.** 0 **25.** 7
27. -2 **29.** false **31.** true **33.** true **35.** false **39.** $\{8, -8\}$ **41.** $\{6, -6\}$
43. $\{6, -6\}$

6. Adding Signed Numbers on a Number Line (*pages 89–90*)

1. $+7$ **3.** $+3$ **5.** 0 **7.** $+4$ **9.** -8 **11.** -2 **13.** 0 **15.** a. -9 b. -9
They are equal. **17.** Commutative property of addition **19.** a. -7 b. -7 They
are equal. **21.** Associative property of addition **23.** 0 **25.** 0 **27.** -8
29. -5 **31.** a rise of $7°$ **33.** 750 kilometers south **35.** a loss of $\$\frac{3}{4}$
37. negative **39.** The sum has the same sign as the larger absolute value.
41. a. yes b. $(-4) + (-6) = -10$

7. Addition of Signed Numbers (*pages 96–98*)

1. $+24$ **3.** -66 **5.** -30 **7.** $+8$ **9.** $+10\frac{1}{2}$ **11.** $18\frac{1}{4}$ **13.** -7.8 **15.** 8.3
17. 14.0 **19.** $+50$ **21.** $+27$ **23.** 0 **25.** $+6\frac{1}{2}$ **27.** -2 **29.** $-13\frac{2}{3}$ **31.** 2.3
33. 2.5 **35.** 0 **37.** $+34$ **39.** -50 **41.** $+25$ **43.** -18 **45.** 0 **47.** 31
49. 54 **51.** 0 **53.** -20 **55.** 0 **57.** 12 **59.** -7 **61.** -2 **63.** $-18\frac{1}{6}$
65. 0 **67.** $+4$ **69.** 0 **71.** -6 **73.** -1.5 **75.** 0 **77.** 0 **79.** -8 **81.** 0
83. -10 **85.** $-15\frac{3}{4}$ **87.** $-C$ **89.** -4 **91.** 0 **93.** $-b$ **95.** $+4$ **97.** -10
99. $+\frac{8}{7}$ **101.** -9 **103.** -4 **105.** $14\frac{1}{2}$ **107.** Commutative property of addition
109. Property of zero (additive identity) **111.** Associative property
113. $15 + (-8) = (7 + 8) + (-8)$ Substitution principle
          $= 7 + [8 + (-8)]$ Associative property of addition
          $= 7 + 0$ Additive inverse
          $= 7$ Additive identity
117. $(8 + 9) + 5 = 8 + (9 + 5)$ Associative property of addition
          $= 8 + (5 + 9)$ Commutative property of addition
          $= (8 + 5) + 9$ Associative property of addition
127. $(x + y) + [(-x) + (-y)] = (x + y) + [(-y) + (-x)]$ Commutative property of
                                                              addition
          $= [x + y + (-y)] + (-x)$ Associative property of
                                      addition
          $= (x + 0) + (-x)$ Additive inverse
          $= x + (-x)$ Additive identity
          $= 0$ Additive inverse
129. true **131.** true

8. Subtraction of Signed Numbers (*pages 101-102*)

1. +4 **3.** -3 **5.** -6 **7.** +20 **9.** 0 **11.** -54 **13.** +35 **15.** -12 **17.** +15
19. +2.2 **21.** -10.6 **23.** +1.6 **25.** +3 **27.** -12 **29.** $-10\frac{1}{6}$ **31.** -11
33. +30 **35.** +1.5 **37.** +2 **39.** $-2\frac{1}{2}$ **41. a.** +29 **b.** -21 **c.** +14 **d.** +3
e. 0 **f.** +9 **43.** +27 **45.** +9 **47.** +19 **49.** -5 **51.** -8.5 **53.** $-1\frac{7}{8}$
55. +20 **57.** +8 **59.** -28 **61. a.** +3° **b.** +28° **c.** -12° **d.** -16°
63. a. false **b.** false **65. a.** false **b.** false **67. a.** true **b.** true

9. Multiplication of Signed Numbers (*pages 109-110*)

1. +72 **3.** -51 **5.** -135 **7.** -3.60 **9.** +4 **11.** $+\frac{1}{6}$ **13.** +48 **15.** -77
17. 0 **19.** +2 **21.** 1 **23.** -3 **25.** +24 **27.** -60 **29.** -120
31. a. +35 **b.** -15 **c.** -45 **d.** +41 **e.** -76.5 **f.** 0 **33.** +16 **35.** +125
37. -125 **39.** $+\frac{1}{4}$ **41.** $+\frac{8}{27}$ **43.** $-\frac{1}{64}$ **45.** $5 \cdot (9) + 5 \cdot (7)$ **47.** $6[(-3) + (-5)]$
49. $8[(5) + (-3)] = (8) \cdot 5 + (8) \cdot (-3)$ **51.** 1500 **53.** -93 **55.** Commutative
property of multiplication **57.** Distributive property of multiplication
59. 1. Multiplication property of zero 2. Addition property of opposites
3. Distributive property of multiplication 4. Substitution principle
5. Addition property of opposites
61. 1. Multiplication property of zero 2. Addition property of opposites
3. Distributive property of multiplication 4. Substitution principle
5. Addition property of opposites

10. Division of Signed Numbers (*pages 114-115*)

1. $\frac{1}{9}$ **3.** 1 **5.** 5 **7.** $\frac{1}{x}$ **9.** +3 **11.** -13 **13.** +5 **15.** +5 **17.** $-\frac{1}{2}$
19. $+1\frac{1}{4}$ **21.** $-2\frac{2}{3}$ **23.** 0 **25.** +32 **27.** -8 **29.** +1.2 **31.** $-\frac{1}{8}$ **33.** -5
35. -2 **37.** $\frac{1}{x-5}, 5$ **39.** $\frac{1}{2x-1}, \frac{1}{2}$ **41. a.** false **b.** false
43. a. false **b.** false **45. a.** true **b.** true **47.** yes

11. Evaluating Algebraic Expressions by Using Signed Numbers
(*page 116*)

1. -48 **3.** +24 **5.** -4 **7.** +64 **9.** -25 **11.** +1 **13.** +2 **15.** +450
17. +54 **19.** -9 **21.** -10 **23.** +12 **25.** +21 **27.** +88 **29.** +9 **31.** +98
33. +9.4 **35.** -4 **37.** +34 **39.** +28 **41.** -2 **43.** -4 **45.** +3 **47.** +24

Chapter 6

2. Adding and Subtracting Like Monomials (*pages 119-120*)

1. +15c **3.** -10a **5.** 0 **7.** +7r **9.** +2q **11.** 0 **13.** +15c **15.** +13c
17. $+11x^2$ **19.** $+6d^2$ **21.** $-\frac{2}{3}c^4$ **23.** +xyz **25.** 0 **27.** $-4xy^2$
29. $-1\frac{1}{4}x^2y^2$ **31.** -2(c+d) **33.** $-2x^2$ **35.** 0 **37.** 0 **39.** false **41.** false

43. $-6b$ **45.** $+8d$ **47.** 0 **49.** $-3y^2$ **51.** $-9t^3$ **53.** $+4(m+n)$ **55.** $+mn$
57. $-10ab$ **59.** $-2(x+y)$ **61.** $-7xy^2$ **63.** $+16c^2d^2$ **65.** $+10(a+b)$
67. $-4y$ **69.** 0 **71.** $-37y^2$ **73.** 0 **75.** $-10cd$ **77.** 0 **79.** $+10y$
81. $-11z$

3. Simplifying, Adding, and Subtracting Polynomials (*pages 123–124*)

1. $10y+9w$ **3.** $3ab-6bc$ **5.** $13a-3b$ **7.** $7x^2-3$ **9.** $-2x^2+x+8$
11. $1.2+2.2z-z^2$ **13.** $6x+6y$ **15.** $2x^2-3x+2$ **17.** $-r$ **19.** $8xy-10cd$
21. $4a^2+3ab$ **23.** $11b-6$ **25.** $-6x^3+4$ **27.** $11xy+7$ **29.** 0
31. $3a+7b$ **33.** $4x^2+9x-16$ **35.** $-5a+2b$ **37.** $19-x$ **39.** $-4x+10$
41. $2x^2-3x-3$ **43.** $2p$ **45.** $6x^2-9x-12$ **47.** $+6y+6$ **49.** a. $19x-6$
b. $11a+9b$ **51.** a. $10x+10$ b. $14x-8$ **53.** $(9x+2y)-(-3x+5y)=$
$12x-3y$ **55.** $(5x^2+7)-(3x^2-1)=2x^2+8$ **57.** $(3x-4)-(9x+5)=-6x-9$

4. Multiplying Powers of the Same Base (*page 126*)

1. a^5 **3.** c^7 **5.** r^{11} **7.** a^7 **9.** t^{14} **11.** a^3 **13.** e^{10} **15.** 5^6 **17.** 2^{10}
19. a^8 **21.** x^4y^6 **23.** r^3s^3 **25.** $(\frac{2}{5})^4\cdot(\frac{1}{3})^{12}$ **27.** y^{c+2} **29.** x^{m+1}
31. true **33.** false **35.** true **37.** false

5. Multiplying a Monomial by a Monomial (*pages 127–128*)

1. $-12a$ **3.** $+30y$ **5.** $-42xyz$ **7.** $-6ab$ **9.** $-15abc$ **11.** $-18cdxy$
13. $-20a^4$ **15.** $-90r^7$ **17.** $+12z^3$ **19.** $-35a^5b^3$ **21.** $-16r^5s^2$ **23.** $-30m^4n$
25. $+9a^3b^3$ **27.** $+49a^2$ **29.** $+.25x^2$ **31.** $-\frac{8}{125}c^6d^3$ **33.** $+16x^2y^2$
35. $+135y^3$ **37.** $15w^2$

6. Multiplying a Polynomial by a Monomial (*page 129*)

1. $18c+9d$ **3.** $-16a-12b$ **5.** $8m-48n$ **7.** $-12c+10d$ **9.** $5d^3-15d^2$
11. m^2n+mn^2 **13.** $15a^3b-21ab^3$ **15.** $-50m^4n^4+30m^6n$
17. $-16x^2+24x+40$ **19.** $-10s^3+30s^2-35s$ **21.** $-10r^4s^2+15r^3s^3-20r^2s^4$
23. $-12t^2+18t-16$ **25.** $9-6x+3x^2$ **27.** $-4y^3+10y^2+6y$
29. $5z(3x+4y)=15xz+20yz$ **31.** a. $4(2x+5)=8x+20$ km b. $8(2x+5)=$
$16x+40$ km c. $20(2x+5)=40x+100$ km d. $h(2x+5)=2xh+5h$ km
e. $x(2x+5)=2x^2+5x$ km **33.** $4(3a+4b)=12a+16b$

7. Using Multiplication to Simplify Algebraic Expressions Containing Symbols of Grouping (*page 130*)

1. $5d+5$ **3.** $-3+14x$ **5.** $-12+17a$ **7.** $10x^2-6x$ **9.** $-c+2d$
11. $29x+14$ **13.** $-2y$ **15.** $7a^2b-5abc+b^2c$ **17.** $49x-14$
19. $-24x^2-20x$ **21.** $36(x+2)+12(2x-1)=60x+60$

8. Multiplying a Polynomial by a Polynomial (*page 132*)

1. a^2+5a+6 **3.** $c^2+2c-48$ **5.** $30+11y+y^2$ **7.** $72+6r-r^2$ **9.** y^2-49
11. $2x^2-11x-6$ **13.** $6a^2+29a+9$ **15.** $4x^2-9$ **17.** $9d^2-64$
19. $a^2-2ab+b^2$ **21.** x^2-16y^2 **23.** $15kr+20ks+6mr+8ms$

25. $36a^2 - 25b^2$ **27.** $x^4 - y^4$ **29.** $4c^3 - 4c^2 - 5c - 1$ **31.** $8a^3 - 26a^2 b +$
$11ab^2 + 10b^3$ **33.** $6x^3 + 13x^2 - 19x - 12$ **35.** $x^3 + 12x^2 + 48x + 64$
37. $2x^3 - 7x^2 + 16x - 15$ **39.** $9b^3 - 9b^2 c - 4bc^2 + 4c^3$ **41.** $12x^2 - 6$
43. $14x + 2$ **45.** $2x^2 + 5xy + y^2$ **47.** $(x + 100)(2x + 3) = 2x^2 + 203x + 300$ km

9. Dividing Powers of the Same Base (*pages 134–135*)

1. x^6 **3.** b^4 **5.** 1   **7.** m^8 **9.** 1   **11.** z^9 **13.** 2^3 **15.** 3^2 **17.** x^{3a}
19. r^{c-d} **21.** 1   **23.** 5^3 **25.** 1   **27.** true   **29.** false

10. Dividing a Monomial by a Monomial (*page 136*)

1. $9x$ **3.** $-5x$ **5.** $11d$ **7.** $4a^2 b$ **9.** $-4c$ **11.** 2   **13.** $3m$ **15.** $-7c^2 b$
17. $-3r$ **19.** $-19a^6 b^6$ **21.** $-19r^{11} s^9$ **23.** $5(x + y)$ **25.** $6(x - 3y)$ **27.** $5x^2$

11. Dividing a Polynomial by a Monomial (*pages 137–138*)

1. $2x + 4y$ **3.** $t - 1$ **5.** $-2c^2 + 3d^2$ **7.** $1 + rt$ **9.** $3d^2 + 2d$ **11.** $3r^3 + 2r$
13. $-3y^6 + 2y^3$ **15.** $3b - 4a$ **17.** $3a + 6b$ **19.** $y^5 - 3y + 5$
21. $4a^4 x^2 - 2a^3 y^2 + 3a^2 z^2$ **23.** $-3r^2 s^2 - 4rs + 1$ **25.** $x + y$
27. a. $12x^2 + 4x$ km   **b.** $3x^2 + x$ km   **c.** $60x + 20$ km   **d.** $6x + 2$ km
e. $3x + 1$ km

12. Dividing a Polynomial by a Polynomial (*pages 141–142*)

1. $b + 2$ **3.** $r - 3$ **5.** $x - 18$ **7.** $11 + x$ **9.** $t - 2$ **11.** $3x - 8$ **13.** $2x + 3y$
15. $15x - 2y$ **17.** $8x - 5$ **19.** $a - b$ **21.** $3a + 3b$ **23.** $x + 8$ **25.** $2m - 7n$
27. $x^2 - 3x + 2$ **29.** $2b^2 - 4b - 3$ **31.** $2y^2 + 3y - 1$ **33.** $4x^2 - 6x + 9$
35. $x - 7 + \dfrac{-7}{x - 2}$ **37.** $x + 2 + \dfrac{-10}{3x + 3}$ **39.** $c^2 - 6c - 18 + \dfrac{-27}{c - 2}$
41. $a^2 - 4a + 2 + \dfrac{-4}{2a + 3}$ **43.** $5x - 4y + \dfrac{13y^2}{2x + y}$ **45.** $a + 9b + \dfrac{26b^2}{a - 6b}$
47. $x - 5 + \dfrac{50}{x + 5}$ **49.** $x - 2$ **51.** $2x + 3$ **53.** $2a^2 - 5b^2$ **55.** $x - 9$
57. No; when you divide by $x - 2$, the remainder is not zero.

13. Non-positive Integral Exponents (*pages 145–147*)

1. $\dfrac{1}{m^6}$ **3.** $\dfrac{5}{x^5}$ **5.** $\dfrac{d^2}{c^3}$ **7.** $\dfrac{1}{(2t)^3}$ **9.** g^2 **11.** $7a$ **13.** $\dfrac{n^2}{m^3}$ **15.** $\dfrac{xz^2}{wy^4}$ **17.** $r^3 s^{-2}$
19. $s^5 t$ **21.** 1   **23.** 1   **25.** 5   **27.** $\frac{1}{9}$ **29.** $-\frac{1}{6}$ **31.** .003   **33.** $1\frac{1}{36}$ **35.** $1\frac{1}{9}$
37. 111.1   **39.** $3\frac{1}{2}$ **41.** 432.79   **43.** y^4 **45.** x^{-4} **47.** a^3 **49.** 1   **51.** xy^3
53. $r^{-2} s$ **55.** m^{-5} **57.** x^{-5} **59.** 2^{-3} **61.** 10^{-7} **63.** x^{12} **65.** d^{-20}
67. 4^{-2} **69.** 10^{-6} **71.** $a^6 y^{-2}$ **73.** $c^{-6} d^{-3}$ **75.** y^3 **77.** 1   **79.** 2
81. 10^7 **83.** 5^6 **85.** 3^4 **87.** 2×10^4 **89.** 7.03×10^{-7} **91.** 2×10^{-8}
93. 6×10^{10} **95.** 3.0×10^9 **97.** 2.0×10^8

14. Scientific Notation (*pages 149–150*)

1. 10^5 **3.** 10^9 **5.** 10^{-6} **7.** 10^{-4} **9.** 10^{-9} **11.** 3.4×10^5 **13.** 6.0×10^6
15. 5.19×10^8 **17.** 1.25×10^{13} **19.** 3×10^{-4} **21.** 3×10^{-9} **23.** .000 084
25. .000 000 0575   **27.** 9999.9   **29. a.** 9×10^{15} **b.** 9,000,000,000,000,000
31. a. 3×10^4 **b.** 30,000   **33. a.** 6.25×10^{-8} **b.** .000 000 0625
35. a. 3.4×10^{-6} **b.** .000 0034   **37. a.** 3.5×10^{-18}
b. .000 000 000 000 000 0035   **39.** .000 0176   **41.** -6 **43.** 6.4
45. 4.85×10^{-7} **47.** 3.0×10^{10} **49,** 40,000,000,000,000
51. 5,900,000,000,000,000,000,000,000

Chapter 7

1. Understanding the Meaning of Solving an Equation (*pages 152–153*)

1. 5   **3.** 14   **5.** 6   **7.** 5.2   **9.** 9   **11.** 10   **13.** yes   **15.** no   **17.** yes
19. no   **21.** yes   **23.** $\emptyset$ **25.** $\{4\}$ **27.** $\{3\}$ **29.** $\{-5\}$ **31.** identity
33. identity   **35.** conditional equation

2. Postulates of Equality (*pages 156–157*)

1. reflexive   **3.** symmetric   **5.** symmetric   **7.** subtraction   **9.** division
11. a. symmetric   **b.** transitive   **13. a.** symmetric   **b.** transitive
15. a. symmetric   **b.** transitive

3. Solving Equations by Using Addition or Subtraction Postulates (*pages 159–160*)

1. $x = 18$ **3.** $t = 26$ **5.** $x = -2$ **7.** $m = -3$ **9.** $r = -14$ **11.** $d = 4$
13. $x = -.4$ **15.** $y = -.4$ **17.** $n = -1\frac{1}{2}$ **19.** $n = 1\frac{1}{4}$ **21.** 14   **23.** 7
25. 0   **27.** $\{7\}$ **29.** $\{-5\}$ **31.** $\{0\}$

4. Solving Equations by Using Division or Multiplication Postulates (*pages 162–163*)

1. $\{5\}$ **3.** $\{-3\}$ **5.** $\{-7\}$ **7.** $\{-2\frac{1}{2}\}$ **9.** $\{-5\}$ **11.** $\{7\}$ **13.** $\{-18\}$
15. $\{18\}$ **17.** $\{-50\}$ **19.** $\{-18\}$ **21.** $\{-5.4\}$ **23.** $\{-1\}$ **25.** $\{-\frac{1}{3}\}$
27. $\{-45\}$ **29.** $\{-6\}$ **31.** 8   **33.** 120   **35.** 3   **37.** $\{-5\}$ **39.** $\{-100\}$
41. $\{-2\frac{1}{2}\}$

5. Writing Verbal Sentences as Equations (*pages 164–165*)

1. Eight times a number x equals 56.
3. A number s decreased by 5 equals 15.
5. A number x divided by 4 equals .8.
7. Negative five times a number y decreased by .7 equals 28.

9. One-half of a number c increased by $\frac{1}{2}$ equals 0.
11. a **13.** d **15.** c **17.** a **19.** $n - 4 = 32$ **21.** $2n - 5 = 25$
23. $5n - 9 = 31$ **25.** $3n + 12 = 2n + (-24)$ **27.** $n + 2n = -45$
29. $\frac{1}{2}n + 8 = n - 4$

6. Solving Problems by Using Variables and Equations (*pages 167–168*)

1. 56 **3.** 15 **5.** 52 **7.** 9 **9.** 18 **11.** 14 **13.** 50 **15.** 400 **17.** 30
19. 11 **21.** $2445 **23.** 12 ft. **25.** 30 km **27.** 5 **29.** 17.5 ft.
31. $119\frac{1}{2}$ lb. **33.** 80 km **35.** $60

7. Solving Equations by Combining Like Terms (*page 170*)

1. $a = 12\frac{1}{2}$ **3.** $b = 12$ **5.** $x = 3$ **7.** $d = -4$ **9.** $y = 7$ **11.** $x = 24$
13. 64 and 32 **15.** 28 and 56
17. Bob earned $18; Dan earned $6.
19. Carl received $19.50; Richard received $13.00.
21. Larry's height is 192 cm; Sam's height is 168 cm.

8. Solving Equations by Using Several Operations (*pages 172–173*)

1. $x = 4$ **3.** $y = 2$ **5.** $t = -6$ **7.** $x = 14$ **9.** $x = -9$ **11.** $x = -1$ **13.** $x = 2\frac{1}{2}$
15. $y = -\frac{1}{2}$ **17.** $c = -6$ **19.** $m = 33$ **21.** $r = -25$ **23.** $c = -20$ **25.** $x = -4$
27. $x = -2$ **29.** $x = 8$ **31.** $x = 10$ **33.** $x = 2$ **35.** $\{-4\}$ **37.** $\{108\}$
39. $\{4\}$ **41.** 8 **43.** 40 **45.** 20.5 **47.** Frank worked 22 hours; Jeff
worked 67 hours.

9. Solving Equations Which Have the Variable in Both Members (*page 175*)

1. $x = 2$ **3.** $c = \frac{2}{3}$ **5.** $x = -9$ **7.** $c = 1$ **9.** $m = 40$ **11.** $y = \frac{1}{3}$ **13.** $x = 96$
15. $x = 36$ **17.** $m = -50$ **19.** $r = 10$ **21.** $s = 5$ **23.** $x = 0$ **25.** $z = \frac{1}{4}$
27. $d = -90$ **29.** $m = -\frac{1}{2}$ **31.** $c = 8$ **33.** $y = 2\frac{1}{2}$ **35.** $n = -10$ **37.** $a = \frac{1}{5}$
39. $x = -12$ **41.** $c = 10$ **43.** $d = -13$ **45.** $z = -1$ **47.** 8 **49.** 22 **51.** 5
53. -8

10. Solving Equations Containing Parentheses (*pages 177–178*)

1. $x = 13$ **3.** $y = 10$ **5.** $x = -\frac{3}{5}$ **7.** $x = -13$ **9.** $y = 19$ **11.** $c = 4$
13. $c = -2$ **15.** $a = -17$ **17.** $x = 9$ **19.** $w = 5$ **21.** $z = \frac{6}{7}$ **23.** $a = 2$
25. $m = 2\frac{1}{3}$ **27.** $v = 3$ **29.** $t = 6$ **31.** $d = 6$ **33.** $x = -\frac{1}{2}$ **35.** $x = -8$
37. $y = 3$ **39.** $r = -5\frac{2}{3}$ **41.** $\{-12\}$ **43.** $\{-4\}$ **45.** $\{-1\}$ **47.** 20 and 18

11. Solving Equations Involving Absolute Values (*page 181*)

1. $y = 7, y = -7$ **3.** $t + 6 = 8, t + 6 = -8$ **5.** $3c + 8 = 29, 3c + 8 = -29$
7. $\dfrac{2c}{3} = 6, \dfrac{2c}{3} = -6$ **9.** $\{14, -14\}$ **11.** $\{12, -12\}$ **13.** $\{9\frac{1}{2}, -25\frac{1}{2}\}$

15. $\{15, -17\}$ **17.** $\{5\frac{1}{2}, -6\frac{1}{2}\}$ **19.** $\{9, -8\frac{1}{2}\}$ **21.** $\{20, -20\}$ **23.** $\{48, -48\}$
25. $\{3, -6\}$ **27.** $\{6, -12\}$ **29.** $\{1, -3\}$ **31.** $\{1\frac{2}{3}, -\frac{1}{3}\}$ **33.** $\{2, -3\}$ **35.** $\emptyset$

12. Solving Equations Containing More Than One Variable (*page 183*)

1. $x = \dfrac{b}{5}$ **3.** $y = \dfrac{s}{r}$ **5.** $x = 7 - a$ **7.** $x = r + 2$ **9.** $x = d + c$ **11.** $x = 9b$

13. $x = \dfrac{c + 5}{b}$ **15.** $y = \dfrac{t - s}{r}$ **17.** $x = s$ **19.** $x = 6a$ **21.** $x = 2a$

13. Properties of Inequalities (*pages 185–186*)

1. $>$ **3.** $>$ **5.** $>$ **7.** $<$ **9.** $>$ **11.** $>$ **13.** $<$ **15.** $>, >$ **17.** $>, >$
19. $>, >$ **21.** $<$ **23.** $<$
25. 1. Order property of number 2. Multiplication property of inequalities
3. Multiplication property of zero 4. Multiplication property of inequalities
5. Multiplication property of zero

14. Finding the Solution Sets of Inequalities Containing One Variable (*pages 189–190*)

1. $\{x \mid x > 6\}$ **3.** $\{y \mid y > 2\frac{1}{2}\}$ **5.** $\{w \mid w < 7\}$ **7.** $\{d \mid d > 2\frac{3}{4}\}$
9. $\{c \mid c < -4\}$ **11.** $\{d \mid d \geq 3\}$ **13.** $\{s \mid s > -2\}$ **15.** $\{y \mid y \geq 5\}$
17. $\{h \mid h \geq -2\frac{1}{2}\}$ **19.** $\{y \mid y > -4\}$ **21.** $\{x \mid x \leq -2\frac{1}{2}\}$ **23.** $\{y \mid y < -6\}$
25. $\{x \mid x > 2\}$ **27.** $\{z \mid z \geq 2\}$ **29.** $\{y \mid y \geq -10\}$ **31.** $\{x \mid x > 3\}$
33. $\{x \mid x > -6\}$ **35.** $\{y \mid y \geq -1\}$ **37.** $\{c \mid c > -2\}$ **39.** $\{h \mid h \geq 3\frac{1}{2}\}$
41. $\{y \mid y \leq 5\frac{3}{5}\}$ **43.** $\{x \mid x > 6\}$ **45.** $\{x \mid x \leq -3\}$ **47.** $\{c \mid c \leq -27\}$
49. $\{x \mid x > 5\}$ **51.** $\{x \mid x > 3\}$ **53.** $\{r \mid r > -2\}$ **55.** $\{x \mid x \geq -2\}$
57. $\{y \mid y \geq -4\}$ **59.** conditional **61.** absolute **63.** absolute
65. $\{x \mid x > 40\}$ **67.** $\{x \mid x < 21\}$ **69.** $\emptyset$; the inequality implies $5 < 0$.
71. $\{x \mid x$ is a real number not equal to zero$\}$

Chapter 8

1. Number Problems

Preparing to Solve Number Problems (*pages 191–192*)

1. $2(x + 8)$ **3.** $12 - 3x$ **5.** $5(2x - 3)$ **7.** $2(3x + 4)$ **9.** $10(2x - 10)$
11. a. $10 - x$ b. $25 - x$ c. $36 - x$ d. $50 - x$ e. $100 - x$ f. $3000 - x$
13. a. $5 - l$ b. $12 - l$ c. $20 - l$ d. $40 - l$ e. $75 - l$ f. $1000 - l$

Solving Number Problems (*pages 193–194*)

1. 6 **3.** 7 **5.** 7 **7.** 32 and 56 **9.** 12 and 33 **11.** 42 and 54 **13.** 7
15. 75 **17.** 19, 18 and 31

2. Consecutive Integer Problems

Preparing to Solve Consecutive Integer Problems (*pages 195-196*)

1. a. 15, 16, 17, 18   b. 31, 32, 33, 34   c. $-10, -9, -8, -7$ d. $-2, -1, 0, 1$
e. $y, y + 1, y + 2, y + 3$ f. $2y + 1, 2y + 2, 2y + 3, 2y + 4$ g. $3y - 2, 3y - 1,$
$3y, 3y + 1$ 3. a. 9, 11, 13, 15   b. 35, 37, 39, 41   c. $-15, -13, -11, -9$
d. $-3, -1, 1, 3$ e. $y, y + 2, y + 4, y + 6$ f. $2y + 1, 2y + 3, 2y + 5, 2y + 7$
g. $2y - 1, 2y + 1, 2y + 3, 2y + 5$ 5. $2x + 7, 2x + 9$ 7. {even integers}
9. {even integers}   11. {integers}   13. even   15. even

Solving Consecutive Integer Problems (*pages 197-198*)

1. a. 30, 31   b. 17, 18   c. 45, 46   d. 62, 63   e. $-9, -8$ f. $-41, -40$
3. 57, 58, 59, 60   5. a. 9, 11, 13   b. 13, 15, 17   c. 51, 53, 55   d. 203,
205, 207   e. $-11, -9, -7$ f. $-37, -35, -33$ 7. 19, 20, 21   9. 14, 15, 16
11. 19, 20   13. 22, 24, 26   15. no   17. none

3. Motion Problems

Preparing to Solve Motion Problems (*pages 200-201*)

1. a. 400 km   b. 280 km   c. $80x$ km   d. $(160x + 80)$ km   e. $(800 - 80x)$ km
3. a. 1000 km/h   b. 600 km/h   c. $\dfrac{4000}{x}$ km/h   d. $\dfrac{4000}{x + 40}$ km/h
e. $\dfrac{4000}{x - 50}$ km/h   5. a. $60x$ km   b. $80x$ km   c. $140x$ km
d. $60x + 80x = 140$ km   7. a. $(x + 1)$ hr.   b. $40(x + 1)$ mi.   c. $50x$ mi.
d. $40(x + 1) = 50x$ 9. a. $40x$ b. $\dfrac{x}{40}$ c. $\dfrac{x}{2}$ d. $50(x + 2)$ e. $\dfrac{150}{x + 1}$
f. $\dfrac{200}{x + 10}$

Solving Motion Problems (*pages 206-208*)

1. 5 hr.   3. $2\frac{1}{2}$ hr.   5. 100 mi.   7. 440 km/h, 880 km/h   9. 45 mph, 60 mph
11. 8P.M.   13. 9:30A.M.   15. 56 mph   17. 12 km   19. 900 km

4. Coin Problems

Preparing to Solve Coin Problems (*pages 208-209*)

1. a. 30 cents   b. 50 cents   c. $5x$ cents   d. $15x$ cents   e. $5x + 15$ cents
f. $10x - 5$ cents   3. a. 150 cents   b. 325 cents   c. $25q$ cents   d. $125q$ cents
e. $25q + 125$ cents   f. $50q - 75$ cents   5. a. 400 cents   b. 1300 cents
c. 550 cents   d. 875 cents   e. 1925 cents   f. 728 cents

Solving Coin Problems (*page 211*)

1. 8 quarters, 2 dimes   3. 7 quarters, 3 dimes   5. 17 quarters, 8 dimes
7. 100 2-cent stamps, 90 10-cent stamps, 50 13-cent stamps

9. 20 2-cent stamps, 60 10-cent stamps   **11.** 10 quarters, 5 dimes, 2 nickels
13. no

5. Percent and Percentage Problems (*pages 214–215*)

1. .72   **3.** 33.6   **5.** 10   **7.** 16   **9.** 6   **11.** 52.5   **13.** 200   **15.** 4.8   **17.** 72
19. 160   **21.** 62   **23.** 50%   **25.** 60%   **27.** $33\frac{1}{3}$%   **29.** 100%   **31.** $\frac{1}{2}$%
33. $517.50   **35.** 52,464   **37.** $60   **39.** $78   **41.** 1600   **43.** 8%   **45.** $7\frac{3}{7}$%

6. Mixture Problems

Preparing to Solve Mixture Problems (*page 216*)

1. a. $1.90   **b.** $9.50   **c.** 95x cents   **d.** 190x cents   **e.** 95(x + 5) cents
f. 95(20 − x) cents   **3. a.** 3100   **b.** 250x + 300(x + 2) = 550x + 600
c. 75x + 65(50 − x) = 10x + 3250   **d.** 350(40) + 250x = 14,000 + 250x

Solving Mixture Problems (*pages 218–219*)

1. 20 lb. of 90-cent nuts, 10 lb. of 75-cent nuts   **3.** 60 lb. of 70-cent candy,
40 lb. of 95-cent candy   **5.** 40 lb. of $1.20 tea, 30 lb. of $1.90 tea
7. a. 8,670 students, 170 faculty   **b.** 40%   **9.** 36   **11.** 125

7. Percent Mixture Problems

Preparing to Solve Percent Mixture Problems (*pages 219–220*)

1. a. 40 lb.   **b.** 24 lb.   **c.** 4.8 lb.   **d.** .4x lb.   **e.** .4(x − 2) lb.   **3. a.** 12 oz.
b. (1) 12 + x oz. (2) 60 + x oz.

Solving Percent Mixture Problems (*pages 221–222*)

1. 20 g of 30% acid, 40 g of 60% acid   **3.** 20 kg   **5.** $2\frac{1}{2}$ g   **7.** 4 g   **9.** 60 kg
11. 10 g

8. Investment Problems

Preparing to Solve Investment Problems (*pages 222–223*)

1. a. $30   **b.** $125   **c.** $.05x   **d.** $.15x   **e.** $.05(x + 500)   **f.** $.05(5000 − x)
3. a. $785   **b.** $507.50   **c.** $480 + .08x   **d.** $.29x   **e.** $.06x + .07(x + 2000)
f. $.05x + .1(8000 − x)   **5. a.** $9000 − x   **b.** $.05x   **c.** $.1(9000 − x)
d. .05x = .1(9000 − x)

Solving Investment Problems (*pages 225–226*)

1. $1000 at 8%, $2000 at 5%   **3.** $500 at 11%, $350 at 6%   **5.** $2000 at 6%,
$5000 at 10%   **7.** $4000 at 6%, $3500 at 10%   **9.** $1500 at 6%, $900 at 10%
11. $8000 at 8%, $10,000 at 10%   **13.** $3000

9. Age Problems

Preparing to Solve Age Problems (*page 226*)

Note: All answers are in years.

1. $x + 10$ **3.** $5y - 4$ **5.** $23 - x$ **7.** $x - y$ **9.** $3x - 1$
11. a. Gloria will be $3x + 6$; Marie will be $x + 6$.
b. Gloria was $3x - 3$; Marie was $x - 3$.

Solving Age Problems (*pages 228–229*)

1. Father is 24; son is 4.   **3.** Father is 40; son is 16.   **5.** Father is 60; son is 20.
7. 2   **9.** 15   **11.** Sanford is 66; Fox is 22.   **13.** Wilbur is 17;   Fred is 3.

10. Perimeter Problems

Preparing to Solve Perimeter Problems (*pages 230–232*)

1. a. $7x + 2$ **b.** $8x - 10$ **c.** $7x + 2$ **d.** $12x - 8$

Solving Perimeter Problems (*pages 230–232*)

1. 16 cm, 64 cm, 64 cm   **3.** Length is 9 m; width is 3 m.   **5.** Width is 16 in.;
length is 20 in.   **7.** 8 cm, 20 cm, 12 cm   **9.** Width is $39\frac{1}{2}$ in.; length is $44\frac{1}{2}$ in.
11. Width is 36 ft.; length is 78 ft.   **13.** Width is 5 in.; length is 16 in.
15. Width is 6 ft.; length is 10 ft.   **17.** 100%

11. Area Problems

Preparing to Solve Area Problems (*pages 232–233*)

1. a. $7x$ **b.** $5(x + 2)$ **c.** $10(2x - 3)$ **d.** $x(x - 1)$ **e.** $x(x + 5)$
f. $(x + 3)(x + 2)$ **3.** $x(x + 10)$ **5.** $x(3x + 2)$ **7. a.** Width is x; length is $x + 2$.
b. Width is $x - 3$; length is $x + 8$.   **c.** $x(x + 2)$ **d.** $(x - 3)(x + 8)$
e. $x(x + 2) = (x - 3)(x + 8)$ **f.** $(x - 3)(x + 8) = x(x + 2) + 6$

Solving Area Problems (*pages 235–236*)

1. Width is 4 cm; length is 12 cm.   **3.** 6 in.   **5.** Width is 4 in.; length is 6 in.
7. Altitude is 8; base is 11.   **9.** Length is 48; width is 10.

12. Lever Problems (*pages 237–238*)

1. 111 lb.   **3.** 40 kg   **5.** 7 ft. from Fred, 5 ft. from Jack
7. $\frac{1}{2}$ m from the object

13. Miscellaneous Problems (*pages 239–240*)

1. 14 women, 22 men   **3.** 2 km by James, 6 km by John, 7 km by Tom
5. 20 km   **7.** House cost $37,200; interior cost $6,000; exterior cost $3,000.
9. $450   **11.** $50

14. Solving Verbal Problems by Using Inequalities (*page 242*)

1. $\{x \mid x < 14\}$ 3. Sue < 20; Carol < 60.   5. \$450   7. \$25   9. 97
11. 280 adults, 80 children   13. 24 and 26

Chapter 9

1. Understanding the Meaning of Factoring (*page 245*)

1. $2, 3, 5, 7$ 3. $23, 29$ 5. $5 \cdot 7$ 7. $2^2 \cdot 3^3$ 9. 2^7 11. $2 \cdot 101$
13. $2 \cdot 5 \cdot 59$ 15. $1, 2, 13, 26$ 17. $1, 2, 3, 4, 6, 9, 12, 18, 36$
19. $1, 2, 4, 5, 10, 20, 25, 50, 100$ 21. a. 72   b. 18   c. 8   d. 4   e. 3
23. 5   25. 7   27. 25   29. 8   31. 4   33. 2   35. $5x$ 37. $9xy^2z$ 39. $6ac^2$

2. Factoring Polynomials Whose Terms Have a Common Monomial Factor (*page 248*)

1. $2(a + b)$ 3. $b(x + y)$ 5. $4(x + 2y)$ 7. $5(3c - 2d)$ 9. $4(2x - 3)$
11. $4(2 - y)$ 13. $x(2x + 5)$ 15. $x(32 + x)$ 17. $a(x - 5b)$ 19. $5x(2 - 3x^2)$
21. $\frac{1}{2}h(b + c)$ 23. $\pi r(r + 2h)$ 25. $3(a^2 - 3)$ 27. $5xy(2 - 3xy)$
29. $3(x^2 - 2x - 10)$ 31. $c(c^2 - c + 2)$ 33. $3a(3b^2 - 2b - 1)$
35. $4a^2b^2c^2(2a^2c + 3)$ 37. $x^n(x^{4n} + 1)$ 39. $w^n(w^{2n} - z)$ 41. $y^{2a}(y - 1)$
43. $x^n(x^2 + x + 1)$ 45. $x(x^{2n} + x^n + 5)$ 47. $(m - n)(c + d)$ 49. $(t - s)(c - d)$
51. 1900   53. 100   55. 28

3. Squaring a Monomial (*pages 249–250*)

1. a^4 3. d^{10} 5. m^4n^4 7. $25y^8$ 9. $100x^4y^4$ 11. $\frac{9}{16}a^2$ 13. $\frac{49}{64}a^4b^4$
15. $\dfrac{x^2}{36}$ 17. $.64x^2$ 19. $.01x^2y^2$ 21. x^{2a} 23. $c^{2x}d^{4y}$ 25. a. $16x^2$
b. $100y^2$ c. $\frac{4}{9}x^2$ d. $2.25x^2$

4. Multiplying the Sum and Difference of Two Terms (*page 251*)

1. $x^2 - 64$ 3. $100 - a^2$ 5. $9x^2 - 1$ 7. $25r^2 - 49s^2$ 9. $a^2 - \frac{1}{4}$ 11. $r^2 - .25$
13. $r^6 - 4s^8$ 15. $a^4 - 625$ 17. $a^4 - b^4$ 19. $x^{2a} - 100$ 21. $a^{2n} - b^{4n}$
23. 396   25. 2491   27. 1596   29. 8096

5. Factoring the Difference of Two Squares (*pages 252–253*)

1. $(y)^2 - (8)^2$ 3. not a difference   5. $(3n)^2 - (4m)^2$ 7. $(p)^2 - (\frac{3}{5}q)^2$
9. y^9 is not a square.   11. $(c + 10)(c - 10)$ 13. $(12 + c)(12 - c)$
15. $(4a + b)(4a - b)$ 17. $(x^2 + 8)(x^2 - 8)$ 19. $(10x + 9y)(10x - 9y)$
21. $(rs + 12)(rs - 12)$ 23. $(s + \frac{1}{10})(s - \frac{1}{10})$ 25. $(7x + \frac{1}{3})(7x - \frac{1}{3})$
27. $\left(\dfrac{1}{3}r + \dfrac{8s}{11}\right)\left(\dfrac{1}{3}r - \dfrac{8s}{11}\right)$ 29. $(.2 + 7r)(.2 - 7r)$ 31. $(8ab + cd)(8ab - cd)$
33. $(5x^3 + 11y^5)(5x^3 - 11y^5)$ 35. $(a + b + c)(a + b - c)$
37. $(x^n + 10)(x^n - 10)$ 39. $(x^{2n} + y^n)(x^{2n} - y^n)$ 41. $(2x^n + 5y^n)(2x^n - 5y^n)$

6. Finding the Product of Two Binomials (*page 255*)

1. $x^2 + 8x + 15$ 3. $9 + 10m + m^2$ 5. $x^2 - 15x + 50$ 7. $z^2 - 8z + 16$
9. $x^2 + 5x - 14$ 11. $m^2 - 13m - 30$ 13. $45 - 4t - t^2$ 15. $3c^2 - 18c + 15$
17. $-7m^2 + 33m - 20$ 19. $10z^2 - 31z + 15$ 21. $25y^2 + 40y + 16$
23. $10c^2 + 11cd - 6d^2$ 25. $25a^2 + 70ab + 49b^2$ 27. $x^{2n} + 2x^n - 8$
29. $y^{4a} - 10y^{2a} + 21$ 31. a. $x^2 + 9x + 20$ b. $2x^2 + x - 3$

7. Factoring Trinomials of the Form $ax^2 + bx + c$ (*page 258*)

1. $(a + 2)(a + 1)$ 3. $(x + 7)(x + 1)$ 5. $(t + 5)(t + 2)$ 7. $(x + 9)(x + 3)$
9. $(a + 9)(a + 2)$ 11. $(16 + c)(1 + c)$ 13. $(z + 5)(z + 5)$ 15. $(x - 11)(x - 1)$
17. $(x - 10)(x - 1)$ 19. $(r - 9)(r - 2)$ 21. $(5 - y)(3 - y)$ 23. $(y - 9)(y - 4)$
25. $(x - 12)(x - 4)$ 27. $(z - 10)(z - 10)$ 29. $(x - 4)(x + 1)$
31. $(z - 13)(z + 1)$ 33. $(b - 4)(b + 2)$ 35. $(t + 3)(t - 2)$ 37. $(z + 12)(z - 3)$
39. $(x + 8)(x - 5)$ 41. $(x - 10)(x + 8)$ 43. $(3x + 1)(x + 3)$
45. $(2x + 3)(x + 4)$ 47. $(2y - 1)(y - 1)$ 49. $(3x + 1)(x - 2)$
51. $(5x - 8)(x + 1)$ 53. $(2x - 5)(2x - 1)$ 55. $(3x + 4)(2x - 1)$
57. $(10x - 1)(x + 5)$ 59. $(x + 2y)(x + y)$ 61. $(3a - b)(a - 2b)$
63. $(4x + 3y)(x - 2y)$ 65. $(a^3 - 7)(a^3 + 4)$ 67. $(x^a + 4)(x^a + 1)$
69. $(x^b - 5)(x^b + 3)$ 71. $(3x^a - 2)(x^a - 3)$

8. Squaring a Binomial (*pages 259–260*)

1. $x^2 + 18x + 81$ 3. $a^2 - 12a + 36$ 5. $4x^2 + 4x + 1$ 7. $16x^2 - 24x + 9$
9. $a^2 + 2ab + b^2$ 11. $4x^2 + 20xy + 25y^2$ 13. $4x^4 + 4x^2 + 1$
15. $25m^4 - 30m^2n + 9n^2$ 17. $a^{2x} + 10a^x + 25$ 19. $x^{4a} + 20x^{2a} + 100$
21. $900 + 2(30)(2) + 4 = 1024$ 23. $4900 + 2(70) + 1 = 5041$ 25. 441
27. 1024 29. 2809 31. $2\frac{1}{4}$ 33. $75\frac{1}{9}$

9. Factoring Perfect Square Trinomials (*page 261*)

1. yes   3. yes   5. yes   7. yes   9. no   11. no   13. $(x + 2)^2$ 15. $(a - 7)^2$
17. $(2x - 1)^2$ 19. not possible   21. $(4m - 7n)^2$ 23. $(10x - 7y)^2$
25. $(8x^2 + 3y)^2$ 27. $(y^{5m} + 2)^2$ 29. $(a - 8)^2$ 31. $[2 - 5(r - s)]^2$
33. $[2(c + d) + 3a]$ 35. a. $10r$ b. $(5r - 1)^2$ 37. a. $56xy$ b. $(7x + 4y)^2$
39. a. $220cd$ b. $(11c + 10d)^2$

10. Factoring by Grouping (*pages 262–263*)

1. $(y + 5)(y + w)$ 3. $(c + 4)(c + d)$ 5. $(x + y)(a + b)$ 7. $(r - s)(a - b)$
9. $(y - 2 + z)(y - 2 - z)$ 11. $(2x - 5y + w)(2x - 5y - w)$
13. $(a + b - 10)(a - b + 10)$ 15. $(7r + s + 7)(7r - s - 7)$
17. $(m - n)(x^{2a} + y^{2b})$ 19. $(x^a + y^b - 7)(x^a - y^b + 7)$

11. Factoring Completely (*page 264*)

1. $2(a + b)(a - b)$ 3. $a(x + y)(x - y)$ 5. $2(x + 4)(x - 4)$
7. $2(3m + 2)(3m - 2)$ 9. $7(3c + 1)(3c - 1)$ 11. $a(2a + b)(2a - b)$
13. $4(a + 3)(a - 3)$ 15. $\pi(R + r)(R - r)$ 17. $a(x + 2)(x + 1)$

19. $4(r - 4)(r + 3)$ **21.** $2a(x - 3)(x + 2)$ **23.** $z^2(z^2 + 1)(z + 1)(z - 1)$
25. $(x^2 + 2)(x + 1)(x - 1)$ **27.** $(y + 3)(y - 3)(y + 2)(y - 2)$
29. $y^{3a}(y + 1)(y - 1)$ **31.** $2(x^a - 1)(x^a - 1)$ **33.** $x^n(x + 6)(x - 3)$
35. $(m - n)(x + 2)(x - 2)$ **37.** $3(2c + d - 2e)(2c - d + 2e)$

Chapter 10

1. The Meaning of an Algebraic Fraction (*page 266*)

1. $\dfrac{x}{7}$ **3.** $\dfrac{15}{y - 3}$, $y = 3$ **5.** $\dfrac{5y + 3}{3y + 1}$, $y = -\frac{1}{3}$ **7.** $x = 0$ **9.** $y = 0$ **11.** $y = -2$

13. $y = -\frac{1}{2}$ **15.** $\dfrac{y}{39}$ **17.** $\dfrac{4x + 9}{x + 1}$ dollars   **19.** $\dfrac{d}{r}$ **21.** $\dfrac{x}{90}$

2. Reducing Fractions to Lowest Terms (*pages 269–270*)

1. $\frac{1}{3}$ **3.** $\dfrac{2c}{3d}$ **5.** $\dfrac{a}{c}$ **7.** $\frac{4}{7}$ **9.** $\dfrac{1}{5x}$ **11.** $\dfrac{3a^3}{4y}$ **13.** $-\dfrac{3ab}{2c}$ **15.** $-\frac{2}{3}$ **17.** $\frac{5}{7}$

19. $\dfrac{m}{n}$ **21.** $\dfrac{a + b}{4x}$ **23.** $\frac{2}{3}$ **25.** $\dfrac{a}{d}$ **27.** $\dfrac{x + 2}{x - 2}$ **29.** $5 + 2x$ **31.** -1

33. $-\dfrac{x + y}{3}$ **35.** $\dfrac{1}{x + 1}$ **37.** $\dfrac{x}{x - 1}$ **39.** $\dfrac{2(x - 5)}{x + 3}$ **41.** $\dfrac{12 - x}{x - 3}$ **43.** $\dfrac{3x - 6}{x + 2}$

45. $\dfrac{2(3c - 4d)}{2c - 3d}$ **47.** $\dfrac{2(5x + y)}{a + b}$

49. No; a is not a factor of the numerator and denominator.
51. No; d is not a factor of the denominator.
53. No; x and y are not factors of the numerator and denominator.

3. Multiplying Fractions (*pages 272–273*)

1. $\frac{21}{40}$ **3.** 12 **5.** $5d$ **7.** $\dfrac{5x^2}{9}$ **9.** $\dfrac{8}{mn}$ **11.** $\frac{6}{5}$ **13.** $\dfrac{y}{x}$ **15.** $\dfrac{2}{s}$

17. $\dfrac{2}{3(x - 2)}$ **19.** $\dfrac{5y}{x(x + y)}$ **21.** $a + 3$ **23.** $-\dfrac{4b^2(a - 2)}{a + 2}$ **25.** $\dfrac{y - 3}{c}$

27. $\dfrac{x + 5}{2x - 3}$ **29.** $\dfrac{1}{5x}$ **31.** -2 **33.** $\dfrac{y + 7}{y - 1}$ **35.** $-\dfrac{(x + 1)(5x + 2)}{3x(3x - 2)}$ **37.** 1

39. $\dfrac{3}{5x}$

4. Dividing Fractions (*page 275*)

1. $\frac{1}{6}$ **3.** $\frac{1}{3}$ **5.** $\dfrac{acd^2}{4b}$ **7.** $\dfrac{s^2}{3}$ **9.** $\dfrac{3(y + 5)}{2}$ **11.** $2y(x + 6)$ **13.** $\dfrac{3(m + 1)}{2}$

15. $y + 2$ **17.** $\dfrac{x - 2}{28x}$ **19.** $2(y - 3)$ **21.** 1 **23.** $\frac{1}{2}$ **25.** $\dfrac{x - y}{x + 2y}$

5. Adding or Subtracting Fractions Which Have the Same Denominator (*pages 277–278*)

1. $\frac{5}{8}$ 3. $\frac{1}{2}$ 5. $\frac{5}{2c}$ 7. $\frac{x-y+z}{2}$ 9. $\frac{a+b-2c}{n}$ 11. $\frac{7c}{3d}$ 13. $\frac{8}{x+2}$

15. $\frac{1}{y+2}$ 17. $\frac{2x-1}{6}$ 19. 1 21. $\frac{1}{x-1}$ 23. $x-y$ 25. $\frac{2}{a+b}$

27. $\frac{2}{a-b}$ 29. $\frac{2m-1}{m+2}$

6. Adding or Subtracting Fractions Which Have Different Denominators (*pages 282–284*)

1. 10 3. $6a$ 5. rs 7. xyz 9. $36x^2y^2$ 11. $(x+3)(x-3)$

13. $12(c+3)$ 15. $3(x+1)(x-1)$ 17. $\frac{9}{15}, \frac{20}{15}$ 19. $\frac{10y}{6}, \frac{7y}{6}$

21. $\frac{10y}{6c}, \frac{7y}{6c}$ 23. $\frac{ab}{bcd}, \frac{md}{bcd}$ 25. $\frac{2(a-6)}{4}, \frac{2a+5}{4}$ 27. $\frac{18(5x-4)}{360y},$

$\frac{5(3x+7)}{360y}$ 29. $\frac{2(5m-1)}{6(m-2)}, \frac{24}{6(m-2)}$ 31. $\frac{4(y+2)}{y(y+2)}, \frac{y(y-1)}{y(y+2)}$ 33. $\frac{-7}{3a-1},$

$\frac{2}{3a-1}$ 35. $\frac{5}{8}$ 37. $\frac{17x}{10}$ 39. $\frac{31x}{20}$ 41. $\frac{39y}{40}$ 43. $\frac{3c-10d}{15}$ 45. $\frac{15}{4x}$

47. $\frac{23x}{6d}$ 49. $-\frac{5r}{12s}$ 51. $\frac{yz+xz+xy}{xyz}$ 53. $\frac{bx+ay}{a^2b^2}$ 55. $\frac{2c-3a}{abc}$

57. $\frac{2cx-3ay}{6abc}$ 59. $\frac{2-3y+7y^2}{y^3}$ 61. $\frac{3y+1}{8}$ 63. $\frac{44-x}{15}$ 65. $\frac{7y-6}{20}$

67. $\frac{a-5b}{12}$ 69. $\frac{50x^2+10x-13}{20x}$ 71. $\frac{12y^2-17y-12}{12y^2}$ 73. $\frac{4a+7}{2}$

75. $\frac{26x+9}{5}$ 77. $\frac{-12x^2-8x+21y}{12x}$ 79. $\frac{ab^2-7a^2-a^2b+6ab-3b^2}{a^2b^2}$

81. $\frac{-7ab-8ab^2+6b+45a}{36a^2b^2}$ 83. $\frac{29}{6(x-2)}$ 85. $-\frac{2}{2x-3y}$ 87. $\frac{11x+23}{12(2x-1)}$

89. $\frac{26-3a}{(a+3)(2-a)}$ 91. $\frac{7c-16}{c(c+8)}$ 93. $\frac{3y+14}{(y+3)(y-3)}$ 95. $\frac{-x+24}{3(x+6)(x-6)}$

97. $\frac{2y^2+11y-30}{3(y-3)(y+4)}$ 99. $\frac{9a^2+7a+5}{(a-1)(a+3)(a+2)}$ 101. $\frac{x^2+xy-2y^2-18x+3y}{3(x+4y)(x-y)}$

103. $\frac{-x}{(3x-1)(2x-1)}$ 105. $\frac{2}{(3b+1)(3b-2)}$

7. Mixed Expressions (*page 285*)

1. $\frac{17}{3}$ 3. $\frac{5x+1}{4}$ 5. $\frac{m^2+1}{m}$ 7. $\frac{7b+7c+2a}{b+c}$ 9. $\frac{s^2-s-1}{s-1}$ 11. $\frac{9c-22}{c-3}$

13. $\frac{a^2+2a+2}{a+1}$ 15. $\frac{2x^2+3x-7}{x+2}$

8. Multiplying and Dividing Mixed Expressions (*page 286*)

1. $\dfrac{m^2 - 16n^2}{n^2}$ **3.** $\dfrac{3(x - 3y)}{y}$ **5.** $\dfrac{21}{-(3b - 1)}$ **7.** $-2a$ **9.** $\dfrac{a^2 + 1}{a + 3}$

9. Simplifying Complex Fractions (*pages 289–290*)

1. $\frac{7}{18}$ **3.** $\frac{5}{2}$ **5.** $\dfrac{1}{nm^2}$ **7.** $\dfrac{a^2}{x + 3y}$ **9.** $\dfrac{c}{c + 5}$ **11.** $\dfrac{y^2 + x^2}{4xy}$ **13.** $\dfrac{-18}{3a + 1}$

15. $\dfrac{(y - 5)(y - 2)}{(y - 6)(y + 2)}$ **17.** $\dfrac{(d + c)(d + c)}{d(d + 3c)}$ **19.** $\dfrac{y^2 + 2y - 3}{2y + 10}$ **21.** $\frac{3}{5}$

23. $\dfrac{(y + 1)(y + 1)}{y(2y + 1)}$ **25.** $\dfrac{1}{y}$ **27.** $\dfrac{y}{x}$ **29.** $\dfrac{x^3}{x^2 + 1}$

10. Studying the Changes in the Value of a Fraction (*pages 291–292*)

1. decreases **3.** decreases **5.** decreases **7.** increases **9.** decreases

11. a. increases **b.** decreases **13.** $\dfrac{x}{y}$ **15.** d **17.** b

Chapter 11

1. Solving Equations Containing Fractional Coefficients or Fractional Constants (*page 295*)

1. $x = 21$ **3.** $x = 25$ **5.** $x = 16$ **7.** $r = -13$ **9.** $x = 4$ **11.** $y = 8$
13. $c = 20$ **15.** $m = -27$ **17.** $x = 21$ **19.** $r = 12$ **21.** $y = 6$ **23.** $s = -75$
25. $y = 1$ **27.** $x = 18$ **29.** $y = 12$ **31.** $v = 2$ **33.** $s = 5$ **35.** $m = 3$
37. $c = 17$ **39.** 60 **41.** $3\frac{1}{2}$

2. Solving Equations Containing Decimals (*page 297*)

1. $x = .3$ **3.** $m = -8$ **5.** $c = 20$ **7.** $t = .03$ **9.** $x = 2$ **11.** $c = 20$
13. $y = 1.3$ **15.** $m = 12$ **17.** $x = 180$ **19.** $x = -20$ **21.** $x = 1500$
23. $x = 40$ **25.** $x = 3000$ **27.** -180

3. Solving Inequalities Containing Fractional Coefficients (*pages 298–299*)

1. $x > 9$ **3.** $c > 6$ **5.** $y \geq 12$ **7.** $t \geq -40$ **9.** $x > 4\frac{4}{9}$ **11.** $x > 11\frac{1}{3}$
13. $d < 1$ **15.** $m \geq 3$ **17.** $x > 2$ **19.** $r \leq 9\frac{1}{2}$

4. Solving Fractional Equations (*page 302*)

1. $x = 2$ **3.** $x = \frac{1}{2}$ **5.** $x = 3$ **7.** $y = -7$ **9.** $x = 2$ **11.** $c = \frac{1}{2}$ **13.** $x = 3$
15. $y = 3$ **17.** $a = 4$ **19.** $x = 1$ **21.** $x = 3$ **23.** $a = -\frac{1}{3}$ **25.** $a = -10$
27. $x = \frac{1}{2}$ **29.** $x = 3$ **31.** $x = -6$ **33.** $y = 6$ **35.** $a = 2\frac{1}{2}$

5. Solving More Difficult Equations Involving Several Variables
(*pages 304–305*)

Note: Where the denominator involves a variable, it cannot equal zero.

1. $x = 5t$　**3.** $x = 3ab$　**5.** $x = 2d + 2c$　**7.** $y = \dfrac{2b}{3}$　**9.** $x = \dfrac{ab}{c}$　**11.** $x = \dfrac{dr - cr}{m}$

13. $x = \dfrac{5}{a}$　**15.** $x = 13c$　**17.** $x = \dfrac{a + b}{c}$　**19.** $y = 12b$　**21.** $y = 18a^3$

23. $y = \dfrac{c - r}{s}$　**25.** $x = 4$　**27.** $x = c + d$　**29.** $x = 2c$　**31.** $x = \dfrac{cd}{c + d}$

33. $x = \dfrac{2ab}{a - b}$　**35.** $x = r - s$

6. Solving Number Problems Involving Fractions (*pages 306–307*)

1. 6 and 18　**3.** 25　**5.** $\frac{20}{50}$　**7.** 29　**9.** 6 and 31　**11.** $\frac{4}{11}$

7. Solving Average Problems Involving Fractions

Preparing to Solve Average Problems (*pages 307–308*)

1. 83　**3.** $\dfrac{2x + 3y}{5}$　**5.** $5x + 5y$

Solving Average Problems (*pages 308–309*)

1. 88　**3.** 140 lb.　**5.** 5 ft. 6 in.　**7.** 16, 33, 44　**9.** 90

8. Solving Motion Problems Involving Fractions (*page 311*)

1. 3 mph
3. James's rate is $342\frac{6}{7}$ mph; Kenton's is $502\frac{6}{7}$ mph.
5. Freight train's rate is 60 km/h; passenger train's is 120 km/h.
7. 30 mph

9. Solving Work Problems Involving Fractions

Preparing to Solve Work Problems (*pages 312–313*)

1. a. (1) $\frac{1}{80}$　(2) $\dfrac{x}{80}$　**b.** (1) $\frac{1}{120}$　(2) $\dfrac{x}{120}$　**c.** $\dfrac{x}{80} + \dfrac{x}{120}$　**d.** 1

e. $\dfrac{x}{80} + \dfrac{x}{120} = 1$　**3. a.** $\frac{1}{4} - \frac{1}{6}$　**b.** $\dfrac{x}{4} - \dfrac{x}{6}$　**c.** $\dfrac{x}{4} - \dfrac{x}{6} = 1$

Solving Work Problems (*pages 316–317*)

1. 4　**3.** 4 min.　**5.** 12　**7.** 12　**9.** 6　**11.** 2 hr.　**13.** $1\frac{1}{3}$

10. Solving Miscellaneous Problems Involving Fractions
(*pages 317-318*)

1. 60   **3.** $\frac{15}{40}$ **5.** $\frac{8}{24}$ **7.** $12,000   **9.** 36 years old   **11.** 18 years old
13. 40 liters of 3.8% fat; 60 liters of 2.8% fat   **15.** $26\frac{2}{3}$ gm   **17.** numerator, 20; denominator, 50   **19.** 18 nickels, 10 dimes

Chapter 12

1. Translating Verbal Sentences Into Formulas (*pages 320-321*)

1. $l = 10f$ **3.** $p = 2l + 2w$ **5.** $M = \dfrac{a+b+c}{3}$ **7.** $A = s^2$ **9.** $S = 6e^2$
11. $F = \frac{9}{5}C + 32$ **13.** $C = \frac{5}{9}(F - 32)$ **15.** $D = dQ + R$ **17.** $T = .08V$
19. $n = 2rs$ **21.** $c = 100m$ **23.** $n = 7w + 5$ **25.** $c = 50 + (n-1)t$
27. $D = 500 + .03(N - 25,000)$

2. Evaluating the Subject of a Formula (*pages 322-328*)

1. a. 26 ft.   **b.** 10 m   **c.** $19\frac{3}{4}$ ft.   **d.** $18\frac{1}{2}$ ft.   **3. a.** 28 in.   **b.** 16 cm
c. 14 m   **d.** 35 in.   **e.** $20\frac{1}{2}$ in.   **5. a.** 44 ft.   **b.** 22 m   **c.** 66 cm   **d.** $9\frac{3}{7}$ ft.
e. $31\frac{3}{7}$ in.   **7. a.** 80 sq. cm   **b.** 25.5 sq. yd.   **c.** 4000 sq. cm   **d.** 104 sq. ft.
9. a. 625 sq. in.   **b.** 1024 sq. ft.   **c.** 81 sq. cm   **d.** $6\frac{1}{4}$ sq. ft.   **e.** 37.21 sq. m
11. a. 68 sq. in.   **b.** 99 sq. in.   **c.** 10 sq. in.   **d.** 2.9 sq. m   **13. a.** 126 sq. cm
b. 318 sq. in.   **c.** 43.28 sq. m   **d.** $91\frac{3}{4}$ sq. in.   **15. a.** 2464 sq. cm
b. 154 sq. ft.   **c.** 1256 sq. m   **d.** 5024 sq. in.   **17. a.** 140 cu. ft.
b. 280 cu. cm   **c.** 214.2 cu. m   **d.** 105 cu. in.   **19. a.** $1437\frac{1}{3}$ cu. ft.
b. $53\frac{19}{81}$ cu. ft.   **c.** $4186\frac{2}{3}$ cu. cm   **d.** 113,040 cu. in.   **21. a.** 90   **b.** 60   **c.** 45
d. 36   **e.** 30   **23. a.** $672   **b.** $7,200   **c.** $1362.50   **d.** $4760   **25. a.** 68°
b. 32°   **c.** 105.8°   **d.** -4°   **e.** -16.6°   **27. a.** 420   **b.** 11.2   **c.** 50   **d.** -72
29. a. 100   **b.** 102.4   **31.** 6   **33.** 20   **35.** $A = 25$, $e = 5$ **37.** $C = 10$, $F = 50$

3. Evaluating a Formula by Solving an Equation (*page 329*)

1. 35   **3. a.** 6   **b.** 8   **5.** 8   **7.** 500   **9.** 6.4   **11.** 5   **13. a.** 41°   **b.** 50°
c. 170.6°   **15.** 14

4. Transforming Simple Formulas (*page 331*)

1. $h = \dfrac{A}{6}$ **3.** $t = \dfrac{D}{r}$ **5.** $h = \dfrac{V}{lw}$ **7.** $p = \dfrac{i}{rt}$ **9.** $B = \dfrac{400}{H}$ **11.** $H = \dfrac{3A}{B}$

13. $g = \dfrac{2S}{t^2}$ **15.** $A = \dfrac{90S}{\pi R^2}$ **17.** $c = l + s$ **19.** $C = \dfrac{5F - 160}{9}$ **21.** $a = \dfrac{2A - hb}{h}$

23. $R = \dfrac{E - Ir}{I}$ **25.** $a = \dfrac{P - b - c}{2}$ **27. a.** $h = \dfrac{2A}{b}$ **b.** 6   **29. a.** $L = \dfrac{P - 2W}{2}$

b. 19   **31.** $A = 4h^2$ **33.** $A = 9b^2$

5. Transforming More Difficult Formulas (*page 333*)

1. $t = \dfrac{s}{v}$ **3.** $A = \dfrac{L}{KV^2}$ **5.** $N = \dfrac{nP}{p}$ **7.** $d = \dfrac{D-r}{q}$ **9.** $n = \dfrac{2S}{a+l}$ **11.** $W = \dfrac{a}{6n+1}$

13. $r = \dfrac{E-IR}{I}$ **15.** $n = \dfrac{CR}{E-rC}$ **17.** $r = \dfrac{lS-a}{S-l}$ **19.** $a = \dfrac{2S}{t^2}$ **21. a.** $B = \dfrac{P}{r}$

b. 2000   **23. a.** $c = \dfrac{2A-hb}{h}$ **b.** 4   **25. a.** $F = \dfrac{gh}{g+h}$ **b.** $\frac{2}{9}$ **27.** $A = 25c^2$

6. Using Formulas to Study Related Changes (*pages 335–336*)

1. increases   **3.** increases   **5.** decreases   **7.** decreases   **9.** decreases
11. divided by 2   **13.** multiplied by 6   **15.** doubled   **17.** multiplied by 6
19. multiplied by 10   **21.** V is multiplied by 1000.

7. More Algebraic Representation (*pages 337–338*)

1. rt **3.** $kf + tm$ cents   **5.** $\dfrac{m}{8}$ dollars   **7.** $\dfrac{rz}{6}$ dollars   **9.** $\dfrac{P+S+T}{3}$ points

11. $\dfrac{k}{h}$ **13.** $\dfrac{W}{W+L}$ **15.** $\dfrac{x+y}{z}$

8. Writing Formulas for Areas (*pages 339–340*)

1. $A = bh$ **3.** $A = s^2$ **5.** $A = \pi r^2$ **7.** $A = mn + ab$ **9.** $A = 7x^2$
11. $A = ab - rs$ **13.** $A = \pi x^2 + \pi y^2$ **15.** $A = \pi R^2 - \pi a^2$ **17.** $A = 15r^2 - \pi r^2$
19. a. $2qp$ **b.** s^2 **c.** πq^2 **d.** $2qp - s^2 - \pi q^2$ **e.** 202 sq. in.

Chapter 13

1. Ordered Number Pairs and Points in a Plane (*pages 343–345*)

1. $A(2, 1)$, $B(-2, 1)$, $C(-2, -1)$, $D(-2, -2)$, $E(2, 0)$, $F(0, 1)$, $G(-1, 0)$, $H(0, -2)$,
$O(0, 0)$ **27.** I   **29.** II   **31.** I   **33.** $(0, -1)$ **35.** at the point, $(1, 0)$ **37.** 0
39. $(0, 0)$ **41. a.** I   **b.** IV   **c.** II   **d.** III   **43.** $x = 10, y = 15$
45. $x = 4, y = 6$ **47.** $x = 8, y = 9$ **49.** $x = y$

2. Finding Solution Sets of Open Sentences in Two Variables
(*pages 347–348*)

1. 6   **3.** 0   **5.** $2a$ **7.** $5\frac{1}{2}$ **9.** -4 **11.** 9   **13.** 4   **15.** $a + 4$ **17.** $5\frac{1}{4}$
19. -12 **21.** no   **23.** yes   **25.** yes   **27.** yes   **29.** yes   **31.** yes   **33.** yes
35. ϕ **37.** ϕ **39.** $\{(10, 2), (10, 6), (10, 10), (12, 2), (12, 6), (12, 10)\}$
41. $\{(x, y) \mid y = 6x\}$ **43.** $\{(x, y) \mid 3x + y = 11\}$ **45.** $\{(x, y) \mid y < 3x - 1\}$

3. Graphing a Linear Equation in Two Variables by Means of Its Solutions (*pages 350–352*)

1. a. no   b. no   c. yes   d. no   5. $y = x + 5$ 7. $y = 4x - 6$ 9. $y = -2x$
11. $y = -2x + 4$ 13. $y = -\frac{3}{2}x - 4$ 15. $y = -2; y = 1; y = 4$ 41. yes   43. no
45. 7   47. 6   49. -11 51. 7   53. -1 55. a. $y = 2x$ 57. a. $y = 3x - 4$
59. a. $2y - 3x = 6$

4. Graphing a Linear Equation in Two Variables by the Intercepts Method (*pages 353–354*)

1. x-intercept: 8; y-intercept: 8   3. x-intercept: -3; y-intercept: 12
5. x-intercept: -3; y-intercept: 4   9. x-intercept: 4; y-intercept: -12
11. x-intercept: 2; y-intercept: 6   13. x-intercept: 3; y-intercept: 2
15. x-intercept: 3; y-intercept: $-1\frac{1}{2}$

5. Graphing Lines Parallel to the X-Axis or the Y-Axis (*page 356*)

15. a. $y = 1$ b. $y = 5$ c. $y = -4$ d. $y = -8$ e. $y = -2.5$

6. The Slope of a Line (*pages 361–362*)

1. a. positive slope   b. no slope   c. slope of zero   d. negative slope
e. positive slope   f. negative slope   3. 1   5. -2 7. -1 9. 0   11. 0
13. yes   15. no

7. The Slope and Y-Intercept of a Line (*page 364*)

1. $m = 3$; y-intercept: 1   3. $m = \frac{1}{2}$; y-intercept: 5   5. $m = -2$; y-intercept: 3
7. $m = 0$; y-intercept: -2 9. $m = -2$; y-intercept: 5   11. $m = \frac{5}{2}$; y-intercept: -2
13. $m = \frac{3}{2}$; y-intercept: $2\frac{1}{4}$ 15. $m = \frac{5}{2}$; y-intercept: $2\frac{1}{2}$ 17. $y = -4x + 2$
19. $y = -2x + 4$ 21. $y = \frac{3}{5}x - 2$ 23. $y = -\frac{4}{3}x - \frac{1}{3}$ 25. $y = 2x; y = 2x + 1;$
$y = 2x + 2$; etc.   27. They have the same slope, 4.   29. They have the same
y-intercept, +1.   31. They are equal.   33. yes   35. yes

8. Graphing a Linear Equation in Two Variables by the Slope-Intercept Method (*pages 365–366*)

1. $m = 2$; y-intercept: 3   3. $m = 1$; y-intercept: -2 5. $m = 3$; y-intercept: 0
7. $m = \frac{2}{3}$; y-intercept: 2   9. $m = \frac{1}{3}$; y-intercept: 0   11. $m = -\frac{3}{4}$; y-intercept: 0
13. $m = -3$; y-intercept: 4   15. $m = -\frac{3}{4}$; y-intercept: 3   17. $m = -\frac{4}{3}$;
y-intercept: 0   19. $m = 2$; y-intercept: 0   21. $m = 5$; y-intercept: 0
23. $m = 2$; y-intercept: 3

9. Writing an Equation for a Line (*page 367*)

1. $y = 2x + 2$ 3. $y = -x - 2$ 5. $y = \frac{1}{2}x$ 7. $y = -\frac{3}{4}x$ 9. $y = -6$
11. $y = 3x - 3$ 13. $y = \frac{4}{3}x + \frac{2}{3}$ 15. $y = -2x + 12$ 17. $y = 3x + 1$
19. a. $y = 2x + 7$ b. $y = 3x - 2$ c. $y = -\frac{2}{3}x$

11. Graphing an Inequality in Two Variables (*page 373*)

1. $y > 2x$ 3. $y < \frac{5}{2}x$ 5. $y \le -2x$ 7. $y \le \frac{3}{4}x + 3$ 9. $y \le -\frac{2}{5}x + 2$
35. a. $y < 4x$ 37. a. $x + y \le 5$ 39. a. $3x + 2y \le 12$

Chapter 14

1. Graphic Solution of a System of Linear Equations in Two Variables (*pages 377–378*)

1. $\{(3, 6)\}$ 3. $\{(2, 2)\}$ 5. $\{(-3, -4)\}$ 7. $\{(-5, -3)\}$ 9. $\{(3, -2)\}$
11. $\{(0, -5)\}$ 13. $\{(0, 0)\}$ 15. $\{(-1, 0)\}$ 17. dependent   19. dependent
21. consistent   23. No; they are dependent.   25. $\{(2, 4)\}$ 27. $\{(1, 6)\}$
29. b. They are parallel.   c. ϕ

2. Algebraic Solution of a System of Simultaneous Linear Equations by Using Addition or Subtraction (*page 381*)

1. $x = 8, y = 4$ 3. $m = 6, n = 4$ 5. $s = -3, r = 3$ 7. $a = \frac{1}{2}, b = 1$ 9. $a = 2$,
$b = 3$ 11. $x = 7, y = -2$ 13. $a = 5, b = 2$ 15. $x = 2, y = 1$ 17. $x = 5, y = 1$
19. $x = -3, y = 1$ 21. $x = 4, y = -2$ 23. $a = 7, b = 2$ 25. $x = -8, y = 3$
27. $x = 12, y = -8$ 29. $a = 10, b = 9$ 31. $x = 200, y = 300$ 33. $x = 500$,
$y = 100$ 35. $x = 6, y = 1$ 37. $c = 5, d = 1$ 39. $a = 3, b = 9$ 41. $x = 4a$,
$y = -2a$ 43. $x = \dfrac{c + d}{2},\ y = \dfrac{c - d}{2}$ 45. $x = \dfrac{ce - bf}{ae - bd},\ y = \dfrac{cd - af}{bd - ae}$ $(ae \ne bd)$

3. Algebraic Solution of a System of Simultaneous Linear Equations by Using Substitutions (*page 384*)

1. $x = 7, y = 7$ 3. $x = 8, y = 2$ 5. $x = 4, y = 5$ 7. $x = 4, y = 7$ 9. $a = -8$,
$b = -3$ 11. $x = 5, y = -5$ 13. $x = 5, y = 4$ 15. $x = -4, y = 3$ 17. $x = 0, y = 1$
19. $x = 6, y = 18$ 21. $t = 2, u = 4$ 23. $x = 400, y = 600$ 25. $x = 8a, y = 10a$
27. $x = \dfrac{r - s}{2},\ y = \dfrac{r + s}{2}$

4. Solving Verbal Problems by Using Two Variables

Number Problems (*page 388*)

1. 35 and 69   3. 18 and 32

Coin Problems (*page 388*)

5. 18 quarters, 12 dimes   7. 38 nickels, 42 dimes

Mixture Problems (*page 388*)

9. 40 lb. of $1.70 nuts, 20 lb. of $1.10 nuts   11. 20 lb. of 80¢ coffee, 10 lb. of 95¢ coffee

Investment Problems (*page 389*)

13. $400 at 5%, $1,000 at 8% **15.** $12,000 at 4%, $8,000 at 6%

Business Problems (*pages 389-390*)

17. $12 per box of oranges, $14 per box of grapefruits
19. Shirt costs $12; shoes cost $8.50.
21. $2.80 for walnuts, $2.50 for pecans
23. $3 on model S, $5 on model R

Preparing to Solve Digit Problems (*page 390*)

1. Value of 3 is 30; value of 9 is 9.
3. 7 is 7000; 8 is 800; 0 is 0; 3 is 3.
5. 2 is 20,000; 5 is 5,000; 0 is 0; 1 is 10; 3 is 3.
7. 57 **9.** $100h + 10t + u$

Solving Digit Problems (*pages 391-392*)

1. 73 **3.** 48 **5.** 41 **7.** 38

Preparing to Solve Motion Problems Involving Currents (*page 393*)

1. a. 4 mph **b.** 2 mph **c.** 1 hr. **d.** 2 hr. **e.** 3 hr. **3.** 3 mph
5. a. $x + y$ mph **b.** $x - y$ mph **c.** $2(x + y)$ mi. **d.** $3(x - y)$ mi.

Solving Motion Problems Involving Currents (*pages 394-395*)

1. 3 hr. **3.** 200 mph
5. Rate in still air is 450 km/h; speed of wind is 50 km/h.
7. Rate in still air is 305 mph; speed of wind is 20 mph.

Miscellaneous Problems (*pages 395-396*)

1. 200 **3.** He hiked for 3 hr. and rode for $\frac{1}{4}$ hr. **5.** 60 cc of 60%; 40 cc of 35%
7. $\frac{6}{9}$ **9.** 42

Chapter 15

1. Ratio (*pages 402-403*)

1. a. $\frac{36}{12}$; 36:12 **b.** $\frac{48}{24}$; 48:24 **c.** $\frac{40}{25}$; 40:25 **d.** $\frac{2}{3}$; 2:3 **e.** $\frac{5}{4}$; 5:4 **3. a.** 2
b. 3 **c.** $\frac{3}{2}$ **d.** $\frac{5}{2}$ **e.** $\frac{5}{3}$ **5. a.** $\frac{1}{3}$ **b.** $\frac{1}{2}$ **c.** $\frac{1}{5}$ **d.** $\frac{2}{3}$ **e.** $\frac{3}{4}$ **7. a.** $\frac{2}{3}, \frac{6}{9}, \frac{50}{75}$
b. 10:8, 20:16, 50:40 **9. a.** $\frac{3}{1}$ **b.** $\frac{3}{1}$ **c.** $\frac{7}{17}$ **d.** $\frac{6}{5}$ **e.** $\frac{2}{3}$ **f.** $\frac{1}{2}$ **g.** $\frac{3}{1}$ **h.** $\frac{3}{10}$
i. $\frac{24}{1}$ **j.** $\frac{5}{1}$ **11. a.** $\frac{3}{1}$ **b.** $\frac{4}{5}$ **c.** $\frac{6}{1}$ **d.** $\frac{12}{1}$ **e.** $\frac{3}{1}$ **f.** $\frac{2}{1}$ **g.** $\frac{1}{4}$ **h.** $\frac{4}{1}$ **i.** $\frac{1}{8}$
j. $\frac{12}{1}$ **k.** $\frac{4}{1}$ **l.** $\frac{4}{1}$ **13. a.** $\frac{3}{2}$ **b.** 3 **15. a.** $4x, 7x$ **b.** $5x, 3x$ **c.** $x, 4x$
d. $3x, 5x$ **e.** $7x, x$

2. Ratios in the Metric System (*page 405*)

1. a. $\frac{5}{1}$ **b.** $\frac{3}{4}$ **c.** $\frac{3}{10}$ **d.** $\frac{1}{2}$ **e.** $\frac{3}{5}$ **f.** $\frac{15}{7}$ **g.** $\frac{2}{3}$ **h.** $\frac{5}{4}$ **i.** $\frac{4}{7}$ **j.** $\frac{6}{5}$ **k.** $\frac{5}{3}$ **l.** $\frac{2}{3}$

3. Using a Ratio to Express a Rate (*page 407*)

1. 2 apples per person   **3.** 8 patients per nurse   **5.** 6 cents per gram
7. 1.09 yards per meter   **9.** .035 ounces per gram   **11.** 3   **13.** .62   **15.** 100

4. Solving Verbal Problems Involving Ratios (*page 409*)

1. 40 and 30   **3.** Gray: $20,000; Charles: $15,000   **5.** 12 cm, 16 cm, 20 cm
7. 245   **9.** 20 and 15   **11.** 12 and 20   **13.** $\frac{6}{14}$ **15.** Sue is 40; Betty is 10.

5. Proportion (*page 412*)

1. no   **3.** no   **5.** yes   **7.** yes   **9.** yes   **11.** $\frac{1}{3} = \frac{10}{30}$ **13.** $\frac{3}{8} = \frac{15}{40}$ **15.** 4
17. 24   **19.** 20   **21.** 36   **23.** $x = 15$ **25.** $x = 4$ **27.** $x = 3$ **29.** $x = 16$
31. $x = 4$ **33.** $x = 5$ **35.** $x = \dfrac{bc}{a}$ **37.** $x = \dfrac{2mr}{s}$

6. Using Proportions to Convert Units of Measure (*page 415*)

Note: In exercises 1–20, the answers are approximate. They depend on the method of solution used.

1. 96.6 km   **3.** 340.2 gm   **5.** 1.8 kg   **7.** 4.75 l   **9.** 5.22 m   **11.** 285 cl
13. 26.25 oz.   **15.** 7.208 qt.   **17.** 9.9 lb.   **19.** 5.635 km

7. Solving Verbal Problems by Using Proportions (*pages 417–418*)

1. $30.80   **3.** 2250 bushels   **5.** $2\frac{1}{2}$ **7.** $4\frac{1}{4}$ in.   **9.** 108   **11.** $\dfrac{nd}{p}$ dollars

8. Direct Variation (*pages 420–422*)

1. Yes; $p = 3s$.   **3.** no   **5.** Yes; $y = -3x$.   **7.** $A = 10$, $h = 5$, $A = 5h$ **9.** $W = 4$,
$L = 14$, $W = \frac{1}{2}L$ **11.** $C = kr$ **13.** $s = kh$ **15.** $I = kn$
17. No; it cannot be put in the form $y = kx$.
19. Yes; the ratio of variables is constant.
21. a. $w = kl$ **b.** $w = 15$ **c.** $l = 25$ **23.** $Y = 140$ **25.** 11   **27.** 3024 lb.
29. 18 kg   **31.** 630 km

9. Inverse Variation (*pages 425–426*)

1. Yes; $nc = 36$.   **3.** no   **5.** Yes; $xy = -36$.   **7.** $w = 3$, $d = 4$, $wd = 24$
9. $w = 16$, $l = 8$, $lw = 64$ **11.** $tr = k$ **13.** $hn = k$
15. a. inversely   **b.** The rectangle will have twice the length.   **c.** W is divided by 3.
17. Yes; it is of the form $xy = k$.
19. No; it cannot be put in the form $xy = k$.
21. a. $nr = k$ **b.** $n = 20$ turns   **c.** 400   **23.** $n = 5$ **25.** $r = .02$ **27.** $N = 2\frac{1}{2}$

Chapter 16

1. The Set of Rational Numbers (*pages 431–432*)

1. $\frac{7}{2}$ **3.** $\frac{5}{6}$ **5.** $\frac{5}{2}$ **7.** $\frac{13}{6}$ **9.** $1\frac{3}{5}$ **11.** $\frac{1}{6}$ **13.** $5\frac{1}{2}$ **15.** $-\frac{1}{2}$ **17.** $\frac{11}{16}$
19. -2.15 **21.** $-1\frac{7}{24}$ **23.** $.625$ **25.** -5.5 **27.** $-.58\overline{3}$ **29.** $.\overline{7}$ **31.** $.\overline{35}$
33. $\frac{1}{2}$ **35.** $-\frac{2}{9}$ **37.** $\frac{25}{99}$ **39.** $3\frac{2}{3}$ **41.** $1\frac{17}{30}$

2. The Set of Irrational Numbers (*page 433*)

1. Increase the number of twos in the sequence by one: 22227.
3. Write the consecutive integers, starting with 95: 99100.
5. rational **7.** irrational **9.** rational **11.** irrational **13.** examples: **a.** $.\overline{78}$
b. .7891011 . . .

3. The Set of Real Numbers (*pages 435–436*)

1. 2.25 **3.** 5353 . . . **5.** $-.\overline{531}$ **7.** $\{.3, .31, .313113111 . . . , .333 . . .\}$
9. $\{.27, .272272227 . . . , .\overline{27}, \frac{2}{7}\}$ **11. a.** positive integers, negative integers,
even integers, rational numbers, irrational numbers, real numbers;
b. even integers, rational numbers, real numbers;
c. positive integers, odd integers, even integers, rational numbers, real numbers;
d. rational numbers, real numbers
13. Every nonzero number has a unique multiplicative inverse.

4. Finding a Root of a Number (*pages 438–439*)

1. index: 2; radicand: 36 **3.** index: 4; radicand: 81 **5.** index: n; radicand: 1
7. 1 **9.** 15 **11.** $\frac{1}{3}$ **13.** .7 **15.** .2 **17.** 9 **19.** -8 **21.** 0 **23.** ± 13
25. -25 **27.** $-\frac{3}{4}$ **29.** $\frac{7}{10}$ **31.** .8 **33.** $\pm.3$ **35.** $\pm.02$ **37.** 3 **39.** -2
41. 8 **43.** .7 **45.** 5 **47.** 36 **49.** 39 **51.** 13 **53.** 24 **55.** $x = \pm 2$
57. $z = \pm\frac{2}{9}$ **59.** $x = \pm 4$ **61.** $x = \pm 5$ **63.** $x = 2$ **65.** $x = 4$ **67.** 6 ft.
69. 40 ft.

5. Square Roots Which Are Irrational Numbers (*page 440*)

1. 2, 3 **3.** 6, 7 **5.** $-4, -3$ **7.** 8, 9 **9.** 11, 12 **11.** $-1, \sqrt{3}, 2$
13. $-4, -\sqrt{15}, -3$ **15.** $\sqrt{21}, 5, \sqrt{30}$ **17.** rational **19.** rational
21. irrational **23.** irrational **25.** rational

6. Estimating Approximate Square Roots (*page 441*)

1. 2 **3.** 5 **5.** -7 **7.** 10 **9.** 13 **11.** 1.4 **13.** 6.7 **15.** -9.3 **17.** 11.2
19. 12.3

7. Using Division to Find Approximate Square Roots (*page 443*)

1. 6 **3.** 12 **5.** 48 **7.** 38 **9.** 8 **11.** 2.4 **13.** 4.2 **15.** -5.8 **17.** 9.5
19. 4.4 **21.** 2.65 **23.** 5.29 **25.** 8.60 **27.** 10.54 **29.** 4.85 **31.** 1.732
33. 9.434 **35.** 5.404 **37. a.** 100 **b.** 10,000

39. greater than 10 but less than 100   **41.** greater than 100 but less than 1000
43. less than 10   **45.** greater than 10 but less than 100
47. greater than 100 but less than 1000

8. Using Another Method for Computing the Square Root of a Number (*page 447*)

1. 17   **3.** -36   **5.** 130   **7.** 9.5   **9.** 1.05   **11.** 1.33   **13.** 3.5   **15.** -7.6
17. 14.1   **19.** 4.3   **21.** -2.9   **23.** 1.41   **25.** 8.77   **27.** 3.08   **29.** 5.4 in.
31. 14.1 in.

9. Using a Table to Find Squares and Square Roots (*pages 448-449*)

1. 729   **3.** 8,836   **5.** 17,424   **7.** 3.6   **9.** -7.9   **11.** -9.3   **13.** 9.5
15. -10.5   **17.** 3.7   **19.** 14.4   **21.** -5.6   **23.** 4.12   **25.** 8.83   **27.** -5.57
29. 10.95   **31.** 12.12   **33.** 34   **35.** 89   **37.** 114   **39.** 137   **41.** 145
43. 43   **45.** -97   **47.** 10   **49.** 39   **51.** 24   **53.** 4   **55.** 10   **57.** 4.9
59. 11.5   **61.** 4.9

10. Finding the Principal Square Root of a Perfect Square Monomial or a Perfect Cube Monomial (*page 451*)

1. $3c$ **3.** $8c^3$ **5.** $9t^4$ **7.** x^2y **9.** x^8y^2 **11.** $2xy$ **13.** $12a^2b$
15. $5r^4s^8t^6$ **17.** $\frac{5}{6}xy$ **19.** $\frac{9}{11}a^3b$ **21.** $.6m$ **23.** $.2xy^3$ **25.** $1.1a^2b^8c^{18}$
27. $5a$ **29.** $\frac{1}{2}a^2b^3$

11. Simplifying a Radical Whose Radicand Is a Product (*pages 453-454*)

1. $2\sqrt{2}$ **3.** $-2\sqrt{6}$ **5.** $-3\sqrt{5}$ **7.** $3\sqrt{7}$ **9.** $7\sqrt{2}$ **11.** $-8\sqrt{2}$ **13.** $10\sqrt{3}$
15. $6\sqrt{2}$ **17.** $-10\sqrt{6}$ **19.** $30\sqrt{2}$ **21.** $\sqrt{5}$ **23.** $\frac{3}{2}\sqrt{2}$ **25.** $2\sqrt{7}$
27. $-2\sqrt{5}$ **29.** $2b^2\sqrt{b}$ **31.** $xy\sqrt{y}$ **33.** $-4ab\sqrt{2b}$ **35.** $10xy\sqrt{xy}$
37. $2xy\sqrt{5y}$ **39.** $2xy^2z\sqrt{z}$ **41.** $15yu^3z^4\sqrt{2y}$ **43.** $3rst\sqrt{2rst}$ **45.** $2\sqrt[3]{3}$
47. $y\sqrt[3]{7y}$ **49.** 17.3   **51.** 25.3   **53.** 33.9   **55.** 10.0   **57.** 5.8   **59.** 10.1
61. a. no   **b.** no   **c.** when a or b equals 0
63. b. yes   **c.** Raising to a power is distributive over multiplication.

12. Simplifying a Radical Whose Radicand Is a Fraction (*page 456*)

1. $\frac{1}{3}\sqrt{5}$ **3.** $\frac{1}{2}\sqrt{2}$ **5.** $3\sqrt{7}$ **7.** $2\sqrt{15}$ **9.** $10\sqrt{2}$ **11.** $\frac{1}{6}\sqrt{21}$ **13.** $\frac{1}{2}\sqrt[3]{4}$
15. $2\sqrt[3]{36}$ **17.** $\frac{1}{3}\sqrt{3a}$ **19.** $4x\sqrt{2}$ **21.** $\frac{1}{a}\sqrt{a}$ **23.** $\frac{1}{\pi}\sqrt{\pi A}$ **25.** $\frac{x}{y}\sqrt{y}$
27. $\frac{3}{4n}\sqrt{2mn}$ **29.** $\frac{1}{3}\sqrt[3]{3x}$ **31.** $\frac{2a}{b}\sqrt[3]{b}$ **33.** .9   **35.** .7   **37.** 6.3   **39.** .7
41. b. yes   **c.** Raising to a power is distributive over division.

13. Adding and Subtracting Radicals (*pages 458-459*)

1. $15\sqrt{2}$ **3.** $12\sqrt{6}$ **5.** $-2\sqrt[3]{7}$ **7.** $6\sqrt{x}$ **9.** $8\sqrt{5}$ **11.** $\sqrt[3]{2}$ **13.** $5\sqrt[3]{3}$
15. $2\sqrt{2}$ **17.** $23\sqrt{2}$ **19.** $8\sqrt{2}$ **21.** $\frac{15}{2}\sqrt{2}$ **23.** $-18\sqrt[3]{3}$ **25.** $5\sqrt{b}$
27. $7\sqrt{3y} - 3\sqrt{3x}$ **29.** $2y\sqrt[3]{5}$ **31.** $y\sqrt{2y}$ **33.** $5x\sqrt{2y}$
35. $7x\sqrt{3x} - 5x\sqrt{3}$

14. Multiplying Radicals Which Have the Same Index (*pages 461-462*)

1. 5 **3.** a **5.** 6 **7.** $2\sqrt{7}$ **9.** $9\sqrt{2}$ **11.** $36\sqrt{2}$ **13.** 48 **15.** $120\sqrt{3}$
17. 140 **19.** $15x$ **21.** $3y$ **23.** 5 **25.** t **27.** $\frac{1}{9}$ **29.** $9a$ **31.** $3a\sqrt{b}$
33. $3ab\sqrt{6}$ **35.** $9r$ **37.** $2x + 1$ **39.** $5x - 3$ **41.** $5 + \sqrt{55}$ **43.** $-8\sqrt{15}$
45. $16 + 4\sqrt{5}$ **47.** $a - b$ **49.** $16 + 6\sqrt{7}$ **51.** $x^2 - 2x\sqrt{y} + y$ **53.** 12
55. 75

Products Involving Irrational Numbers (*page 462*)

1. rational **3.** irrational

15. Dividing Radicals Which Have the Same Index (*page 464*)

1. 6 **3.** 16 **5.** $42\sqrt{2}$ **7.** $\frac{7}{3}$ **9.** 2 **11.** $6\sqrt[3]{2}$ **13.** 3 **15.** 1 **17.** $10\sqrt{3}$
19. y **21.** a **23.** $\sqrt{3}$ **25.** 4.8 **27.** 14.9 **29.** .3

Quotients Involving Irrational Numbers (*page 465*)

1. rational **3.** irrational

16. Rationalizing an Irrational Radical Denominator (*pages 466-467*)

1. $\frac{1}{7}\sqrt{7}$ **3.** $\frac{5}{3}\sqrt{3}$ **5.** $\frac{8}{11}\sqrt{11}$ **7.** $3\sqrt{3}$ **9.** $\sqrt{6}$ **11.** $3\sqrt{2}$ **13.** $6\sqrt{2}$
15. $3\sqrt{2}$ **17.** $3\sqrt{2}$ **19.** $\frac{1}{5}\sqrt{30}$ **21.** $3\sqrt[3]{3}$ **23.** $\frac{6}{5}\sqrt[3]{15}$ **25.** $\frac{5}{21}\sqrt[3]{18}$
27. $\frac{1}{s}\sqrt{rs}$ **29.** $\frac{4}{a}\sqrt{2a}$ **31.** 5 **33.** $\dfrac{12 + 2\sqrt{3}}{3}$ **35.** 6.9 **37.** 2.8 **39.** .3

17. Rationalizing a Binomial Radical Denominator (*pages 468-469*)

1. $\dfrac{2(4 + \sqrt{3})}{13}$ **3.** $\dfrac{11(\sqrt{2} + 2)}{-2}$ **5.** $\dfrac{5(3\sqrt{2} - 2)}{14}$ **7.** $3 + 2\sqrt{3}$ **9.** $\dfrac{89 - 24\sqrt{5}}{71}$
11. $6 - \sqrt{35}$ **13.** $\dfrac{4\sqrt{2} - 4}{1}$ **15.** $\dfrac{2\sqrt{5} + \sqrt{15} - 2\sqrt{3} - 4}{1}$ **17.** $\dfrac{a + \sqrt{ab}}{a - b}$

18. Solving Radical Equations (*page 472*)

1. $x = 25$ **3.** no root **5.** $b = \frac{1}{16}$ **7.** $x = 32$ **9.** $x = 9$ **11.** $y = \frac{1}{4}$
13. no root **15.** $z = 24$ **17.** $x = 20$ **19.** $b = 65$ **21.** $a = 11$ **23.** $x = 25$
25. $r = \frac{1}{2}$ **27.** $y = \frac{49}{16}$ **29.** $y = 2$ **31.** $x = 10$ **33.** $x = 3$ **35.** $y = 2$
37. $A = s^2$ **39.** $s = 6e^2$

19. Rational Exponents (*pages 474–475*)

1. $\sqrt{3}$ **3.** $\sqrt[4]{a}$ **5.** $\sqrt[3]{-27}$ **7.** $\sqrt{49ab}$ **9.** $\sqrt[4]{(2y)^3}$ **11.** $\dfrac{1}{\sqrt[3]{(27x)^4}}$ **13.** $3^{\frac{1}{2}}$

15. $x^{\frac{1}{4}}$ **17.** $x^{-\frac{1}{5}}$ **19.** $(x^3z^4)^{\frac{1}{5}}$ **21.** 2 **23.** 4 **25.** $\frac{1}{2}$ **27.** $\frac{1}{25}$ **29.** 7

31. $38\frac{1}{5}$ **33.** 1 **35.** -1 **37.** $2560\frac{1}{4}$ **39.** $\dfrac{y^a}{3}$ **41.** $\dfrac{c^6}{729}$ **43.** $\dfrac{1331}{8y^9}$

45. $\dfrac{8c^{2b-a}}{d^4}$

20. Applying the Laws of Exponents to Fractional Exponents
(*page 477*)

1. x^3 **3.** $10^{\frac{1}{6}}$ **5.** x^2 **7.** x **9.** $x^{\frac{1}{4}}$ **11.** $y^{-\frac{3}{2}}$ **13.** $x^{\frac{4}{3}}y^{-2}$ **15.** $x^{-3}y^{-2}$

17. $\dfrac{x^2}{y^3}$ **19.** $x^{20}y^2$ **21.** $\dfrac{x^4}{y^3z^5}$ **23.** $\dfrac{100}{y^{\frac{1}{3}}z^{\frac{5}{4}}}$ **25.** $\sqrt[12]{x^{12}y^{18}}$ **27.** $\sqrt[12]{x^9y^6}$

29. $\sqrt{x}$ **31.** $\sqrt{9x^3y^2}$ **33.** $\sqrt{4xy^2}$ **35.** $\sqrt[12]{648}$ **37.** $\sqrt[6]{(3x)^7}$ or $3x\sqrt[6]{3x}$

39. $\sqrt[6]{108x^{11}y^7}$ or $xy\sqrt[6]{108x^5y}$

Chapter 17

1. The Standard Form of a Quadratic Equation (*page 479*)

1. yes **3.** no **5.** no **7.** yes **9.** yes **11.** $2x^2 + 4x = 0$ **13.** $x^2 - 4x - 3 = 0$

15. $x^2 - 3x - 10 = 0$ **17.** $2x^2 - x + 12 = 0$

2. Using Factoring to Solve a Quadratic Equation (*pages 482–483*)

1. $\{1, 2\}$ **3.** $\{4\}$ **5.** $\{-5, -1\}$ **7.** $\{-8, -3\}$ **9.** $\{-5, 7\}$ **11.** $\{-5, 3\}$

13. $\{-7, 7\}$ **15.** $\{-3, 3\}$ **17.** $\{0, 2\}$ **19.** $\{0, -3\}$ **21.** $\{\frac{1}{2}, 2\}$ **23.** $\{-\frac{3}{2}, 1\}$

25. $\{-\frac{5}{2}, 2\}$ **27.** $\{-2, 3\}$ **29.** $\{-4, 7\}$ **31.** $\{-5, 5\}$ **33.** $\{0, 6\}$

35. $\{-2, 10\}$ **37.** $\{-\frac{5}{2}, 3\}$ **39.** $\{\frac{1}{2}, 3\}$ **41.** $\{4, 7\}$ **43.** $\{-3, -1\}$

45. $\{-\frac{2}{3}, 3\}$ **47.** $\{-1, 4\}$ **49.** $\{-6, 4\}$ **51.** $\{3, 9\}$ **53.** $\{-5, 8\}$

55. $\{-5, 4\}$ **57.** ϕ **59.** $\{-2, 5\}$ **61.** $\{0, 7\}$ **63.** $\{\frac{1}{5}, 2\}$ **65.** $\{-9, 4\}$

67. $\{-1, 6\}$ **69.** $\{3, 5\}$ **71.** $\left\{-\dfrac{c}{2}, \dfrac{c}{2}\right\}$ **73.** $\{0, c\}$ **75.** $\{2b, 3b\}$

77. $\{-a, a\}$

3. Solving Incomplete Quadratic Equations (*pages 484–486*)

1. $\{-2, 2\}$ **3.** $\{-5, 5\}$ **5.** $\{-7, 7\}$ **7.** $\{-2, 2\}$ **9.** $\{-12, 12\}$ **11.** $\{-9, 9\}$

13. $\{-5, 5\}$ **15.** $\{-3, 3\}$ **17.** $\{-3, 3\}$ **19.** $\{-6, 6\}$ **21.** $\{-5, 5\}$

23. $\{-2\sqrt{5}, 2\sqrt{5}\}$ **25.** $\{-5\sqrt{2}, 5\sqrt{2}\}$ **27.** $\{-2\sqrt{3}, 2\sqrt{3}\}$

29. $\{-3\sqrt{2}, 3\sqrt{2}\}$ **31.** $\{-2\sqrt{7}, 2\sqrt{7}\}$ **33.** $\{-3\sqrt{3}, 3\sqrt{3}\}$

35. $\{-\sqrt{61}, \sqrt{61}\}$ **37.** $\{-\sqrt{15}, \sqrt{15}\}$ **39.** $\{-3\sqrt{3}, 3\sqrt{3}\}$ **41.** $\{-7, 7\}$

43. 2.6 **45.** 9.6 **47.** 6.3 **49.** 5.7 **51.** 6.3 **53.** 3.2 **55.** 7.4 **57.** 13.1

59. $\{-6, 2\}$ 61. $\{-5, 7\}$ 63. $\{2 + \sqrt{15}, 2 - \sqrt{15}\}$ 65. $\{-5a, 5a\}$

67. $\left\{-\dfrac{a}{2}, \dfrac{a}{2}\right\}$ 69. $\{-\sqrt{c^2 - b^2}, \sqrt{c^2 - b^2}\}$ 71. $\{-\frac{1}{6}\sqrt{6S}, \frac{1}{6}\sqrt{6S}\}$

73. $\left\{-\dfrac{1}{2\pi}\sqrt{\pi S}, \dfrac{1}{2\pi}\sqrt{\pi S}\right\}$ 75. $\left\{-\dfrac{1}{\pi h}\sqrt{\pi h V}, \dfrac{1}{\pi h}\sqrt{\pi h V}\right\}$

77. $\left\{-\dfrac{1}{m}\sqrt{gmrF}, \dfrac{1}{m}\sqrt{gmrF}\right\}$

4. Completing a Perfect Square Trinomial (*page 487*)

1. $k = 4$ 3. $k = \frac{9}{4}$ 5. $49; (c + 7)^2$ 7. $\frac{25}{4}; (r + \frac{5}{2})^2$ 9. $\frac{1}{4}; (x - \frac{1}{2})^2$
11. $\frac{1}{36}; (y - \frac{1}{6})^2$ 13. $6, -6; (x + 3)^2, (x - 3)^2$ 15. $16, -16; (x - 8)^2, (x + 8)^2$
17. yes 19. no 21. no 23. $(x + 2)^2$, yes 25. $(x + 6)^2$, yes
27. $(x - 8)^2$, yes

5. Solving Quadratic Equations by Completing the Square (*page 490*)

1. $\{-2, 12\}$ 3. $\{-6, 14\}$ 5. $\{-\frac{5}{3}, -\frac{1}{3}\}$ 7. $\{-1, 3\}$ 9. $\{5 + 5\sqrt{2}, 5 - 5\sqrt{2}\}$
11. $\{-5, 2\}$ 13. $\{-4, 2\}$ 15. $\{1, 3\}$ 17. $\{-2, 7\}$ 19. $\{2\}$ 21. $\{-\frac{1}{2}, 2\}$
23. $\{-\frac{1}{3}, 2\}$ 25. $\{-1 + \sqrt{2}, -1 - \sqrt{2}\}$ 27. $\left\{-\dfrac{3}{2} + \dfrac{\sqrt{29}}{2}, -\dfrac{3}{2} - \dfrac{\sqrt{29}}{2}\right\}$

29. $\{3 + 2\sqrt{7}, 3 - 2\sqrt{7}\}$ 31. $\left\{2 + \dfrac{\sqrt{21}}{3}, 2 - \dfrac{\sqrt{21}}{3}\right\}$

33. $\left\{\dfrac{3}{10} + \dfrac{\sqrt{29}}{10}, \dfrac{3}{10} - \dfrac{\sqrt{29}}{10}\right\}$ 35. $\{-3.7, -.3\}$ 37. $\{-.2, 8.2\}$

39. $\{-.4, 1.7\}$

6. Solving Quadratic Equations by Formula (*pages 493–494*)

1. $\{-6, 4\}$ 3. $\{3\}$ 5. $\{-5, 6\}$ 7. $\{\frac{1}{2}, 2\}$ 9. $\{-\frac{2}{5}, 1\}$ 11. $\{-3, 3\}$

13. $\{-1 + \sqrt{2}, -1 - \sqrt{2}\}$ 15. $\left\{-\dfrac{3}{2} + \dfrac{\sqrt{29}}{2}, -\dfrac{3}{2} - \dfrac{\sqrt{29}}{2}\right\}$

17. $\left\{-\dfrac{5}{2} + \dfrac{\sqrt{33}}{2}, -\dfrac{5}{2} - \dfrac{\sqrt{33}}{2}\right\}$ 19. $\left\{\dfrac{3}{4} + \dfrac{\sqrt{17}}{4}, \dfrac{3}{4} - \dfrac{\sqrt{17}}{4}\right\}$

21. $\left\{\dfrac{1}{3} + \dfrac{\sqrt{10}}{3}, \dfrac{1}{3} - \dfrac{\sqrt{10}}{3}\right\}$ 23. $\left\{\dfrac{1}{5} + \dfrac{\sqrt{6}}{5}, \dfrac{1}{5} - \dfrac{\sqrt{6}}{5}\right\}$

25. $\{3 + \sqrt{13}, 3 - \sqrt{13}\}$ 27. $\left\{\dfrac{5}{4} + \dfrac{\sqrt{57}}{4}, \dfrac{5}{4} - \dfrac{\sqrt{57}}{4}\right\}$ 29. $\{.6, 3.4\}$
31. $\{-3.2, 1.2\}$ 33. $\{.1, 3.9\}$ 35. $\{-2.6, .6\}$ 37. $\{-.8, 1.8\}$
39. $\{-10.2, 1.2\}$ 41. $\{-4.8, .3\}$

7. Using the Theorem of Pythagoras (*pages 496–498*)

1. $c = 5$ 3. $a = 8$ 5. $c = 8$ 7. $c = \sqrt{13}$ 9. $b = 4\sqrt{3}$ 11. $a = 2\sqrt{3}$
13. $c = 8.6$ 15. $b = 21.2$ 17. $c = 9.9$ 19. $x = 4\sqrt{2}$ 21. $x = 4\sqrt{3}$
23. 36 ft. 25. 100 km 27. 25 cm 29. 26 m 31. 8 ft. 33. 2.8 in.

35. 7.1 in. **37.** 9.9 in. **39.** 1.4 in. **41.** 7.1 in. **43.** 3.5 cm **45.** 6.9 cm
47. 4.3 cm **49.** 13 cm **51.** 15 cm, 20 cm **53.** 26 **57.** no **59.** no

10. Solving Quadratic Equations by Using Graphs (*page 502*)

1. b. $\{-2, +2\}$ **3. b.** $\{0, 3\}$ **5.** $\{-4, 2\}$ **7.** $\{-5, +5\}$ **9.** $\{-3, 0\}$
11. $\{-2, 4\}$

11. Solving Verbal Problems by Using Quadratic Equations

Number Problems (*pages 504–505*)

1. 4 or $^-7$ **3.** 7 or $^-3$ **5.** 4 and 9 **7.** 2 and 7 **9.** 4 and 6 **11.** 2 or $-1\frac{3}{5}$
13. 9, 11, 13 **15.** 5 and 8 or $^-8$ and $^-5$ **17.** $\frac{2}{3}$ or $\frac{3}{2}$

Geometric Problems (*pages 505–507*)

1. width, 6 in.; length, 12 in. **3.** base, 30 cm; height, 40 cm **5.** 2 in.; 8 in.
7. 6 cm **9.** width, 10 ft.; length, 12 ft. **11.** 3 in. **13.** altitude, 7 cm;
base, 12 cm **15.** 66.8 ft. **17.** legs, 6 cm and 8 cm; hypotenuse, 10 cm

Miscellaneous Problems (*page 507*)

19. 2 hr. **21.** Stuart, 9 km/h; Perry, 12 km/h **23.** 2 mph **25.** 50 mph
27. Tom, 3 hr.; Bill, 6 hr. **29.** 4 and 3 or $^-21$ and 28

Chapter 18

1. The Angle (*page 511*)

1. a. $60°$ **b.** $120°$ **c.** $90°$ **d.** $40°$ **e.** $125°$ **f.** $50°$ **3.** right angle
5. $\angle D$ and $\angle F$ are acute angles; $\angle E$ is an obtuse angle.
7. a. $\angle BOA$ **b.** $\angle y$ **c.** $\angle COB$ or $\angle BOA$ **d.** $\angle COA$ **8. a.** $30°$ **b.** $54°$
9. a. $360°$ **b.** $180°$ **c.** $15°$ **d.** $1°$

2. The Triangle (*pages 513–514*)

1. yes **3.** yes **5.** $60°$ **7.** $74°$ **9. a.** no **b.** no **c.** no
d. The sum of the measures of the angles of a triangle is $180°$.
11. The third pair is equal because the sum of the measures of three angles of a
triangle is $180°$.
13. $m\angle S = 40°, m\angle R = 20°, m\angle T = 120°$ **15.** $35°, 65°, 80°$ **17.** $80°, 10°$
19. $24°, 60°, 96°$ **21.** $20°, 100°, 60°$

3. Similar Triangles (*pages 516–518*)

1. Yes; the measures of two pairs of corresponding angles are equal.
3. $\triangle ABC \sim \triangle LMN$
5. Yes; the measure of each angle is $60°$.

7. $DF = 8, EF = 10$ **9. a.** $\dfrac{x}{15}$ **b.** $\frac{5}{4}$ **c.** $\dfrac{x}{15} = \dfrac{5}{4}$, $\triangle LMN \sim \triangle DEF$ **d.** $18\frac{3}{4}$
11. $17\frac{1}{2}$ m   **13.** $\frac{5}{4}$

4. Using Similar Triangles in Indirect Measurement (*page 519*)

1. 20 ft.   **3. a.** Yes; $m\angle B = m\angle D$ and $m\angle ACB = m\angle DCE$.   **b.** 8 m
5. a. 150 m   **b.** 90 m

5. The Tangent Ratio

The Table of Tangents (*pages 523-524*)

1. AB is hypotenuse; $\angle A$: BC is opposite, AC is adjacent; $\angle B$: AC is opposite,
BC is adjacent.
3. RT is hypotenuse; $\angle R$: ST is opposite, RS is adjacent; $\angle T$: RS is opposite,
ST is adjacent.
5. $\tan A = 1$, $\tan B = 1$ **7.** $\tan G = \frac{5}{6}$, $\tan I = \frac{6}{5}$ **9.** $\tan A = \frac{4}{3}$
11. $\tan 15 = .2679$ **13.** $\tan 32 = 1.0000$ **15.** $\tan 89 = 57.2900$ **17.** $19°$
19. $45°$ **21.** $77°$ **23.** $38°$ **25.** $13°$ **27.** $67°$ **29. a.** 1.0000 **b.** $45°$

Using the Tangent Ratio to Solve Problems (*pages 526-527*)

1. 23 ft.   **3.** 27 ft.   **5.** 29 ft.   **7.** $63°$ **9.** 11 m   **11.** 14 ft.   **13.** $45°$
15. $69°$

6. Trigonometry of the Right Triangle Involving the Sine Ratio

The Table of Sines (*pages 528-529*)

1. $\sin A = \frac{3}{5}$, $\sin B = \frac{4}{5}$ **3.** $\sin L = \dfrac{\sqrt{2}}{2}$, $\sin N = \dfrac{\sqrt{2}}{2}$ **5.** $\frac{3}{5}$ **7.** $.3090$
9. $.8480$ **11.** $.9998$ **13.** $57°$ **15.** $11°$ **17.** $7°$ **19. a.** $.5000$ **b.** $30°$

Using the Sine Ratio to Solve Problems (*page 531*)

1. 7 ft.   **3.** $30°$ **5.** 23 ft.   **7.** 100 m   **9.** 6600 ft.   **11.** $64°$

7. Trigonometry of the Right Triangle Involving the Cosine Ratio

The Table of Cosines (*page 533*)

1. $\cos A = \frac{4}{5}$, $\cos B = \frac{3}{5}$ **3.** $\cos N = \dfrac{\sqrt{2}}{2}$, $\cos L = \dfrac{\sqrt{2}}{2}$ **5.** $\frac{4}{5}$ **7.** $.9336$
9. $.3907$ **11.** $.0349$ **13.** $69°$ **15.** $13°$ **17.** $73°$ **19. a.** $.5000$ **b.** $60°$

Using the Cosine Ratio to Solve Problems (*pages 535-536*)

1. 24 ft.   **3.** 14 ft.   **5.** 6 ft.   **7.** 38 ft.   **9.** 137 ft.   **11.** $13°$

8. Using All Three Trigonometric Ratios (*pages 537–540*)

1. $\sin A$ **3.** $\sin A$ **5.** $\tan A$ **7.** $\tan A$ **9.** $\frac{15}{8}$ **11.** $\frac{15}{17}$ **13.** $\frac{8}{15}$ **15.** 26 ft.
17. 10 ft. **19.** 38 ft. **21.** 59 ft. **23.** 19° **25.** 34° **27.** 135 ft.
29. 50 m **31.** 5600 ft. **33.** 34° **35.** 650 ft. **37.** 32° **39. a.** 16.4 in.
b. 11.5 in. **c.** 189 sq. in. **41. a.** 35.3 cm **b.** 1765 sq. cm **43. a.** 145 ft.
b. 26 ft.

Chapter 19

1. Understanding the Meaning of a Relation (*pages 544–545*)

1. a. $\{1, 2, 3, 4\}$ **b.** $\{3, 6, 9, 12\}$ **3. a.** $\{2, 3, 4, 5\}$ **b.** $\{-10, -8, -6, -4\}$
5. $\{(0, 0), (1, 2), (2, 4), (3, 6)\}$ **7.** $\{(0, 2), (4, 3)\}$ **9.** $\{(4, 0), (5, 2), (6, 4)\}$
11. $\{(0, 2), (1, 3), (2, 6)\}$
13. $\{(0, 1), (0, 2), (0, 3), (0, 4), (0, 5), (0, 6), (1, 2), (1, 3), (1, 4), (1, 5), (1, 6),$
$(2, 5), (2, 6)\}$
15. a. $y = 2x + 1$ **b.** $\{(x, y)|y = 2x + 1\}$ **c.** example: $(3, 7)$
17. a. $x - y = 5$ **b.** $\{(x, y)|x - y = 5\}$ **c.** example: $(5, 0)$
19. a. $3y - x = 6$ **b.** $\{(x, y)|3y - x = 6$ **c.** example: $(0, 2)$

21. a. $y < \dfrac{x}{2}$ **b.** $\{(x, y)|y < \dfrac{x}{2}\}$ **c.** example: $(3, 1)$

23. a. $y < 2x - 5$ **b.** $\{(x, y)|y < 2x - 5$ **c.** example: $(4, \frac{1}{3})$
25. a. $\{5, 6, 7, 8\}$ **b.** $\{10, 12, 14, 16\}$ **d.** $\{(x, y)|y = 2x\}$
27. a. $\{1, 2, 3, 4\}$ **b.** $\{0, 2, 4, 6\}$ **d.** $\{(x, y)|y = 2x - 2\}$
29. a. $\{-4, -3, -2, -1\}$ **b.** $\{1, 4, 9, 16\}$ **d.** $y = x^2$
31. a. $\{(-1, -3), (0, 0), (1, 3)\}$ **b.** $\{-1, 0, 1\}$ **c.** $\{-3, 0, 3\}$
33. a. $\{(0, -2), (1, 1)\}$ **b.** $\{0, 1\}$ **c.** $\{-2, 1\}$
35. a. $\{(-1, -3), (0, -2), (1, -1), (2, 0), (3, 1)\}$ **b.** $\{-1, 0, 1, 2, 3\}$
c. $\{-3, -2, -1, 0, 1\}$
37. a. $\{(-1, 1), (0, 0), (1, 1)\}$ **b.** $\{-1, 0, 1\}$ **c.** $\{0, 1\}$

2. Understanding the Cartesian Product of Two Sets (*pages 546–547*)

1. a. $\{(1, 2), (1, 3), (1, 4), (2, 2), (2, 3), (2, 4)\}$
3. a. $\{(2, 3), (2, 5), (4, 3), (4, 5), (6, 3), (6, 5)\}$
5. a. $\{(3, -3), (3, -2), (5, -3), (5, -2), (7, -3), (7, -2)\}$
7. a. $\{(1, 1)\}$
9. a. $\{(1, 1), (1, 2), (1, 3), (1, 4), (2, 1), (2, 2), (2, 3), (2, 4), (3, 1), (3, 2), (3, 3),$
$(3, 4), (4, 1), (4, 2), (4, 3), (4, 4)\}$
11. a. $\{(1, 1), \ldots, (1, 6), (2, 1), \ldots, (2, 6), (3, 1), \ldots, (3, 6), (4, 1), \ldots, (4, 6),$
$(5, 1), \ldots, (5, 6), (6, 1), \ldots, (6, 6)\}$
19. a. $\{(1, 2), (1, 4), (3, 2), (3, 4)\}$ **b.** $\{(2, 1), (2, 3), (4, 1), (4, 3)\}$
c. no; $(1, 2) \in A \times B, (1, 2) \notin B \times A$ **21.** r^2

3. Understanding the Meaning of a Function (*pages 550–552*)

Note: In questions 1–8, the reason for each answer is derived from the definition of a function.

1. yes 3. no 5. no 7. yes 9. b. a function 11. b. not a function
13. b. a function 15. b. not a function 17. b. a function
19. b. a function 21. yes 23. yes
25. b. yes c. $\{x|-3 \le x < 3\}$ d. $\{y|-3 \le x \le 3\}$
27. b. yes c. $\{x|-1 < x \le 2\}$ d. $\{y|-2 < y \le 7\}$
29. b. no c. $\{x|x = 2\}$ d. $y \in \{\text{real numbers}\}$
31. b. no c. $\{x|0 \le x \le 3\}$ d. $\{y|-3 \le y \le 3\}$
33. a. $\{-1, 0, 1, 2\}$ b. $\{-1, 0, 1, 2\}$ c. yes
35. a. $\{-1, 0, 1, 2\}$ b. $\{-2, -1, 0, 2\}$ c. yes
37. a. $\{x|-2 < x < 2\}$ b. $\{-2\}$ c. yes
39. a. $\{x|-2 \le x \le 2\}$ b. $\{y|-2 \le y \le 2\}$ c. no
41. a. $\{x|0 \le x < 2\}$ b. $\{y|-2 < y < 2\}$ c. no
43. a. $\{x|-2 \le x \le 2\}$ b. $\{y|-2 \le y \le 2\}$ c. no
45. a. $\{x|0 \le x < 2\}$ b. $\{y|0 \le y < 2\}$ c. yes
47. a. $\{x|-2 \le x \le 2\}$ b. $\{y|-1 \le y \le 0\}$ c. yes

4. Understanding Function Notation (*page 554*)

	$f(-2)$	$f(-1)$	$f(0)$	$f(1)$	$f(2)$	$f(|-3|)$	$f(\tfrac{1}{3})$	$f(\tfrac{3}{2})$	$f(\sqrt{3})$
1.	-10	-5	0	5	10	15	$\tfrac{5}{3}$	$7\tfrac{1}{2}$	$5\sqrt{3}$
3.	4	3	2	1	0	-1	$\tfrac{5}{3}$	$\tfrac{1}{2}$	$2 - \sqrt{3}$
5.	8	3	0	-1	0	3	$-\tfrac{5}{9}$	$-\tfrac{3}{4}$	$3 - 2\sqrt{3}$
7.	-16	-4	0	-4	-16	-36	$-\tfrac{4}{9}$	-9	-12
9.	-5	-4	-5	-2	11	40	$-\tfrac{128}{27}$	$\tfrac{23}{8}$	$3\sqrt{3} + 1$
11.	2	0	0	0	2	6	$-\tfrac{2}{9}$	$\tfrac{3}{4}$	$3 - \sqrt{3}$

13. a. 19 b. 3 c. $\tfrac{79}{25}$ d. 4 e. 12 f. 12 g. $6 - 2\sqrt{2}$ h. 14
i. $b^2 - 2b + 4$ j. $9a^2 - 6a + 4$ k. $b^2 + 4b + 7$ l. $4b^2 - 8b + 7$
15. a. $\{1\}$ b. $\{-1\}$ c. $\{3\}$ d. $\{-3\}$ e. $\{\tfrac{1}{3}\}$ f. $\{\tfrac{1}{2}\}$ g. $\{-2\}$ h. $\{7\}$
i. $\{1\}$ j. $\{x|x > 1\}$ k. $\{x|x > -1\}$ l. $\{x|x \ge \tfrac{1}{3}\}$ 17. $\{0\}$ 19. $\{-1, +1\}$
21. $\{-2\}$

5. Graphs of Linear Functions (*page 556*)

3. yes 5. no 7. yes 9. no 11. a. $3x - 3$ b. (1) -9 (2) -3 (3) 3
e. (1) $\{1\}$ (2) $\{5\}$ (3) $\{-2\}$

6. Graphs of Quadratic Functions (*pages 558–559*)

1. a. -2 b. -4 c. 23 d. 5 e. $-\tfrac{5}{8}$ f. 10 g. $2r^2 + 3r - 4$
h. $32s^2 + 12s - 4$ i. $2a^2 + 7a + 1$ j. $8a^2 - 2a - 5$ k. $2a^4 + 3a^2 - 4$
l. $8a^2 + 6a - 4$ m. $4a^2 + 6a - 8$ n. $2a^2 + 3a - 2$ o. $2a^2 + 11a + 10$

INDEX